Dirr's
Encyclopedia
of Trees and
Shrubs

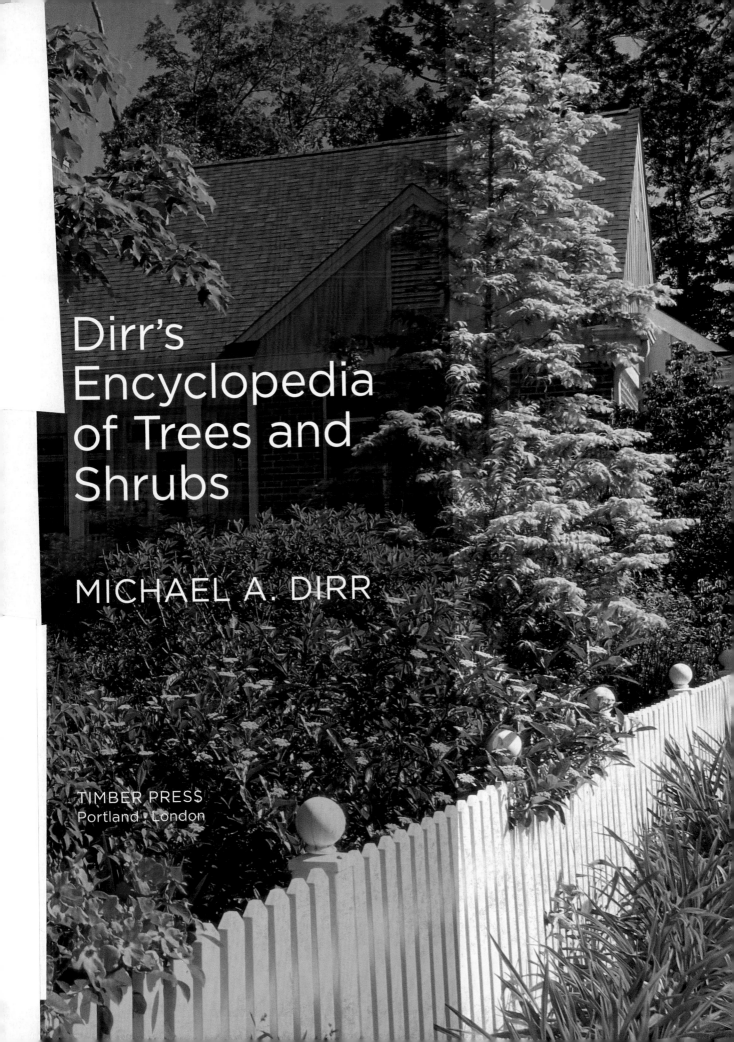

Dirr's Encyclopedia of Trees and Shrubs

MICHAEL A. DIRR

TIMBER PRESS
Portland · London

To Roger Milliken—
mentor, friend, and advocate for Noble Trees

Frontispiece: Chapel Hill garden, late May 2008.

Pages 14–15: *Daphniphyllum macropodum*

All photographs are by the author.

Published in 2011 by Timber Press, Inc.

The Haseltine Building
133 S.W. Second Avenue, Suite 450
Portland, Oregon 97204-3527
www.timberpress.com

2 The Quadrant
135 Salusbury Road
London NW6 6RJ
www.timberpress.co.uk

Printed in China

Library of Congress Cataloging-in-Publication Data

Dirr, Michael.
Dirr's encyclopedia of trees and shrubs/Michael A. Dirr.—1st ed.
p. cm.
Includes indexes.
ISBN 978-0-88192-901-0
1. Ornamental trees—Encyclopedias. 2. Ornamental shrubs—Encyclopedias.
I. Title. II. Title: Encyclopedia of trees and shrubs.
SB435.D57 2011
635.9'7603—dc22 2011007951

Catalog records for this book are available from the British Library.

Contents

Introduction

Timber Press and I have developed a symbiotic relationship in our quest/journey to produce worthy books that gardeners would embrace and enjoy. *Dirr's Hardy Trees and Shrubs* (1997), *Dirr's Trees and Shrubs for Warm Climates* (2002), *Hydrangeas for American Gardens* (2004), and *Viburnums* (2006) have found niches in the garden and nursery circles. This encyclopedia builds on the foundations of the *Hardy* and *Warm Climate* books, with more than 3,500 photographs of species and cultivars in 380 genera, with an emphasis on the best new introductions of the past ten to 15 years.

The garden and nursery worlds have changed dramatically in that time. Independent garden centers have waned, while Home Depot, Lowe's, Wal-Mart, and other mega-chains command greater percentages of green good sales. Be advised that the mass merchandisers are actively pursuing new plants to entice customers. Reflecting these advances are the increases in plant patents, which allow the owner to control the licensing of the product. In 1996 (66 years after the Plant Patent Act was instituted), approximately 10,000 plant patents were granted; in 2010, the number was over 21,000. This increase reflects the desire of breeders and introducers to protect their intellectual property. Also, many plants are not patented, but introduced for the greater good. The new plant tsunami literally swamps horticulturists' and gardeners' will and ability to stay current.

The rush to market is based on competition among breeders and introducers who have similar plants. The financial advantage is often weighted toward the first mover. Testing and trialing for many woody plants are minimal, and marketing supersedes the reality of performance. In this tome, I provide the best assessment possible based on testing data, research reports, performance in nurseries and gardens, and evaluations at our breeding company in Watkinsville, Georgia, Plant Introductions, Inc. (www.plantintroductions.com).

Take variegated leaf cultivars of *Abelia* ×*grandiflora*, now numbering about 17. Many are unstable, producing green, albino, and other shoot permutations not typical of the original cultivars. I have bred, evaluated, tested, trialed, selected, grown, and introduced abelias, and 'Hopleys' ('Aghop'), rebranded Twist of Lime™, has been one of the most stable, consistently true to type. Does this mean that someone else could have a different experience? Absolutely!

Cross-referencing the *Hydrangea*

Lagerstroemia Cherry Dazzle®, a superior red-flowered, genetically compact selection from the author's breeding program.

paniculata cultivar trials at the Royal Horticultural Society (www.rhs.org.uk) with my Georgia evaluations reflects dichotomies of results. For example, *RHS Trials Bulletin* 23 (December 2008) evaluated more than half of the more than 80 known cultivars. Best (three stars) were 'Big Ben' (lousy in Georgia), 'Dolly' (lousy in Georgia), 'Kyushu' (lousy in Georgia), Limelight™ (very good in Georgia), Pinky Winky™ (poor in Georgia), and so forth. The take-home lesson: biology is shades of gray, and dogmatic acceptance of anyone's results is foolish. Use these data as guides to the superior introductions.

"Show me your garden and I shall tell you what you are." This Alfred Austin quote captures Bonnie's and my love of garden-making. As an introduction to the *Warm Climate* book, I textually and photographically walked the reader through our then 23-year-old garden, and many readers commented positively about "seeing" it.

Unfortunately, the home and garden in the 2002 book are no more, as we sold and moved to Chapel Hill, North Carolina, for medical reasons, to care for our youngest daughter, Suzanne. After existing in an apartment for six months (no garden), we decided to purchase a home, develop a garden, and live a normal life. The landscape (initially with bargain-basement butterflybushes, abelias, and Indian hawthorns—all eliminated) was transformed into a garden with color, fragrance, diversity, and seasonality. In part, it was also a test site for many new plants from our breeding program and those of colleagues.

The neighbors noticed, commented, queried about the roses (Knock Out®), dwarf crapemyrtles (Razzle Dazzle® series), and lantanas (Chapel Hill series), and others. With delight, I watched Knock Out® move around the cul-de-sac and throughout the neighborhood.

This garden was spiritually and psychologically essential to Bonnie's, my, and Susy's well-being. Susy, who carried the gene for cystic fibrosis, was blessed to have two double-lung transplants at UNC-CH and live a rich, full, vibrant, and meaningful life. We lost our beloved Susy to chronic rejection in January 2008.

Books are written on dealing with grief, but Bonnie and I find inner peace with each other and in the garden. Bonnie stated it best—there is joy in nurturing and loving living things to their greatest genetic potential. We sold our place in Chapel Hill and returned to Athens, where in 2009 we purchased a new home on an acre and started the garden journey anew. Realizing that planting space was being rapidly consumed, we pur-

Hydrangea macrophylla hybrid selections at Plant Introductions, Inc.

chased the contiguous lot as well. It was choked with Chinese privet (*Ligustrum sinense*), kudzu (*Pueraria montana* var. *lobata*), and muscadine (*Vitis rotundifolia*), all quickly cleared; a specimen white oak (*Quercus alba*), a 50-ft.-high, four-trunked black tupelo (*Nyssa sylvatica*), and flowering dogwood (*Cornus florida*) were preserved. We are enjoying pencil farming this and the home site, dreaming about what may metamorphosize.

In autumn 2010, we planted a sinuous shrub border that effectively screens the new lot from the street. Neighbors commented and asked about the identity of the plants. I mentioned that 14 different viburnums were utilized. They were mystified for, in the South, "viburnum" simply does not resonate. Hopefully, they will enjoy and learn as the border matures.

Plant Introductions, Inc., continues to develop. My two partners are Jeff

Lantana camara 'Chapel Hill Yellow' in production; note flower quantity.

Knock Out® roses planted over a French drain between drive and neighbor's fence, four years after planting: Blushing Knock Out®, 'Carefree Sunshine', and Knock Out®, the original red. Chapel Hill, North Carolina.

Chapel Hill garden border, first year planted, August 2004.

Chapel Hill garden border, four years later, July 2008.

Plant Introductions, Inc., before clean-up of the pig farm.

Beasley of Transplant Nursery in Lavonia, Georgia, and Mark Griffith, Griffith Propagation Nursery, also in Watkinsville. Together we bring a total of 80 years' experience to the venture—breeding, evaluating, propagating, producing, and marketing new woody (and a few herbaceous) garden plants. Most new introductions are presented in this work. We started with a dream, planned and strategized, leased/purchased a dilapidated pig (yes) farm, cleaned (spit-polished), built growing and greenhouse facilities, and four years later have 40 plants in various stages of evaluation. Our breeder, Josh Kardos, Ph.D., a University of Georgia horticulture graduate, is the epicenter of the company.

As you, the reader, peruse the book, please take special note of genera emphasized in PII's breeding:

Lantana camara 'Chapel Hill Yellow' growing between 'Pink Crush' and 'Orange Crush', late September 2008; note quantity of flowers on 'Chapel Hill Yellow', a self-sown seedling in Susy's garden, now patented, with 30 percent of royalties donated to UNC-CH. Plant Introductions, Inc., has utilized this selection in breeding for improved flower colors, hardiness, superior foliage, and lower growth habit; 'Chapel Hill Gold', 'Sunny Side Up', 'Apricot Sunrise', and 'Sunset Orange' are the current introductions.

1849 Heather Lane, new home and garden.

Abelia, *Berberis*, *Buddleia*, *Clethra*, *Cryptomeria*, *Distylium*, *Gardenia*, *Hydrangea*, *Hypericum*, *Illicium*, *Lagerstroemia*, *Lantana*, *Loropetalum*, *Punica*, *Quercus*, *Ulmus*, and *Viburnum*. The ultimate goal is to breed superior ornamental plants that perform as promised (Promised Performance™) for growers, retailers, and gardeners.

May the book provide inspiration and education, and guide you to the best of the new (and perpetually reliable) woody garden plants.

MICHAEL A. DIRR, PH.D.
Oconee County, Georgia

Red-flowered *Lagerstroemia* seedlings in the evaluation phase at Plant Introductions, Inc. Red flowers are difficult to consistently breed; PII has developed a protocol to breed primarily *red* flowers.

Lagerstroemia hybrid seedling selections at Plant Introductions, Inc.

A–Z
Encyclopedia
of Trees and
Shrubs

Abelia

abelia

Many gardeners yawn when *Abelia* is mentioned, but for 15 years I have been evaluating and breeding this taxonomically topsy-turvy genus and grow fonder each year. A recent study at Kew Gardens, England, separates the 30 species into four genera, a move that will confuse even more gardeners. New cultivars, especially from *Abelia* ×*grandiflora* have proliferated,

with over 30 in the literature. The best of these are described and shown herein along with seven additional species.

Abelias require minimal care and make superb garden companions in containers, borders, groupings, masses, and hedges. In Urbana, Illinois, *Abelia* ×*grandiflora* was a half-hardy shrub but regrew and flowered every summer into fall. In the South, I observed a 70-year-old specimen, 18

ft. by 20 ft.! To be sure, abelias will never replace hydrangeas but have a place in every garden. May one of the following taxa grace your garden.

Abelia chinensis

Chinese abelia

The Chinese abelia is a great biological butterfly magnet. In the Dirr garden (zone 7), flowers open in June, continuing until frost. Small white fragrant flowers are borne in rounded panicles

Abelia chinensis, Chinese abelia

Abelia chinensis

Abelia floribunda, Mexican abelia

on the new growth of the season. The ¾- to 1½-in.-long, lustrous dark green leaves provide background to the flowers. Habit is rounded, spreading, loose. Prospers in moist, acid, well-drained soil. Full sun to half shade. Makes a great shrub border plant combined with butterflybushes and lantana. Prune in late winter, and by June and July, flowering is in high gear. A parent of many of the new hybrids, imparting the essential attribute of continuous flowering. Grows 5 to 7 ft. high and wide. Zones (5)6 to 9. China.

Abelia floribunda
Mexican abelia

The most beautiful of all abelias, especially when the trumpet-shaped flowers, 1½ to 2 in. long, ¾ to 1 in. wide at mouth, open cerise-red from cherry-red buds. Flowers open in June (as I observed them), but California literature cites January and summer. The corolla interior is cerise-red to white. Flowers dangle from the stems like small ornaments. The beautiful evergreen leaves, lustrous dark green, ½ to 1½ in. long, are the perfect contrast to the flowers. First observed in 1996, and I thought, Wow, what a breeding partner! Unfortunately, the species is difficult to culture in the Southeast and resisted hybridizing with other abelias. In California, 20°F caused severe damage. Possibly a conservatory plant, or move to California, which actually might be worth it. Grows 5 to 8 (to 10) ft. tall. Zones 9 and 10. California, Mexico.

Abelia ×grandiflora
glossy abelia

No other flowering evergreen (to deciduous) shrub displays the resiliency of this hybrid species (*Abelia chinensis* × *A. uniflora*). Originated in Italy before 1866 and in cultivation for more than a century, it is still one of the most popular shrubs for gardens.

White, flushed pink, ¾- to 1-in.-long tubular flowers open on new growth from May to frost. Individual flowers do not overwhelm, but a shrub in full flower is quite effective. The five sepals that subtend the flower age gracefully from green to rose-purple and literally smother the foliage canopy by late summer. Habit is rounded to spreading, densely foliated with ½- to 1½-in.-long lustrous dark green leaves that color bronze-red-purple in cold weather. Wonderfully serviceable shrub that prospers in sun and shade and in acid, well-drained soil. Recent years of drought and heat in Athens showed *A. ×grandiflora* to be one of the most durable shrubs. Effective as border plant, mass, hedge, and butterfly attractant. One of my favorite shrubs. Many new introductions from the University of Georgia and Plant Introductions, Inc. (www.plantintroductions.com) are described. Grows 3 to 6 ft. high and wide; plants to 8 ft. occur; 18 ft. by 20 ft. at Keith Arboretum, Chapel Hill, North Carolina. Zones 6 to 9.

CULTIVARS AND VARIETIES

'Canyon Creek' sports bronze new growth, maturing to gold and yellow, and turning coppery pink to rose in cold weather. It is striking in spring when all colors are present but becomes green in the heat of summer if not watered and fertilized. Produces large, 2-in.-long, fragrant, pink flowers.

Confetti™ ('Conti') is a compact form to 2½ ft. high, 3 ft. wide, with cream-margined leaves that turn rose in winter; flowers (sparse) are white. Not a particularly vigorous plant. Will revert to green.

'Edward Goucher', a hybrid between *Abelia ×grandiflora* and *A. parvifolia* (*A. schumannii*), produces lavender-pink flowers and is less cold hardy than *A. ×grandiflora*. Flowers open earlier than those of *A. ×grandiflora*. Grows 4 to 5 ft. high and wide.

'Francis Mason' produces copper-

MORE ▶

Abelia ×grandiflora, glossy abelia

Abelia ×*grandiflora*

Abelia ×*grandiflora*

Abelia ×*grandiflora* 'Canyon Creek'

Abelia ×*grandiflora* 'Canyon Creek'

Abelia ×*grandiflora* Confetti™

Abelia 'Edward Goucher'

Abelia ×*grandiflora* 'Francis Mason'

Abelia ×*grandiflora* Golden Fleece™

Abelia ×grandiflora CONTINUED

colored new shoots that mature yellow to yellow-green, fading to green in hot climates, and pink to white flowers. Grows 5 to 7 ft. high. Originated in the 1950s at Mason's Nurseries, New Zealand. About the first variegated selection.

Golden Fleece™ ('PIIAB-I') has beautiful, butterscotch-yellow emerging leaves that turn yellow, then green. Leaves do not bleach (turn white) in heat of zone 7. Abundant early white flowers and pink sepals cover the foliage. A vigorous grower, 3 to 6 ft. high and wide, from Plant Introductions, Inc.

'Kaleidoscope' has leaves with a wide, bright yellow to gold margin and irregular green center that turn rose to rose-red in cold weather. Excellent heat and sun tolerance in zone 7. Flowers are primarily white.

'Little Richard' (best), 'John Creech'

(middle), and 'Sherwoodii' (worst) are compact forms, 3 to 4 ft. high or less; I have observed reversion shoots on all.

Mardi Gras™ is a compact form with silvery to cream-margined, gray-green-centered leaves that turn a rose color in cold weather. New stem growth is dark pink. Flowers are pink in bud, opening pink and fragrant. Grows 2 to 3 ft. high and 4 to 5 ft. wide.

'Rose Creek' is the first compact form from the Georgia breeding program. Grows 2 to 3 ft. high and wide, with broad-ovate lustrous dark green leaves and copious fragrant white flowers and rose-pink sepals.

Twist of Lime™ ('Hopleys', 'Aghop') is a branch sport of 'Francis Mason' with gold-margined, green-centered leaves. Flowers are pink-white. Grows 3 to 4 ft. high and 5 to 7 ft. wide. Among the most stable of all variegated leaf types. Many of the 16 cur-

rent selections for yellow-, white-, and gold-margined leaves revert to green and are not worthy. See my *Manual of Woody Landscape Plants* (2009) for specifics.

Abelia macrotera

A most unusual species, with thickish, shiny dark green leaves that turn burgundy-maroon in winter. Leaves are semi-evergreen in Athens. Youthful outline is rather wild, with spreading-arching branches, but ultimate shape is unknown. Flowers, rose-lavender with an orange throat, 1½ in. long, no fragrance, develop on new growth, June into late summer. Flowers are not as prolifically produced as those of *Abelia chinensis*, *A. ×grandiflora*, and *A. parvifolia*. Outplanted in the Georgia trials since 2007, it has survived heat, drought, and cold (13°F). Appears well-drained soil, full sun to

MORE ▶

Abelia ×grandiflora 'Kaleidoscope'

Abelia ×grandiflora Mardi Gras™

Abelia ×grandiflora 'Rose Creek'

Abelia ×grandiflora Twist of Lime™

Abelia macrotera CONTINUED

partial shade, suit it best. Potential for breeding and, indeed, Plant Introductions, Inc., has a beautiful hybrid that develops bronze-purple winter foliage on a compact framework. Estimate the species will grow 3 to 5 ft. high and wide. Zones 6 to 8? Collected by Maurice Foster near Boaxing, China. Given to Plant Introductions, Inc., by British nurseryman Peter Catt.

Abelia mosanensis
Korean abelia

My great enthusiasm for this species is grounded in its reported –30°F cold hardiness. First witnessed the red-budded, opening white, fragrant flowers at the JC Raulston Arboretum (Raleigh, North Carolina) in April. Such a sensual pleasure. Flowers open with the emerging matte-green leaves, then the plant settles into obscurity.

Fully deciduous in our Georgia trials and does not prosper in zone 7 heat. Requires full sun. Flowers on old wood, so prune after flowering. Grows 6 to 10 ft. high, less in spread. A four-year-old plant was 7 ft. by 5 ft. in our trials. Tatty and disheveled by mid to late summer. Best in zones 3 to 6. Korea.

CULTIVARS AND VARIETIES

'Bridal Bouquet' is, based on my observations, nothing more than a marketing name for the species.

Abelia parvifolia
  syn. *Abelia schumannii*

Certainly not an everyday garden species; however, the lilac-pink flowers of May twinkle into late summer–autumn. The leaves, lustrous dark green, are smaller (½ to 1 in.) than those of *Abelia ×grandiflora*. Habit is somewhat loose and open but gracefully elegant.

Sepals are in twos (sometimes more), while those of *A. ×grandiflora* are typically in fives. Foliage varies from evergreen to semi-evergreen in zone 7 with approximately 35 percent leaf retention into March. Leaves may turn bronze-purple in cold weather. Tolerates heat and drought. Requires full sun for best flowering. Disease- and insect-resistant. A sleeper, worthy of sanctuary in most gardens. Prune to tidy. Flowers on new growth. Largely unassailable. Grows 6 to 10 ft. high and wide. Grew 7 ft. by 8 ft. in six years in Georgia trials. Zones 6 and 7. Western China.

Abelia serrata

A smallish shrub with white, orange-throated flowers. Wonderful specimen, 5 ft. by 7 ft., in full flower in late April at Keith Arboretum, Chapel Hill, North Carolina. Worth a look by gardeners

Abelia macrotera

Abelia mosanensis, Korean abelia

Abelia parvifolia

and breeders. Flowers are fleeting.
Zones 6 and 7. Japan.

Abelia spathulata

I first sighted this species at Hillier
in 1999. The Hillier plant was beautiful, broad-rounded, 6 ft. by 8 ft., with
scattered white, marked with yellow

MORE ▶

Abelia serrata

Abelia parvifolia

Abelia serrata

Abelia spathulata

Abelia spathulata

Abelia spathulata CONTINUED
flowers in May. Leaves, mid-green, have a purple rim around the margin and are slightly toothed. Has suffered in the heat of Athens, Georgia. Zone 6, perhaps better on West Coast. Japan.

Abeliophyllum distichum
Korean abelialeaf, white forsythia
Many years past, in mid March, I would bundle up my Illinois students and take them south to Bernheim Arboretum, in Clermont, Kentucky, and Cave Hill Cemetery, in Louisville, Kentucky. Consistently, we would find Korean abelialeaf in full white flower, long before true forsythia ever considered thrusting its yellow head from the buds. Students would ask its identity and then invariably add, "Gosh, it's ugly." True, overgrown specimens and mass plantings of Korean abelialeaf tend to assume the appearance of an

old brush pile. The habit is rounded with arching branches. The white or faintly pink-tinged, four-petaled, fragrant flowers open before the leaves. The 2- to 3½-in.-long, medium to dark green leaves offer no fall color. Plants are easily transplanted and grown. Suitable for massing in full sun. Might be used in a winter-garden border with hellebores, witchhazels, winterhazels, winter honeysuckle, and bulbs. Grows 3 to 5 ft. high, 3 to 4 ft. wide or more. Zones (4)5 to 8. Korea.
CULTIVARS AND VARIETIES
Roseum Group is a taxonomic designation that includes forms with pink flowers. Have observed several times, rather delicate soft pink, not overwhelming.

Abies
fir
In the grand scheme of everyday landscaping, firs are probably utilized less

than any other needle evergreens. Their sensitivity to extremes of soil and climate translates to mediocre performance. Most require cool climates, but a few exceptions, like *Abies firma*, are known. Where adaptable, they are noble, formal, elegant, aesthetic components in the landscape. Many produce beautifully colored cones. Unfortunately, cones (scales) shatter at maturity and do not persist. Numerous cultivars have been selected for growth habit and needle colors. *Conifers for Gardens* (2007) by Richard Bitner presents the newer selections. During sabbatical at Hillier Arboretum, many new (to me) firs entered my vocabulary. *Abies bornmuelleriana* (now *A. nordmanniana* subsp. *equitrojanii*), *A. borisii-regis*, *A. delavayi*, and for the South, *A. nebrodensis* (from Sicily) and *A. vejarii* (from Mexico) are worth considering.

Abeliophyllum distichum, Korean abelialeaf

Abeliophyllum distichum

Abeliophyllum distichum Roseum Group

Abies balsamea

balsam fir

A symmetrically pyramidal tree, balsam fir has ½- to 1-in.-long, lustrous dark green needles, each with two silver bands on the underside, and the fragrant Christmas-tree scent when bruised. The 2- to 4-in.-long cones are dark violet when young, turning gray-brown and resinous with maturity. The species requires well-drained, moist, acid soils and some protection from desiccating winds. Use for Christmas tree production, as a specimen, or in groupings. Grows 45 to 75 ft. high, 20 to 25 ft. wide. The balsam woolly adelgid has wreaked havoc on the species throughout its native range. Zones 3 to 5(6). Labrador to Alberta, south to Pennsylvania.

CULTIVARS AND VARIETIES
Hudsonia Group (f. *hudsonia*) is a cute, diminutive, 1- to 2-ft.-high, broad mound with numerous short branches, needles radially arranged, dark green above, silvery below, about ½ in. long.

Abies cilicica

Cilician fir

Seldom offered in U.S. commerce and limitedly represented in arboreta, yet a noble stand at Spring Grove, Cincinnati, Ohio, has prospered and even produced seedlings in the neighboring woods. Several trees are now 70 ft. high with narrow-columnar-pyramidal outlines. From a distance, the ¾- to 1¼-in.-long needles are gray-green compared to the dark green of most fir species. Cones are 6 to 10 in. long, 2 to 2½ in. wide, cylindrical and reddish brown. In the wild, grows in association with cedar-of-Lebanon on calcareous, limestone-based rocky soils in areas of hot, dry summers and mild, rainy winters. Estimate 30 to 50 ft. by 8 to 15 ft. in 20 to 30 years. Zones 5 and 6(7). Southern Turkey, northwest Syria, Lebanon.

MORE ▶

Abies balsamea, balsam fir

Abies balsamea Hudsonia Group

23

Abies cilicica, Cilician fir

Abies concolor 'Candicans'

Abies concolor
white fir

No doubt, this is one of the most adaptable and beautiful firs for landscape work, particularly in the Northeast and Midwest. Under the hot, dry conditions of the Midwest and East, white fir is the most prosperous fir for general use. The habit is strongly spire-like to narrow-conical, with tiered branches. The 1½- to 2½-in.-long needles vary from green to blue-green to almost silver-blue. In the wilds of Arizona, the silver-blue forms are mixed with the green types. Grows 30 to 50 ft. high, 15 to 20 ft. wide; can grow to 100 ft. or more. Zones 3 to 7. Western United States.

CULTIVARS AND VARIETIES
'Blue Cloak', 'Candicans', and 'Violacea' have silver-blue needles of great beauty, especially when the new growth emerges.

Abies concolor, white fir, silver-blue form

Abies firma
Momi fir

Firs and heat are akin to cats and dogs; they simply do not socialize well. However, the Momi fir is succeeding in Athens, Georgia, and Mobile, Alabama. Habit is pyramidal-conical in youth and maturity. The lustrous dark green needles are sharply notched at their ends. Cones are 3½ to 5 in. long, 1½ to 2 in. wide, and brown at maturity. Slight foliage discoloration may result from the winter sun. A plant in the Dirr garden, sited on the north side of deciduous woods, has prospered. Best performance occurs in moist, well-drained, acid soils. Slow to initiate strong growth—kind of stares at the gardener for several years, then decides to leap. In zone 7, some trees display significant vigor; others creep along. Worthy specimen fir and, to my knowledge, the only viable candidate for the South. Grows 40 to 50 ft. high, 10 to 15 ft. wide. Observed 70-ft.-high specimens at Longwood Gardens, Kennett Square, Pennsylvania. Zones 6 to 9. Japan.

Abies fraseri
Fraser fir

Mentioned here because of its similarity to *Abies balsamea* and its importance as a Christmas tree. The actual differences between this species

MORE ▶

Abies concolor 'Blue Cloak'

Abies firma

Abies firma, Momi fir

Abies fraseri, Fraser fir

Abies fraseri CONTINUED

and *A. balsamea* are minimal, and it could be considered a southern extension. Bracts extend beyond the cone scales, while those of *A. balsamea* are not visible. Common along the Blue Ridge Parkway in North Carolina. Grows 30 to 40 ft. high, 20 to 25 ft. wide. Zones 4 to 7. Mountains of West Virginia, North Carolina, and Tennessee.

Abies homolepis
Nikko fir

The few Nikko firs I have observed were quite handsome specimens. They are typically spire-like and conical in habit. Needles are glossy dark green with two white bands on the lower surface. Beautiful 20-ft.-tall trees at Shadow Nursery in Winchester, Tennessee. Slow-growing but one of the handsomest firs in youth.

Grows 30 to 50 ft. high in cultivation; can grow 100 to 130 ft. high in its native habitat. Zones 4 to 6. Japan.

Abies koreana
Korean fir

Lustrous dark green, ½- to ¾-in.-long needles, two whitish bands below, densely set along the branches, create a superb nesting site for rich violet-purple to blue-purple, 2- to 3-in.-

Abies fraseri

Abies koreana, Korean fir

Abies koreana

Abies homolepis, Nikko fir

Abies koreana 'Silberlocke'

26

long, 1-in.-wide cones. Cones may develop on young trees in the 3- to 5-ft. height range. Habit is that of a stout, dense pyramid. Appears slightly more heat-tolerant than many firs but still best in cold climates. Eye-catching as a specimen, accent, or in a grouping. Grows 15 to 30 ft. high, half or less that in width. Zones (4)5 and 6. Korea.

CULTIVARS AND VARIETIES
Many, but 'Silberlocke' ('Horstmann's Silberlocke'), the needles curving upward displaying the bright silver-white lower surface, is quite common. Have observed as a sprawling, irregularly branched shrub and a 30-ft.-high, perfectly shaped pyramid. May set abundant cones.

Abies lasiocarpa
Rocky Mountain fir
A narrow, conical, slender outline with branches draping the ground as observed in Olympic National Park. Hiking the ridgeline to Dege Peak (7,000 ft.), trees dotted the slopes, narrow in stature to shed the heavy snow. Needles, bluish green with silver-gray bands below, 1 to 1½ in. long, crowded and directed forward and upward along the stem. Dark purple

cones, 2 to 4 in. long, are oblong-cylindric in shape. Beautiful in its native state. Not easily adapted to culture in eastern United States. National champion is 130 ft. by 26 ft. Zones 5 and 6. Alaska to Oregon, Utah and northern New Mexico.

CULTIVARS AND VARIETIES
Variety *arizonica*, cork fir, is smaller, forming a blue-green pyramid that is amenable to culture in the East and Midwest.

Abies nordmanniana
Nordmann fir
A magnificent fir. At its best, this species forms a dense, uniform pyramid of lustrous black-green needles. May be more adaptable than *Abies balsamea* and *A. fraseri* to general landscape conditions. Grows 40 to 60 ft. high in cultivation; can reach 200 ft. in the wild. Zones 4 to 6. Caucasus, Asia Minor.

CULTIVARS AND VARIETIES
'Golden Spreader' is a genuine conversation piece with striking golden yellow needles turning burnished gold in winter. Best in cooler climates. Forms a haystack outline, 3 to 5 ft. high and wide.

Abies nordmanniana, Nordmann fir

Abies nordmanniana

Abies lasiocarpa, Rocky Mountain fir

Abies nordmanniana 'Golden Spreader'

27

Abies pinsapo
Spanish fir

The rigid, ½-in.-long, green to blue needles of this species radiate from the branches in bottlebrush fashion. One of two firs with this radiating needle disposition; the other is *Abies cephalonica*. The habit is broad pyramidal with stiff secondary branches extending outward and upward at the tips. More open than most firs discussed herein. Cones, 4 to 6 in. long, are purplish brown when young. Observed on East and West Coasts performing well. Considered one of the best species for limestone (high pH soils). Usually 20 to 30 (to 40) ft. at landscape maturity in United States. Zones 6 and 7. Mountains of southern Spain.

CULTIVARS AND VARIETIES
'Glauca', with bluish gray needles, appears more common than the species in cultivation.

Abies veitchii
Veitch fir

Another handsome dark green species that has performed reasonably well in the Midwest. The dark green needles average 1 in. long and have two silver-white bands on the underside. Cones are 2 to 3 in. long, bluish purple in youth, the tips of the bracts exserted. Considered more urban-tolerant. Grows 50 to 75 ft. high, 25 to 30 ft. wide. Zones 3 to 6. Japan.

Abutilon pictum
flowering maple, Chinese bell flower, Chinese lantern

Almost better known for container culture and bedding schemes, particularly in European gardens, than as a flowering shrub in the United States. Approximately 150 species of trees, shrubs, and herbaceous perennials native to tropical and subtropical regions. Typically a dieback shrub that rejuvenates from the roots with accelerated growth and flowers in summer. Leaves are maple-like, typically three-lobed, yellow-green, and assume a slightly reflexed, graceful posture. The flowers develop from the leaf axils and are semi-pendulous, bell-shaped, 2 in. long, with crepe-papery petals. Colors of the numerous cultivars are kaleidoscopic, from white and yellow to pink, orange, and red, opening from sum-

Abies pinsapo 'Glauca'

Abies pinsapo 'Glauca'

Abies veitchii underside of needles

Abies veitchii, Veitch fir

mer until frost. Adaptable, but requires well-drained soil. Do not overfertilize, as this results in rampant vegetative growth at the expense of flower production. About four to six hours of sun suit plants best, yet they flower reasonably in partial shade. Wonderful plant for summer flowers. Useful as a filler in borders and containers.

Abutilon vitifolium

Abutilon megapotamicum, trailing abutilon

Abutilon pictum 'Variegatum'

Foliage on the variegated types, like 'Thompsonii' (yellow-streaked and -flecked), adds sparkle. Expect 3 to 4 ft. of growth in zone 7, more in warmer areas. Zones 8 to 11. Brazil.

The related species *Abutilon megapotamicum*, trailing abutilon, is a finely branched shrub with leaves to 3 in. long, rarely lobed, and pendulous, 1-in.-long, red flowers (red calyx, yellow petals, and purple anthers) on 1- to 2-in.-long, red stalks. Refined and delicate in flower. Fine container or bedding plant. Zones 8 and 9. Brazil.
CULTIVARS AND VARIETIES
'Variegatum' has mottled yellow leaves and is relatively common in commerce.

Abutilon vitifolium

A much larger shrub (small tree) than *Abutilon pictum*, *A. vitifolium* has gray-green leaves. Flowers are large, saucer-shaped, pale to deep lavender-mauve in late spring into summer. Grows 10 to 15 ft. high. Zones 9 and 10 on West Coast. Chile.
CULTIVARS AND VARIETIES
'Album' has white flowers, as does 'Tennant's White'.

Acacia dealbata
silver wattle, mimosa
I have chased *Acacia* species throughout my travels and have yet to even partially understand this diverse genus, with estimates of 700 to 1,200 species. Silver wattle is one of the more common species in English gardens and also one of the hardiest (to 14°F). Typically an evergreen tree, loose and architectural in habit, with bipinnate leaves ranging from blue-green to medium green. Each leaf is 3 to 5 in. long, with eight to 20 pinnae (branches), each with 20 to 40 pairs of ⅙-in.-long, 1/24-in.-wide leaves. Fragrant, ball-shaped clusters of yellow flowers are borne in large racemes in late winter to early spring. Outside the library window at the Hillier Arboretum, England, a large *Acacia dealbata* provided great botanical interest during my sabbatical. Green and reticent upon my arrival in February, it blossomed in March and April, settling down by May, retreating to green. Provide well-drained, acid soil in sun or partial shade. Flowers develop from previous season's wood, so prune

MORE ▶

Abutilon vitifolium 'Tennant's White'

29

Acacia dealbata CONTINUED

after flowering. Reliable only in warmer West Coast gardens and south Florida, otherwise a conservatory plant. Grows 20 to 30 ft. high, although listed to 100 ft. Zones 8 to 10(11). Tasmania, Australia.

Acca sellowiana
pineapple guava

This handsome gray-leaved evergreen shrub is a common element in coastal southeastern and Florida landscapes. Rounded and shrubby in outline but can be grown as a small tree. The broad, ovate, 1- to 3-in.-long leaves are reminiscent of juvenile *Eucalyptus* foliage, except whitish-felted below. Their upper surfaces are dark green. The flowers are like fuchsias, with four reflexed sepals, four petals red in center and whitish at margins, stamens numerous, ¾ to 1 in. long and rich crimson. Flowers in May and June. Fruit are 1- to 3-in.-long, egg-shaped berries, green, tinged red, turning yellow. Edible with taste likened to pineapple with overtones of spearmint. Full sun to partial shade in light, loamy soil. Tolerates salt spray. Prune after flowering. Use for foliage effect as a screen, hedge, mass, or cut-back shrub. Grows 10 to 15 ft. high, 10 ft. wide. Zones (7)8 to 10(11). Southern Brazil and Uruguay.

CULTIVARS AND VARIETIES
'Variegata' has pretty cream-white-margined leaves, the center more gray-green; slower growing than the species.

Acer buergerianum
trident maple

Small, dapper, handsomely clothed trees are a rarity, and trident maple qualifies as one of the best. The habit is oval to rounded. The pest-free, lustrous dark green, 1½- to 3½-in.-wide leaves are three-lobed (hence, trident). They change to rich yellow and red in fall. Bark on old trunks is quite striking, coloring gray, orange, and brown and developing an exfoliating, platy, scaly character. This species withstands drought and infertile soils and displays excellent cold and heat tolerance. Unlike many maples, does not develop leaf scorch under drought stress. A fine choice for the small residential landscape, as a street tree, or under utility wires. Many dwarf and variegated types are known. Grows 25 to 35 ft. high, 15 to 25 ft. wide. Zones 5 to 8(9). China.

CULTIVARS AND VARIETIES
'Angyo Weeping', a promising new introduction from Japan, has gracefully arching branches.

MORE ▶

Acacia dealbata, silver wattle

Acacia dealbata

Acacia dealbata

Acca sellowiana, pineapple guava

Acca sellowiana

Acca sellowiana

Acca sellowiana 'Variegata'

Acer buergerianum, trident maple

Acer buergerianum 'Angyo Weeping' fall color

Acer buergerianum CONTINUED

'Mino-yatsubusa' is a cute, graceful, dwarfish form; leaves have long slender lobes that extend to narrow apices. Observed 4-ft. and 10-ft. trees; usually rounded in outline.

Raising Blaze™ ('EOAB-1') has red new growth, brilliant orange to red fall color, superior heat tolerance, and reduced fruit set.

Acer campestre
hedge maple

The common name is appropriately derived from the use of this species for hedging purposes, especially in Europe, where it occurs naturally in the famed hedgerows along highways. As a medium-sized lawn tree, it has few rivals. The habit is rounded and dense. The dark green leaves, 2 to 4 in. long and wide, are composed of five rounded lobes. Leaves usually die off late in fall but on occasion turn yellow. Displays excellent tolerance to drought and heat. Good for use along streets, in lawns and parks, and fashioned into a hedge. Grows 25 to 35 ft. high and wide; can reach 75 ft. high. Zones 4 to 7, 8 and 9 on West Coast. Europe, Near East, Africa.
CULTIVARS AND VARIETIES
'Carnival' develops green, pink, and

Acer buergerianum Raising Blaze™

Acer buergerianum 'Mino-yatsubusa'

Acer campestre

Acer campestre, hedge maple

Acer campestre fall color

white leaves that age to green with a white margin; slow-growing and will revert.

Metro Gold® ('Panacek') develops an upright, tightly branched, pyramidal habit. Not as fruit-ful as Queen Elizabeth™. Dark green foliage turns bright yellow in autumn; 35 ft. by 20 ft.

'Nanum' ('Compactum') is dense, multi-stemmed, of compact habit, typically broader than high. Usually grafted on a standard, forming a small lollipop tree. Listed as a 4- to 6-ft. shrub, but I've observed a specimen that was 12 ft. by 15 ft.

Queen Elizabeth™ ('Evelyn') is more vigorous than the species. Its branches angle at 45°. The dark green leaves are larger than those of the species and develop yellowish fall color. Matures to a medium-sized tree with a flat top and rounded outline. Sets abundant fruit that turn brown in late summer.

'Royal Ruby' has red-purple new leaves that fade to green. Others like 'Red Shine' and Sparkling Burgundy® are similar.

Acer carpinifolium
hornbeam maple
A favorite of the author; smallish, refined, gracefully vase-shaped in youth, with dark green leaves resembling hornbeam, *Carpinus*, in shape and venation. Leaves turn rich gold to brown in autumn, similar to color of American beech leaves. Pretty understory and edge-of-woods tree; acid, well-drained soil suits it best. Tolerates moderate shade to full sun but not heat: 90 days of 90°F in summer 2010 ruined the expression of greatness. Grows 20 to 25 ft. high, slightly wider. Zones (4)5 to 7. Japan.

Acer campestre 'Nanum'

Acer campestre 'Carnival'

Acer carpinifolium fall color

Acer carpinifolium, hornbeam maple

Acer circinatum

Oregon vine maple

In my academic youth, while teaching/researching at the University of Illinois, Urbana, I accumulated myriad trees and shrubs for testing. This West Coast species was in my purview, secured, planted, observed, and died in less than a year. Not exactly an uplifting experience for a young assistant professor. Subsequent trips to the Pacific Northwest introduced me to the species contentedly thriving in the shade of Douglas-fir, bigleaf maple, western arborvitae. The lesson learned: some species are best left at home! Almost always shrubby, low-branched, multi-stemmed in habit. Leaves are seven- to nine- (occasionally five- to 11-) lobed, 3 to 5 in. long and wide, medium green, turning yellow, orange, and red in fall. The new spring growth is reddish tinged.

Typically found in moist woods, along stream banks, and the dry Oregon summers do not adversely affect performance. In August, plants are already showing fall color impulses. Best in shady border, naturalizing situation, and grouping. Observed 20-ft.-high plant in the Hoh Rain Forest, Washington; specimen at Hillier was 20 ft. by 25 ft.; national champion is 64 ft. by 37 ft. Zones 6 to 8 on West Coast. British Columbia to northern California.

CULTIVARS AND VARIETIES
Several smallish selections, like 'Monroe', with deeply cut leaves and good orange-red fall color. May grow 10 ft. high, less in spread.

Pacific Purple® ('JFS-Purple') has new growth bronze over green and intensifies to deep purple, the colors deeper in full sun; orange-bronze fall color. J. Frank Schmidt & Son Nursery, Boring, Oregon, introduction; 12 ft. high and wide.

Acer cissifolium subsp. henryi

Rare, small-statured maple with upright-oval habit, eventually rounded at maturity. Emerging leaves are red to purple, eventually medium green, then yellow-orange-red in fall. Leaves are trifoliate, each leaflet toothed, unlike *Acer cissifolium*, which has essentially entire leaflets. Flowers, yellow-green, are borne in 2- to 4-in.-long racemes with the unfolding leaves. Adapted to extremes of soil and climate except permanently wet. Withstood −24°F in Louisville, Kentucky, area while *A. cissifolium* was killed to the main trunk. Worthy maple for smaller properties. Movement toward selection of superior types by J. Frank Schmidt & Son; I observed a rich red-

Acer circinatum

Acer circinatum, Oregon vine maple

Acer cissifolium subsp. *henryi* new growth

purple foliage selection that is close to release. Grows 20 to 30 ft. high and wide. Zones (4)5 to 7, 8 on West Coast.

Acer griseum
paperbark maple

If more widely available in commerce, paperbark maple would be a common plant in American gardens. Its paucity may be related to the difficulty associated with propagation—poor seed quality, slow growth, and very difficult to root. As an element in a winter landscape, however, it has few peers. The rich cinnamon to reddish brown exfoliating bark commands center stage, especially when framed by snow. Habit is that of a small tree, ranging from oval to rounded in outline. The dark bluish green, 3- to 6-in.-long, trifoliate leaves often turn brilliant red in fall,

MORE ▶

Acer griseum, paperbark maple

Acer cissifolium subsp. *henryi*

Acer griseum

Acer griseum CONTINUED

but superior fall color is more common in the East than in the Midwest. The species is extremely tolerant of acid or alkaline clay soils, as long as they are well drained. No two specimens are exactly alike, and such individuality provides for excellent landscape effect. Serves well as a specimen or small lawn tree, in a shrub border, or in groupings. No finer tree could be rec-ommended. Grows 20 to 30 ft. high and wide. Zones 4 to 8. Central China.

Other trifoliate maples that offer excellent fall color and/or bark include *Acer mandshuricum*, Manchurian maple, with fluorescent, pinkish red fall color and smooth gray bark; *A. maximowiczianum* (*A. nikoense*), Nikko maple, with yellow, red, or purple (often muted red) fall color and smooth gray bark; and *A. triflorum*, threeflower maple, with orange-red fall color and ash-brown to golden amber, loose, vertically fissured and lightly exfoliating bark. This is the most cold hardy of the trifoliates and is growing in Minnesota.

CULTIVARS AND VARIETIES
'Cinnamon Flake' and Gingerbread™ ('Ginzam') are beautiful hybrids between *Acer griseum* and *A. maximowiczianum* with cinnamon-stick exfoliat-

Acer griseum fall color

Acer triflorum fall color

Acer mandshuricum, Manchurian maple, fall color

Acer triflorum, threeflower maple

Acer maximowiczianum, Nikko maple

ing bark and blue-green leaves that turn rich red in autumn. A plant in the Dirr garden displayed great vigor and increased heat tolerance over either parent.

Acer japonicum
fullmoon maple

Although not as popular as its close relative *Acer palmatum*, Japanese maple, this small, rounded tree offers excellent fall foliage and has several outstanding cultivars. The 3- to 6-in.-wide, rich green leaves are composed of seven to 11 lobes. The sinuses are not as deeply cut as those of *A. palmatum*. In autumn, the leaves change to vibrant yellows and reds. Purplish red flowers, ½ in. in diameter, appear in great numbers on long-stalked, nodding corymbs in April. The smooth gray bark is quite handsome. Culture is similar to that of *A. palmatum*, except *A. japonicum* does not appear to be quite as heat-tolerant. Grows 20 to 30 ft. high and wide. Zones 5 to 7. Japan. CULTIVARS AND VARIETIES 'Aconitifolium' has nine- to 11-lobed leaves that are cut to within ¼ to ½ in. of the petiole. Each major lobe is again divided and sharply toothed, producing a fern-like texture. Fall color

MORE ▶

Acer japonicum, fullmoon maple

Acer japonicum 'Aconitifolium' fall color

Acer japonicum 'Vitifolium'

Acer shirasawanum 'Aureum'

Acer japonicum 'Vitifolium' fall color

Acer japonicum CONTINUED

is spectacular orange to crimson. Rounded and shrubby in habit. Grows 8 to 10 ft. high.

'Aureum' is a pretty yellow-leaved cultivar. The color holds quite well, except in intense heat. Fall color is a handsome golden yellow. It has a distinct upright, vase-shaped habit, with the branches suspended in cloud-like strata. Now placed as a selection of

Acer shirasawanum. Grows 10 to 20 ft. high.

'Vitifolium' has grape-like leaves, 4 to 6 in. long and wide, that turn rich shades of yellow, orange, red, and purple in autumn. Grows 20 to 25 ft. high and wide.

Acer miyabei
Miyabe maple

Always had a fascination with the species and questioned its absence from gardens. A kindred spirit with *Acer campestre*, but larger in leaf and stature. Habit, in youth, is upright-oval, becoming rounded with age. Leaves, five-lobed, 4 to 6 in. wide, 3 to 5 in. long, are flat to semi-glossy dark green, pale to rich yellow in autumn. Flowers, greenish yellow, are borne in slender-stalked, 10- to 15-flowered corymbs in May with the expanding leaves. Culturally, prefers moist, well-drained soils on the acid side but appears suitable for neutral soils. Successful culture in Minnesota, Illinois, Missouri, and South Carolina cor-

roborates adaptability. Excellent lawn, park, and potential street tree. Grows 30 to 40 ft. high and wide. Zones 4 to 7. Japan.

CULTIVARS AND VARIETIES
State Street™ ('Morton') is an upright-oval form, 40 ft. by 25 ft., with dark green foliage turning yellow in fall. Handsome corky bark, fast growth, and distinct ascending, full branching in youth. Performed superbly in zone 7, and the original tree was housed in the Morton Arboretum, Lisle, Illinois.

Several hybrids, such as *Acer ×hillieri* (*A. miyabei* × *A. cappadocicum*) and *A. miyabei* × *A. campestre*, have the potential for landscape acceptance.

Acer negundo
boxelder

For those areas of the country where tree culture is fraught with difficulty, this species can be recommended. The ornamental attributes are limited, but boxelder's adaptability to dry or wet soils and to inhospitable climatic

Acer miyabei, Miyabe maple

Acer miyabei fall color

Acer miyabei State Street™

conditions provide a legitimate basis for utilization. Habit is rounded to broad-rounded, but there is no constancy to this character, and *Acer negundo* may appear as an unkempt shrub, a gaunt tree, or a biological fright. The light green leaves are composed of three to five (seven to nine), 2- to 4-in.-long leaflets that turn yellowish in fall but are not particularly striking. It is dioecious (sexes separate), and female trees set prodigious quantities of fruit, which leads to supra-optimal quantities of seedlings. Wood is subject to breakage, insects, and diseases. Temperance is the rule when considering this species. Grows 30 to 50 ft. high, variable spread. Zones 2 to 9. United States, Canada.

CULTIVARS AND VARIETIES
Several variegated cultivars are known, the best being 'Variegatum', with cream-margined leaves. It is

MORE ▶

Acer negundo 'Kelly's Gold'

Acer negundo, boxelder

Acer negundo 'Variegatum'

Acer negundo 'Auratum'

Acer negundo 'Flamingo'

Acer negundo CONTINUED

Acer negundo var. *violaceum*

spectacular for summer foliage color, but it requires partial shade. A female, and the wings of the samaras are also variegated. 'Auratum' and 'Kelly's Gold' (male) have yellow leaves, and 'Flamingo' (male) has brilliant pink new leaves that mature to green with a white border.

Variety *violaceum* has bloomy (waxy) violet stems and beautiful lavender-purple pendent stamens before the leaves; new growth is bronze. The 60-ft.-high, oval-rounded tree at Hillier was as close to "noble" as any box-elder will ever achieve.

'Winter Lightning' with saturated yellow-bug-light stems makes quite a winter show; probably best to cut back and encourage vigorous young shoots, which develop the maximum winter color.

Acer palmatum, Japanese maple

Acer palmatum

Japanese maple

True aristocrats are rare among people and trees, but Japanese maple is in the first order. It is difficult to imagine a garden that could not benefit from one of the many forms of *Acer palmatum*. The normal habit is round to broad-rounded, with the branches assuming a layered, almost stratified architecture, similar to *Cornus florida*, flowering dogwood. The five- to nine-lobed, finely serrated, 2- to 5-in.-long and -wide leaves vary from light green to dark green; variety *atropurpureum* offers shades of reddish purple. Fall color is sensational, with rich yellows and reds developing consistently each autumn. The color persists and may be effective as late as November. The winter silhouette is also attractive and, coupled with the smooth gray bark, provides interest during the "off season." Landscape uses for the spe-

cies and its many cultivars are limited only by the imagination of the gardener. Soils should be evenly moist, acid, organic-laden, and well drained. Grows 15 to 25 ft. high and wide; 40-ft. specimens are known. Zones 5 to 8. Japan, central China, Korea.

CULTIVARS AND VARIETIES

Hundreds of selections have been made. For a detailed and meticulous accounting, refer to *Japanese Maples* (2010) by Peter Gregory and J. D. Vertrees. I have grown seedling populations with dissected green and purple leaves as well as normal green and purple. Herein utilized a new designation to partition the cultivars. I have grown/observed all presented.

GREEN GROUP Five- to nine-lobed green leaves.

'Bihou' has beautiful yellow, apricot, orange winter stems on an upright habit.

'Glowing Embers' has small dark

green leaves that turn orange-red-purple in fall. Vigorous, heat-tolerant selection for the South. Introduced by the author.

'Katsura' is a beautiful form with new leaves opening apricot-gold-yellow, maturing to green, and turning apricot-gold in the fall.

'Osakazuki' produces bright green leaves that turn a rich crimson in the fall; one of the best for fall color. Becomes a round-topped 15- to 20-ft.-high tree at maturity.

'Ryusen' is a true weeping selection with cascading, pendulous branches clothed with typical green leaves that turn yellow-orange-red in autumn.

'Sango Kaku' is an upright, vase-shaped form. It has green leaves, yellow to orange fall color, and coral-orange-red winter stems.

ATROPURPUREUM GROUP Five- to seven-lobed, red to red-purple leaves.

MORE ▶

Acer palmatum

Acer palmatum samaras

Acer palmatum 'Glowing Embers' fall color

Acer palmatum 'Katsura'

Acer palmatum CONTINUED

Acer palmatum fall color

Acer palmatum 'Sango Kaku'

Acer palmatum 'Bihou'

Acer palmatum 'Osakazuki' fall color

Acer palmatum 'Glowing Embers'

Acer palmatum 'Bloodgood'

Typically tree-like, but compact forms are included here.

'Bloodgood' has large, deep red-purple leaves that turn an excellent red in autumn. One of the best for retaining deep reddish purple foliage. Slow-growing, small tree maturing in the 15- to 20-ft. range. Among the most cold hardy purple-leaf types.

'Emperor I' has red leaves that are large like 'Bloodgood' but with more blue pigment, akin to purpleleaf plum. It grows more rapidly than 'Bloodgood' but still matures in the 15- to 20-ft.-high and -wide range.

'Hefner's Red' is a recent introduction with excellent red-purple pigment retention in zone 7.

'Moonfire' is another excellent purple-red leaf form that holds color during the summer and turns crimson in the fall; grows approximately 15 ft. high. Will lose color in heat of zone 7.

DISSECTUM GROUP Leaf lobes finely dissected to varying degrees; green- and purple-leaf types. Typically small and mounded-arching, but 'Seiryu' forms a tree.

GREEN: 'Seiryu' is an upright vase-shaped form, atypical for the Dissectum Group, maturing 10 to 15 (to 20) ft. high, 8 to 10 (to 15) ft. wide. Rich green summer leaves turn brilliant gold-orange to orange-red in fall.

'Viridis' has beautiful, green, seven- to nine-lobed, dissected leaves; fall color is yellow-gold to red. Probably a catch-all term for all green leaf dissected types.

'Waterfall' is considered the best green leaf dissected form. The rich green foliage holds up well in heat of zones 7 and 8; fall color is golden with reddish suffusions. Will grow 10 ft. high and 12 to 14 ft. wide.

PURPLE: 'Crimson Queen' produces bright crimson-red new foliage that may hold in cooler climates, but I have grown it, and it becomes more bronze-green to red in zone 7; red fall color. Develops handsome cascading

MORE ▶

Acer palmatum 'Moonfire'

Acer palmatum 'Seiryu' fall color

Acer palmatum 'Waterfall'

Acer palmatum 'Hefner's Red'

Acer palmatum 'Waterfall' fall color

Acer palmatum 'Tamukeyama'

Acer davidii

Acer pensylvanicum, striped maple

Acer pensylvanicum fall color

branches and eventually grows 8 to 10 ft. high by 12 ft. wide.

'Garnet' is a vigorous form that will grow 10 ft. high. The rich gemstone garnet is most evident in plants grown in full sun; when grown in shade, leaves maintain a greenish cast; fall color is a good red. Grew one in our Chapel Hill garden, and leaves became reddish green by mid summer.

'Inaba Shidare' produces large leaves, up to 6 in. long and wide, that begin purple-red and hold their color reasonably well in the heat; red to crimson fall color. Faster growing than many of the red dissectums and considered one of the most cold hardy.

'Tamukeyama' has deep crimson-red young foliage that matures purple-red and holds quite well. Considered the best of the purple-leaf dissecteds for the Southeast. Still, in zone 7 (Athens), the color is greatly diminished.

Acer pensylvanicum
striped maple

This species belongs to a group of maples termed "snake-barks." The unflattering nickname refers to the whitish vertical fissures that develop on the bark, which when set against the greenish background conjure visions of a snake's skin. Habit is upright-oval to oval-rounded. The bright green leaves, 5 to 7 in. long and wide, turn soft yellows in fall and provide a candle glow from the northern woods into the southern Appalachians. *Acer pensylvanicum* occurs as an understory species in the wild and does not compete well when transported to cultivation. The vagaries of domesticated environments often wreak havoc. Cool, evenly moist, acidic soils are optimal. Grows 15 to 20 (to 30) ft. high, similar spread. Zones 3 to 7; use only at higher elevations farther south. Quebec to Wisconsin, south to northern Georgia.

Other species with somewhat similar traits include *Acer capillipes*, *A. davidii* (David maple), *A. rufinerve* (redvein maple), and *A. tegmentosum* (Manchu striped maple). These four are better suited to cultivation than *A. pensylvanicum*.

CULTIVARS AND VARIETIES
'Erythrocladum' receives high accolades for bright coral-red, first-year stems, the white striations intervening on older stems. Older branches and trunk become yellow-amber-brown; upright vase-shaped habit.

'White Tigress', with large, three-lobed leaves and green-white striated bark, is beautiful. Plant in the Dirr garden was plagued by tip borer and canker, and succumbed; better in the North.

MORE ▶

Acer davidii, David maple

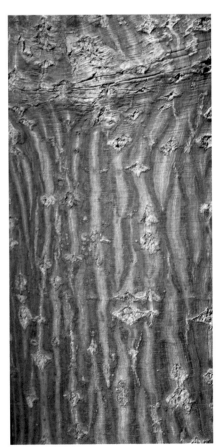

Acer davidii

Acer capillipes

Acer tegmentosum

Acer platanoides
Norway maple

Commonality breeds contempt, and many gardeners have tired of Norway maple, long a staple for street and urban use—street after street is planted with this maple species. Stress tolerances of the tree are also now being questioned. The rounded outline is common to young and mature trees. In spring, lovely yellow flowers smother the as-yet-leafless branches. The dark green, 4- to 7-in.-wide leaves may turn rich yellow in fall and, when environmental conditions are optimal, can be spectacular. Generally quite tolerant of extremes of soil and climate. In some areas has become invasive, with seedlings overtaking native woodlands. Grows 40 to 50 ft. high, similar spread. Zones 3 to 7. Europe.

Acer capillipes

Acer pensylvanicum 'Erythrocladum' first-year stems

Acer tegmentosum, Manchu striped maple

Acer pensylvanicum 'Erythrocladum'

CULTIVARS AND VARIETIES
Numerous cultivars have been selected over the centuries, and some, such as 'Crimson King' (reddish purple leaves) and 'Schwedleri' (reddish purple in spring, fading to green), have become more com-

MORE ▶

Acer platanoides fall color

Acer platanoides, Norway maple

Acer platanoides 'Crimson King'

Acer platanoides 'Cleveland'

Acer platanoides 'Schwedleri'

Acer platanoides CONTINUED

mon than the species. 'Cleveland', 'Emerald Queen', and 'Summershade' offer the greatest hope for the landscape. Limited new introductions over the last ten to 15 years due to the ascendancy of red and sugar maple cultivars, the latter two being native species and less prone to the nasty invasive invective.

Acer pseudoplatanus
planetree or sycamore maple

A weed in Europe and some portions of the eastern United States, *Acer pseudoplatanus* has never received the acceptance of the native maple species because it lacks their dignity and excellent fall color. The branching pattern is distinctly upright-spreading, the ultimate silhouette approaching oval to oval-rounded. The five-lobed,

Acer pseudoplatanus, planetree maple

Acer pseudoplatanus

Acer pseudoplatanus

Acer pseudoplatanus 'Brilliantissimum'

Acer pseudoplatanus 'Leopoldii'

3- to 6-in.-wide, dark green leaves seldom display good fall color. Bark on mature trees becomes brown or grayish, with rectangular exfoliating scales exposing the orangish brown inner bark. Tolerates sandy or clay-based soils and saline conditions. Grows 40 to 60 ft. high, 25 to 40 ft. wide. Zones 4 to 7. Europe, western Asia.

CULTIVARS AND VARIETIES
'Atropurpureum' has leaves that are purplish on their lower surface.

Acer pseudoplatanus

'Brilliantissimum' thrusts forth shrimp-pink leaves, later pale cream to yellow-green and maturing off-green. Slow-growing, round-headed tree; requires consistently cooler climates; usually grafted on a standard; grows 15 to 20 ft. high and wide.

'Esk Sunset' has leaves speckled, streaked, and splotched salmon-pink, green, and yellow; white on upper surface, purple-red underside. From New Zealand.

'Leopoldii' has white-speckled leaves in a pattern reminiscent of marble cake and spider mite infestations.

Acer pseudosieboldianum
Korean maple

Underappreciated and largely ignored because of cult-like devotion to *Acer palmatum, but* an alternative to Japanese maple for colder parts of the country. In Maine, Minnesota, and South Dakota has survived −30°F and lower. Leaves, deep green, nine- to 11-lobed, 4 to 6 in. across, pubescent below, turn orange, scarlet, crimson, and purple in fall. Adaptable. Many landscape uses akin to *A. palmatum*. Has been hybridized with that species to produce wider range of colorful foliage trees and cold hardiness. Naturalized along the Stillwater River near the University of Maine, Orono, campus. Grows 15 to 25 ft. high and wide. Zones 3 to 6(7). Had a small plant in the Dirr garden which, although inching along, wanted to move north. China, Korea, Manchuria.

CULTIVARS AND VARIETIES
'Northern Glow' is the first U.S. cultivar. Develops outstanding red fall color. Observed in Oregon, where the tree was low-branched with pretty green-tinged red leaves in August. Introduced by Dr. Ed Hasselkus, retired, University of Wisconsin.

Acer rubrum
red maple

A red maple from Florida is not the same as a red maple from Maine. The name may be the same, but leaf shape, degree of leaf retention, fall color, and cold hardiness are distinctly different. A red maple from Florida will die in Maine, and vice versa. In either locale, *Acer rubrum* forms a pyramidal or elliptical outline in youth, becoming ovoid, rounded, or irregular at maturity. Reddish flowers appear in early spring and are followed by red fruit. The smooth gray bark is quite attractive, particularly on young plants; often ridged and furrowed with scaly ridges on large trunks. Emerging leaves are reddish tinged, changing to medium or dark green, and reaching 2 to 5 in. in length. Foliage often develops glorious yellows and reds in fall. In the wild, a pure yellow fall-colored specimen will rub branches with a rich red plant. The colors of New England

MORE ▶

Acer pseudosieboldianum, Korean maple

Acer pseudosieboldianum 'Northern Glow'

Acer rubrum CONTINUED

autumns are a spectacular mix of red maple, sugar maple, and birch—no sight is more magnificent or more memorable. *Acer rubrum* is a cosmopolitan species and can be found in swamps, mixed forest situations, and rocky uplands. When correctly utilized, it makes a fine tree for lawns, streets,

Acer rubrum, red maple

Acer rubrum 'Armstrong'

Acer rubrum fall color

Acer rubrum 'Columnare' fall color

or parks. Grows 40 to 60 ft. high, variable spread. Zones 3 to 9. Newfoundland to Minnesota, south to Florida and Texas.

CULTIVARS AND VARIETIES
'Armstrong', 'Autumn Spire', 'Bowhall' ('Scanlon'), 'Columnare', 'Karpick', and 'Red Rocket' are upright, columnar-pyramidal forms. 'Armstrong' and 'Bowhall' are the most common of these and arguably the best, but 'Columnare' is still my favorite. New columnar types are under evaluation at West Coast nurseries.

'Autumn Blaze' is a cultivar of *Acer ×freemanii* (*A. rubrum* × *A. saccharinum*). Displays excellent red fall color. Have observed breakage (splitting) on trees in Minnesota and South Carolina. Grows almost too fast. Other hybrids are Autumn Fantasy® ('DTR 102') with reliable red fall color in the South; 'Marmo' with red-green fall

MORE ▶

Acer rubrum fall color

Acer rubrum Red Sunset® fall color

Acer rubrum Autumn Flame® fall color

Acer ×freemanii 'Autumn Blaze' fall color

Acer ×freemanii Redpointe®

Acer rubrum 'Sun Valley' fall color

51

Acer rubrum CONTINUED

color in zone 5, yellow in zone 7; and Redpointe® ('Frank Jr.') with smaller dark green leaves and red fall color, even in zones 7 and 8.

October Glory® and Red Sunset® ('Franksred') are the most widely known and utilized selections, offering excellent orange-red to red fall color. October Glory® develops reliable red

Acer saccharinum fall color

fall color in the heat of the Southeast. Autumn Flame® (male), with smaller leaves, colors red two weeks ahead of Red Sunset®, four weeks ahead of October Glory®.

Dr. Townsend, U.S. National Arboretum, bred 'Brandywine', 'Somerset', and 'Sun Valley' using Autumn Flame®, October Glory®, and/or Red Sunset®. All are males, with 'Sun Valley' a pleasantly pyramidal-rounded tree, 40 ft. by 35 ft., with peach-orange-red fall color. I consider it the best of the three.

Acer saccharinum
silver maple

Once the most widely planted native maple, silver maple has fallen into disfavor with nursery people and gardeners. Broken limbs, limited ornamental attributes, and a gross-feeding root system that buckles sidewalks and clogs drains have inhibited its planting. The fastest growing maple spe-

cies, it is at the same time the most susceptible to breakage in storms. Habit is oval to rounded, with strongly upright, spreading branches. The five-lobed, deeply cut, 3- to 6-in.-long leaves are dark green with silvery backs, creating a rather attractive effect when the wind buffets and exposes the undersides. The flowers often open before those of *Acer rubrum* and range in color from yellowish to a good red. The species is extremely adaptable to varied soils. A reasonable choice where few other species will grow or where there is need for a truly fast-growing shade tree. Grows 50 to 70 ft. high, 30 to 45 ft. wide. Zones 3 to 9. Quebec to Florida, west to Minnesota, Oklahoma, and Louisiana.

CULTIVARS AND VARIETIES
'Silver Queen' represents an improvement on the species because of its better habit and its minimal fruit, reducing the nuisances of litter and

Acer saccharinum, silver maple, fall color

Acer saccharinum 'Silver Queen'

invasiveness. Amazingly, has held up in ice storms much better than Autumn Blaze®.

Acer saccharum
sugar maple

The true nobility of fall-coloring trees —challenged by many, rivaled by none. Traveling on a quiet country lane in Massachusetts, Indiana, or Pennsylvania on an October day yields a spectacular experience: the yellow, orange, and red palette of sugar maple. The soul is soothed, and one is able to cope with the tribulations of daily life. The habit of this tree is distinctly upright-oval to rounded. Displays attractive gray-brown bark. The five-lobed, 3- to 6-in.-long and -wide leaves range from medium to dark green in summer. Greenish yellow flowers emerge before the leaves and from a distance appear as a soft haze. Well-drained, evenly moist, acid soils suit

MORE ▶

Acer saccharum fall color

Acer saccharum, sugar maple, fall color

Acer saccharum 'Legacy' fall color

Acer saccharum

Acer saccharum Caddo ecotype

Acer saccharum 'Green Mountain' onset of fall color

Acer saccharum 'Monumentale'

it best. *Acer saccharum* does tolerate less-than-ideal conditions, although it is not a tree for high-stress environments. Makes a great lawn, park, campus, golf-course, or large-area tree. Grows 60 to 75 ft. high, 40 to 50 ft. wide. Zones 3 to 8. Eastern Canada to Georgia, west to Texas.

CULTIVARS AND VARIETIES
'Commemoration', 'Green Mountain', and 'Legacy' have thick, waxy textured leaves, rapid growth rates, yellow-orange fall color, and excellent heat tolerance. 'Legacy' has proven the toughest of the cultivars in Kansas and South Carolina tests.

'Monumentale' ('Temple's Upright') is a handsome broad-columnar form.

Newer introductions include several derived from the Caddo ecotype (naturally occurring in the western part of range, thus more heat-tolerant) such as Flashfire® ('JFS-Caddo2') with excellent red fall color and 'John Pair' with early red fall color. From Georgia comes Harvest Moon® ('Sandersville'), with orange-red fall color and significant heat and drought tolerance.

The most cold hardy (zones 3 and 4) are Apollo®, 'Fairview', Fall Fiesta®, 'Green Mountain', and Unity®.

Acer saccharum subsp. floridanum

syn. *Acer barbatum*, *Acer saccharum* subsp. *barbatum*

southern sugar maple

The true sugar maple, *Acer saccharum*, often struggles in the heat of zone 7 and higher. This southern native is a worthy alternative. I have observed thriving specimens in coastal South Carolina, north Florida, and near Nacadoches, Texas, that attest to its heat tolerance. The habit is oval-rounded, densely branched, and foliated with dark green leaves. One of the best ways to separate this species from the closely allied *A. saccharum* subsp. *leucoderme* is by the grayish underside of the leaf, compared to green for subsp. *leucoderme*. Fall color varies from yellow to orange-red. Fall colors develop in mid November and are still effective in early December in zone 7. Leaves have remained alive and colorful after 23°F. No serious insects or diseases. A terrific candidate for bringing rich fall color to warm climates. More drought-tolerant than *A. saccharum*. Grows 20 to 30 ft. high, similar spread. Have observed trees over 60 ft. high in Texas. Zones (6)7 to 9. Virginia to Florida, southeastern Missouri, Arkansas, eastern Oklahoma, and Texas.

Acer saccharum subsp. leucoderme

syn. *Acer leucoderme*

chalkbark maple

In the Piedmont forests of Georgia, this wonderful maple resides in anonymity until autumn, when its flamboyant yellows, oranges, and reds vie for attention. Almost always an understory plant, usually single-stemmed

MORE ▶

Acer saccharum subsp. *floridanum*, southern sugar maple, fall color

Acer saccharum foliage comparison, subsp. *floridanum* (right) and subsp. *leucoderme*

Acer saccharum subsp. *leucoderme*, chalkbark maple, fall color

Acer saccharum subsp. *leucoderme* CONTINUED
and low-branched, sometimes multi-stemmed, it develops a roundish outline. Bark with ashy gray patina (hence, chalkbark maple). The leaves are lighter green than those of subsp. *floridanum*. Several Georgia nurserymen have tried to commercialize the species, but the growth rate is slower than subsp. *floridanum*, and the variation in fall color maddening. Found as an understory plant in drier, upland woods throughout its native range. Worthy of consideration in the South, but selections for desirable characteristics (habit, fall color) are necessary to bring the plant to everyday commerce. Grows 20 to 30 ft. high and wide. Zones 5 to 9. Native to Georgia, the panhandle of Florida, Louisiana, eastern Oklahoma, and Texas.

Acer saccharum subsp. *leucoderme* fall color

Acer tataricum

Acer tataricum

Acer tataricum
Tatarian maple

In many respects, this species is a carbon copy of *Acer tataricum* subsp. *ginnala*, Amur maple, except the leaves do not develop the strong lobing found in those of the latter. The habit is also more tree-like and the fruit more consistently red than those of subsp. *ginnala*. Fall color of *A. tataricum* is seldom pronounced and does not rival Amur maple's. Displays tolerance to dry and high pH soils. A good small specimen tree for the residential landscape. Grows 15 to 20 ft. high and wide. Zones 3 to 8. Southeast Europe, western Asia.
CULTIVARS AND VARIETIES
More tree-like habit, yellow to red fall color, and red samaras are found in Hot Wings® ('GarAnn'), Pattern Perfect™ ('Patdell'), Rugged Charm® ('JFS-KW2'), and Summer Splendor™ ('Actar').

Acer tataricum subsp. ginnala
syn. *Acer ginnala*
Amur maple

Among the most cold hardy maples, and certainly one of the most adaptable. Grown as a large shrub or small tree, it serves many landscape purposes. In its finest form, the tree is limbed up, exposing the smooth gray bark and creating an artistic, sculp-

Acer tataricum, Tatarian maple

tural element. The three-lobed, 1½- to 3-in.-long leaves change from a rich dark green to excellent shades of yellow, orange, and red in fall. Fragrant, creamy white flowers appear with the new foliage in April and May, and the wings of the fruit often turn a handsome red in August and September. It is the first maple, and one of the first woody plants, to leaf out in the spring. Displays excellent tolerance to dry and alkaline soils. Fine plant for raised planters, narrow tree lawns, and difficult sites. Grows 15 to 18 ft. high and wide. Zones 3 to 8. Central to northeastern China, Japan.

CULTIVARS AND VARIETIES
Many selections, particularly suited to northern states. See my *Manual of Woody Landscape Plants* (2009) for specifics.

'Bailey Compact' grew for many years in the Dirr garden, where it

MORE ▶

Acer tataricum subsp. *ginnala*

Acer tataricum subsp. *ginnala*

Acer tataricum subsp. *ginnala*, Amur maple

Acer tataricum subsp. *ginnala* 'Flame' fall color

Acer tataricum subsp. *ginnala* 'Bailey Compact' fall color

Acer tataricum subsp. *ginnala* Red November™ fall color

Acer tataricum subsp. *ginnala* CONTINUED reached 10 ft. by 15 ft. in ten years. Lustrous dark green foliage and rich red-purple fall color are principal assets. It colored well in Georgia, but I observed even more intense coloration in Maine.

'Flame' is more tree-like, with good orange-red fall color. Originally introduced as a seed-grown cultivar, so expect variation in fall color.

Red November™ ('JFS-UGA') produces reliable red-purple fall color in the heat of zone 7. Selected by the author from a tree growing in the University's Botanical Garden; now 20 ft. by 30 ft. with five main trunks.

Acer truncatum
Shantung or purpleblow maple

This is another small maple that could be effectively utilized in urban situations. It is a small, round-headed tree with a neat outline and a regular branching pattern. The five-lobed, 3- to 5-in.-wide, lustrous dark green leaves turn yellow-orange and red in fall. Bright yellow flowers emerge before the leaves in April. It is tolerant of acid, alkaline, and dry soils, making it well suited to the rigors of the urban landscape. Fine specimens in Iowa and on the campus of the University of Maine at Orono attest to the northern adaptability of the tree. In situations where *Acer platanoides* and *A. rubrum* would be too large, this is a fine choice. Grows 20 to 25 ft. high, similar spread. Zones 4 to 8. Northern China.

CULTIVARS AND VARIETIES
Considerable enthusiasm for this species because of its adaptability and smaller stature. Hybrids with *Acer platanoides*, Norway maple, including Crimson Sunset™ ('JFS-KW202') with red-purple leaves and increased heat tolerance over 'Crimson King', one of the parents. Norwegian Sunset® ('Keithsform') and Pacific Sunset® ('Warrenred') are both smaller statured than Norway with yellow-orange fall color in the South.

Main Street® ('AT-WF1'), with oval-rounded habit and beautiful orange-red fall color, is a selection of *Acer truncatum*.

Actinidia arguta
bower actinidia

This vigorous twining vine, with beautiful lustrous dark green foliage, appears restricted only by the structure to which it is attached. I have seen 30-ft.-high plants climbing downspouts on large buildings and 8-ft.-high plants on small trellises. The 3- to 5-in.-long leaves have undulating surfaces and red petioles. Leaves hold late and may develop yellow fall color. Whitish, ¾-in.-wide, fragrant flowers develop from the axils of the stems in May and June, after the leaves have emerged, and are essen-

MORE ▶

Acer truncatum, Shantung maple

Acer Norwegian Sunset® fall color

Acer truncatum

Acer truncatum fall color

Acer Crimson Sunset™

Acer Pacific Sunset® fall color

Actinidia arguta, bower actinidia

Actinidia arguta

Actinidia arguta

tially hidden from view. Edible, greenish yellow berries, 1 to 1¼ in. long and ¾ in. wide, ripen in fall. This is an excellent vine for difficult sites. Tremendously adaptable to acid or high pH soils, and withstands sun or partial shade. Obviously a rampant grower and should be considered for large-area use. Requires support. Grows 25 to 30 ft. high. Zones 3 to 8. Japan, Korea, northeastern China.

CULTIVARS AND VARIETIES
Many for fruit size and quality are available, with 'Ananasnaya' frequently listed.

'Silver Lining' has a cream-white irregular border to the mid-green interior of the leaf. Vigorous, and I have not noticed reversions. Rate this one of the best new introductions for variegated foliage.

Actinidia arguta fall color

Actinidia arguta 'Silver Lining'

Actinidia deliciosa

syn. *Actinidia chinensis*

kiwi, Chinese gooseberry

Unique, rapid-growing, twining vine producing edible "berry." The New Zealanders were the first to successfully commercialize the plant and make it a household word worldwide. The fuzzy young leaves emerge bronze to purplish green, changing to dark green. The 1½-in.-wide creamy white fragrant flowers open in April and May. The famous brownish green, hairy, 1- to 2-in.-long fruit ripen in fall. Susceptible to late spring frosts in zone 7, and the emerging foliage is often killed. Provide full sun, moist, well-drained soils. Male ('Chico Male') and female ('Hayward') vines are required for effective fruit set. Grows 40 to 50 ft. or limited by structure. Zones (7)8 to 10. China.

Actinidia kolomikta

kolomikta actinidia

This species is less rampant than *Actinidia arguta* and offers exquisite white- to pink-blotched foliage. Typically the coloration occurs from the middle of the leaf to the tip. The 3- to 6-in.-long leaves emerge purplish tinged and develop the white, pink, and dark green combinations. Young plants do not have the strong coloration of mature plants. Supposedly, males are more strongly colored than females. The vividness of the color is reduced by hot weather, excess fertility, and shade. Ideally plants should be purchased in leaf to assure trueness. Fragrant white flowers, ½ in. wide, appear in the leaf axils during May and June. The fruit are sweet, edible, greenish yellow, 1-in.-long berries that ripen in September and October. As adaptable as *A. arguta* and probably better suited to the smaller landscape. Grows 15 to 20 ft. high or more. Zones 4 to 8; plants can survive zone 2 temperatures (−45°F). Northeastern Asia to Japan, central and western China.

CULTIVARS AND VARIETIES
Several Russian cultivars for fruit production. Pasha™ with pink-, white-, green-variegated leaves is utilized as a male pollinator. Specialty nurseries like Northwoods Nursery (One Green World), www.northwoodsnursery.com, Molalla, Oregon, and Edible Landscaping, www.ediblelandscaping.com, Afton, Virginia, offer these selections via mail order.

Actinidia deliciosa, kiwi

Actinidia deliciosa

Actinidia deliciosa

Actinidia deliciosa 'Chico Male'

Actinidia kolomikta, kolomikta actinidia

Actinidia kolomikta

Actinidia kolomikta

Actinidia pilosula

Actinidia pilosula is the most refined of the *Actinidia* species discussed in this book. The lance-shaped leaves, ending in a taper point, are dark green with prominent silver-white marking at the apex or covering half to most of the leaf. The leaf margins have bristle-like teeth. Some leaves are totally green, so the variegation pattern is inconsistent. Flowers are pink, ¾ in. wide, nonfragrant, borne singly in small clusters in the leaf axils in May and June. I consider this one of the most beautiful twining vines. Certainly not well known. Grows 10 to 20 ft. Zones 6 and 7? China.

Actinidia polygama
silver-vine

Extremely rare in cultivation, and in all my travels I have encountered the plant on only two or three occasions. It is the weakest growing of the *Actinidia* species presented here. The 3- to 5-in.-long leaves are marked with a silver-white to yellowish color on male plants. Fragrant white flowers, ½ to ¾ in. wide, open in June and July. The 1-in.-long, greenish yellow berries are edible; fruiting selections are offered by the nurseries listed under *Actinidia kolomikta*. The chief advantages of this species are its less-vigorous nature and smaller stature. Like the other actinidias discussed, it is a twining vine and requires support. Grows 10 to 15 ft. high. Zones 4 to 7. Japan, central and northeastern China.

Adina rubella
Chinese buttonbush

Beautiful shiny-leaved shrub that, for foliage alone, is recommended for warmer climate gardens. The habit is loose, arching-spreading, and refreshingly fine-textured. The 1- to 2-in.-long, lustrous dark green leaves provide mirror-like reflections. Leaves hold late; in Athens they are still a pristine green in late December. Flowers, akin to miniature sputniks, ½ to ¾ in. in diameter, initiate in June and July and continue into October in zone 7. Soft and creamy in color, they spew a slight fragrance. Unique and almost unknown plant for shady nooks and crannies. Worthy filler in the shady border, north and east side of structures. Will also grow in sun. Any well-drained, acidic soil is suitable. Grows 8 to 10 ft. high and wide. Plant was

Actinidia polygama

Actinidia pilosula

Actinidia polygama, silver-vine

Actinidia pilosula

Adina rubella

killed to the ground after exposure to −24°F in Bernheim Arboretum, Clermont, Kentucky, and produced 3 to 4 ft. of new growth in a single season. Zones (6)7 to 9. China.

Aesculus californica
California buckeye
Rather crafty buckeye, prospering in the warm, moist California spring, then shedding its leaves in the dry summer season. In Europe, leaves persist into fall. The leaves are composed of five lustrous green leaflets, each 3 to 6 in. long. Bark is beautiful, light to pale silver, reminiscent of the bark of *Fagus grandifolia*, American beech. Small, rounded to broad-rounded, low-branched tree of stunning elegance in flower. Numerous 4- to 8-in.-long, 2-in.-wide, cylindrical panicles of fragrant white flowers open in June. The smooth, pear-shaped cap-

MORE ▶

Adina rubella

Adina rubella, Chinese buttonbush

Aesculus californica

Aesculus californica

Aesculus californica, California buckeye

Aesculus californica 'Canyon Pink'

63

Aesculus californica CONTINUED

sule contains one or two, 1½- to 2-in.-wide, pale orange-brown seeds. Have observed on dry hillsides in California and the moist soils of the English landscape. A collector's trophy plant, not for everyone. A tree has performed reasonably well at the JC Raulston Arboretum, Raleigh, North Carolina, with defoliation in hot, dry summers but strong floral potency. Grows 15 to 20 ft. high and wide. Zones 7 to 9(10). California.

CULTIVARS AND VARIETIES
'Canyon Pink', a fragrant, true pink-flowered selection, flowers earlier than the species, in early May.

Aesculus ×carnea
red horsechestnut

A hybrid between *Aesculus pavia* and *A. hippocastanum* that is superior to either parent for general landscape use. The habit is rounded to broad-rounded, with the stout, close-knit branches creating a dense canopy. The leaves are composed of five to seven lustrous dark green leaflets. In May, 6- to 8-in.-long and 3- to 4-in.-wide panicles of rose-red flowers cover the tree. For flower effect, it is spectacular. Red horsechestnuts are susceptible to a fungal blight that causes a browning of the leaves in summer and fall. This tree prefers moist, deep, well-drained soils, but it is widely adaptable to soil types. Worth considering for parks, campuses, golf courses, and other large-area uses. It is widely planted in Europe in parks, on residential lots, and along streets. Grows 30 to 40 ft. high and wide. Zones 4 to 7.

CULTIVARS AND VARIETIES
'Briotii' has flowers that are deeper red and held in longer panicles (to 10 in.).

'Fort McNair', with rose-pink flowers, is considered more resistant to leaf blight but is still susceptible. Has performed reasonably well in Georgia and North Carolina gardens.

'O'Neil's Red' produces 10- to 12-in.-long panicles of rose-red flowers in early to mid May (zone 7).

Aesculus flava
syn. *Aesculus octandra*
yellow buckeye

Of the native tree buckeyes, this species is certainly the most spectacular and, from a landscape standpoint, the most trouble-free. In the mountains of north Georgia, 80- to 100-ft.-high specimens can be found in moist coves. In a comparable environment,

MORE ▶

Aesculus ×carnea, red horsechestnut

Aesculus ×*carnea*

Aesculus ×*carnea*

Aesculus ×*carnea* 'Fort McNair'

Aesculus ×*carnea* 'Briotii'

Aesculus flava, yellow buckeye, fall color

65

Aesculus flava CONTINUED

Aesculus flava appears less prone to disease than *A. ×carnea*, *A. glabra*, and *A. hippocastanum*. The habit is upright-oval, and the upper branches develop a slight spreading outline. The dark green leaves are composed of five 4- to 6-in.-long leaflets that turn yellow to pumpkin-orange in fall. Greenish yellow flowers appear in May and, like those of *A. glabra*, are

Aesculus flava

Aesculus flava

Aesculus flava

somewhat masked by the foliage. The smooth, pear-shaped, brownish capsules house one or two buckeyes. The bark is a rather curious combination of gray and brown, with large, flat, smooth plates and scales on old trunks. Common along the Blue Ridge Parkway in North Carolina and Virginia. Grows 60 to 75 ft. high, 30 to 50 ft. wide. Zones 4 to 8. Has been hardy in North Dakota (zone 3). Pennsylvania to Illinois, south to Tennessee and northern Georgia.

Aesculus glabra
Ohio buckeye

This native species is commonly found in moist soils and there makes its best growth. As a general landscape plant, it offers limited promise. Mildew, leaf blight, and scorch often disfigure the trees. If native in an area, it should be protected and worked into the framework of the landscape.

Generally rounded in habit, the plant appears quite coarse in winter. The dark green leaves are composed of five to seven, 3- to 6-in.-long leaflets. Foliage may change to pumpkin-orange in fall, but fall color is variable and seldom consistent from tree to tree. The greenish yellow flowers, borne in 4- to 7-in.-long, 2- to 3-in.-wide terminal panicles during May, are almost lost among the leaves. The fruit are prickly, dehiscent capsules that contain the shiny, rich brown seeds known as buckeyes. Grows 20 to 40 ft. high and wide. Zones 3 to 7. Pennsylvania to Alabama, west to Kansas.

CULTIVARS AND VARIETIES
Variety *arguta*, Texas buckeye, is similar to Ohio buckeye but smaller in all its parts; typically 15 to 20 ft. high and wide. Occurs in Arkansas, Missouri into east Texas.

Aesculus flava

Aesculus glabra fall color

Aesculus glabra, Ohio buckeye

Aesculus glabra

Aesculus glabra var. arguta

Aesculus glabra var. arguta, Texas buckeye

Aesculus glabra var. arguta

Aesculus glabra CONTINUED

Variety *nana* is a cute, compact-rounded shrub with typical flowers and fruit. Great under pine shade. Early leafing and flowering in the Dirr garden.

Aesculus hippocastanum
common horsechestnut

A common species in the Midwest and New England that is seldom planted anymore in the United States. In Europe, it graces parks and gardens and is one of the dominant landscape species. Like *Aesculus glabra*, it is afflicted (at least in the United States) with a blotch that causes an unsightly browning of the leaves by summer. When unadulterated, it can command a kingly presence. Trees vary in shape from upright-oval to rounded. The dark green leaves are composed of seven (occasionally five) 5- to 10-in.-long leaflets that turn a respectable yellow in fall. White flowers are borne in May in 5- to 12-in.-long, 2- to 5-in.-wide terminal panicles. The spiny, capsular, 2- to 2½-in.-wide fruit each contain one or two rich brown seeds. Grows 50 to 75 ft. high, variable spread. Zones 3 to 7. Greece, Albania.

CULTIVARS AND VARIETIES
'Baumannii' is the best for the garden of the many that have been selected. It has double white sterile flowers, blotched with red or yellow (no fruit are produced).

Aesculus glabra var. *nana*

Aesculus glabra var. *nana*

Aesculus hippocastanum, common horsechestnut

68

Aesculus hippocastanum

Aesculus hippocastanum 'Baumannii'

Aesculus indica
Indian horsechestnut

A rarity in the United States and easily cultured only along the West Coast into Vancouver, British Columbia. Large, rounded, densely foliated tree with seven (occasionally five or nine) lustrous dark green leaflets and a distinct, wavy leaf margin. In fall, leaves may develop auburn to orange-red coloration. Smooth gray bark develops on old specimens, and the trunk becomes scaly with unique puzzle-like pieces and patterns. Flowers, which appear in late May and June,

MORE ▶

Aesculus indica, Indian horsechestnut

Aesculus hippocastanum

Aesculus indica 'Sydney Pearce'

69

Aesculus indica CONTINUED

Aesculus indica

Aesculus parviflora, bottlebrush buckeye

Aesculus parviflora

are eyepoppers, in panicles of pinkish white to pinkish rose, 12 to 16 in. long, 4 to 5 in. wide. The magnificent specimen trees at Kew Gardens, England, inspire casual and serious visitors alike. Fruit are 2- to 3-in.-wide, rounded, roughened capsules. Grows to full genetic potential, 50 to 60 ft. high and wide, in moist soil, cool climate, and full sun. Zones 7 to 10 on the West Coast; not suitable for warm southeastern United States, although a small plant in the Dirr garden survived but did not flower. Northwestern Himalayas.

CULTIVARS AND VARIETIES
'Sydney Pearce' has deeper pink flowers in tighter panicles that are freely borne. An old tree at Kew Gardens is magnificent.

Aesculus parviflora
bottlebrush buckeye

Over my career, I have given hundreds of garden and nursery talks, and this species has probably appeared in 90 percent of them. Truly one of the best native shrubs for late-spring and early-summer flower. This broad-mounded,

suckering shrub can colonize a large piece of real estate. The wonderful coarse-textured, dark green leaves are composed of five to seven, 3- to 8-in.-long leaflets that turn rich butter-yellow in fall. The 8- to 12-in.-long, bottlebrush-shaped inflorescences contain hundreds of white, four-petaled flowers with pinkish white stamens that stand out an inch from the petals. The inflorescences occur at the ends of the branches and are held upright. Interestingly, this species flowers almost as prolifically in shade as in sun. Smooth, 1- to 3-in.-long, pear-shaped, light brown capsules contain one or two shiny, light brown seeds. Bottlebrush buckeye requires moist, well-drained soils for best growth, although quality specimens are found in every conceivable situation. Transplant balled and burlapped or from a container. Ideal for underplanting in woodlands or for use in shrub borders and large masses. Grows 8 to 12 ft. high, 8 to 15 ft. wide. Zones 4 to 8. South Carolina to Alabama and Florida.

CULTIVARS AND VARIETIES
Variety *serotina* flowers two to three

Aesculus parviflora fall color

Aesculus parviflora var. *serotina*

weeks later than the species. 'Rogers' is a selection of var. *serotina* with inflorescences fully 18 to 30 in. long.

Aesculus pavia
red buckeye

Another native buckeye that inhabits woodlands and spends its life in the shadows of large trees. When grouped or massed in light shade provided by pines, the effect can be spectacular. The brilliant dark green leaves, each with five to seven, 3- to 6-in.-long leaflets, are among the handsomest of the native buckeyes. Leaves emerge in March in Athens. Rich red flowers appear above the foliage in April and May, in panicles 3 to 6 in. long and 1½ to 3 in. wide. The smooth brown capsules harbor one or two lustrous dark brown seeds. Habit is rounded, but there is significant variation, and at times the plant appears almost shrub-like. This is a fine plant for

MORE ▶

Aesculus pavia

Aesculus pavia

Aesculus pavia, red buckeye

71

naturalizing in moist soils and where there is a modicum of shade. Like *Aesculus glabra*, it abhors dry soils and tends to develop leaf scorch or to defoliate, often by August or September. Grows 15 to 20 ft. high and wide. Zones 4 to 8. Virginia to Florida, west to Texas.

Aesculus sylvatica
painted buckeye
Imagine northern slopes of southern woodlands covered with the bronze, brown, and red-purple early maturing leaves, typically mid to late March in Athens. What a great native plant for those understory situations in the garden. Almost always small, shrubby, wide-spreading, it occasionally reaches small tree status. My observations provide concrete data that this is a favorite landscape plant of squirrels—willy-nilly it emerges from the forest duff in the same pattern as a squirrel crossing the road. The five dark green leaflets produce a sprinkle of yellow fall color. Leaves may abscise early if summers are hot and dry. Yellow-green flowers, in 4- to 8-in.-long panicles, crown the foliage in April and May. Fruit, smooth, 1 to 2 in. in diameter, contain one to three shiny brown-black seeds. Wonderful for naturalizing in the understory. Grows 6 to 15 ft. high and wide. Zones 6 to 9. Virginia to Georgia, west to Tennessee and Alabama.

Aesculus turbinata
Japanese horsechestnut
Worth a place in this tome? . . . debatable . . . but it's a beautiful large tree at its best. Habit similar to that of *Aesculus hippocastanum* with dark green leaves composed of five to seven, 8- to 14-in.-long leaflets. Occasionally touted as resistant to foliar anthrac-nose, and I followed this dictum until witnessing severe infection. The white flowers occur in 6- to 10-in.-long, upright panicles in May and June. Fruit are 2-in.-wide, broad pear-shaped capsules, usually without spines. The seed averages 1 in. or more in length, with the hilum covering nearly half the surface. Successfully grown at the Arnold and Raulston arboreta. Estimate 40 to 50 ft. under cultivation. Zones 5 to 7. Japan.

Agarista populifolia
syn. *Leucothoe populifolia*
Florida leucothoe
Graceful, arching, upright, and dense in structure, with bamboo-like clumping habit. The emerging leaves, tinged red to bronze-purple, turn glossy rich green and hold this color through winter. Fragrant cream-colored flowers, about ⅓ in. long, appear in axillary

MORE ▶

Aesculus sylvatica

Aesculus sylvatica, painted buckeye

Aesculus sylvatica

Aesculus turbinata, Japanese horsechestnut

Aesculus turbinata

Agarista populifolia new growth

Agarista populifolia

Agarista populifolia, Florida leucothoe

Agarista populifolia CONTINUED

clusters from each node in May and June. Great plant for shady, moist sites in the garden. May languish if sited in full sun and dry soils. Fast-growing and requires pruning to keep it small. A 12-ft. plant in our garden was cut back to 1½ ft. and completely rejuvenated. Excellent in groupings in shady settings, to screen and shape vistas. Stems are densely set, so pedestrian traffic is reduced. Typically grows 8 to 12 ft. high and wide. Have observed 15- to 18-ft.-high plants in South Carolina. Zones (6)7 to 9. South Carolina to Florida.

CULTIVARS AND VARIETIES
Leprechaun™ ('Taylor's Treasure') is a dense, compact form with smaller rich green leaves than the species; grows 4 ft. by 4 ft. I thought this introduction would prove outstanding but have been less than impressed by performance.

Agave americana
century plant

Certainly not a woody plant in the classical definition but a collection of rosetted, large, fleshy (rawhide), spiny-margined leaves that adds impact to any garden. Forms a rounded outline, the large leaves splaying in all directions from the center. Leaves are blue-green, with hooked spines along the margin and a sharp spine at the tip. Leaves are formidable, so use with discretion. Flowers occur in an elongated stalk (variable length) in paniculate fashion, each about 3 in. long and yellow-green. It supposedly flowers only once every hundred years, hence the common name. Actually flowers when physiologically mature at variable intervals. Have observed in a garden in Wrightsville, Georgia, in dry, sandy soil. Any well-drained soil in sun is suitable. Excellent drought and salt tolerance. Makes a striking container plant, particularly the variegated forms. Margin leaf spines are dangerous, so site with some thought

to safety. Individual leaves to 6 ft. long; entire plant grows 3 to 6 ft. high, 10 to 12 ft. wide. Zones (8)9 and 10. Mexico.

CULTIVARS AND VARIETIES
The literature mentions at least four variegated leaf forms; the most common is 'Marginata', with yellow-white margins and a more restrained habit.

Agave americana, century plant

Agave americana 'Marginata'

Ailanthus altissima
tree-of-heaven

The tree that grows in Brooklyn could be none other than this species. Tough, persistent, and durable to a fault, it has few redeeming landscape features. Asphalt, sidewalks, or construction seldom deter it from making an appearance. If its genes could be transferred to our agronomic crops, the need for pesticides would nearly disappear. In its finest form, the habit is upright-spreading, open, and coarse, with clubby branches. The dark green, 18- to 24-in.-long, compound pinnate leaves, composed of 13 to 15 leaflets, display no propensity to develop fall color. Yellow-green flowers appear in June, and male flowers have a particularly vile odor. Unfortunately, female plants set prodigious quantities of fruit, and the resulting seedlings can be troublesome. For impossible landscape situations, this might be an acceptable choice. Grows 40 to 60 ft. high. Zones 4 to 8. China, naturalized over much of the United States.

Akebia quinata
fiveleaf akebia

I have a strong love-hate relationship with this most vigorous twining vine. When restrained by proper pruning, the bronzy purple new leaves, which mature to rich blue-green, the rosy purple flowers, and the purple-violet

MORE ▶

Ailanthus altissima, tree-of-heaven

Ailanthus altissima

Ailanthus altissima

Akebia quinata, fiveleaf akebia

Akebia quinata

Akebia quinata CONTINUED

pods add up to a spectacular ornamental vine. Left to its own devices, however, it will colonize an area, twining around, over, and through other plants, shading them like kudzu. The leaves, composed of five 1½- to 3-in.-long leaflets, emerge early, often by March, and then persist, often into December. The flowers are hidden beneath the foliage and are curiously interesting. The three-sepaled, 1-in.-wide, chocolate-purple, slightly fragrant female flowers occur separately from the smaller, lighter-colored males. The 2¼- to 4-in.-long fruit resemble fattened, violet-purple sau-

sages. Fruit set is dependent upon another clone being available for cross-pollination. Adaptable to sun or shade, moist or dry soils, low or high pH, *Akebia quinata* is difficult to kill once in place. It is somewhat stoloniferous, which allows it to colonize and cover large ground areas. On a fence or other suitable structure, it is a respectable plant. I have also observed it as a groundcover. Use with the knowledge that it can transcend the boundaries imposed. There are white- and pink-flowered forms, as well as a white-fruited form. Grows 20 to 40 ft. Zones 4 to 8. Central and northeastern China, Korea, Japan.

Alangium platanifolium
lobed-leaf alangium

Although a relative newcomer to the gardens of the United States, the species offers large textured leaves, yellow fall color, yellow-white flowers, and small tree/large shrub habit. The 4- to 8-in.-long, dark green leaves are thick-textured and meld to soft yellow in fall. Cream-yellow flowers appear in May and June in a loose pendent inflorescence. Fruit are ½-in.-long, egg-shaped, thinly fleshy, blue drupes. Soils should be moist and well drained, although a specimen in the Dirr garden has prospered in the heat and drought of the Georgia summers. When grown as a small tree the habit is pyramidal-rounded; as a shrub, more spreading and vase-shaped. Among the most unrecognized plants in our garden. Also, tends to sucker and develop wandering shoots. Grows 6 to 10 (to 15) ft. high and wide. Zones (6)7 to 9. China.

Albizia julibrissin
silk tree, albizia, mimosa

Certainly a handsome small tree when the flowers appear like rosy pink brushstrokes across a green canvas. Unfortunately, this member of the legume family is extraordinarily susceptible to a wilt disease that causes gradual decline and eventual death. The habit is vase-shaped with

MORE ▶

Akebia quinata

Alangium platanifolium fall color

Akebia quinata

Alangium platanifolium

Alangium platanifolium, lobed-leaf alangium

Alangium platanifolium

Albizia julibrissin, silk tree

Albizia julibrissin CONTINUED

a broad-spreading, flat-topped crown. Rich green, almost tropical-looking, bipinnately compound leaves, to 20 in. in length, hold late in autumn and develop no appreciable fall color. This is one of the last trees to leaf out in spring. The fragrant, pink, brush-like flowers appear from June through August and are followed by 5- to 7-in.-long, gray-brown pods. Extremely tolerant of droughty, alkaline soils. At one time considered a choice small flowering tree, it is questionable in today's landscapes because of its disease susceptibility and invasive tendencies. Grows 20 to 35 ft. high and wide. Zones 6 to 9; low temperatures around –5 to –10°F result in some stem dieback. Iran to central China. CULTIVARS AND VARIETIES Merlot Majik™ ('Nurcar10') holds the rich merlot foliage color better than 'Summer Chocolate' in the heat of the South. Introduced by Ted Stephens, Nurseries Caroliniana.

'Pendula' is a green-leaf, weeping selection with pink flowers. It has been hybridized with the purple-leaf selections to produce a purple-leaf weeping form.

Variety *rosea* ('Ernest Wilson') is considerably more cold hardy than the typical species and tolerates –15°F; leaves are green, flowers pink.

'Summer Chocolate' was the first of the purple-leaf types and, indeed, is quite striking. Young shoots are bronze-green, maturing to purple and maintaining that color into fall. Flowers are a light pink-white. Seedling populations often contain purple-leaf types.

Variegated selections. White- and yellow-variegated leaf types are in various stages of testing.

Allamanda cathartica
golden trumpet or yellow allamanda

A fence, trellis, and mailbox plant, vining in character, that is hardy only in the deep coastal South and West but is widely available in the North and South for color in the summer landscape. The glossy, leathery, broadleaf evergreen leaves, 4 to 6 in. long, occur in twos (up to five) at each node. Flowers develop on new growth over the entire growing season. Each five-lobed flower is shaped like a morning glory, 3 to 6 in. long and wide; red-brown buds open golden yellow. Best flowering in full sun in fertile, well-drained soil. Prune to keep tidy, and since flowers are formed on new growth, greater production will occur. Wonderful color element around pools and high traffic areas; requires support to climb. Grows 10 ft. high or more. Zones 9 to 11. South America.

Albizia julibrissin

Albizia julibrissin

Albizia julibrissin 'Summer Chocolate'

Allamanda cathartica, golden trumpet allamanda

CULTIVARS AND VARIETIES
'Hendersonii' has attractive, large, orange-yellow flowers.

Alnus
alder

Shunned, rejected, and unloved . . . the fate of alders, both shrubs and trees, but in my assessment, worthy subjects for difficult situations. About 35 species with most harboring the ability to fix nitrogen, thus ensuring survival where lesser plants languish. Typically native to watery habitats but adaptable to drier situations. Male flowers in slender catkins, usually before leaves although a few flower summer into fall; female flowers in cone-like structures containing many papery or leathery winged samaras. Seeds germinate on moist medium and require no special stratification

MORE ▶

Catkins on *Alnus glutinosa*

"Cones" of *Alnus cordata*

Alnus rhombifolia, water alder

Allamanda cathartica 'Hendersonii'

Alnus incana 'Pendula'

Alnus CONTINUED

treatment. Distributed across the northern hemisphere, to Central America into the Andes. Two western U.S. species, *Alnus rhombifolia*, water alder, and *A. rubra*, are large trees. *Alnus japonica*, Japanese alder, bears beautiful, deeply veined, lustrous dark green leaves. *Alnus hirsuta*, Manchurian alder, with dull, dark gray-green leaves yielded Prairie Horizon® ('Harbin'), a rapid-growing tree for dry sites. A most beautiful weeping tree is *A. incana* 'Pendula', which crossed my path in several European gardens. Difficult to locate an alder in American commerce, yet I remain hopeful that a few species will see the light of landscape day.

Alnus cordata
Italian alder

In landscape status, the Italian alder most assuredly plays second fiddle to its close relative *Alnus glutinosa*, common alder. Ornamentally, however, this species is superior, attractive throughout the seasons. In early spring, the yellowish brown, pendulous catkins sway in the soft breeze. The large (1 in. long), egg-shaped fruit look like small pine cones. Habit is pyramidal to pyramidal-oval, and after the lustrous dark green, 2- to 4-in.-long leaves fall, a clean, finely branched winter silhouette is evident. An excellent choice near water, but it is also at home in drier soils. Withstands infertile, high pH soils. Deserves a longer look by American gardeners. Grows 30 to 50 ft. high, 20 to 40 ft. wide. Zones 5 to 7(8). Corsica, southern Italy.

Alnus glutinosa
common or European alder

This dark, somber broadleaf tree is often found in the English landscape, especially along watercourses. In America, it has naturalized along stream banks to the point of weediness. In youth the outline is pyramidal, becoming ovoid or oblong and somewhat irregular with maturity. It has often been grown multi-stemmed and makes an attractive specimen. The dark green, 2- to 4-in.-long, 3- to 4-in.-wide leaves offer no hint of fall color and die off green or brown. One

Alnus cordata, Italian alder

Alnus glutinosa, common alder

of the best trees for wet soils, it can endure standing water for a time. It fixes atmospheric nitrogen and is able to survive infertile soils. Tent caterpillars can be a problem. Grows 40 to 60 ft. high, 20 to 40 ft. wide. Zones 3 to 7. Europe, western Asia, northern Africa.

CULTIVARS AND VARIETIES
'Imperialis' bears finely dissected leaves and provides a much finer-textured imprint on the landscape.

'Pyramidalis' ('Fastigiata') is a distinct columnar form not unlike Lombardy poplar, *Populus nigra* 'Italica'. It can be used for screening in areas where *Alnus glutinosa* would spread out of bounds.

Alnus serrulata
tag or hazel alder
Considered the southern counterpart of *Alnus rugosa*, speckled alder, and common along watercourses throughout the South although native as far

north as Maine. I find this a most attractive, large spreading shrub or small pyramidal tree. The dark green, 2- to 4-in.-long leaves die off green to brown in autumn. The male flowers

open in February and March and dangle like worms from the branches. On the same plant, the reddish purple female flowers open at the same

MORE ▶

Alnus cordata

Alnus glutinosa

Alnus glutinosa 'Pyramidalis'

Alnus glutinosa 'Imperialis'

Alnus serrulata

Alnus serrulata, tag alder

81

Alnus serrulata CONTINUED

time. The female flowers produce fruit that mature in fall and are ½ in. long, resembling brownish pine cones in shape. Adaptable to drier soils as well as flooding, it is a great plant for naturalizing along stream banks, rivers, and troublesome erosion areas. Grows 10 to 20 ft. high and wide. Zones (4)5 to 9. Maine, south to Florida and Louisiana.

Amelanchier alnifolia
Saskatoon serviceberry

A shrubby species that has been domesticated for fruit production, with superior cultivars like 'Regent', 'Smokey', 'Success', 'Thiessen', and others now available. Leaves, sharply and coarsely toothed compared to eastern species, are dark green and may develop orange-red fall color. White flowers on naked stems are followed by ⅓- to ½-in.-wide, bluish purple, sweet, juicy berries in June (Minnesota). Tolerates harsh climates and alkaline soils. Entomosporium leaf spot is problematic in the Midwest, East, and South. I typically see 6- to 10-ft.-high shrubs, but national champion in Washington State is 41 ft. high and wide. Zones 2 to 5(6). Great Plains, from Manitoba and Saskatchewan to Nebraska.

Amelanchier arborea
downy serviceberry, Juneberry, shadbush, service-tree, sarvis-tree

One of the finest native North American species for naturalizing at the edge of woodlands. In the wild, it occurs along streams and on rocky slopes as a small tree or a large, multi-stemmed shrub of rounded outline. The emerging leaves are covered with numerous hairs, which impart an almost pussy-willow effect. Leaves mature to a rich green, 1 to 3 in. long, and in October they color yellow, orange, and apricot to dull, deep, dusty red. White flowers, in fleecy 2- to 4-in.-long racemes, appear slightly before or with the leaves in April. In June, the ¼- to ⅓-in.-wide fruit mature from green to red and finally to purple-black. The fruit taste much like those of highbush blueberry (*Vaccinium corymbosum*) but are slightly sweeter, and they make outstanding pies. Birds are particularly fond of the fruit, so it is often a race between homeowner and feathered creature. With the annual rites of winter, the beautiful smooth, grayish streaked bark assumes center stage and provides an excellent effect. Downy serviceberry is adaptable to acid and high pH soils, and to moist or relatively dry situations. Many cultivars have

Amelanchier alnifolia, Saskatoon serviceberry

Amelanchier arborea, downy serviceberry

Amelanchier alnifolia

Amelanchier arborea

been introduced, including several notable selections of the hybrid of *Amelanchier arborea* and *A. laevis*, *A. ×grandiflora* (which see). Its cosmopolitan nature should endear this species to more gardeners. At home in Chicago, Boston, and Atlanta. Grows 15 to 25 ft. high, variable spread; can grow to 40 ft. Zones 4 to 9. Maine to Iowa, south to northern Florida and Louisiana.

Amelanchier canadensis
shadblow serviceberry

The true *Amelanchier canadensis* is hopelessly confused in the landscape trade. In general, it is an upright, suckering, tightly multi-stemmed shrub with a dome-shaped crown. The leaves, 1½ to 2½ in. long, are similar to those of *A. arborea*, but the white flowers come in more compact, 2- to 3-in.-long racemes and are held in a more upright position. To this author, the fruit do not have the flavor of those of *A. arborea* or *A. laevis*. In flower, shadblow serviceberry is not as dominant as the other species, but it is still an effective landscape element. It occurs naturally in bogs and swamps along the eastern seaboard, but under cultivation, it performs well in drier soils. A wonderful plant to use around ponds, lakes, and streams,

MORE ▶

Amelanchier arborea

Amelanchier canadensis, shadblow serviceberry

Amelanchier arborea fall color

Amelanchier canadensis fall color

or in boggy or marshy ground. It will never disappoint. Grows 6 to 20 ft. high. Zones 3 to 7(8). Maine to South Carolina, along the coast.

Amelanchier ×grandiflora
apple serviceberry
A naturally occurring hybrid between *Amelanchier arborea* and *A. laevis*, it exhibits characteristics intermediate between those of the parent species. Absolute identification is difficult. The newly emerging leaves are purplish

Amelanchier ×grandiflora 'Ballerina'

Amelanchier ×grandiflora 'Autumn Brilliance' fall color

Amelanchier ×grandiflora 'Princess Diana'

tinged and slightly pubescent, traits that distinguish the hybrid from its parents. Grows 20 to 25 ft. high, similar spread. Zones (4)5 to 8(9).

CULTIVARS AND VARIETIES

Several interesting cultivars have been selected. The best of the influx include 'Autumn Brilliance', with red fall color, 'Ballerina', with brick-red fall color, and 'Princess Diana', with red fall color. 'Robin Hill' and 'Rubescens' have pink buds that fade upon opening.

Amelanchier laevis

Allegheny serviceberry

Another serviceberry not too different from the other species, especially *Amelanchier arborea*, in flower, fruit, bark, and growth habit. The principal differences are the purplish to bronze color of the emerging leaves and the lack (almost) of hairs on the leaves and flower stalks. When the leaves mature to summer green, it is virtually impossible to distinguish this from the three previous serviceberries; for most purposes, they are interchangeable in the landscape. Grows 15 to 25 (to 40) ft. high, similar spread. Zones 4 to 8. Newfoundland to Georgia and Alabama, west to Michigan and Kansas.

An enigmatic species is *Amelanchier lamarckii*, with rich bronze-red (coppery red) new growth and abundant white flowers. Typically a loose, elegant shrub with dark green leaves turning orange and red in fall. Fruit are blue-black. Resistant to leaf spot.

Amorpha canescens

leadplant amorpha

Although seldom used in contemporary landscapes, this gray-leaved shrub provides worthwhile summer foliage color. The leaves are composed of 15 to 45 grayish leaflets, each ⅓ to 1 in. long, resulting in a fine texture. Purplish flowers occur in 1- to 2-in.-long, cylindrical terminal panicles in June and July. Prospers under hot,

MORE ▶

Amelanchier laevis, Allegheny serviceberry

Amelanchier laevis

Amelanchier laevis

Amorpha canescens, leadplant amorpha

Amorpha canescens CONTINUED

dry conditions. Observed growing on a dry, sandy hillside above the Mississippi floodplain in Minnesota. Grows 2 to 4 ft. high and wide. Zones 2 to 6. Manitoba and Saskatchewan, south to Iowa and New Mexico.

Amorpha fruticosa
indigobush amorpha

My first encounter with this shrub provided convincing evidence that I would never use it in the garden. The habit is upright-spreading, rather unkempt and untidy. In winter, the gray-brown stems look as if they were dead. The bright green foliage is rather pleasing and probably the shrub's most noteworthy attribute. Flowers are purplish blue with orange anthers and occur in 3- to 6-in.-long upright spikes in June. Adaptable to infertile, dry, sandy soils as well as moist, damp areas. Once

planted, it remains for life. Utilize in dry soils and full sun where precious few plants will prosper. Grows 6 to 20 ft. high, 5 to 15 ft. wide. Zones (3)4 to 9. Observed in the wild along a marsh at Middleton Place, Charleston, South Carolina and on the banks of Crooked Creek, southwest Virginia. Connecticut to Minnesota, south to Florida and Louisiana.

Ampelopsis brevipedunculata
porcelain ampelopsis, porcelain-vine

As much as this plant is ballyhooed for its excellent yellow to pale lilac to bright blue fruit, the species makes a minimal contribution to the smaller garden. I grew a plant on a downspout of my Illinois home and had to wade through five or six viburnums to even see the fruit of this vine. Porcelain-vine climbs by twining and

tendrils; unless provided a structure, it becomes a viny heap. The dark green, 2½- to 5-in.-long, three- (rarely five-) lobed leaves seldom develop fall color. Greenish flowers open in June, July, and August, followed by ¼- to ⅓-in.-wide fruit in September and October. Adaptable to varied soils, but site in full sun for best fruiting. Japanese beetles love the foliage. Use in a semi-naturalized way by allowing it to scramble over a rock pile or wall, or perhaps a lattice or open fence. Exceptionally vigorous and aggressive, shows invasive tendencies. Grows 10 to 20 ft. high or more. Zones 4 to 8. China, Korea, Japan, Russian Far East.

CULTIVARS AND VARIETIES
'Elegans', which appears to be a selection of var. *maximowiczii*, displays greenish white and pink leaf color when young, maturing to green

Amorpha canescens

Amorpha fruticosa

Ampelopsis brevipedunculata, porcelain ampelopsis

Ampelopsis brevipedunculata var. *maximowiczii* 'Elegans'

and white. Not as vigorous as the species.

Variety *maximowiczii* has leaves with lobes more deeply cut than those of the species. More common in commerce than the species.

Andrachne colchica
andrachne
Resides in the Never Never Land of deciduous shrubs, and even when one reads the label indicating such,

stunned disbelief is the result. I have observed this wispy shrub only in arboreta, its long, arching branches forming a fountain-like outline. Leaves, rich green, ¼ to ¾ in. long, half as wide, assume sporadic yellow tints in fall. Flowers (yellow-green) and fruit are not showy. Prune in late winter to induce the elongated shoots. Another quiz-your-friends species, perhaps useful as a filler in a sunny border. Appears to thrive with neglect. Grows 2 to 3

(to 5) ft. high and wider at maturity. Large, old, archaic, creaky specimen at Missouri Botanical Garden. Zones 5 to 7. Asia Minor.

Andromeda polifolia
bog-rosemary
Diminutive evergreen shrub with creeping rootstock and upright, minimally branched stems. The dark green, 1- to 1½-in.-long, ⅛- to ⅓-in.-wide leaves are silver-tomentose on the lower surface. Pretty white tinged pink flowers, in two- to eight-flowered umbels, open in May and June. Found in cool, moist peat/sphagnum bogs. Chanced upon the species in an Orono, Maine, bog, some plants with silver-blue foliage. Beautiful, finicky, bog- and rock-garden plant for northern gardens. Grows (6 in.) 1 to 2 ft. by 2 to 3 ft. Zones 2 to 5. Northern

MORE ▶

Amorpha fruticosa, indigobush amorpha

Andrachne colchica, andrachne

Andromeda polifolia, bog-rosemary

Andromeda polifolia

Andromeda polifolia CONTINUED

hemisphere, in North America south to New York and Idaho.

CULTIVARS AND VARIETIES
Many compact cultivars have been selected. My question . . . How much smaller can the compact version be than the typical species?

'Blue Ice' has silver-blue leaves and a uniform compact-mounded habit; 'Nana' is a perfect broad mound of rich green leaves. Both are 1 ft. high, 2 ft. wide.

Antigonon leptopus, coral vine

Antigonon leptopus

Antigonon leptopus
coral vine

Jogging around Brownsville, Texas, in October, I kept passing this rich pink-flowered vine. I tracked its identity and did the necessary taxonomic homework. The next time I witnessed it was in Charleston, South Carolina. A rampant twining deciduous vine, climbing by tendrils and requiring support. The bright green, heart- to arrow-shaped leaves, 3 to 4 in. long, are coarsely veined with wavy margins. The flowers open in summer; their showy portion, the reddish pink sepals, literally hides the foliage. As long as new growth continues, flowers will be produced. Prefers full sun and warm temperatures, well-drained soil, and low to moderate fertility. I have observed it draped over walls and fences to the degree the structures are hidden. The floral effect is overwhelming. Use with caution. Can become weedy and invasive. Fast-growing to 20 (to 40) ft. or more. Zones 8 to 10. Mexico.

CULTIVARS AND VARIETIES
'Alba' is a white-flowered form.

Aralia elata
Japanese angelica tree

Truly one of the great plants for foliage texture, this species provides a rare opportunity to bring the tropics to the north temperate zone. The gigantic compound leaves are 3 to 5½ ft. in length, slightly less in width. One leaf provides shade for an entire garden party. The 2- to 5-in.-long, dark green leaflets may turn yellow to reddish purple in fall. The habit varies from an irregularly shaped tree to a large, spreading, suckering shrub. White, 12- to 18-in.-wide inflorescences appear in August and are followed by purplish fruit. Not particular as to soils and tolerates partial shade or full sun. Grows 20 to 30 ft. high, variable spread. Zones (3)4 to 8. Japan, Korea, China, Russia.

CULTIVARS AND VARIETIES
'Variegata', with creamy white leaf margins, and 'Aureo-variegata', with yellow-margined leaves, are great color elements in garden corners. 'Silver Umbrella' parallels 'Variegata' in characteristics. All are slow-growing.

Aralia spinosa
devil's-walkingstick, Hercules'-club

Very similar to *Aralia elata*, differing in its smaller size and more vigorous suckering habit. A great native species for textural effect, but it needs to be restrained in the landscape to prevent rampant spread. The rich dark blue-green leaves are free of pestiferous nuances and may turn yellow to purplish in fall. Prominent white flowers occur in 12- to 18-in.-wide inflorescences in mid to late summer. The light brown, clubby stems are armed with prominent prickles, providing the basis for the common names. Often seen in the eastern states in moist soils along highways. Grows 10 to 20 ft. high, spreads almost indefinitely unless restrained. Zones 4 to 9. Southern Pennsylvania to eastern Iowa, south to Florida and east Texas.

CULTIVARS AND VARIETIES

A cream-margined leaf selection will be offered by Broken Arrow Nursery, Hamden, Connecticut.

Aralia spinosa fall color

Aralia spinosa, devil's-walkingstick

Aralia spinosa

Aralia elata, Japanese angelica tree

Aralia elata

Aralia elata 'Variegata'

89

Araucaria araucana
monkey puzzle

A wild and rather "scary" tree with open splaying branches and spirally arranged, 1- to 2-in.-long, sharp-pointed, dark green leaves that cover the branches like armor plates. The habit is pyramidal-oval in youth, later with a slender bole and ascending branches near the top. The tree is associated with the Victorian era in England, where it was planted in great numbers. Male flowers occur in 3- to 5-in.-long cylindrical catkins; female in 5- to 8-in.-wide, pineapple-shaped cones that take two years to mature. Cones are about twice the size of hand grenades and hurt even worse. Tolerates extremes of soil, except permanently moist. Useful as a specimen, or for groupings or accent. Have observed on the West Coast in reasonable numbers; seldom grown in southeastern United States. Grows 50 to 80 ft. high. Zones (7)8 to 11. Chile, Argentina.

Araucaria angustifolia has been successful at the Atlanta Botanical Garden and is now 50 ft. high.

Arbutus menziesii
madrone

At its most beautiful, a one-of-a-kind evergreen tree with striking cinnamon-brown bark. The habit varies from cloud-like and low-branched to tall, slender trees. I have observed both types on Vancouver Island, British Columbia. The younger branches shed the brown bark in scales and sheets, exposing the red-brown to red inner bark. The leaves are lustrous dark green, 2 to 6 in. long. Flowers, urn-shaped, ¼ to ⅓ in. long, white, occur in 3- to 9-in.-long, 6-in.-wide terminal panicles in May. The ½-in.-wide red fruit color in fall and persist into winter. Transplant from containers into well-drained, dryish soils. Excessive irrigation may prove lethal. Have noticed leaf spot susceptibility, particularly on plants in English gardens. Remarkable for the beauty of its bark. The tree would almost be more beautiful without foliage. Grows 20 to 50 ft. high, 15 to 30 ft. wide in gardens; 75 to 100 ft. in native habitat. Zones 7 to 10. British Columbia to San Francisco area.

Arbutus unedo
strawberry tree

I was privileged to experience the species in the Killarney National Park, Ireland, where it exists as a large shrub to small tree. The evergreen foliage is 2 to 4 in. long and provides a dark green contrast to the ¼-in.-long, urn-shaped white flowers that open from October through December. The ¾-in.-wide, orange-shaped

MORE ▶

Araucaria araucana

Araucaria araucana, monkey puzzle

Araucaria angustifolia

Arbutus menziesii

Arbutus menziesii, madrone

Arbutus menziesii

Arbutus unedo, strawberry tree

Arbutus unedo

Arbutus unedo

Arbutus unedo

Arbutus unedo CONTINUED

fruit ripen the year following flowering. Fruit are orange-red, almost fluorescent, and will definitely turn heads. Moist, well-drained soil, in sun or shade is suitable. Once established, will tolerate drier soils. Great accent or novelty plant and certainly a plant for the collector. Plants have come and gone in Athens, yet a particular 12-ft. specimen prospers in the University's Botanical Garden. Grows 10 to 15 ft. high, 8 to 12 ft. wide; to 30 ft. high in the wild. Zones 7 to 10. Southwestern Ireland to the Mediterranean region.

Arbutus ×andrachnoides, a hybrid between *A. unedo* and *A. andrachne*, is more common in cultivation than the latter parent. Unique for its rich reddish brown bark, smaller size, and easier culture. Zones 7 to 10.

CULTIVARS AND VARIETIES
Several of garden interest, including 'Compacta' with contorted, picturesque branching; 5 ft. by 5 ft.

'Elfin King' bears abundant flowers and fruit and grows 5 to 10 ft. high.

'Rubra' produces red-budded, dark pink flowers.

Arctostaphylos uva-ursi
bearberry, kinnikinnick

At its best, among the most beautiful of broadleaf evergreen groundcovers. Unfortunately, excessive moisture and fertilizer are anathema. On Cape Cod, in "pure" sand and maritime conditions, plants form ever-widening circles of lustrous dark green. The obovate leaves, ¼ to 1¼ in. long, ¼ to ½ in. wide, may assume bronze to reddish purple tints in winter. Flowers, white tinged pink, urn-shaped, ⅙ to ¼ in. long, are present April to May. Fruit are bright red, ¼- to ⅓-in.-wide, fleshy drupes, ripening in July and August and persisting into winter. Certainly where it can be grown, an outstanding and beautiful groundcover. Grows 6 to 12 in. high, 2 to 4 ft. wide. Zones 2 to 5. Circumboreal.

CULTIVARS AND VARIETIES
'Massachusetts' is one of the best and most widely grown selections because of resistance to leaf spot and gall.

Ardisia japonica
Japanese ardisia, marlberry

An evergreen groundcover planting of this species under a massive live oak, *Quercus virginiana*, at Live Oak Gardens, New Iberia, Louisiana, made a believer out of me. Beautiful lustrous dark green leaves blanket the ground as thoroughly as *Pachysandra terminalis*. The 1½- to 3½-in.-long leaves, tapered at their ends, are crowded at the end of the stems and appear whorled. The white to pink,

MORE ▶

Arbutus ×andrachnoides

Arbutus ×andrachnoides

Arbutus unedo 'Compacta'

Arctostaphylos uva-ursi, bearberry

Arctostaphylos uva-ursi

Arctostaphylos uva-ursi

Arctostaphylos uva-ursi 'Massachusetts'

Ardisia japonica, Japanese ardisia

Ardisia japonica

Ardisia japonica

Ardisia crenata, coralberry

Ardisia japonica CONTINUED

star-shaped, ½-in.-wide flowers are borne two to six together in July and August and sporadically thereafter. Fruit, ¼-in.-wide red drupes, mature in fall and persist through winter. Cultur-ally, acid, organic, moist, well-drained soils are ideal. Site in partial to full shade. Have tried the species and cul-tivars in our zone 7 garden; only 'Chiri-men' survived. Foliage is often injured by late spring frosts. Grows 8 to 12 (to 16) in. high and spreads indefinitely by rhizomes. Zones 8 and 9(10). Japan, China.

The related species *Ardisia crenata*, coralberry, spiceberry, has shiny, dark green, toothed, evergreen leaves to 8 in. long, white to pink flowers, and bright red fruit. Requires well-drained soils and partial to full shade. A sturdy plant grew in a protected pocket by our home; flowered and fruited every year until 10°F and an up/down winter elimi-nated it. Grows 2 to 4 (to 6) ft. high. Zones 8 to 10. Japan to northern India.

Ardisia crenata

Aristolochia macrophylla

syn. *Aristolochia durior*

Dutchman's pipe

Older residences throughout the Mid-west and East often used this vine as a kind of sun shield or venetian blind to shade porches. Typically, a set of strings or trellis was attached to the porch, and the twining nature of Dutch-

Aristolochia macrophylla

Aristolochia macrophylla, Dutchman's pipe

Aronia arbutifolia, red chokeberry

man's pipe would take the leaves to the top in about six to eight weeks. The 4- to 12-in.-long, dark green leaves may stand out like elephant ears but serve a functional purpose. The flowers, which bloom from the leaf axils in May and June, resemble a meerschaum pipe. In order to see the flowers, the foliage must be parted. Extremely adaptable. Withstands full sun or partial shade. Relatively common along Blue Ridge Parkway from Cherokee to Asheville, North Carolina. Grows 20 to 30 ft. high. Zones 4 to 8. Pennsylvania to Georgia, west to Minnesota and Kansas.

Aronia arbutifolia
red chokeberry

Red chokeberry labors in obscurity and is seldom available in commerce. The shrub's bright red fruit are long persistent, and they are shunned by birds, as is suggested by the name "chokeberry." A mature specimen or colony can be spectacular in October as the leaves turn brilliant red. The 1½- to 3½-in.-long, lustrous dark green leaves, handsome throughout the spring and summer, are free of serious insects and diseases. White flowers occur in May in 1- to 2-in.-wide clusters of nine to 20. The ¼-in.-wide, rounded, bright red fruit start to ripen in September and persist through winter. Unfortunately, the habit is somewhat leggy, and old specimens appear disheveled. Proliferates in well-drained, acid, and organic-laden soils, but it is quite adaptable. Use in borders or masses, or as a bank cover along streams and ponds. Grows 6 to 10 ft. high, variable spread; usually wider at maturity. Zones 4 to 9. Massachusetts to Minnesota, south to Florida and Texas.

CULTIVARS AND VARIETIES
'Brilliantissima' has waxier, more lustrous leaves and more vivid red fall foliage. On occasion, it rivals *Euonymus alatus*, winged euonymus, for fall color.

Aronia melanocarpa
black chokeberry

This species is generally considered inferior to *Aronia arbutifolia*, although it does offer several worthwhile ornamental attributes, including large, long-persistent black fruit and wine-red fall color. Fruit are made into juice, with 'McKenzie', 'Nero', and 'Viking' selected for fruit qualities. Habit is similar to that of *A. arbutifolia*, perhaps less leggy. The 1- to 3-in.-long leaves are a rich, lustrous dark green. The small, white flowers do not overwhelm. Adaptable to many soils, in sun or partial shade. Use in borders, masses, or large groupings. Can colonize large areas. Grows 3 to 5 (to 10)

MORE ▶

Aronia arbutifolia

Aronia arbutifolia

Aronia arbutifolia 'Brilliantissima' fall color

Aronia melanocarpa CONTINUED
ft. high. Zones 3 to 8(9). Nova Scotia to Florida, west to Michigan.
CULTIVARS AND VARIETIES
'Autumn Magic' and Iroquois Beauty™

('Morton') are more compact versions of the species although the former at the Minnesota Landscape Arboretum was leggy, loose, open, and ugly.

Variety *elata* is superior to the spe-

cies from a landscape perspective because of its greater stature, 6 to 10 ft. high and wide, with larger leaves, flowers, and fruit. Certainly worth considering where an aronia is to be used.

Asimina triloba
pawpaw

Simply a great plant for foliage effect. The droopy, 6- to 12-in.-long leaves lend a sleepy, "shut-eye" aura to the summer landscape. This beautiful native tree is often found as an understory plant in cool, moist, alluvial soils along streams. Lurid purple flowers creep out of hairy brown buds before the leaves in April and May. They are followed by edible, waxy, irregularly shaped berries, 2 to 5 in. long. The fruit are greenish yellow maturing to black and have a slight banana-like taste. The rich green leaves turn spectacular yellow to golden hues in fall.

Aronia melanocarpa, black chokeberry

Aronia melanocarpa fall color

Asimina triloba, pawpaw

Asimina triloba

It prefers moist, well-drained soils, in shade to full sun. Difficult to transplant; gardeners should opt for small container-grown seedlings. Will sucker and produce colonies that have an almost eerie, enchanted-forest quality. Unfortunately, this species is virtually nonexistent in the retail nursery trade, but it can be obtained from specialty mail-order firms that offer fruit crops. Grows 15 to 20 ft. high and wide; can grow 30 to 40 ft. in favorable locations. Zones 5 to 9. A favorite of the author, especially in fall in its native haunts. New York to Florida, west to Nebraska and Texas.

Asimina parviflora, dwarf pawpaw, is a reduced-in-stature version of *A. triloba*. I find it in the Piedmont of Georgia, always in the shade. Grows 6 to 8 ft. high. Zones 7 to 9. Virginia to Mississippi and east Texas.

Aucuba japonica
Japanese aucuba

Considered old-fashioned, dated, tired, and dinosauristic, but the infusion of new cultivars has brought the species a rejuvenated lease on landscape life. Typically, haystack to rounded evergreen shrub, consisting of a thicket of erect or arching, limitedly branched shoots. The

MORE ▶

Asimina triloba fall color

Asimina triloba

Asimina triloba

Aucuba japonica, Japanese aucuba

Aucuba japonica male flowers

97

Aucuba japonica CONTINUED
species has lustrous leathery dark green leaves, 3 to 8 in. long and either entire or coarsely toothed. Leaves hold their color throughout the seasons when sited in shade. Flowers, male and female, open in March and April on separate plants, lurid purple on both, the former in large terminal panicles, the latter in clusters from the axils of the leaves. Female flowers yield shiny scarlet ellipsoidal drupes, ½ in. or longer, that ripen in fall and persist into winter. Grows in almost any well-drained soil, but should be sited in shade. Young leaves may blacken (burn) when exposed to full sun. Good choice for the shadowy area of the garden. The variegated leaf cultivars provide color to heavily shaded areas. Grows 6 to 10 ft. high and wide. Zones 7 to 10. Japan.

CULTIVARS AND VARIETIES
Numerous recent introductions with striking leaf shapes, variegation patterns, and fruit color and abundance. The best collection I observed resides at Hawksridge Nursery, Hickory, North Carolina.

'Crotonifolia' (female) and 'Marmorata' (female) are superb gold-variegated leaf forms, each richly endowed with vibrant gold markings consuming 70 percent of the leaf surface.

Aucuba japonica

Aucuba japonica 'Rozannie'

Aucuba japonica 'Crotonifolia'

Aucuba japonica 'Hosaba Hoshifu'

Aucuba japonica 'Variegata'

'Hosaba Hoshifu' (male) has narrow, lance-shaped leaves, to 9 in. long, 2½ in. wide, dark green and covered with yellow-gold blotches/spots.

'Mr. Goldstrike' (male) and 'Golden King' (male) are beautiful gold-speckled leaf forms that serve as pollinators for the female forms.

'Pink Champagne' has large, leathery, lustrous dark green leaves and champagne-pink fruit; grows 5 to 6 ft.

'Rozannie' (female) is a compact, 3- to 4-ft.-high and -wide form with lustrous dark green foliage.

'Variegata' (female), gold dust plant, the common form in cultivation, is less gold-speckled than 'Crotonifolia' and 'Marmorata'.

Azara microphylla

The genus umbrellas ten species of evergreen trees and shrubs, native to South America, with fragrant, mustard-yellow flowers in spring and summer. My observations point to *Azara microphylla* as the most common, at least in European gardens. Develops into a large shrub or small tree clothed with ½- to ⅝-in.-long, ⅓-in.-wide, lustrous dark green leaves. Flowers, yellow, chocolate fragrance, appeared in early March (Hillier). Light shade and moist, well-drained, reasonably fertile soils suit it best. Worthy plant for espalier in a courtyard, container plant, or accent. Grows 15 to 20 ft. high and wide. Zones (8)9 and 10 on West Coast. Chile, Argentina.
CULTIVARS AND VARIETIES
'Variegata', with yellow-cream-margined leaves, is quite pretty.

Baccharis halimifolia

groundsel-bush

So nondescript that its presence is undetected until the female plants develop their cottony white fruit, akin to dandelion seed heads, in late summer and fall. I have observed entire fields and marshy areas in Georgia and Louisiana literally invaded by the species. The habit is loose, lax, and arching, with occasional compact, oval to rounded forms evident. The bright to soft green foliage is attractive and may remain evergreen to semi-evergreen in the South; deciduous in the North. Species is dioecious, sexes

MORE ▶

Azara microphylla

Baccharis halimifolia, groundsel-bush

Baccharis halimifolia

Baccharis halimifolia CONTINUED
separate, with flowering and fruiting occurring in summer and fall, respectively. In Georgia, fruit persist into December. Grows in dry and moist soils; extremely salt-tolerant and easily maintained by cutting to the ground in late winter. Best as a filler in the border for foliage contrast. Aggressive and has taken over abandoned fields and dump sites. Plant a male to avoid seed production. However, the showy white fruit will be absent. Grows 5 to 12 ft. high and wide. Zones 5 to 9. Massachusetts to Florida and Texas.

Bauhinia variegata
orchid tree
No *Bauhinia* species is truly hardy below 20°F, but during travels to Orlando, Florida, I see *Bauhinia variegata* (pale purple to white flowers) and *B. ×blakeana* (pink to pinkish purple flowers) more than any other. Although tree-like in habit, most grow as large shrubs. Leaves are light green and deeply cleft at the apex and base, producing a twin-leaf effect. Leaves may drop in fall or persist into winter. The great beauty is allocated to the orchid-like flowers with five unequal petals, each narrowed to a claw. The 2- to 3-in.-wide, light pink to orchid-purple flowers open in January and February. The 1-in.-

Bauhinia variegata, orchid tree

Bauhinia variegata

Bauhinia ×blakeana, Hong Kong orchid tree

Bauhinia ×blakeana

Berberis candidula

long, flat, sharp-beaked pods form after flowering. Place in full sun, well-drained soil, and stake for tree habit. *Bauhinia* species are listed as deer-resistant. Flowers on old wood, so reserve pruners until after flowering. Beautiful specimen shrub or tree, best located in a border. Grows 15 to 25 ft. high, more often 10 to 15 ft. as a shrub. Zones (9)10 and 11. India, China.

Bauhinia ×*blakeana*, Hong Kong orchid tree, has larger flowers, 5 to 6 in. across, in a range of colors from reddish to orchid-pink in late fall to spring. The gray-green foliage is tardily deciduous. Grows 20 ft. high. Zones 10 and 11. China.

CULTIVARS AND VARIETIES
'Candida' has white flowers.

Berberis
barberry

Over 400 species of evergreen and deciduous shrubs with typically yellow to orange flowers and a range of fruit colors. *Berberis thunbergii* is the species of major importance in garden commerce. Thirty new cultivars were added to the 2009 revision of the *Manual* and more are on the way. This species is under assault for its aggressive invasive nature. New Hampshire and Massachusetts have banned its sale, and considerable breeding research is focused on developing sterile cultivars. The new, compact, colorful cultivars are eye-catching garden plants and possible low fruit producers. *Berberis thunbergii* and cultivars are utilized by the millions in the United States and worldwide. Stay tuned.

Berberis candidula
paleleaf barberry

This diminutive evergreen species makes a handsome addition to any perennial border or rock garden, and it can serve as a functional mass or large groundcover plant. Broad-mounded in habit, the branches are rigidly arching and covered with three-parted spines. The 1- to 2-in.-long leaves are lustrous dark green above, silver below. Bright yellow, 5/8-in.-wide flowers appear in May and June. I have never observed fruit set, although it is described as a grayish purple, 1/2-in.-long berry. Transplant from a container into any well-drained soil, in sun or

MORE ▶

Berberis candidula, paleleaf barberry

Berberis verruculosa, warty barberry

Berberis verruculosa

partial shade. In northern areas, protect from extreme wind and sun. Numerous evergreen barberries are available, but identification is quite difficult. *Berberis candidula* is one of the best. Grows 2 to 4 ft. high, to 5 ft. wide. Zones 5 to 8. China.

Berberis verruculosa, warty barberry, is similar to and often confused with *B. candidula*. I have studied many specimens and have yet to discover a reliable method of distinguishing the two species. Supposedly, the stems of *B. verruculosa* are warty (bumpy), the undersides of the leaves not as silvery, and the ultimate size larger (3 to 6 ft. tall). Having grown the two plants side by side in my Illinois garden, I know *B. verruculosa* is less hardy than *B. candidula*. Best in zone 6.

Berberis ×*gladwynensis* 'William Penn'

A hybrid evergreen barberry that has become popular in the Mid-Atlantic states. The spiny, 1- to 2-in.-long, lustrous dark green leaves turn bronzed-red in winter. Yellow flowers open in April and May. The habit is mounded-spreading. Makes an effective ground-cover or mass. Grows 3 to 4 ft. high and wide. Zones 6 to 8.

Berberis julianae
wintergreen barberry

Probably the best-known garden representative of the evergreen barberries, this species develops into a large, rounded, impenetrable mass of heavy, rich dark green leaves and three-parted, spiny stems. Abundant golden yellow flowers appear in March and April, followed by rather inconspicuous small, grayish, waxy-coated fruit. Easily transplanted and grown. The most common evergreen barberry in gardens on the East Coast. A great foliage and barrier plant, wintergreen

Berberis ×*gladwynensis* 'William Penn'

Berberis julianae

Berberis julianae, wintergreen barberry

Berberis julianae 'Spring Glory'

barberry has kept many college students in bounds on their way to and from classes. Grows 6 to 8 (to 10) ft. high and wide. Zones 5 to 8. China.

CULTIVARS AND VARIETIES

'Nana' is more compact and suitable for smaller gardens. It has all the attributes of the species but is half the size. Plants that I have seen are mounded-spreading.

'Spring Glory' has bronze-red new shoots that provide an unusual color addition to the spring garden.

Berberis koreana

Korean barberry

I have always wondered why this species was not more abundant in American gardens. Perhaps its rather aggressive, suckering nature is offensive to many gardeners. An upright-branched, colonizing shrub, Korean barberry requires occasional thinning to keep in bounds. The medium to dark green (almost blue-green) leaves turn rich shades of yellow, orange, and reddish purple in autumn. In the Boston area (zone 6), the leaves persist into November. The bright yellow flowers occur in 3- to 4-in.-long, pendulous racemes in May and provide a delicate floral beauty that is foreign to the common landscape barberries. The egg-shaped, reddish fruit, ¼ to ⅜ in. long, are effective through fall and into winter. The species is easy to grow and prospers in anything but wet soils. Use in a border, as a barrier, or in a mass. Probably not a good choice for the small garden, where *Berberis thunbergii* cultivars would be more appropriate. Suckering nature may result in large colonies. Grows 4 to 6 (to 8) ft. high, generally less in spread. Zones 3 to 7. Korea.

Berberis ×mentorensis

Mentor barberry

I can still remember perusing the old Wayside Garden catalogs as a horticulture student at Ohio State and reading about the best hedge plant ever developed—and that label has stayed with the plant to this day. Mentor barberry is often used as a hedge or barrier, especially in the Midwest. Purportedly a hybrid between *Berberis thunbergii* and *B. julianae*, it develops into a dense, rounded, spiny shrub. It has heavy-textured, 1- to 2-in.-long, dark green leaves that hold later than those of *B. thunbergii* and often turn yellow, orange, and red in fall. Flowers are yellow; fruit, red. Of easy culture, it is a solid, functional performer, never flashy or gauche. Easily pruned into any configuration. Grows 5 to 7 ft. high and wide; I have seen specimens

MORE ▶

Berberis julianae

Berberis koreana, Korean barberry

Berberis koreana

Berberis koreana fall color

Berberis ×mentorensis CONTINUED
5 to 7 ft. high and 10 to 12 ft. wide.
Zones 5 to 8.

Berberis thunbergii
Japanese barberry

Worldwide, this is the most popular landscape barberry, and the number of cultivars that originated in Europe, particularly the Netherlands, is astronomical. In my travels through European gardens, I saw selections that I did not even know existed. The species is not an unworthy plant, form-ing a dapper mound of single-spined branches. The spatulate, ½- to 1¼-in.-long leaves have entire margins, a feature that separates this species from *Berberis ×mentorensis*. The ⅓- to ½-in.-wide, yellow flowers occur in small clusters on the undersides of the stems in April and May. The ⅓-in.-long, ellipsoidal, bright red berries ripen in October and persist through the winter. Quite adaptable. Prefers full sun but will tolerate partial shade. Used as a hedge or barrier in many older gardens. The newer cultivars are utilized in all types of situations. Grows 3 to 6 ft. high, 4 to 7 ft. wide. Zones 4 to 8. Japan.

CULTIVARS AND VARIETIES
ATROPURPUREA GROUP 'Admiration' is a compact, 12- to 20-in.-high mound of red-centered, yellow-cream-margined leaves. To date, has held color in heat of South. One of the more colorful new introductions.

'Atropurpurea' (var. *atropurpurea*) has spawned a whole race of purple-leaf forms that are among the most common barberry cultivars. Differing in growth habit and in the intensity of purplish red leaf color, these cultivars generally grow about the same size as the species. Useful in the summer or fall garden for the color of the foliage.

Berberis ×mentorensis, Mentor barberry

Berberis ×mentorensis

Berberis thunbergii, Japanese barberry, fall color

Berberis thunbergii

For best leaf color, the plants should be grown in sun. The yellow flowers are tinged with purple, but the fruit are the same bright red (sometimes darker) as those of the species.

'Bagatelle' is a small, compact form. It is similar to 'Crimson Pygmy'

Berberis thunbergii

Berberis thunbergii 'Admiration'

Berberis thunbergii 'Atropurpurea'

but much slower growing, reaching perhaps 2½ ft. in 15 years. Makes a great filler in rock garden or perennial borders. Almost too slow for commercial production. Purple leaf color is diminished in heat of zone 7. Low seed producer.

'Concorde' is a relatively slow-growing form with a compact habit, probably 2 ft. by 3 ft. Small, deep red-purple leaves hold color in heat; performed well in Georgia trials, beating out many other Atropurpurea Group forms for retention of deep color. Minimal to no fruit set.

'Crimson Pygmy' is the most popu-

Berberis thunbergii 'Bagatelle'

Berberis thunbergii 'Concorde'

lar of the purple-leaf forms because of its excellent reddish purple leaves and compact, mounded habit. Often used in mass plantings, almost as a tall groundcover. Grows 1½ to 2 ft. high, 2½ to 3 ft. wide.

Golden Ruby™ ('Goruzam') has pretty leaves etched in gold, centered with bright red-purple. Compact, mounded habit and quite slow-growing; estimate 15 in. by 30 in.

'Helmond Pillar' is a distinct upright form with reddish purple leaves. Leaf color fades in heat of summer; good red autumn color. Probably grows 4

MORE ▶

Berberis thunbergii 'Crimson Pygmy'

Berberis thunbergii Golden Ruby™

Berberis thunbergii 'Helmond Pillar'

Berberis thunbergii 'Rose Glow'

Berberis thunbergii 'Aurea'

Berberis thunbergii Golden Nugget™

to 5 ft. high by 2 ft. wide; narrower at base than top.

'Rose Glow' may be the best reddish purple form. The first leaves emerge from clustered buds a rich purple, followed by new shoots with rose-pink leaves, mottled and speckled with deeper red-purple splotches. These shoots eventually turn reddish purple. Fall color can be a good red. Grows 5 to 6 ft. high and wide.

Royal Burgundy™ ('Gentry Cultivar', 'Gentry') has new spring foliage that beads water droplets like a freshly waxed car. Small velvety leaves hold the deep burgundy color throughout summer, changing to black-red in autumn. In Georgia trials, foliage color is diminished compared to 'Concorde'. Forms a low-mounding shrub, 3½ ft. by 5 ft.; larger than 'Crimson Pygmy' but similar in growth habit. Moderate fruit set. Certainly a worthy form. YELLOW AND GREEN FORMS Numerous selections with yellow-gold leaves, both compact and upright. See the *Manual* (2009) for specifics.

'Aurea' provides knockout golden yellow foliage color. Practice restraint when using this shrub; perhaps plant it as a decoy to divert attention away from garbage cans. Grows 3 to 4 ft. high and wide, sometimes larger. Low seed producer.

'Golden Divine' has held yellow-gold leaf color in zone 7 and was reported to develop *no* seed.

Golden Nugget™ ('Monlers') has orange new growth that matures to golden yellow; more sun-tolerant than other golden barberries. Compact-mounded habit, 15 in. by 24 in.

'Kobold' is reminiscent of a green boxwood, with rich green foliage and densely mounded habit. Makes a good low hedge and has been used in mass plantings with great success. Grows 2 to 2½ ft. high and wide. Flowers and fruit are sparsely produced.

'Sparkle' should rank among the leaders of the green barberry revolution but, unfortunately, it has not been promoted like other forms. The plants, even when young, have arching horizontal branches and maintain a dense constitution into old age. The leathery, glossy dark green foliage turns fluorescent reddish orange in fall. Abundant yellow flowers are followed by persistent bright red fruit. Grows 3 to 4 ft. high, slightly greater in spread.

Sunjoy™ Gold Pillar (upright) and Sunjoy™ Gold Beret (compact mounded), both with yellow foliage, were less than satisfactory in 2010 trials at PII. The former splayed; the latter bleached and browned.

Betula albosinensis var. septentrionalis
Chinese paper-birch

The great plant explorer E. H. Wilson stated, "The bark is singularly lovely, being a rich orange-red or orange-brown and peels off in sheets, each no thicker than fine tissue paper, and each successive layer is clothed with a white glaucous bloom (wax)." Difficult to supersede Wilson's spot-on description. Habit is pyramidal-rounded, eventually rounded, often low-branched. The matte-green leaves, up to 5 in. long, are silky

MORE ▶

Betula albosinensis var. *septentrionalis*, Chinese paper-birch

Berberis thunbergii 'Kobold'

Berberis thunbergii 'Sparkle'

107

Betula albosinensis var. *septentrionalis*

Betula alleghaniensis, yellow birch, fall color

pubescent on veins below with axillary tufts of hairs. Have yet to witness fall color but suspect the normal yellow. Appears to prefer a cool, more even climate, and I observed magnificent trees in Europe, 40 to 45 ft. high, 40 to 50 ft. wide. Nowhere common in the United States but worth the effort in cooler habitats. Zones 5 and 6. Central and western China.

Betula alleghaniensis
syn. *Betula lutea*
yellow birch
Truly a native treasure, this species is not in vogue because its bark is not white. In fall, however, the brilliant golden yellow foliage compensates a thousandfold. Summer leaves are dark green and average 3 to 5 in. long. The leaves are highly resistant to leaf miner, a severe problem for many of the white-barked species. The bark on young trees is a polished brown or bronze, with thin, papery, shaggy shreds; with age, the bark becomes gray-brown and breaks into large, ragged-edged plates. Bruised stems emit the heady aroma of wintergreen. The habit on young trees is pyramidal-oval, becoming rounded at maturity. Prefers cool, moist soils and cool summer temperatures. Grows 60 to 75 ft.

Betula alleghaniensis

Betula lenta, sweet birch, fall color

Betula lenta

Betula lenta

sweet, black, or cherry birch

Not unlike *Betula alleghaniensis* in garden attributes and cultural require-ments—indeed, side by side, older trees of the two species appear quite similar. This species is possibly more heat-tolerant and has performed admi-rably in the Midwest for many years. The fall color, regardless of environ-mental conditions, is a consistent rich golden yellow. The reddish brown bark on young branches does not peel like that of *B. alleghaniensis*, but sweet birch offers similar mature bark, and the stems emit a wintergreen odor when bruised. A superb birch for naturalizing. Best growth is realized in deep, moist, slightly acid, well-drained soils; however, it is often found on dry, rocky sites. Grows 40 to 55 ft. high, 35 to 45 ft. wide. Zones 3 to 7. Maine to Alabama, west to Ohio.

Betula uber (*B. lenta* subsp. *uber*) is a close relative with small, lustrous dark green leaves that turn rich yellow in fall. Leaves are rounded, approxi-mately 2 in. by 2 in., and finely ser-rated. Known only from a remnant population in Virginia. Observed a 35-ft. specimen in Marion, Virginia; a small plant is growing in the Univer-sity's Botanical Garden. Zones (5)6 and 7.

Betula uber fall color

109

Betula maximowicziana
monarch birch

This species was touted as the savior of the white-barked birches because of its suspected resistance to bronze birch borer. Unfortunately, when the true species finally arrived in America, the tree was neither uniformly white-barked nor borer-resistant. The bark may be whitish to brown and is seldom uniform among seedlings. The habit is coarsely pyramidal to rounded, with perhaps the stiffest secondary branches of any birch. The 3- to 6-in.-long, dark green leaves are the largest of the cultivated birches. In autumn, the leaves turn lovely butter-yellow and have the size and consistency of notebook paper when they fall. Provide deep, moist soils, and avoid heat and drought stress. The Arnold Arboretum had many different seedling accessions; some were large, robust, thriving trees growing over 30 ft. high in 14 years, while others were riddled with borers. Perhaps this species is best reserved for the collector. Be leery when purchasing, for its identity is confused. Grows 40 to 50 ft. high, can be as wide at maturity. Zones 5 and 6. Japan.

Betula nigra
river birch

The most heat-tolerant of all North American birch species. The habit is pyramidal to oval in youth, often rounded at maturity. Large, multi-stemmed specimens are inherently more aesthetic than the single-stem specimens because the attractive rich cinnamon-brown exfoliating bark is more visible on the former. In fact, this particular birch is more spectacular without leaves. The medium green, 2- to 3½-in.-long leaves seldom color in fall (at best they turn yellow). In extremely rainy seasons, the leaves

Betula maximowicziana

Betula maximowicziana, monarch birch

Betula nigra

may develop significant leaf spot, and under drought conditions, they may drop prematurely, but neither problem is sufficiently serious to discourage use. Found in moist soils along watercourses throughout its native range. For best growth, soils should be moist and acidic; in high pH soils, chlorosis can be serious. River birch is not afflicted by the bronze birch borer. I see this species being planted more than the white-barked species, even in Maine, where *Betula papyrifera* is native. Grows 40 to 70 ft. high, 40 to 60 ft. wide. Zones 4 to 9. Massachusetts to Florida, west to Minnesota and Kansas to Texas.

CULTIVARS AND VARIETIES
City Slicker® ('Whit XXV') is notable for its large, darker green, lustrous foliage, early white bark, borer resistance and superior drought and cold tolerance. May prove more adaptable to higher pH soils.

Dura-Heat® ('BNMTF') has glossy dark olive-green leaves that are smaller than those of the species and good yellow fall color. Bark exfoliates early and is whitish. Have observed this next to Heritage® in September and October in the Athens area: Dura-Heat® fully clothed with leaves, Heritage® largely defoliated.

Fox Valley® ('Little King') exhibits a dense, compact, oval-rounded

MORE ▶

Betula nigra City Slicker®

Betula nigra, river birch

Betula nigra Fox Valley®

Betula nigra Dura-Heat®

Betula nigra CONTINUED

growth habit with branches to the ground. Glossy medium green foliage is densely borne. Exfoliating bark like the species makes a pleasing winter effect; 10 ft. high and 12 ft. wide after

Betula nigra Heritage®

Betula nigra 'Summer Cascade'

15 to 20 years, will prove useful as a shrub mass along watercourses and in perpetually moist soils. Observed 20-ft.-high plant with a 30-ft. spread on the West Coast.

Heritage® ('Cully') is an excellent selection with superior vigor and larger leaves. It displays salmon-white bark, especially in the early years of growth (two to five years).

Northern Tribute™ ('Dickinson') has dark green leaves that turn yellow in fall and ivory-colored bark that exfoliates to copper-bronze. Upright-oval habit. Matures 35 to 40 ft. by 30 to 35 ft. Resistant to bronze birch borer. Selected for superior adaptability to stresses of the Upper Midwest and Northern Plains; rated zone 3.

'Summer Cascade' is a true weeper that must be staked to produce a trunk or grafted on a standard. Have a plant in our Georgia garden—great showstopper; almost more beautiful in winter with the shiny brown, slender stems and the cream-salmon-cinnamon-brown exfoliation of the main trunk.

Betula papyrifera
paper or canoe birch

This superb white-barked native birch offers greater resistance to the borer than either *Betula pendula* or *B. populifolia*. The loosely pyramidal outline of youth gives way to an oval to rounded crown at maturity. The dark green, 2- to 4- (to 5½-) in.-long leaves turn rich butter-yellow to golden yellow in fall. The chalky white bark is outstanding in the winter landscape. This species is excellent when used in groupings, in groves, or even as a single specimen. Performs best in moist, acid, sandy, or silty loams, but will grow in a wide range of soil conditions. A cool-climate tree that deserves the title "Lady of the North American Forest." Grows 50 to 70 ft. high, 25 to 45 ft. wide. Zones 2 to 6(7). Labrador to British Columbia, south to Pennsylvania, Nebraska, and Washington.

CULTIVARS AND VARIETIES

Prairie Dream® ('Varen') develops broad-oval outline, 50 ft. by 40 ft., dark green leaves and snow-white bark. Bronze borer resistance and zone 2 adaptability.

Renaissance series resulted from 30 years of hybridization, testing, and selection. Highly resistant to bronze birch borer.

Renaissance Compact™ ('Cenci') is a tight compact pyramidal form; 30 ft. by 15 ft. with semi-glossy rich green leaves.

Renaissance Oasis® ('Oenci') is broad pyramidal, 60 ft. by 30 ft. Dark green leaves turn yellow in fall and rich-mahogany-reddish bark matures white and exfoliates.

Renaissance Reflection® ('Renci') is pyramidal and fast-growing, maturing 50 to 70 ft. by 20 to 25 ft. Other desirable traits include white bark, yellow fall color, and heat tolerance.

Renaissance Upright™ ('Uenci') becomes a narrow pyramid with a strong central leader. Exhibits white semi-exfoliating bark and semi-glossy leaves.

Betula papyrifera Renaissance Reflection®

Betula pendula
European white birch

At one time, this was the most popular white-barked birch because the bark color develops at an early age. Unfortunately, bronze birch borer reduces European white birch to rubble, especially when the tree is under stress, and now many gardeners and nurseries shy away from the species. In youth the habit is gracefully pyramidal; at maturity, oval to rounded. The triangular to diamond-shaped, 1- to 3-in.-long, dark green leaves turn yellow in fall. Tolerant of extremely moist and dry soils, but the tree should not be stressed—you might as well send a formal dinner invitation to the bronze birch borer. Grows 40 to 50 ft. high, 20 to 30 ft. wide. Zones 2 to 6(7). Europe, especially high altitudes, northern Asia.

MORE ▶

Betula papyrifera, paper birch

Betula papyrifera fall color

Betula pendula CONTINUED

CULTIVARS AND VARIETIES

'Dalecarlica' has finely cut leaves and gracefully pendulous branches on a full-sized framework.

'Fastigiata' is an erect, columnar form that becomes columnar-oval with age. Foliage holds later than that of other cultivars. Appears to possess some resistance to the bronze birch borer.

'Purpurea' is an umbrella that covers several purple-leaf cultivars like 'Burgundy Wine', 'Dark Prince', Purple Rain®, 'Purple Splendor', and 'Scarlet Glory'.

'Youngii' has normal leaves but a strong weeping tendency. Grows 15 to 20 ft. high and wide.

Betula platyphylla var. japonica

Japanese white birch

Along with the *szechuanica* variety (now *Betula szechuanica*) of *B. platy-*phylla, this beautiful variety was hailed as the replacement for *B. pendula* because of early (and false) reports of resistance to the bronze birch borer. In 1957, Dr. John Creech, of the U.S. National Arboretum, collected the seed of the original *B. platyphylla* var. *japonica* in a remote alpine meadow in Japan. One seedling raised from seeds planted at the University of Wisconsin proved borer-resistant, and this selection, 'Whitespire', was introduced; unfortunately, faulty record keeping gave credit to the wrong taxon: the original 'Whitespire' is a selection of *B. populifolia*, which see. Almost 30 years after the original seed was collected, *B. platyphylla* var. *japonica* was made available to the gardeners of the world. The tree offers a lovely pyramidal outline, leathery, dark green, 1½- to 3-in.-long leaves, and white bark at an early age. It has proven exceptionally adaptable to the vagaries of the midwestern climate; but borers and leaf miners have manifested themselves on both it and *B. szechuanica*, and the *B. platyphylla–B. szechuanica* complex has performed miserably in the South, zone 7 and higher. Grows 40 to 50 ft. high, 20 to 30 ft. wide. Zones 4 to 7(8). Japan, northern China.

CULTIVARS AND VARIETIES

'Crimson Frost' and Royal Frost® ('Penci-2') are red-purple-leaf selections with rather mixed parentage. The latter is a better grower than 'Crimson Frost'.

Dakota Pinnacle® ('Fargo') is a narrow pyramidal-columnar form; 30 ft. high and 8 ft. wide in ten years. Average tolerance to bronze birch borer.

Prairie Vision® ('VerDale') has an upright-oblong to semi-pyramidal habit, broadening with age; high

MORE ▶

Betula pendula, European white birch

Betula pendula

Betula pendula 'Dalecarlica'

Betula pendula 'Fastigiata'

Betula pendula 'Youngii'

Betula pendula 'Purpurea'

Betula platyphylla var. japonica

Betula platyphylla var. japonica, Japanese white birch

Betula platyphylla var. japonica CONTINUED

Betula Royal Frost®

bronze birch borer resistance. Grows 35 to 45 ft. high, 20 to 25 ft. wide.

Betula populifolia
gray birch

Always treated as a distant land-scape cousin of the more popular *Betula pendula* and *B. papyrifera*, but certainly worthwhile in its native haunts. A weedy species through-out the Northeast, gray birch grows in the poorest of acid, sterile soils, from sand and gravel to rock, form-ing a narrow, irregularly open, conical crown. The glossy dark green, 2- to 3½-in.-long leaves turn yellow in fall. The bark drifts to a dirty off-white and does not glisten like that of its rich relatives. Leaf miner can be particu-larly serious on this species, but it is

not as susceptible to the borer as *B. pendula*. Develops leaf chlorosis in high pH soils. Best in cooler areas of eastern North America. Grows 20 to 40 ft. high, 10 to 20 ft. wide. Zones 3 to 6(7). Nova Scotia to Ontario, south to Delaware.

CULTIVARS AND VARIETIES
'Whitespire', long misidentified as a *Betula platyphylla* derivative, resides herein. It displays resistance to the borer but was originally seed-grown, so variation in characteristics is the only constant. If purchasing a 'Whitespire' clone, make abso-lutely certain it was not seed-grown but vegetatively propagated from 'Whitespire Senior', the original tree in Madison, Wisconsin. See comments under *B. platyphylla*.

Betula platyphylla var. japonica Dakota Pinnacle®

Betula populifolia, gray birch

Betula utilis var. jacquemontii

whitebarked Himalayan birch

Although a certain amount of taxonomic confusion surrounds this tree, the certainty of its early and pure milk-white bark is absolute. Like *Betula pendula*, European white birch, this species is not heat-tolerant, but the distinct pyramidal habit, the dark green leaves (2 to 3 in. long), and the bright yellow fall color, together with the exquisite bark, make it a choice specimen in colder climates. Whitebarked Himalayan birch has received attention from nursery people as a possible borer-resistant substitute for European white birch, but unfortunately, it too has proven susceptible. One of the most susceptible birches to Japanese beetle feeding. Grows 30 to 50 ft. high, 20 to 35 ft. wide. Zones 4 to 7. Western Himalayas.

CULTIVARS AND VARIETIES

Many cultivars with superior bark have been introduced. 'Doorenbos' ('Snow Queen'), 'Grayswood Ghost', 'Jermyns', 'Kashmir White', 'Kyelang', 'Ramdana River', and 'Silver Shadow' among others, were chosen for their white bark. All are of European origin and limitedly available in the United States.

Variety *utilis* represents the eastern distribution, and bark is orange to

MORE ▶

Betula populifolia

Betula populifolia 'Whitespire'

Betula utilis var. *jacquemontii*

Betula populifolia 'Whitespire'

Betula utilis var. *jacquemontii*, whitebarked Himalayan birch

117

Betula utilis var. jacquemontii

copper-brown, eventually peeling to expose waxy, glaucous, grayish pink coloration.

Bignonia capreolata

syn. *Anisostichus capreolatus*

crossvine

Although not well known in gardening circles, the crossvine offers worthwhile attributes. The semi-evergreen to evergreen, 2- to 6-in.-long leaves are lustrous dark green in summer,

Bignonia capreolata

Bignonia capreolata 'Atrosanguinea'

Bignonia capreolata, crossvine

Bignonia capreolata 'Jekyll'

turning bronzy red in winter. Broad trumpet-shaped, brownish orange to orange-red flowers, 1½ to 4 in. long and ¾ to 1½ in. wide, open in May. Flowers on old wood but sporadic flowers may develop on new growth. The flowers have a distinct mocha fragrance. Although found in the shade in its native setting, crossvine achieves best growth and flowering in full sun. Prefers moist, acid, well-drained soils, but can also be found along rivers and streams where it is periodically flooded. A true clinging vine, it also twines. A plant in our garden cemented itself to a wood fence and climbed, with gusto, toward the heavens. Requires pruning under cultivation to keep it in check. A handsome vine for walls, trellises, and structures. Depending on the support structure, it will climb 30 to 50 ft. Zones (5)6 to 9. Virginia to southern Illinois, south to Florida and Louisiana.

CULTIVARS AND VARIETIES
'Atrosanguinea' produces red-purple flowers, although a plant I grew as such had orange-red flowers.

'Jekyll' has orange outer corolla, yellow inner, nonfragrant flowers. Vigorous and cold hardy. Discovered by the author on Georgia's Jekyll Island.

'Tangerine Beauty' combines vigor with orange-red flowers, orange interior.

Bougainvillea glabra

syn. *Bougainvillea spectabilis*
bougainvillea, tissue paper plant
Every gardener who witnesses the plant in flower—bright, vivid, vibrant, and fluorescent—hopes to grow one of the many cultivars. A wicked, spiny, scandent shrub or vine that has scissored my arms on several occasions; handle with leather gloves, for it requires a structure to climb and occasional nipping to keep it in check. The lustrous medium to dark green, 1- to 3-in.-long leaves are little more than the "food" factory that supports the overindulgent floral production engine.

The showy portions of the flowers are the paper-like bracts, three together, 1 to 2 in. long, that surround the true flowers. Colors span the rainbow, and in late March, I stopped at a nursery in the Florida Keys to buy red and coppery salmon forms while salivating over 30 other cultivars. Requires sun, heat, and well-drained, acid soil. Typically, flowers in summer and fall in zone 7 when grown as a container plant. Refrain from overfertilizing, as this leads to excessive vegetative growth. Great trellis, wall, fence, and container plant. A trip to Disney in Florida will make a Minnesotan a believer. Grows willy-nilly, 40 ft. or more. Zones 9 to 11. South America.

CULTIVARS AND VARIETIES
'Barbara Karst' is often listed as one of the hardiest, with red flowers over a long period. 'Sanderiana', with magenta bracts, is common.

Bougainvillea glabra, bougainvillea

Bougainvillea glabra

Broussonetia papyrifera
paper mulberry

An aggressive, intimidating, invasive species that colonizes waste areas and never lets go. In Athens, it is the biological glue that keeps the railroad embankment from eroding. In its best manifestation, however, the species develops into a round-headed tree of respectable attractiveness. The dull dark green leaves, 4 to 8 in. long, are covered with soft "furry" hairs on the lower leaf surfaces; the upper surfaces have the consistency of sandpaper. Leaves are variously lobed to entire with coarsely dentate teeth along the margins. Male and female flowers are borne on separate plants, the female producing ¾- to 1-in.-wide, orange-red drupes. Certainly not a tree for the average garden but perhaps for impossible sites. Old, gnarly, picturesque trees at Monticello and Williamsburg in Virginia. Full sun locations in well-drained, acid soils are best. Grows 30 to 50 ft. high and wide. Zones 6 to 10. China, Japan.
CULTIVARS AND VARIETIES
'Golden Shadow' ('Aurea'), with rich yellow to yellow-gold leaves, holds the color through the growing season. Introduced by Don Shadow, Winchester, Tennessee.

Broussonetia papyrifera, paper mulberry

Broussonetia papyrifera

Broussonetia papyrifera

Brugmansia ×candida

syn. *Brugmansia suaveolens*

angel's trumpet

Recent weather "patterns" continue to produce surprises relative to outdoor plant survival. In August, I spied an 8-ft.-high, yellow-flowered angel's trumpet in the front garden of an Atlanta residence. Driving (by myself), I tend to verbalize to the imaginary garden friend in the passenger's seat: "Is this possible?" Plants are rounded, with thickish stems. Leaves are large, 6 to 12 in. long, irregularly lobed with entire to coarsely serrated margins, and bright green. Flowers are head-knockers, white, 6 to 9 in. long, fragrant, trumpet-shaped, arching-pendulous, developing on new growth in summer and fall. Well-drained soil in sun to light shade is acceptable. Provide supplemental water in droughts, fertilize lightly. A dieback shrub into coastal Florida and Louisiana, at temperatures of 20 to 25°F and below. Regenerates quickly. Used in borders and containers. Plant parts are poisonous. Have observed 15-ft.-high, freestanding shrubs in St. Francisville, Louisiana. Grows (6 to) 10 to 15 ft. high and wide. Zones (8)9 to 11. Peru, Ecuador, Chile.

CULTIVARS AND VARIETIES

Numerous cultivars, both singles and doubles, in white, yellow, pink, and peach colors.

Brunfelsia pauciflora

yesterday-today-and-tomorrow

In coastal Southeast and Florida, occasionally used as a container plant for the beautiful violet (on the outside) flowers that open to a flat disk and, over a three-day period in spring and summer, age to pale violet or white. Has an irregular shrub-like habit and requires pruning. The oval to obovate, evergreen leaves are 3 to 6 in. long

MORE ▶

Brunfelsia pauciflora, yesterday-today-and-tomorrow

Broussonetia papyrifera 'Golden Shadow'

Brugmansia ×*candida*

Brugmansia ×*candida*, angel's trumpet

Brunfelsia pauciflora CONTINUED
and dull dark green. Not winter hardy in most of the Southeast, where it is best grown as a container plant. Prefers full sun and fertile, well-drained soil high in organic matter. Use as a massing shrub in zones 10 and 11. Grows 4 to 5 ft. high and wide. Zones (9)10 and 11. Brazil, Paraguay.

Buddleia alternifolia
alternate-leaf butterflybush
This is such a great plant but so rarely used in modern gardens. To be sure, it can become mammoth, the long supple branches often reaching out to consume precious garden real estate. The overall texture is quite refined because of the gray-foliaged branches that sway in the faintest breeze. The habit is that of a large shrub or small tree. The 1½- to 4-in.-long leaves are dull green above and grayish below, almost willow-like in composition.

Buddleia alternifolia

Buddleia alternifolia 'Argentea'

Bright lilac-purple, fragrant flowers appear in dense clusters from the axils of the previous season's growth, usually in June. Does not rebloom like *Buddleia davidii* and cultivars. Prefers loose, loamy soils and a sunny position. Makes a great addition to the border. Can be used tree-form (single stem). Grows 10 to 20 ft. high. Zones (4)5 to 7. China.
CULTIVARS AND VARIETIES
'Argentea' is a fine selection, with appressed silky hairs that impart a silvery sheen to the leaves.

Buddleia davidii
orange-eye butterflybush
This delicate, at times thuggish, flowering shrub is culturally adapted to virtually any landscape site in full sun. Peering through a bus window in Edinburgh, Scotland, I spied a vacant, rubble-strewn lot alive with seedling butterflybushes; I have also seen this plant growing out of mortar joints in walls. These are old-fashioned garden plants, and their popularity has ebbed and flowed. With a new wave of cultivars, the plant is currently in vogue. The habit is rounded-arching with long,

slender branches. The 4- to 10-in.-long leaves vary from gray-green to dark green above and are silver and pubescent beneath. The leaves hold late and do not develop any fall color. Fragrant flowers appear in 4- to 10- (to 14-) in.-long panicles on new growth of the season from June and July to fall. The flowers range in color from white, pink, lavender, blue, and purple to near red. Spent inflorescences must be removed to foster new shoot growth and flower development. Easily transplanted from containers. Prefers well-drained, moist, loamy soils; pH adaptable and at home in calcareous soils. Once established, the plant tolerates heat and drought. If plants become overgrown, cut back to 12 to 18 in. from the ground in late winter and fertilize—a handsome flowering shrub will be evident by mid summer. A great border plant. Attracts butterflies and bees in profusion and imparts a pastoral tranquility to the garden. Also makes a good cut flower. Grows 5 to 10 ft. high and wide. Zones 5 to 9. China.
CULTIVARS AND VARIETIES
Buddleia davidii can be invasive. In

Buddleia alternifolia, alternate-leaf butterflybush

2010 the Oregon Department of Agriculture prohibited the sale of non-approved selections of *B. davidii* within the state of Oregon. Approved sterile cultivars of *Buddleia* are not regulated under this ruling. Breeders continue to select for sterility, and numerous new cultivars from Europe and America are swamping the market. In the *Manual* (2009), 118 are treated, and recent literature describes another 41 I never encountered when revising the *Manual*.

'Asian Moon' is the first true sterile introduction, from Dr. John Lindstrom, Arkansas. Rich blue fragrant flowers, perhaps with a hint of purple, in inflorescences 4 to 6 in. long that are more cylindrical than tapering. Checked this for seed production and was unable to find a single viable fruit.

'Attraction' is an improvement on 'Royal Red' with red-purple flowers in slightly smaller inflorescences, superior foliage, and a more restrained habit. Introduced by the author.

'Bicolor' produces beautiful purple buds that open lavender-purple with

Adonis Blue™ ('Adokeep') has richly saturated blue-purple, fragrant flowers 10 to 12 in. long. Listed as 4 to 5 ft. in height.

MORE ▶

Buddleia davidii, orange-eye butterflybush

Buddleia davidii 'Attraction'

Buddleia davidii 'Bicolor'

Buddleia davidii CONTINUED

butterscotch-orange eye. Flowers are fragrant, foliage a pretty gray-green. A loose, lax grower that matures 8 to 10 ft. high. Introduced by the author.

'Black Knight' has extremely dark purple, wonderfully fragrant flowers in 10-in.-long panicles. An old cultivar, still common in commerce, that should be replaced by newer introductions like 'Guinevere' and Adonis Blue™.

'Blue Chip' is a compact spreading, mounding form with dark green foliage and abundant bluish flowers in smaller panicles. A true genetic dwarf; I estimate 18 to 24 in. by 36 in. Male sterile but female fertile and does set viable seed.

Buzz™ series offers plants ideally suited to container gardening and shrub borders. All are 4 to 5 ft. high and wide, with fragrant, tapering inflorescences in various colors. From Thompson and Morgan.

'Dubonnet' is one of the best garden types. It is an early-flowering form with violet-purple flowers with an orange eye and sweet fragrance. Large dark gray-green leaves and an upright-rounded, vigorous habit, to 7 ft. by 9 ft.

'Ellen's Blue' has deeply saturated blue flowers with a bright orange eye and pleasing fragrance; grayish silver leaves.

Flutterby™ series from Ball Ornamentals includes 15 introductions. My only question concerns the use of *Buddleia crispa* in the breeding, as it is not cold- or heat-tolerant based on Georgia trials. See ballhort.com for complete descriptions.

'Guinevere' has deep purple flowers, lustrous dark green leaves, and vigorous demeanor; 8 to 10 ft. high. A Georgia introduction.

'Honeycomb' is a yellow-flowered cultivar of *Buddleia* ×*weyeriana*, the hybrid between *B. davidii* var. *mag-*

nifica and *B. globosa*. Flowers, with cream-yellow buds, an orange eye, and sweet fragrance, occur in interrupted panicles. Medium-green foliage. Introduced by the author.

'Lochinch' has sweetly scented, lavender-blue flowers in 12-in.-long panicles. It may be confused in the trade, for I have observed at least two forms: one vigorous, the other less so. The form that I grew was more compact and smaller in all its parts, with attractive grayish, felted leaves. The large form may grow 12 to 15 ft. high; the compact form, half this size.

'Miss Ruby' is a rich rose-red hybrid with beautiful foliage from Dr. Denny Werner at North Carolina State University. Estimate 5 to 6 ft. high in the landscape. Voted best in a 2008–09 trial of more than 75 butterflybushes at RHS Garden, Wisley. In fact, the top five or six cultivars were red-purple flowered. 'Miss Molly' is a new sangria-red-flowered Werner introduction.

Buddleia davidii 'Dubonnet'

Buddleia davidii 'Guinevere'

Buddleia 'Honeycomb'

Buddleia davidii 'Nanho Purple'

Nanho series comprises forms with white, mauve-blue, and purple flowers on a more compact, finely textured framework, 5 to 6 ft. high and wide. 'Nanho Purple' is slower growing and has smaller flowers and leaves than those of the species types. It reached 8 ft. by 6 ft. in two years in the Georgia trials.

'Pink Delight' has deep pink, fragrant flowers in 12- to 15-in.-long panicles. I consider this the best pink-flowered butterflybush.

'Royal Red' has rich purple-red flowers in 10- to 15-in.-long panicles. The habit is quite large, and a plant can grow as much as 12 to 15 ft. high and wide.

'Silver Frost' is a Georgia introduction with white flowers and silver-gray foliage; 6 to 8 ft. high.

'Summer Rose' produces large 8- to 12- (to 18-) in.-long inflorescences of iridescent mauve-rose; excellent fragrance. Large, robust, dark blue-green, densely foliaged shrub maturing 8 to 10 ft. high. One of the best. 'Raspberry Wine' is similar if not the same based on Georgia evaluations.

'Sun Gold' ('Sungold'), another *Buddleia* ×*weyeriana* cultivar, has yellow-orange flowers on a large shrub, to 6 ft.

MORE ▶

Buddleia davidii 'Lochinch'

Buddleia davidii 'Pink Delight'

Buddleia davidii 'Silver Frost'

Buddleia davidii 'Summer Rose'

Buddleia 'Violet Eyes'

Buddleia davidii CONTINUED

'Violet Eyes' is an evergreen (zone 7) hybrid with lustrous blue-green, mite-resistant foliage. Flowers dusty-violet on outside, violet-purple inside, and nonfragrant. Butterflies are attracted in great numbers. Vigorous to 10 ft. high and wide. *Buddleia globosa*, *B. davidii*, and *B. lindleyana* are the parents.

'White Bouquet' and 'White Profusion' are among the best of the many white-flowered forms. 'White Bouquet' has fatter panicles than the others. 'Peace', 'Ornamental White', and 'Snowbank' are other worthy white-flowered forms.

'Windy Hill' is the only truly cold hardy form, with strong regrowth year to year—probably 5 to 8 ft. in a single season. Purple flowers and narrow, delicate blue-green leaves. From the beautiful garden of Dennis and Judy Mareb, Great Barrington, Massachusetts.

Buddleia davidii 'Peace'

Buddleia lindleyana

Buddleia lindleyana
Lindley butterflybush

An anomaly among typical *Buddleia* species in that the flowers are not fragrant, yet attract copious quantities of butterflies. I was introduced to the species over 30 years ago when a specimen was brought to me for identification. Perusal of the literature indicated that it, like *Buddleia davidii*, had escaped from cultivation in the South.

Buddleia davidii 'Windy Hill'

Buddleia lindleyana, Lindley butterflybush

The evergreen, rounded-arching, suckering habit is not everyone's cup of tea. The lustrous dark green, 2- to 4-in.-long leaves are handsome year-round. From May and June until frost, flowers are produced on new growth. Each flower is 1 to 1½ in. long, tubular, four-lobed at the mouth, dusty lavender on the outside, deep violet on the interior, and borne in 3- to 8-in.-long panicles. The inflorescence is indeterminate, meaning it continues to elongate while the basal flowers are opening, resulting in structures 2 ft. or longer by summer's end. A tough, durable plant that requires full sun. Displays high mite resistance. Grows 4 to 6 ft. high, wider at maturity. Have observed a 10- to 12-ft.-high plant. Zones 7 to 9. Eastern China.

CULTIVARS AND VARIETIES

'Gloster' is a 6-ft.-high, strong-growing form with larger foliage and 2-ft.-long inflorescences.

'Miss Vicie' is smaller in stature (4 ft.) with smaller leaves and inflorescences.

Buddleia loricata

Remarkable evergreen species from South Africa that is virtually unknown in American gardens but worthy of consideration. Along with *Buddleia salviifolia*, this was a foliage favorite of visitors to the University's *Buddleia* trials. The dense rounded habit and non-invasive nature make it one of the tidiest garden species. The narrow, 3- to 5-in.-long, lustrous dark green leaves are covered on the lower surface with cottony pubescence. The fragrant white flowers open in June and July

from previous year's wood. This and *B. salviifolia* should be pruned after flowering; any earlier pruning results in flower bud removal. Superb performer in the heat, drought, and blanketing humidity of zone 7, requiring full sun and well-drained soil. Terrific foliage in the border or when utilized in groupings and masses. Grows 6 to 8 ft. high and wide. Zones 7 to 9. South Africa.

CULTIVARS AND VARIETIES

Silver Anniversary™ ('Morning Mist') with narrow, silver-white leaves on a compact framework was bred by the great Peter Moore in England. The parentage appears to be *Buddleia loricata* and *B. crispa*.

Buddleia salviifolia

South African sage wood, South African sage butterflybush

Who would have thought a butterfly-bush from South Africa could prosper in the heat and humidity of the South? For starters, not this author, but over six seasons, this evergreen shrub grew into an upright-arching, densely foliaged shrub over 10 ft. high. The leaves are the most beautiful asset,

MORE ▶

Buddleia loricata

Buddleia Silver Anniversary™

Buddleia salviifolia, South African sage wood

Buddleia loricata

Buddleia salviifolia

Buddleia salviifolia CONTINUED

2 to 5 in. long, wavy-surfaced, sage-textured, gray-green above, gray-brown below. The flowers, pale lavender-lilac, open on last season's wood in April. They are not particularly showy and have only a slight fragrance. The species prospers in full sun, heat, and drought. Wonderful foliage plant for the borders, especially when pruned to the ground to force new shoots. Best thought of as a structural foliage plant for garden-making. All visitors to our *Buddleia* trials were enamored of the foliage. Grows 10 ft. high, 8 ft. wide. Grew 7 ft. high and 5 ft. wide in two years in Georgia trials. Zones 7 to 9. South Africa.

Buxus
boxwood

For functionality, few broadleaf evergreens approach the boxwoods. The name is synonymous with hedging, and the intricate parterres of many formal European gardens come to mind. Cultivars of *Buxus microphylla* and *B. sempervirens* fit numerous geographic and climatic niches. Boxwoods prefer loamy, loose, well-drained soils. Root systems are near the surface and should not be disturbed. Full sun or partial shade situations are suitable. Display superb deer resistance. Nomenclature has been kicked around like an old can. Names herein reflect "current" scientific status.

Buxus harlandii, Harland boxwood

Buxus microphylla var. *japonica*

Buxus harlandii

Harland boxwood

Although not well known in southern landscapes, this broad, vase-shaped, densely branched form is unique because of its larger leaves, to 2 in. long. The lustrous dark green leaves are broadest above the middle, almost spatulate, with a distinct notch at the apex. The foliage color is a richer, brighter green than *Buxus sempervirens*. In the Dirr garden, the plant prospers in full sun and well-drained soil. Leafs out early; late spring frosts occasionally nip the foliage. Excellent for evergreen effect in the border or in groupings. One of my favorite plants in the winter landscape—always vibrant, rich green, and reassuring. Grows 6 ft. high and wide. Requires minimal pruning to keep it garden-worthy. Zones 7 to 9. China.

CULTIVARS AND VARIETIES

'Richard' appears to belong here because of leaf shape and color. Smaller in all its parts compared to the species, although listed to 6 ft. high. Hardiness is targeted to 0°F.

Buxus microphylla

littleleaf boxwood

Buxus microphylla is a compact, mounded-rounded, densely branched shrub. The ⅓- to 1-in.-long, oval leaves are medium green in summer and turn yellow, brown, or bronze in winter, especially in cold climates. It is less troubled by insects and diseases than *B. sempervirens*, common boxwood, but it is not as handsome in leaf or stature. Utilize for large masses or as accents in borders, rock gardens, and perennial gardens. The numerous cultivars lend themselves to specialized uses. Grows 3 to 4 ft. high and wide. Zones 6 to 8. Japan, Korea.

CULTIVARS AND VARIETIES

'Golden Dream' has dark green leaves with prominent yellow-gold margin; matures 2 ft. by 3 ft.

Variety *japonica*, although more common in the Southeast and Southwest, is adaptable in zone 6. The leaves are as long as those of the species and almost as broad, but they are a much darker green color. I have not observed severe discoloration of winter foliage. Appears more sun and shade adaptable than typical *Buxus microphylla*. Grows 3 to 6 ft. high and wide. A 10 ft. by 25 ft. specimen was reported.

Buxus sinica var. *insularis* (formerly *B. microphylla* var. *koreana*) is a true cold hardy stalwart, surviving –20 to –25°F or lower (zone 4 or 5). Leaves are smaller than those of *B. microphylla*, but other characteristics are similar. More common in cultivation than *B. microphylla*.

'Justin Brouwers', a selection of var. *insularis* with forest-green foliage, the color largely retained in winter, grows 3 to 4 ft. high and wide.

Sheridan Hybrids resulted from crossing *Buxus sinica* var. *insularis* and *B. sempervirens*, and the hybrids embody the best characteristics of the parents. 'Green Gem', 'Green Mound', 'Green Mountain', and 'Green Velvet' are compact forms of varying growth habits, with excellent dark green winter color reminiscent of that of *B. sempervirens* and cold hardiness paralleling that of var. *insularis*. Somewhat slow-growing. A visit to Blandy Arboretum, Virginia, opened my eyes relative to size and performance of this group. 'Green Mountain' was 7 ft. by 6 ft., 'Green Mound'

MORE ▶

Buxus 'Green Mountain'

Buxus sinica var. insularis

Buxus microphylla CONTINUED

was 6½ ft. by 5½ ft., 'Green Velvet' and 'Green Gem' were 6 ft. by 6 ft. All showed leaf miner damage, with 'Green Mountain' the worst.

'Wintergreen' represents a seedling selection from var. *insularis* with smaller leaves and green winter color. The leaves are light green, but they hold color reasonably well, even in climates like that of Chicago.

Buxus sempervirens
common, American, or English boxwood

One of the most functional plants in garden history, it has been used for screens, hedges, and foundations in the great gardens of the world. In habit, common boxwood is a behemoth; specimens 15 to 20 ft. high and wide prospered in Cincinnati, Ohio, until the devastating freezes (−20°F and lower) of 1976–77. Compared to *Buxus microphylla* or *B. sinica* var. *insularis*, this boxwood offers neither outstanding cold nor heat tolerance. The ½- to 1-in.-long, ½-in.-wide leaves are dark green above, yellowish green below. Prospers in virtually any well-drained soil, in sun or quite dense shade. Plants can become unkempt as the result of climatic and insect problems. Cut older plants in late winter to within 18 to 36 in. of the ground; by the end of summer, the foliage will have covered the exposed stems. Psyllid, leaf miner, mites, and nematodes may cause significant damage. Grows 15 to 20 ft. high and wide. Zones (5)6 to 8. Europe, northern Africa, western Asia.

CULTIVARS AND VARIETIES

The many cultivars are preferable to the species, although no perfectly cold hardy forms exist for all conditions.

'Dee Runk' is upright, tightly narrow-columnar-pyramidal, with a slight taper toward the base. Dark green leaves. A great accent plant, but I would hate to make a hedge of it. About 5 ft. by

Buxus 'Green Velvet'

Buxus sempervirens 'Suffruticosa'

Buxus sinica var. *insularis* 'Wintergreen'

Buxus sempervirens 'Vardar Valley'

1 ft.; possibly higher and wider at maturity.

'Suffruticosa' (true English boxwood) is a dense, compact, slow-growing form ideal for edging. Leaves quite fragrant and considered the least susceptible to box leaf miner; susceptible to nematodes. It can be kept a few inches high or will reach 4 to 5 ft. after many years.

'Vardar Valley' develops deep blue-green foliage. Low-growing, flat-topped, mounded form; 2 to 3 ft. by 4 to 5 ft. although can reach 8 ft. by 15 ft.

MORE ▶

Buxus sempervirens, common boxwood, tightly pruned

Buxus sempervirens 'Dee Runk'

Buxus sempervirens CONTINUED
Beautiful at its best, and one of the more cold hardy cultivars. Others frequently listed or quoted for hardiness include 'Inglis', 'Northern Beauty', 'Northern Find', 'Northland', 'Pullman', and 'Welleri'.

Calia secundiflora
syn. *Sophora secundiflora*
Texas mountain laurel, mescal bean
When I first saw it, during a visit to San Antonio, Texas, I thought this was one of the most beautiful flowering plants I had ever laid eyes upon. Attempts to grow the plant in Athens, Georgia, met with disaster. Often, plants native to areas with dry climates and soils perform inadequately in humid climates. Evergreen large shrub or small tree, upright-spreading and low-branched. The leaves, compound pinnate, 4 to 6 in. long, are composed of seven to nine, rich green, oblong or obovate, notched leaflets, each to 2 in. long. The great aesthetics are embodied in the fragrant, violet-blue, 1-in.-long flowers, borne in a wisteria-like raceme in late winter to spring. Fruit are 6- to 9-in.-long, silver-gray, woody pods with ½-in.-wide red seeds. Transplant from containers into well-drained, drier soils; best suited for the Southwest. Tolerates alkaline soils. Use as an accent plant and small street tree, and in courtyards, containers, and groupings. Grows (15 to) 20 to 30 ft. high. Zones 8 to 10. Texas, New Mexico, northern Mexico.

Callicarpa
beautyberry
The *Callicarpa* species (about 140 worldwide) are dieback shrubs that flower on new growth of the season. Breeding research conducted by Dr. Ryan Contreras at the University of Georgia advanced knowledge of the genus. I have tested many species in Athens and found none better than those featured herein. *Callicarpa acuminata* (shiny dark purple fruit) and *C. kwangtungensis* (deep purple-red new shoots) are also rather attractive, but they become ratty and unkempt with age. The best remedy is to cut them to within 6 to 12 in. of the ground in winter. Flowers and fruit are still guaranteed later in the growing season. The latter has not fruited well in Athens, but I observed photos of striking purple-magenta fruit on plants in Dr. John Ruter's Georgia trials.

Callicarpa americana
American beautyberry, French mulberry
Spectacular in fruit but coarse-textured in habit, *Callicarpa americana* is suitable for massing in large areas. The 3½- to 6-in.-long, medium green leaves have no appreciable fall color; yellow at best. Dense, lavender-pink cymes develop from the axils of the

Calia secundiflora

Calia secundiflora, Texas mountain laurel

Callicarpa americana 'Lactea'

leaves, and the fruit set that follows is so abundant that the stems are encircled with the brilliant violet to magenta, ¼-in.-wide, rounded drupes. It is a great thrill to experience the plant in the wild, particularly in September and October when the fruit are at their best. This shrub thrives with neglect. It fruits more abundantly in full sun, but it is probably the best for shade of the species treated here. Grows 4 to 8 ft. high and wide. Zones (6)7 to 10. Southwest Maryland to Arkansas, south to the West Indies and Mexico.

CULTIVARS AND VARIETIES
'Lactea' has white fruit and is available from specialty nurseries.

'Welch's Pink' is a pink-fruited selection. I grew many seedlings of this hoping for bright pink fruit, but all were similar to the species.

Callicarpa bodinieri
Bodinier beautyberry
From a landscape point of view, I do not see great differences between this species and *Callicarpa japonica*, Japanese beautyberry. The habit is erect, loose, and somewhat unkempt. Admittedly, the rich magenta-lilac fruit are lovely. The fruiting clusters are much more open and loose than those of either *C. americana* or *C. dichotoma*. Leaf color is a dull dark green, and on occasion, the leaves turn pinkish purple in fall. Culture and care are similar to that of *C. americana*. Grows 6 to 10 ft. high and wide. Zones (5)6 to 8. China.

CULTIVARS AND VARIETIES
'Profusion' is a Dutch selection with ⅙-in.-wide, violet fruit that occur in clusters of 30 to 40. Fruit are more abundant, even on young plants.

Callicarpa dichotoma
purple beautyberry
Purple beautyberry is the most refined of the beautyberries. It has a graceful, arching, spreading habit and 1- to 3-in.-long, light to medium green leaves. Small, rather inconspicuous, light lavender-pink flowers emerge from the leaf axils in June, July, and August. The ⅛-in.-wide, lilac-violet fruit start to ripen in September and persist into November. The fruit are borne in clusters above the foliage,

MORE ▶

Callicarpa americana, American beautyberry

Callicarpa americana

Callicarpa americana 'Welch's Pink'

Callicarpa bodinieri 'Profusion'

Callicarpa dichotoma CONTINUED

and the branches appear studded with brightly colored jewels. The species will prosper in any well-drained soil and in full sun. If plants become tatty, cut to within 6 to 12 in. of the ground in late winter and fertilize. Regrowth is rapid, and flowers and fruit will occur the same year. For maximum effect, use in masses or large groups. Grows 3 to 4 (to 6) ft. high, slightly greater in spread. Zones 5 to 8. China, Japan.
CULTIVARS AND VARIETIES
'Albifructus' is a pretty white-fruited form with lighter green foliage and white flowers. It reaches 6 to 8 ft. in height.

'Duet' has medium green leaves with cream-yellow to white margins. I see minimal reversions and the variegation does not burn in the heat of zone 7. Fruit are white and sparsely produced. Grew 6 ft. by 6½ ft. in four years in Georgia trials. Among the better variegated shrubs for heat and drought tolerance.

'Early Amethyst' and 'Issai' fruit more abundantly than the species. I have grown both and see *no* differences in landscape magnitude.

Callicarpa japonica
Japanese beautyberry
At one time, I rated this species as my favorite, but after growing and carefully observing all the species described here, I judge *Callicarpa dichotoma* the best garden plant.

Callicarpa japonica is certainly a fine plant, but it grows much larger and more open than *C. dichotoma*. Leaves, medium blue-green, 2 to 5 in. long, 1½ to 2 in. wide, are disease- and insect-free. Habit is bushy and rounded with arching branches. Requires pruning to keep it well groomed. Fruit color varies from violet to metallic purple. Grows 4 to 6 ft. high and wide; can grow 10 ft. high. Zones (5)6 to 8. Japan.
CULTIVARS AND VARIETIES
'Leucocarpa' offers attractive white fruit.

Callistemon citrinus
lemon bottlebrush
As a group, the bottlebrushes cause me more confusion in identification than about any other genus. This species is a large, evergreen shrub or small tree with coppery new growth, maturing to bright green. The leaves have a lemon odor when bruised. Leaves are 1 to 3 (to 4) in. long, ¼ to ⅝ in. wide, with a prominent ribbed midvein. The garden beauty resides in the bright crimson flowers, which develop on new growth in 4- to 5-in.-long, 2- to 2½-in.-wide, erect, terminal

Callicarpa dichotoma 'Albifructus'

Callicarpa dichotoma, purple beautyberry

Callicarpa dichotoma 'Early Amethyst'

Callicarpa japonica, Japanese beautyberry

inflorescences. I have observed flowers in December, March, and summer in Orlando, Florida. Potential to develop flowers at the base of each new growth flush. Grow in a well-drained soil, provide supplemental moisture and full sun. Makes a great container plant in northern areas. Excellent for flower color in the border or as an accent plant. Grows 10 to 15 ft. high and wide; 20 to 25 ft. high if staked and grown as a tree. Zones 8 to 11. Australia, New South Wales, Victoria, and Queensland.

Related species *Callistemon linearis* (narrow-leaved bottlebrush), *C. rigidus* (stiff bottlebrush), *C. speciosus*, and *C. viminalis* (weeping bottlebrush) produce red flowers. *Callistemon salignus* and *C. pityoides* (*C. sieberi*) have light yellow to pink, and cream to yellow flowers, respectively. The latter has been the hardiest species at Hillier Arboretum.

MORE ▶

Callicarpa japonica

Callicarpa japonica 'Leucocarpa'

Callistemon citrinus, lemon bottlebrush

Callistemon rigidus, stiff bottlebrush

Callistemon citrinus CONTINUED
CULTIVARS AND VARIETIES
'Little John' is a compact bushy hybrid with blue-green narrow leaves, soft pubescent young shoots, and blood-red flowers in spring and summer. Grows 3 ft. by 5 ft.

'NCSU Hardy' and 'Woodlanders Red' are more cold hardy selections with red flowers; but the foliage discolors, red-brown, in winter, and plants are large, loose, and disheveled.

Calluna vulgaris
Scotch heather, ling
During late summer in England and Scotland, the fields are ablaze with mauve-pink to rose-pink heathers—a sight that both inspires and humbles. *Calluna vulgaris* makes a splendid groundcover in full sun and can be effectively combined with dwarf conifers and deciduous shrubs to produce a magnificent landscape tapestry. The needle-like, soft-textured leaves range from light to dark green in the species, although the many cultivars provide offerings of gray, silver, yellow, and red foliage. Flowers appear in elongated racemes up to 12 in. long. Each flower is urn-shaped, ¼ in. long, with a four-parted corolla and the large, showy, four-parted calyx. Remove old flowers after they fade. Provide well-drained, acid, sandy soils that are low in fertility. Observed in the wilds of England and Scotland, where they carpet moors and sandy, infertile soils.

Good drainage is critical; one authority reported a 20 to 25 percent loss of plants in heavy clay soils and humidity in zone 7. Grows ⅓ to 2 ft. high, much greater in spread. Zones 4 to 6. Europe, Asia Minor.
CULTIVARS AND VARIETIES
Within the genetic plasticity of this single species, over 700 cultivars have been selected for foliage, flower color, and habit. Every conceivable foliage and flower color is available. Flowers also come in singles and doubles. Great fun for the collector.

Calocedrus decurrens
syn. *Libocedrus decurrens*
California incensecedar
I have always considered this a most elegant and formal evergreen, but it is seldom used in contemporary landscapes. The form typically found in

Callistemon viminalis, weeping bottlebrush

Callistemon salignus

Calluna vulgaris, Scotch heather

cultivation is possibly 'Columnaris', an upright, telephone pole–shaped, columnar cultivar; the species form is more broadly conical. The seed-bearing cones are interesting, with scales arranged in opposite pairs, and the shiny dark green foliage is handsome year-round. The gray-green to red-brown bark is scaly and exfoliating and provides winter interest. Prefers moist, acid, well-drained soils, although based on successful plantings in Massachusetts, Ohio, Georgia, Oklahoma, and South Carolina, the plant is tremendously adaptable. Grows 30 to 50 ft. high, 8 to 10 (to 15) ft. wide; can grow 100 to 125 ft. high in the wild. A healthy 80-ft.-high specimen with deeply ridged and furrowed, rich brown bark resides in Athens, Georgia. Zones 5 to 8. Oregon to Nevada and lower California.

Species possibly better suited to the Southeast are *Calocedrus formosana* (bright green needles, yellowish green below) and *C. macrolepis* (sea-green needles, glaucous below). Have grown *C. macrolepis* for years and the refined, fern-spray texture is a welcome addition to the garden. Slight bronzing to foliage at about 10°F in the Dirr garden.

CULTIVARS AND VARIETIES
'Aureo-variegata' is an unusual form, with yellow variegation ranging from a small splash to an entire spray.

'Berrima Gold' is a broad-columnar form with yellow-green foliage; rich golden orange in winter. Prefers cooler temperatures. Slow-growing.

MORE ▶

Calocedrus decurrens

Calocedrus decurrens, California incensecedar

Calluna vulgaris collection

Calocedrus decurrens cones

Calocedrus decurrens CONTINUED

Calocedrus decurrens mature trunk

Calocedrus formosana

Calocedrus macrolepis

Calocedrus decurrens 'Aureo-variegata'

Calocedrus decurrens 'Berrima Gold'

Calycanthus chinensis

Calycanthus chinensis
Chinese sweetshrub

Introduced into the United States as *Sinocalycanthus chinensis*, but a 2001 taxonomic revision folded it into *Calycanthus*. Nothing changed, and the species forms a large upright rounded shrub, relatively coarse in texture, with lustrous dark green, somewhat bumpy-surfaced, 4- to 6-in.-long leaves that turn soft yellow in autumn. The nodding flowers, 2½ to 3 in. across, are white, sometimes tinged pink on the outer tepals, the inner smaller with pale yellow to white at the base with maroon markings. The nonfragrant flowers open over a month's time, typically in April and May. Adaptable and amenable to sun and partial shade. Based on performance in the Dirr garden, moist, well-drained soils rich in organic matter are ideal. Drought may induce premature defoliation. Something of a collector's plant, but hybrids with American *Calycanthus* species are notably garden-worthy. Estimate 6 to 10 ft. high and wide. Zones 6 to 8, 9 and 10 on West Coast. China.

CULTIVARS AND VARIETIES
'Hartlage Wine' produces nonfragrant, red-maroon flowers, 3 to 3½ in. across, in copious quantities from mid April to mid May (zone 7). The habit is upright-rounded with attractive dark green leaves. Will grow 8 to 10 ft. high.

Venus™ is a complex hybrid with shiny dark green leaves, soft yellow buds, opening white and resembling star magnolia in shape. Sterile, and flowered over a long period from May to August in our garden in Chapel Hill. Tepals are disfigured by a brown fungal spotting. Somewhat loose and open habit, wider than high. Literature says 8 ft. by 12 ft., but I estimate 5 to 6 ft. high.

Calycanthus chinensis, Chinese sweetshrub

Calycanthus chinensis

Calycanthus 'Hartlage Wine'

Calycanthus Venus™

Calycanthus floridus
sweetshrub, Carolina allspice

One of the great treasures of eastern North America, especially the open-grown specimens that develop into large, roundish shrubs and offer wonderfully fragrant, brown-maroon flowers in April and May. Truly an old-fashioned heirloom plant, gracing many old gardens, it offers a sense of permanence and purpose. The lustrous dark green, 2- to 5-in.-long leaves turn respectable yellow in autumn. Flowers appear on short stalks from the nodes of naked stems and continue to open as the leaves unfurl. The fragrance is reminiscent of a mélange of ripening melons, strawberries, pineapples, and bananas. Unfortunately, seed-grown plants are unpredictable as to degree of fragrance, and some actually smell like vinegar. Always buy the plant in flower to ensure pleasing fragrance. Site in any well-drained soil, in sun or partial shade. Although found in the wild on dry slopes as an understory plant, it performs more satisfactorily in good light. Great for the shrub border, and I have used it as a welcoming plant by the front door. Grows 6 to 10 ft. high, 6 to 12 ft. wide. Zones (4)5 to 9. Virginia to Florida.

CULTIVARS AND VARIETIES

I have grown all listed herein. 'Athens'

Calycanthus floridus, sweetshrub, fall color

Calycanthus floridus

Calycanthus floridus 'Athens'

Calycanthus floridus 'Michael Lindsey'

Calycanthus occidentalis, California sweetshrub

('Katherine') is a deliciously fragrant, yellow-flowered clone, with heavier-textured, dark green leaves that turn good golden yellow in autumn. Grew for many years in the Dirr garden. Tepals may develop a brown spotting. A trait that has been passed to Venus™.

'Edith Wilder' offers the species' flower color but with guaranteed floral fragrance. Larger, duller blue-green leaves than 'Athens' or 'Michael Lindsey'.

'Michael Lindsey' produces deliciously fragrant maroon flowers and lustrous spinach-green and -textured leaves on a more compact framework. Still the best of the red-maroon flowered forms.

Calycanthus occidentalis
California sweetshrub

Calycanthus occidentalis has larger leaves (to 8 in.) and exposed buds. Those of *C. floridus* are hidden by base of petiole. Flowers are lighter (more red) but lack the sweet fragrance of *C. floridus*. In fact, odor is akin to vinegar. Develops into a large shrub, 10 to 15 ft. high. Plant at the JC Raulston Arboretum, Raleigh, North Carolina, is contented. Zones 6 and 7 on East Coast. California.

Camellia japonica
Japanese camellia

Over the centuries, this woody species has probably had more cultivar selections than any other broadleaf evergreen shrub or tree—an enormous number, with estimates from 3,000 to 30,000 worldwide. The habit is a dense pyramid, some selections almost columnar-pyramidal, rather stiff, stodgy, and formal. The 2- to 4-in.-long, leathery, lustrous dark green serrated leaves serve as the perfect foil for the flowers, 3 to 5 (to 6) in. in diameter, which span the rainbow in coloration. Flowers open in November and December (zone 7) with selected cultivars flowering in April. Provide moisture-retentive acidic soil and partial shade (pine shade is ideal), and protect from sweeping winds. Flowers are frost sensitive, and the petals turn to brown mush after cold nights. When scattered about and mingled with other shrubs, it provides beauty and flowers for the home. Ask the local garden center about the best cultivars for your area; in Athens, one garden center stocks 40 to 60 cultivars, a daunting number. Grows 10 to 15 ft. high, 6 to 10 ft. wide. Zones 7 to 9, 10 on the West Coast. China, Japan.

CULTIVARS AND VARIETIES
The American Camellia Society (www. camellias-acs.com) is located in Fort Valley, Georgia. The collections and displays are extensive. Great purveyor and breeder of camellias is Camellia Forest Nursery, Chapel Hill, North Carolina (www.camforest.com).

Camellia japonica, Japanese camellia

Camellia japonica floral diversity

Camellia oleifera
tea-oil camellia

First time I spied the species, the beautiful golden brown bark was forever etched in my mind. The uniqueness of the species resides in its cold hardiness (zone 6) and use as a breeding parent. The lustrous dark green leaves, 1 to 3 in. long, are serrated from the middle to apex. The 2- to 2½-in.-wide, five-petaled white flowers open from October through January. Flowers are not spectacular. In China, seeds from the greenish fruit are processed for their oil. Culture is as for *Camellia sasanqua*. Dr. William Ackerman, U.S. National Arboretum, crossed this with *C. hiemalis* and *C. sasanqua* to produce October- and November-flowering, cold hardy cultivars like 'Frost Prince', 'Frost Princess', 'Pink Icicle', 'Polar Ice', 'Snow Flurry', 'Spring Frill', 'Winter's Beauty', 'Winter's Charm', 'Winter's Hope', 'Winter's Interlude', 'Winter's Rose', 'Winter's Star', and 'Winter's Waterlily'. I grew 'Polar Ice' and 'Snow Flurry' in our Georgia garden and found them not as satisfactory as *C. sasanqua* types. Grows 12 to 15 ft. high and wide. Zones 6 to 9. China.
CULTIVARS AND VARIETIES
'Lu Shan Snow' is the original plant of *Camellia oleifera* at the U.S. National Arboretum that is described above. Average white flowers.

Camellia reticulata

Flowers the size of salad plates are part of the genetic soup of this species. Even at the American Camellia Society headquarters in Fort Valley, Georgia, plants are protected in a greenhouse. My observations have been of a rather loose, open broadleaf evergreen shrub, the leaves to 4 in. long, leathery dark green, and net-veined (hence, *reticulata*). The flowers are 6 to 10 in. across with curly, wavy petals. Most are semi-double and literally weight the stem to an arching disposition. Flowers open in winter to early spring. Culture is similar to other species, except protect *Camellia reticulata* under pines or a large broadleaf evergreen tree, like live oak. Beautiful for large flowers and a worthy conservatory plant in the North. Grows 8 to 12 ft. high and wide. Zones (8)9 and 10(11). China.

Camellia saluenensis

Camellia saluenensis is a parent of the *C.* ×*williamsii* hybrids and, to my knowledge, virtually unknown in the Southeast. Suspect it is only adapted to the West Coast. The shiny dark green leaves are narrow-elongated. The flowers are cupped, slightly nodding, pink, single, and are produced in great abundance. Witnessed 20 ft. by 20 ft. plants in England flowering

Camellia oleifera, tea-oil camellia

Camellia oleifera

Camellia 'Snow Flurry'

Camellia reticulata

in April. 'Cornish Snow', a beautiful hybrid (*C. cuspidata* × *C. saluenensis*) with white, cup-shaped flowers, is at its best in February. Zones 9 and 10 on West Coast. Yunnan, western China.

Camellia sasanqua
sasanqua

For the everyday gardener, this evergreen species offers more aesthetic growth habit, finer texture, and reliable flowers (because of earlier fall flowering). Typically, less formal in habit than *Camellia japonica*, but still dense and oval-rounded to rounded with looser, arching branches. The 1½- to 3-in.-long, lustrous dark green, finely serrated leaves are beautiful through the seasons. The young shoots are covered with fine hairs, which distinguishes the species from the nonhairy *C. japonica*. The 2- to 4-in.-wide flowers (singles, doubles, whites to reds) appear from September (zone 7) into early December. Petals abscise individually rather than as the entire floral tube in *C. japonica*. Culture is similar to *C. japonica*; however, *C. sasanqua* is more sun-tolerant, and in field nurseries is grown in full sun for four to six years before being sold. Used in

MORE ▶

Camellia saluenensis

Camellia sasanqua, sasanqua

Camellia sasanqua

Camellia sasanqua

Camellia sasanqua

Camellia sasanqua CONTINUED
groupings, masses, and espaliers. In the Dirr garden, the plant is liberally sprinkled throughout the shady borders. Scale is the major insect problem on all camellias. Grows 6 to 10 ft. high and wide. Zones 7 to 9, 10 on the West Coast. China, Japan.

Camellia sinensis
tea
Tea as an ornamental, who would have thought?! For over 30 years, Bonnie and I have grown the species in our Georgia garden. Remarkably resilient, it rewards us with 1- to 1½-in.-wide, five-petaled, white, fragrant flowers with a mass of yellow stamens in late summer to fall. Bees love the nectar and provide a regular stage-show. The lustrous dark green, serrated, reticulate-veined leaves, 2 to 4½ in. long, are beautiful. Requires a modicum of shade, well-drained soil, and occasional pruning to keep it in bounds. Scale, as is true for all *Camellia* species, may occur. Mix with other broadleaf evergreens for foliage color and textural effects. Self-sown seedlings are more common under and around *Camellia sinensis* than any other *Camellia* species. Grows 4 to 6 (to 10)

ft. high and wide. Zones 6 to 9. China.
CULTIVARS AND VARIETIES
Many new variegated ('Shirotae', 'Silver Dust') and contorted ('Unryu') selections have been introduced in recent years. Have read that more than 3,000 genotypes (clones) of tea are known.

'Rosea' ('Rubra') has pink flowers and rich reddish purple new growth. It is not as vigorous as the species.

Camellia ×williamsii
Camellia ×williamsii (*C. japonica* × *C. saluenensis*) offers superb winter-flowering shrubs with supra-abundant, single and double, white, pink, and red flowers over a month's period in February and March. Plants reach 15 ft. with looser, more refined habit than *C. japonica*. Observed a prosperous plant at the JC Raulston Arboretum, Raleigh, North Carolina. Suspect zones 7 to 9.

Campsis grandiflora
Chinese trumpetcreeper
In its own right, a spectacular apricot-orange flowered vine, but commercially outdistanced by one of its hybrids, 'Madame Galen'. Dr. J. C. Raulston often touted this species, and a fine

specimen at the JC Raulston Arboretum, Raleigh, North Carolina, when in flower, does justice to his beliefs. The foliage is lustrous dark green, each leaf consisting of seven to nine, 1½- to 3-in.-long, serrated leaflets. The 2- to 3-in.-long and -wide flowers open in June (zone 7) and do not reflower like *Campsis radicans*. Will tolerate any soil except permanently wet. Vigorous, requires pruning to keep it in check. Great for hiding unsightly structures, fences, or rusting automobiles. Grows 15 to 25 ft. or more. Zones (6)7 to 9. Japan, China.

Campsis radicans
common trumpetcreeper
Common trumpetcreeper is a rampaging, clinging and twining vine that will scale a 60-ft. tree or snake along the ground until it meets something to ascend. In my travels, I have never seen a specimen that did not need pruning. The lustrous dark green

Camellia sinensis

Camellia sinensis, tea

Camellia sinensis 'Rosea'

Camellia ×*williamsii*

Campsis grandiflora, Chinese trumpetcreeper

Campsis radicans, common trumpetcreeper

leaves are composed of seven to 11 coarsely serrated leaflets, ¾ to 4 in. long. Fall color is at best yellow-green. Orange to red, 2½- to 3-in.-long, trumpet-shaped flowers open from June and July into September. The 3- to 5- (to 8-) in.-long, pod-like capsules contain numerous winged seeds. Trumpetcreeper tolerates virtually any soil condition, except permanently wet.

MORE ▶

Camellia ×*williamsii*

Campsis radicans

Campsis radicans

Campsis radicans CONTINUED

Campsis radicans

Campsis radicans 'Flava'

Maximum flowering occurs in full sun. Prune in late winter, since flowering occurs on new growth. Grows 30 to 40 ft. high. Zones 4 to 9. Pennsylvania to Florida, west to Missouri and Texas.
CULTIVARS AND VARIETIES
'Crimson Trumpet' is a strong-growing form, with glowing, pure red flowers that lack any trace of orange.

'Flava' is a handsome yellow-flowered form (actually more orange-yellow), that displays vigor similar to that of the species. 'Apricot' is similar and may, in fact, be a rename.

Campsis ×tagliabuana 'Madame Galen'
Madame Galen Tagliabue trumpetcreeper

This hybrid between *Campsis grandiflora* and *C. radicans* is less rampant and slightly less hardy than the latter parent, but it offers orange, tuba-shaped flowers, each 2 to 3 in. long and wide, in six- to 12-flowered panicles. The flowers are spectacular, and the growth habit is more restrained than that of *C. radicans*. I have seen it flowering heavily in full sun or in half

Caragana arborescens, Siberian peashrub

Campsis ×tagliabuana 'Madame Galen'

Campsis ×tagliabuana Hot Lips®

shade. Like *C. radicans*, it displays great heat tolerance. Grows 20 to 30 ft. high. Zones (5)6 to 9.
CULTIVARS AND VARIETIES
Several, including Madame Rose® ('HOMR') with rose-red flowers and Hot Lips® ('RUTCAM') with velvety reddish orange flowers.

Caragana arborescens
Siberian peashrub

Several peashrubs crop up in the strangest places, although none are common, and in the great flowering shrub sweepstakes, this plant would never survive the first round of cuts. For impossibly harsh northern conditions and heavy, dry soils, however, it has a place. Siberian peashrub becomes a massive, wide-spreading, irregularly rounded shrub, with pea-green leaves that develop before or with the yellow flowers in May. The effect is not overwhelming, as some of the flower effect is diminished by the foliage. The 1½- to 3-in.-long leaves are composed of eight to 12 leaflets. Fruit are narrow, 1½- to 2-in.-long, pencil-like pods that make a popping sound as they open in July and August. Easy to culture. It also fixes atmospheric nitrogen. Useful as a hedge, screen, or windbreak. Grows 15 to 20 ft. high, 12 to 18 ft. wide. Zones 2 to 6(7). Siberia, Mongolia.
CULTIVARS AND VARIETIES
'Lorbergii' has feathery leaflets that provide a ferny texture.

'Nana' is a rather dwarf, stunted form with stiff, contorted branches. Grows 6 ft. by 3 ft. in 15 to 18 years.

'Pendula' is a stiffly weeping form that is often grafted on a standard, resulting in a respectable weeping tree.

'Walker' is similar to 'Lorbergii' in leaf texture but strongly weeping in habit.

Caragana arborescens

Caragana arborescens 'Lorbergii'

Caragana arborescens 'Pendula'

Caragana frutex
Russian peashrub

This species is an upright, suckering shrub. Unarmed, this plant does not bear the spines that are found on several other peashrub species. The leaves are composed of four ¼- to 1-in.-long, dark green leaflets. Bright yellow, 1-in.-long flowers appear in May and June. Grows 6 to 9 ft. high. Zones 2 to 6. Russia.

CULTIVARS AND VARIETIES
'Globosa' is a diminutive, globe-shaped form. Grows 2 ft. high and wide.

Carissa macrocarpa
syn. *Carissa grandiflora*
Natal plum

Broadleaf evergreen shrub, usually rounded, densely branched, with two- to four-pronged spines, and impenetrable. The opposite, leathery dark green leaves are 3 in. long and 2 in. wide. At the petiole base, sharp-branched stipular spines develop, giving the entire shrub a porcupine-like countenance. The five-petaled, star-shaped, fragrant white flowers, each 1½ to 3 in. across, open from spring into summer and thereafter. Red, plum-shaped fruit, 1 to 1½ in. long, ripen in late summer to fall and are utilized for jams and jellies. Adaptable, requires well-drained soil in sun to partial shade. Good mass or barrier plant, also used for hedges, foundations, and screens. Tolerant of salt spray and wind. Grows 5 to 10 ft. high and wide. Zones 9 to 11. South Africa.
CULTIVARS AND VARIETIES
Several low-spreading and compact forms grow less than 5 ft. high. 'Boxwood Beauty' grows 2 ft. high and wide with deep green leaves and no thorns.

Caragana frutex 'Globosa'

Carissa macrocarpa

Carissa macrocarpa, Natal plum

Carissa macrocarpa

'Prostrata' grows 2 ft. high, greater in spread. Makes a good groundcover.

Carpinus
hornbeam

A favorite genus of the author, probably 30 to 40 species worldwide, with only *Carpinus betulus* and *C. caroliniana* common in American commerce. I was privileged to study the superb *Carpinus* collection at Hillier and believe the opportunities abound for other species in contemporary landscapes. Most are smaller trees, 20 to 40 ft. high. The species tolerate acid and calcareous soils, sun to partial shade, and may be pruned and shaped (even into hedges). All are monoecious, with males in yellow-green-brown catkins before the leaves in spring, followed by fruits (nutlets) subtended or enclosed by leafy bracts. Significant *Carpinus* breeding by the Landscape Plant Development Center. I walked the seedling populations at their Oregon Research Station in Canby and witnessed fastigiate to weeping types. Exciting!

Carpinus betulus
European hornbeam

In the garden-making process, this species should find a place of prominence. A superb medium-sized, oval to rounded, dapper tree of uniform proportions, it functions equally well as a single specimen, in groupings, as a screen, in the understory, or as a magnificent hedge. Furthermore, the steel-gray, smooth, sinewy bark is a welcome addition to the winter landscape. The deep green, prominently ribbed, 2- to 5½-in.-long leaves hold late in fall and may turn golden yellow, although exceptional fall coloration is rare. The reddish brown buds are angular-conical and much larger than those of *Carpinus caroliniana*, American hornbeam. Displays excellent tolerance to acid, high pH, moist, or dry soils and withstands full sun or heavy shade. A

MORE ▶

Carpinus betulus, European hornbeam

Carpinus betulus

Carpinus betulus CONTINUED

well-grown specimen is a superb garden treasure. Grows 40 to 60 ft. high, 30 to 40 (to 60) ft. wide; I have seen gigantic 80-ft. specimens in Europe. Zones 4 to 7(8). Europe, Asia Minor.

CULTIVARS AND VARIETIES
'Columnaris' maintains a central leader and relatively upright-ascending secondary branches. The branches are so closely spaced that it serves as an effective screen even in winter.

Emerald Avenue™ ('JFS-KW6') is a superb, tightly pyramidal introduction with large dark green leaves from J. Frank Schmidt & Son Nursery. I observed this tree on many West Coast trips and believe it has a great landscape future.

'Fastigiata' is a fine form with upright branching and a pyramidal-oval outline. Grows 30 to 40 ft. high, 20 to 30 ft. wide. More narrow in youth, becoming wider with maturity; definitely not fastigiate in old age, more chubby, much like the author.

'Frans Fontaine' is another upright-columnar form that was touted as more fastigiate than 'Fastigiata', but older trees I observed were quite wide; 30 to 35 ft. by 15 to 18 ft.

'Monument' ('Columnaris Nana') is a miniature version of 'Fastigiata': about 8 to 10 ft. by 2 to 3 ft. at Hillier.

'Pendula' is not well known in the United States, but it is reminiscent

Carpinus betulus

Carpinus betulus

Carpinus betulus fall color

Carpinus betulus 'Fastigiata' fall color

150

of *Fagus sylvatica* 'Pendula', weeping European beech. The branches arch, dip, and dive to produce a singular specimen plant. Grows 30 to 40 ft. high, 35 to 45 ft. wide.

Carpinus caroliniana

American hornbeam, ironwood, musclewood

The North American counterpart of the European hornbeam is smaller in size and has distinct brownish black buds. Some of the best gardeners in the world have confused the two species. *Carpinus caroliniana* is distinctly upright-spreading with a round (often irregular) to flat-topped crown. The bark is similar to that of *C. betulus*. The dark green, 2½- to 5-in.-long leaves color yellow, orange, and red in the fall. American hornbeam usually grows along streams in moist, alluvial soils throughout its range. In the wild,

MORE ▶

Carpinus betulus 'Columnaris'

Carpinus caroliniana

Carpinus caroliniana fall color

Carpinus betulus 'Pendula'

Carpinus caroliniana, American hornbeam

151

Carpinus caroliniana CONTINUED

it occurs primarily as an understory tree, but it can be grown successfully in full sun under landscape conditions. Maximum growth is achieved in deep, moist, acid soils, although the species performs remarkably well in the more hostile environments of the Midwest. Great tree for naturalizing along the edges of woodlands and streams. Also makes a fine small street or lawn tree. Grows 20 to 30 ft. high and wide. Zones 3 to 9. Nova Scotia to Minnesota, south to Florida and Texas.
CULTIVARS AND VARIETIES
Worthy new introductions with red fall color include Ball O'Fire™ ('J. N. Globe'), Firespire™ ('J. N. Upright'), and Palisade™ ('CCSQU'), with a narrow oval outline.

Carya
hickory

Hickories are seldom available in the trade because of transplanting difficulties and the public's perception of them as less-than-desirable landscape plants because of large fruit. The large, compound pinnate leaves are dark yellow-green, often lustrous, and on many species turn brilliant yellow to golden yellow in fall. Flowers are monoecious, male in long green catkins appearing with emerging leaves; fruit is a nut, enclosed in a dehiscent, four-valved husk, ripening in fall. The leaves, as well as the fruit, are messy however, and in general, the trees grow too large for contemporary landscapes. But if hickories are present on a building site or around the home, do not disturb or remove. The assets far outweigh the liabilities. The trees will provide seasonal interest, and several species produce edible nuts. Hickories grow in deep, moist, well-drained soils, as well as dry, upland soils. The approximately 18 species are distributed in North America, Mexico, and eastern Asia, with majority centered in the United States.

Carya aquatica
water hickory

What a surprise . . . a hickory that is relatively easy to transplant. Select Trees, Athens, Georgia, trialed this species extensively and transplanted trees around the nursery without any losses. Young trees are reminiscent of green ash, with pyramidal habit and finer texture than other hickories. The leaves consist of nine to 11 dark green leaflets, 3 to 5 in. long; they turn yellow-green in fall, not as vibrant as *Carya glabra*, *C. ovata*, and *C. tomentosa*. Bark is light brown, splitting into plate-like scales. Mature trees are vase-shaped, and a beautiful specimen is 70 ft. high in the Coker Arboretum, Chapel Hill, North Carolina. Native in swamps and watercourses but prospers in ordinary soils. Estimate 50 to 70 ft. high at landscape maturity. Zones 6 to 9. Southern Virginia to southern Illinois, eastern Oklahoma and Texas.

Carya cordiformis
bitternut hickory

Bitternut hickory is a slender tree, usually with an irregular, cylindrical

Carya aquatica, water hickory

Carpinus caroliniana

Carya cordiformis, bitternut hickory

crown of stiff, ascending branches, often widest at the top. The compound pinnate leaves contain five to nine medium green, 3- to 6-in.-long leaflets that turn yellow in fall. Bark is gray-brown and shallowly furrowed. The seeds are bitter, and supposedly even the squirrels ignore them. Grows 50 to 75 ft. high. Zones 4 to 9. Quebec to Minnesota, south to Florida and Louisiana.

Carya glabra
pignut hickory

Generally smaller than *Carya cordiformis*, and when open grown, it develops an oblong to round-headed outline. Usually this species is a tree with a regular, rather open, oval head of slender, contorted branches. The lustrous dark green leaves contain five 3- to 6½-in.-long leaflets, which turn a gorgeous, often brilliant yellow in

fall. The seeds are bitter and astringent. In the wild, it grows along hillsides and ridges in well-drained to dry, fairly rich soils. Grows 50 to 60 ft. high, 25 to 35 ft. wide. Zones 4 to 9. Maine to Ontario, south to Florida and Mississippi.

Carya illinoinensis
pecan

Economically, this species is a most important member of the genus *Carya*—the production of pecans is a multimillion-dollar industry in the United States—but again there are limitations in the average landscape. This massive, upright-spreading tree can consume an entire city lot. The lustrous dark olive-green leaves, composed of 11 to 17 leaflets, each 4 to 7 in. long, do not develop appreciable fall color. Additionally, leaf scab can cause premature defoliation. The nuts

MORE ▶

Carya glabra, pignut hickory, fall color

Carya glabra fall color

Carya illinoinensis, pecan

Carya glabra

153

Carya illinoinensis

Carya illinoinensis

Carya illinoinensis

are outstanding, but they ripen consistently only in the warmer regions of the country. The species is quite difficult to transplant—a 6-ft. tree may have a 4-ft. taproot. Best growth occurs in deep, moist, well-drained soils; it follows the river valleys closely in its native range. Grows 70 to 100 ft. high, 40 to 75 ft. wide. Zones 5 to 9. Indiana to Iowa, south to Alabama, Texas, and Mexico.

Carya ovata
shagbark hickory

Perhaps the most widely recognized of all hickories because of its large, shaggy strips of exfoliating gray bark, which provide the basis for the common name. Shagbark hickory develops a straight, cylindrical trunk and an oblong crown of ascending and descending branches. The leaves consist of five deep yellow-green, 4- to 6-in.-long leaflets that assume rich yellow and golden brown tones in fall. The seed is sweet and edible. Grows best in rich, well-drained, loamy

Carya illinoinensis

soils but is extremely adaptable. The closely related *Carya laciniosa*, shellbark hickory, differs primarily in that its leaves are composed of seven leaflets. Grows 60 to 80 ft. high, 30 to 40 ft. wide. Zones 4 to 9. Quebec to Minnesota, south to Georgia and Texas.

Caryopteris ×clandonensis
blue-mist shrub, blue spirea

A valuable shrub for its soft gray-green foliage color and light blue, late summer flowers. For years, I have grown it in a sandy vein of soil and have never witnessed anything less than

Carya ovata, shagbark hickory

Carya laciniosa, shellbark hickory

Carya ovata fall color

Caryopteris ×clandonensis, blue-mist shrub

excellent performance. It thrives with neglect. Leaves average 1 to 2 in. long, and from the axils arise cymose clusters of soft blue flowers in August and September. Flowers occur on the new growth of the season, and plants should be tidied lightly and/or cut back in late winter to promote vigorous new growth. The habit is mounded-rounded. Great in a perennial border or for foliage effect. In our garden, it grew next to rosemary and santolina in a rather harmonious arrangement. Grows 2 to 3 ft. high and wide. Zones (5)6 to 9.

CULTIVARS AND VARIETIES
Increasingly popular in recent years, with many new introductions. In 2007, RHS Garden, Wisley, published the results of trials with 41 taxa of *Caryopteris*. Report can be downloaded at www.rhs.org.uk.

MORE ▶

Caryopteris ×clandonensis 'Dark Knight'

Caryopteris ×clandonensis 'Kew Blue'

Caryopteris ×*clandonensis* CONTINUED

'Dark Knight', 'Kew Blue', and 'Longwood Blue' have dark blue flowers.

'First Choice' is more compact with deeper blue flowers; best performer in Georgia and RHS trials.

Hint of Gold™ ('Lisaura'), 'Summer Sorbet', 'Worcester Gold', Lil' Miss Sunshine™ ('Janice'), and Sunshine Blue® ('Jason') are yellow-foliaged, blue-flowered selections. The first three were best in RHS trials. The cooler, more even British climate is kinder to most yellow-foliage plants. None of these hold their color in Athens, Georgia, heat.

Sterling Silver™ ('Lissilv') with silver-gray foliage and bright blue flowers is unique among the caryopteris.

'White Surprise' has irregular white-margined, gray- to blue-green-centered leaves and blue flowers. Unstable and apt to revert to green or cream.

Cassia
senna

Try as I have to grow the various species for their summer and fall yellow flowers, most have proven minimally hardy with the exception of *Cassia marilandica* (now *Senna marilandica*), wild senna, which still dies to the ground during winter and regrows 4 to 6 ft. each year. The habit is bushy, rounded, with compound pinnate, bright green leaves and clusters of yellow flowers in summer. All species prefer well-drained soil, moderate fertility, and full sun. Great plants for the border and late-season flowering; a 6- to 8-ft. specimen at the Atlanta Botanical Garden was just entering the flower cycle in mid August. Grew large seedling population and all flowered the first season. No variation evident in any characteristics. Zones 7 to 10 (dieback shrub). Midwest and southeastern United States.

Cassia bicapsularis produces spectacular brown-yellow to golden yellow flowers in October in the Dirr garden. Unfortunately, it is killed to the ground each winter but regrows 6 to 8 ft. In Charleston, South Carolina, specimens over 10 ft. high are common. Great for late-season color. Zones 9 to 11. Tropical regions worldwide.

Castanea mollissima
Chinese chestnut

This species is acceptable as a substitute for American chestnut, but as an outstanding ornamental, it falls short. *Castanea mollissima* is typically rounded in outline with a short trunk and wide-spreading branches. The lustrous dark green, 3- to 6- (to 8-) in.-long, coarsely serrated leaves assume a respectable yellow to golden brown fall color. The exceptionally foul-smelling flowers appear in May and June

MORE ▶

Caryopteris ×*clandonensis* 'First Choice'

Caryopteris ×*clandonensis* 'White Surprise'

Caryopteris ×*clandonensis* 'Summer Sorbet'

Cassia bicapsularis

Cassia marilandica, wild senna

Castanea mollissima, Chinese chestnut

Cassia bicapsularis

Castanea dentata, American chestnut

Castanea mollissima

Castanea mollissima

Castanea mollissima CONTINUED

and can ruin a late-spring barbecue. The edible nuts are borne two or three together in a prickly structure not unlike a mini-porcupine. The burrs litter the ground, and hence, trees should be located away from trafficked areas. Chestnut weevils lay their eggs in the burrs, and the larvae feed on the nuts. Grows 40 to 60 ft. high, similar spread. Zones 4 to 9. Northern China, Korea.

Castanea dentata, American chestnut, once a magnificent and noble tree of the eastern North American forests, was largely devastated by a blight, but isolated trees survive. By means of back-crossing, a hybridizing technique, seedlings that are $^{15}/_{16}$s American chestnut with blight resistance are now a reality. Breeding for resistance continues, and anyone interested in the latest progress should check www.acf.org.

Castanea pumila
Allegheny chinkapin

The southeastern mountains are rich with this smaller cousin of the more famous *Castanea dentata*. During my hikes in Rabun County, Georgia, the tree, sometimes shrub, is a common sight. The telltale identification feature is the lustrous dark green leaf with the silver underside. The cream flowers occur in terminal panicles in June. The 1½-in.-wide prickly fruit covering houses one or two, ¾- to 1-in.-long, dark brown, sweet edible nuts. Requires full sun for best growth and tolerates drier soils. I often see it growing in the shade of the understory. Resistant to chestnut blight. Grows 20 to 25 ft. high, usually smaller. Zones 5 to 9. Pennsylvania to Florida, west to Oklahoma and Texas.

Catalpa bignonioides
southern catalpa, Indian bean

Ever ask the local nursery for a catalpa? Chances are it has none to offer. Southern catalpa and the related species nearly qualify for dinosaur status in the landscape world. The flowers are quite attractive, however, and the bold coarseness of the large leaves adds textural interest. *Catalpa bignonioides* is a rounded to broad-rounded tree, with an irregular crown composed of short, crooked branches. The 4- to 8-in.-long and -wide leaves are light green and seldom display a hint of fall color. Leaves hold late in fall before coloring and are still green in October during the annual pilgrimage Bonnie and I make to Maine. White, tubular-flaring, 2-in.-long and -wide flowers occur in 8- to 10-in.-long and -wide panicles in June, about two weeks after those of *C. spe-*

Castanea dentata fall color

Castanea pumila, Allegheny chinkapin, fall color

Castanea pumila

Castanea pumila

ciosa, northern catalpa. Each flower has two ridges and two rows of yellow spots and numerous purple spots on the tube and lower lobe. The 6- to 15-in.-long, bean-like (capsule) fruit occur in prodigious quantities and provide the basis for the common name "Indian bean." Tremendously tolerant of adverse soil conditions. Generally, the cultivars are more suitable than the species for contemporary landscaping. Grows 30 to 40 ft. high and wide. Often shows up as a guest without ever being touched by the gardener. Zones 5 to 9. Georgia to Florida and Louisiana.

CULTIVARS AND VARIETIES

'Aurea' has new leaves of a rich yellow color, holding same until flowering, becoming yellow-green to green.

'Nana' is an old dwarf, bushy form that is grafted on a standard to produce a mushroom or globe shape.

Catalpa speciosa
northern or western catalpa

A common sight on farmsteads of the Midwest, abundant in the New England countryside, a presence in the Southeast, and certainly not without merit because of its inherent toughness and adaptability. It differs from *Catalpa bignonioides* in its narrow, open, irregular, oval crown, and its flowers open several weeks earlier. No genuine advantage over southern catalpa other than hardiness and size. Grows 40 to 60 ft. high, 20 to 40 ft. wide. Zones 4 to 8. Southern Illinois and Indiana, south to western Tennessee and northern Arkansas.

Two related species, *Catalpa ×erubescens* (*C. bignonioides* × *C. ovata*) and *C. fargesii*, Farges catalpa, are worthy of mention. The first has purple new leaves (with 'Purpurea', dark

MORE ▶

Catalpa bignonioides, southern catalpa

Catalpa bignonioides

Catalpa bignonioides

Catalpa bignonioides 'Aurea'

159

Catalpa speciosa CONTINUED
chocolate-purple leaves) and white flowers with inflorescence stalks deep purple. The second, particularly in its forma *duclouxii*, has purplish pink flowers. Neither is common; they are typically warehoused in arboreta.

Ceanothus
California lilac
The 50 to 55 evergreen species of this genus, principally centered in California but found from Canada south to Mexico and Guatemala, are not adapted to the eastern United States. Both species and cultivars receive limited attention in the Southeast but are mainstays in West Coast gardens. I have tested many in Athens, with 'Victoria' the last to perish. The magnificent blue flowers are coveted by all gardeners. *Ceanothus* (2006) by David Fross and Dieter Wilken is the best read on the subject.

Ceanothus americanus
New Jersey tea, redroot
Along I-80 in Pennsylvania on a June day, thousands of *Ceanothus americanus* plants appear as billowy white cushions. Unfortunately, this species has never found its way into commerce, possibly because of transplanting difficulties. The habit is a refined broad-mounded cushion. The rich, glossy green, 2- to 3-in.-long leaves may develop yellowish hues in fall.

Catalpa speciosa, northern catalpa

Catalpa ×*erubescens* 'Purpurea'

Catalpa fargesii, Farges catalpa

Catalpa speciosa

White flowers appear in 1- to 2-in.-long panicles at the end of the shoots in June and July. Transplant from a container. Will grow in infertile, dry soils. Also has the ability to fix atmospheric nitrogen. Use as a tall groundcover or mass on banks, cuts, and fills, and in difficult dry, sunny locations. Have grown many seedlings that flowered (white) in the second year and displayed no variation. Grows 3 to 4 ft. high, 3 to 5 ft. wide. Zones 4 to 8.

Quebec to Manitoba, south to South Carolina and Texas.

Ceanothus ×delileanus
French hybrid ceanothus
This hybrid, a cross between the tender *Ceanothus coeruleus* of Mexico and *C. americanus*, has given rise to beautiful blue-flowered forms. Habit is variable; some grow as mounding shrubs, others as tall, upright shrubs. The lustrous dark green leaves are evergreen to semi-evergreen. Flowers are light blue to deep blue and mask the foliage during May and June.

MORE ▶

Ceanothus americanus, New Jersey tea

Catalpa fargesii

Ceanothus americanus

Ceanothus ×delileanus 'Gloire de Versailles'

Ceanothus ×delileanus 'Henri Desfosse'

Ceanothus ×delileanus 'Henri Desfosse'

Ceanothus ×delileanus CONTINUED

Perhaps the bluest flower range of all woody shrubs is inherent in this group. Prefers drier conditions; thrives in California and for some reason most of Europe. Not as happy in the Southeast, but evaluations over the past ten years provide a window to successful culture. Grows 3 to 5 (to 15) ft. high; often espaliered on walls. Zones 8 to 10.

CULTIVARS AND VARIETIES

Plant Introductions, Inc., grew numerous seedlings with nothing better than the two described here.

'Gloire de Versailles' with large leaves and soft blue flowers grew 7 ft. by 8 ft. in the Georgia trials. Tardily deciduous; flowers heavily in May and June, sporadically into late summer.

'Henri Desfosse' is almost evergreen depending on degree of cold, with finer textured leaves than 'Gloire de Versailles'. Flowers are soft blue in smaller inflorescences. More compact habit, 6 ft. by 6 ft.

Ceanothus ×pallidus

This hybrid species is beautiful in flower. Of its many representatives, I have observed and grown 'Marie Simon' and 'Roseus' from Boston to Athens. Both are loosely branched shrubs with soft pink flowers developing on new growth of the season. 'Marie Simon', with slower growth, was essentially deciduous in the Georgia trials; grew 3 ft. by 3 ft. 'Roseus' was killed to ground but regrew and flowered. The foliage is lustrous dark green and holds late in fall, with no appreciable fall color. Requires full sun and well-drained soil, erring toward the drier side. Works well as a filler in herbaceous and woody borders. Grows 3 to 4 ft. high and wide. Zones 6 to 8.

CULTIVARS AND VARIETIES

Marie Bleu™ ('Minmari'), with the hardiness of 'Marie Simon', has light blue flowers.

Ceanothus ×pallidus 'Marie Simon'

Ceanothus ×pallidus 'Roseus'

Ceanothus ×pallidus 'Roseus', seed capsules

Cedrus atlantica

Cedrus atlantica

Cedrus atlantica

Atlas cedar

The true cedars are in the first rank of needle evergreens, and the Atlas cedar is, with maturity, truly magnificent. The Glauca Group (var. *glauca*), blue Atlas cedar, is more common than the species and will be discussed here. The habit in youth is pyramidal and sparsely branched; in ten to 20 years, denser and acquiring character; by year 50, a grand and noble, broadly horizontal-branched specimen. The ¾- to 1½-in.-long needles are rich frosty blue, particularly on the new spring growth. In a crowd, this form shouts for attention. The male cones are 2- to 3-in.-long, finger-shaped structures that release clouds of golden yellow pollen in September. Female cones, on the same tree (monoecious condition), are 3 in. long, 2 in. wide, and egg-shaped. They are glaucous blue-green, maturing to rich brown. Female cones take two years to develop and occur only on older trees. Transplant as a container-grown or balled-and-burlapped plant into any reasonably moist, well-drained soil. It is tolerant of acid and alkaline conditions and, once established,

MORE ▶

Cedrus atlantica, Atlas cedar

Cedrus atlantica 'Glauca Pendula'

Cedrus atlantica, blue Atlas seedling

Cedrus atlantica CONTINUED

is more tolerant of heat and dry soil than *Cedrus deodara* or *C. libani*. The least cold hardy of the tree cedars. Ideally *C. atlantica* var. *glauca* should be used as a specimen plant where there is ample room for it to spread its feathery, blue boughs; anything less is a sin. Has been used beside lakes, ponds, and reflecting pools, where it appears as blue-green water cascad-ing over rocks—a magnificent sight! Grows 40 to 60 ft. high, 30 to 40 ft. wide; trees over 100 ft. high are common in Europe. Zones 6 to 8. Atlas Mountains of northwest Africa.

CULTIVARS AND VARIETIES

'Glauca Pendula', a weeping form, can be trained and shaped to resemble a daddy-long-legs, a potato beetle, or a geodesic dome framework.

Cedrus deodara
deodar cedar

The most popular landscape cedar, principally because of its fast growth and branch density in youth. The habit is fluffy and dense, becoming more open and artistic with age. The 1- to 2-in.-long, sharply pointed, blue-green needles are the longest of the true cedars. Cones are similar to those of *Cedrus atlantica*, only larger. A top decline (possibly from canker or cold) often results in multiple leader formation and, in some cases, dieback. The easiest true cedar to transplant. Commonly used as an understock. Extremely adaptable, it has survived on the high, dry, alkaline plains of west Texas. Most common species in the Southeast. Grows 40 to 70 ft. high. Zones 6 to 8(9). Himalayas.

CULTIVARS AND VARIETIES

Numerous with yellow, white, gray, blue, and green needles from compact buns to weepers to large trees.

Blue Velvet™ ('Sander's Blue') is a graceful pyramidal form with beautiful blue needles.

'Kashmir' and 'Kingsville' are often listed as cold hardy forms, but they are really no better than −5°F cold tolerant.

'Shalimar', an Arnold Arboretum introduction, displays good blue-green needle color and is hardy to at least Boston (zone 6). It survived −15°F in Winchester, Tennessee.

Cedrus deodara, deodar cedar

Cedrus deodara

Cedrus deodara

Cedrus libani

cedar-of-Lebanon

Considered the patriarch of the true cedars because of biblical associations and its dominating landscape presence. A fully developed specimen provides cause for reflection and inspiration. In youth the habit is tightly pyramidal; with age it develops horizontally disposed branches and a flat-topped crown. The ¾- to 1½-in.- long needles are lustrous dark green. Culture is similar to that of *Cedrus atlantica*. At the species level, this is the most cold hardy of the cedars. Grows 40 to 60 ft. high. Zones 5 to 7. Asia Minor.

CULTIVARS AND VARIETIES

'Pendula' is a weeping, green-needled selection.

Variety *stenocoma* is a cold hardy

MORE ▶

Cedrus libani female cone

Cedrus libani male cones

Cedrus deodara Blue Velvet™

Cedrus libani, cedar-of-Lebanon

Cedrus libani

165

Cedrus libani CONTINUED
(–20°F) form, more stiff and rigid than the species. The habit is pyramidal-columnar. Observed in Cincinnati after –24°F with no needles but complete regrowth by summer.

Celastrus orbiculatus
oriental bittersweet

Oriental bittersweet is closely related to *Celastrus scandens*, American bittersweet, but differs in the flowers and fruit that develop in the axils of the leaves. The leaves are more rounded and slightly larger (2 to 5 in. long). This species is a significant weed in the Northeast, where it has crowded out native vegetation. Use with caution in any cultivated situation. Grows 20 to 40 ft. high. Zones 4 to 7. Japan, China.

Celastrus scandens
American bittersweet

American bittersweet offers beautiful yellow-orange and red fruit that have long been a staple of the dried-flower market, particularly for fall arrangements. The species is a vigorous twining vine or scandent shrub. The 2- to 4-in.-long, lustrous dark green leaves turn greenish yellow in fall. Non-showy, yellowish white flowers open in May and June in 2- to 4-in.-long panicles at the ends of the branches. The species is dioecious, and male and female plants are needed for good fruit set. The ⅓-in.-wide, three-lobed,

Cedrus libani 'Pendula'

Cedrus libani var. *stenocoma*

Celastrus orbiculatus, oriental bittersweet

capsular fruit open in October to display the yellow-orange inside and crimson seeds. The species is adaptable to a wide range of soils and pH, even dry conditions. Site where the plant will not engulf other plants. Best in a semi-naturalized situation on a fence or rock pile. Grows 15 to 20 ft. high. Zones 4 to 8. Quebec, south to North Carolina and New Mexico.

CULTIVARS AND VARIETIES
Autumn Revolution™ ('Bailumn') is a hermaphrodite selection with large marble-like fruit in grape-like clusters, self-fruitful, spectacular. Have observed the plant at Bailey's, St. Paul, Minnesota. Anyone who likes bittersweet will love this.

Celtis laevigata
sugar hackberry
Certainly never on any list of the ten most desirable trees, but sugar hackberry is as handsome as any when properly grown. The city of Savannah, Georgia, has splendid specimens used in street plantings. The habit is distinctly upright-spreading, not unlike that of *Ulmus americana*, American elm, but without the elegance of the latter. The bark on the best forms is a smooth, rich gray, very similar to that of *Fagus grandifolia*, American beech. The lustrous dark green, 2- to 3½-in.-long leaves do not color particularly

MORE ▶

Celastrus orbiculatus

Celastrus orbiculatus

Celastrus scandens, American bittersweet

Celastrus scandens

Celtis laevigata, sugar hackberry

Celtis laevigata CONTINUED

well in fall. The small, ⅓-in.-wide, orangish to blue-black fruit have a sweet date-like taste and are relished by many birds. *Celtis laevigata* will grow in wet or dry soils. Has been utilized in the South and, to some degree, the Midwest with great success. Selection of superior trees is the key to wider use. Grows 40 to 50 ft. high, similar spread. Zones 5 to 9. Southern Indiana and Illinois, south to Florida and Texas.

Celtis occidentalis
common hackberry

The fierce, drying winds of the Midwest and Plains states do not faze this tough hombre. Its tolerance is legendary, and it can be found in floodplains, in open fields, along roadsides, and in fencerows. The best forms approach the dignity of an American elm; the worst, a worn-out broom. In youth the habit is weakly pyramidal; in old age the broad crown is composed of ascending-arching branches, often with drooping branchlets. The gray bark is covered with corky warts and ridges. Unfortunately, the light to medium green foliage is not particularly attractive and is often covered with a nipple gall. Witch's-broom (clusters of twiggy growths) also often develops in common hackberry. Trees with superior characteristics are evident in any population. For areas where few trees will prosper, it is a reasonable choice. Grows 40 to 60 ft. high, similar spread. Zones (2)3 to 9. Quebec to Manitoba, south to Georgia and Oklahoma.

CULTIVARS AND VARIETIES

'Prairie Pride' offers good glossy foliage and no gall or witch's-broom.

Prairie Sentinel® ('JFS-KSU1') is a

Celtis laevigata

Celtis laevigata

Celtis occidentalis, common hackberry

168

tight-columnar form with ascending branches discovered in Kansas. Have seen photos and young nursery-grown trees. Holds great promise for the Midwest and Plains states. Grows 45 ft. by 12 ft. Zone 4.

Cephalanthus occidentalis
buttonbush

In a naturalized landscape where excess moisture is present, the buttonbush is a reliable performer. Short on ornamental attributes—except for its 2- to 6-in.-long, lustrous green leaves and the curious 1- to 1¼-in.-wide, rounded, creamy white flowers in summer—the plant labors in obscurity. A wonderful butterfly attractant. I have observed it growing with its trunks submerged in fresh water ponds in Georgia and on Cape Cod,

MORE ▶

Celtis occidentalis

Celtis occidentalis

Celtis occidentalis

Cephalanthus occidentalis, buttonbush

Celtis occidentalis

169

Cephalanthus occidentalis CONTINUED
Massachusetts. The habit is rounded, rather lax and loose, and variable in size. Grows 3 to 6 ft. high and wide; can reach 10 to 15 ft. high and wide. Zones 5 to 11. Always attached to moist to wet habitats in the wild. United States, Cuba, Mexico, eastern Asia.

CULTIVARS AND VARIETIES
I may be a degree harsh in my discussion for, with selection, particularly dwarf forms, the plant has merit. Have grown many seedlings with minimal variation.

Sputnik™ ('Bieberich') has pinkish white flowers and glossy foliage, and grows 8 to 10 ft. high and wide. I have only witnessed photos, which showed white flowers.

The Landscape Plant Development Center has a compact selection with shorter internodes and abundant white flowers; developed from northern plant provenances by treating seeds with mutagenic agents.

Cephalotaxus fortunei
Fortune's plum-yew
Certainly not as well known as *Cephalotaxus harringtonia* but worthy of consideration in warm-climate gardens. Habit is more loose and open, with significantly longer needles, to 3½ in. long. The undersides of the needles are streaked with two prominent silver bands. The reproductive structures are similar to those of *C. harringtonia*, only larger. Requires shade and moist, well-drained soil. Useful for needle texture and accent but not preferable to *C. harringtonia* for everyday garden use. Grows 15 to 20 ft. high and wide. Zones 7 to 9. Eastern and central China.

Cephalotaxus fortunei, Fortune's plum-yew

Cephalanthus occidentalis

Cephalotaxus fortunei

Cephalotaxus fortunei 'Prostrate Spreader'

CULTIVARS AND VARIETIES
'Grandis' has longer needles and graceful arching habit.

'Prostrate Spreader' is a wide-spreading, long-needled, densely branched form, 5 ft. high, 8 to 10 ft. wide.

Cephalotaxus harringtonia
Japanese plum-yew

What a wonderful needle evergreen, in many respects resembling *Taxus*, yew, yet offering deer resistance and heat tolerance. The variation is phenomenal: 45 clones were collected for testing at the University of Georgia, including prostrate, shrubby, and tree-type forms. The lustrous dark green needles are 1 to 2 in. long with two grayish bands on the lower side. Male and female reproductive structures occur on separate plants in March and April with the female producing ¾- to 1-in.-long, olive-like seeds. Provide moist, well-drained soil in partial to heavy shade. The short-needled forms are acceptable in sun once established. Excellent for massing, grouping, and foundation plantings. Maintenance-free and one of the most serviceable needle evergreens for the South. Grows 5 to 10 ft. high and wide. Zones 6 to 9. Japan.

CULTIVARS AND VARIETIES
Variety *drupacea* is an elusive taxonomic entity but typically shrubby, bushy and spreading, with shorter dark green needles than the type. See my *Manual* (2009) for an expanded discussion. RHS Garden, Wisley, in England, recorded an 18 ft. by 30 ft. female plant.

'Duke Gardens' is a short-needled, shrubby form with wide, vase-shaped growth habit. Grows 3 to 5 ft. high, wider at maturity. Male.

'Fastigiata' is distinctly upright-columnar, broadening with age to 10 ft. high, 6 to 8 ft. wide. Needles are whorled around the stem, creating a bottlebrush-like composition.

'Norris Johnson' is a handsome shrubby form, the branches ascending at 30° angles, needles whorled in bottlebrush fashion around the stems. One of the best cultivars, and a stalwart in the Dirr garden. Grows 3 to 4 ft. high and wide.

MORE ▶

Cephalotaxus harringtonia, Japanese plum-yew

Cephalotaxus harringtonia 'Duke Gardens'

Cephalotaxus harringtonia

Cephalotaxus harringtonia CONTINUED

'Prostrata' in its best form is low-growing and long-needled, 1½ to 2 ft. high, 4 to 6 ft. wide. Male.

Yewtopia™ is a great name from the Southern Living Plant Collection. As I view it, not much different from 'Norris Johnson', and there is no royalty or marketing fee with the latter. Grows 3 to 4 ft. high and wide.

Cephalotaxus harringtonia 'Fastigiata'

Cephalotaxus harringtonia 'Norris Johnson'

Cercidiphyllum japonicum
katsuratree

Understated elegance is evident in this species through the seasons—never gauche, gaudy, or noisy, always in elegant landscape fashion. Habit is pyramidal in youth, pyramidal-oval to rounded with maturity. Flowers, reddish purple, dioecious, before the leaves in March and April. Fruit, brownish, banana-shaped pods with small winged brown seeds that germinate upon sowing. Leaves average 2 to 4 in. long and wide, with a uniform crenate-serrate margin. The young leaves emerge a beautiful bronzy purple, fading to light green and then blue-green, and turn rich yellow to apricot hues in fall. The senescing (fall-coloring) leaves give off a delightful, spicy odor reminiscent of cotton candy. Emerging leaves may be injured by spring freezes. The brown, slightly shaggy bark is lovely through the seasons. No serious insect or disease problems, but trunks of young trees may sun-scald or split in cold climates. Requires ample moisture in the early years of establishment. A superb species for large lawns, parks, and streets. One of my favorite trees; I added two to the new garden. Grows 40 to 60 ft. high and wide; often variable in spread. Zones 4 to 8. China, Japan.

CULTIVARS AND VARIETIES
'Amazing Grace' ('Pendula') is a small, gracefully weeping form. From a graft, it will grow 10 to 15 ft. high and wide in five years. Typically wider than high at maturity. Ultimate size is 25 ft. Male.

'Heronswood Globe' is a refined, globe-shaped, 15-ft.-high selection for smaller properties. Had a 10-ft.-high plant in the Georgia garden that developed only yellow fall color.

MORE ▶

Cephalotaxus harringtonia 'Prostrata'

Cercidiphyllum japonicum, katsuratree

Cercidiphyllum japonicum fall color

Cercidiphyllum japonicum

Cercidiphyllum japonicum

Cercidiphyllum japonicum 'Red Fox'

Cercidiphyllum japonicum CONTINUED

Cercidiphyllum japonicum 'Amazing Grace'

Cercidiphyllum japonicum 'Heronswood Globe'

Cercidiphyllum japonicum 'Morioka Weeping'

'Morioka Weeping' is a beautiful form, the habit more upright and tree-like than 'Amazing Grace'. Observed 30-ft.-high trees in the Northeast. Originally listed as *Cercidiphyllum magnificum* 'Pendulum', but DNA freed it from this moniker. Male.

'Peach', 'Raspberry', 'Ruby', and 'Strawberry' were selected for these early-season foliage colors.

'Red Fox' ('Rotfuchs'), with beautiful red-purple leaves, first crossed my path at the great Spinners Nursery in Hampshire, England. Color fades in the heat. Leaves are more frost-resistant than those of the species.

Cercis canadensis
eastern redbud

A treasure in the March–April landscape, when its clustered magenta buds unfold a blanket of rosy pink. No equal, no competitor, can be found among small flowering landscape trees—the stage is reserved for this native species. The flowers appear on leafless branches and are followed by waxy, bronzy to reddish purple new leaves that soon turn dark, almost bluish green and may assume yellow tints in fall. The 3- to 5-in.-long and -wide leaves are a unique heart shape. This is a small, dapper, low-branching tree with a spreading, flat-topped to rounded crown. Leaves may develop spotting or discoloration in late summer, and along with the excess baggage of abundant 2- to 4-in.-long seed pods, may prove less than aesthetic. The bark, especially when moist, is glistening black, with rust-colored patches resulting from the exfoliation of the outer scales and plates. Not the easiest plant to transplant, it should be moved balled and burlapped or from a container in the dormant season. Adaptable to acid, calcareous or high pH, moist or dry soils. In highly stressed situations, redbuds may decline from diseases; botryosphaeria canker and verticillium wilt are the

MORE ▶

Cercis canadensis, eastern redbud

Cercis canadensis

Cercis canadensis fall color

Cercis canadensis

Cercis canadensis 'Ace of Hearts'

Cercis canadensis CONTINUED

most troublesome diseases. Can be used for every imaginable landscape situation, from the front yard of a Florida residence to the slopes of a New England freeway. Planted ten different redbuds in the new Dirr garden. Grows 20 to 30 ft. high, 25 to 35 ft. wide. Zones 4 to 9. Massachusetts to northern Florida, west to Missouri, Texas, and northern Mexico.

CULTIVARS AND VARIETIES

'Ace of Hearts' is typically a shrubby form; parent plant is 12 ft. by 11 ft. Shiny green leaves, half species size, overlap each other along the stem. Flowers are lavender-rose-pink and borne in abundance.

'Alba' and 'Royal White' offer white flowers; 'Royal White' is the more cold hardy.

'Appalachian Red' is supposedly close to red, but the plant in my possession has deep red-purple buds that open to bright (neon) pink; more eye-catching than the species. Habit akin to the species.

'Flame' is an attractive, rather interesting, double rose-pink form. Flowers are atypical as stamens are largely petaloid. Fruitless. A vigorous grower but less cold hardy than species.

'Floating Clouds' is a white-variegated leaf selection, the white speckling more prominent than 'Silver Cloud' and less subject to burning in hot climates. Pink flowers. 'Alley Cat' is a recent discovery with even more prominent white markings on a green background.

'Forest Pansy' has shimmering, reddish purple young foliage that fades with the heat of late spring. Flowers are more intense red-purple than the species.

'Hearts of Gold' produces yellow new leaves tinted with red-purple that mature pure yellow. Will keep much of the yellow if well watered; drought-stressed plants become green. Flowers are rose-pink.

Lavender Twist™ ('Covey') is a small weeping form with shoots arching from a contorted stem to produce an umbrella-shaped crown; original tree was 5 ft. high by 8 ft. wide at 30 years; must be staked to produce a trunk. Rose-pink flowers.

'Little Woody' produces thick, rugose, bumpy-surfaced dark green leaves closely spaced along the stem, on a shrubby, tightly branched, 10- to 12-ft.-high framework. Flowers are deeper pink than those of 'Ace of Hearts' but not as heavily produced.

'Merlot' is a vase-shaped form with thick, glossy, wavy-margined leaves that transform from purple to burgundy to green later in summer. Hybrid of 'Forest Pansy' and 'Texas White'. Rose-pink flowers.

'Ruby Falls' is a weeping red-purple leaf selection with rose-pink flowers. Lavender Twist™ × 'Forest Pansy'.

'Silver Cloud' has leaves that are

MORE ▶

Cercis canadensis 'Royal White'

Cercis canadensis 'Appalachian Red'

Cercis canadensis 'Floating Clouds'

Cercis canadensis 'Forest Pansy'

Cercis canadensis 'Alba'

Cercis canadensis 'Hearts of Gold'

Cercis canadensis subsp. *texensis* 'Traveller'

Cercis canadensis 'Flame'

Cercis canadensis Lavender Twist™

Cercis canadensis 'Little Woody'

Cercis canadensis 'Silver Cloud'

177

Cercis canadensis CONTINUED
splotched, blotched, and speckled with creamy white. Variegation not as pronounced as 'Floating Clouds' in the heat of lower zone 7, and branch reversions may occur. Less floriferous than species. Best grown in some shade. Pink flowers.

'Tennessee Pink' has potent, abundant, true clear pink flower, almost neon pink.

Subspecies *texensis* 'Oklahoma' has deeper rosy magenta flowers and waxy, thick-textured, dark green leaves. Grows 15 to 25 ft. high and wide.

Subspecies *texensis* 'Texas White' has milk-white flowers; the leaves are leathery lustrous green with undulating margins.

Subspecies *texensis* 'Traveller' is stiffly arching-weeping and builds on itself without staking to form a broad dome 8 to 10 ft. high by 8 to 12 ft. wide. Produces exceptionally glossy

dark green, leathery leaves that start out rich copper-red. Flowers are a deep rose-pink.

The Rising Sun™ has new growth that is golden-orange, maturing to yellow and eventually typical redbud green unless maintained in an active state of growth; more potent color than 'Hearts of Gold' when first emerging. Rose-pink flowers. 'Solar Eclipse' is a variation with wide green margin and yellow-orange center.

Cercis chinensis
Chinese redbud
Almost always a strongly multi-stemmed, upright-rounded to oval-rounded shrub; occasionally it is trained as a small tree. The 5- to 6-in.-long and -wide, lustrous dark green leaves possess the typical heart shape, but they are somewhat thicker in texture than those of *Cercis canadensis*. Rosy-purple flowers occur up and down the stems about the time

forsythia blooms in March and April. Easy to transplant and grow, it is now more common in American gardens. Makes a wonderful specimen plant, but better used in borders or groupings. A combination with spring bulbs like *Leucojum* would prove lovely. Grows 6 to 10 ft. high and wide; I have encountered 15-ft.-high specimens. Zones 6 to 8(9). China.
CULTIVARS AND VARIETIES
'Avondale' is an attractive small tree or large shrub with vivid magenta-pink flowers in great profusion; grew for many years in the Dirr garden and was always delighted by the floral profusion as flower buds are formed from the smallest stem to the largest branches. Grows 10 ft. and larger.

'Don Egolf' is a more diminutive selection with copious deep rose-mauve flowers in late March in Athens. Does not set fruit. Estimate 5 to 6 ft. high and wide. Named after Dr. Donald Egolf, U.S. National Arboretum.

Cercis canadensis 'Tennessee Pink'

Cercis canadensis subsp. *texensis* 'Oklahoma'

Cercis canadensis The Rising Sun™

Cercis chinensis 'Don Egolf'

'Shibamichi Red' produces neon-rose flowers and thickish, deeply veined dark green leaves with pretty red petioles. A small plant in the Dirr garden is thick-stemmed with soft gray-brown bark. Flowers open in late March. New introduction from Japan via Hawksridge Nursery.

'Shirobana' ('Alba') is an attractive, white-flowered form.

Chaenomeles japonica
Japanese floweringquince

This species is seldom available in commercial horticulture, having been largely superseded by the many *Chaenomeles speciosa* cultivars and hybrids. Frequently a denizen of older gardens, Japanese floweringquince offers a compact framework of interlacing, often spiny stems that seem to attract bottles, cans, and papers. Five-petaled, 1½-in.-wide, orange to orange-red flowers occur on naked stems in late winter and often remain colorful after the leaves have unfurled. The lustrous dark green, 1- to 2-in.-long leaves seldom develop anything more than subdued yellow fall color. The greenish yellow, 1½-in.-wide, rounded, hard-as-a-bullet fruit make

MORE ▶

Cercis chinensis 'Shibamichi Red'

Cercis chinensis 'Shirobana'

Chaenomeles japonica

Cercis chinensis, Chinese redbud

Chaenomeles japonica, Japanese floweringquince

Chaenomeles japonica

179

Chaenomeles speciosa

Chaenomeles speciosa

Chaenomeles speciosa 'Cameo'

ideal ammunition. Provide moist, acid, well-drained soils, in full sun or partial shade. Use in mass plantings or as a filler in the shrub border. Grows 2 to 3 ft. high and wide. Zones 4 to 8. Japan.

Chaenomeles speciosa
common floweringquince

At their best, the flowers are spectacular; at the least hint of winter warmth, however, the buds swell and flowers open, which results in cold-damaged, ugly brown petals. The habit is rather oafish and clumsy, lacking the grace and dignity of the viburnums. Strongly multi-stemmed with a tangled mass of stems, it requires frequent pruning and tidying. The lustrous dark green leaves, 1½ to 3½ in. long, are susceptible to a fungal disease that causes premature defoliation, usually leaving only the youngest leaves present by summer's end. Flowers range from white to pink to scarlet and every conceivable shade in between, in singles and doubles. The fruit average 2 to 2½ in. long and wide, are yellow to rose-blush in color, and have the firmness of a rock. An adaptable species, but chlorosis in high pH soils is a problem. Use in a shrub border, under pines, or in a mass. Often used as a single specimen, where it can become a hummocky mass of unmanageable proportions. Grows 6 to 10 ft. high and wide. Zones 4 to 8(9). China.

Chaenomeles speciosa, common floweringquince

Chaenomeles speciosa 'Jet Trail'

Chaenomeles speciosa 'Texas Scarlet'

Chaenomeles speciosa 'Toyo-Nishiki'

CULTIVARS AND VARIETIES

'Cameo' offers large, double, fluffy, peach-pink flowers in profusion. Holds its rich green foliage into fall better than most other cultivars. One of my favorite quinces and long a prized plant in the Dirr garden.

'Jet Trail' is a white-flowered sport of 'Texas Scarlet' with a similar growth habit.

'Orange Storm', 'Pink Storm', and 'Scarlet Storm' are thornless, fruitless, many-petaled doubles from Dr. Tom Ranney, North Carolina State University.

'Texas Scarlet' presents tomato-red flowers on a spreading shrub that matures between 3 and 4 ft. high. Profuse flowers and a long flowering period.

'Toyo-Nishiki' is a strong, upright grower to 8 ft. high and wide. White, pink, red, and combination-colored flowers appear on the same or different branches.

Chamaecyparis lawsoniana
Lawson's falsecypress

This species is not common in eastern, midwestern, or southern gardens, primarily because of its intolerance to heavy, wet, inadequately drained soils. In Europe and in the Pacific Northwest, it is quite common. The species develops into a pyramidal to conical tree, with a massive, buttressed trunk and short, ascending branches that droop at the tips and end in flat, glaucous green to deep green sprays. Provide well-drained soils. Although respectable specimens of this species occur on Long Island, New York, for most of the eastern half of the United

MORE ▶

Chamaecyparis lawsoniana, Lawson's falsecypress

Chamaecyparis lawsoniana

Chamaecyparis lawsoniana

Chamaecyparis lawsoniana CONTINUED

States, *Chamaecyparis obtusa, C. pisifera*, and *C. thyoides* and their cultivars are preferable. It is worthwhile to relate that the two largest West Coast wholesale container conifer producers did not list a single form of *C. lawsoniana* in their catalogs, whereas the *RHS Plant Finder 2010* lists more than 200 commercially available culti-vars. Grows 40 to 60 ft. high, 10 to 15 ft. wide. Zones 5 to 7. Southwestern Oregon, isolated parts of northwestern California.

CULTIVARS AND VARIETIES
'Alumii', with strongly vertical sprays of rich blue-green foliage, shows up more often than any other large, tree-type cultivar in the Midwest and East.

Chamaecyparis obtusa
Hinoki falsecypress

Cultivars are abundant in landscapes, but the species itself is virtually an enigma. The few representatives I have seen were softly pyramidal trees with spreading branches and droop-ing, frond-like branchlets. The needles are dark green above, with silvery markings on the undersides, and the

Chamaecyparis lawsoniana collection

Chamaecyparis obtusa, Hinoki falsecypress

Chamaecyparis obtusa

foliage is almost fern-like in overall form and texture. The ⅓- to ½-in.-wide cones are composed of eight to ten scales. For positive identification of this species as distinct from *Chamaecyparis pisifera*, the large cone size is a reliable trait. Soils should be moist, well drained, and acidic, although this species is the most climatically adaptable of the genus. Full sun to partial shade is suitable. Use as an accent or specimen plant, or use the dwarf forms in rock gardens, borders, and foundation plantings. Grows 50 to 75 ft. high, 10 to 20 ft. wide. Zones 4 to 8. Japan, Taiwan.

CULTIVARS AND VARIETIES
Numerous cultivars are known. Consult a specialty reference book, such as *Conifers: The Illustrated Encyclopedia* (1996) by D. M. van Gelderen and J. R. P. van Hoey Smith or Richard Bitner's *Conifers for Gardens* (2007), for additional listings.

'Crippsii' is an old standard, yellow foliage, tree type; observed 50-ft.-high trees.

'Filicoides' is a small tree of open, irregular habit, with long, extended branches clothed in semi-pendulous sprays of dark green foliage.

'Nana Gracilis' has dark green foliage in artistic clusters. Grows about 6 ft. high, 3 to 4 ft. wide.

Chamaecyparis pisifera
Japanese or Sawara falsecypress
Like *Chamaecyparis obtusa*, this species is seldom found in the United States. General characteristics are much like those of *C. obtusa*, except for the smaller, ¼-in.-wide, globose cones. Prefers cooler climates. Grows 50 to 70 ft. high, 10 to 20 ft. wide. Zones 4 to 8. Japan.

CULTIVARS AND VARIETIES
'Boulevard' has silvery blue-green, soft-textured foliage on a broad columnar framework. Grows 10 ft. high or more.

'Filifera' forms a gigantic, pyramidal haystack and displays atypical stringy, green foliage. Can grow 15 to 20 ft. high and has actually prospered in heat and drought. A golden-foliaged form, 'Filifera Aurea', offers the same growth habit.

MORE ▶

Chamaecyparis pisifera, Japanese falsecypress

Chamaecyparis obtusa 'Nana Gracilis'

Chamaecyparis obtusa 'Crippsii'

Chamaecyparis pisifera CONTINUED

'Golden Mop', 'Lemon Yellow', and 'Paul's Gold' (excellent in zone 7) are compact gold-leaf types.

'Plumosa' is a standard tree type with soft-textured, feathery foliage. Plants in the Midwest have grown over 30 ft. high. A golden form, 'Plumosa Aurea', is also available.

'Squarrosa' is called the moss falsecypress because of its feathery,

Chamaecyparis pisifera 'Boulevard'

Chamaecyparis pisifera

Chamaecyparis pisifera 'Golden Mop'

Chamaecyparis pisifera 'Filifera'

Chamaecyparis pisifera 'Squarrosa'

Chamaecyparis pisifera 'Filifera Aurea'

gray-green to blue-green, needle-like foliage. Tree-like in habit. Grows 30 to 40 ft. high.

Chamaecyparis thyoides
Atlantic whitecedar
What a thrill it was to view this tree for the first time in the White Cedar Swamp in Cape Cod National Seashore—growing in a swamp along with blueberry and *Clethra alnifolia*. A tall, slender column, the plant looks more like a juniper than a falsecypress. The green to bluish green, soft-textured, needle-like foliage may develop an off color (bronze) in winter. The ¼-in.-wide

cones are about the smallest of the genus. Probably does not have great landscape appeal, but for naturalizing in wet areas it is acceptable. Grows 40 to 50 ft. high, 10 to 20 ft. wide. Zones 4 to 8. Maine to Florida, along the coast to Alabama and Mississippi.
CULTIVARS AND VARIETIES
In Georgia work, over 50 accessions were assembled for examination. Most performed well in youth but aged disgracefully or died. 'Emily' and 'Rachael' were two of the greenest and longest-lived.

'Red Star' ('Rubicon') develops a compact, dense columnar habit, 15

to 25 ft. Needles blue-green, turning plum-purple in winter. Persistent in the Georgia trials.

Chamaedaphne calyculata
leatherleaf
Fortunate are the few who have experienced this humble evergreen member of the Ericaceae that inhabits wet, boggy areas. It is a shrub of sparse, open habit with thin, wiry branches and dull green scaly leaves, ½ to 2 in. long, half as wide. Flowers, ¼ in. long, white, urn-shaped, occur in 1½-

MORE ▶

Chamaecyparis thyoides

Chamaecyparis thyoides, Atlantic whitecedar

Chamaecyparis thyoides 'Red Star' winter color

Chamaedaphne calyculata CONTINUED
to 5-in.-long terminal racemes in April to June. Obviously not a mainstream plant, but for naturalizing, stabilizing pond edges, and watercourses, it has a place. Only author sightings were in Connecticut and Maine, and neither induced great commercial excitement. Grows 2 to 5 ft. high, wider at maturity. Zones 3 to 5. Europe, Asia, and North America.

CULTIVARS AND VARIETIES
'Verdant' is a 20-in.-high, thicket-like groundcover with shiny, dark green foliage and white, blueberry-like flowers. Discovered by Dr. Richard Lighty in the New Jersey Pine Barrens.

Chilopsis linearis
desert willow
Great expectations in the Southeast for this southwestern species; unfortunately, mildew and minimal tolerance for wet soil equated with miserable garden performance. In Texas, where I witnessed flowering plants, the habit was upright, loose, open, and lax. Since it flowers on new growth, the possibility of a cut-back shrub would offer promise. The rich green, willow-like leaves are 6 to 12 in. long, only ¼ to ½ in. wide. In June and into summer, the fragrant flowers, 1 to 1½ in. long and wide, funnelform-campanulate, with two upper and three lower lobes, open in shades of white, pink, rose, and lavender with interior purple markings. In Nagodoches, Texas,

plants were still flowering in October. Fruit are 6- to 12-in.-long, ¼-in.-wide, two-valved capsules. Trunks are often twisted, with shaggy bark. Full sun, well-drained, higher pH soils. Excellent heat tolerance. Not the easiest plant to incorporate into the landscape. Back of the border plant for airy texture. Cut back to promote new growth and flowers. Grows 15 to 25 ft. high, 10 to 15 ft. wide. Zones 7 to 9. Southern California to Texas, south to Mexico.

CULTIVARS AND VARIETIES
A number were introduced by Texas A&M University; 'Alpine' (white-amaranth), 'Burgundy' (burgundy), 'Dark Storm' (lavender, wine-red) 'Marfa Lace' (semi-double, blush pink-rose),

'Regal' (pale lavender to deep burgundy), and 'Tejas' (rose to pink to amaranth) are in cultivation.

Chimonanthus praecox
fragrant wintersweet
Each December, I wait for the wintersweet to spread its sweet, somewhat spicy fragrance across the Georgia campus. The transparent yellow tepals, stained purple in the center, mingle with the tardily deciduous leaves. Never floral dynamite, like forsythia, but opening over an extended period into February and early March. Leaves, 2½ to 6 (to 8) in. long, lustrous dark green with sandpaper-like upper surface, turn yellow in fall and

Chamaedaphne calyculata, leatherleaf

Chilopsis linearis, desert willow

Chilopsis linearis

winter. Fruit is a brown achene, several, held inside a skinny, wrinkled, fig-shaped brown receptacle. Full sun to partial shade in well-drained, acid and calcareous soil, make for an easy-to-grow plant. Great in the border or where people walk. Many times I have been asked where the fragrance is coming from. Grows 10 to 15 ft. high and wide. Zones (6)7 to 9. China.

Chimonanthus nitens is rank-growing, semi-evergreen, with lustrous dark green, 3- to 4-in.-long, 1½-in.-wide leaves, and ¾-in.-wide, weakly fragrant, off-white flowers borne in the leaf axils in October and November. About 8 to 10 ft. high, wider at maturity. Zones 6 to 8. China.

CULTIVARS AND VARIETIES
'Luteus' is a pure bright yellow-flowered form with excellent fragrance. Flowers are not as large as those of the species.

Chionanthus retusus
Chinese fringetree
Like its American cousin *Chionanthus virginicus*, Chinese fringetree is one of the most beautiful large shrubs or small trees for North American gardens. The habit varies from a large, multi-stemmed, rounded to broad-rounded shrub to a small, rounded tree. The bark is a pleasing gray and with maturity becomes ridged and furrowed. The 3- to 8-in.-long, lustrous

dark green leaves hold late, often into December in southern climes, and may show reasonable yellow fall color. Two forms are in cultivation in the United States: one is shrub-like with rounded, leathery, dark green leaves; the other is tree-like and has thinner, more elongated leaves. White, lightly fragrant flowers occur in 2- to 3-in.-long, 2- to 4-in.-wide panicles at the end of the current season's growth in May and June. The flowers smother the foliage and create a fleecy, snow-like dome. Fruit are ovoid, ⅜- to ½-in.-long, bluish drupes. Since the species is effectively dioecious, the fruit occur in prodigious quantities only on female plants. Extremely easy to grow. Chinese fringetree withstands acid or high pH, sandy loam or clay soils. It prospers in sun and also withstands a modicum of shade. Use as an elegant specimen plant, in groupings, in the

MORE ▶

Chimonanthus praecox, fragrant wintersweet

Chimonanthus praecox

Chimonanthus praecox

Chimonanthus nitens

187

Chionanthus retusus CONTINUED

back of a shrub border, or as a small street tree. I have observed it in gardens from Massachusetts to California to Georgia and Florida. Grows 15 to 25 ft. high and wide. Zones 5 to 8. China, Korea, Japan.

CULTIVARS AND VARIETIES
'Arnold's Pride' is the great tree along the Chinese Walk at the Arnold Arboretum. Observed on many occasions, none more beautiful. Vase-shaped, perfectly proportioned with elongated, oval-elliptic, dark green leaves, abun-

dant flowers and fruit. I estimate 30 ft. by 20 ft.

'China Snow' coincides with the plant offered in southern commerce. Almost rounded, plastic-elastic, lustrous dark green leaves. Shrubby, wide-spreading habit; beautifully ridged and furrowed bark. Named by Don Shadow.

'Tokyo Tower' ('Ivory Tower') is a new columnar introduction. Was told the parent plant was 15 ft. by 6 ft. Lustrous dark green leaves; a white column when flowering. Leaves coincide with 'China Snow'.

Chionanthus retusus

Chionanthus retusus

Chionanthus retusus

Chionanthus retusus, Chinese fringetree

Chionanthus retusus 'Arnold's Pride'

Chionanthus retusus

188

Chionanthus virginicus
white fringetree

An extremely variable species: no two seedlings are alike in all characteristics. One of the great challenges in my research career has been to propagate this native species from cuttings. To date, the plant has resisted most advances, but several nurserymen have been successful. Found in a variety of habitats throughout the southeastern United States, it is perfectly cold hardy to at least −30°F. Habit varies from an oval or wide-spreading shrub to a small tree. The bark is light gray-brown. The 3- to 8-in.-long leaves vary from medium to dark green, with various degrees of gloss. In fall, leaves turn muted yellow to yellow-brown. Slightly fragrant, strap-shaped, four- to five-petaled, white flowers are borne in 6- to 8-in.-long, fleecy panicles that open on the previous year's wood in May and June. The ½-in.-long, bluish drupes ripen in September. Culturally, it prefers moist, acid, well-drained soils, but like *Chionanthus retusus*, it is extremely adaptable. Prospers in full sun to moderate shade. Makes a great woodland or understory naturalizing plant. Flowers at a young age; two- to three-year-old seedlings will produce flowers. Grows 12 to 20 ft. high and wide; can grow larger. Zones 4 to 9. Southern New Jersey to Florida, west to Texas.

Cultivars and Varieites. 'Emerald Knight' (male) was selected for long glossy dark green foliage and upright habit; vegetatively propagated; 15 to 20 ft. high.

Prodigy® ('CVSTF') develops a rounded habit with masses of cloud-like white flowers, female, leathery dark green leaves. Introduced by Tree Introductions, Inc., Athens, Georgia.

'Spring Fleecing' is a nifty name and quite appropriate around tax time. Loose, graceful habit, shiny dark green narrow leaves, abundant flowers, male. Had a small plant in our Chapel Hill garden, extremely floriferous. Introduced by Sam Allen, Tarheel Native Trees, North Carolina.

×*Chitalpa tashkentensis*

A most rare intergeneric hybrid that I knew the Dirr garden could not live without. Well, after about five years

MORE ▶

Chionanthus virginicus, white fringetree, fall color

Chionanthus virginicus

Chionanthus virginicus

Chionanthus virginicus

×Chitalpa tashkentensis CONTINUED
serving as a mildew farm, it was removed. In that time, it grew 15 ft. high and formed a loose, open, rounded outline. The medium green leaves are 4 to 6 in. long, 1 to 2 in. wide. Lavender flowers, which developed in summer, were less than exciting. Flowers on new growth. This hybrid is sterile; I never witnessed a single fruit. Requires full sun and well-drained soil. Responds to water and fertility and quickly overgrows its allotted boundaries. Use as a cut-back shrub in the border. Too many better deciduous shrubs to justify chasing it down (like I did). A hybrid between *Catalpa bignonioides* and *Chilopsis linearis*; initial crosses were made at the Tashkent Botanical Garden in Uzbekistan in 1964. Have observed it in the vicinity of Portland, Oregon, in late August, where it was mildew-free and still producing a few flowers. Greater than 20 ft. high and wide at maturity. Zones 6 to 9.

CULTIVARS AND VARIETIES
'Morning Cloud' produces white to pale pink flowers with rich purple streaks in the interior.

'Pink Dawn' has light pink flowers with a pale yellow throat. Flower color is deeper than that of 'Morning Cloud'.

Summer Bells™ ('Minsum'), frilly pink flowers with a yellow throat, develops a rounded habit, 15 to 30 ft.

Choisya ternata
Mexican-orange
A Mexican species that is a common shrub in England and Europe but almost absent in zones 7 to 10, although with some attention to culture, it can be successfully grown. About as perfect in habit as a prescription for same could read—broad-rounded, dense but not bulletproof, with lustrous dark green foliage. The opposite, trifoliate leaves, 3 to 6 in. long, are composed of 1½- to 3-in.-long, almost as wide, lustrous dark green leaflets. Leaves, when bruised,

emit a pungent citrus odor. The flowers, white, fragrant, 1 to 1¼ in. wide, appear in three- to six-flowered corymbs at the ends of the shoots in May and June. The combination of glistening white flowers against the dark green foliage is spectacular. Partial shade to shade, well-drained, acid to neutral soils suit it best. I suspect high night temperatures in the South diminish performance. Excellent border, foundation, or grouping plant. Grows 6 to 8 ft. high and wide. Zones 7 to 9, more robust on the West Coast.

CULTIVARS AND VARIETIES
'Aztec Pearl' (*Choisya arizonica × C. ternata*) is a finer-textured shrub than *C. ternata*, with narrow leaflets and pink flushed to white (open), fragrant flowers. Grows 3 to 4 ft. high, slightly wider at maturity. Bred by Peter Moore, England.

Goldfingers™ ('Limo') represents a breakthrough in color and texture, with the gold of Sundance™ and the fine foliage of 'Aztec Pearl' commingled into a single genotype.

Moonshine™ ('Walcho') has broader

×Chitalpa tashkentensis

Choisya ternata, Mexican-orange

leaflets and larger flowers. Recorded a 4-ft.-high plant with 3-in.-wide white flowers at RHS Garden, Wisley, England, in mid April.

Sundance™ ('Lich'), a golden yellow leaf form with white flowers, is one of the most popular selections. Almost as vigorous as the species. Kind of like spackling mustard on the landscape.

White Dazzler™ ('Londaz') is more compact, densely foliaged, with uniform branching and abundant white flowers ahead of 'Aztec Pearl'.

Cinnamomum camphora
camphor tree

Beautiful broadleaf evergreen tree that from the coast of Georgia to south Florida makes a successful shade tree. Also well adapted to California. In its finest form, a rounded to broad-rounded broadleaf evergreen with fine branches and a thick, stout, gray-brown trunk. The new leaves emerge bronze, finally lustrous dark green, 3 to 4 in. long, with three or four prominent veins. Inconspicuous, greenish white flowers yield copious amounts of shiny black, 1/3-in.-wide fruit in fall and winter. At Leu Gardens in Orlando, Florida, the ground was covered with

MORE ▶

Choisya ternata

Choisya ternata

Choisya ternata 'Aztec Pearl'

Choisya ternata 'Aztec Pearl'

Choisya ternata Goldfingers™

Choisya ternata Sundance™

191

Cinnamomum camphora CONTINUED

fruit in December. Full sun to partial shade in moist, well-drained soil. The aggressive root system competes with surrounding vegetation. Handsome tree when well grown. Grows 40 to 60 ft. high and wide. Zones (8)9 to 11. At 11°F on the Georgia coast, large trees were killed outright. Japan, China, Taiwan.

Cistus

rock rose

Many of the known species are common garden fixtures in European gardens, but, with a Mediterranean heritage, they are best reserved for San Francisco–type climates into Vancouver, British Columbia. Have tried to grow *Cistus laurifolius*, with white, yellow-spotted fragrant flowers, but excessive moisture derailed the effort. Typically, broadleaf evergreen groundcovers to 3- to 6-ft.-high shrubs with dark green leaves that are sticky on both surfaces. Leaves are 1 to 3 in. long, dark green above, gray-tomentose below. Flowers occur in great profusion in June and July (and occasionally August), each five-petaled, 1 to 3 (to 4) in. wide, in shades of white, pink, reddish, often with a deeper colored spot at the base of the petal. Locate in full sun in well-drained, reasonably dry, limy soils. Transplant as container-grown plants, since they do not move readily bare root. In flower, they are knockouts; during our Euro-

Cinnamomum camphora, camphor tree

Cistus ×purpureus, orchid rock rose

Cinnamomum camphora

Cistus ×purpureus

192

pean garden tours, fellow travelers ask the inevitable: "Will it grow in South Carolina?" For groupings, borders, masses, simply terrific choices. Grows 1 to 3 (to 6) ft. high and wide. Zones 8 to 10. Mediterranean region.

Cistus ×*purpureus*, orchid rock rose, produces reddish purple flowers, 3 in. and wider in diameter, with a darker spot at the petal base, on a 3- to 4-ft.-high and -wide, rounded, evergreen shrub.

When revising the *Manual*, I consulted the *RHS Plant Finder 2008–2009*, which listed 20 species, 27 hybrid combinations, and too many cultivars to count. In European gardens, they thrive. The West Coast, from British Columbia to California, offers greatest opportunity for successful culture.

Cladrastis kentukea

syn. *Cladrastis lutea*

American yellowwood

The blossoms of American yellowwood, cascading like white rain from the pea-green shrouded canopy on a spring day, produce one of the most spectacular shows among large flowering trees. This native species, nowhere very common, is a low-branching tree with a broad-rounded crown of delicate branches. The older branches and trunk are smooth and gray—very beech-like in appearance. The emerging leaves are covered with silky hairs, which impart a gray haze, but they soon mature to rich pea-green and turn yellow to golden brown in fall. Fragrant, creamy flowers occur in pendulous, 8- to 14-in.-long pani-

cles in May and June and are followed by small, 2½- to 4-in.-long, light brown pods. Best growth occurs in calcareous, limestone-based soils, but splendid specimens throughout the Northeast grow in distinctly acid soils. An excellent specimen tree, it deserves a prominent position in the landscape. Grows 30 to 50 ft. high, 40 to 55 ft. wide. Zones 4 to 8. North Carolina to Kentucky and Tennessee. Was able to touch the species along the Little River in the Great Smoky Mountains National Park.

CULTIVARS AND VARIETIES

'Perkins Pink' ('Rosea') is a handsome pink-flowered form. Seedlings of this produce pink-flowered trees. Bonnie and I had two in our garden.

MORE ▶

Cladrastis kentukea, American yellowwood

Cladrastis kentukea

Cladrastis kentukea fall color

Cladrastis kentukea CONTINUED

Cladrastis kentukea

Cladrastis kentukea

Clematis 'Jackmanii'

Clematis
clematis

Difficult to categorize as *woody* so . . . purchase a good book on *Clematis* because anything I present can and will be held against me in a garden court-yard. Circa 300 species, deciduous and evergreen, exist as climbers, shrubs, and herbaceous perennials. The climbing species utilize clasping petioles to ascend. The potential for hybridization transcends sanity, and a quick count of species and cultivars in the *RHS Plant Finder 2010* totaled approximately 1,200. I have grown several species and a few hybrids ('Jackmanii', 'Nelly Moser', 'Henryi'). *Clematis armandii* (white, winter–spring, evergreen); *C. montana* var. *rubens*, anemone clematis (rose-pink, abundant, June); *C. tangutica*, golden clematis (yellow, summer, with fluffy achenes); *C. terniflora*, sweetautumn clematis (white, summer, rampant); *C. texensis*, scarlet clematis (carmine, urn-shaped, summer–fall); and *C. viticella*, Italian clematis (purple, violet, summer, extremely dainty) proved successful in both the Illinois and Georgia Dirr gardens.

Clematis require full sun for best flowering and a cool, moist, well-drained root run, succeeding, as I observed, in acid to neutral soils. Ideally provide a structure, trellis, mailbox, fence, or string for climbing. 'Crimson Star' was allowed to snake throughout *Itea virginica* in the Dirr garden. Mailboxes are the norm, and 'Jackmanii', a rich violet-purple, summer-flowering cultivar dating from 1858, is commonly attached. 'Jackmanii' flowers on new growth as do many other large-flowered types, so pruning to shape and control direction can be accomplished in spring. Flowers typically open in May in Athens.

This discussion will end where it started: buy a good book. Any with the name Raymond Evison attached is a good start.

MORE ▶

Clematis 'Nelly Moser'

Clematis 'Henryi'

Clematis armandii

Clematis armandii

Clematis montana var. *rubens*

Clematis tangutica

Clematis tangutica fruit

Clematis terniflora

Clematis texensis

Clematis viticella

Clerodendrum trichotomum

Clerodendrum trichotomum

Clerodendrum trichotomum

harlequin glorybower

I was never particularly enamored of harlequin glorybower until I observed the excellent flower and fruit set, which provided cause for reassessment. The habit is rounded and shrubby, but some plants, particularly those located further south, develop into small trees. In the North, plants should be treated as partial dieback shrubs. *Clerodendrum trichotomum* flowers on new growth, so the principal ornamental characteristics are not lost. The fragrant, white flowers occur in long-stalked, 6- to 9-in.-wide cymes during July and August. Each 1- to 1½-in.-wide flower has a tubular base and five spreading lobes. The pea-shaped, ¼- to ⅜-in.-wide, bright blue drupe is subtended by a leathery, reddish calyx, ½ to ¾ in. wide, five-angled, and five-lobed. Fruit and

Clerodendrum trichotomum, harlequin glorybower

Clerodendrum trichotomum var. *fargesii*

flowers are often present at the same time. The 4- to 9-in.-long, 2- to 5-in.-wide, dark green leaves develop no fall color. When bruised or cut, they release a potent off-odor. Provide moist, organic-laden, acid, well-drained soils, in sun or partial shade. Wilting occurs in extremely dry soils. Makes a good filler in a border. Grows 10 to 15 ft. high and wide. Zones (6)7 to 9. Eastern China, Japan.

CULTIVARS AND VARIETIES
'Carnival' ('Variegata', I suspect, is the same) produces yellowish to creamy-margined leaves and is a vigorous grower. Leaves do not "burn" in the heat of the South. Will revert, and a plant in the Georgia trials ended its useful life totally green.

Variety *fargesii* is a hardier, shrubbier form that flowered heavily in Georgia trials.

Clethra acuminata

cinnamon clethra

Arguably, this species is so specialized that it may belong in a more ethereal reference. Although cinnamon clethra is hard to access in the commercial trade, work at North Carolina State University's Mountain Horticultural Crops Research and Extension Center has provided some keys to successful commercial culture, and the species is becoming more widely available. I have observed *Clethra acuminata* on the tallest mountain in Georgia and marveled at the rich cinnamon-brown, flaky bark. Bark color varies from almost purplish or bluish to flat brown. The species develops a suckering habit and tends to slowly colonize. In the North, it is much more shrub-like and slower growing. The 3- to 6- (to 8-) in.-long, dark green leaves develop yellow fall color. White flowers occur in 3- to 8-in.-long terminal racemes in July and August. Although often listed as fragrant, the scent is rather faint; in repeated nose-to-flower confrontations, I could not detect much. Appears to prosper under less-than-ideal conditions; in the wild, it is commonly found in dry, rocky terrain. In the Dirr garden (zone 7), the species succumbed to heat and drought. Good plant for a semi-shaded garden nook. Grows 8 to 12 ft. high, wider at maturity. Zones 5 to 7. Mountains from Virginia to West Virginia, south to Georgia and Alabama. Common in north Georgia, almost always in shade, where its cinnamon-brown bark is readily identifiable.

Clerodendrum trichotomum 'Carnival'

Clethra acuminata fall color

Clethra acuminata, cinnamon clethra

Clethra acuminata

Clethra alnifolia

summersweet clethra

During June (Athens), July, and August, the sweet floral fragrance of summersweet can permeate an entire garden. The habit is densely rounded and often suckering, resulting in large colonies. The 1½- to 4-in.-long, sharply serrated, lustrous dark green leaves turn pale yellow to rich golden yellow in fall. Fragrant white flowers occur in 2- to 6-in.-long, ¾-in.-wide racemes and are effective for four to six weeks. Provide acid, moist, well-drained soils, in full sun to relatively heavy shade. It has proven more heat- and drought-tolerant than *Clethra acuminata*. An amazingly adaptable plant. Great choice in a shrub border, along streams and ponds, or in large masses by the edge of woodlands. Grows 3 to 8 ft. high, variable spread. Zones 4 to 9. Maine to Florida to coastal Texas.

CULTIVARS AND VARIETIES
Instituted a *Clethra* trial at Georgia and assessed performance of all discussed herein. Longwood Gardens also trialed many cultivars.

Several compact forms, including 'Compacta' ('Nana') and 'Hummingbird', are available. They grow 2½ to 3½ ft. high. 'Hummingbird' forms

Clethra alnifolia

Clethra alnifolia fall color

Clethra alnifolia 'Hummingbird'

Clethra alnifolia 'Rosea'

Clethra alnifolia 'Ruby Spice'

Clethra alnifolia 'Sixteen Candles'

198

Clethra alnifolia, summersweet clethra

Clethra alnifolia 'Compacta'

Clethra alnifolia 'Tomentosa'

large colonies and becomes floppy with age, whereas 'Compacta' is more shrubby. The latter, introduced by Tom Dilatush, is still the most uniformly compact cultivar as well as the highest rated in Longwood trials.

'Fern Valley Pink', 'Hokie Pink', 'Pink Spires', and 'Rosea' offer pink buds and pink (or light pink) flowers as fragrant as those of the white form. Habits are similar to that of the species.

'Ruby Spice' is an introduction with deep rose-colored, non-fading, fragrant flowers. Grows 6 to 8 ft. high. An outstanding selection from Broken Arrow Nursery, Connecticut.

'Sixteen Candles' has lustrous dark green foliage and 4- to 6-in.-long, racemose, white flowers that are held upright like candles on a birthday cake. Introduced by the author.

Sugartina™ ('Crystalina') has lustrous dark green leaves and inflorescences that appear broader and fuller than typical. Listed as growing 30 in. high and wide. Plant in my possession is already over 4 ft. high.

'Tomentosa' (var. *tomentosa*) leaves, with varying degrees of hairiness on the lower surface, emerge two to three weeks ahead of the species and drop later in the fall. Individual flowers are larger than the species, about ½ in. across, and open later than the northern clones.

Vanilla Spice® ('Caleb') has glossy dark green leaves and larger individual flowers. Grows 3 to 6 ft. high.

Clethra arborea
lily of the valley tree, evergreen clethra

One of my most significant dreams (after, of course, two pieces of chocolate cake, a glass of milk, and a double cheeseburger at 11:30 p.m.) conjured the possibility of hybridizing this magnificent evergreen species with the native *Clethra alnifolia*, a deciduous species, and producing cold hardy, evergreen, large-flowered

MORE ▶

Clethra arborea CONTINUED

progeny. Still only a dream, as had to grow *C. arborea*, a large shrub/small tree, in the greenhouse in Athens. The emerging leaves are bronze-red-green, maturing to lustrous dark green, and 4 to 6 in. long. Flowers, summer to fall, occur in large panicles at the end of the shoots. Each flower is cup-shaped, pure white, 1/3 in. long, and slightly fragrant. Requires moist, well-drained soils and at least partial shade. Even in England, the plant grows well only in the mild southwest (Devon and Cornwall). Grows 10 to 20 ft. high. Zones 9 to 11. Madeira Islands.

Clethra barbinervis
Japanese clethra

Seldom available in nursery commerce but remarkable for the large panicles of white flowers in July and August and the richly colored exfoliating bark. Most commonly grown as a large shrub but also makes a handsome small tree. Bark is a beautiful, smooth, polished, rich gray-brown to cinnamon-brown, and displays an exfoliating character. Dark green leaves are 2 to 6 in. long and turn bronzered to maroon in fall. The slightly fragrant white flowers occur in 4- to 6-in.-long and -wide, terminal, rac-

Clethra arborea, lily of the valley tree

Clethra arborea

Clethra barbinervis, Japanese clethra

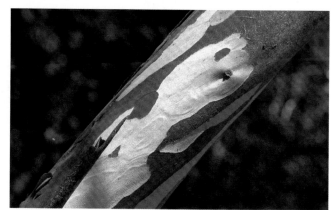

Clethra barbinervis

Clethra barbinervis fall color

Clethra barbinervis 'Takeda Nishiki'

emose panicles. I have grown and killed the species numerous times in our zone 7 garden, ultimately concluding that shade and moisture-retentive soil are prerequisites for success. The lone plant in the garden, located in a shady, moist border, told me the secret. Beautiful in a mixed shrub border. Great plants at the Arnold Arboretum, Smith College Botanic Garden, and the Barnes Foundation. Grows 10 to 20 ft. high. Zones 5 to 7. Japan.
CULTIVARS AND VARIETIES
'Takeda Nishiki' is a variegated leaf selection, pink-bronze, speckled white, on a green background, as I saw it. May be unstable.

Cleyera japonica
Japanese cleyera

Terribly confused with *Ternstroemia gymnanthera* and often marketed as that species. An easy way to separate this species is by the extended apex of the leaf and the terminal bud, which is crooked like the little finger. Habit can be dense and wide-spreading or loose and open, like a small tree. Plants grown in full sun tend toward the former. Leaves are 1 to 3 in. long, lustrous dark green in summer maintaining the color through winter, although in cold winters assuming a bronze-purple-green cast. The ½-in.-wide, cream-white flowers, borne one to five from the leaf axils and underneath the leaves, open in June. The fruit are globose and black. Easy to culture but not well known. Two established plantings in Athens lend credence to heat and soil adaptability. Requires occasional pruning to maintain respectable shape. Worthy hedge, screening, and buffer plant but suffers from second cousin status to *T. gymnanthera*. Grew many plants from seed, shared and planted liberally, but noticed a consistent leaf spot that tempered my enthusiasm. Also not as cold hardy as originally estimated, as 0 to 10°F injures/kills leaves. Grows 10 to 15 ft. high. Zones 7 and 8(9). Japan, Korea, China.
CULTIVARS AND VARIETIES
'Fortunei' ('Tricolor') with thin, bright green leaves, cream, golden yellow, and rose along the margins, maturing to white margins and green centers.

Cleyera japonica, Japanese cleyera

Cleyera japonica

Cleyera japonica

Cleyera japonica 'Fortunei'

Cliftonia monophylla
buckwheat-tree, titi

A relatively unknown southern native shrub or tree that produces 2½- to 3½-in.-long racemes of fragrant white flowers in March and April. The habit is loose and open with evergreen, 1- to 2-in.-long, dull medium green leaves. Fruit are three- to four-winged and similar to the buckwheat fruit in shape (hence, buckwheat-tree). Grows in the same habitats as *Cyrilla racemiflora*. Tolerates full sun to partial shade. I have not found it as garden-worthy or adaptable as *C. racemiflora*. Grows 6 to 12 (to 18) ft. high, slightly less in spread. Zones 7 to 9. Georgia, Florida to Louisiana.
CULTIVARS AND VARIETIES
'Chipolo Pink' and 'Vancleave' produce medium pink–budded, opening lighter pink flowers. Very delicate and attractive.

Cocculus carolinus
Carolina moonseed

Sprinkled liberally with red fruit in September through November, this viney member of the moonseed family was frequently brought to my office for identification. A twining vine, not as thuggy as *Wisteria* species, for example; dovetails neatly with chain-link fences and trellises, and scrambles among shrubs. The 2- to 4-in.-long, lustrous dark green leaves turn yellowish in fall. The dioecious flowers are an inconspicuous yellow-green in spring. Gradually the greenish fruit turn to red, and soon the entire length of the vine appears decorated. Fruit are ¼-in.-wide, rounded drupes that occur in 2- to 4-in.-long racemes. Each fruit contains a single crescent moon–shaped seed. Adaptable to both sun and shade, and to moist or dry, acid soils. Occurs in the wild in sandy soils. Respectable, quick, chain-link fence eliminator. Grows 10 to 15 ft. Zones 6

Cliftonia monophylla, buckwheat-tree

Cliftonia monophylla

Cocculus carolinus

Cocculus carolinus, Carolina moonseed

to 9. Virginia to Illinois and Kansas to Florida and Texas.

The related species *Cocculus laurifolius*, laurel-leaved snailseed, is a rounded-arching, broadleaf evergreen shrub with shiny, leathery leaves, up to 6 in. long, each with three deeply impressed veins running from the base to the apex. Have observed in Mobile, Alabama, as a 4- to 6-ft.-high shrub, but best in central Florida and south. Grows 6 to 10 ft. high; further south to 20 ft. high. Zones (8)9 to 11. Himalayas to southern Japan.

Colutea arborescens
common bladder-senna

An essentially unknown shrub in American gardens and, to my knowledge, not particularly prized in any country. The sum of its ornamental parts, however, makes it worth considering. It is a large, rounded, sometimes scruffy shrub that requires pruning to keep it tidy. The bright green, compound pinnate leaves are composed of nine to 13 leaflets, each ½ to 1 in. long. The pea-green foliage color is distinct from that of many other shrubs, and

it seems to jump out and identify the plant. The ¾-in.-long, pea-shaped flowers are yellow with red markings and appear in six- to eight-flowered racemes from May to July. The flowers do not overwhelm, but they are curiously pretty—with the right amount of imagination they conjure visions of Yosemite Sam. The inflated, pea-like fruit, 3 in. long and 1½ in. wide, range in color from green to reddish to brown at maturity. Transplant from a container into any soil short of per-

MORE ▶

Cocculus laurifolius

Colutea arborescens, common bladder-senna

Cocculus laurifolius, laurel-leaved snailseed

Colutea arborescens

Colutea arborescens

Colutea arborescens CONTINUED

manently wet. Use the species on hot, dry sites; it might be a decent choice for highway right-of-ways. Grows 6 to 8 ft. high and wide. Zones 5 to 7. Mediterranean region, southeastern Europe.

Colutea ×media (C. arborescens × C. orientalis) is similar, but new leaves are brownish red to coppery; the inflated fruit lime-green, pink or bronze, reddish to reddish purple; flowers yellow with tints of copper, pink, reddish brown. Grows 6 to 10 ft. high.

Comptonia peregrina
sweetfern

I have loved this denizen of sandy, acid soil since my days as a graduate student at the University of Massachusetts, where the nearby highway verges were covered with the shrub. Small, dainty, wispy, spreading and colonizing, it forms broad, flat-topped colonies. The 2- to 4½-in.-long, dark green, deeply incised leaves give the plant a woodsy, ferny appearance. Transplant only as a container specimen. Thrives in low-fertility soils, in sun or light shade. Good "no maintenance" groundcover for naturalistic plantings. Grows 2 to 4 ft. high, 4 to 8 ft. wide or more. Zones 2 to 6. Nova Scotia to Manitoba, south to North Carolina.

Cornus alba
Tatarian dogwood

I had forgotten how spectacular this species can be, but a most magnificent planting of Cornus alba 'Sibirica' and C. sericea 'Flaviramea' at the John F. Kennedy Arboretum in Ireland (seen during a January visit) ignited the senses. Their bright red and yellow stems (respectively) set against

Comptonia peregrina, sweetfern

Comptonia peregrina

Cornus alba

Cornus alba, Tatarian dogwood

a steel-gray winter sky provide a tremendous psychological lift. The habit is distinctly upright, with many slender branches arching to form a rounded outline. In leaf, the plant looks like every other deciduous shrub. The typical dogwood leaves, 2 to 4½ in. long, may turn reddish purple in autumn. White flowers occur in 1½- to 2-in.-wide, flat-topped inflorescences in May and June and are followed by whitish or slightly blue-tinted, ⅜-in.-wide, rounded fruit in summer. The species will grow in acid or alkaline, dry or wet soils, in full sun or heavy shade. Canker can be a problem, especially in zones 7 and 8. Use in mass plantings where the winter stem color will be effective. Young stems have the most intense coloration. To foster maximum stem color, remove one-third of the oldest canes each year or cut the plants to the ground in late winter. Grows 8 to 10 ft. high, 5 to 10 ft. wide. Zones 2 to 6(7). Eastern Russia to northeast China and North Korea.

CULTIVARS AND VARIETIES
Many of the 23 cultivars I described in the *Manual* (2009) are minimalist variations on the following.

'Argenteo-marginata' ('Elegantissima') has leaves with an irregular, creamy white border and a subdued grayish green center. Stems are red in winter. This is a fine plant for brightening shady areas of the garden. A form with crisp, white margins and a green middle is occasionally available.

'Aurea' offers uniform, soft yellow leaves during the growing season that turn birch-yellow in autumn. Reports

MORE ▶

Cornus alba

Cornus alba fall color

Cornus alba

Cornus alba Ivory Halo™

Cornus alba 'Sibirica'

Cornus alba 'Spaethii'

Cornus alba CONTINUED

indicate it is resistant to sun scorch. Stems are red in winter.

'Bud's Yellow' is a yellow-stemmed form with clean summer foliage and yellow fall color. Grows 6 to 8 ft. by 5 to 6 ft., although plants I witnessed at Hillier were wider than tall.

Ivory Halo™ ('Bailhalo') is a compact, rounded form that matures 5 to 6 ft. high and wide. Variegated foliage with whitish margins and a green center. Red stems in winter.

'Kesselringii' produces bold, deep

Cornus alba 'Aurea'

Cornus alternifolia, pagoda dogwood

Cornus alternifolia

Cornus alternifolia fall color

red-purple fall color and stems that turn dark brownish purple in winter.

'Sibirica' is smaller in stature than the species and has bright coral-red stem color. Genuinely confused in the trade, and what I perceive as the true selection may or may not be so.

'Spaethii' has golden-edged leaves that do not scorch. Several clones of 'Spaethii' are flashing around in commerce. The real entity is quite colorful.

Cornus alternifolia
pagoda dogwood

In most situations, this species develops into a large, multi-stemmed shrub, although single-stemmed tree specimens are common. Pagoda dogwood has a spreading habit, with horizontal branches that create a layered look. Young stems are deep purplish brown; older stems and the trunk turn gray. The 2- to 5-in.-long, dark green leaves may turn reddish purple in fall, but fall color is seldom spectacular. White flowers are borne in 1½- to 2½-in.-wide clusters above the foliage during May and June. The ¼- to ⅓-in.-wide, rounded, purplish black fruit ripen in July. The fruit stalks are rich pinkish red and more ornamental than the fruit. In theory, the species is more stress-tolerant than *Cornus florida*, flowering dogwood, but in actual landscape practice, few trees withstand the test. Moist, acid, well-drained

MORE ▶

Cornus alternifolia Gold Bullion™

Cornus controversa, giant dogwood

Cornus alternifolia Golden Shadows®

Cornus controversa

Cornus alternifolia CONTINUED

soils and partial shade are ideal. Use the strong horizontal lines to soften sharp architectural features. Grows 15 to 25 ft. high, 10 to 17 ft. to equal in spread. Zones 3 to 7. Abundant in the southern Appalachians at about 2,000 ft. elevation, in some areas as thick as grass, especially along highway embankments. New Brunswick to Minnesota, south to Georgia and Alabama.

Cornus controversa, giant dogwood, is similar but larger in all its parts. Although promoted as stress adaptable, it has not lived up to the press. Its selections June Snow™ and 'Pagoda' are vigorous, with accentuated horizontal branching, abundant white flowers, and blue-black fruit. 'Variegata' is the strongest variegated-leaf grower. Grows 30 to 35 ft. high, and I experienced a 40- to 50-ft.-high tree in England. Zones 5 to 7. China, Japan.

CULTIVARS AND VARIETIES
'Argentea' has smallish cream-green leaves. The habit is more compact and the stems thinner and finer textured.

Gold Bullion™ ('Bachone') has golden yellow foliage that fades to green in the heat. Slow-growing.

Golden Shadows® ('Wstackman') sports yellow-margined leaves, eventually cream-margined at maturity.

Cornus amomum
silky dogwood

This rather pleasant species takes a commercial backseat to the red-stemmed species. In fact, I doubt if it could be purchased from more than five nurseries in the United States. At its best, a large, robust, rounded shrub. The medium to dark green, 2- to 4-in.-long leaves may turn reddish purple in fall. The creamy flowers occur in flat-topped, 1½- to 2½-in.-wide cymes in May and June, seldom raising an eyebrow. Fruit, on close inspection, are spectacular shades of blue, almost porcelain-blue, with white blotches. Birds are attracted to the fruit and can empty a shrub in a short time. It is adaptable to extremes of soil, in sun or shade. Great for the shrub border or for massing and naturalizing. Grows 6 to 10 ft. high and wide. Occurs along

Cornus amomum, silky dogwood

Cornus amomum, red-stemmed seedling

Cornus amomum fall color

Cornus amomum

stream banks and in low swampy habitats, in places so abundant that it forms a monoculture. Discovered a red-stemmed seedling in Virginia. This allows for successful culture in zones 7 and 8, where *Cornus alba* and *C. sericea* disappoint. Zones 4 to 8. Massachusetts to New York, south to Georgia and Tennessee.

Cornus capitata
Bentham's cornel

Little-known evergreen dogwood that is suited only for the mildest areas of the western United States. Small rounded tree with typical dogwood leaves and beautiful cream-yellow flowers arching upward at their mid-dle, forming a cup-like composite. Have only observed flowering trees in Europe, particularly at the great Hillier Arboretum in Hampshire. Too beautiful to adequately describe. The fleshy, rounded, 1-in.-wide fruit turn brilliant red in fall. Have tried to grow the species in our zone 7 garden with no success. Grows 20 ft. high and wide. Zones 7 to 10 on the West Coast. China.

Occasionally encounter *Cornus emeiensis* (*C. omeiensis*) and *C. hongkongensis*, both evergreen, with white flowers shaped like those of *C. kousa*. Recently noted *C. emeiensis* is included in *C. hongkongensis*. Have

MORE ▶

Cornus capitata

Cornus hongkongensis

Cornus 'Norman Hadden'

Cornus capitata, Bentham's cornel

Cornus 'Porlock'

Cornus capitata 'Mountain Moon'

209

observed/grown all and also been confused trying to identify them.

CULTIVARS AND VARIETIES

Hybrids between *Cornus capitata* and *C. kousa*, notably 'Norman Hadden' and 'Porlock', are noteworthy for the cream-white bracts that age to rose and pink.

'Mountain Moon' is allied with *Cornus capitata*; Summer Passion™ with *C. emeiensis*.

Cornus florida
flowering dogwood

Many gardeners consider this species the aristocrat of small flowering trees, a claim that is not unjustified. Normally a low-branched tree with a rounded to flat-topped crown and strong horizontal or tiered branching. The dark green, 3- to 6-in.-long leaves provide excellent red to reddish purple fall color. The handsome 3- to 4-in.-wide, white flowers (actually bracts;

true flowers are yellow) open in April and May, usually before the leaves, and are the envy of every landscape plant. Glistening red, ovoid, ⅓- to ½-in.-long fruit ripen in September

Cornus florida

and October. Bark on older branches develops an alligator-hide appearance, which is particularly distinctive and attractive in the winter landscape. *Cornus florida* has suffered in the

Cornus florida fall color

Cornus florida, flowering dogwood

Midwest, East, and South from cold and drought cycles, which predisposed plants to insects and diseases; mildew, anthracnose, and borers are major problems for cultivated dogwoods. If provided evenly moist, acid, well-drained soils and partial shade, this species should prove a reasonably long-lived plant. Unfortunately, it is often placed in the most inhospitable situations imaginable, without the necessary drainage, moisture, or shade. When grown in full sun, the species tends to be denser and loses a measure of the character that is evident on specimens grown in shadier sites. A superb landscape tree that will never go out of style. Grows 20 ft. high and wide; can reach 30 to 40 ft. high. Zones 5 to 9. Massachusetts to Florida, west to Ontario, Texas, and Mexico.

CULTIVARS AND VARIETIES
Numerous selections, both white- and pink- to red-bracted. The best reference is *Dogwoods* (2005) by Paul Cappiello and Don Shadow.

Appalachian series from the University of Tennessee is considered resistant to anthracnose. 'Appalachian Blush' proved outstanding in Georgia trials. 'Appalachian Spring' has white, non-overlapping bracts, dark green leaves, red fall color, and an upright habit, 20 to 30 ft. high.

Cherokee Brave™ ('Comco No. 1') is

MORE ▶

Cornus florida

Cornus florida

Cornus florida

Cornus florida 'Appalachian Blush'

Cornus florida Cherokee Brave™

Cornus florida 'Cherokee Chief'

211

Cornus florida CONTINUED

one of the red (var. *rubra*) forms producing reddish pink (burgundy) flowers with a white center. New leaves bronze-red-green. Grows 20 to 25 ft. high and wide. Good resistance to mildew.

'Cherokee Chief' is a garden-tested, deep red-bracted form.

'Cherokee Princess' sets numerous buds at an early age that expand to large white-bracted flowers.

Cherokee Sunset™ ('Sunset') has pinkish red-tipped new growth, maturing to green with a broad irregular margin of yellow that will not burn in the heat of summer; fall color ranges from pink through red to purple. The bracts are a good red.

'Cloud Nine' offers good hardiness, and flowers profusely (white) at a young age.

'First Lady' has variegated yellow-green foliage and white flowers.

'Pluribracteata' has double white flowers that last longer and open later than those of the species. Large shiny dark green leaves turn red-purple in fall. Appears more resistant to mildew and anthracnose.

Red Pygmy® ('D-383-22', 'Rutnut') produces numerous rose-red bracted flowers even at a very young age. A genetic dwarf from Dr. Elwin Orton, Rutgers University, with a round-

Cornus florida 'Cherokee Princess'

Cornus florida Cherokee Sunset™

Cornus florida 'First Lady'

Cornus florida Red Pygmy®

Cornus florida 'Rubra'

Cornus florida subsp. *urbiniana*

headed habit, matures about 5 to 6 ft. high.

'Rubra' (var. *rubra*) produces pink flowers; this is the forerunner of all pink/red-flowered types. Not as cold hardy as the best whites. Tends to open slightly later than the whites.

Spring Grove® ('Grovflor') has large, white, 5-in.-wide bracts, often two or three terminal flower buds, and abundant fruit. Medium green leaves turn reddish purple in fall. Parent plant 22 ft. by 32 ft. at 45 years of age. Good cold hardiness; survived –26°F. One of the most beautiful trees at Spring Grove Cemetery and Arboretum, Cincinnati, Ohio.

Subspecies *urbiniana* is unique because the white bracts are fused at their tips in a Chinese-lantern shape. Leaves bluish green; beautiful flowers. Witnessed a 20-ft.-high tree in Washington, D.C.; 60-ft. tree in Seattle.

Cornus kousa
kousa dogwood

A most elegant dogwood, but often lost in the landscape shadow of *Cornus florida*. For many parts of the country, however, *C. kousa* is probably a better choice. In youth the habit is stiffly upright, almost vase-shaped, but with age it becomes rounded to broad-spreading, with distinct horizontal branches. Multicolored mosaics of gray, tan, and rich brown develop on older trunks, and the jigsaw-puzzle-like pattern becomes graphically evident when the bark is wet. The dark green, 2- to 4-in.-long leaves are slightly smaller than those of *C. florida* and may develop respectable deep red fall color. The creamy white, 2- to 4-in.-wide flowers, which are composed of four long-pointed bracts, open two to three weeks later than those of *C. florida*. Raspberry-shaped, ½- to 1-in.-wide, red fruit appear in September

and October. Prefers moist, acid, well-drained soils, in sun or partial shade, although it is probably more adaptable to extremes of soil than *C. florida*. Makes a choice specimen plant and can be incorporated into borders or used in groupings. Resistant to *Discula destructiva*, the organism that causes dogwood anthracnose. Grows 20 to 30 ft. high and wide. Probably a half zone more cold hardy than *C. florida* (i.e., zone 4). Zones (4)5 to 8. Japan, Korea, China.

CULTIVARS AND VARIETIES
The many selections of *Cornus kousa* are seldom available in commerce. Be leery when buying the old cultivar 'Milky Way', for it is seed-produced and generally does not deliver on its promises. Every August in Oregon I study the selection trials at J. Frank Schmidt & Son and am befuddled by the endless stream of green-leaf and

MORE ▶

Cornus kousa, kousa dogwood, fall color

Cornus kousa CONTINUED

variegated hopefuls (50 in 2011). Cappiello and Shadow list 136; *RHS Plant Finder 2010* 110, many never grown in U.S. nurseries. The following selections have passed the Dirr "look" test.

Variety *angustata* has narrow-ovate to ovate evergreen leaves; can be quite shabby in winter, however, as leaves assume purple-red-green coloration and are windburned even in zone 7. A plant at Atlanta Botanical Garden, 30 ft. by 30 ft., usually with about 50 percent of leaves in January, may be *Cornus elliptica*. Flowers and fruit like the species. Not evergreen or fully hardy in zone 6 and colder; best in zones 7 to 9. Taxonomically confusing and has been listed as *C. angustata*. Most recent taxonomy places "angustata" as a species, *C. elliptica*. Few gardeners are tuned to var. *angustata* and its merits, so do not expect the adoption of *C. elliptica* by nurseries in the near future.

'China Girl' is an early-flowering form with very large bracts, good fall color, and large fruit. I thought this was the most beautiful *Cornus kousa* in Hillier's collection; cream-yellow bracts mature glistening milk white, numerous flowers.

Empress of China® ('Elsbry'), a var.

Cornus kousa

Cornus kousa fall color and fruit

Cornus kousa var. *angustata*

Cornus kousa 'China Girl'

Cornus kousa 'Lustgarten Weeping'

Cornus kousa 'Satomi'

angustata selection, sets abundant flower buds as a young plant.

Galilean® ('Galzam') has large dark green leaves, white flowers, and red fruit. Increased cold hardiness (zone 4) over the species. Matures 20 to 25 ft. by 15 to 20 ft.

'Lustgarten Weeping' is a beautiful weeping form, with flowers positioned along the weeping stems so that they are directly in view. Needs to be grafted on a standard to produce a small weeping tree. Flowers effective but not as abundant. Excellent yellow to red-purple fall color.

'Satomi' ('Rosabella', 'New Red', Heart Throb® ['Schmred']) was a respectable rose-pink in England; however, it has not been as vibrant in the United States. Various nurseries list bract color as red, rich pink, pink to red, carmine red, "red," deep pink, bright rose red. Slower growing than the species.

'Summer Fun' produces white flowers and sage-green leaves with wide cream-white margins; margins may develop pink hues. Small, dense, vase-shaped habit, 8 ft. by 4 ft. in ten years. Pretty foliage in early part of growing season.

'Wolf Eyes' has prominent white-margined leaves on a compact spreading plant and outstanding pink to red fall color. Less susceptible to burning than most variegated dogwoods.

MORE ▶

Cornus kousa var. *angustata* Empress of China®

Cornus kousa

Cornus kousa 'Wolf Eyes'

Cornus kousa 'Summer Fun'

Cornus ×*rutgersensis* Aurora®

215

Cornus kousa CONTINUED

Slower growing, more shrubby; parent plant 6 ft. high and wide, larger at maturity. Does best in partial shade.

Cornus ×*rutgersensis* (*C. kousa* × *C. florida*), Rutgers hybrids, developed by Dr. Elwin Orton, Rutgers University, include Aurora®, Celestial®, Constellation®, Ruth Ellen®, Saturn™, Stardust®, and Stellar Pink®. They exhibit characteristics intermediate between those of the parents and are resistant to dogwood anthracnose. 'Celestial Shadow' is a pretty variegated yellow-margined sport of Celestial® discovered and named by Don Shadow.

Dr. Orton also hybridized *Cornus nuttallii* with *C. kousa*, producing Starlight™ ('KN4-43'), with cream-white bracts up to 5 in. in diameter, and Venus™ ('KN30-8'), with 5- to 6-in.-wide, white bracts.

Cornus macrophylla
bigleaf dogwood

In the late '70s, I was introduced to this species during sabbatical at the Arnold Arboretum. Rare then, but beautiful. Still beautiful, and rare. Why? I am not sure. Habit is round-headed with horizontal, layered branches and smooth gray bark that becomes shallowly ridged and furrowed with age. The 4- to 7-in.-long, 2- to 3½-in.-wide, dark green leaves show no signs of mildew and anthracnose. Have not witnessed notable fall color. Flowers, in 4- to 6-in. cymose panicles, yellowish white, reasonably fragrant, open in June and are quite showy. The reddish purple, eventually blackish purple, ¼-in.-wide fruit ripen in August and September. Appears adaptable, and large trees I observed in Massachusetts, North Carolina, Georgia, and

Cornus ×*rutgersensis* Celestial® fall color

Cornus ×*rutgersensis* Constellation®

Cornus macrophylla, bigleaf dogwood

Cornus ×*rutgersensis* Stellar Pink®

Cornus macrophylla

England reflect this. Full sun and any well-drained soil serve it well. Estimate 25 to 35 ft. high and wide, although noted 30- and 40-ft.-high trees. Useful for small properties. Zones 5 to 7. Himalayas, China, Japan.

Cornus mas
corneliancherry dogwood

Few dogwoods are as durable as this underutilized yellow-flowered, red-fruited species. In the Midwest, it is the longest lived of all *Cornus* species. The habit is oval-rounded to rounded, with a dense network of rather fine stems. Used as a hedge, the branches grow so close-knit as to be impenetrable. The 2- to 4-in.-long, lustrous dark green leaves hold late into fall and may develop a semblance of purple-red fall color. Bright yellow flowers open on naked branches in March and are the only show in town. The $5/8$-in.-long, ovoid, bright cherry-red fruit ripen in June and July. They serve as snacks for the birds or can be used for preserves and syrup. Many clones for fruit production have been selected in Europe and Russia and its former satellites. The species tolerates acid and high pH, as well as heavy clay soils, better than any dogwood. It usually

MORE ▶

Cornus mas, corneliancherry dogwood

Cornus mas

Cornus mas

217

Cornus mas CONTINUED

suckers and develops large colonies, although some plants do not show this tendency. Great in groupings or for screens, hedges, or the border. Grows 20 to 25 ft. high, 15 to 20 ft. wide. Zones 4 to 8. Central and southern Europe, western Asia.

CULTIVARS AND VARIETIES

'Aurea' (yellow), 'Aureoelegantissima' ('Elegantissima') (green center, yellow border; pink shading on young leaves), and 'Variegata' (green center, white border) are the best available cultivars for colorful foliage.

'Flava' (var. *flava*) has yellow fruit that are larger, sweeter, and ripen earlier than those of the typical species.

'Golden Glory', an upright form with abundant flowers, has proven its mettle in the Midwest, particularly in the Chicago area.

'Spring Glow' is a bright yellow-flowered form with excellent, leathery dark green foliage. Sets abundant flower buds on small plants. Minimal fruit.

Spring Grove® ('Grovas') is a tree-like form with a broad-rounded outline and non-suckering habit. Exceptional lustrous, leathery dark green leaves and abundant bright yellow flowers.

Cornus mas 'Aurea'

Cornus mas 'Aureoelegantissima'

Cornus mas 'Variegata'

Cornus mas 'Flava'

Cornus mas 'Spring Glow'

218

Cornus nuttallii
Pacific dogwood

The West Coast equivalent of *Cornus florida* but typically larger and more upright in habit, almost oval-rounded. The dark green leaves are 3 to 5 in. long, 1½ to 3 in. wide, and develop yellow to red autumn tints, not as potent as *C. florida*. Flowers, April to May, sporadically in summer, although I observed trees in August in heavy flower. Each flower is composed of four to eight (usually six) bracts, each 1½ to 3 in. long, 1 to 2 in. wide, cream-white, then white flushed pink. Fruit are ellipsoidal, ⅓-in.-long, orange-red drupes. Bark develops a scaly-blocky texture not unlike that of *C. florida*. Prefers West Coast conditions (i.e., cool nights, dry summers, wet winters). Susceptible to dogwood anthracnose. Occasionally bump into a tree on the East Coast. Dr. Elwin Orton, Rutgers, the great *Cornus* breeder, noted that flowers "blasted" in zone 6 and plants were not vegetatively hardy. Grows 20 to 30 ft. high, less in spread. Zones 7 to 9 on West Coast. British Columbia to southern California.

CULTIVARS AND VARIETIES
'Goldspot' has leaves that are splashed, spotted, and mottled with cream-yellow and 5-in.-wide flowers composed of six overlapping bracts. Flowers in May and again in summer.

Cornus officinalis
Japanese cornel dogwood

Many gardeners who glimpse the true species develop a lifelong passion to acquire it. Unfortunately, the true species is difficult to locate in commerce. In many respects, *Cornus officinalis* is similar to *C. mas*, although it flowers earlier (the species will overlap) and the fruit ripen later. Other primary differences are the tufts of brownish hairs in the leaf axils (although this trait is variable) and the exquisite gray, orange, and brown bark, which exfoliates in large scales and plates. Landscape uses and culture are similar to that of *C. mas*. The size also approximates *C. mas*, but a 46-year-old tree at the Secrest Arboretum, Wooster, Ohio, grew 22 ft. high and 35 ft. wide. Has performed quite contentedly in Athens and is slightly more heat-tolerant. Flowers open in mid March in

MORE ▶

Cornus mas Spring Grove®

Cornus officinalis, Japanese cornel dogwood

Cornus nuttallii, Pacific dogwood

Cornus nuttallii 'Goldspot'

Cornus officinalis CONTINUED

Athens. Noted abundant flower production in moderate shade. Zones (4)5 to 7(8). Japan, Korea.
CULTIVARS AND VARIETIES
'Kintoki' is a heavy-flowering, perhaps smaller-statured plant. Observed many times and always impressed with floral profusion. Was able to procure one for the new garden and an 18-in.-high plant had ten to 15 flowers.

Cornus officinalis

Cornus racemosa
gray dogwood

Like *Cornus amomum*, silky dogwood, this is a sleeping giant in the world of deciduous shrubs, and one day it will emerge with a vengeance. A pleasant shrub with excellent blue-green foliage, creamy white flowers, and whitish fruit, it prospers in sun or shade and under varied cultural conditions. Use as a filler in the shrub border or in a naturalized situation. Can become a massive suckering shrub that will easily overgrow its boundaries. Grows 10 to 15 ft. high and wide. Zones 4 to 8. Maine to Ontario and Minnesota, south to Georgia and Nebraska.
CULTIVARS AND VARIETIES
Amazing number in the past ten years. Perhaps the best are in the Counties of Ohio™ series from Lake County Nursery, Perry, Ohio, one of which is Muskingum® ('Muszam'), a tight, low-mounded selection with gray-

Cornus officinalis 'Kintoki'

Cornus officinalis

Cornus racemosa

green foliage that turns brick-red in fall. Grows 2 ft. by 4 ft.; others in the series are larger.

Snow Lace® ('Emerald') is somewhat more compact than the species, still 6 to 9 ft. high and wide, with emerald-green leaves, purple fall color, and abundant white fruit on red pedicels. Introduced by North Dakota State University.

Cornus sanguinea
bloodtwig dogwood

Like *Cornus amomum* and *C. racemosa*, bloodtwig dogwood labors in landscape obscurity, and, in general, serves similar landscape purposes. Its large, round-topped, spreading outline is sloppy and unkempt, and the few specimens noted always left me cold. Translation: "Why waste garden space?" The 1½- to 3-in.-long, dark green leaves seldom develop respectable fall color, although blood-red is described. The young stems are blood-red where exposed to the sun; older branches are greenish gray. For winter stem color, cut to the ground in late winter to foster long shoot extensions. Quite adaptable and may be worthy for difficult sites. Grows 6 to 15 ft. high and wide. Zones 4 to 7. Europe.
CULTIVARS AND VARIETIES
'Midwinter Fire' ('Beteramsii')

MORE ▶

Cornus racemosa, gray dogwood

Cornus racemosa

Cornus racemosa fall color

Cornus sanguinea, bloodtwig dogwood, fall color

221

Cornus sanguinea CONTINUED

Cornus sanguinea Winter Flame™

Cornus sanguinea 'Viridissima'

Cornus sericea, redosier dogwood

develops beautiful yellow, orange, red-at-base stems that glow like a campfire. Plant may reach 10 ft. in height. Striking addition to winter garden; fall color is a respectable yellow. Cut back to encourage new shoots, which offer the best color. Some confusion as to whether this is one clone with multiple names or multiple clones, but an English evaluation of colored-stemmed cultivars showed that 'Winter Beauty', Winter Flame™ ('Anny'), 'Magic Flame', 'Anny's Winter Orange', 'Green Light', and 'Cato' were indeed different. 'Anny's Winter Orange', with good vigor and bright coral-red stems, was the best of the lot.

'Viridissima' is a rather attractive selection with yellowish green winter stems.

Cornus sericea
syn. *Cornus stolonifera*
redosier dogwood

In most respects quite similar to *Cornus alba*, although this species is more suckering, stoloniferous, and colonizing. Even the seasoned pro has difficulty separating the two. This species may be more tolerant of wet soils. Often growing in low, wet areas in the wild. Grows 8 to 10 ft. high, 10 ft. wide or more. Zones 2 to 7. Newfoundland to Manitoba, south to Virginia and Nebraska.

Cornus sericea

CULTIVARS AND VARIETIES

'Cardinal' was released by the Minnesota Landscape Arboretum. Reasonably resistant to leaf spot. Stem color, although listed as red, is not good in zone 7; color was yellowish, perhaps with a trace of orange. Grows 8 to 10 ft. high and wide.

'Flaviramea' has forever graced midwestern and northeastern gardens. Yellow stems with a hint of green brighten the winter landscape.

'Garden Glow' has yellow foliage and a relatively compact habit, 4 to 5 ft. by 6 to 7 ft. Better foliage color retention in the shade.

'Kelseyi' is a neat, compact, mounded form, 2 to 2½ ft. high and wide. Frequently encountered in the Midwest. It is quite susceptible to leaf spot.

'Silver and Gold' has cream-margined leaves and yellow stems. 'White Gold' is similar.

MORE ▶

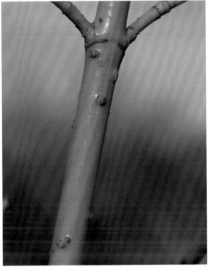

Cornus sericea 'Flaviramea'

Cornus sericea 'Kelseyi'

Cornus sericea

Cornus sericea 'Silver and Gold'

Cornus sericea 'Silver and Gold'

Cornus sericea 'Sunshine'

223

Cornus sericea CONTINUED

'Sunshine' forms a large 10- to 12-ft.-high shrub with a general pale yellow or chartreuse foliar glow. Leaves are variable in variegation and may be all of one hue (yellow) or have yellow margins and an irregular green center; more rarely they are creamy white-margined with a central green blotch. On young shoots, they average 4 to 6 in. long and 2 to 2½ in. wide. Stem coloration is red.

'White Gold' ('White Spot') has leaves edged gold, turning cream-white, with bright gold stems.

Corokia cotoneaster
wire-netting bush

A curious novelty with the most artistic branching . . . contorted, bent, misshapen, and intertwined. Stems, black with maturity, are quite thin, hence the common name. Leaves, evergreen, ½ to 1 in. long, almost as wide, are dark maroon-green to bronze. Flowers, yellow, ½ in. across, star-shaped, open in May and June. Fruit is a ¼- to ⅓-in.-wide, oblong to rounded, orange-red drupe. Requires perfect drainage. For several years, maintained a plant in a container, then it left for no logi-cal reasons. Successfully cultured on the West Coast. A useful analogy to visualize the plant is to imagine rusted barbed wire rolled into messy tangles. Grows 5 to 8 ft. high and wide. British reference noted a plant 8 ft. high and 60 ft. in circumference in Northern Ireland. Zones 7 to 9. New Zealand.

Corylopsis
winterhazel

The winterhazels are quite confused taxonomically. To provide some concept of the potential for confusion, a 1977 article in the *Journal of the Arnold Arboretum* reduced the then-described 33 species to seven. *Hillier Manual* (2007) listed 30 species of deciduous or semi-evergreen shrubs and small trees, native to eastern Himalayas, China, and Japan. Nomenclature has been changed more often than bed sheets, so what the gardener buys as *Corylopsis spicata* is anyone's guess. *Corylopsis* species prefer organic, acid, well-drained soils, in partial shade. Plants do prosper in full sun, however, and in less-than-ideal sites. They are excellent plants for the shrub border or in mass plantings. All produce yellow flowers on naked stems in late winter to early spring. Flowers open in March in Athens. Prune after flowering.

Corylopsis glabrescens
fragrant winterhazel

Fragrant winterhazel can be spectacular in flower, although it tends to become a massive, wide-spreading, dense shrub. It is somewhat flat-topped to rounded in outline and multi-stemmed. The dark green, 2- to 4- (to 5-) in.-long leaves may turn yellow in fall. Fragrant, pale yellow flowers occur in 1- to 1½-in.-long, pendulous racemes in March and April, before the leaves. Same requirements as *Corylopsis spicata*. Grows 8 to 15 ft. high and wide. Zones 5 to 8. Japan.
CULTIVARS AND VARIETIES
Variety *gotoana* is becoming more

Corokia cotoneaster, wire-netting bush

Corylopsis glabrescens, fragrant winterhazel

common in commerce. It is considered less cold hardy than the species but superior to it for general landscape use, although the individual flowers are smaller. The true botanical differences are trivial, and some experts do not recognize it as a distinct entity. Grows 8 to 15 ft. high and wide. Zones 5 to 8. Japan.

'March Jewel' is a low-spreading form, free-flowering and opening earlier than var. *gotoana*. Grew 1½ ft. by 5 ft. in ten years; the habit is so dense and low, it appears to have been woven from willow stems.

Corylopsis pauciflora
buttercup winterhazel

Gardeners will argue the merits of this species over the rest because of its small size, spreading habit, fragrant primrose-yellow flowers, and overall neatness. Flowers open in March in Athens. Like *Corylopsis spicata*, this is a great plant for the woodland garden.

Protect from incessant wind and sun. Grows 4 to 6 ft. high and wide. Witnessed a 15-ft.-high plant in England. Zones 6 to 8. Japan, Taiwan.

Corylopsis sinensis var. *calvescens*

syn. *Corylopsis platypetala*
The garden version of this variety is the largest of the cultivated winterhazel species. It forms a multi-stemmed, rounded shrub. The 2- to 4- (to 5-) in.-long, blue-green leaves die off green or brown in fall. Bright yellow flowers occur in 1- to 2-in.-long racemes in April. Combine with dwarf conifers and broadleaf evergreens for

MORE ▶

Corylopsis pauciflora, buttercup winterhazel

Corylopsis glabrescens

Corylopsis pauciflora young leaves

Corylopsis glabrescens var. *gotoana*

Corylopsis pauciflora

225

Corylopsis sinensis var. *calvescens* CONTINUED

Corylopsis sinensis var. *calvescens*

Corylopsis sinensis var. *calvescens* f. *veitchiana*

Corylopsis spicata, spike winterhazel

maximum effect. Grows 10 to 15 ft. high and wide. Zones 6 to 8. China.
CULTIVARS AND VARIETIES
Forma *veitchiana* is distinctly upright, vase-shaped, with bright green leaves, edged with incurved teeth, glaucous below. Flowers primrose-yellow in 2- to 3-in.-long racemes in March in Athens. A pretty, vigorous form that has performed well in zone 7. Resides between 10 and 15 ft. at maturity.

Corylopsis spicata
spike winterhazel

In my April forays through the Arnold Arboretum, I found that spike winterhazel appeared to be the best behaved and most floriferous of the winterhazels. The delicate flowers hang like yellow tassels from the naked branches and shift with every breath of the wind. New foliage emerges rich, vinous purple, eventually changing to blue-green. The 2- to 4-in.-long,

Corylopsis spicata

Corylopsis spicata 'Ogon'

strongly serrated leaves tend to hold late and are rendered brown by fall freezes. Becomes a mass of crooked, flexible, wide-spreading branches at maturity. A great plant for the shrub border or in mass plantings. Flowers about the same time as Korean rhododendron (*Rhododendron mucronulatum*). Grows 4 to 6 (to 10) ft. high. Zones 5 to 8. Japan.

CULTIVARS AND VARIETIES
'Ogon' ('Golden Spring') is a yellow-foliage introduction that is quite pretty in spring, losing the color with leaf maturity and heat. Possibly best sited in partial shade.

'Spring Purple', with plum-purple young shoots that eventually turn green, is now included in the Willmottiae Group; formerly allied to *Corylopsis willmottiae* and then *C. sinensis* var. *calvescens*.

Corylus americana
American filbert

American filbert is a fine plant for naturalizing, yet it is scarce in commerce. Although no single feature attracts attention, the dark green leaves, yellowish brown catkins, and interesting fruit provide multi-season interest. Flowers are monoecious: the male in brown pendulous catkins; the female only with red stigmas protruding from tips of the buds, in March in Athens. Fall color is yellow-green but occasionally pleasing orange-red-bronze. Prospers in shade or sun and in moist or dry, acid or high pH soils. Although often listed as a smallish shrub, it can easily grow larger, devouring large tracts of garden real estate. Use with discretion and the knowledge that it will outgrow the space. Grows 8 to 10 ft. high and wide; may grow 15 to 18 ft. high and wide. Zones 4 to 9. New England to Saskatchewan, south to Florida.

CULTIVARS AND VARIETIES
A rather exciting red-leaf selection is in the plant evaluation process; holds color more intensely in cooler climates. Has been difficult to propagate.

Corylus avellana
European filbert

An immense shrub or small tree often cultivated for its nuts. Oregon is the center of filbert production in the United States. The species is seldom planted, and the cultivars represent the species in garden cultivation. Grows 12 to 20 ft. high and wide. Zones 4 to 8. Europe, western Asia, northern Africa.

CULTIVARS AND VARIETIES
'Aurea' is a slow-growing form, with yellow leaves that become green with the heat of summer.

'Contorta', aka Harry Lauder's walk-

Corylus americana, American filbert

Corylopsis spicata 'Spring Purple'

Corylus americana fall color

MORE ▶

Corylus avellana CONTINUED

ingstick, is the most popular cultivar. It has artistically contorted stems that provide great interest in the winter garden. Leaves are also slightly twisted. Numerous male catkins are present during fall and winter. Fruit production is minimal. Often grafted, and the understock will sucker. Buy plants that are on their own roots. Grows 8 to 10 ft. high and wide, although plants to 20 ft. are known.

'Heterophylla' ('Laciniata', 'Quercifolia') presents deeply incised leaves of finer texture than the species.

Corylus avellana, European filbert

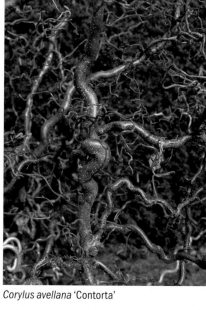
Corylus avellana 'Contorta'

Corylus avellana

Corylus avellana 'Aurea'

Corylus avellana 'Contorta'

Corylus avellana 'Red Majestic'

'Pendula' has distinctly weeping branches and forms a large, cascading, arching shrub. Could be grafted onto *Corylus colurna*, Turkish filbert, to form a small weeping tree.

'Red Dragon' is a red-leaf, contorted-stem selection with complete resistance to eastern filbert blight; grows 10 to 12 ft. high, 6 to 8 ft. wide. Developed at Oregon State University.

'Red Majestic' is a red-leaf, contorted-stemmed introduction. Not as colorful as *Corylus maxima* 'Purpurea' in leaf. Color fades in the heat of zone 7; suspect more intense in cooler zones. Estimate 5 to 6 ft. high and wide.

Corylus colurna
Turkish filbert

A notably underutilized species in northern landscapes, although such neglect is not justified. *Corylus col-*urna is densely pyramidal in youth, pyramidal-oval to almost rounded at maturity. The brown bark exfoliates in small, scaly plates. The best forms offer lustrous dark green, 2½- to 6-in.-long leaves that are resistant to insects and diseases. No appreciable fall color develops. In March, the male flowers appear in 2- to 3-in.-long,

MORE ▶

Corylus avellana 'Heterophylla'

Corylus avellana 'Pendula'

Corylus colurna, Turkish filbert

Corylus colurna

Corylus colurna

229

Corylus colurna CONTINUED

Corylus colurna

Corylus fargesii, Farges hazelnut

Corylus fargesii

brownish catkins, hinting that spring is just around the corner. Nuts develop inside a rather unusual deeply divided involucre. Turkish filbert will grow in a variety of soils and, once established, displays excellent drought tolerance. Superb as a single specimen or in groupings; use along streets, in parks, on golf courses, and on campuses. Grows 40 to 50 ft. high, 15 to 35 ft. wide. Zones 4 to 7. Southeastern Europe, western Asia.

CULTIVARS AND VARIETIES
A unique hybrid, *Corylus ×colurnoides* (*C. avellana* × *C. colurna*), has the common name "trazel." A red-leaf selection, 'Te-Terra Red', has red-purple leaves that fade to green, red-purple catkins, and red-purple involucres that enclose the nuts. Have observed only at Hillier Arboretum. Certainly a worthy candidate for the United States.

Corylus fargesii
Farges hazelnut
My excitement for this species continues to increase exponentially. Virtually unknown except to a few arboretum keepers. Probably a small tree under cultivation, although described as reaching 75 ft. in its native China. Habit is softly pyramidal-rounded, low-branched on most trees I have observed. Leaves, 2 to 4 in. long, 1 to 2 in. wide, medium green, coarsely and doubly serrate, do not resemble the typical hazelnut; they develop soft

Corylus fargesii

yellow fall coloration. Spectacular sheathing, salmon-brown bark. Male flowers, two to eight together, 1 to 2½ in. long; female, two to four in a cluster, bracts forming a tubular sheath, 1 to 2 in. long, enclosing ½-in.-wide nuts. Appears adaptable to acid and high pH soils. Best in full sun. Resistant to eastern filbert blight. Could prove a specimen tree to rival river birch, *Betula nigra*. To date growing in Chicago, Boston, Philadelphia, Washington, D.C., and Raleigh vicinities. If my premonitions are correct, *Corylus fargesii* has the moxie to become a landscape stalwart. Probably 20 to 40 ft. high and wide. Zones (4)5 to 7. China.

Corylus maxima 'Purpurea'
purple giant filbert

The species is not sufficiently different from *Corylus avellana* to warrant giving detailed characteristics (and has in fact been merged by one taxonomic resource into *C. avellana*); however, the involucre encloses and protrudes beyond the nut. The vivid dark red-purple leaves of this taxon are beacons in the early spring, turning dark green in summer. A large shrub on the Georgia campus would burst forth in brightest red-purple in April, becoming green by early June. Even in late summer and fall, the male catkins and fruit involucres have a purplish tint. Grows 15

to 20 ft. high and wide. Zones 4 to 8. Species is native to southeastern Europe, western Asia.

Cotinus coggygria
common smoketree, smokebush

One of the more common shrubs in the Midwest and East into zone 7 in the Southeast. This species has tremendous visual appeal in May and June (and sometimes July; later in the North) when the plumy, pink, smoke-like panicles are at their peak. The "smoke" effect is provided by the silk-like hairs that develop on the inflorescences. Actual flowers are ⅓ in. in diameter, yellowish green, and

MORE ▶

Corylus maxima 'Purpurea', purple giant filbert

Cotinus coggygria, common smoketree

Corylus maxima 'Purpurea'

Corylus maxima 'Purpurea'

231

Cotinus coggygria CONTINUED

five-petaled. The bluish green leaves, 1½ to 3½ in. long and wide, turn rich yellows, reds, and purples in autumn. The habit of this immense, rounded shrub is often unkempt, and hard pruning results in long, buggy-whip branch extensions. Several major gardens cut the plants, particularly the purple-leaf cultivars, to within 6 to 12 in. of the ground to promote colorful, long shoot extensions. *Cotinus coggygria* grows in anything but wet soils. Plant in full sun. Use in borders or groupings. Grows 10 to 15 ft. high and wide. Zones 4 to 8. Southern Europe to central China and the Himalayas.

CULTIVARS AND VARIETIES

Many new cultivars from Europe; most unavailable in the United States.

'Daydream' produces an abundance of dense, ovoid, fluffy inflorescences that mature rich brownish pink. Bears green leaves and has a smaller stature, possibly 10 to 12 ft. high.

Golden Spirit™ ('Ancot') with bright yellow leaves that fade to green-yellow or green, depending on heat. Certainly not at its best in zone 7.

'Nordine', 'Notcutt's Variety', 'Royal Purple', and 'Velvet Cloak' are cultivars with maroon to reddish purple leaves. 'Royal Purple' and 'Velvet Cloak' may be the same plant masquerading under two names.

Cotinus coggygria Golden Spirit™

Cotinus coggygria

Cotinus coggygria fall color

Cotinus coggygria 'Daydream'

Cotinus coggygria 'Royal Purple'

Cotinus obovatus

syn. *Cotinus americanus*

American smoketree

A choice native species that occurs in limestone soils. In the wild, it is often a large shrub rather than a tree, but most cultivated specimens are small trees. The habit is oval to rounded, with a dense crown. The gray-black bark develops a fish-scale constitution that is particularly noticeable in the winter landscape. The rich blue-green, 1½- to 3½-in.-long, oval leaves turn magnificent yellow, orange, red, and reddish purple in fall, with no two trees exactly alike. In fact, a single tree may display all these colors. Makes an excellent small lawn tree and offers possibilities for street and urban planting in dry soils. No serious insect or disease problems. Should become more commonly used in gardens as people discover its many virtues. Grows 20 to 30 ft. high, variable spread. Zones 4 to 8. Tennessee to Alabama, west to the Edwards Plateau of Texas. Don Shadow showed me a

MORE ▶

Cotinus obovatus

Cotinus obovatus

Cotinus obovatus fall color

Cotinus coggygria 'Notcutt's Variety'

Cotinus obovatus, American smoketree

Cotinus 'Grace'

233

Cotinus obovatus CONTINUED

native stand near his Winchester, Tennessee, nursery with all manner of fall color variation.

CULTIVARS AND VARIETIES

'Grace', a hybrid ('Velvet Cloak' × *Cotinus obovatus*) with exceptional vigor, has red-purple leaves when young, losing color as leaves mature, becoming dusky blue-green; red, orange, and yellow in fall. Raised and named (after his wife) by Peter Dummer, Hillier Nurseries, whom I had the privilege to meet, at which time, he shared a plant of 'Grace'. Large plant, 15 to 20 ft.

Cotinus szechuanensis

My antennae were sent skyward when Peter Moore, a wonderful British plant breeder, showed me this species, a small shrub, with red young shoots, red petioles, and blue-gray-green leaves, wavy-edged, rounded, 1½ to 1¾ in. wide, with red margins. Peter was utilizing it for breeding. Witnessed it only at Hillier and at Peter Moore's home, have yet to see in the United States. Will grow 5 to 10 ft. high. Zones 7 and 8.

Cotoneaster

A difficult genus to wrap one's arms around, both taxonomically and horticulturally. About 400 species, and a new reference, *Cotoneaster* by Jeanette Fryer and Bertil Hylmö (2009), is a difficult read. Not for weak-kneed

gardeners. Many name changes, and herein I make the best of a confusing situation.

Cotoneasters have decreased in garden acceptability, and I cannot remember a plant lecture in the past ten years that mentioned a single cotoneaster. Best adapted in the North and West, with only *Cotoneaster franchetii* and *C. lacteus* worth three hoots in the Southeast. Lace bugs, mites, fireblight have wreaked havoc on the common garden-variety types like *C. apiculatus*, *C. dammeri*, and *C. salicifolius*.

Cotoneaster adpressus
creeping cotoneaster

This species and *Cotoneaster apiculatus*, cranberry cotoneaster, are among the most popular of all groundcover and massing cotoneasters because of their handsome dark green foliage and large, lustrous red fruit. The habit is low-spreading, compact, and rigidly branched. The ¼- to ⅝-in.-long leaves turn reddish purple in fall. The pinkish flowers are rather inconspicuous, but the ¼-in.-wide, dark red fruit persist into winter. Transplant as a container-grown plant into any well-drained soil. Quite tolerant of high pH soils. Makes a great groundcover or mass planting, in full sun to partial shade. Grows 1 to 1½ ft. high, 4 to 6 ft. wide. Zones 4 to 6. Western China.

CULTIVARS AND VARIETIES

Variety *praecox* is larger than the spe-

cies in all its parts and offers better fruit display.

Cotoneaster apiculatus
cranberry cotoneaster

Much like *Cotoneaster adpressus*, but more common in cultivation. Tends toward a stiffer habit, with the branches forming impenetrable tangles. The ¼- to ⅓-in.-wide, cranberry-red fruit are often spectacular, and they persist into November and later. The lustrous dark green, ¼- to ¾-in.-long and -wide leaves have wavy margins. Habit is perhaps more shrubby than that of *C. adpressus*. Grows 3 ft. high, 3 to 6 ft. wide. Zones 4 to 7. Western China.

Cotoneaster dammeri
bearberry cotoneaster

Bearberry cotoneaster achieved commonality in landscapes in the 1980s and '90s. In northern gardens, the leaves are usually persistent, unless winter temperatures drop below −10°F. The initial growth habit is relatively prostrate; branches build up, however, layer upon layer, resulting in a sizable plant. The ¾- to 1¼-in.-long leaves are lustrous dark green, turning reddish purple with cold weather. The ⅓- to ½-in.-wide, five-petaled, white flowers appear in profusion during May, followed by globose to top-shaped, ¼-in.-wide, red fruit. Fruit set is often sparse. Adaptable and extremely fast-growing, it is a popular choice for

Cotinus szechuanensis

Cotoneaster adpressus, creeping cotoneaster

quick cover. Tends to become ratty with time and requires pruning to maintain neatness. Fireblight, a bacterial disease, and lace bugs, which cause spotting and yellowing of the leaves, may be problematic. Grows 1 to 1½ ft. high, 6 ft. wide or more. Zones 5 to 8. Central China.

CULTIVARS AND VARIETIES

'Coral Beauty' ('Royal Beauty') is described as a free-fruiting clone, but it is not much different from 'Skogholm'. It sets reasonable quantities of red fruit. Grows 2 to 2½ ft. high.

'Mooncreeper' and var. *radicans* have a more rounded, lustrous dark green leaf and are 4 to 6 in. high.

'Skogholm' is a most vigorous, widespreading form that covers the ground as fast as any cotoneaster. Grows 1½ to 3 ft. high. Listed as a *Cotoneaster* ×*suecicus* selection.

'Streib's Findling' is a dull dark blue-green, small-leaf form of prostrate

MORE ▶

Cotoneaster adpressus var. *praecox*

Cotoneaster adpressus

Cotoneaster apiculatus

Cotoneaster apiculatus, cranberry cotoneaster

Cotoneaster dammeri, bearberry cotoneaster

235

Cotoneaster dammeri CONTINUED

Cotoneaster dammeri var. *radicans*

Cotoneaster dammeri 'Skogholm'

Cotoneaster dammeri 'Skogholm'

habit that sets heavy crops of bright red fruit. Grows 4 to 6 in. high with carpeting-like tendencies.

Cotoneaster divaricatus
spreading cotoneaster

Spreading cotoneaster is an extremely vigorous, upright-spreading form that eventually develops into a rather refined shrub. The ⅓- to 1-in.-long, lustrous dark green leaves may turn rich, almost fluorescent reddish purple in autumn. The fall color can persist for as long as four to six weeks. Small, rose-colored flowers produce handsome red to dark red fruit, ⅓ in. long and ¼ in. wide, that persist into November. It is tremendously adaptable. Makes a serviceable screen,

Cotoneaster divaricatus fall color

Cotoneaster dammeri 'Streib's Findling'

mass, grouping, or hedge. In fact, I have observed numerous *Cotoneaster divaricatus* hedges that outperform the ubiquitous privet (*Ligustrum*). Grows 5 to 6 ft. high, 6 to 8 ft. wide. Zones 4 to 7. Central and western China.

Cotoneaster horizontalis
rockspray cotoneaster

This plant of great beauty is used as a groundcover and espalier plant in gardens the world over. The flat, fan-like, herringbone branching pattern distinguishes this species from the others.

The ⅓- to ½- (to ¾-) in.-long, rounded, flattish leaves are lustrous dark green and often turn excellent reddish purple in fall, holding into November. The branches mound upon one another, forming a horizontal, tiered effect. Rose-colored flowers in May and June are followed by abundant red fruit that often persist into winter. May be slightly more susceptible to fireblight than *Cotoneaster adpressus* or *C. apiculatus*. Grows 2 to 3 ft. high, 5 to 8 ft. wide. Zones (4)5 to 7. Western China.

CULTIVARS AND VARIETIES
'Hessei' is purportedly a hybrid between *Cotoneaster horizontalis* and *C. adpressus* var. *praecox*. It has ¼- to ⅗-in.-long and -wide leaves, pinkish red flowers, and ¼-in.-wide, globose, red fruit.

'Tom Thumb' is a dense, closely branched, broad-spreading mound. Makes a handsome rock garden plant. Taxonomy is confused, and it might be placed under *Cotoneaster adpressus*.

MORE ▶

Cotoneaster divaricatus

Cotoneaster divaricatus, spreading cotoneaster

Cotoneaster horizontalis

Cotoneaster horizontalis, rockspray cotoneaster

Cotoneaster horizontalis

Cotoneaster horizontalis CONTINUED

'Variegatus' has leaves edged with cream and is one of the daintiest of variegated shrubs. The leaves turn lovely rose-red in fall. Northern Borders™ appears nothing more than a marketing name for 'Variegatus'.

Cotoneaster lacteus

syn. *Cotoneaster parneyi*

Parney cotoneaster

Cotoneasters in the southeastern United States are decimated by fireblight, lace bugs, and mites. Many have been trialed and grown, and none, except for this species and *Cotoneaster franchetii*, display staying power.

Parney cotoneaster is a lax, loose, upright-spreading evergreen shrub. The 1- to 2-in.-long, dark green leaves are cloaked with woolly pubescence on the undersides. White flowers, somewhat ill-scented, occur in 2- to 3-in.-wide corymbs in May. The red, football-shaped fruit are ¼ to ⅓ in. long and persist through winter. Grow in full sun or partial shade in average soil. Not a "fussy" cotoneaster and definitively more resistant than the typical commercial species. Lace bug resistance is predicated on the thick woolly pubescence on the lower leaf surface. Excellent choice for large mass plantings, to screen areas of the garden and define property boundaries, and for single plant use in the border. Wonderful for espaliers. Consistently produces abundant red fruit in the Southeast and is obviously self-fertile since there are no other cotoneasters for cross pollination. Grows 6 to 10 ft. high and wide. Zones 6 to 8. Western China.

Cotoneaster horizontalis 'Variegatus'

Cotoneaster lacteus

Cotoneaster horizontalis 'Tom Thumb'

Cotoneaster lacteus, Parney cotoneaster

Cotoneaster lacteus

Cotoneaster lucidus
hedge cotoneaster

Unfortunately, hedge cotoneaster is often totally confused with *Cotoneaster acutifolius*, Peking cotoneaster, in the trade, but it is easily distinguished by its glossy dark green leaves, as compared to the dull green of the latter species. This large, rounded shrub is ideal for pruning and manipulating into geometric shapes—the common name was derived quite honestly. The leaves, ¾ to 2 in. long, turn yellow to red in fall. Pinkish white flowers appear in May and are followed by rounded, ⅖-in.-wide, black fruit; neither are showy. Easily grown, it is encountered on college campuses in the Midwest as a hedge. Many plants are better for hedging, and this species is actually more aesthetic when left unpruned. Grows 6 to 10 ft. high and wide. Zones 3 to 7. Siberia, northern Asia.

Cotoneaster multiflorus
manyflowered cotoneaster

In flower, *Cotoneaster multiflorus* is reminiscent of a white froth, but unfortunately, the flowers are malodorous. Locate the plant at a safe distance from trafficked areas. A massive shrub with upright-arching branches, it requires ample space. The blue-green, ¾- to 2½-in.-long leaves develop before the flowers and provide a handsome foil for the five-petaled, ½-in.-wide, white flowers that appear in May. The ⅓-in.-wide, rounded, red fruit ripen in late August and persist into October. It thrives in heavy clay soils and full sun. Excellent for massing or large-area use. Grows 8 to 12 ft. high, 12 to 15 ft. wide. Zones 3 to 7. Western China.

Cotoneaster lucidus

Cotoneaster multiflorus

Cotoneaster multiflorus

Cotoneaster lucidus, hedge cotoneaster

Cotoneaster multiflorus, manyflowered cotoneaster

Cotoneaster salicifolius
willowleaf cotoneaster

Somewhat of an enigma in American gardening, willowleaf cotoneaster is principally represented by the smaller selections and hybrids. The species is a broadleaf evergreen shrub of spreading, arching habit. The 1½- to 3½-in.-long, leathery, lustrous dark green leaves are pubescent on their undersides. White flowers occur in 2-in.-wide, flat-topped inflorescences in May and June and are followed by bright red fruit, ¼ in. in diameter. Same cultural requirements as for the other cotoneasters. Use in a shrub border for winter foliage and fruit effect. Grows 10 to 15 ft. high, slightly less in spread. Zones 6 to 8. Western China.

CULTIVARS AND VARIETIES
Many low-growing, 1- to 2½-ft.-high types appear to be hybrids between this species and *Cotoneaster dam-meri*, bearberry cotoneaster. Among these are 'Autumn Fire', 'Gnom' ('Gnome'), 'Repens' ('Repandens'), and 'Scarlet Leader'. 'Repens' has 1- to 1½-in.-long, lustrous dark green leaves that turn reddish purple in winter. It is the most common cultivar in American gardens. All are tremendously susceptible to lace bugs and decline rapidly when infested.

Crataegus
mayhaw, hawthorn

Difficult to discuss a genus so vaguely defined yet so similar in characteristics. The three principal fruit-producing species (i.e., mayhaws) are *Crataegus aestivalis*, *C. opaca*, and *C. rufula* (20 to 30 ft. high and wide; zones 7 to 9). All are small, oval to round-headed trees with dark green leaves, white flowers, and red fruit. Bark is often mottled, exfoliating, in gray, green, orange, and brown. Fruit are utilized to make a rich rose-colored jelly. The species occur in many habitats from river bottoms to thin soils of rock outcrops. Extremely important food source for wildlife, particularly birds. Thorns are irritating and dangerous. All are susceptible to cedar-quince and cedar-hawthorn rusts (*Gymno-sporangium* spp.). Various references list as many as 1,000 species, others 200, 35 for the Southeast alone (including the three aforementioned). Northern hemisphere.

Cotoneaster salicifolius, willowleaf cotoneaster

Cotoneaster salicifolius 'Gnom'

Cotoneaster salicifolius 'Repens'

Crataegus crus-galli
cockspur hawthorn

One of the most popular species in the East and Midwest for its legendary tolerance to hot, dry conditions. Forms a low-branched tree, with wide-spreading, horizontal branches that are armed with 1½- to 3-in.-long thorns. The lustrous dark green, 1- to 4-in.-long leaves have variable bronzed-red to purplish red fall color. White, disagreeably scented flowers occur in 2- to 3-in.-wide clusters (corymbs) in May. The ½-in.-wide, rounded, deep red fruit ripen in late September and October and persist into winter. Cedar-hawthorn rust can disfigure leaves and fruit. No special soil requirements, although the tree prefers well-drained, slightly acid soils and full sun. Excellent plant to use in mass plantings, screens, groupings, or as a general barrier. The thorns do present problems where there is significant pedestrian traffic or where children play. Grows 20 to 30 ft. high, 20 to 35 ft. wide. Zones 3 to 7. Quebec to North Carolina, west to Kansas.

CULTIVARS AND VARIETIES
Variety *inermis* 'Crusader' ('Cruzam') is a thornless form with the same high-quality ornamental attributes as the species.

Crataegus laevigata
English hawthorn

A very beautiful species commonly found in English and continental European landscapes. It is common in hedgerows throughout Great Britain and can be observed in open pastures, on rocky mountain slopes, and in waste areas. In this country, however, English hawthorn is not without its problems. The species and several cultivars are affected by leaf spot (caused by a blight), which may defoliate the tree by July or August. Low-branching, round-topped habit, with a close, dense head of ascending branches. The stiff, zig-zag branches are well armed with thorns to 1 in. in length. The lustrous dark green, three- to five-lobed leaves, ½ to 2½ in. long, develop no appreciable fall color. White flowers emerge with the leaves in May and turn the plant into a cloud of snow. The small, red fruit ripen in

MORE ▶

Crataegus crus-galli, cockspur hawthorn

Crataegus laevigata, English hawthorn

Crataegus crus-galli

Crataegus crus-galli fall color

241

Crataegus laevigata

Crataegus laevigata

Crataegus laevigata 'Crimson Cloud'

Crataegus laevigata 'Paul's Scarlet'

Crataegus ×lavalleei, Lavalle hawthorn

Crataegus ×lavalleei

September and October but are not as showy as those of the American species *Crataegus crus-galli*, *C. phaenopyrum*, and *C. viridis*. Same soil requirements as *C. crus-galli*. Grows 15 to 20 ft. high and wide. Zones 4 to 7. Europe, northern Africa.

CULTIVARS AND VARIETIES

'Crimson Cloud' offers single red flowers with a white center. It is resistant to leaf spot.

'Paul's Scarlet' ('Paulii') displays beautiful double, rose-red flowers, but unfortunately, it is tremendously susceptible to leaf spot.

Crataegus ×lavalleei
Lavalle hawthorn

This hybrid between *Crataegus crus-galli* and an unknown species has an oval-rounded habit, rich silver-gray branches, and minimal thorns. The 2- to 4-in.-long leaves are lustrous dark green in summer, followed by bronzy or coppery red colors in fall. White flowers occur in 3-in.-wide clusters in May. The ½- to ¾-in.-wide, brick-red to orange-red fruit persist into winter. As with *C. crus-galli*, this species prefers well-drained, slightly acid soils. It is more resistant to hawthorn leaf rusts than the parental species. Grows 15 to 30 ft. high, variable spread. Zones 4 to 7.

Crataegus ×mordenensis

This complex hybrid resulted from crosses between *Crataegus laevigata* 'Paul's Scarlet' and *C. succulenta*, fleshy hawthorn. Grows 20 ft. high and wide. Zones 4 to 6.

CULTIVARS AND VARIETIES

I tested both commercial introductions, 'Snowbird' and 'Toba', at Milliken Arboretum, Spartanburg, South Carolina. They failed miserably. I have not seen a quality specimen of either, but perhaps in the northern part of the range the trees are less afflicted by the leaf blight that is so troublesome to *Crataegus laevigata*.

'Snowbird' is a double white form that originated as an open-pollinated seedling of 'Toba'. Performed satisfactorily in North Dakota State University evaluations.

'Toba' has fragrant, double white flowers that age to pink, and its two- to four-lobed leaves are larger and darker green than those of typical *Crataegus laevigata*.

Crataegus nitida
glossy hawthorn

In the Midwest and East, this species is often spectacular in flower, fruit, and foliage, but it is never common in commerce. Its wide-spreading branches form a broad, dome-shaped outline. The extremely lustrous, 1- to 3-in.-long, dark green leaves turn orangish to red in fall. Small, white flowers appear in 1- to 2-in.-wide clusters in May and are followed by ½-in.-wide, dull red fruit, which persist into

MORE ▶

Crataegus ×mordenensis

Crataegus nitida, glossy hawthorn

Crataegus nitida fall color

Crataegus nitida CONTINUED

winter. The rich orange-brown bark is somewhat exfoliating and quite attractive. Relatively free of diseases, this might be a good choice in lieu of the more susceptible types. Grows 20 to 30 ft. high and wide. Zones 4 to 7. Illinois to Missouri and Arkansas.

Crataegus phaenopyrum
Washington hawthorn

The most popular landscape hawthorn species for its clean foliage and persistent, brilliant red fruit; and one of the most adaptable hawthorns, more comfortable in the heat of the South, along with 'Winter King', than any of the other commonly cultivated species. The habit is broadly oval to rounded, and the tree is densely thorny, bearing 1- to 3-in.-long spines. The three- to five-lobed, 1- to 3-in.-long, lustrous dark green leaves color orange and scarlet to purplish in fall. Creamy white, tolerably fragrant flowers appear in May and June and are followed in September and October by the ¼-in.-wide, glossy red fruit, which persist all winter. Grows 25 to 30 ft. high, 20 to 25 ft. wide. Zones (3)4 to 8. Virginia to Alabama, west to Missouri.

Crataegus phaenopyrum, Washington hawthorn

Crataegus phaenopyrum

Crataegus phaenopyrum

Crataegus viridis 'Winter King'

244

Crataegus punctata
thicket hawthorn

A rather unheralded species that has yielded a fine cultivar, 'Ohio Pioneer', an essentially thornless type with good vigor, growth, and fruiting characteristics. Abundant white flowers are followed by dark red fruit. Grows 20 to 30 ft. high. Zones 4 to 7. Quebec to Georgia, west to Ontario and Illinois.

Crataegus viridis 'Winter King'
Winter King green hawthorn

No other hawthorn cultivar has received as much attention as 'Winter King', selected by Robert Simpson of Vincennes, Indiana, in 1955. The lovely rounded habit, almost vase-shaped branching structure, and distinct gray-green stems provide ideal architecture. The lustrous dark green foliage, white flowers, and ⅜-in.-wide red fruit are outstanding. Has become extremely popular in the Midwest and East. Will contract some rust in wet weather, and leaves and fruit can be infected. Excellent choice as a small ornamental tree or for use against an evergreen background, where the gray stems and persistent red fruit are more prominent. Bark on older stems exfoliates and exposes grays, greens, and orangish browns. Grows 20 to 25 ft. high, 20 to 30 ft. wide. Zones 4 to 7. Maryland to Florida, west to Iowa and Texas.

Croton alabamensis
Alabama croton

Quite a captivating species—the crushed leaves emit the fragrance of apples, grapes, or a banana-apple compote. As I have observed the species, it is a loose, open, flopsy, mopsy shrub. The leaves, semi-evergreen to deciduous, 2 to 4 in. long, are rich green with silver scales above, silvery and shiny beneath. The senescent older leaves turn brilliant orange in fall. Flowers are yellow-green and appear in 1- to 1½-in.-long racemes in March and April. Best sited in partial shade in moist, well-drained root run laden with organic matter. At its best, a collector's plant and nifty native that

MORE ▶

Crataegus viridis 'Winter King'

Crataegus viridis 'Winter King'

Crataegus viridis 'Winter King'

Croton alabamensis, Alabama croton

245

Croton alabamensis CONTINUED
will taxonomically confound even the best plantspeople. Grows 6 to 8 ft. high, wider at maturity. Zones 6 to 8. Alabama.

Croton alabamensis fall color

Croton alabamensis

Croton alabamensis undersides of foliage

Cryptomeria japonica
Japanese cryptomeria

Possibly the finest U.S. planting of this species is housed at the National Arboretum in Washington, D.C., framing the entrance to the bonsai collection. A tall, lofty, pyramidal or conical tree with a stout trunk, it makes an effective screen or grouping. The rich blue-green, ¼- to ¾-in.-long needles point toward the ends of the stems, clothing the branches in a foxtail effect. Needles tend to develop a bronzy or purple-bronze color in cold climates. The rich reddish brown bark peels off in shreds and strips. Provide moist, well-drained, acid soils, in full sun to partial shade. Certainly a beautiful evergreen, and worth considering as an alternative to pines, spruces, and firs. Has become quite common in the Southeast for screening, partially replacing the ubiquitous Leyland cypress. Grows 50 to 60 ft. high, 20 to 30 ft. wide. Zones (5)6 to 8(9). China, Japan.

Cryptomeria japonica, Japanese cryptomeria

Cryptomeria japonica

CULTIVARS AND VARIETIES

'Black Dragon' is a compact, extremely dark green-needled form, somewhat irregular-pyramidal, 10 ft. by 4 to 6 ft. Sets abundant male cones.

Chapel View™ originated as a witch's-broom, about 60 ft. above the ground in a mature *Cryptomeria japonica* in the Sarah P. Duke Gardens, Durham, North Carolina. Beautiful blue-green foliage that maintains the color through winter. The small shoots sweep upward and toward the center of the plant creating a full, dense pyramid, about 7 to 8 ft. by 5 to 6 ft. in 12 years.

'Elegans' is a juvenile form of tall bushy habit, 9 to 15 (to 30) ft. Have seen large plants in Europe. The soft, feathery, ½- to 1-in.-long, green summer needles turn brownish red in winter. Less hardy than the species.

'Globosa Nana' is a neat, dense, dome-shaped form that grows 2 to 3 ft. high and 2½ to 3½ ft. wide in ten to 15 years; may mature between 4 and 8 ft. The bluish green adult needles assume a rusty red color in winter.

'Gyokuryu(a)' forms a dense broad pyramid to almost broad column, 10 to 15 ft. high, probably half as wide. Needles shorter and darker green than species and hold color better in winter.

'Little Diamond' is a perfect mound of mint-green needles, probably 1½

MORE ▶

Cryptomeria japonica Chapel View™

Cryptomeria japonica 'Elegans'

Cryptomeria japonica

Cryptomeria japonica 'Black Dragon'

247

Cryptomeria japonica CONTINUED

Cryptomeria japonica 'Globosa Nana'

Cryptomeria japonica 'Gyokuryu'

Cryptomeria japonica 'Sekkan'

to 3 ft. high and wide. Utilized on Georgia campus and held the green color through winter better than most cryptomerias.

'Lobbii' is an upright, pyramidal-columnar form, with denser and less-pendulous branching than the species. The needles are deeper green and will bronze in cold weather.

'Radicans' is a pretty glaucous blue-green form with a tree-like habit. One of the better summer foliage types. Beautiful tight pyramidal habit as a young plant; matures 40 to 45 ft. by 15 ft.

'Sekkan' ('Sekkan-sugi') is a vigorous grower with yellow-green new growth that fades to green in the heat of summer. Maintains a pyramidal-conical habit, 20 ft. high in ten years.

'Yoshino' is a handsome blue-green form, with foliage turning slightly bronze-green in cold weather. Growth rate is fast (2 to 3 ft. per year), and the plant becomes quite dense without extensive pruning.

Cunninghamia lanceolata
common chinafir

Throughout the Southeast, in the remotest locations, one is apt to chance upon this prehistoric-appearing needle evergreen. Often broad-pyramidal in outline, the branches are cloaked with 1- to 2½-in.-long, sharp-pointed needles. The dead needles persist, contributing to the disheveled appearance. Needles range from lustrous dark green to blue-green and in their finest manifestations are quite handsome. The globose, pendent cones, 1½ in. across, look like artichokes. Bark is rich reddish brown, stringy, and seldom seen, since the lower branches remain into old age. Tolerates excessive heat and drought, full sun to partial shade. When cut back, regenerates by developing numerous shoots. Strictly a specimen plant and seldom available in modern commerce. Grows 30 to 75 ft. high, 10 to 30 ft. wide. Zones 7 to 9. China.

248

CULTIVARS AND VARIETIES

'Glauca' is unique because of the waxy deposits on the needles, resulting in bluish coloration. Holds blue color during winter. Preferable to the species and somewhat slower growing.

×*Cupressocyparis leylandii*

syn. ×*Cuprocyparis leylandii*

Leyland cypress

This species has become popular as a Christmas tree in the South and is used for screening and hedges from coastal Massachusetts (Cape Cod) to Florida to the West Coast. The habit is tightly columnar, with feathery, blue-green foliage sprays. The foliage does not discolor in winter to the degree of *Cryptomeria* and *Thuja*. Without extensive pruning, Leyland cypress makes a very dense plant, and it should be restrained at an early age before pruning becomes impossible. Transplant from a container or as a small, balled-and-burlapped specimen. Expect 3 ft. of vertical growth per year if soils are moist and fertile. Displays excellent salt tolerance and is a choice evergreen for protecting the garden from salt spray. Bagworms and canker can prove troublesome. Diseases have caught up with the species, so be

MORE ▶

×*Cupressocyparis leylandii*, Leyland cypress

Cunninghamia lanceolata

Cunninghamia lanceolata, common chinafir

Cunninghamia lanceolata

Cunninghamia lanceolata 'Glauca'

×*Cupressocyparis leylandii* CONTINUED
leery about extensive use. Grows 60 to 70 ft. high, 6 to 12 ft. wide; can reach 70 to 100 ft. high. Zones 6 to 9.
CULTIVARS AND VARIETIES
The cultivars of Leyland cypress are numerous and somewhat confused taxonomically. Thirty-two are described in the *Manual* (2009).

'Gold Rider' has branchlets that are yellow with green tips in winter, changing to deeper yellow with dark yellow

×*Cupressocyparis leylandii*

×*Cupressocyparis leylandii* 'Haggerston Grey'

×*Cupressocyparis leylandii*

×*Cupressocyparis leylandii*

×*Cupressocyparis leylandii* 'Gold Rider'

×*Cupressocyparis leylandii* 'Silver Dust'

margins in summer. I rate this the best yellow-needled form.

'Green Spire' is densely narrow-columnar in habit and has rich green foliage.

'Haggerston Grey' has a more open habit (still dense and columnar), with bluish green (to gray-green) foliage.

Irish Mint™ has lighter green foliage than the species, and a root system superior to what is typical. Slow-growing and densely branching; 20 to 25 ft. high by 6 ft. wide.

'Jubilee' and 'Star Wars' have yellow and cream-yellow sprays, respectively.

'Leighton Green' is a tall, columnar form with a central leader and rich green foliage. In Georgia trials, I noted little difference between this and 'Haggerston Grey'.

'Naylor's Blue' is the most open, loosely branched form. It has distinct glaucous blue-green foliage. Beautiful when young, and the bluish foliage distinguishes it from the many cultivars.

'Silver Dust' offers cream-splotched and -streaked foliage. It is considered a branch sport of 'Leighton Green'. Slower growing but still 1½ to 2 ft. per year.

×*Cupressocyparis ovensii*

This hybrid (*Cupressus lusitanica* × *Chamaecyparis nootkatensis*) has finely dissected, bluish green sprays, more fine-textured than Leyland cypress. In Georgia trials, it has grown faster than ×*C. leylandii* and, from a distance, is grayer green and slightly more loose and open. In six years it averaged 3 ft. per year. Given the name Murray cypress in the South. Possibly will reach heights of ×*C. leylandii*. Zones 6 to 8.

Cupressus arizonica var. *glabra*

smooth cypress

The delineation of this variety, with its exfoliating, papery, purple to red bark and bright blue-green needles, from the type (coarsely shredding, gray-brown bark and dull gray-green needles) is not clear-cut. What I meet in the Southeast favors *Cupressus arizonica* var. *glabra*. Typically, habit is pyramidal becoming more open and feathery with age, but near Tucson, Arizona, as I ascended Mount Lemmon, the variation in its needled forms from green to bright blue was a feast for the collector's eyes. Instead of the flat, planar foliage common to arborvitae and falsecypress, the stems form dendritic configurations, like stereoisomers from your college chemistry days. The oblong, 1- to 1¼-in.-wide cones are six- to eight-scaled, each scale with a sharp point. Transplant from containers into well-drained, dryish soils in full sun. Several canker diseases are troublesome. Makes an unusual container plant. The rich blue needles provide contrast in southern

MORE ▶

×*Cupressocyparis leylandii* 'Naylor's Blue'

Cupressus arizonica var. *glabra*, smooth cypress

Cupressus arizonica var. *glabra* CONTINUED
and western gardens; do not expect
long life in the Southeast, where it is
now grown as a Christmas tree. More
amenable for the Southwest and California. Grows 40 to 50 ft. high, 25 to
30 ft. wide. Zones 7 to 9, 10 on the
West Coast. Central and southern
Arizona.

CULTIVARS AND VARIETIES
'Blue Ice' has icy-blue foliage, mahog-
any-red stems, and tight, conical-pyramidal outline, particularly in youth.

'Blue Pyramid' is similar in appearance to 'Blue Ice', and both, growing
side by side in my Georgia trials, look
like blue rockets on the launch pad.

'Carolina Sapphire' is loose and airy

Cupressus arizonica var. *glabra* 'Carolina Sapphire'

Cupressus arizonica var. *glabra*

Cupressus arizonica var. *glabra*

Cupressus arizonica var. *glabra* 'Blue Ice'

Cupressus arizonica var. *glabra* 'Raywood Weeping'

Cupressus arizonica var. *glabra* 'Sapphire Skies'

even as a young plant, with silver-blue, closer to silver-gray, needles.

'Limelight' has light yellow to lime-green foliage. Narrow, conical outline and compact, although I observed fatter, chunkier plants.

'Raywood Weeping', with irregular, strongly weeping habit and blue-green foliage, makes a potent "look-at-me" accent plant.

'Sapphire Skies' is a tall, straight, full, conical-pyramidal selection. When I discovered it in an abandoned tree farm, the original plant was 20 to 24 ft. by 5 to 6 ft.; Bonnie subsequently named it.

Cupressus macrocarpa
Monterey cypress

Leaning, literally, along the Monterey Peninsula, over the Pacific Ocean, is this most famous needle evergreen, celebrated for being one of the parents of Leyland cypress, ×*Cupressocyparis leylandii*. Habit is narrow and pyramidal in youth, becoming picturesque with age. Massive trees, 100 ft. high, grow in the moist atmosphere of Ireland; at Powerscourt and Emo Court, the trunks alone captivate the passerby. Foliage is rich dark green through

MORE ▶

Cupressus macrocarpa, Monterey cypress

Cupressus macrocarpa

Cupressus macrocarpa CONTINUED

the seasons. The eight- to 14-scaled cones are 1 in. or more in diameter. Relishes the moisture-laden atmosphere of the California coast around the Monterey Peninsula. Seiridium canker has killed many trees in California, especially those planted away from the coast. Coastal plants I witnessed were 30 to 40 (to 50) ft. high and broad, sculpted by the wind. Zones 7 to 9, 10 on the West Coast. California.
CULTIVARS AND VARIETIES
Several yellow- to gold-foliaged selec-

tions, among them 'Golden Cone', 'Donard Gold', and 'Goldcrest'. Often sold for container use in the eastern United States.

Cupressus sempervirens
Italian cypress

Both the species and 'Stricta' in particular have been a part of garden-making since time immemorial. A Mediterranean species that is variable in habit but usually upright, with green to bluish needles. The cones are ovoid, 1 to 1½ in. long. Prefers hot, dry cli-

mates and well-drained soils but survives in the heat and humidity of the Southeast. Use as an accent plant, in formal landscapes, allées, and containers. Grows 20 to 30 ft. high, 5 to 10 ft. wide. Zones 7 to 9, 10 in California. Southern Europe, western Asia.
CULTIVARS AND VARIETIES
'Glauca' has rich blue-green foliage and columnar habit.

'Stricta' is narrow-columnar with green foliage, and 20-ft.-high rockets are "everywhere." A blue-green form is more common than the green. Sets abundant cones (branches may splay under their weight) and is susceptible to canker. Not long-lived in the Southeast.

'Swane's Gold' ('Swane's Golden') is a slow-growing, narrow-columnar form with golden needles.

Cycas revoluta
Sago palm

Not a true palm but a gymnosperm, with naked seeds produced on female plants and cone-like structures on the male. Single-stemmed initially; side shoots (offsets) develop with age, creating a multi-stemmed effect. Leaves occur in a pseudo-whorl and produce a feathery texture. Each leaf is 4 to 5 ft. long, with fern-like, lustrous dark green pinnae, each up to 6 in. long, with a sharp apex. Seeds are plum-shaped, 1 to 1½ in. wide, hard-shelled, with a fleshy, brownish orange

Cupressus macrocarpa 'Goldcrest'

Cupressus sempervirens 'Stricta'

Cupressus sempervirens 'Stricta'

outer covering. Provide well-drained soil and full sun to partial shade. Noticed significant scale infestation in recent years, on both the upper and lower surfaces. Leaves appear yellow to irregularly spotted. On the Georgia coast, plants grow in sand and in pine shade. Beautiful architectural plant, particularly in containers. Grows 4 to 6 (to 8) ft. high and wide. Zones 8 to 11. Temperature of 11°F defoliated plants in coastal Georgia but did not injure buds, and regrowth was normal. Southern Japan.

Cyrilla racemiflora
swamp cyrilla, leatherwood

The wet areas of the Coastal Plain of Georgia are rich with this species, and the spectacular flowers make one question the lack of garden use. In June, frothy white flowers cover the previous season's growth and, in composite with the lustrous dark green leaves, are effective for a month and longer. Habit is sprawling-spreading, loose, and open, with branches bent, gnarled, and contorted. Plants sucker from roots to form large colonies.

Leaves, 1½ to 4 in. long, are evergreen in the Deep South to deciduous further north, lustrous dark green, turning orange and scarlet with age. The fragrant white flowers are borne in 3- to 6-in.-long racemes in a horizontal whorl at the base of the current season's growth. The ½-in.-long, round-

MORE ▶

Cycas revoluta

Cycas revoluta, Sago palm

Cyrilla racemiflora fall color

Cyrilla racemiflora, swamp cyrilla

Cyrilla arida

255

Cyrilla racemiflora CONTINUED

ish, two-celled capsular fruit mature in August and September and persist into winter. Grows wild in swamps but will succeed in moist, well-drained, drier soils. Full sun to partial shade. Good native plant for the wild look. Tolerant of prolonged flooding and therefore ideal for wet areas in the landscape. Utilized it in the Dirr garden, but it grew too large. Years after removal, shoots were still developing from roots. Grows 10 to 15 ft. high and wide. To afford a concept of maximum growth potential, the national champion is 50 ft. by 12 ft. Zones 6 to 11. Virginia to Florida.

Cyrilla arida is a microcosm of *C. racemiflora*, smaller in all its parts and growing only 6 ft. high and wide. Requires well-drained soils, preferably sandy. Grew 4 ft. high and wide in seven years in Georgia trials with about 30 percent leaf retention into early March. Evergreen where winter temperatures are warmer. Zones (7)8 and 9(10). Central Florida.

Cyrtomium falcatum
Japanese holly fern
One of the best evergreen, heat-tolerant ferns for use in zones 8 and 9, with protection into zone 7. Common in commercial landscapes throughout the region, particularly in shady nooks and crannies where few other plants survive. Habit is leafy, like a fine dark green leaf lettuce, somewhat rhizomatous, forming dense clumps. Leaves, 20 to 30 in. long, 8 in. wide, emerge the softest yellow-green, settling down to lustrous dark green. Leaves have wavy margins, a feature that imparts a rich texture to large plantings. Provide shade and moist, acid soils rich in organic matter. Fertilize with all-purpose (i.e., 8-8-8) fertilizer in late winter. Remove old fronds. Terrific filler, tall groundcover, and massing plant. Largely insect- and disease-free. Grows 2 ft. high, 3 ft. wide. Zones (7)8 and 9. Killed outright at −3°F in

the Dirr garden. China, Malaysia, Taiwan, India, eastern and south Africa, Hawaii.

Cytisus battandieri
syn. *Argyrocytisus battandieri*
Moroccan or pineapple broom
About 35 species of *Cytisus* are known, but few are prominent in modern gardens. It is not easy (for me) to distinguish among them, and I suspect many cultivars are hybrids. This particular taxon has been transferred by some to the related genus *Argyrocytisus*; most references I checked maintain it in *Cytisus*. It is a curious shrub with cone-like inflorescences of bright yellow, pineapple-fragrant, pea-shaped flowers in summer (June and July). Habit is upright-oval to rounded, rather stiff but softened by the pretty, silky, gray-green leaves in threes, recalling *Laburnum*. Amenable to fashioning into a small tree, but suckers (sprouts)

Cyrtomium falcatum, Japanese holly fern

Cytisus battandieri, Moroccan broom

need to be removed. Inflorescences average 4 in. long and are produced in significant quantities. Requires well-drained soil and sunny location. Does well on West Coast, where leaves persist through winter. Gossler Farms Nursery, Springfield, Oregon, reported the species surviving −12°F. Beautiful in flower and foliage. Grows 10 to 15 (to 20) ft. high; 15 ft. high in ten years in Oregon. Zones 6 and 7, 8 and 9 on West Coast. Morocco.

CULTIVARS AND VARIETIES
'Yellow Tail', with inflorescences to 6 in. long, was introduced by Hillier Nurseries.

Cytisus scoparius
Scotch broom
In Europe, Scotch broom, with its bright yellow flowers, is abundant along roadsides and in waste areas. The habit is rounded-mounded, with erect, slender, angled, grass-green stems. The species becomes unkempt with age and requires renewal pruning. European literature suggests that old hard wood should not be pruned, only the younger green stems. Leaves are much reduced, about ¼ to ⅝ in. long, and sparingly evident. The stems function as the principal photosynthesizing organ. Flowers are magnificent, ranging in color from white to shades of yellow, orange, pink, and red, and

MORE ▶

Cytisus battandieri

Cytisus ×praecox 'Allgold'

Cytisus scoparius 'Boskoop Ruby'

Cytisus scoparius, Scotch broom

Cytisus scoparius 'Burkwoodii'

Cytisus scoparius CONTINUED

bicolors. The entire shrub truly lights up in mid to late April (Athens), May, and June. Unfortunately, the species and cultivars are not persistent and simply die out over time; and new seedlings, when they appear, are generally inferior to the parent plant. Occasionally, self-sown seedlings pop up in Georgia landscapes—always the yellow-flowered! Broom thrives with neglect, and sandy, infertile, drier soils are most suitable. May prefer slightly acid to neutral pH soils. Transplant from a container. Use along highways, in mass plantings, or in a shrub border, with caution: the species has escaped in the western states and is considered invasive. Grows 5 to 6 ft. high and wide. Zones 5 to 8. Europe.
CULTIVARS AND VARIETIES
Hundreds are known, the greatest concentration originating in the Netherlands. Some of the smaller types may be suitable for pockets in perennial or rock gardens. The following are a few of the most common cultivars and/or ones that I have observed in my travels.

'Allgold' is a form of *Cytisus ×praecox* (*C. multiflorus* × *C. purgans*) with dark yellow flowers. It is a relatively compact, 5- to 6-ft.-high shrub. Also considered quite cold hardy.

'Boskoop Ruby', with profusely borne, rich garnet flowers and small rounded habit, is one of the best.

'Burkwoodii' is a vigorous, bushy form with garnet-red flowers; standards are red-carmine, and the wings are red-brown with a narrow gold border.

'Hollandia', with rose-pink flowers, grows 5 to 8 ft. high.

'Lena' is a compact, comparatively dwarf form, 3 to 4 ft. high. Its flowers have ruby-red standards and wings and pale yellow keels.

'Moonlight' produces cream-white flowers on nodding shoots; grows 5 to 6 ft. high and wide.

Daboecia cantabrica
Irish heath

Resembles *Calluna vulgaris* and *Erica* species in foliage and floral traits. Seldom cultivated in the United States, but I've observed it on many occasions in Scottish gardens, where the flowers appear on 3- to 5-in.-long, terminal racemes on new growth of the season from June to November. The ⅓- to ½-in.-long, urn-shaped flowers are typically rose-purple. The dark green, needle-like, evergreen foliage is ¼ to ⅝ in. long, 1/10 to ¼ in. wide, and forms mats and hummocks from which the flowers arise. Requires full sun, acid, sandy, well-drained soils, and cooler temperatures. Beautiful in rock gardens, drifts, and masses. Reserved for Northeast and Pacific

Cytisus scoparius 'Hollandia'

Cytisus scoparius 'Lena'

Cytisus scoparius 'Moonlight'

Daboecia cantabrica, Irish heath

Northwest. Grows 12 to 20 in. high. Many selections (and hybrids) with white, pink, rose, purple, and ruby-red flowers are in cultivation. Zone (5)6. Western Europe including Ireland.

Danae racemosa
Alexandrian-laurel

A striking amalgamation of gracefully arching evergreen shoots with shimmering, shiny green "leaves" that brighten shady areas of the garden. Seldom available in commercial quantities, it is most often passed from gardener to gardener via division. It is a member of the lily family, and the leaves are actually modified stems. Typically, it must be propagated by division or seed. The orange-red, ⅜- to ½-in.-wide, rounded berries are attractive but occur only on female plants. Seeds are tricky to germinate. Magnificent shade plant that requires moist, well-drained soils laden with organic

matter. Observations indicate it is extremely shade- and drought-tolerant once established. In sunny locations, leaves may become yellowish and appear nitrogen deficient. Grows 2 to 4 ft. high, wider at maturity. Zones 7 to 9. Northern Iran and Asia Minor.

Daphne

The daphnes are great garden plants, and several species offer the sweetest fragrance. They are fickle, however, and many die for no explicable reason (although it is often attributed to a virus). *Daphne* culture is akin to voodoo medicine, and many different recommendations are given. From my experience, it is best to provide well-drained soils with adequate organic matter and even moisture, in shade or partial sun. A pH range of 6 to 7 is recommended, but daphnes will grow in soils with pH of 4.5. Once planted, do not move, prune, or abuse in any

way. Robin White's *Daphnes* (2008) is a must read for daphnophiles. I visited his Blackthorn Nursery, where he collects, grows, and breeds *Daphne*. From my visits and his literature, successful culture hinges on drainage, drainage, more drainage, and limestone-based medium.

Daphne bholua

Probably for the West Coast only, as attempts by colleagues in zone 7 were unsuccessful. Great pleasure, during sabbatical at Hillier Arboretum, was derived from the intoxicatingly sweet perfume that literally permeated the garden in late February, early March. Typically an upright shrub, deciduous to evergreen depending on provenance; leaves 1¾ to 4 in. long, ½ to 1 in. wide, narrow elliptic to oblanceolate, shiny green. Flowers, white, pink, purple-pink, are eight to 15 per inflo-

MORE ▶

Danae racemosa, Alexandrian-laurel

Danae racemosa

Daphne bholua

Daphne bholua 'Peter Smithers'

259

Daphne bholua CONTINUED

rescence. Grows 6 to 10 ft. high, less in spread. Zones (7)8 and 9 on West Coast. Himalayas.

Cultivars and Varieites. I tried 'Jacqueline Postill' in the Athens garden without success.

'Alba' is a white-flowered selection.

'Peter Smithers' has deep purple-pink flowers and evergreen to semi-evergreen leaves.

Daphne ×burkwoodii
Burkwood daphne

This dapper, densely branched, compact-rounded form might be the toughest of all the daphnes. The narrow, 1- to 1½-in.-long, blue-green leaves persist into November and December (at least in Boston). Pink-budded flowers open pinkish white to white and are borne in 2-in.-wide umbels in May. The flowers nestle in the foliage and are lovely on close inspection. The sweet fragrance is fantastic, and this alone makes the plant a candidate for virtually any garden (although the finicky requirements of daphnes, aforementioned, may preclude use in certain environments). Makes a great filler in any border or rock garden, particularly where people walk. Grows 3 to 4 ft. high and wide. Zones 4 to 8. Hybrid

Daphne ×burkwoodii, Burkwood daphne

Daphne ×burkwoodii

Daphne ×burkwoodii 'Briggs Moonlight'

Daphne ×burkwoodii 'Carol Mackie'

Daphne ×burkwoodii 'Somerset'

of *Daphne cneorum* and *D. ×transatlantica* (*D. caucasica*).

CULTIVARS AND VARIETIES
Many; see my *Manual of Woody Landscape Plants* (2009).

'Briggs Moonlight' is the reverse variegation of 'Carol Mackie' with pale yellow centers and green margins. Eye-catching but will revert and "cook" in intense sun and heat.

'Carol Mackie' has delicate cream edges on the leaves and fragrant flowers, light pink maturing to white. It grows about as large as the species, possibly broader but typically 3 ft. by 3 ft., and shows the same adaptability. Excellent for a touch of color in a shady niche of the garden.

'Somerset' is probably the most common representative of *Daphne ×burkwoodii* in cultivation. Two seedlings resulted from the original cross, and this form is the one described in the main entry.

Daphne cneorum
rose daphne

My attempts to grow this species have been unsuccessful, but on occasion handsome plantings have crossed my path. *Daphne cneorum* has a groundcover-like habit, with trailing and ascending branches forming low, loose masses of evergreen foliage. Bright rose-pink, fragrant flowers smother the dark green foliage during May. Overall, the flowering habit is reminiscent of candytuft. Culture is similar to that of *D. ×burkwoodii*, although this species may be more sensitive to inadequate drainage: the best specimens usually develop in rock, scree, or wall gardens. Grows 6 to 12 in. high, 2 ft. wide or more. Zones 4 to 7. Europe.

CULTIVARS AND VARIETIES
'Eximia' ('Eximea') and 'Ruby Glow' with deep rose-red buds, open rose-pink on a dark green, evergreen background. Grows 6 to 12 in. high, 2 to 3 ft. wide. Beautiful when healthy.

'Variegata' has delicate, cream-margined leaves and flowers like the species.

Daphne genkwa
lilac daphne

Few woody shrubs can measure up to lilac-colored flowers that open along naked stems in April (zone 7). Flowers are not fragrant, although this is the subject of debate among my gardening friends. Leaves, dull green, 1 to 2½ in. long, ½ to 1 in. wide, impart a feathery, refined texture. A plant in the Dirr garden flowered reliably in early April. Witnessed deeper and lighter flowered forms but am unsure of their presence in U.S. commerce. Grows 3 to 4 ft. high and wide with a somewhat billowy outline. Zones (4)5 to 7. China, Korea.

Daphne cneorum, rose daphne

Daphne cneorum 'Eximia'

Daphne genkwa, lilac daphne

Daphne mezereum

February daphne

During a late-January trip to Ireland, I observed the naked stems of *Daphne mezereum* adorned with vivid rose-purple, fragrant flowers. In Boston, the plant flowered in late March—so the common name doesn't always fit the flowering response. February daphne lacks the grace of many species because of its large size, leggy, upright habit, and large, dark blue-green leaves (1½ to 3½ in. long). Fruit are bright red, ½-in.-long drupes. Utilize in a shrub border. Possibly a good plant for cut-branch production because of its early flowering date. Grows 3 to 5 ft. high and wide. Zones 4 to 6(7). Europe, Siberia.

CULTIVARS AND VARIETIES
Forma *alba* offers dull white flowers and yellowish white fruit. The several other white-flowered forms include 'Paul's White' and 'Bowles' Variety'.

'Rubra', 'Rubra Plena', 'Ruby Glow', and 'Rosea' offer rose-pink to red flowers.

Daphne mezereum

Daphne mezereum f. *alba*

Daphne mezereum, February daphne

Daphne odora

fragrant or winter daphne

A southern landscape without fragrant daphne is really not a garden. Over our 30 years in Athens, probably 30 have been planted, with three large, magnificent specimens extant. In our garden, the alluring fragrance is released in January and is often still wafting in early March. Truly a sign from the Head Gardener that all is right with the world, certainly the gardening world. Typical mature habit approaches a broad mound with dense, lustrous dark green evergreen foliage, each leaf 1½ to 3½ in. long. Flowers occur at the end of the shoots, nestled in the pseudo-whorl of foliage. The rose-purple buds open to rose-pink, 1- to

Daphne odora, fragrant daphne

Daphne odora 'Alba'

1½-in.-wide inflorescences. *Remarkable* for fragrance! Plant in well-drained soil in shade; do not disturb after planting. I have observed healthy plants on one day turn up their root tips and die the next. Biological truth is stranger than fiction. Spot plants throughout shady borders and woods, almost like breadcrumbs. Has been my great pleasure to lose more than I can count on fingers and toes, but I continue to plant. The nose knows and will follow the scent. Grows 3 to 4 ft. high, slightly wider. Zones 7 to 9. China.

CULTIVARS AND VARIETIES
'Alba' has fragrant cream-white flowers and polished dark green leaves.

'Aureomarginata' is slightly hardier than the species with yellow-margined leaves and reddish purple flowers.

'Mae-Jima' ('Mae Jima') is unique: large shiny green leaves with prominent yellow margins; rose flowers, opening pink-white, develop from the nodes; extremely fragrant. Have grown this in Athens. May revert and tends to be loose in habit.

Daphne ×transatlantica
syn. *Daphne caucasica*
fragrant daphne

This hybrid and its cultivars are all the rage in the Mid-Atlantic and New England states. It flowers sporadically throughout the summer and provides a sweet, delicate perfume. Habit is rounded and reasonably dense, with 1- to 1¾-in.-long, glaucous blue-green leaves. Foliage does not develop fall color. Four-sepaled, fragrant, white flowers occur in groups of four to 20 in small inflorescences in May and June, and sporadically thereafter. Prefers well-drained soils and partial shade. Appears more amenable to garden culture, yet I had a plant collapse in the container before making it to the garden. Observed in Bangor, Maine, in early September, and is more cold hardy than would be expected. Grows 4 to 5 ft. high and wide. Zones (4)5 to 8. Caucasus.

CULTIVARS AND VARIETIES
'Beulah Cross' has semi-evergreen, matte green leaves with a thin white margin. Larger than typical.

Eternal Fragrance™ ('Blafra') has

MORE ▶

Daphne odora 'Aureomarginata'

Daphne ×transatlantica, fragrant daphne

Daphne odora 'Mae-Jima'

Daphne ×transatlantica

Daphne ×transatlantica CONTINUED
fragrant white flowers, blush-pink in cooler climates. Flowers sporadically through summer and is semi-evergreen. Bred by Robin White.

Daphniphyllum macropodum

I listened to garden lecturers tout this Asiatic species for its wonderful rhododendron-like foliage and refused to buy into its uniqueness. Since 1990, a 15-ft.-high, haystack-shaped specimen has prospered at the University's Botanical Garden. The 5- to 6-in.-long, polished dark green leaves have red petioles, with the color extending to the midrib of the leaf blade. The leaf underside is glaucous-silver. The plant is unbelievably sun-tolerant and exhibits no discoloration. Pale green (female) and purplish (male) flowers are not particularly showy, and the 1/3-in.-long

bluish black drupes occur on female plants. Germinates readily from seed, and I attempted to give seedlings to visitors, who turn me down more often than bed sheets. Anytime the casual visitor asks, "What is it? What does it do?"—I know the plant does not have a chance. In the South, a wonderful substitute for large-leaf rhododendrons for textural qualities. Beautiful plantings in Aiken, South Carolina, that beg the question, "Why isn't it more common?" Tolerates shade and sun, provide only well-drained soil. Listed as deer-resistant. Difficult to root from cuttings and, to my knowledge, only seedling material is offered. Several variegated clones of great beauty are known but difficult to propagate, and I have yet to witness them in commerce. Grows 10 to 15 ft. high and wide. Zones 7 to 9. China, Japan, Korea.

Davidia involucrata
dove-tree

One of the most fabled of all garden plants because of the heroic collecting efforts of Ernest H. Wilson in the late 1800s and early 1900s. Wilson eventually collected numerous fruit and sent them to England. Dove-tree is distinctly pyramidal in youth; with age it is pyramidal-oval, although certain trees become rounded. The deep green, 2- to 5½-in.-long, strongly serrated leaves typically do not color in fall, although a British authority noted red. The most famous characteristic of the species is the two large, creamy white bracts, which subtend the true flower and give the appearance of white dove tails or handkerchiefs fluttering in the breeze. The flowering may not be prolific every year, but a tree in full flower is a spectacle that will be carried through a lifetime of memories. Fruit, an ovoid

Daphniphyllum macropodum

Daphniphyllum macropodum

Daphniphyllum macropodum variegated form

Davidia involucrata, dove-tree

1½-in.-long drupe, covered with a purplish bloom when young, russet-colored and -speckled when ripe. Fruit suspended on 2-in.-long stalks. Seeds are recalcitrant germinators, taking from two to eight years to germinate completely. Even the orange-brown bark is attractive, developing a handsome scaly, exfoliating character. Prefers moist, well-drained soils, in full sun or partial shade. A splendid specimen tree worthy of greater use in American gardens. Attempted many times in Dirr garden and lost all to canker. Grows 20 to 40 ft. high, variable spread. Zones (5)6 and 7. China.

CULTIVARS AND VARIETIES
Observed a purple-leaf selection that fades to green, and a variegated leaf type with a broad cream margin and green center.

'Sonoma' is a heavy-flowering selection that produces abundant flowers on young trees. A small tree may have 15 to 25 flowers. Consistent flowers in zone 7 but also canker susceptible.

Decaisnea fargesii
blue-bean

One of those rare plants, first time observed, never forgotten, because of bean-like, cylindrical (2 to 4 in. long, ¾ in. wide), metallic blue fruit. Tried, and I have, to culture it in Athens, and watched the heat mercilessly beat up container plants, sapping my persistence. A handsome shrub with a tropical appearance, its 20-to 32-in.-long leaves are composed of 13 to 25 leaflets, each 2 to 6 in. long and rich blue-green. The yellow-green flowers appear in 8- to 18-in.-long panicles in May and June. Provide semi-shade to shade and moist, acid soils high in organic matter. Great adventure for the advanced gardener. Best on West Coast. Persisted as root-hardy, dieback shrub at the Morton Arboretum, Lisle,

MORE ▶

Davidia involucrata

Decaisnea fargesii, blue-bean

Davidia involucrata variegated leaf type

Decaisnea fargesii

Illinois. Grows 10 to 15 ft. high and wide. Zones 6 and 7(8). Western China.

Decumaria barbara

wild hydrangea vine, wood vamp

A common, true-clinging native vine, found growing in floodplains and banks along southeastern watercourses. Climbs trees with the root-like holdfasts that originate from the stems. Beautiful lustrous dark green leaves, 3 to 5 in. long, up to 3 in. wide, turn pale cream-yellow in autumn. The fragrant white flowers are borne in 2- to 3-in.-high and -wide terminal corymbs in May and June. Flowers are attractive but do not overwhelm like those of *Hydrangea anomala* subsp. *petiolaris*, climbing hydrangea. Site in shade, provide moisture in dry periods. Have observed in full sun where it flowers more abundantly. Trouble-free vine that offers beautiful foliage and fragrant flowers. Grows 30 to 40 ft. or limited by structure. Zones 5 to 9. Virginia to Florida to Louisiana.

CULTIVARS AND VARIETIES

'Barbara Ann' is a superior selection from the wilds of Madison County, Georgia, discovered by former University of Georgia football coach Vincent J. Dooley, Dr. Dongling Zhang, and me, and named after Coach Dooley's wife. Leathery, thickish, lustrous dark green leaves outshine all seedling-grown plants. Spectacular for foliage and flower.

Desfontainia spinosa

On a miserable, cold, damp March day in Benmore Botanic Garden, Scotland, I circled, stalked, mused, meditated, and attempted to identify the shrub with oppositely arranged, spiny, lustrous dark green leaves. A weird *Osmanthus* species I opined; the label said *Desfontainia* . . . I will never forget. The funnel-shaped, waxy corolla is orange-scarlet with five rounded lobes. Flowers are spectacular and open from June and July into fall. Requires well-drained, moist soil and relatively cool climate. Only for the collector but is reported as satisfactory in Oregon. Grows 6 to 8 (to 10) ft. high with greater spread. A plant 10 ft. high and 32 ft. wide grew in Rowallane Garden, Ireland. Zones 7 and 8 on West Coast. Found in cool mountain cloud forests of the Andes, South America.

Decaisnea fargesii

Decumaria barbara, wild hydrangea vine

Decumaria barbara 'Barbara Ann'

Deutzia

Perhaps because deutzias were as common as mud and about as aesthetic when not flowering in the Midwest landscape, I never afforded them the respect they deserve. On too many occasions, the massive *Deutzia scabra*, fuzzy deutzia, and *D. ×magnifica* lumbered across even the smallest of landscapes and offered floral interest only in May and June—a pile of leaves and brush the rest of the year.

Fruit are small, brown capsules with no intrinsic beauty. My opinions have changed, however, and some of the smaller types, like *D. gracilis*, are certainly garden-worthy. Deutzias (about 70 species) across the board thrive with neglect, but they require full sun and well-drained soil for maximum flowering. Occasional renewal pruning or selective branch removal is necessary to keep the plants presentable. All flower on previous season's

wood, so prune after flowering. They are not the easiest plants to identify, and the many hybrids are difficult to pigeon-hole.

Deutzia gracilis
slender deutzia

This lovely species develops into a low, graceful, free-flowering, broad-mounded shrub with slender, ascending branches. The 1- to 3-in.-long, flat, deep green leaves may develop a hint of maroon in fall. The real show is on in April and May, when the pure white, ½- to ¾-in.-wide flowers smother the plant in a billowy white foam. For floral effect, it is a great overachiever. Use slender deutzia as a filler in rock gardens, in perennial and shrub borders, and for mass plantings. Grows 2 to 4 ft. high, 3 to 4 ft. wide. Zones 4 to 8. Japan.

CULTIVARS AND VARIETIES
Chardonnay Pearls™ ('Duncan') with

MORE ▶

Desfontainia spinosa

Deutzia gracilis, slender deutzia

Desfontainia spinosa

Deutzia gracilis Chardonnay Pearls™

Deutzia gracilis CONTINUED

yellow to lime-yellow foliage, white flowers, grows 20 to 36 in. by 18 to 24 in. New growth is attractive, but summer heat discolors foliage.

'Nikko' (var. *nakaiana*) is a graceful, compact, small-leaved shrub. It offers clean white flowers, dark blue-green foliage, and deep burgundy fall color. Almost serves as a groundcover. Grows 1½ ft. high, 3 to 5 ft. wide.

Deutzia ×hybrida

syn. *Deutzia ×kalmiiflora*

On first inspection, it is difficult to recognize the flower of this hybrid (*Deutzia discolor* × *D. longifolia*) as that of a deutzia. The good pink (or darker), five-petaled flowers are more open and saucer-shaped than those of other *Deutzia* species, occurring in loose inflorescences of five to 12 blossoms. Flowers open in May and June. Foliage is light green. Grows 4 to 5 ft. high and wide. Zones 5 to 8.

CULTIVARS AND VARIETIES

Selected cultivars include 'Contraste', 'Mont Rose', 'Perle Rose', and 'Pink Pompon', all in shades of pink to fuchsia-purple.

'Magicien' ('Strawberry Fields') has fuchsia-purple flowers edged in white. A plant in the Georgia trials is rather pretty in flower; for most of the year little more than an organized brush pile. West Coast literature noted magnificent flowers on a 10 ft. by 10 ft. shrub.

Deutzia ×lemoinei

Lemoine deutzia

The great French nurseryman Victor Lemoine produced many hybrids between *Deutzia gracilis* and *D. parviflora*. Most of these produce abundant white flowers on 1- to 3-in.-long, pyramidal corymbs. The habit is typically quite twiggy, dense, erect-branched, and ultimately rounded in outline. Considered one of the hardiest deutzias, able to survive −30°F. Grows 5 to 7 ft. high and wide. Zones 4 to 7.

Deutzia scabra

fuzzy deutzia

Essentially a dinosaur in modern landscapes, but very much a part of older gardens. *Deutzia scabra* forms an oval or obovate, round-topped shrub, taller than broad, with spreading, somewhat arching branches and brown, peeling bark. The dull green leaves are 1 to 4 in. long and have a sandpapery texture on the upper surface. The white flowers, often tinged with pink, are the only salvation of this shrub. The flowers, each about ½ to ¾ in. long and wide, occur in 3- to 6-in.-long panicles in May and June. Easy to grow. Grows 6 to 10 ft. high, 4 to 8 ft. wide. Zones 5 to 7. Japan, China.

CULTIVARS AND VARIETIES

'Plena' is a form with double, pure white flowers.

'Pride of Rochester' has double flowers that are tinged with pink.

Deutzia gracilis 'Nikko'

Deutzia ×hybrida 'Perle Rose'

Deutzia ×hybrida 'Magicien'

Deutzia setchuenensis

I'm casually excited by this refined, rounded shrub, which bears corymbose clusters of small, star-like white flowers in June. Flowers gracefully engulf the mid-green foliage. Grows 4 to 6 ft. high and wide. Zones 6 and 7. China.

CULTIVARS AND VARIETIES
Variety *corymbiflora* appears more common in cultivation. The flowers akin to the species; the leaves wider.

Have observed in flower—certainly showy.

Dichroa febrifuga

Allied to *Hydrangea* (and included therein by DNA analysis), but this species is evergreen and minimally cold hardy (zones 8 to 10 on West Coast). Flowers on old wood, so cold pretty much eliminates the potential; a few sporadic, eccentric flowers later in season, blue, occasionally

pink, without showy sepals. Fruit are fleshy, blue, gentian-blue, indigo-blue, purple-blue, ¼ to ⅓ in. in diameter. Excited about breeding the unique fruit characteristics into *Hydrangea macrophylla*; Dr. Josh Kardos, Plant Introductions, Inc., produced hybrids in the hundreds but without the large sepals typical of *H. macrophylla*. Certainly hardiness has been increased. A full-grown shrub, as I've witnessed

MORE ▶

Deutzia ×lemoinei, Lemoine deutzia

Deutzia setchuenensis var. *corymbiflora*

Deutzia scabra, fuzzy deutzia

Deutzia scabra 'Pride of Rochester'

Deutzia setchuenensis var. *corymbiflora*

Dichroa febrifuga CONTINUED

in Portland, Oregon, is a beautiful experience. Requires moist, acid, well-drained soil, shade, and wind protection. Grows 3 to 4 (to 5) ft. high and wide. Eastern Asia.

Dichroa versicolor is similar but larger in all its parts. Less cold hardy than *D. febrifuga*. The two species were subjected to 15°F in Athens one November: *D. febrifuga* was still evergreen; all leaves dead on *D. versicolor*.

Dichroa febrifuga

Dichroa febrifuga

Dichroa versicolor

Dicksonia antarctica
Australian tree fern

This genuine arborescent fern is a common occurrence in conservatories in the North and grows, typically, 15 to 20 ft. high under outdoor cultivation in warmer climates (in Irish gardens, this species grew like a shade tree). A stout trunk is topped by a uniform head of evergreen fronds, often 4 ft. long or more. Leaves dark green; the trunk is covered with brown fibrous roots. Reproduces by spores in moist climates. Requires shade and a moist environment. Unique architectural plant or container plant; groupings create a mini-forest. Zones 9 to 11. Australia, Tasmania.

Diervilla sessilifolia
southern bush-honeysuckle

This species will doubtfully make anyone's list of the top 50 flowering shrubs, but it can be a serviceable filler in sun or shade and in inhospitable soils. Forms a low-growing, wide-spreading,

Dicksonia antarctica, Australian tree fern

flat-topped shrub. The 2- to 6-in.-long leaves emerge bronze-purple in spring, change to lustrous dark green, and may develop tints of red-purple in autumn. Sulfur-yellow flowers appear at the ends of the shoots from June into August. The floral display is not potent and is really only noticeable if one stumbles into the shrub. An extremely adaptable and versatile plant. Could be used for large-area coverage on banks. Grew a large population of seedlings hoping for compact habit, bronze-red foliage, larger flowers, and was rewarded with nothing special. Some plants all green, others with bronze new growth; all flowered yellow the first year; all were pitched. Grows 3 to 5 ft. high and wide. Zones 4 to 8. Common on Rabun Bald, Georgia's second-highest mountain at 4,696 ft. elevation, a hike I take on a regular basis. North Carolina to Georgia and Alabama.

CULTIVARS AND VARIETIES

'Butterfly' has deep yellow flowers and glossy green foliage that turns purple in fall. I see little difference between this and the everyday species.

Cool Splash™ ('LPDC Podaras') is a chance seedling with pretty cream-white-margined, dark gray-green-centered leaves. Quite a handsome shrub, 2½ to 4½ ft. high and wide. Observed reversion shoots.

Summer Stars™ ('Morton') is a compact, 2- to 3-ft.-high shrub with yellow, trumpet-like flowers; attached to *Diervilla rivularis*.

Diospyros kaki
Japanese persimmon
Thirty years past, traveling through south Georgia, I spied a small round-headed tree dripping with peaches, or so I thought. The tree was actually a *Diospyros kaki* laden with orange fruit 3 to 4 in. in diameter. Habit is rounded with thick-textured, lustrous dark green, 3- to 7-in.-long leaves, changing to vibrant shades of yellow, orange, and red. Fruit are edible; cultivars

often require complete maturity to lose astringency. Prefers moist, well-drained soils, full sun but grows, once established, in droughty, heavy-textured soils. Always thought the male trees would make good drought-tolerant street trees. Good plant for the backyard fruit garden. Fruit are beautiful, ripening in fall and persisting into December in the Piedmont of Georgia. Many fruiting selections; trees in the

MORE ▶

Diervilla sessilifolia, southern bush-honeysuckle

Diervilla sessilifolia

Diervilla sessilifolia fall color

Diospyros kaki, Japanese persimmon, fall color

Diervilla sessilifolia Cool Splash™

Diospyros kaki CONTINUED
Athens trials produce great quantities of orange fruit. Grows 15 to 20 (to 30) ft. high and wide. Zones 7 to 9. China.

Diospyros virginiana
common persimmon
This native species will never win a landscape beauty contest, but it possesses an inherent toughness that assures survival under difficult conditions. Common persimmon is seldom available in commerce, so gardeners must be satisfied with transplanting seedlings from the wild. Pyramidal to oval-rounded in outline, with dark green, 2- to 5½-in.-long leaves, yellow to reddish purple fall color, and squarish, blocky, gray-black bark. The foliage may contract a disfiguring blackish leaf spot. Fragrant, white, blueberry-shaped flowers occur in May and June, with male and female on separate trees. The 1- to 1½-in.-wide, yellowish red to pale orange, edible berries ripen in fall. Astringent before ripening, which is usually predicated on frost(s). The species is adaptable to extremely dry soils, and numerous cultivars have been selected for fruiting qualities. Superior selections of male (i.e., nonfruiting) trees might be utilized for urban plantings. Grows 35 to 60 ft. high, 20 to 35 (to 50) ft. wide. Zones 4 to 9. Connecticut to Florida, west to Kansas and Texas.

Dipelta floribunda
rosy dipelta
Difficult to locate in commerce (not sure I have ever seen) and even more so in gardens. So why discuss? Remi-

Diospyros kaki

Diospyros kaki

Diospyros virginiana, common persimmon, fall color

Diospyros virginiana

Diospyros virginiana

niscent of an out-of-control, steroidal weigela—and the funnel-shaped, rounded-spreading, five-lobed, pale pink, yellow in throat, flowers, 1 to 1¼ in. by 1 in., do bear a resemblance. Four, ¾-in.-long, ½-in.-wide, shield-shaped, greenish white bracts subtend the flower. Innocuous, 2- to 5-in.-long, ⅝- to 1½-in.-wide, mid to dark green leaves do not develop fall color. Bark is ash-brown to brown and exfoliates in elongated strips. Adaptable, and flowers best in full sun. Perhaps best sited in a shrub border for May and June flowers. Typically 10 to 15 ft. high, round-headed, and open-leggy at the base. Zones 5 to 7. Central and western China.

Dirca palustris
leatherwood

A great, restrained, dapper, shade-loving native shrub that simply cannot find its way out of the shadows into commerce. This is a choice plant for those impossible shady garden areas; in fact, it performs more admirably in shade than in full sun, where the leaves bleach. The habit is oval to rounded, with light brown stems that are almost leathery. The egg-shaped, 1- to 3-in.-long, light green leaves are among the first to emerge in spring. In fall, they turn clear yellow. Pale to bright yellow flowers occur on leafless stems in March and April and provide a barometer for spring. Fruit are ⅓-in.-long, oval, (reddish) green drupes that ripen in June and July. Provide organic-laden, moist, acid soils. Use in a woodland garden, in a naturalized

MORE ▶

Dipelta floribunda, rosy dipelta

Dipelta floribunda

Dirca palustris, leatherwood

Dirca palustris

Dirca palustris

273

Dirca palustris CONTINUED
situation, or in combination with ericaceous plants. Grows 3 to 6 ft. high
and wide. Zones 4 to 9. New Brunswick to Ontario, south to Florida and
Missouri.

Disanthus cercidifolius
disanthus

Virtually unknown in American gardens, this shrub is worthy of use
because of its excellent wine-red fall
color. The specimens I have encountered invariably were located at
botanic gardens and arboreta. Disanthus forms a broad, spreading shrub
with slender branches, and it requires
room to develop. The lustrous, dark
bluish green, 2- to 4½-in.-long leaves
are heart-shaped, like those of redbud (*Cercis*). In fall, the foliage turns
combinations of claret-red and purple,
often suffused with orange. Four-

petaled, dark purple flowers occur in
October into December (Athens) and
are, at best, curiously interesting. Provide moist, acid, organic, well-drained
soils. Light shade is preferable,
although I have observed plants that
were prosperous in full sun. Grows 6
to 10 (to 15) ft. high and wide. Zones
5 to 7. Japan.
CULTIVARS AND VARIETIES
'Seiju Yamaguchi' may be the correct
name of a cream-margined, gray-green
centered, variegated-leaf form with
red petioles. Leaves smaller and plant
slower growing that species. A collector's item.

Distylium myricoides
blueleaf isu tree

Mystical representative of this virtually
unknown, broadleaf evergreen genus
of the Hamamelidaceae. First plants in
Athens arrived via Piroche Plants, Pitt
Meadows, British Columbia. Habit is
layered, spreading, flat-topped initially,
the branches arching at their extremities. Leaves, refined, matte blue-green,
3 to 3½ in. long, ¾ to 1 in. wide, linear
in outline. Leaves do not discolor in
winter. Red, apetalous flowers in (January) February and March in quantity
from the leaf axils. Not overwhelming, but pretty, making excellent cut

Disanthus cercidifolius

Disanthus cercidifolius, disanthus

Disanthus cercidifolius fall color

Disanthus cercidifolius 'Seiju Yamaguchi'

branches for floral arrangements. Fruit is a two-valved, gray-brown, dehiscent capsule with brown seeds. Scintillatingly resilient: full sun, partial shade, moist to dry soils, pH adaptable. Excellent grouping, mass-planting element. Roots readily from cuttings, and seeds germinate without pretreatment. Gets bigger than advertised, 5 ft. by 8 ft. in four years in Georgia trials. Can be pruned to 6 to 12 in. from the ground and completely rejuvenates. True for the other species and hybrids. Zones (6)7 to 9. China.

CULTIVARS AND VARIETIES

A lone plant in the Piroche shipment was intermediate in characteristics between *Distylium myricoides* and *D. racemosum*. I segregated, tagged, and outplanted next to the two suspected parents. Plant grew 7½ ft. by 8 ft. in five years, and its seedlings showed magical variation. Selected three, all of which, at five years, are low-mounded to small-statured shrubs. All who see verbalize . . . "Wow!" Something in the broadleaf evergreen crowd that is not named holly, cherrylaurel, or boxwood. Introduced by McCorkle Nursery, Dearing, Georgia, and Plant Introductions, Inc.

Blue Cascade™ ('PIIDIST-II') has pretty bronze-red new growth, maturing matte blue-green; compact spreading habit, 2 to 3 ft. high, 3½ to 4½ ft. wide.

Emerald Heights™ ('PIIDIST-I') is a worthy alternative to 'Schipkaensis' cherrylaurel, with bright green new leaves turning lustrous, almost black-green, holding color through winter; 5 to 6 ft. high and wide.

'Vintage Jade' is the most unique of the three with a spreading, spidery, cushion-like, layered branching habit; leaves lustrous dark green; 2 ft. high, 5 ft. wide.

Distylium racemosum
isu tree

An evergreen member of the witch-hazel family that, in leaf, appears totally unrelated; however, flowers and fruit do not lie. In Athens and

MORE ▶

Distylium Emerald Heights™

Distylium myricoides, blueleaf isu tree

Distylium Blue Cascade™

Distylium 'Vintage Jade'

Distylium racemosum CONTINUED

Distylium racemosum

Distylium racemosum 'Akebono'

Distylium racemosum 'Guppy'

Distylium racemosum 'Ogisu'

Savannah, Georgia, and Asheville, North Carolina, old plants are upright and shrubby. The 1- to 1½-in.-long leaves are shiny dark green. The subdued reddish maroon flowers open in March and April (Athens), somewhat inconspicuously, and are followed by two-beaked woody capsules. Moist, acidic soils, laden with organic matter, are best; however, a plant in full sun and heavy soil at the Horticulture Farm in Athens has performed at the highest level for 20 years. At best, 10 to 15 ft. high, although the literature mentions 60-ft.-high plants in the wild. Zones 6 to 9. Southern Japan.

CULTIVARS AND VARIETIES
'Akebono' has cream-white (slightly yellow) new shoot growth that matures to green. Reasonably vigorous.

'Guppy' has small leaves, compact habit; largest observed was 3½ ft. by 2½ ft., upright and formidably dense. Still not a "take home to the garden" candidate.

'Ogisu' has white-margined leaves.

Duranta erecta
syn. *Duranta repens*
pigeon berry, golden dewdrop

H. P. Leu Gardens, Orlando, Florida, displayed fruiting specimens that had me checking identity. The ⅜- to ½-in.-wide, yellow globose drupes ripen in late summer to fall. Excellent for fruit effect! Typically a dieback shrub, broad-spreading, on the Coastal Plain of Georgia but growing up to 18 ft. in central and south Florida gardens. Shiny rich green leaves (evergreen in Deep South) are quite handsome. Bluish flowers develop on new growth of the season in 6-in.-long panicles. Full sun and loose, well-drained soils are suitable. Grows 4 to 6 ft. high and wide. Zones 8 to 11. Tropical America.

CULTIVARS AND VARIETIES
'Golden Edge' is similar to 'Variegata' but with flashy gold patterns.

'Variegata' has leaves margined and irregularly splashed with cream and white.

Distylium racemosum, isu tree

Edgeworthia chrysantha

syn. *Edgeworthia papyrifera*

paperbush

During our daily walks through the garden, Bonnie and I *always* remarked about the oversized, beautiful bluish green leaves that combine so seamlessly with the leaves and flowers of *Hydrangea arborescens* 'Annabelle'. This unique plant is reserved for the shady nooks and crannies of the garden, where ample moisture is available. It is a suckering shrub, growing 3 to 4 ft. high. The lithe, spotted, and stippled stems, lustrous red-brown with permanent light gray crescent-shaped leaf scars, are handsome in winter. The dark blue-green leaves are typically 6 in. long, although leaves from the plant in our garden measured 10 in. long. Flowers are unique, opening on naked stems in February, March, and April, fragrant, silky white and yellow, in 1- to 2-in.-wide umbels. Flowers open over long periods, at least four to six weeks. Flower buds are evident from leaf drop until they open. Wonderful plant to combine with shade-tolerant broadleaf evergreens and wildflowers. Becoming available in nursery commerce. Grows 3 to 4 (to 7) ft. high, spreads by rhizomes. Referenced to 10 ft. on West Coast. Zones 7 to 9. China.

Edgeworthia papyrifera is often

MORE ▶

Duranta erecta, pigeon berry

Edgeworthia chrysantha, paperbush

Duranta erecta

Duranta erecta

Duranta erecta 'Golden Edge'

Edgeworthia chrysantha CONTINUED
listed but taxonomically was folded into *E. chrysantha*. Most of the former are smaller statured than *E. chrysantha*.

CULTIVARS AND VARIETIES
'Gold Rush' has larger flowers and is overall more robust than typical.

'Grandiflora' has large flowers and leaves.

'Jitsu Red', 'Red Dragon', and 'Rubra'—probably all the same—have reddish tinted flowers.

'Snow Cream' is large-flowered and vigorous, with tree-like attributes; 6 ft. high and wide. Introduced by Tony Avent, Plant Delights Nursery, Raleigh, North Carolina.

'Winter Gold' is attached to a large-leaved, large-flowered, easier-to-grow selection introduced by Ted Stephens, North Augusta, South Carolina.

Ehretia dicksonii

Little-known, small flowering tree with broad-spreading habit; leaves are shining dark green, 4 to 8 in. long, with no appreciable fall color. The fragrant white flowers occur in 2- to 4-in.-wide, flattish terminal panicles in May and June. Fruit are small blackish drupes. The gray-brown bark is deeply ridged and furrowed. Prospers in full sun and well-drained soil. For the

Edgeworthia chrysantha

Edgeworthia chrysantha 'Rubra'

Ehretia dicksonii

Ehretia dicksonii

Elaeagnus angustifolia

obsessed collector only. Grows 20 to 25 ft. high and wide. Zones (7)8 and 9. China, Taiwan, Japan.

Elaeagnus angustifolia
Russian-olive

An excellent plant for its silvery gray foliage effect, as well as its salt tolerance. Utilized along highways in the Midwest, where de-icing salts are common. The habit is quite loose, of light texture, and generally rounded in outline. The elliptical, 1- to 3-in.-long, silvery leaves hold late in fall and do not color. The silvery white to yellowish, fragrant flowers and the silver-scaled fruit, which eventually turn reddish, are lost among the foliage. Tolerates acid, high pH, saline, and dry soils; also fixes atmospheric nitrogen. Unfortunately, verticillium wilt can severely injure the tree. A respectable plant for difficult sites or where a change in foliage color is warranted.

Has lost much of its appeal and is difficult to locate in everyday nursery commerce. Grows 12 to 15 (to 20) ft. high and wide; can grow 30 to 40 ft. National champion is 47 ft. by 61 ft. Zones 2 to 7. Southern Europe, Asia.

Elaeagnus ×ebbingei

A hybrid evergreen species, similar to and often difficult to distinguish from *Elaeagnus pungens*. In general, this is the better garden plant, with larger

MORE ▶

Elaeagnus ×ebbingei

Elaeagnus angustifolia, Russian-olive

Elaeagnus ×ebbingei 'Gilt Edge'

Elaeagnus ×ebbingei 'Limelight'

leaves and less rampant growth. In truth, it is still quite vigorous and requires pruning to remove the extraneous shoots. Leaves, flowers, and fruit similar to *E. pungens*. The differences are most manifest in the cultivars. Grows 8 to 10 ft. high and wide. Zones 7 to 9.

CULTIVARS AND VARIETIES

Eleador™ ('Lannou') is green-margined, yellow-centered but prone to reversion, which limits its usefulness.

'Gilt Edge' has soft yellow-gold margins and light green centers.

'Limelight' is the reverse, with pale to deep gold centers and green margins.

Elaeagnus macrophylla

One of the parents, along with *Elaeagnus pungens*, of *E. ×ebbingei*. As I witnessed the species in Europe, a robust rounded shrub not as wild as *E. pungens*. Leaves lustrous dark green above, silvery below. Flowers and fruit similar to *E. pungens*. Same uses as *E. pungens*. The new leaves appear coated with silver fur. When the leaves first emerge in spring the entire plant is attractive. Grows 8 to 12 ft. high and wide. Zones 8 and 9. Korea, Japan.

Elaeagnus multiflora
cherry elaeagnus

Many gardeners are wary of *Elaeagnus* species because of the weedy nature of *Elaeagnus umbellata*, autumn-olive, and this species too will "jump the fence" and develop invasive tendencies. *Elaeagnus multiflora* makes a handsome rounded shrub, however. The 1½- to 2½-in.-long leaves are dark green above and silvery brown below. Dirty white or silvery brown, tubular, fragrant flowers occur from the leaf axils in April and May. The scaly, ovoid, ½-in.-long, red fruit ripen in June and July. Selections for fruit size and flavor are known and available in U.S. commerce. Adaptable to infertile soils, in full sun to half shade. Nitrogen-fixing species. Good plant to use for screening or massing. Definitely not for the small garden. Grows 6 to 10 ft. high and wide. Zones 5 to 7. China, Japan.

Elaeagnus pungens
thorny elaeagnus

Truly the cowboy of evergreen shrubs —wild, woolly, unkempt, and tough

Elaeagnus macrophylla

Elaeagnus macrophylla

Elaeagnus multiflora, cherry elaeagnus

Elaeagnus multiflora

as rawhide. Grows anywhere and a remarkable plant for the location where nothing else prospers. Rounded, more or less, in outline with long, supple, buggy-whip shoots that wander in disarray. Silver leaves emerge in spring, the upper surface becoming lustrous dark green, the lower silver-brown. Stems, buds, and all other plant parts are covered with brownish scales. Flowers, tubular-flaring, white with brownish scales, fragrant, ½ in. long, open from September through November and are lost among the leaves. Often the only indication of flowering is the gardenia-esque fragrance saturating the autumn air. The ½- to ¾-in.-long, oval drupes are red with brownish scales and ripen in April of the year following flowering. They serve as bird food, for I see many seedlings in places that only birds travel. Grows in any soil except wet, in sun or in shade. Fixes atmospheric nitrogen and is apt to grow in the most infertile soils. Significant barrier or massing plant because of the density of the branches and thorns. Almost impenetrable even to a porcupine. Grows 10 to 15 ft. high and wide. Plant literally "climbs," and I observed it 30 ft. high in trees. Zones 6 to 9(10). Japan.

CULTIVARS AND VARIETIES
'Dicksonii' produces leaves bordered with a broad gold margin, with some leaves completely gold toward the apex. Witnessed a 15-ft.-high plant in England.

MORE ▶

Elaeagnus pungens, thorny elaeagnus

Elaeagnus pungens 'Fruitlandii'

Elaeagnus pungens undersides of foliage

Elaeagnus pungens

Elaeagnus pungens

Elaeagnus pungens CONTINUED

Elaeagnus pungens 'Frederici'

Elaeagnus pungens 'Hosoba Fukurin'

Elaeagnus pungens 'Maculata'

'Frederici' has small, narrow, 1- to 1¾-in.-long leaves, the cream-colored or pale yellow center bordered with a thin margin of green. Not particularly striking, appears sick.

'Fruitlandii' more compact and not as wild.

'Hosoba Fukurin' is more refined and does not throw the wild shoots of the species. Smaller, wavy leaf with yellow margins, silver-white beneath.

'Maculata' has leaves with deep yellow blotches and staining in their centers; unstable and may revert to all-green or -gold leaves.

Elaeagnus umbellata
autumn-olive

This introduced species has become a pernicious invasive pest of woodlands on the southeast and east coasts. It has crowded out many of the better native understory species because of its tolerance of shade and infertile, dry soils. By no means a wee lad, autumn-olive becomes a massive shrub or small tree. The 2- to 4-in.-long leaves are bright green above, silver-white beneath. Fragrant, silvery white, ½-in.-long, funnel-shaped flowers occur in May and June, after the leaves have emerged. Numerous globose, ⅓-in.-wide, red fruit develop in September and October. Birds are the great disseminators of the species, and stray seedlings are evident everywhere. Use only with the knowledge that it can become an ineradi-

Elaeagnus umbellata, autumn-olive

Elaeagnus umbellata

Elaeagnus umbellata

cable liability. In and around Athens it is "everywhere," formidable even in shady environments. Grows 12 to 18 ft. high and wide. Zones 3 to 8. China, Korea, Japan.

CULTIVARS AND VARIETIES
Many cultivars selected for fruit and juice-making potential. Fruit are high in lycopenes, which are reported to help prevent prostate and other cancers.

'Titan' has no redeeming qualities other than habit; grows 12 ft. high, 6 ft. wide.

Eleutherococcus sieboldianus

syn. *Acanthopanax sieboldianus*
fiveleaf aralia
This is one of the toughest shrubs available, virtually indestructible. Almost impossible to locate in commerce, it is frequently found in older landscapes as a hedge or massing plant. By no means dainty, open-grown specimens become massive, rounded shrubs. The dark green (could argue rich green) leaves are composed of five to seven, 1- to 2½-in.-long, serrated leaflets. The light brown stems have one (two) prickle(s) beneath each narrow leaf scar. The greenish white flowers are undistinguished, and the black fruit seldom, if ever, set. Noted abundant, coal-black fruit on plants at the University of Maine. Easily cultured, it will prevail in urban situations and appears quite tolerant of air pollution. Grows where little else will. Use in hedges, groupings, masses, in shade or full sun, on clay or rock scrabble. Grows 8 to 10 ft. high and wide. Zones 4 to 8. Japan.

CULTIVARS AND VARIETIES
'Variegatus', more commonly available than the species, has leaflets with irregular creamy white margins. Good for brightening a shady corner of the garden. Grows more slowly than the species, to 6 to 8 ft. high and wide. May revert to green or albino shoots, which should be removed.

Elliottia racemosa
Georgia plume
The more fickle the plant, the greater the desire to grow it in the garden. This Georgia native certainly fits the bill as it is nowhere common in gardens. Found wild in the sandy soils of Georgia and South Carolina, the species suckers and forms 8- to 12-ft.-high colonies. Isolated specimens make small trees; the national champion is 47 ft. high, 20 ft. wide. The 2- to 5-in.-long, dark blue-green leaves may develop bronze-red shades in November. The fragrant white flowers occur in 4- to 10-in.-long terminal racemes (panicles) in mid June and early July. Well-drained soil, full sun to partial shade, and possibly mycor-

MORE ▶

Eleutherococcus sieboldianus

Eleutherococcus sieboldianus 'Variegatus'

Eleutherococcus sieboldianus, fiveleaf aralia

Elliottia racemosa CONTINUED

rhizae (fungal associations with roots) are necessary for good growth. The Arnold Arboretum germinated many seedlings, but subsequent growth was poor. Not for the once-a-year putterer, and a challenge to the embattled gardener. Zones 6 (once established) to 8(9).

Elsholtzia stauntonii
Staunton elsholtzia

One can debate its relative garden merits, but this shrubby member of the mint family offers fragrant foliage and purplish pink flowers on terminal panicles in September and October, when few shrubs are in flower. The strongly toothed, 2- to 6-in.-long leaves are bright green in summer. Provide loamy, well-drained soils, in full sun. Cut back old branches in late winter, since flowers occur on new growth of the season. Use in a perennial or shrub border for late-season color. Grows 3 to 5 ft. high and wide. Zones 4 to 8. Northern China.

CULTIVARS AND VARIETIES
'Alba' is a white-flowered selection.

Emmenopterys henryi

E. H. Wilson, the great plant explorer, described this as one of the most strikingly beautiful trees of the Chinese forests, reaching heights of 80 ft. Typically, in cultivation, it forms a rounded, spreading canopy. The oppositely arranged leaves, 6 to 9 in. long, lustrous dark green, with red to red-purple petioles, are beautiful.

The leaves are red-bronze when first emerging. The exquisite, fragrant, white flowers appear in corymbose panicles, 6 to 8 in. long, up to 10 in. wide, in June and July. The individual 1-in.-wide flowers are long funnel–shaped, with spreading, rounded lobes. The urn-shaped calyx (collection of sepals) has five rounded, hairy lobes, occasionally one lobe enlarging into a 2-in.-long, 1½-in.-wide white "bract." Provide deep, moist soils laden with organic mat-

Elsholtzia stauntonii, Staunton elsholtzia

Elliottia racemosa, Georgia plume

Emmenopterys henryi

ter, in sun, although partial shade in the South is advisable. One-of-a-kind specimen tree. Grew in Georgia trials, never flowered but leaves were beautiful . . . until Easter freeze (25°F) of 2007 cut it back to earth. Rebounded but multi-stemmed now. Yet to flower. I witnessed beautiful specimens at Raulston and Scott arboreta in June flower. Grows 30 to 50 ft. high and wide. Zones (6)7 and 8. China.

Enkianthus campanulatus
redvein enkianthus

For some reason, I have had limited success with *Enkianthus* species. They sit in the garden and look at me, never prospering. Mature specimens, however, are superb, particularly in glorious fall color. Redvein enkianthus is the most popular and the easiest member of the genus to cultivate, and it is also the most commonly available in commerce. The habit is upright in youth, becom-

ing more open and layered (stratified) with age. The 1- to 3-in.-long, sharply serrated, blue-green leaves turn brilliant yellow to orange and red in fall. The ⅓- to ½-in.-long, bell-shaped flowers are creamy yellow or light orange, veined with red. Flowers open in May and June and have a curious, rather unpleasant odor. Provide acid, organic, moist, well-drained soils, in partial shade or sun. Excellent choice for flower and fall color. Combines

MORE ▶

Emmenopterys henryi

Emmenopterys henryi

Enkianthus campanulatus, redvein enkianthus

Enkianthus campanulatus

Enkianthus campanulatus fall color

285

Enkianthus campanulatus CONTINUED
well with other ericaceous plants, such as rhododendrons and azaleas. Grows 6 to 8 ft. high in the Midwest; 12 to 15 ft. high in the Northeast. Zones 4 to 7. Japan.
CULTIVARS AND VARIETIES
Albiflorus Group has flowers that are creamy white.

'Red Bells' has cream to deep pink flowers, corolla veined pink, on an upright plant.

Enkianthus cernuus

Although not as robust as *Enkianthus campanulatus*, *E. cernuus* bears ¼-in.-long, white flowers in ten- to 12-flowered racemes, providing a lovely accent in May. Generally smaller in all its parts than *E. campanulatus*. Similar cultural requirements. Grows 5 to 10 ft. high. Zones 5 to 7. Japan.
CULTIVARS AND VARIETIES
Forma *rubens* has deep red flowers;

beautiful, rich color. Observed an 8-ft.-high plant at Hillier Arboretum.

Enkianthus perulatus
white enkianthus

Possibly the most refined and elegant enkianthus, but nowhere common in gardens. The bright green leaves, the fine-textured, slender stems, and the dainty rounded habit contribute to its garden worthiness. Urn-shaped, ⅓-in.-long, white flowers open with or before the 1- to 2-in.-long leaves in May. As with the other *Enkianthus* species, the flowers are somewhat ill-scented. Fall color is often brilliant scarlet. Use as an accent plant in a border or rock garden, or in a prominent position. Grows 6 ft. high and wide. Zones 5 to 7. Japan.
CULTIVARS AND VARIETIES
'J. L. Pennock' represents the 9 ft. by 15 ft., 60- to 70-year-old plant at the Morris Arboretum. Abundant white flowers; brilliant red fall color.

Enkianthus serrulatus

What a scintillating flowering shrub! The waxy, cream-white, ½-in.-long, broad urn-shaped flowers, the lobes reflexed, appear three to six together in arching umbels in April. Witnessed in flower in early April at Sarah P. Duke Gardens just as the leaves were emerging. Leaves, deep green, yellow, orange, and red in autumn, are 1½ to 3 (to 4) in. long, serrulate, and elliptic-oblong. Best in partial shade in acid, well-drained, organic-laden soil. Habit is rather sparse, with coarser branches than the other *Enkianthus* species treated here. Listed to 20 ft. high; plants I experienced were 5 ft. high, about as wide. Zones 6 and 7. China.

Epigaea repens
trailing arbutus

Somewhat of a stretch to include this evergreen groundcover, but its understated, subtle beauty provides legiti-

Enkianthus campanulatus Albiflorus Group

Enkianthus campanulatus 'Red Bells'

Enkianthus cernuus f. *rubens*

Enkianthus perulatus, white enkianthus

macy. The plant has followed Bonnie and me from our graduate student days at the University of Massachusetts, Amherst, to Athens. Always evident during walks in Massachusetts; similarly so in north Georgia, where it is abundant. Almost have to look, see, and focus to discover. The glossy dark green leaves are covered with persistent stiff hairs on both surfaces. Flowers, which open in March and April in Georgia, are ⅝ in. long, ½ in. wide, fragrant, white to deep pink. Several cultivars with deeper pink flowers are described, but one can find such forms in almost any native population. Fruit are whitish, berry-like, ½-in.-wide capsules that I have yet to observe. Best sited in acid, sandy, gravelly soil, mulched with decayed oak leaves or pine needles. Locate in wildflower garden. A true gardener's plant, not for the Big Box crowd. Grows 2 to 4 (to 6) in. high, spreading along the ground.

Zones 4 to 9. Massachusetts to Florida, west to Ohio and Tennessee.

Erica carnea
spring heath

The heaths are a most difficult group to discuss since some 700 species are known, and most of these are not cold hardy. They range from dwarf shrubs to small trees. Spring heath makes a fine evergreen groundcover in well-drained, acid soils and a sunny exposure. The ½-in.-long, lustrous green, needle-like leaves provide a delicate texture. Each flower is composed of an urn-shaped corolla, ¼ in. long, constricted at the end of the lobe. Flowers appear from January to March. The principal flower colors are white to rose-pink to rose-fuchsia. Remove spent inflorescences. Plant in sandy, acid, loamy soils in full sun to partial shade. Does not appear as sensitive to high pH soils as other

MORE ▶

Enkianthus perulatus fall color

Enkianthus serrulatus

Erica carnea, spring heath

Epigaea repens, trailing arbutus

287

Erica carnea CONTINUED

ericaceous genera. Lovely for color in the winter garden. Grows 1 ft. high, variable spread. Zones 5 to 7. Europe.

Erica ×*darleyensis* (*E. carnea* × *E. erigena*) flowers about the same time as *E. carnea*, forming broad mounds. I noted a healthy planting in full flower on a mid February day in Chapel Hill, North Carolina. Has persisted and flowered profusely on the Georgia campus. Many larger cultivars tied to this hybrid. 'Dunwood Splendour' was 4 ft. high at Hillier Arboretum. Zones 6 and 7.

CULTIVARS AND VARIETIES
Scarily numerous, with 'Springwood Pink', clear rose-pink flowers, and 'Springwood White', considered the finest white, the most common in U.S. commerce.

Eriobotrya japonica
loquat

Great architectural plant for the warm-climate garden, with "cabbagey," leathery-textured, dark green leaves that are covered on the lower surface with grayish brown indumentum. Typically, somewhat cold-sensitive in Athens, it develops into a large shrub to small rounded tree along the coast and farther south. A plant that was

Erica ×*darleyensis* 'Dunwood Splendour'

Eriobotrya japonica, loquat

Eriobotrya japonica

Eriobotrya japonica

Eriobotrya japonica 'Variegata'

killed to the ground at −3°F in the mid 1980s regrew to a 20-ft.-high and -wide specimen by 2010. Bark is a beautiful cinnamon-brown on older trunks. Leaves, particularly on vigorous shoots, are up to 12 in. long and 5 in. wide. Flowers, which appear September through January, are off-white, fragrant, and five-petaled, borne in 3- to 6-in.-long, stiff, terminal panicles. The edible yellow to orange, oblong to pear-shaped, 1- to 2-in.-long pome ripens from April through June. Tolerates extremes of soils, sun, and shade. Requires well-drained soil situation. Makes a great espalier against a wall or structure. Because of drought tolerance, serves as a great container plant. Grows 15 to 25 ft. high and wide. Zones 8 to 10. China, Japan.
CULTIVARS AND VARIETIES
'Variegata', a pretty form with cream-margined leaves, would be useful for brightening dark shadowy areas of the garden.

Erythrina ×bidwillii
coral-bean
Cardinal-red flowers in immense, elongated spires crown the foliage of this evergreen hybrid species. Terrific, almost epiphanic, surprise in the shrub or perennial border. Typically, in zones 7 and 8, the species is a dieback shrub, growing into a large shrub in central and south Florida. Leaves have sharp prickles on the midrib and are as nasty as blackberry prickles. Flowers occur in 16- to 24-in.-long racemes on new growth of the season. Spectacular and almost always greeted by "Wow! What is it?" Full sun and drier soils suit it best. A hybrid between the southeastern U.S. native *Erythrina herbacea*, Cherokee-bean or coral-bean, 3 to 5 ft. high in a single growing season with 1½-ft.-long racemes laden with deep scarlet flowers, and *E. crista-galli*, cockspur coral-tree, an evergreen tree species with cardinal-red flowers from Brazil. Zones 9 to 11 for woody structures above ground, 7 and 8 for dieback shrubs.

Escallonia rubra
Terrific evergreen shrub with beautiful lustrous dark green leaves and red flowers in June. Typically a large, rounded shrub, the red flowers appearing in 1- to 4-in.-long, leafy panicles; however, I have yet to observe this or any of the 50 to 60 *Escallonia* species thriving in the Southeast. Best suited to a climate with less humidity and cooler nights. Full sun to partial shade in moist, well-drained, fertile soils are best. Excellent salt tolerance. Useful as large screen or hedge or combined in a shrub border. Grows 10 to 15 ft. high and wide; less in the Southeast. Zones 8 to 10, ideally utilized on the West Coast. Chile.

Escallonia rubra

Escallonia rubra

Erythrina ×bidwillii, coral-bean

Eubotrys racemosa

syn. *Leucothoe racemosa*

sweetbells leucothoe

What a beauty! Unfortunately, well known only by native plant aficionados. Bonnie and I were hiking the Bartram Trail in Rabun County, Georgia, and spied a plant with elongated racemes and cylindrical flowers. Had to key it out to be sure. A small, refined shrub that produces a suckering colony. The rich green, ½- to 2½-in.-long leaves turn shades of red in autumn. The red-budded flowers are visible the year prior to flowering and are quite handsome in mid April (Athens). The ⅓-in.-long, urn-shaped, white flowers open along the entire 4-in.-long raceme. Definitely a woodland plant for moist soils. Grows 4 to 6 ft. high. Zones 5 to 9. Massachusetts to Florida and Louisiana in moist to wet areas.

Eucalyptus

eucalyptus

Enormous genus—500 to 600 species most often listed; 800 in *Hillier Manual* (2007); over 900 in *New Trees* (2010) by John Grimshaw and Ross Bayton. None completely cold hardy in zone 7 but common in Florida and the West, zones 8 to 10. Large trees (shrubs also) have juvenile leaves that are paired, rounded; mature leaves alternate in shades of gray, glaucous

Eubotrys racemosa, sweetbells leucothoe

Eubotrys racemosa

Eubotrys racemosa fall color

Eucalyptus gunnii

Eucalyptus gunnii adult foliage

blue to dark green. Leaves contain high levels of oils (volatiles) and burn quite quickly. Flowers range from cream to red, often spectacular. Bark often exfoliates to expose white, gray-green, rich brown inner bark. Stunning in their best forms. Prospers in heat and drought. Early fall or late spring freezes may injure tissues. Handsome specimen tree, common in California. In the Southeast, often grown as a cut-back plant for the beautiful foliage. Grows 60 to 100 ft. high in the West; 8- to 10-ft.-high shrub in Atlanta to medium-sized tree in Orlando, Florida. The best garden choices for zones 7 to 9 of the Southeast include *Eucalyptus gunnii*, *E. pauciflora* subsp. *niphophila*, and *E. urnigera*. Do not believe nursery catalogs, as ratings for the cold hardiness of *E. gunnii* were listed as +10°F, 0°F, and –10°F by various nurseries. From 2000 to present, has not dropped below 5°F in Athens, and 30-ft.-high trees are extant. Most appear to be *E. gunnii*. I cut several trees to about 12 in. from the ground, and the quantity of latent shoots was astronomical. Rubbed them off, a second multitude; again the same treatment and finally the plants died. Australia, Tasmania, Malaysia, New Guinea, Philippines, and Java.

Eucommia ulmoides
hardy rubber tree

A most unusual tree because of the high latex content (3 percent) in the leaves and stems; strands of latex are evident when a leaf is torn apart. A rounded to broad-spreading tree of rather uniform outline at maturity. The 3- to 6-in.-long, lustrous dark green leaves do not color in fall. Flowers dioecious with males in clusters of brown-green stamens, females a single pistil that develops into a 1½-in.-long, oval-oblong, winged capsule-like structure. Tolerant of a wide range of soils and pH. At one time considered a possibility for street and urban use, but this tree never jumped the hurdle. Nice for lawns, parks, golf courses, or commercial grounds. Grows 40 to 60 ft. high and wide. Zones 4 to 7. China. CULTIVARS AND VARIETIES Emerald Pointe™ ('Empozam'), with upright, columnar habit and thick, heavily serrated, emerald-green leaves, grows 40 ft. by 5 ft.; and, to my knowledge, is the first cultivar of the species.

Eucommia ulmoides

Eucalyptus urnigera

Eucommia ulmoides, hardy rubber tree

Eucryphia glutinosa
nirrhe

Nowhere in evidence in the Southeast, but a large shrub to small tree that prospers in the Pacific Northwest into British Columbia. The July and August flowering period brings color when most trees and shrubs are green. Flowers, four-petaled, white, with numerous yellow stamens, fragrant, 1½ to 2 in. across, occur singly or in pairs from the leaf axils. During sabbatical at the Sir Harold Hillier Gardens and Arboretum, I was privileged to photograph and observe most of the common species and hybrids. All prefer a cool, moist climate and thrive in shade to full sun. Utilized in shrub borders and mixed tree and shrub plantings. The Keith Arboretum, Chapel Hill, North Carolina, has trialed most *Eucryphia* species without any success. Grows 10 to 25 ft. high, 5 to 15 ft. wide. Zones 8 to 10, West Coast. Chile.

Euonymus alatus
winged euonymus

Truly one of the great aesthetic and functional shrubs available for American gardens. Too often, it is pruned into oblivion; an open-grown specimen is much more appealing and retains an aura of elegance. The medium green, 1- to 3-in.-long leaves, finely and sharply serrated, become

Euonymus alatus 'Compactus' fall color

Eucryphia glutinosa, nirrhe

Euonymus alatus, winged euonymus

Eucryphia glutinosa

Euonymus alatus

fluorescent pinkish red to vibrant red in fall. Coloration is as intense and consistent as that provided by any shrub. Flowers are a rather insignificant greenish yellow. Fruit are reddish with an orange-red seed. The large, corky wings are arranged at 90° separations around the stem. The wings are ¼ to ½ in. wide, and if plants are severely pruned, the wings on the new growth extensions may average ¾ in. or greater. Easily transplanted and culturally adaptable. Develops premature fall color if summer or early-fall drought occurs. Great plant for massing or grouping. Ideally do not prune. I have observed tree-form specimens in New England and the Midwest. Escaped in some areas of the United States. Grows 15 to 20 ft. high and wide. Zones 4 to 8. Northeastern Asia to central China.

CULTIVARS AND VARIETIES
Counted 20 cultivars; habit the major difference, with fall color consistently red.

'Compactus' lacks the prominent corky wings of the species. It is used for hedging, grouping, or massing. Beautiful red fall color. Grows 5 to 10 ft. high and wide.

Fire Ball® has tighter branching, increased hardiness, and rich red fall color. Grows 5 to 7 ft. high and wide.

'Rudy Haag' is more compact than 'Compactus', about 5 ft. high and wide in 15 years. The fall color is more pinkish red.

Euonymus americanus
American euonymus, strawberry-bush, hearts-a-burstin'
Obviously a schizophrenic shrub when burdened with such a ragtag litany of common names. Missed by most individuals until the red fruit and red seeds ripen in September and October. A loose (not all-together), suckering, fine-textured, green-stemmed shrub that grows in woods over much of the eastern United States. Leaves are medium green, 1½ to 3½ in. long, finely serrated, turning yellow-green (occasionally reddish purple) in fall. The ⅓-in.-wide, greenish, five-petaled flowers open in May and June. The ½- to ¾-in.-wide, three- to five-lobed, warty, red capsule opens to expose the bright red seeds that hang from the interior. Grows best in a degree of shade in dry soil. Scale is a major pest; mildew is common in extended,

late-season, rainy weather. Good naturalizing plant that should be left to its own foibles. Grows 4 to 6 ft. high and wide. Witnessed a "tree form" in north Florida, 12 to 15 ft. high, with slender branches, narrow leaves, and an obovate crown. Zones (5)6 to 9. New York, south to Florida, west to Texas.

Euonymus bungeanus
winterberry euonymus
Although not common in landscapes, tree-type *Euonymus* species, including this one, can be spectacular for fruit display. Unfortunately, most of these tree types are horrendously susceptible to scale, so one that appears healthy one year may be heavily infested or dead the next. The gardener is largely powerless to stop scale infestations. Weigh the orna-

MORE ▶

Euonymus bungeanus, winterberry euonymus

Euonymus americanus, American euonymus

Euonymus bungeanus CONTINUED

mental features against this admonition. The habit is distinctly rounded with fine-textured, almost pendulous branches. Bark is deeply ridged and furrowed; the ridges flat gray-brown. The light green, 2- to 4-in.-long leaves turn yellowish, occasionally a beautiful soft pink, in fall. The yellowish green flowers are inconspicuous, but in fall, the pinkish fruit capsules open to expose showy orange seeds—this is possibly the only reason to grow the species. Tolerant of most soils and hot, dry, windy exposures. Grows 18 to 24 ft. high and wide. Witnessed a 50-ft.-high tree at Missouri Botanical Garden. Zones 4 to 8. Northern and northeastern China.
CULTIVARS AND VARIETIES
Several. 'Pink Lady' and Prairie Radiance™ ('Verona'), neither of which I have observed in commerce, have showy pink fruit.

Euonymus carnosus
fleshy-flowered spindletree

First observed 20 years past at the Arnold Arboretum in vibrant red-purple fall color. Thought to myself . . . another tree euonymus . . . but have yet to witness scale. Small, stiff, rigid habit, a tad ragged as it shuffles to maturity. The foliage is early emerging, showy yellow-green, maturing lustrous dark green. Four-petaled, yellow-green flowers, in upright cymose clusters, peek through or above the foliage in May and June. Shiny, waxy, pink-rose, ½ in. by ½ in., four-valved capsules split to expose the orangish seeds in October and November. Adaptable and has flourished in the heat of zone 7. Estimate 20 ft. by 15 ft. at landscape maturity. Zones 4 to 7(8). China.

Euonymus europaeus
European euonymus

Not unlike *Euonymus bungeanus* in susceptibility to scale, and not as amenable to garden culture, but with prettier fruit, which range in color from pink to red and have orange seeds. Grows 12 to 30 ft. high, 10 to 25 ft. wide. Zones 3 to 7. Europe, western Asia.
CULTIVARS AND VARIETIES
'Red Cascade' has proven respectable in the Midwest, with its abundant rosy red capsules and orange seeds.

Euonymus fortunei
wintercreeper euonymus

The species itself is seldom grown; its many cultivars provide the major representation in cultivation. Habit varies from an evergreen groundcover to a 3- to 4-ft.-high and -wide shrub. The 1- to 2-in.-long leaves are dark green with lighter colored veins. Greenish white flowers appear in June and July, followed by pinkish to reddish capsules that dehisce to expose the orange-red seeds. Prefers moist, loamy soils, in

Euonymus bungeanus fall color

Euonymus bungeanus

Euonymus carnosus, fleshy-flowered spindletree

Euonymus carnosus

sun or shade, and is largely indestructible. Scale can be devastating. A good choice in borders; combine with junipers and green meatball shrubs to provide color and texture. Zones 5 to 8(9). China.

CULTIVARS AND VARIETIES

Abundant and redundant; many with variegated leaves, cream-yellow margins and green centers, or the reverse.

Blondy® ('Interbolwi') has prominent yellow center, green margin; 18 to 24 in. high, wider at maturity; terrible reversion tendencies.

'Coloratus' (var. *coloratus*), possibly the most common form, is used for groundcover purposes. In winter, the glossy deep green leaves turn a lurid plum-purple. This variety has the advantage of being very tolerant of sun and shade. Grows 9 to 12 in. high, spreads indefinitely.

'Emerald Gaiety' is a shrubby form that develops into a large mound of silver-edged leaves. Leaves average ¾ to 1¾ in. long and almost as wide. Grows 4 to 5 ft. high, slightly greater in spread.

'Emerald 'n Gold' offers 1- to 1½-in.-long, glossy dark green leaves with yellow margins. Although often listed as smaller than 'Emerald Gaiety', it will grow as large.

MORE ▶

Euonymus europaeus, European euonymus

Euonymus europaeus

Euonymus fortunei, wintercreeper euonymus

Euonymus fortunei 'Emerald Gaiety'

Euonymus fortunei 'Emerald 'n Gold'

Euonymus fortunei CONTINUED

Frosty Pearl™ with cream-white, irregular wide margins, deep green centers, develops frosted pearl capsules that turn pinkish red, opening to expose orange-red seeds. Grows 4 to 5 ft. high, less in width.

'Kewensis' has ¼- to ⅝-in.-long leaves and makes an excellent, dainty groundcover; leaves are green in winter.

'Longwood' and 'Minimus' are small-leaf forms akin to 'Kewensis'.

'Sunspot' with yellow centers, green margins, grows 3 ft. by 6 ft.; will revert as do most of the yellow/cream-centered cultivars.

'Vegetus' is a robust shrub form used extensively in the Midwest. The 1- to 2-in.-long, dull green leaves are almost rounded. It is a free-fruiting clone. More susceptible to scale than other clones. Grows 4 to 5 ft. high and wide.

Euonymus japonicus
Japanese euonymus

A much-overutilized evergreen shrub, particularly the variegated leaf selections. Has become synonymous with fast-food establishment landscaping and Big Box garden centers. Upright-oval in outline, densely branched and foliated. Sheeny, polished leaves are indeed beautiful, but the true species is seldom planted. Creamy, four-petaled, vinegary-smelling flowers emerge in June, followed by ⅓-in.-wide, four-valved, pinkish capsules with orange seeds. Grows anywhere except in wet soils. Astoundingly salt-tolerant and

Euonymus fortunei 'Coloratus'

Euonymus japonicus, Japanese euonymus

Euonymus fortunei 'Sunspot'

Euonymus fortunei 'Vegetus'

Euonymus japonicus 'Chollipo'

is a common hedge plant in English seaside gardens. Mildew and scale are serious problems. Grows 5 to 10 ft. high, less in spread. Noted a tree form in California. Literature gives size to 25 ft. high. Zones (6)7 and 8, 9 and 10 on the West Coast. Japan.

CULTIVARS AND VARIETIES
Those with colored foliage flood the market.

'Aureomarginatus' has yellow margins, green center.

'Aureus' has a bright yellow center bordered with green but tends to revert.

'Chollipo' is an upright, vigorous form with rich gold-margined leaves; about the largest leaves of the variegated selections. Habit more upright and robust.

'Green Spire' ('Emerald Towers', 'Benkomasaki') is decidedly columnar with extremely dark green leaves. A 15-ft.-high, fruiting plant grows at the Keith Arboretum, Chapel Hill, North Carolina.

'Microphyllus' has smaller leaves, ½ to 1 in. long, and is fashionably outfitted in green, yellow-margined, and cream-margined forms. It and variegated forms are less hardy than the species. Grows 1 to 3 ft. high and half as wide. A scale's best friend.

'Silver King', with cream-white margins and pale green large leaves, is common in older landscapes.

Euonymus kiautschovicus
spreading euonymus

In the past, this species was about as common as soil in many northern gardens, but it has lost favor. It is rounded in habit and has semi-evergreen (evergreen in the South), 2- to 3-in.-long, lustrous dark green leaves. Flowers and fruit are somewhat similar to those of *Euonymus fortunei*. Adaptable to virtually any soil, in sun or shade. Susceptible to scale. Use for hedges, screens, or masses. Grows 8

MORE ▶

Euonymus japonicus 'Microphyllus'

Euonymus kiautschovicus 'Manhattan'

Euonymus japonicus 'Green Spire'

Euonymus japonicus 'Silver King'

297

Euonymus kiautschovicus CONTINUED

to 10 ft. high and wide. Zones 5 to 8. Eastern and central China.
CULTIVARS AND VARIETIES
'Manhattan' is the most common cultivar. It has more rounded foliage and is smaller in stature than the species. Probably not as cold hardy; –15°F temperatures will likely reduce it to rubble. Grows 4 to 6 ft. high and wide; I have seen plants 8 ft. high, 12 ft. wide.

Eurya japonica

Eurya emarginata

Euscaphis japonica

Eurya japonica

Rare broadleaf evergreen member of the tea family that is represented in select arboreta and botanical gardens but seldom ventures into commerce. A small spreading shrub with lustrous dark green leaves that turn bronze to purple-green in winter. Each leaf is 1 to 3 in. long and ½ to 1 in. wide. The axillary, ¼-in.-wide, white flowers open in winter. In fact, I witnessed them fully open in late February at the Hillier Arboretum. The ⅕-in.-wide, globose, black fruit ripen in late summer to fall. Tolerates full sun and heavy shade. Best performance in moist, acid, well-drained soils. Could be utilized for hedges, groupings, mixed borders. Grows 4 to 6 ft. high and wide (my

Euscaphis japonica, sweetheart tree

observations), although literature mentions to 30 ft. high. Zones (7)8 and 9. Japan.

The related species *Eurya emarginata* has 1- to 1½-in.-long, ½-in.-wide, lustrous dark green, crenate-serrate leaves, blackish malodorous flowers, and ⅕-in.-wide, globose, purple-black fruit. Forms a small mound, 2 to 3 ft. high. Available cultivars include 'Meadow Snow', with a tantalizing array of white-splashed leaves, and 'Moutiers' ('Thinly Green Margined'), with gray-green center and thin dark green margin. Zones 7 to 9. Japan.
CULTIVARS AND VARIETIES
'Winter Wine' is smaller, slower growing, more spreading than *Eurya japonica*, with burgundy winter foliage.

Euscaphis japonica

Euscaphis japonica
sweetheart or euscaphis tree

In the plant introduction business, hyperbole often overshadows reality. The gardening world is still debating the merits of this small tree, originally advertised as heat- and drought-tolerant. In our garden, it flagged at the first hint of drought and was not to be trusted without moist medium. Lustrous dark green, compound pinnate leaves, composed of seven to 11 leaflets, each 2 to 4 in. long, are engaging and turn mahogany-purple in fall. Yellowish white flowers in 4- to 9- (to 12-) in.-wide terminal panicles appear in May and June. The nifty fruit are rose to ruby-red and open to expose the shiny, steel-blue to black seeds. Quite spectacular at their best. Reddish brown stems are also beautiful, developing vertical gray-brown fissures that produce striated (snakeskin) patterns. Moist, organic-laden soils and partial shade to full sun maximize performance. Possible use as an accent or novelty plant. Will *never* become an everyday tree! Several 20-ft. specimens in shady environments in Athens have flowered and fruited. Grows 15 to 25 ft. high and wide. Zones 7 and 8. China, Korea, Japan.

Exochorda racemosa
common pearlbush

To see one pearlbush species is to see them all. Common pearlbush is a large, irregular shrub that becomes floppy and often unkempt with age. White, 1½-in.-wide flowers occur in 3- to 5-in.-long racemes before the leaves in April. The expanding buds look like small pearls—hence, the common name. Broad, turbinate, winged, five-valved, ⅓-in.-wide, persistent capsule is a great identification feature. The 1- to 3-in.-long, medium green leaves are not troubled by insects or diseases. The gray to orange-brown bark on older branches develops a scaly constitution. Adaptable and easy to grow. Once established, it tolerates drought. Excellent for flower effect, and best reserved for the shrub border. Grows 10 to 15 ft. high and wide. Zones 4 to 8. Eastern China.

CULTIVARS AND VARIETIES
Snow Day™ series offers larger flowers and stronger habit than 'The Bride'.

'The Bride' is a hybrid (*Exochorda* ×*macrantha*) between *E. racemosa* and *E. korolkowii*. It has a delicate, arching branch structure and broad-rounded habit. The 1¼-in.-wide flowers occur in 3- to 4-in.-long racemes of six to ten flowers. Grows 3 to 4 ft. high, slightly wider.

Exochorda serratifolia

My early schooling in this species left considerable doubts about its merits. At the Arnold Arboretum, it was the least impressive of *all* pearlbushes in flower. More restrained in habit, leaves 2 to 3 (to 4) in. long, 1¼ to 2 in. wide, medium green, sharply serrate particularly near apex, entire below middle. White flowers in terminal racemes in April and May. Grows 6 to 10 ft. high, less in width. Zones 4 to 7. Manchuria, Korea.

CULTIVARS AND VARIETIES
'Northern Pearls' is a compact selection, 6 to 8 ft. by 4 to 6 ft., which produces masses of 2-in.-wide white flowers.

'Snow White' is a vigorous, upright form with early flowers. Witnessed in England.

Exochorda racemosa, common pearlbush

Exochorda racemosa 'The Bride'

Fagus grandifolia

American beech

Described by Florence Bell Robinson as "'The Beau Brummel' of trees but clannish and fastidious as to soil and atmosphere, magnificent specimen, casting shade which does not permit undergrowth." The accolades continue. "If the word 'noble' had to be applied to only one kind of tree, the honor would probably go to the beech," writes James U. Crockett.

"A sturdy, imposing tree often with a short trunk and wide-spreading crown, a picture of character" (from my *Manual of Woody Landscape Plants*). A beech forest is perhaps the most awe-inspiring sight in the natural world, especially when the shimmering green leaves emerge in spring and again in fall, when the leafy mantle assumes a rich golden hue. The 2- to 5-in.-long, coarsely serrated, lustrous dark green leaves turn yellow to golden brown to

brown in fall and persist, in ghostly ash-gray, on the tree's lower extremities into winter. In winter, the silver-gray trunks and branches are outstanding. Unfortunately, the American beech is seldom available in the trade. Transplant as a small container or balled and burlapped. Reputation as difficult to transplant may be unwarranted. Over many year of consulting, I recommended planting American beech and have yet to lose a single

Fagus grandifolia, American beech, fall color

Fagus grandifolia

Fagus grandifolia

300

tree. It prefers well-drained, acid, moist soils but is amazingly tolerant to a variety of soil conditions, and in the wild across its native range, it is found in soils from acid to calcareous, wet to dry. Will grow in sun or shade. Grows 50 to 70 ft. high, equal or slightly less in spread. National champion is 112 ft. by 103 ft. Zones 4 to 9. New Brunswick to Ontario, south to Florida and Texas.

Fagus sylvatica
European beech

Considerably more amenable to garden culture than *Fagus grandifolia*, *F. sylvatica* has been widely planted in Europe and North America for centuries. Its numerous cultivars have gained even greater popularity, but the species is a star in its own right, with a densely pyramidal to oval outline in youth, branching to the ground. It becomes more rounded in age but never loses the stately elegance. The lustrous dark green, 2- to 4- (to 5-) in.-long, entire-margined leaves hold late in fall before developing the rich russet and golden brown colors. The smooth, gray, elephant hide–like bark is absolutely stunning in the winter landscape. Should be reserved for large-area planting because of its massive mature size. Possibly more tolerant than *F. grandifolia* to extremes of soil. Not so well adapted to heat of South and, although it grows in zone 7, it does so incrementally, slowly. Grows 50 to 60 ft. high, 35 to 45 (to 60) ft. wide, often larger. Zones (4)5 to 7. Europe.

CULTIVARS AND VARIETIES

'Asplenifolia' is a delicate, fine-textured form, with gracefully cut (dissected) leaves that impart a fern-like texture. Makes a soft, billowy impression in the landscape. Will mature into a large tree.

'Fastigiata' is an elegant, upright, columnar to slightly columnar-oval form. In a landscape setting, the tree makes a strong vertical element. Fastigiate forms with yellow foliage ('Dawyck Gold') and purple foliage ('Dawyck Purple') are available.

'Pendula' has a personality all its own: most are certainly weeping, but also dipping, diving, arching, and permutating in all directions. No two are alike. Several purple weeping types and a golden weeping form ('Aurea Pendula') are available.

Purpurea Group ('Atropunicea', 'Purpurea') is a catchall term for the purple-leaf forms. On many of these, new leaves emerge coppery purple and mature to dark purple-maroon. The foliage fades in the heat of summer to green with tinges of the original purplish pigmentation. The best forms are possibly 'Spaethiana' and 'Riversii'.

MORE ▶

Fagus sylvatica, European beech

Fagus sylvatica 'Dawyck Gold'

Fagus sylvatica 'Asplenifolia' fall color

Fagus sylvatica 'Roseomarginata'

Fagus sylvatica 'Pendula'

Fagus sylvatica 'Aurea Pendula'

Fagus sylvatica 'Atropunicea'

Fagus sylvatica 'Tortuosa'

Fallopia baldschuanica, silver-vine fleeceflower

'Roseomarginata' ('Tricolor', 'Purpurea Tricolor') is a purple-leaf type with an irregular rose and pinkish white border. Beautiful in spring but requires protection from intense sun, and even then will lose the potent color.

'Rotundifolia' is a most beautiful form, with ½- to 1½-in.-wide, rounded, black-green leaves. It leafs out about two weeks later than the species and is also more tightly branched.

'Tortuosa', with uniquely twisted branches, forms a spreading dome of foliage; 10 to 15 ft. high, wider at maturity.

Fallopia baldschuanica

syn. *Fallopia aubertii*, *Polygonum aubertii*

silver-vine fleeceflower

Gritty, street-savvy twining vine, surviving cracks in concrete and becoming thuggish under good garden culture. Redeeming feature is the fragrant, snowy floral mantle that engulfs the bright green leaves from July through September. Emerging leaves bronze-red before greening. Flowers smallish, only ⅕-in.-wide, and produced on new growth of the season. Prospers in acid, neutral, alkaline, dry soils in full sun. Spreads rapidly by underground stems. May produce 10 to 15 ft. of linear growth in a single season. Perhaps useful to hide the ramshackle shed, woodpile, or offensive detritus. Observed many times and have *never* been tempted to utilize. Zones 4 to 7(8). Western China, Tibet, Russia.
CULTIVARS AND VARIETIES
'Summer Sunshine' has yellow leaves with red stems and white flowers; have only seen photos, so do not know if yellow coloration persists.

×*Fatshedera lizei*

Remarkable intergeneric hybrid between *Fatsia japonica* 'Moseri' and *Hedera helix* 'Hibernica' with scandent growth habit and evergreen leaves.

MORE ▶

×*Fatshedera lizei* CONTINUED

Loose and snaky on its own. Makes a terrific espalier when trained on a wall, tree, or fence. Develops (like *H. helix*) root-like holdfasts that permit attachment to porous materials. Leathery, lustrous dark green, five-lobed, 4- to 10-in.-wide leaves are intermediate between the parents. The pale green-white flowers are held in a terminal panicle, 8 to 10 in. long, up to 4 in. wide, composed of 1-in.-wide, 12- to 36-flowered hemispherical umbels. Flowers in October in the Dirr garden. Shade (some degree) and moist, well-drained soils suffice. Have grown it for many years with only cold (−3°F) killing it to the ground. Resprouted and became its vigorous self. Allow it to wind through multi-stemmed shrubs. Grows 3 to 5 ft. high; larger on a wall. Zones (7)8 to 10.

CULTIVARS AND VARIETIES
'Angyo Star', the leaves with wide yellow to white margins, is the most potent variegated selection to date. A consistent cold winter, lows of 13°F, knocked it back to the ground.

'Annemieke' ('Anna Mikkels', 'Lemon and Lime', 'Maculata') has irregular yellowish markings in center of leaf.

'Variegata' is splashed and bordered with white.

×*Fatshedera lizei* 'Angyo Star'

×*Fatshedera lizei* 'Annemieke'

×*Fatshedera lizei* 'Variegata'

×*Fatshedera lizei*

Fatsia japonica, Japanese fatsia

Fatsia japonica

Fatsia japonica 'Spider Web'

Fatsia japonica 'Variegata'

Ficus carica, common fig

Fatsia japonica
Japanese fatsia

Beautiful, seven- to nine- (to 11-) lobed, 6- to 14-in.-wide, lustrous dark green leaves bring bold texture to shady areas of the garden. In fact, even in England, the plant *requires* a shady environment to prevent leaf discoloration. Dense and rounded in habit. Flowers, white, appear in 1- to 1½-in.-wide rounded umbels, in a 15- to 20-in.-long and -wide terminal panicle. Opening times vary, October or November, with full flower in early January in Savannah. Fruit are ⅓-in.-wide, subglobose, blackish drupes. Transplant from containers into moist, acid soils high in organic matter. Provide adequate fertilizer, or leaves show nitrogen deficiency. Tolerant of air pollution and salt spray. One of the prized plants in our many gardens—nothing compares for a textural accent. Grows 6 to 10 ft. high and wide. Zones (7)8 to 10. Japan.

CULTIVARS AND VARIETIES
'Spider Web' is an intriguing addition to the garden, with white web-like pattern to newly emerging leaves. Needs protection, and mature leaves lose the variegation.

'Variegata' has white margins and streaks and "shows" even better than the species in shade.

Ficus carica
common fig

Common in old homesteads throughout the South, often outlasting the house itself. Massive rounded shrub—bold leaves and coarse stems (winter) make it difficult to miss. The sandpapery, dark green leaves, more or less three- to five-lobed, are 4 to 8 in. long and wide, even larger on vigorous shoots. Flowers are produced inside a concave structure that, when mature, enlarges and becomes fleshy. The tapering, top-shaped fruit, 2 to 4 in. long, 1 to 2½ in. wide, are green-purple-brown at maturity. Inexplicably, the fig in our garden, so beautiful in leaf, produces a fruit with the texture and taste of a dishrag. Tolerates about any well-drained soil and full sun. Plant it for foliage texture, fruit, and as a conversation piece. Good as a cut-back shrub for foliage. Grows 10 to 15 ft. high and wide. I observed a 30-ft.-high and -wide rounded tree with a 14- to 16-in.-wide trunk at Mompes-

MORE ▶

Ficus carica

305

Ficus carica CONTINUED
son House, Salisbury, England. Could not believe it was a fig at first. Zones (7)8 to 10. Western Asia and Mediterranean regions.

Ficus pumila
climbing fig

A rambunctious, true-clinging, evergreen vine that is famous for covering structures throughout the Southeast and West. The juvenile leaves, ¾ to 1¼ in. long, are appressed to the structure. Adult leaves, 2 to 4 in. long, are borne on woody stems that grow in all directions. Have observed the adult form pruned into a hedge in Savannah. Best growth occurs in shade and protected areas. Winter sun in zone 7 has discolored leaves. Will grow in virtually any soil. Requires pruning to keep it neat. For a small-leaf vine, it is quite tenacious. Limited by structure: have seen it 3 ft. high on 3-ft. walls and 40 ft. up on columns. Typically the leaves are injured/killed between 10 and 15°F; stems are largely unscathed, and new growth ensues in spring. Zones 7 to 10. China, Taiwan, Japan.

CULTIVARS AND VARIETIES
'Variegata' has leaves with a creamy white margin.

Ficus pumila, climbing fig

Firmiana simplex, Chinese parasol tree, fall color

Ficus pumila 'Variegata'

Firmiana simplex

Firmiana simplex
Chinese parasol tree

I love this most unusual large, tropical-motif tree, the rich green leaves, 6 to 8 (to 12) in. long and wide, turning respectable yellow in autumn. The large shrubby stems and branches, as well as the trunk, are gray-green and attractive. Yellow-green flowers, in 10- to 20-in.-wide, terminal panicles (June and July) are followed by pea-sized fruit that are attached to the edges of the leaf-like carpels. Adaptable, and I mean adaptable, except in standing water. Sun or shade. Great textural element in the garden. Multiple-trunked specimens are more effective than the single-stemmed tree because of the bark effect. Grows 30 to 45 ft. high and about as wide. Great 40- to 50-ft.-high tree at Coker Arboretum, Chapel Hill, North Carolina. Escaped in Louisiana, where I observed its mighty leaves among the native vegetation. Zones (6)7 to 9. China, Japan.

Firmiana simplex

Fontanesia philliraeoides subsp. fortunei

Fontanesia philliraeoides subsp. fortunei
syn. *Fontanesia fortunei*
Fortune's fontanesia

Rare and "Jurassic" shrub with nail-like durability. I remember seeing in my travels a pristine planting near Clinton, Oklahoma, where the wind never stopped blowing. For some unearthly reason, the plant was taught in the woody plant course during my Ohio State days. Upright, multi-stemmed, graceful, almost unperturbable shrub. Leaves, opposite, willow-like, 1 to 4½ in. long, and lustrous dark green, hold late in fall without appreciable fall color. Foliage, from a distance, resembles a fine-textured bamboo and is a sensible alternative, especially since it does not "run." The greenish white flowers, in 1- to 2-in.-long panicles, do not inspire. Fruit is a ⅜-in.-long, flat, oblong samara with winged margins and a notched apex. Adaptable to varied soils and climatic conditions. Perhaps for massing and screening, where few other plants would thrive. Grows 10 to 15 ft. high. Zones 4 to 8. China.
CULTIVARS AND VARIETIES
'Titan' is more upright in habit with prettier foliage; a 3-in.-high cutting grew 76 in. high, 65 in. wide, in three

growing seasons in Georgia trials. About as disappointing a cultivar as I have ever tested. The ugliness factor was overwhelming.

Forestiera acuminata
swamp privet

What is it? Who cares. Why is it here? Large shrub or small tree, loose, open, often wider than high. Mid-green, 1- to 4-in.-long leaves, oblong- to ovate-lanceolate. Stems gray with prominent lenticels. A dioecious species, flowers greenish (yellow) in axillary clusters before the leaves in March and April. Fruit are curved-ovoid, purple-black, ½- to ¾-in.-long drupes. Apparently a favorite of ducks. Tolerates dry soils but in the wild is found in moist to wet habitats. Probably useful only for naturalizing, and I can count the number of times on one hand that I observed it in cultivation. Takes several painful minutes to correctly identify the species. Grows 10 to 30 ft. high. National champion is 46 ft. by 29 ft. Zones 5 to 8(9). Illinois to Missouri, south to Florida and Texas.
CULTIVARS AND VARIETIES
'Pendula', a nifty stiff, arching, pendulous form with spidery connotations,

MORE ▶

Fontanesia philliraeoides subsp. *fortunei*, Fortune's fontanesia

Forestiera acuminata CONTINUED
is allied to *Forestiera angustifolia*.
Appears evergreen with lustrous rich
green, linear leaves, ½ to ¾ in. long,
1/16 in. wide. Sets abundant blue fruit,
⅜ in. wide. When leaves abscise, the
silver-gray stems and bark are formidably showy. Now 6 ft. by 10 ft. in
Georgia trials. More questions about
this than any other from visitors. From
Woodlanders, Aiken, South Carolina.

Forsythia

Several cold hardy *Forsythia* cultivars
have been introduced, with buds hardy

to at least −20°F. None measure up
to the *Forsythia ×intermedia* types for
floral quality, but where temperatures
drop below −15°F, their use is justified. After a −20°F Illinois winter, *F.
×intermedia* types flowered only below
the snowline; the cultivar 'Meadowlark' (a cross between *F. ovata* and
F. europaea), however, flowered to
the tips of the branches. The new
cold hardy selections may be somewhat difficult to locate. Try northern-
based, specialty mail-order firms. Ask
for 'Happy Centennial', 'Meadowlark',
'New Hampshire Gold', 'Northern Sun',

'Sunrise', and 'Vermont Sun'. 'Meadowlark' is the most flower-bud hardy
based on North Dakota evaluations.

Forsythia 'Arnold Dwarf'

This hybrid cultivar (*Forsythia ×interme-
dia* × *F. japonica* var. *saxatilis*) can be
used effectively for mass or groundcover. I have even seen it covering 45°
banks. Habit is mounded with long,
trailing branches. Flowers are somewhat greenish yellow and sparingly
produced, although older specimens
flower quite abundantly. Has lost favor
with the introduction of the brighter
yellow, more abundantly flowered *F.
×intermedia* cultivars. Grows 3 (to 6)
ft. high, 7 ft. wide. Zones 5 to 8.

Forsythia ×intermedia
border forsythia

My horticultural development was
hampered by this species, since it
seemed to be the only flowering shrub
on the planet. Widely planted because

Forestiera angustifolia 'Pendula' winter habit

Forsythia 'Arnold Dwarf'

Forsythia 'Arnold Dwarf'

Forsythia ×intermedia 'Beatrix Farrand'

of its vivid golden yellow flowers, border forsythia is truly a harbinger of the spring season. A large, at times wild and woolly shrub with intricate tangles of branches, it forms a broad-rounded outline. The 3- to 5-in.-long, sharply serrated, medium to dark green leaves die off green or with a hint of burgundy. Four-petaled, yellow flowers, 1¼ to 1½ in. long and often as wide, open on naked branches in March and April. The flower effect is spectacular, making this the most recognized and beloved of garden shrubs. It offers ironclad adaptability to soils and climates. Prune after flowering, or remove the largest canes each year. This applies to all forsythias discussed herein, since flower buds

are formed on previous year's wood. Use in mass plantings, shrub borders, parking lot islands, and other inhospitable places. Grows 8 to 10 ft. high, 10 to 12 ft. wide. Zones 5 to 8.

CULTIVARS AND VARIETIES
'Beatrix Farrand' offers 1½- to 2-in.-wide, vivid golden yellow flowers on a robust, 8- to 10-ft.-high shrub. Petals are thick-textured, waxy, and overlapping.

Gold Tide™ ('Courtasol', 'Marée d'Or'), with abundant grapefruit-yellow flowers and moss-green leaves, is a worthy compact introduction, approximately 1½ to 2½ ft. by 4 to 5 ft. Witnessed a 3 ft. by 4 ft. plant at Hillier.

'Karl Sax' is bushier in habit and not

MORE ▶

Forsythia ×*intermedia* 'Lynwood'

Forsythia ×*intermedia*, border forsythia

Forsythia ×*intermedia* 'Spring Glory'

Forsythia ×*intermedia* Magical® Gold

Forsythia ×*intermedia* 'Fiesta'

Forsythia ×intermedia CONTINUED
as tall as 'Beatrix Farrand'. It bears golden yellow flowers, and the buds are considered slightly more cold hardy.

'Lynwood' has lighter yellow flowers, more open and better distributed along the stem. Petals are strap-shaped and do not overlap like those of 'Beatrix Farrand'.

Magical® Gold ('Kolgold') is a more compact, upright, strong-stemmed introduction with rich golden-yellow flowers the size of a quarter. Grows 4 to 5 ft. high and wide. Witnessed in flower in late March (Athens), and the more restrained habit is a perfect fit for smaller landscapes.

'Spring Glory' offers abundant soft yellow flowers on a robust shrub. The color is lighter than that of 'Lynwood' and not as harsh and obtrusive as that of 'Beatrix Farrand'. 'Primulina' is similar. Grows 10 ft. high, 12 ft. wide.

Variegated selections. Most with a yellow or cream margin; not particularly stable. 'Fiesta', 'Golden Times', and 'Variegata' are but a few.

Forsythia suspensa var. sieboldii
weeping forsythia

This pretty, gracefully arching shrub can be used creatively on banks, walls, or any place the long, trailing branches are able to stretch and arch. Unfortunately, the golden yellow flowers are smaller, 1 to 1¼ in. across, and not as profuse as those of many of the *Forsythia ×intermedia* types. Leaves vary from simple to trifoliate, a trait that further permits separation from *F. ×intermedia*. Forms a large, upright-spreading, almost fountain-like shrub. Grows 8 to 10 ft. high, 10 to 15 ft. wide. Zones 5 to 8. China.

Forsythia viridissima 'Bronxensis'
Bronx greenstem forsythia

A compact, flat-topped, spreading form, quite common in northern gardens. The bright green, ¾- to 1½-in.-long leaves are sharply serrated and

Forsythia suspensa var. *sieboldii*, weeping forsythia

Forsythia viridissima Citrus Swizzle™

Forsythia viridissima 'Bronxensis', Bronx greenstem forsythia

Forsythia viridissima 'Kumson'

handsome through the growing season. Primrose-yellow flowers appear in late March or early April and are effective, but not to the degree of those of *Forsythia* ×*intermedia* types. Use as a groundcover or in mass plantings, rock gardens, and borders. Grows 1 ft. high, 2 to 3 ft. wide. Zones 4 to 8. CULTIVARS AND VARIETIES Citrus Swizzle™ ('McKCitrine') is a golden leaf form of 'Bronxensis', leaves with an irregular green center and a showy yellow margin. I am minimally impressed, as variegation fades with heat.

Variety *koreana* 'Ilgwang' has leaves edged and mottled with gold.

'Kumson' has silver-yellow veins with green interveinal areas, effective on young leaves, lost with maturity/shade. Typical yellow flowers; 4 to 6 ft. high.

Fothergilla gardenii
dwarf fothergilla

Fothergillas have assumed their rightful place in American gardens as magnificent shrubs that offer superb flowers and foliage, in both summer and fall, as well as sun and shade tolerance. They do not have a bad season. The habit of dwarf fothergilla is significantly variable, from a small, finely twiggy, rounded shrub to a more open, suckering, colonizing form. The 1- to 2½-in.-long, dark blue-green leaves turn shades of fluorescent yellow, orange, and red in fall, with all colors present in the same leaf. The leaves hold late, and fall color is expressed over a long period. White, fragrant flowers occur in 1- to 2-in.-long, bottle-brush-like inflorescences in April and May, before or as the leaves develop. The flowers appear about the same time as those of Kurume azaleas and make a handsome complement to the often gaudy-colored azaleas. Much has been written about the adaptability of fothergillas, but the greatest success is guaranteed with acid, moist, organic-laden, well-drained soils. Plants flower and color best in full sun but respond quite nicely to half shade. Use in shrub borders, perennial borders, groupings, or foundation plantings. Grows 2 to 3 ft. high and wide; 5- to 6-ft.-high plants are not uncommon. Zones (4)5 to 9. Southeastern United States.
CULTIVARS AND VARIETIES
'Blue Mist' has rich, glaucous blue foliage and disappointing yellow or bronze fall color. Flowers are slightly smaller than typical. It is a rather wispy grower, probably maturing about 3 ft.

high. Disappeared in the Dirr garden; it is simply not a competitive plant.

'Jane Platt' has narrow blue-green leaves and a cascading habit, reaching 3 ft. high. Considered outstanding for yellow, orange, and red fall colors by Roger, Eric, and Marjory Gossler in their *Best Hardy Shrubs* (2009), but my eastern/southeastern experiences reflect so-so fall color, yellow-green to brown.

Fothergilla major
large fothergilla

Virtually everything mentioned under *Fothergilla gardenii* can be applied to this species, with the exception that it is larger in all its parts. Grows 6 to 10 ft. high and wide; 15-ft.-high specimens are known. Zones 4 to 8. Mountains of southeastern United States.
CULTIVARS AND VARIETIES
Recent DNA work showed that 'Eastern', 'Mt. Airy', and 'Red Licorice' are

MORE ▶

Fothergilla gardenii 'Blue Mist'

Fothergilla major, large fothergilla

Fothergilla gardenii, dwarf fothergilla

Fothergilla major CONTINUED

Fothergilla ×intermedia selections and, as such, theoretically intermediate in characteristics.

'Blue Shadow' is a glaucous blue branch sport of 'Mt. Airy'. Have tested for five years in Georgia. In full sun makes a perfect mound, 3 ft. by 4 ft., with abundant flowers, beautiful glaucous-blue leaves, yellow-orange-red fall color. All who witness the plant ask its identity. Has shown some reversion tendencies to green. From Gary Handy, Boring, Oregon, who first showed me a branch at the 2000 Farwest Show.

'Eastern' ('Eastern Form'), offered by Gossler Farms Nursery, has better fall color than 'Jane Platt'.

'Mt. Airy' ('Mount Airy') is vigorous, with large flowers, 2 in. long by 1¾ in. wide, and consistent yellow, orange, and red fall color, even under mediocre environmental conditions.

Heavy-textured, rich blue-green leaves with whitish undersides make this a superb selection. This introduction by the author from Mt. Airy Arboretum, Cincinnati, Ohio, forced others to consider the landscape attributes of this most beautiful native genus. It is now the standard in the U.S. nursery trade and a staple of American gardens. Grows 5 to 6 ft. high and wide.

'Red Licorice' is receiving some press for its red fall color but trends closer to 'Mt. Airy' in coloration in Georgia trials. Was with Paul Cappiello, the introducer, when a gaggle of plantsmen spotted the plant. For me has yet to live up to that great day of discovery.

Frangula alnus

syn. *Rhamnus frangula*

glossy buckthorn

The habit of this species is upright-spreading with long, arching branches, resulting in a gangly appearance. The 1- to 3-in.-long, glossy dark green leaves develop, at best, greenish yellow fall color. The creamy green flowers are not showy. The ¼-in.-wide fruit pass from red to purple-black as they mature. Birds devour the fruit, and stray seedlings are common. Glossy buckthorn is easy to transplant and grow, but compacted soils and other high-stress situations should be avoided. Grows 10 to 12 (to 18) ft. high and wide. Zones 2 to 7. Europe, eastern Asia, North Africa.

CULTIVARS AND VARIETIES

Although the species has minimal appeal in contemporary landscapes, the cultivars are worth considering.

'Asplenifolia' offers a fine-textured, almost fern-like appearance. The leaves are reduced to elongated ribbons with an irregular margin. Grows 10 to 12 ft. high, 6 to 10 ft. wide.

'Columnaris' is a narrow, columnar shrub that has been overused for

Fothergilla major 'Blue Shadow'

Fothergilla major 'Eastern'

Fothergilla major 'Mt. Airy'

hedges and screens (particularly in the Midwest), but canker and other stress-related maladies have slowed its advance. Grows 10 to 15 ft. high, 5 ft. wide.

Fine Line® ('Ron Williams') has a distinctly upright habit, with graceful, narrow, arching, lustrous dark green leaves. Appears to be a 'Columnaris' × 'Asplenifolia' hybrid. Low seed producer.

Fothergilla major 'Red Licorice'

Frangula alnus Fine Line®

Frangula alnus, glossy buckthorn

Frangula alnus

Frangula alnus 'Asplenifolia'

Frangula caroliniana

syn. *Rhamnus carolinianus*

Carolina buckthorn

This was among the first of the unknown plants I agonized over upon arriving in Athens. Looked like a buckthorn, but I had never seen one so rich and vibrant with red fruit, ripening to black, and the darkest of green leaves. Often planted by the birds, it appears in the oddest places, usually as a large shrub or small tree. The 2- to 6-in.-long leaves have eight to ten, deeply impressed vein pairs, resulting in a corrugated appearance. Flowers, inconspicuous yellowish green, open in spring, followed by the ⅓-in.-wide globose, red to black fruit. Prefers shady, moist soils but is quite adaptable. Worthy naturalizing species, particularly in the understory. Simply not well known but rivals a good deciduous holly in rich red fruit. Grows 10 to 15 ft. high and wide. Zones 5 to 9. New York to Florida, west to Nebraska and Texas.

Franklinia alatamaha

franklinia, Franklin tree

Originally found by John Bartram along the banks of the Altamaha River in Georgia in 1770 and last sighted in the wild in about 1790, *Franklinia alatamaha* has perhaps engendered more folklore than any shrub or small tree. Bartram's foresight resulted in a most handsome and somewhat persnickety landscape plant. The branching pattern is upright-spreading, giving the plant an open, airy appearance. The smooth gray bark is broken by irregular vertical fissures. The 5- to 6-in.-long, lustrous dark green leaves turn orange and red in fall. Five-petaled, fragrant, white, yellow-stamened flowers, 3 in. in diameter, open from late July into August, with a smattering in September. Transplant from a container into acid, organic-laden, moist, well-drained soils. Poorly drained soils generally prove lethal. Use as an accent or specimen, or in borders.

Frangula caroliniana, Carolina buckthorn

Frangula caroliniana

Franklinia alatamaha fall color

Frangula caroliniana

Grows 10 to 20 (to 30) ft. high, 6 to 15 ft. wide. Zones 5 to 8. Georgia.

Related is the exciting intergeneric (with *Gordonia*) hybrid, ×*Gordlinia grandiflora*, by Dr. Tom Ranney, North Carolina State University. Large, 3-in.-wide

Franklinia alatamaha

×*Gordlinia grandiflora* winter color

Franklinia alatamaha

flowers, lustrous dark green leaves, red-purple winter color, vigorous constitution. Time will tell its garden worthiness. Another intergeneric hybrid, ×*Schimlinia floribunda* (*Franklinia alatamaha* × *Schima argentea*), was also engineered by Dr. Ranney.

Fraxinus
ash

About 65 species, with opposite, largely pinnately compound leaves, dioecious flowers, samara-type fruit, yellow to red-maroon fall color, and cultural adaptability. Sounds terrific until I mention the emerald ash borer that decimated native ash stands in Michigan and is creeping into neighboring states. Ash sales declined as much as 80 percent and, to date, essentially no resistance resides in the genus. The borer situation is acute in the North; to date less so in the South, but has shrouded the future of ash tree planting in a dense fog.

Fraxinus americana
white ash

This wide-ranging, eastern North American species appears to reach its greatest development in fertile midwestern soils, but it is just as likely to occur on a rocky slope in Connecticut or in an overgrown field in Georgia. Young trees are irregularly pyramidal to upright-oval, and with maturity become rounded. The compound pinnate leaves contain five to nine dark green, 2- to 6-in.-long, ovate leaflets. In fall, the leaves turn rich shades of yellow to reddish purple and almost maroon. The pattern of fall coloration is fascinating: at the extremities of the canopy the color is often reddish purple, and it grades to yellow toward the center. The grayish brown bark is ridged and furrowed into close, diamond-shaped patterns. Performs best in deep, moist, well-drained soils of varying pH. Scale and borer can be

MORE ▶

Fraxinus americana, white ash

Fraxinus americana CONTINUED

problems. A splendid large shade tree. Give ample room to develop. Grows 50 to 80 ft. high, similar spread. Zones 3 to 9. Nova Scotia to Minnesota, south to Florida and Texas.

CULTIVARS AND VARIETIES

'Autumn Purple' has beautiful, lustrous dark green foliage that turns red to reddish purple in the fall. Environment plays a significant role in the expression of fall color: in Maine, it is knockout red; in Athens, Georgia, it is significantly less intense.

Northern Blaze® ('Jefnor') develops an oval crown, 50 to 60 ft. by 25 to 30 ft., mid-green leaves turn purple in fall; the hardiest white ash, zone 3.

Fraxinus ornus
flowering ash

Better adapted to West Coast conditions and into British Columbia, where it is utilized in street tree plantings. Round-headed with smooth gray bark, unlike most ash, it also surprises with fragrant, showy white flower panicles above the foliage in May and June (Boston). Leaves, dull dark green, composed of five to nine leaflets, seldom develop appreciable fall color, although yellow to purple-tinted is mentioned. Adaptable, particularly to calcareous, high pH soils in full sun. Where suitable, a pretty, medium-sized, flowering tree. Grows 40 to 50 ft. high and wide. Zones 5

and 6. Southeastern Europe, western Asia.

Fraxinus pennsylvanica
green ash

A major reason for the widespread popularity of this species is its unbelievable native range. Landscapes in the West, Midwest, and East cannot escape the clutches of this everyman's tree. Its tolerance of hot, dry, sweeping winds, wet and dry soils, and high pH environments makes it universally functional. As a young tree, the habit is irregularly pyramidal; with age it becomes upright-spreading, with several large main branches and many coarse, twiggy branchlets, which

Fraxinus americana

Fraxinus ornus

Fraxinus americana 'Autumn Purple'

Fraxinus ornus, flowering ash

bend down and then up at the ends. More or less oval to rounded in outline at maturity. Summer leaf color is variable, from medium to dark green. Respectable to superb yellow fall color. Each leaf is composed of five to nine lustrous, 2- to 5-in.-long leaflets. Female trees bear 1- to 2-in.-long, ¼-in.-wide fruit (samaras), which can become a nuisance. Use as a street tree or in lawns, parks, commercial plantings, or planters. Displays excellent heat and cold tolerance, but plants can contract borer and scale. The emerald ash borer has largely turned this species and *Fraxinus americana* into firewood. Grows 50 to 60 ft. high, variable spread. Zones 3 to 9. Nova Scotia to Manitoba, south to northern Florida and Texas.

CULTIVARS AND VARIETIES

Georgia Gem™ ('Oconee') was discovered by the author growing in a sandbar in McNutt's Creek, which separates Clarke and Oconee counties in Georgia. Softly pyramidal-rounded, large shiny green leaflets, yellow fall color, fast-growing. First green ash selection of southern provenance. Performing well in Athens and Augusta, Georgia, and Spartanburg, South Carolina.

'Marshall's Seedless' is a male form with glossy dark green foliage, good yellow fall color, and no fruit.

MORE ▶

Fraxinus pennsylvanica, green ash, fall color

Fraxinus pennsylvanica Georgia Gem™

Fraxinus ornus

Fraxinus pennsylvanica 'Summit' fall color

317

Fraxinus pennsylvanica CONTINUED

Common but confused in the trade. Observed so-termed trees with variable habits and prodigious fruit.

'Patmore' is a hardier male selection, with upright branching and a more uniform outline than 'Marshall's Seedless'.

'Summit' produces a central leader, displays better growth habit than 'Marshall's Seedless', and has good yellow fall color and no fruit. From Summit Nursery, Stillwater, Minnesota.

Fraxinus quadrangulata
blue ash

One of the most beautiful ash species with seven to 11 (occasionally five), lustrous dark green leaflets, each 2 to 5 in. long, changing to pale yellow in autumn. The habit is narrow-rounded, often irregular with a crown of spreading branches. Bark is gray-brown and broken into irregular scaly plates.

Inner bark contains a mucilaginous substance that turns blue on exposure to air, hence, the common name. Stems are four-sided, slightly winged, squarish. Native in well-drained soils and found on limestone outcrops and in rich valleys. I always considered this among the most beautiful of the ashes. Unfortunately, nowhere is it common in commerce. In Georgia trials, it was considerably slow-growing compared to *Fraxinus pennsylvanica* Georgia Gem™ and *F. caroliniana*. Grows 50 to 70 ft. high and as wide. National champion is 120 ft. by 132 ft. Zones 4 to 7. Michigan to Arkansas and Tennessee.

Fuchsia magellanica
hardy fuchsia

Although nowhere common in zones 7 to 10, this small to medium-sized shrub produces an attractive arrangement of pendulous red flowers in sum-

mer. The habit is oval-rounded with slender branches clothed in lustrous dark green, ¾- to 2-in.-long, prominently toothed leaves. The beautiful flowers, solitary or paired and originating from the leaf axils in summer, average 2 in. long and range from deep crimson to occasionally white or pale pink. The red-purple, ¾-in.-long, oblong fruit are seldom produced on plants that I have observed. Best performance in moist, well-drained soils and cooler air temperatures. Almost weed-like in Ireland, England, and continental Europe, and one of the most asked about plants during our garden tours. Great border and container plant. Have tried to cultivate in Athens with the idea of breeding superior flower colors but could not keep the plant alive. Grows 2 to 10 ft. high and wide. Zones 7 to 9, 10 on the West Coast. Chile, Argentina.

Fraxinus quadrangulata, blue ash

Fraxinus quadrangulata

Fraxinus quadrangulata

Galphimia gracilis

syn. *Thryallis glauca*

shower of gold, spray of gold

During a walk in Orlando, Florida, I went (almost) crazy trying to identify this evergreen shrub, which was endowed with bright yellow flowers in October. A utilitarian, rounded shrub that is used in foundations, groupings, and mass plantings in central Florida and south. Leaves, opposite, gray-green, to 2 in. long, turn reddish pur-ple in winter. The ½- to 1-in.-wide, yellow flowers open throughout the warm periods. Each flower is composed of five, free-clawed, bright yellow petals surrounding the ten, red, stalked stamens. Requires full sun and well-drained soil. Easily pruned and maintained. Flowers on new growth, so removing old flowers encourages new shoot development. Grows 4 to 6 ft. high and wide. Zones 9 to 11. Central America.

Gardenia jasminoides

syn. *Gardenia augusta*

gardenia, cape jasmine

Fortuitous that this prose is penned just after sniffing a double-flowered gardenia in the garden. Powerful, heady aroma, equatable with a walk through the perfume section of a major department store. Wow! For the better half of May into June, sporadically thereafter, waxy, white flowers twinkle in the garden and cast their floral fragrance for meters. Shiny, dark green leaves, either opposite or in threes, grace the lustrous green stems. The entire evergreen shrub, oval-rounded to rounded in outline, is elegant. Each flower, 2 to 3 (to 4) in. wide, with six (occasionally seven) wedge-shaped petals, lasts a brief time and ages to yellow. Fruit are 1- to 1½-in.-long, six-winged (ridged), fleshy berries that color a beautiful rich orange in November and persist into

MORE ▶

Fuchsia magellanica, hardy fuchsia

Fuchsia magellanica

Galphimia gracilis, shower of gold

Galphimia gracilis

Gardenia jasminoides, gardenia, double form

Gardenia jasminoides

Gardenia jasminoides

Gardenia jasminoides Pinwheel™

Gardenia jasminoides Crown Jewel™

winter. Seeds are readily extracted and will germinate upon sowing. Have observed plants prospering in shade and sun. Tolerant of dry soils; intolerant of wet soils. Whiteflies and scale can be bothersome. Bonnie and I grew four different cultivars and have never had any problems. Makes a good container plant, shrub border component, entrance plant. Grows 4 to 6 ft. high and wide. Zones 7 to 10. China, Taiwan, Japan.

CULTIVARS AND VARIETIES
Numerous, embracing such double-flowered forms as 'Aimee Yoshida', 'August Beauty', 'Billie Holiday', 'Chuck Hayes' (semi-double), 'Fortuniana', 'Michael', and 'Mystery'. Single, hardier forms include 'Daisy', 'Daruma', 'Grif's Select', 'Kleim's Hardy', 'Shooting Star', and 'White Gem'.

Crown Jewel™ is a cold hardy double that flowers in May and June without any significant reflowering.

Jubilation™ is a double-flowered, reblooming type, 3 to 4 ft. high and wide.

'Radicans' is a compact rounded form, 1 to 2 ft. high, with 1- to 2-in.-wide double white flowers. Not particularly cold hardy, wet soils are anathema, and 10 to 15°F results in leaf injury.

'Radicans Variegata' has restrained cream-margined leaves that often revert to the species type. Same liabilities as 'Radicans'.

Since the mid 1980s I have been breeding for cold hardiness, superior foliage, compactness, reblooming, and the pretty orange fruit. Heaven Scent™ ('Madga 1') and Pinwheel™ meet these criteria. The former is more upright with small, lustrous dark green leaves and supernumerary flowers; the latter rounded, 3 ft. by 4 ft., with larger flowers, 2½ to 2¾ in. across, larger lustrous dark green leaves, and excellent cold hardiness.

Garrya elliptica
wavyleaf silktassel

Evergreen shrub native to the West Coast and amenable to culture only there. The lustrous dark green leaves, 2 to 2½ in. long, have undulating margins, and woolly undersides. Typically an 8- to 10-ft.-high and -wide shrub but may develop small-tree stature, 20 to 30 ft. high. The ornamental aspect is the male flower, yellowish to

MORE ▶

Garrya elliptica, wavyleaf silktassel

Garrya elliptica

Garrya elliptica

Garrya elliptica CONTINUED

greenish gray, 3 to 8 in. long, opening in winter. Adaptable as long as soil is well drained. Sun to partial shade. Beautiful foliage and intriguing flowers. Useful in mass plantings, borders, and hedges. Prune after flowering. Have yet to witness on East Coast. Relatively common in England. Zone 8. Pacific Coast Range from southwest Oregon to southern California.

Gaultheria mucronata

syn. *Pernettya mucronata*
Suitable only to the West Coast of the United States, but what a stunner! My first introduction occurred at Royal Botanic Garden Edinburgh, where these wiry-stemmed, evergreen shrubs with small, sharp-pointed, glossy dark green leaves, were studded with marble-sized berries in gorgeous high-definition colors of white, pink, rose, red, and purple. Fruit are often blushed and not a solid color.

Flowers are white, heath-like, and produced in great quantities. Requires well-drained soil and sun. For maximum fruiting, mix clones for improved cross-pollination. Excellent massing plant; 2 to 3 ft. high and wide. Zones 7 to 9 on West Coast. Chile to Magellan Region.

CULTIVARS AND VARIETIES
Numerous introductions for fruit color. 'Wisley Pearl' (*Gaultheria* ×*wisleyensis*), a hybrid (*G. shallon* × *G. mucronata*), produces larger leaves and deep purple fruit. On the West Coast, withstood −12°F with minimal injury.

Gaultheria procumbens
checkerberry, wintergreen

A low-growing, 6-in.-high, creeping, evergreen groundcover, the leaves lustrous dark green, turning reddish with the touch of low temperatures. Bruised or crushed leaves emit a wintergreen fragrance. Perfect, pinkish white flowers, ¼ in. long, nodding,

solitary, occur in May through September. Fruit are the real deal: red, usually ⅜ in. long in the typical species, with superior selections producing giant marble-sized fruit that persist through winter. Culturally, acid, moist, high-organic-matter soils in full sun to partial shade prove optimum. Utilized on Georgia campus in heavy wet soils where it could not perish fast enough. Zones 3 to 5. Newfoundland to Manitoba, south to Georgia and Michigan.

Gaylussacia brachycera
box huckleberry

An unknown treasure among the broadleaf evergreens, box huckleberry offers lustrous dark green foliage that turns deep bronze to reddish purple in winter. The habit is low, mounded, almost suckering, and with time, large colonies are formed. One stand in Pennsylvania covered 300 acres and was estimated to be over 12,000 years old. Urn-shaped, white to pink,

Gaultheria mucronata

Gaultheria mucronata

Gaultheria procumbens, checkerberry

Gaylussacia brachycera, box huckleberry

¼-in.-long flowers open in May and June. Leaves are ⅓ to 1 in. long. Provide acid, organic-laden, well-drained soils and partial shade. Plants will grow in full sun. Use in combination with other ericaceous plants. Grows 6 to 18 in. high, spreads indefinitely. Zones 5 to 7. Pennsylvania to Virginia, Kentucky, and Tennessee.

Gaylussacia ursina
bear huckleberry

Huckleberries are not the easiest members of the Ericaceae to identify, but this 2½- to 5-ft.-high suckering shrub is the one I encounter most often during my hikes through north Georgia. Forms low thickets, suckering in all directions, of rather nondescript medium green leaves, 2 to 4 in. long, with tiny resinous dots on the lower leaf surface. The fall color is beautiful; leaves turn reddish purple, the effect lasting long into the season. The small rose flowers are mixed with the foliage and not greatly effective. The ⅓-in.-wide shiny black drupe ripens in late summer. Grows in acid soils, often rocky, dry, and well drained. Have observed only in the shade in the wild. Great naturalizing plant. Zones 6 and 7. Tennessee, North Carolina, and Georgia.

Gelsemium sempervirens
Carolina yellow jessamine

The Head Gardener turns the light switch on in late March and April in the Southeast, for shrubs and trees are crawling with this glowing yellow-flowered vine, evergreen and twining, that appears to embrace every structure, yet never smothers a plant

MORE ▶

Gaylussacia ursina, bear huckleberry

Gaylussacia ursina

Gaylussacia ursina fall color

Gelsemium sempervirens, Carolina yellow jessamine

Gelsemium sempervirens CONTINUED
like kudzu or wisteria. The shiny green leaves are 1 to 3½ in. long and may discolor (yellow) in winter sun. The 1½-in.-long, 1-in.-wide, funnel-formed, fragrant, yellow flowers are effective for a full month, opening from February into April across the South, depending on the return of warm temperatures. Grows in any well-drained soil in sun to partial shade. Used on trellises, walls (with support), mailboxes, and as a groundcover. Beautiful early spring flowering vine. Grows 10 to 20 ft. on structures. Zones 6 to 9, probably to 10 and 11. Virginia to Florida westward to Texas and Arkansas, south to Central America.

Gelsemium rankinii, swamp jessamine, differs from *G. sempervirens* by flowering in fall and spring and having no floral fragrance. Also grows in swamps in North Carolina to Florida to Louisiana. Zones 7 to 9.

CULTIVARS AND VARIETIES
Lemon Drop™ ('Conrop') is more compact with shrub-like habit and softer yellow flowers.

'Pale Yellow' has cream-yellow flowers, larger than the type but not as cold hardy. Florida provenance, zone 8 and higher. From Woodlanders, Aiken, South Carolina.

'Pride of Augusta' produces double yellow flowers with the appearance of miniature rose buds.

Genista lydia

This low-growing groundcover species has become quite popular, particularly in the West and Northeast. It forms a prostrate, small-leaved (⅜ in. long), dark olive-green carpet. The stems are four- to five-angled. In May and June, bright yellow flowers explode from each node to form a sea of gold. A great plant for rock walls and dry, sandy pockets. Requires full sun for best flowering. Grows 6 to 12 in. high.

Zones 6 to 8(9). Southeastern Europe, western Asia.

Genista pilosa
silkyleaf woadwaxen
Silkyleaf woadwaxen offers grayish green leaves and bright yellow flowers that appear in 2- to 6-in.-long racemes. Reports indicate that this species is more reliable than *Genista lydia*. Grows 1 to 1½ ft. high. Zones 5 to 7(8). Europe.
CULTIVARS AND VARIETIES
'Vancouver Gold' is a heavy-flowering, golden yellow form. Grows 1 ft. high, 3 ft. wide.

Genista tinctoria
Dyer's greenwood
When adorned with bright yellow flowers in summer, *Genista tinctoria* stirs the soul and landscape imagination. During the rest of the year, the plant blends in with the woodwork. Develops into a wispy, rounded shrub with

Gelsemium sempervirens

Gelsemium rankinii, swamp jessamine

Gelsemium sempervirens 'Pale Yellow'

Gelsemium sempervirens 'Pride of Augusta'

Genista lydia

Genista pilosa, silkyleaf woadwaxen

Genista pilosa

slender, almost vertical, green stems and limited branching. The bright green, ½- to 1-in.-long leaves are sharp-pointed. Yellow, ½- to ¾-in.-long flowers occur in erect, 1- to 3-in.-long racemes in June (May, zone 7) and sporadically thereafter. Dead-head to allow new flowers to develop. Considered difficult to transplant; it should be container-grown and then

MORE ▶

Genista lydia

Genista tinctoria, Dyer's greenwood

Genista tinctoria

Genista tinctoria CONTINUED

transplanted to a permanent location. Performs best in dryish, well-drained soils and in full sun. Use where few other plants will provide summer color. Grows 2 to 3 ft. high and wide. Zones (4)5 to 7. Europe, western Asia.
CULTIVARS AND VARIETIES
'Flore Pleno' ('Plena') is a dwarf, semi-prostrate shrub with numerous petals of a brilliant yellow.

'Royal Gold' with golden yellow flowers in terminal and axillary racemes, erect stems. Grows about 2 ft. high.

Ginkgo biloba
ginkgo

The ginkgo has existed, unchanged, for millions of years on planet Earth. This long history and the plant's unique fan-shaped leaf make it perhaps the most widely recognized of all shade and ornamental trees. Every child who has ever made a leaf collection included a leaf from a ginkgo. In addition to its history, *Ginkgo biloba* has much to offer as an ornamental plant. In youth the habit is somewhat gaunt and open; with age it becomes full and dense, an imposing, beautiful specimen. Male and female flowers are borne on separate trees, and it often takes 20 years or more before flowers develop. Purchase male trees whenever possible; female trees can be quite objectionable—the orangish, 1- to 1½-in.-long, plum-like seeds drop to the ground and, when the outer flesh decomposes, give off a rancid butter odor that is the scourge of the neighborhood. The bright green, fan-shaped leaves, 2 to 3 in. long and wide, turn brilliant yellow in fall. If faced with a hard freeze, virtually all the leaves will cascade to the ground in a single day. Tolerates extremes of soil, except permanently wet. Great park or large-area tree. I have observed it from Minnesota to Florida and from Massachusetts to California, which provides some idea of its adaptability. Grows 50 to 80 ft. high, variable spread. Zones 4 to 9. China.
CULTIVARS AND VARIETIES
'Autumn Gold' is a handsome male form, broad-spreading in habit.

'Fastigiata' is an upright, columnar form, of which 'Princeton Sentry' is a

Ginkgo biloba, ginkgo, fall color

Ginkgo biloba 'Autumn Gold' fall color

Ginkgo biloba 'Princeton Sentry'

male selection. Observed seeds on this cultivar.

Golden Colonnade™ ('JFS-UGA2') is a narrow oval-columnar, male form with strongly ascending branches at a 45° angle to the central leader. Excellent yellow fall color, 45 ft. by 20 ft., introduced by the author.

Presidential Gold™ ('The President') has bright yellow fall color and an upright oval-rectangular outline, developing a full, denser habit at an early age; 60 ft. by 40 ft.; male; introduced by the author.

Gleditsia triacanthos f. *inermis*

thornless common honeylocust

A popular lawn and street tree in the Midwest and East, it offers a graceful habit and fine-textured leaves. Can be spectacular in fall when the ½-in.-long leaflets turn rich golden yellow. Usually develops a short trunk and an open, spreading crown with a delicate and sophisticated silhouette. The light shade it casts permits grass to grow next to the trunk. The bright green summer foliage is quite handsome, and in autumn the fallen leaflets sift their way through the grass and understory litter, requiring little raking. Most trees, however, produce brownish, 7-

Ginkgo biloba

MORE ▶

Ginkgo biloba Golden Colonnade™ fall color

Ginkgo biloba Presidential Gold™ fall color

327

Gleditsia triacanthos f. *inermis* CONTINUED to 8-in.-long pods, which drop off in fall and winter and create a mess. The cultivars do not produce as much fruit as the typical species. In the Midwest, webworm, mites, galls, and various cankers have wreaked havoc on a number of plantings. On the University of Illinois campus, many trees planted in the 1950s were removed in the 1980s because of these problems. Very adaptable to soils, and displays excellent salt tolerance. Grows 30 to 70 ft. high and wide. Zones 4 to 9. Pennsylvania to Nebraska, south to Mississippi and Texas.

CULTIVARS AND VARIETIES
'Majestic', 'Moraine', 'Shademaster', and 'Skyline' are superior to the species.

Northern Acclaim® ('Harve') is broad-pyramidal, more upright in youth, spreading with age. Yellow fall color, seedless, zone 3 adaptability, 45 ft. by 35 ft.

Street Keeper™ ('Draves') is a new broad-columnar introduction with a dominant leader, dark green foliage, 45 ft. by 18 ft. Has fruited on only two occasions. A photo I witnessed showed heavy fruit.

'Sunburst' offers golden yellow new foliage, which eventually matures to bright green.

Gordonia lasianthus
loblolly-bay

Native evergreen tree or shrub that grows in swamps but has a difficult time transitioning into garden culture.

Gleditsia triacanthos f. *inermis*, thornless common honeylocust, fall color

Gleditsia triacanthos f. *inermis* fall color

Gleditsia triacanthos f. *inermis*

In central Florida, nursery plants grew contentedly in the sandy soils, supplemented only by drip irrigation. The habit is pyramidal-conical, somewhat open, with 4- to 6-in.-long, glossy dark green leaves. Flowers open in late May and continue sporadically into October. Each flower is 2½ in. across, five-petaled, with a central mass of yellow stamens. In cultivation, does best in well-drained soils. Fickle, and plants on the Georgia campus have inexplicably died. Probably no mass commercial appeal but a pretty tree, resembling *Franklinia alatamaha* in flower. Abundant, appearing as pyramidal-columnar sentinels in Georgia's Okefenokee Swamp. Possibly 30 to 40 ft. high in cultivation, but generally

MORE ▶

Gordonia lasianthus, loblolly-bay

Gleditsia triacanthos f. *inermis* 'Moraine'

Gordonia lasianthus

Gleditsia triacanthos f. *inermis* 'Sunburst'

Gordonia lasianthus 'Variegata'

Gordonia lasianthus CONTINUED

doesn't live long enough under same. National champion in Florida is 102 ft. by 61 ft. Zones 7 to 9. Virginia to Florida to Louisiana.

CULTIVARS AND VARIETIES
'Variegata' has irregular creamy white margins that turn rose-pink in cold weather. This is a weak grower and needs protection from sun and wind to keep it looking good. Maintained for many years in the lath house at Georgia, where visitors would ask the identity. Once in the garden, it had no identity.

Grevillea robusta
silk oak

Tried to grow this in Athens but the first fall freeze deep-sixed any hopes. A warm-climate tree, picking up steam in central Florida and south. Beautiful soft pyramidal habit with fernlike leaves, gray-green above, silvery beneath, up to 12 in. long. Flowers, like many members of the Proteaceae, are showy by virtue of the stamens, in this case orange-yellow, in comblike, 4-in.-long racemes borne on short shoots in spring. Best in full sun and well-drained soil. Handsome specimen, shade, and street tree. Somewhat messy, with considerable leaf abscission in spring, sporadically thereafter. Grows 50 to 75 ft. high, about half as wide. Larger in its native haunts. Zones 9 to 11. Australia.

Grevillea rosmarinifolia, a needle-like evergreen shrub to 5 ft. high, produces lovely crimson-red flowers in spring and summer; 'Canberra Gem' is a vigorous, rounded shrub, 6 ft. by 8 ft. high and wide, with waxy bright rose-pink flowers, which open in March and April in Athens, beautiful lustrous dark green foliage, and refined texture. A yellow-flowered form, *G. juniperina* 'Sulfurea', is also available; the species has been successfully grown near Commerce, Georgia (zone 7). Provide well-drained soil on the dry side in full sun. Have killed many in containers. Zones 7 to 9. Australia.

Gymnocladus dioicus
Kentucky coffeetree

To know her is to love her. Among my top Noble Trees. A wonderful native species that tolerates the worst stresses nature and humanity can impose, yet it is nowhere very common in the landscape. As a young tree, the shape is irregular and the texture is coarse, especially in the winter months. The rich bluish green, bipinnately compound leaves, composed of 1½- to 3-in.-long leaflets, soon cover the blemishes of winter, however. Emerging leaves are pink to bronze-tinted, finishing the growing season with a cloud of yellow. With age the habit becomes more uniform, producing a picturesque, obovate crown of rugged branches.

MORE ▶

Grevillea robusta, silk oak

Grevillea rosmarinifolia 'Canberra Gem'

Grevillea juniperina 'Sulfurea'

Gymnocladus dioicus

330

Gymnocladus dioicus, Kentucky coffeetree

Gymnocladus dioicus

Gymnocladus dioicus

Gymnocladus dioicus

Gymnocladus chinensis

Gymnocladus dioicus 'Variegata'

Gymnocladus dioicus CONTINUED

Scaly, recurving ridges develop on the gray-brown bark and provide additional seasonal interest. Male and female flowers appear on separate trees. The females produce 5- to 10-in.-long, leathery, brownish black pods. The fruitless male trees are preferable, and they can be grown from root cuttings, grafting/budding, or through micropropagation (tissue culture). Kentucky coffeetree tolerates drought, city conditions, and a wide range of soils. Particularly well adapted to limestone soils. A superb tree for large-area use. Grows 60 to 75 ft. high, 40 to 50 ft. wide. Zones 4 to 8. New York to Minnesota, south to Tennessee and Oklahoma.

Gymnocladus chinensis is a beautiful, more refined tree, with smaller blue-green leaflets. A small specimen in the Keith Arboretum, Chapel Hill, North Carolina, provides incentive for me to test.

CULTIVARS AND VARIETIES

'Stately Manor' is a grand male selection. As I viewed it, 40 ft. by 35 ft. at the Minnesota Landscape Arboretum. Hardy in North Dakota. Best of the current male cultivars; others are Espresso™ ('Espresso-JFS') and Prairie Titan® ('J. C. McDaniel').

'Variegata' has cream-white leaflets and is slower growing.

Halesia carolina

syn. *Halesia tetraptera*

Carolina silverbell

A great tree for understory planting along stream banks, in the back of the shrub border, against a background of large conifers, or as a single specimen, yet not common in American gardens. The species develops a low-branched profile, often with several trunks, and forms a rounded crown. Single-trunked specimens are more pyramidal to oval in outline. The bark on young stems is brown and stringy, becoming gray with darker striations, and finally developing flattened, scaly ridges of gray, brown, and black colors. The dark yellowish green, 2- to 5-in.-long leaves seldom color spectacularly in fall, at best showing glimpses of muted yellow. In April and May, slightly before or with the leaves, ½- to 1-in.-long, white, bell-shaped flowers appear in clusters from the axils of the branches. The flowers, in a subtle, not boisterous way, are among the most beautiful of all flowering trees. The 1- to 1½-in.-long, ovoid fruit, with four distinct wings, ripen in September and October. Prefers cool, moist, acid, well-drained soils, in shade or sun. Will develop chlorosis in extremely high pH soils. Resists transplanting especially balled-and-burlapped material; utilize container-grown plants. Found along streams, on the banks above watercourses, and in sheltered coves throughout its native range. Grows 30 to 40 ft. high,

Halesia carolina, Carolina silverbell

Halesia carolina

Halesia carolina fall color

20 to 35 ft. wide; national champion is 116 ft. by 39 ft. Zones 5 to 8(9). West Virginia to Florida, west to eastern Texas.

CULTIVARS AND VARIETIES

'Lady Catherine' is the first weeping selection (semi-pendulous as I observed it) and, based on two years of evaluation, a must-have for the *Halesia* aficionado and other iconoclastic gardeners. Introduced by Dr. Ken Tilt, Auburn University, and named for his daughter.

'Rosea' (var. *rosea*) is a pink-flowered form of great beauty. The pink forms may crop up in seedling populations. Monitor the flowers before buying, because the pinkness varies from near white to almost rose. Cooler spring weather fosters deeper pink corollas. 'Arnold Pink' and 'Rosy Ridge' pink-flowered forms belong here, the latter introduced by Hawksridge Nursery, Hickory, North Carolina.

Halesia diptera
two-wing silverbell

A round-headed small to medium-sized tree, bearing white flowers with four deeply cut lobes and two-winged fruit. Leaves broader than *Halesia carolina*, and fall color often a pleasing yellow; otherwise similar to Carolina silverbell in its traits, including its resistance to transplanting. Very delicate in flower and certainly worth considering when available. Difficult to propagate from cuttings, so grafting or seed is the only choice. Grows 20 to 30 ft. high; 50-ft.-high specimens are known. Zones 5 to 9. South Carolina and Tennessee to Florida and Texas.

CULTIVARS AND VARIETIES

Variety *magniflora* produces more abundant and larger flowers than the species, as seen in 'Southern Snow', a magnificent medium-sized tree introduction from Don Shadow.

Hamamelis
witchhazel

Flowering in Athens as I put these letters on paper: Bonnie and I walked the University's Botanical Garden on Sunday, February 21, 2010, where 'Jelena' (coppery, fragrant) and 'Palida' (soft sulfur-yellow, sweetly fragrant) were in regal flower. Pleasant,

MORE ▶

Halesia carolina 'Rosea'

Halesia diptera var. *magniflora*

Halesia diptera, two-wing silverbell

Halesia diptera var. *magniflora* 'Southern Snow'

sunny, 68°F day, and the fragrance wafted. Great plants and so many wonderful choices, but few customers are in the garden centers to purchase them. A dilemma, to be sure. Every garden *needs* a witchhazel. Allow me to show and tell . . .

Quite adaptable plants, with minimal expectations of well-drained, preferably acid soils, full sun to partial shade. Flower on old wood, initiating in fall through late winter, depending on the species. Chris Lane's *Witch Hazels* (2005) is an excellent reference.

Hamamelis ×intermedia

With such a pedigree—this is a hybrid between *Hamamelis japonica* and *H. mollis*—it is obvious why the offspring are so handsome. For color in the winter garden, this group of hybrids ranks among the best shrubs. The soft yellow to bronzy red flowers occur in clusters of two to four, each bud opening to expose four strap-shaped, often slightly twisted petals from January to March, depending on the cultivar. Flowers persist for as long as one month and resist the vagaries of the winter weather. Most are wonderfully fragrant, an attribute that makes them useful near trafficked areas. The 2- to 4-in.-long, dark green to blue-green leaves are intermediate between those of the parents. In fall, the foliage develop gorgeous yellow to deep red tints. Transplant container- or field-grown plants into moist, organic-laden, well-drained soils. Appears quite pH adaptable. Maximum flowering is achieved in full sun, but will produce a reliable show in partial shade. Plants are much slower growing in hot, dry, exposed locations. Great element for the shrub border, or as an artistic specimen, combined with a dark green groundcover-like *Pachysandra*, *Sarcococca hookeriana* var. *humilis*, or *Vinca minor*. Grows 10 to 20 ft. high and wide. Zones 5 to 8.

CULTIVARS AND VARIETIES
Cultivars are variable in habit, ranging from broad-spreading to upright vase-shaped. Most are grafted, and the understock, usually *Hamamelis vernalis* or *H. virginiana*, may sucker and overgrow the scion. Be observant and remove the basal shoots.

'Angelly' produces abundant, clear light yellow flowers with a faint fragrance in late February and March. Bright yellow fall color; vigorous upright-spreading habit. Among the most beautiful. Raised in the Netherlands.

'Arnold Promise' is one of the best, oldest, and deservedly most popular cultivars. Its fragrant flowers, bright yellow with a reddish calyx cup, appear in February and March. Fall color is a rich yellow to orange-apricot. Grows

Hamamelis ×intermedia 'Arnold Promise'

Hamamelis ×intermedia 'Arnold Promise' fall color

Hamamelis ×intermedia 'Barmstedt Gold'

Hamamelis ×intermedia 'Birgit'

over 20 ft. high. Raised at the Arnold Arboretum and named in 1963.

'Barmstedt Gold' has sweetly fragrant, rich golden yellow flowers, suffused with red at the base, in late January and February. Vigorous shrub with narrowly ascending branches; yellow fall color. Excellent and consistent for flower production.

'Birgit' has slightly shorter red-purple petals and a dark purple calyx cup. Overall effect is dark red. Slight scent.

'Diane' is red, actually deep bronzy red, with faint fragrance. Habit is medium-spreading. Old leaves may persist and require removal to maximize flower effect. A 35-year-old plant in Oregon was approximately 14 ft. by 15 ft.

'Jelena' is a great favorite of mine because of its strong horizontal habit and coppery colored, fragrant flowers. Excellent yellow-orange-red fall color. A 35-year-old plant in Oregon was 12 ft. by 15 ft.

'Pallida' is an early-flowering form with soft sulfur-yellow, sweetly scented flowers. Reddish purple calyx cup. Probably not as large as 'Arnold Promise' at maturity, and better suited to smaller gardens. Another of my favorites.

'Primavera' has flowers that are primrose-yellow, stained purple-red at base, glossy wine-red calyx, and a sweet scent. It is exceedingly floriferous in late January and February. A

MORE ▶

Hamamelis ×intermedia 'Pallida'

Hamamelis ×intermedia 'Diane'

Hamamelis ×intermedia 'Jelena'

Hamamelis ×intermedia 'Rubin'

Hamamelis ×intermedia 'Sunburst'

Hamamelis ×intermedia CONTINUED
wide-spreading shrub with yellow fall
color.

'Rubin', with red petals, red-purple
calyx, faint fragrance, is the truest red
I have experienced; however, a plant
at RHS Garden, Wisley, was more cop-
per-orange than red.

'Sunburst' produces abundant
lemon-yellow, largely scentless flowers
in January and February; petals up to
1 in. long, $\frac{1}{12}$ in. wide, wine-red calyx
cup. Vase-shaped habit, vigorous
grower, 10 to 15 ft. high.

Hamamelis japonica
Japanese witchhazel

I have seen this large, spreading
shrub with criss-crossing, architecturally sculptured branches in European
gardens but only sporadically in America. It is much wider spreading than
Hamamelis mollis or *H. ×intermedia*
and requires ample room. The flowers
have thin, wrinkled-crinkled petals
and appear in February and March.
Color ranges from yellow to coppery
red, with a deep purple calyx cup. Fragrance is generally not as potent as

Hamamelis japonica, Japanese witchhazel

Hamamelis japonica 'Superba'

Hamamelis mollis, Chinese witchhazel

Hamamelis mollis fall color

that of *H. mollis* or the better *H. ×inter-media* forms. This species is probably too large and too florally inferior to compete with the other types for average landscape use, but a large specimen in full flower is a sight to appreciate. Grows 10 to 15 ft. high and wide. Zones 5 to 8. Japan.

CULTIVARS AND VARIETIES
'Superba' produces bright yellow crinkled petals, claret sepal cup. Awe-inspiring specimen, 15 ft. by 30 ft., at the RHS Garden, Wisley.

Hamamelis mollis
Chinese witchhazel

In late January, this is often the first Asian witchhazel to spread its petals. It is a robust, rounded, densely branched shrub, with dull dark green, 3 to 6 in. long, 2 to 5 in. wide, roundish leaves that are covered with grayish, woolly pubescence on their undersides. (The other species included here are sparingly pubescent.) Fall color is vivid yellow to almost orange-yellow. Flowers are often bright yellow with a reddish brown calyx cup and

extremely fragrant. Culture is as for *Hamamelis ×intermedia*. Grows 10 to 15 (to 20) ft. high and wide. Zones 5 to 8. Central China.

CULTIVARS AND VARIETIES
'Early Bright', with bright yellow flowers that open three to four weeks ahead of the species (mid January in Swarthmore, Pennsylvania). Parent plant, 15 ft. high and wide, was 37 years old.

'Goldcrest' produces large, fat, rich golden yellow petals suffused claret at base; sweetly scented. Spectacular yellow-gold fall color. Wide vase-shaped habit, 8 to 10 ft. high.

Hamamelis vernalis
vernal witchhazel

This fine native shrub pales by floral comparison with *Hamamelis mollis*, but it offers several desirable ornamental traits. The habit is mounded-rounded, often suckering and coloniz-

MORE ▶

Hamamelis vernalis, vernal witchhazel, fall color

Hamamelis vernalis

Hamamelis vernalis

Hamamelis vernalis 'Sandra' fall color

Hamamelis vernalis CONTINUED

ing. The 2- to 5-in.-long, dark green leaves turn rich butter-yellow to golden yellow in autumn. The pungently fragrant flowers, each petal about ½ in. long, are the smallest of the species discussed here. Color varies from yellow and orange to red, and the flowers open in January and February. A great plant for massing, naturalizing, or grouping, in quite moist or dry soils. A tough plant with an alley-cat tenacity. Grows 6 to 10 ft. high, generally wider at maturity. Zones 4 to 8. Missouri to Louisiana and Oklahoma.

CULTIVARS AND VARIETIES
'Amethyst', with abundant light purple flowers, is a distinctly different color.

'Sandra' produces yellow-tinged-orange, fragrant flowers. Excellent orange-red fall color. Color is best expressed in cold climates. My experiences in zone 7 reflect minimalist fall color. Plant at Hillier was 18 ft. by 15 ft. Discovered there in a seedling population by propagator Peter Dummer in 1962.

Hamamelis virginiana
common witchhazel

Another wonderful native plant that displays excellent climatic and cultural adaptability. In the wild, *Hamamelis virginiana* is often found as an understory plant in moist soils along stream banks, but I have also found it on drier hillsides and mountainsides. Forms a large, multi-stemmed shrub or a small tree, with several crooked, spreading, gray-brown branches. The 3- to 6-in.-long, medium to dark green leaves turn handsome yellow in autumn. Fragrant yellow flowers appear from October to as late as December. Unfortunately, fall foliage color develops as the flowers open, and much of the floral effect is lost. Use like the previous

Hamamelis virginiana, common witchhazel

Hamamelis virginiana fall color

Hamamelis virginiana 'Lemon Lime'

338

species, although this shrub is much more massive than *H. vernalis*. Grows 15 to 20 (to 30) ft. high and wide. Zones 3 to 8(9). Canada to Georgia, west to Nebraska and Arkansas.
CULTIVARS AND VARIETIES
'Green Thumb' and 'Lemon Lime' are variegated selections: the first with 3 in. by 1¾ in., yellow-margined, green-blotched leaves and pale sulfur-yellow flowers, 8 ft. by 8 ft.; the second with delicately beautiful normal-sized leaves, speckled light yellow, light green, and green. Introduced by Hidden Hollow Nursery, Belvidere, Tennessee.

'Harvest Moon' flowers about two weeks later than the typical species; the flowers lemon-yellow, fragrant, showier than the type. Yellow fall color; 18 ft. high after 15 years. From Broken Arrow Nursery, Hamden, Connecticut.

Hebe
shrubby veronica
Essentially unknown in eastern U.S. gardens (I tested several taxa and all succumbed) but successfully cultured on the West Coast. During my many European garden tours, they were relatively common elements, thriving with little maintenance. From evergreen groundcovers to medium-sized shrubs to the occasional tree, the variation in characteristics is remarkable. Many produce racemose, white, pink, and deep purple-blue flowers from spring into late summer. Over 100 species and many hybrids; the *RHS Plant Finder 2010* lists over 500 taxa, primarily cultivars. Well-drained soil, full sun, avoiding excess moisture are keys to success. *Phytophthora*, *Fusarium*, and *Verticillium* species cause root rot and dieback. Zones 9 and 10 on West Coast. New Zealand, a few species in Australia and South America. *Hebes* (2006) by Lawrie Metcalf provides in-depth information.

Hedera canariensis
Algerian ivy
Another ivy, but not just another ivy. Large glossy dark green leaves with red petioles rise 8 to 10 in. above the ground to form a beautiful groundcover carpet. The leaves are 2 to 6 (to 8) in. long. Prefers partial shade and moist, organic, well-drained soil. Excellent salt tolerance. Have witnessed terrific injury (kill) to plantings on the coast of Georgia after exposure to 11°F. Best above 20°F. Excellent groundcover plant for warmer climates. Grows 10 to 20 ft. or more on a tree or structure. Zones 9 and 10. Canary Islands, Madeira, the Azores, Portugal, and northwest Africa.

Hebe, shrubby veronica

Hedera canariensis, Algerian ivy

Hebe foliage and flower

Hedera colchica

Colchis ivy

I consider this one of the most beautiful ivies; could be likened to English ivy on Kickapoo Joy Juice, as it has a more robust constitution. The leathery dark green evergreen leaves are 3 to 7 in. across. Observed many times in Europe; in a test planting at Griffin, Georgia, in full sun, it performed magnificently. Grows 6 to 8 in. high, spreading indefinitely. Will also climb structures. Zones (6)7 to 9, possibly 10 on West Coast. Caspian Sea region, Caucasus to Asiatic Turkey.

CULTIVARS AND VARIETIES
'Dentata Variegata' has a cream-white-margined leaf and performed well in the Dirr garden.

Hedera helix

English ivy

Without equivocation, English ivy is one of the dominant groundcovers, but it also produces a viny green covering on trees and structures—another invasive species poster child. It will climb trees to great heights, as high as 90 ft., but does not grow over and shade the foliage like kudzu. The three- to five-lobed, 1½- to 4-in.-long, maple-like evergreen leaves are lustrous dark green with lighter colored veins. As the plant ascends, the leaves mature and lose the distinct lobing and the veinal mosaic pattern. In this adult stage, greenish white flowers develop in September and October, followed by ¼-in.-wide, blackish fruit. English ivy prefers shade and moist, well-drained soils, but it is remarkably adaptable. The plant faces no serious problems, although mites and bacterial leaf spot crop up occasionally. Zones 5 to 9. Caucasus Mountains.

Hedera colchica, Colchis ivy

Hedera colchica 'Dentata Variegata'

Hedera helix, English ivy

Hedera helix vines encrusting a tree trunk

CULTIVARS AND VARIETIES
See www.ivy.org for the many available. Check with a local nursery for those best adapted in a given area. 'Baltica', 'Bulgaria', 'Thorndale', and 'Wilson' are reasonably cold hardy selections.

Helianthemum nummularium
sunrose
Smallish wee-plants, with no charisma until they burst forth with white, yellow, orange, and red flowers, like starburst fireworks. Witnessing their beauty is the lure that entices the gardener to take the bait. I succumbed and have little to show for trying except the knowledge that heat and humidity wreak havoc. A small spreading evergreen, almost groundcover-like, is covered with 1-in.-wide, single or double flowers in May and June. Flowers persist for a month. Individual open flowers last but a day, but buds are produced by the hundreds, even on small plants. Leaves, ½ to 1 in. long, vary from dark green above, grayish below, to gray on both surfaces. Requires well-drained soil on the dry side, preferably in low to moderately fertile soils, slightly acid to neutral in full sun. A common rock garden or wall plant where drainage is excellent. Numerous cultivars are available in European commerce. Remove spent flowers to encourage new foliage. Grows 6 to 12 in. high, 2 to 3 ft. wide

in rather uniform circles. Zones (7)8 to 10 on the West Coast. Mediterranean region.

Heptacodium miconioides
seven-son flower
Introduced from China by the Sino-American Botanical Expedition in 1980, this shrub was, for a time, the horticultural rage in the Northeast, and the Arnold Arboretum did more than any other agency to popularize the species. A handsome plant, but one that I initially was not enamored of. After observing it over several years, however, I planted one in the Georgia garden. The habit is multi-stemmed and upright-spreading with a cloud-like canopy. The 3- to 4-in.-long, dark green leaves emerge early in spring, around mid to late April, and persist into November, but they do not develop appreciable fall color. The bark exfoliates to expose ash-cream to light brown underbark. Pale, creamy white, fragrant flowers are borne on seven-tiered panicles from August into October. The real show occurs in October and November when the

MORE ▶

Helianthemum nummularium, sunrose

Heptacodium miconioides, seven-son flower

Helianthemum nummularium double form

341

Heptacodium miconioides CONTINUED
calyces (sepals) turn reddish—the
effect is spectacular and long lasting.
Best growth occurs in moist soils and
full sun, but the species is adaptable
to dry, acid soils and at least semi-
shade. Use as an accent, in shrub borders, or in groupings. Grows 10 to 20
ft. high, slightly less in spread. Zones
(4)5 to 8. China.

Heptacodium miconioides

Heptacodium miconioides

Heptacodium miconioides

Hibiscus mutabilis
Confederate rose
This large, oafy, coarse-stemmed,
rounded shrub appears in late summer, almost like a mushroom after a
rainstorm. What is truly remarkable
is the dieback (herbaceous) nature of
the species and its spirited growth in
a single season, resulting in a large,
rounded form. Plants in Athens, Georgia, have reached 10 to 12 ft. high. The
three- to seven-lobed, 4- to 10-in.-long,
dark green leaves serve as the perfect
foil for the 1½- to 3- (to 4-) in.-wide,
five-petaled white, aging to pink, rose,
and red, flowers. Flowers initiate on
new growth in summer and continue
until hard frosts. Fruit are hairy, subglobose, 1-in.-wide capsules with rounded
seeds. Ideally, remove capsules to
keep plants in active growth. Prefers
moist, well-drained, fertile soils in full
sun to maximize growth. May require
supplemental fertilizer during active
growth to maintain good green foliage
color and flower production. Lovely for
flower color in perennial and shrub borders. Could be used as a specimen
plant but takes on the appearance of

a large bundle of gray-brown sticks
in winter. Grows 8 to 10 ft. high and
wide. Zones 7 to 10(11). China.
CULTIVARS AND VARIETIES
Variety *flore-pleno*, the double form
with cottonball-shaped flowers,
inspired the common name.

Hibiscus rosa-sinensis
Chinese hibiscus
Strictly a herbaceous perennial in
zone 8, becoming above-ground woody
about central Florida into the Keys
and on lower West Coast. Shrub or
small tree, often used for container
planting in the North or in conservatories. Leaves are waxy, rich green,
6 in. long and 4 in. wide. Remarkable
flowers in a spectrum of colors and
shapes (single to double). The flowers,
5 to 8 in. in diameter in white, yellow,
pink, salmon, red, and combinations,
cause shortness of breath. Numerous cultivars are known. Full sun, any
well-drained soil, and ample nutrition
keep plants vigorous. Flowers on new
growth of season, so remove spent
flowers. Grows 8 to 15 ft. high. Zones
9 to 11. Tropical Asia.

Hibiscus mutabilis var. *flore-pleno*, Confederate rose

Hibiscus syriacus
rose-of-sharon, shrub althea

Often found at older residences, this shrub had fallen out of fashion; however, in recent years, the species has been reinvigorated via a wave of new cultivars. The habit is stiffly upright and strongly multi-stemmed. The three-lobed, medium green, 2- to 4-in.-long leaves do not color appreciably in fall. The flowers range in color from white, pink, red, and purple to almost blue, and come in singles and doubles. Flowers appear from June and July into September on new growth of the season, and so it is prudent to remove old branches in late winter to encourage best flowering. Grows in any soil, except those that are extremely dry or wet. Requires full sun. Quite pH adaptable. Use in the border, in groupings, or perhaps as an accent in the summer garden. The plant essentially fruits itself out of

MORE ▶

Hibiscus syriacus, rose-of-sharon

Hibiscus mutabilis var. *flore-pleno*

Hibiscus rosa-sinensis

Hibiscus rosa-sinensis, Chinese hibiscus

Hibiscus syriacus CONTINUED

flower; several of the new sterile types (which are triploids) are everblooming. Grows 8 to 12 ft. high, 6 to 10 ft. wide. Zones 5 to 8(9). China, India.

CULTIVARS AND VARIETIES

Antique nursery catalogs listed numerous cultivars of this species. Unfortunately (or fortunately, depending on your perspective), most have disappeared from cultivation.

'Aphrodite' (dark pink with prominent dark red eye), 'Diana' (pure white and large), 'Helene' (white with maroon eye), and 'Minerva' (lavender-pink with prominent dark red eye) were bred by Dr. Don Egolf, U.S. National Arboretum, for floral quality and non-stop flowering. These should be given first consideration. They are not completely sterile; I have grown seedlings of 'Diana' and 'Helene'.

'Blue Bird' ('Oiseau Bleu') is an older introduction (1958) with single, lilac-blue flowers and a small red center. Flowers average 4 to 5 in. across. It is a vigorous grower. Flowers close in rainy weather. Grew seedling populations looking for improved true blue flowers and greater vigor. Ended up with white, pink, lavender, and muddy blue seedlings. Pitched all!

Chiffon™ and Satin™ series offer

Hibiscus syriacus 'Aphrodite'

Hibiscus syriacus 'Diana'

Hibiscus syriacus 'Helene'

Hibiscus syriacus 'Minerva'

Hibiscus syriacus 'Blue Bird'

Hippophae rhamnoides

singles and semi-doubles in a variety of rich colors, some with ruffled anemone center and contrasting eye. Observed several of these, and they are quite attractive; perhaps too many, and I don't have a handle on the best.

Hippophae rhamnoides
seabuckthorn

Although seldom available in the United States, this species has potential for use in sandy soils where oceanic salts are prevalent. It is an extremely irregular, multi-stemmed, rounded small tree or shrub with 1- to 3-in.-long leaves. The attractive grayish foliage, like that of *Elaeagnus angustifolia*, Russian-olive, serves as a pleasant diversion from the typical shades of green. The yellowish, dioecious flowers, which open before the leaves in March and April, are not particularly showy. The ¼- to ⅓-in.-long, orange fruit ripen in September and persist into fall and winter. The species languishes under high fertility and should be used only in infertile soils. I have tried to grow it on several occasions without any success. In Europe, particularly the Netherlands and Germany, seabuckthorn is used in highway plantings. Grows 8 to 30 ft. high, 10 to 40 ft. wide. Zones 4 to 7. Europe, China, Himalayas.
CULTIVARS AND VARIETIES
Several fruit cultivars from Russia or its former satellites are offered by Northwoods Nursery, Molalla, Oregon.

'Sprite' is a dense, compact, gray-leaf form, 15 in. by 34 in. in three years. It has landscape potential, as witnessed at the University of Maine. Offered by Forestfarm, Williams, Oregon.

Holboellia latifolia

A twining, monoecious, evergreen vine with pretty, compound palmate, dark green leaflets, each 3 to 7 in. long, and campanulate, 1-in.-long, lavender-purplish tinged female flowers in few-flowered racemes in May. Greenish white male flowers, on approximately 1-in.-long pedicels, are somewhat hidden among the foliage. Fruit, a purple, sausage-shaped, 2- to 3-in.-long pod, is considered edible. Prefers full sun and well-drained soils. Requires a structure to climb, otherwise it's just a heap of tangled foliage and stems. Grows 12 to 20 ft. high. Zones 7 to 9 on West Coast. Have observed only a few times, primarily in botanical gardens. An unprotected plant in a container was undamaged at 13°F in Athens. Himalayas.

Hippophae rhamnoides, seabuckthorn

Hippophae rhamnoides 'Sprite'

Holboellia latifolia

Hovenia dulcis

Japanese raisin tree

A little-known tree with several outstanding attributes, including lustrous green, pest-free foliage, greenish white flowers in June and July, and edible fruiting structures in September and October. The reddish, fleshy fruiting branches have a pleasant sweet taste. The habit is oval to rounded, with uniform, ascending main branches and a paucity of lateral branches. Leaves are 4 to 6 in. long and 3 to 5 in. wide. The gray to gray-brown bark develops wide, flat ridges and shallow, darker furrows. Adaptable to varied soils and presents no cultural problems. Grows 30 ft. high under cultivation; 40- to 45-ft.-tall specimens are occasionally seen. Zones (5)6 and 7(8); severe damage was evident after exposure to –22°F. Japan.

Hydrangea

hydrangea

This genus—known, grown, and loved worldwide—is not without some rare, unique species, all grown in Georgia trials and/or Dirr garden.

Hydrangea angustipetala has narrow, serrated, lustrous dark leaves; white (cream) lacecap flowers; great variation in size to 5 ft. Observed evergreen forms in snow in Wales. Many different selections from the wild. Best lumped with *H. scandens* subsp. *chinensis*. Zones 7 and 8. Japan, China, Taiwan.

Hydrangea aspera is a vexing species with significant foliar variation. Leaves are typically dull dark green; hairy above, densely so beneath. The typical species leaf is narrow-ovate, 4 to 5 in. long, 1½ to 2 in. wide; subspecies *macrophylla* and *sargentiana* with leaves to 10 in. by 4 in. The lacecap flowers are comprised of white to mauve sepals, lavender to muted pur-

ple fertile flowers. Flowers open in late June and July (Athens). Bark, brown, is exfoliating, often in papery sheets. Best in partial shade, moist well-drained, slightly acid to high pH (calcareous) soils. Certainly, best adapted to West Coast but flowered in Athens and Atlanta, Georgia; Mentor, Ohio; and Louisville, Kentucky. Species grows 6 to 12 ft. high; subspecies, 15 to 18 ft. high and wide. Available from specialty and hydrangea purveyors. Many cultivars and varieties; 'Burgundy Bliss' with rich burgundy new growth, maturing to green on upper surfaces, burgundy on lower, appears promising. Zone (6)7, 8 and 9 on West Coast. China, Taiwan.

Hydrangea involucrata has 3- to 6-in.-long, 1- to 2½-in.-wide, mid-green leaves with bristle-tipped serrations. Lacecap flowers, white-, pink-, blue-sepaled, appear in 3- to 5-in.-wide inflorescences in June. Flowers originate from large, peony-shaped buds.

Hovenia dulcis, Japanese raisin tree

Hovenia dulcis

Hovenia dulcis

Hovenia dulcis

Flowers are produced on new growth of the season, and I observed plants killed to ground that regrew and flowered in summer. Several mophead, double forms, with showier flowers are in cultivation. 'Hortensis' is most common in the United States. Grows 3 to 4 (to 5) ft. high and wide. Zones 7 to 9, 10 on the West Coast. Japan, Taiwan.

Hydrangea scandens and *H. luteovenosa* appear shades-of-gray different. Both small-leaved, thin-stemmed, with small lacecap flowers, the sepals white-yellow, resembling Mickey Mouse ears. *Hydrangea luteovenosa* has been one of the hardiest in Georgia trials. Both species flower early, mid to late April in Athens. Flowers are fragrant and occur at the nodes, often along the length of the stem. Useful for breeding and the true collector. Estimate 2 to 3 ft. high, potential to 6 ft. and as wide. By some authori-

MORE ▶

Hydrangea aspera

Hydrangea angustipetala

Hydrangea involucrata 'Hortensis'

Hydrangea scandens

Hydrangea luteovenosa

Hydrangea CONTINUED

ties, *H. luteovenosa* is treated as *H. scandens* subsp. *liukiuensis*. Zone 7. Japan, Taiwan.

Hydrangea anomala subsp. *petiolaris*

climbing hydrangea

Considered the supreme flowering vine because of its beautiful foliage, flowers, and habit. The lustrous dark green leaves, 2 to 4 in. long and almost as wide, serve as a background for the 6- to 10-in.-wide corymbs of fragrant, white flowers, which open in late May (Athens), June, and July. Fall color is variable but on occasion soft to bright yellow. The inflorescence is composed of showy white, sterile outer sepals that surround the dull white, fertile inner flowers. Flowers persist for four to six weeks, the sepals aging from white to green to brown. Climbing hydran-

gea is a true clinging vine, cementing itself to any structure. With time, the vine becomes woody, and the cinnamon-brown bark exfoliates. Tolerates shade or sun and is adaptable to a variety of soils. Somewhat slow in

the early years of establishment. It is a long-lived and almost trouble-free vine, except for Japanese beetles, which enjoy an occasional free leafy lunch. Use on walls, trees, fences, or over rocks; it has also been used as

Hydrangea anomala subsp. *petiolaris*, climbing hydrangea

Hydrangea anomala subsp. *petiolaris*

Hydrangea anomala subsp. *petiolaris* fall color

Hydrangea anomala subsp. *petiolaris* Mirranda™

Hydrangea anomala subsp. *petiolaris* Moonlight Magic™

348

a groundcover and a shrub. Almost unlimited in its ability to climb tall trees. Grows 60 to 80 ft. high; can be maintained at a lesser size. Zones 4 to 8. Japan, China.

CULTIVARS AND VARIETIES
Mirranda™ ('Firefly') was highly touted as a yellow-margined, green-centered leaf form. Unfortunately, variegation fades (to green) faster than invisible ink. Grew in our Chapel Hill garden, be leery.

Moonlight Magic™ ('Kuga Variegated') with emerging leaves pink, bronze, white, and green, mature green; grew for a time.

Small-leaf forms are rather confusing introductions, about one-half the size of the species leaf. 'Brookside Littleleaf', 'Cordifolia', and subsp. *quelpartensis* belong here. Have observed 'Tillaefolia' with normal-species-sized leaves.

Hydrangea arborescens
smooth hydrangea

To witness this species in the wild makes one wonder how it could ever be a popular garden plant. When brought from the shady nooks and crannies of the wild to a relatively fertile garden setting, the transformation brings to mind the story of the beauty and the beast, and the prince he turned out to be. Plants in the wild are often loose and open in habit, but when provided with moisture and moderate fertility, plants become impressive dense, mounded specimens. In cultivation, it forms a clumpy, rounded mound, often broader than high at maturity. The 2- to 8-in.-long, strongly serrated, dark green leaves seldom develop appreciable fall color, except in more southerly locales, where they turn almost lemon-yellow in November. The flowers are not overwhelming, often consisting of nonshowy creamy, fertile flowers with an outer whorl of showy white sepals. Flowers appear in June and are at their showiest for three to four weeks when they pass

from apple-green to white to brown. If spent flowers are removed, the new growth will produce a second flush of flowers, generally in August and September. Provide moist, organic-laden, well-drained, acid or higher pH soils. The plant is well adapted to full sun in the North, opting for degrees of shade farther south. Cut to within 6 in. of the ground in late winter and fertilize or thin out older stems. Use in masses or groupings. Combine with cultivars of *Spiraea japonica*, Japanese spirea, for a real summer show as they flower

at the same time. Grows 3 to 5 ft. high and wide. Zones 3 to 8(9). New York to Iowa, south to Florida and Louisiana. Abundant in the North Georgia mountains in the shady understory; so thick, in fact, in places on Rabun Bald that it forms a monoculture.

CULTIVARS AND VARIETIES
'Annabelle' is a superb selection with large, uniform, broad-rounded inflorescences. The individual inflorescences, typically 4 to 6 in. across but up to 12 in. in diameter on vigorous shoots,

MORE ▶

Hydrangea arborescens, smooth hydrangea

Hydrangea arborescens 'Annabelle'

Hydrangea arborescens CONTINUED
are more uniformly symmetrical than those of 'Grandiflora'.

Bella Anna™ ('PIIHA-I') represents ten years of breeding effort by the author to produce a pink-flowered 'Annabelle'-type. In 2008, 31 pink mopheads were selected with Bella Anna™ the ultimate selection; photo speaks to its beauty. Developed at Plant Introductions, Inc., licensed to Bailey Nurseries, and marketed under the Endless Summer® brand. Stronger stems; fuller, larger inflorescences; richer persistent pink sepal coloration; and greater heat tolerance than Invincibelle™ Spirit.

'Bounty' (U.S. version) is stronger stemmed than 'Annabelle' but with less uniform mophead inflorescences. Plant Introductions, Inc., utilized 'Bounty' to breed stronger-stemmed, uniform mophead types.

'Grandiflora' is the standard large-flowered form, with rather lumpy, 6- to 8-in.-wide clusters of white flowers. Particularly common around older homesteads, and there forming large colonies.

'Hayes Starburst' is a double-flowered form, initially apple-green, then white, aging green-white to parchment. I thought it had a shot at landscape greatness, but the stems are thin and weak-kneed, so the plant becomes a floppy mess.

'Mary Nell' is the best lacecap, with sterile flowers (sepals) interspersed among the central fertile flowers and forming an almost double ring around the periphery. Inflorescences to 6 in. across. Named after the wife of J. C. McDaniel, a professor of horticulture at the University of Illinois and one of my mentors.

Pinks are represented by the fertile, largely non-showy, pink, fading white, 'Chestatee', 'Eco Pink Puff', 'Pink Pincushion', and 'Wesser Falls'. 'Eco Pink Puff' and 'Wesser Falls' provided the genes to breed Bella Anna™.

Hydrangea macrophylla
bigleaf hydrangea

Perhaps no flowering plant commands greater attention than bigleaf hydrangea, particularly in June, July, and August, when the hortensia types, with their pink to blue snowballs, all but tackle passersby. The habit is rounded-mounded with thickish, waxy ash-brown, unbranched stems. The often thickish, 4- to 8-in.-long leaves are lustrous medium to dark green. Typically not known for great fall color, but yellow, bronze, and red hues occur during extended falls. Flowers are displayed in two forms: the lacecaps, with showy sterile outer sepals and fertile inner flowers (often sepals mixed with fertile flowers); and the hortensias (mopheads), with mostly showy sepals in rounded to broad-rounded inflorescences. Depending on temperatures, flowers last for four weeks or longer, generally metamorphosing through several colors. The

Hydrangea arborescens Bella Anna™

Hydrangea arborescens 'Hayes Starburst'

Hydrangea arborescens 'Mary Nell'

Hydrangea macrophylla Endless Summer®

350

Hydrangea macrophylla, bigleaf hydrangea

Hydrangea macrophylla 'Ami Pasquier'

Hydrangea macrophylla 'Générale Vicomtesse de Vibraye'

flowers occur primarily on old wood, so do not prune until after flowering. Provide either sun or partial shade, in deep, moist, organic-laden, well-drained soils. Plants require abundant moisture. Flowers are blue in acid soils, pink in high pH soils, a function of aluminum availability. Withstands salt spray and is a good seashore garden plant—the abundance of plants from Cape Cod, Massachusetts, south to Cape May, New Jersey, provides proof of its salt tolerance. Also abundant on West Coast. Countless (about 1,000) cultivars have been named, and it is difficult to buy true-to-name selections in the everyday nursery trade; it is best to purchase these plants from a specialty nursery. Grows 3 to 6 (to 10) ft. high, wider at maturity. Zones 6 to 9(10). Japan.

CULTIVARS AND VARIETIES

Hydrangea macrophylla has experienced a 21st-century rebirth thanks to Martha Stewart's championing; new books on the genus; the American Hydrangea Society's efforts; and Endless Summer® ('Bailmer'), a remontant mophead. "Remontant" means plants will continue to produce flowers on new growth. To facilitate new flowers, remove old, fertilize, maintain watering to encourage growth flushes.

Countless new introductions, often branded series like Cityline™, Edgy™, Forever and Ever™, Kaleidoscope®, Mystical™, and others. Most are

MORE ▶

Hydrangea macrophylla 'Blue Wave'

Hydrangea macrophylla 'Nikko Blue'

Hydrangea macrophylla 'Lanarth White'

Hydrangea macrophylla 'Lilacina'

Hydrangea macrophylla 'Mme. Emile Mouillère'

Hydrangea macrophylla 'White Wave'

derived from pot-plant, florist-type breeding programs in Europe and Asia. The marketing is sunny; the reality of performance, cloudy.

I have grown, observed, tested over 250 cultivars, with the following the first choices for gardeners (mh = mophead; lc = lacecap).

HISTORICAL 'All Summer Beauty' (mh), 'Ami Pasquier' (mh), 'Blue Wave' (lc), 'Frillibet' (mh), 'Générale Vicomtesse de Vibraye' (mh), 'Lanarth White' (lc), 'Lilacina' (lc), 'Mme. Emile Mouillère' (mh), 'Mousseline' (mh), 'Nikko Blue' (mh), 'Veitchii' (lc), and 'White Wave' (lc).

REMONTANT 'Blushing Bride' (mh), 'David Ramsey' (mh), 'Decatur Blue' (mh), Endless Summer® (mh), 'Mini Penny' (mh), 'Oak Hill' (mh), 'Penny Mac' (mh), and Twist-n-Shout™ (lc).

Hydrangea paniculata 'Grandiflora'
peegee hydrangea

The species form of panicle hydrangea is seldom planted, but the cultivar 'Grandiflora', peegee hydrangea, is common throughout the northern and western states. It forms a coarsely spreading, low-branched large shrub or small tree. The 3- to 6-in.-long, dark green leaves show hints of yellow to reddish purple fall color. The flowers of 'Grandiflora' average 6 to 8 in. long, although flower panicles on vigorous shoots may reach 12 to 18 in. long and 6 to 12 in. wide. The fertile flowers are hidden beneath the outer showy sepals. Flowers open white in June, July, and August, aging to a blushed purplish pink. Flowers occur on new growth of the season, so prune in late winter. Probably the most culturally adaptable of the hydrangeas. Tolerates any soil condition, except wet. I was never enamored of this species and find it hard to blend into any landscape, although it is certainly showy in flower. A shrub border is probably the most logical place for it. Grows 15 to 25 ft. high, 10 to 20 ft. wide. Zones 3 to 8.

MORE ▶

Hydrangea macrophylla 'Penny Mac'

Hydrangea macrophylla Twist-n-Shout™

Hydrangea macrophylla 'Blushing Bride'

Hydrangea macrophylla 'Oak Hill'

Hydrangea paniculata 'Grandiflora' CONTINUED
Japan, Sakhalin Island, Taiwan, eastern and southern China.
CULTIVARS AND VARIETIES
Over 80, with Baby Lace™ ('PIIHP-I'), 'Bombshell', 'Little Lamb', and Little Lime™ ('Jane') all less than 10 ft. high with full white inflorescences.

'Dharuma' is an early-flowering form; in full expression in late May at the JC Raulston Arboretum in Raleigh, North Carolina. Smaller habit, to about 4 ft., stout stems, dark green leaves, and white sepals that age to pink/rose. Some thinking that this may be a hybrid between *Hydrangea paniculata* and *H. heteromalla*. Does not flower on new growth.

Limelight™ is promoted as producing bright lime-green flowers; however, in my experience, flowers are white, with emerging sepals light green. Has energized gardeners because small container plants produce copious flowers on upright stems. Estimate 8 to 10 ft. high and wide.

'Phantom' has spectacularly large (immense) inflorescences, the sepals forming a full, glistening, white panicle. Large shrub, coarser than many paniculatas; listed as 10 ft. by 10 ft.

Pinky Winky™ ('DVP Pinky'), as I witnessed in Europe, has an upright habit with large, conical inflorescences 12 to 16 in. long, that open white, aging pink, creating a two-toned effect. Plants in Georgia have not developed such large inflorescences, actually about 6 in. long, with sepals not covering fertile flowers. Matures 6 to 8 ft. high. Stronger-stemmed than Vanille Fraise (Vanilla Strawberry™).

Quickfire™ ('Bulk') flowers early, late May and June in Athens, producing smallish inflorescences that are white to pink and not particularly full; sepals are rather sparse and fertile flowers evident, sepals turn pink by July in Athens. Mature size 6 to 8 ft. high and wide. Possibly a hybrid (*Hydrangea paniculata* × *H. heteromalla*).

'Silver Dollar' produces beautiful,

Hydrangea paniculata 'Grandiflora', peegee hydrangea

Hydrangea paniculata 'Dharuma'

Hydrangea paniculata Limelight™

354

Hydrangea paniculata Quickfire™

Hydrangea paniculata 'Tardiva'

Hydrangea paniculata White Diamonds™

full, white inflorescences on rather strong stems that hold the flowers upright. I have been impressed by quality of flowers, foliage, and habit. Estimate mature size as 8 ft. high and wide, perhaps larger.

'Tardiva' provides a mixture of sterile and fertile flowers that open in September. This is a common cultivar in commerce. Will grow 10 ft. high and larger.

MORE ▶

Hydrangea paniculata 'Grandiflora'

Hydrangea paniculata Pinky Winky™

Hydrangea paniculata 'Silver Dollar'

Hydrangea paniculata 'Grandiflora' CONTINUED

White Diamonds™ is a compact form, 5 to 6 ft. high and wide, with large, broad-ovate, dark green leaves. Strong stems hold 6- to 8-in.-long, 4-in.-wide panicles with large, white sepals covering most of the fertile flowers; sepals age light green to parchment color. Introduced by the author.

Hydrangea quercifolia
oakleaf hydrangea

One of the most handsome plants that landscape designers have at their disposal, yet it is not utilized to its fullest potential in American gardens. The full, rounded-mounded outline, lobed leaves, and magnificent white flowers provide full measure for the landscape dollar. The dark green, three- to seven-lobed, oak-shaped leaves, 3 to 8 in. long and wide, turn rich red to burgundy in fall and may persist into December. The 4- to 12-in.-long, paniculate inflorescences are composed of 1- to 1½-in.-wide, showy sepals interspersed with fertile flowers. The flowers open in June and last for three to four weeks, often developing purplish pink coloration with age. Flowers are formed on previous year's growth, so prune after flowering. The bark peels off in papery, light brown to cinnamon-brown strips. Provide moist, acid, organic-laden, well-drained soils, in full sun to partial shade. Some degree of shade is best in the South (zones 7 to 9). Easily transplanted from a container or the field. Grows rapidly if ample moisture and fertilizer are provided. Use in mass plantings, groupings, or the border. One of the best landscape plants for use at the edge of woodlands. Grows 4 to 6 (to 8) ft. high, equal or greater in spread. Zones 5 to 9. Georgia to Florida and Mississippi.

CULTIVARS AND VARIETIES
'Alice' produces 10- to 14-in.-long inflorescences composed of half-dollar-sized sepals that age to rosy pink.

Hydrangea quercifolia, oakleaf hydrangea

Hydrangea quercifolia 'Alice'

Hydrangea quercifolia 'Snow Queen'

Grows 12 ft. high and wide. Introduced by the author.

'Amethyst' is a handsome, compact selection by the author. Parent plant 5 ft. by 6 ft.; with dark green leaves, red-purple fall color, and white panicles, about 6 in. long, held upright above the foliage. The white sepals turn burgundy-rose and hold color; color retained upon drying.

'Harmony' and 'Roanoke' have large, mostly sterile inflorescences, up to 12 in. long, so heavy as to cause the branches to arch.

Little Honey™ ('Brihon') is a yellow-leaf selection from 'Pee Wee', potent April to June, less so later in heat. Loses color in shade; orange-red fall color. Flowers like 'Pee Wee'; unfortunately quite susceptible to cercospora leaf spot.

'Munchkin' is a compact selection, 3 ft. by 4½ ft. in nine years, with upright, 6½-in.-long, white-aging-pink inflorescences. Dr. Sandy Reed 2010

introduction, U.S. National Arboretum.

'Pee Wee' is a dwarfish, broad-mounded form, with leaves and flowers about half the size of those of the species. Rose to red-purple fall color in the Dirr garden. Grows 3½ to 4½ ft. by 6 ft.

'Ruby Slippers' is compact, 3½ ft. by 5 ft. in seven years, with 9-in.-long, upright inflorescences, white, turning to pale pink to rose. The sepals develop the rose coloration by July and August in Athens. A beautiful introduction (2010) from Dr. Sandy Reed.

'Snowflake', always a favorite, has multiple white sepals emerging on top of the older ones, creating a double-flowered appearance. The large, 12- to 15-in.-long inflorescences may cause the branches to arch, although usually not to the degree of 'Harmony' and 'Roanoke'. Introduced by Aldridge Nursery, Birmingham, Alabama.

'Snow Queen' was only a photograph in a nursery catalog to me until

the real thing flowered at the University's Botanical Garden. What a beauty. Large, showy white sepals cover the fertile flowers, producing an 8-in.-long cone of white, maturing to pretty pink. The inflorescences are not excessively large, and they remain upright. Fall color is potent red with a hint of burgundy. May prove more compact in habit than the others; I estimate 6 ft. by 6 ft. at maturity.

Hydrangea serrata
mountain hydrangea

Definitely second banana to the big-leaf hydrangea, *Hydrangea macrophylla*, but more refined in habit, leaf, and flower. Develops a mounded outline of slender, graceful stems. The leaves are generally narrower, 2 to 6 in. long, 1 to 2½ in. wide, mid to dark green, and finely to coarsely serrate. Flowers, in 2- to 3- (to 4-) in.-wide inflorescences ahead of *H. macrophylla*,

MORE ▶

Hydrangea quercifolia fall color

Hydrangea quercifolia 'Amethyst'

Hydrangea quercifolia 'Roanoke'

Hydrangea quercifolia 'Snowflake'

357

Hydrangea serrata CONTINUED

early to mid May in Athens. Flowers (primarily) on old wood, so prune after flowering. Moist, well-drained, acid soil in partial shade maximize the species' qualities. Grows 2 to 3 (to 5) ft. high, slightly wider. Zones (5)6 and 7, 8 and 9 on the West Coast. Japan, Korea.
CULTIVARS AND VARIETIES
Hundreds of cultivars, lacecap and mopheads, are in cultivation. Best in Georgia trials were 'Amagi-amacha', 'Benigaku', 'Blue Deckle' (rebloom-

Hydrangea serrata 'Amagi-amacha'

Hydrangea serrata 'Blue Billow'

Hydrangea serrata 'Bluebird'

Hydrangea serrata 'Benigaku'

Hydrangea serrata 'Miyama-yae-Murasaki'

Hydrangea serrata 'Tiara'

ing), 'Miyama-yae-Murasaki' (double), 'Miranda', 'Tiara', and 'Woodlander'. 'Blue Billow', 'Bluebird', 'Geisha Girl', and 'Tokyo Delight' are also solid choices.

Hypericum
St. Johnswort

A varied group of evergreen to deciduous shrubs, usually small in stature, with rich green leaves, needle-like in some species, and ⅓- to ½-in.-wide, five-petaled, yellow flowers from May or June through September. Several of the following species, although largely unknown to cultivation, are easy to cultivate and provide compactness, handsome foliage, and beautiful yellow flowers. Observed many insects, particularly butterflies, visiting the flowers. Acid, well-drained, moist soil in full sun results in maximum performance. All are easy to grow from seed (sow on moist medium, do not cover) and root from softwood cuttings. St.

Johnswort is hardly a household word in American gardens, though *Hypericum* 'Hidcote' and *H. calycinum*, Aaronsbeard St. Johnswort, do enjoy popularity. The latter is an evergreen groundcover with 3-in.-wide, screaming bright yellow flowers; 'Brigadoon'

has uniform golden yellow leaves, but in zone 7 they "cook," and branch reversions to green are common.

With about 400 *Hypericum* species worldwide, the choices are nearly infinite. In addition to the featured

MORE ▶

Hypericum calycinum, Aaronsbeard St. Johnswort

Hydrangea serrata 'Geisha Girl'

Hypericum calycinum

Hydrangea serrata 'Tokyo Delight'

Hypericum calycinum 'Brigadoon'

Hypericum CONTINUED

species, I've developed a reasonable working knowledge and appreciation for the following: *Hypericum addingtonii*, with 2- to 3-in.-wide, rich yellow flowers, semi-evergreen foliage, 4 ft. high; *H. pseudohenryi*, 2-in.-wide golden-yellow flowers, 4 to 6 ft. high and wide; and the new, brightly colored fruit types like the Mystical™ series. I am doubtful about the latter's adaptability because of *H. androsaemum*, *H. ×inodorum*, and *H. hircinum*

parentage. This translates to inadequate cold and heat tolerance as well as rust susceptibility.

Hypericum brachyphyllum

Lustrous green, needle-like leaves, less than ½ in. long, $\frac{1}{24}$ in. wide, occur in clusters along the two-winged stems. The flower buds are red and conical, opening to ½-in.-wide yellow flowers. Grows 3 to 5 ft. high. Inhabits wet areas in the wild. Zones 7 to 9. Georgia to Florida and Louisiana.

Hypericum densiflorum

A rounded deciduous shrub with 1- to 2-in.-long, ⅛- to ⅓-in.-wide lustrous dark green leaves that occasionally develop yellow-orange fall color. Habit is oval-rounded to rounded with fine-textured, lax-arching shoots. The ½-in.-wide yellow flowers occur in corymb-like panicles at the ends of the shoots from June through August. Variable habitats in the wild from mountain balds to swamps and bogs. Observed growing in standing water at

Hypericum densiflorum

Hypericum densiflorum

Hypericum frondosum 'Sunburst'

Hypericum fasciculatum, sand-weed

Hypericum 'Hidcote'

4,000 ft. elevation in Highlands, North Carolina. Grows 1 to 3 (to 6) ft. high and wide. Zones 5 to 9. New York to Georgia, west to Missouri, Louisiana, and Texas.

Hypericum fasciculatum
sand-weed

Lustrous dark green, needle-like, evergreen leaves, ½ in. long, about $\frac{1}{12}$ in. wide, with many clustered at the nodes, producing a juniper-type texture. Habit is dense and compact to

3 ft. high and wide. The ½- to ⅔-in.-wide yellow flowers open from May through September. Grows in moist soils (low pinelands, swamps). Zones 7 to 9. North Carolina to Florida, west to Mississippi.

Hypericum frondosum
golden St. Johnswort

This species is a rounded-mounded shrub with reddish brown exfoliating branches and distinct, glaucous bluish green leaves. The 1- to 2-in.-wide,

five-petaled, bright yellow flowers have a dense, brushy, ¾-in.-wide mass of stamens in the center. Prefers well-drained soils and full sun. Great plant for grouping or for a spot of color in the border. Grows 3 to 4 ft. high and wide. Zones 5 to 8. South Carolina and Tennessee to Georgia, west to Texas.

CULTIVARS AND VARIETIES
'Sunburst' is lower growing than the species and has more-glaucous blue foliage and larger (3 in. in diameter) flowers. A fine performer in tests at the University of Illinois, Urbana (zone 5). Grows 3 ft. high. Has succeeded admirably in mass plantings on the University of Georgia campus (zone 7).

Hypericum galioides
bedstraw St. Johnswort

Similar to *Hypericum fasciculatum* with longer and wider, lustrous dark green evergreen leaves to 2 in. long. Forms a loose, lax cushion, 1 to 1½ ft. high, 3 ft. wide. Golden yellow flowers, ½ to ¾ in. in diameter, open in June and July. Grows in moist soils in the Coastal Plain from North Carolina to Louisiana. Zones 7 to 9.

CULTIVARS AND VARIETIES
'Brodie' is a uniform, broad-mounded selection with lustrous dark green leaves and ¾-in.-wide flowers. Some thinking this may be a *Hypericum densiflorum* selection. Has been deciduous in Athens. 'Creel's Gold Star' is similar.

Hypericum 'Hidcote'

'Hidcote' is a hybrid cultivar of confusing parentage, but at its best, it is the benchmark for the other landscape hypericums. It forms a mounded, arching framework of rich blue-green leaves, which are followed by 2½- to 3-in.-wide, golden yellow flowers from June and, sporadically, into fall. Unfortunately, the petals brown with age and become unsightly. Flowering occurs on new growth of the season,

Hypericum galioides 'Brodie'

Hypericum 'Hidcote'

MORE ▶

Hypericum 'Hidcote' CONTINUED

so treat the plant as a herbaceous perennial and cut back in winter. Provide well-drained soils, in sun or partial shade. Use as a mass or grouping. In my Georgia garden, every 'Hidcote' plant succumbed to a wilt-type phenomenon. Grows 3 ft. or more high and wide. Zones (5)6 to 9.

Hypericum kalmianum
Kalm St. Johnswort

Small, compact, finely branched shrub with 1- to 2-in.-long, ⅛- to ⅓-in.-wide, bluish green leaves; produces bright yellow, 1- to 1½-in.-wide flowers in three-flowered cymes, in June and July. Fruit is a five- (four-) valved, ovate, yellow to brown, dehiscent capsule. Adaptable to any well-drained, acid to neutral soil. Grows 2 to 3 ft. high and wide. Zones 4 to 6(7). Quebec and Ontario to Michigan and Illinois.

CULTIVARS AND VARIETIES

'Ames' is a uniform mounded form, 2 to 3 ft. high, with 1-in.-wide yellow flowers and improved hardiness.

Blue Velvet™ ('Cfflpc-1') is a dense, rounded shrub, 2 to 3 ft. by 3 to 4 ft., with beautiful, 2-in.-long, narrow-linear, blue-green leaves, and ¾- to 1-in.-wide yellow flowers in five- to seven-flowered cymes in June and July. Have grown seedlings of Blue Velvet™, and all had rich blue-green to glaucous blue leaves. I cannot reconcile that this is a pure *Hypericum kalmianum* selection. Intro-

Hypericum kalmianum 'Ames'

Hypericum lissophloeus

Hypericum prolificum

Hypericum kalmianum, Kalm St. Johnswort

Hypericum prolificum, shrubby St. Johnswort

duced by Paul Cappiello and John Wachter.

Hypericum lissophloeus

A wonderful textural plant for borders, airy and feathery, with asparagus-like leaves and exfoliating copper-brown bark. The habit is upright, 3 to 5 ft. high, loose and arching, and the gray-green, ½- to 1-in.-long, needle-like evergreen leaves are elegant. The ½-in.-wide yellow flowers twinkle among the needles, producing just enough color to entice. Grows in wet depressions in north Florida. Zones 7 to 9.

Hypericum lloydii

Can be confused with *Hypericum reductum* but has longer, notched, evergreen leaves and sepals. Growth habit is decumbent and groundcover-ish. Needle-like leaves are more lustrous than *H. reductum*. The ⅓-in.-wide yellow flowers open in August and continue until frost. Found in dry pine woods and rock outcrops, North Carolina to Alabama. Zones 7 to 9.

Hypericum prolificum

shrubby St. Johnswort

Seldom seen in contemporary land-scaping, but this species offers ¾- to 1-in.-wide, bright yellow flowers in June, July, and August. It develops into a dense little shrub with stout, stiff, erect stems. Provide well-drained soils, in sun or partial shade. Useful in the shrub border. Grows 1 to 4 ft. high and wide. Zones 3 to 8. New Jersey to Iowa, south to Georgia.

Hypericum reductum

An evergreen groundcover species, about 1 to 1½ ft. high and spreading to form a carpet of dull green, needle-like leaves less than ½ in. long. Flowers are ⅓ in. in diameter, yellow, and open in August and beyond. Grows in drier soils (dunes, sand hills) from North Carolina to Florida and Alabama. Zones 7 to 9.

Idesia polycarpa

igiri tree

Quite an iconoclastic biological specimen that, although outlandish, has not attracted attention from gardeners. Becomes a rounded tree with coarse branches and 5- to 10-in.-long, deep green leaves. Bark is almost grayish white, and several multi-stemmed specimens in the University's Botanical Garden are about as close to white-bark birches as is possible in the South. Flowers (June) are dioecious, yellow-green, male in 5- to 6-in.-long panicles, female in up to 8-in.-long panicles. A fruiting tree is *spectacular* with dangling panicles of ¼- to ⅓-in.-wide, bright red fruit. My fondest memories conjure fruiting trees, in a grove type planting, at the U.S. National Arboretum. Tolerates heat, drought, and substandard soils. Extremely fast-growing in youth; seedling trees fruited at six years of age in Georgia trials. Easily grown from freshly planted seed. Grows 40 to 60 ft. high and wide. Witnessed a 60-ft.-high tree in Brooklyn Botanic Garden. Zones 6 to 9. Southern Japan, central and western China.

MORE ▶

Idesia polycarpa, igiri tree

Hypericum reductum

Idesia polycarpa

Idesia polycarpa

Idesia polycarpa

Ilex
holly

A garden-worthy group of plants of the first order of magnitude with beauty of foliage, fruit, and habit. Some 400 species, probably more, are recognized worldwide. They exist as wind-sculpted mountaintop to swampy shrubby denizens, 12 in. to 60 ft. high. Leaves are either evergreen or deciduous and, although usually depicted with spiny margins, can be lightly serrated to entire. Flowers open in late winter to spring, usually white, four-petaled or more, either quite fragrant or nondescript. Sexes are separate, with male flowers generally having four extended stamens; female flowers, with the green ovary in the center, recall a green basketball. Fruit are botanically drupes, not berries as often stated. Colors range from white to yellow, orange, red, purple, and black. The seed-like structures in the fleshy fruit pulp are called pyrenes. Various numbers are present per fruit depending on species. For ideal pollination and fruit set, it is best to have a male and female from the same species that flower at the same time. Bees are the primary purveyors of pollen. In truth, according to discussions with experts and personal observations, any male can pollinate any female if flowering overlaps. Holly boughs, particularly *Ilex aquifolium*, make beautiful Christmas decorations. Prune holly in winter to rejuvenate entire plants. I witnessed 20-ft.-high 'Nellie R. Stevens' cut within 3 ft. of the ground with new shoots emerging from the large trunk the following spring. Sun- and moderately shade-tolerant. Any soil (preferably acid) except permanently wet; several species withstand wet feet. Minimal diseases and insects with root rot, spittlebugs, scale, leaf miner, and mites most prominent.

Fred C. Galle's *Hollies: The Genus Ilex* (1997) will forever stand as the classic reference on the large genus. *Hollies for Gardeners* (2006) by Christopher Bailes, although British in origin, translates accurately to American gardens.

Ilex ×altaclerensis
altaclera holly

A hybrid group of hollies with *Ilex aquifolium* and *I. perado* (and subsp. *platyphylla*) as parents. Medium-sized pyramidal trees with lustrous dark green, entire (almost) to spiny-

Ilex ×altaclerensis, altaclera holly

margined leaves. Flowers white (early spring), and fruit bright red. Not the most cold- or heat-tolerant but adaptable in the Mid-Atlantic states and on the West Coast. Over 50 cultivars are known. Good collection at VanDusen Botanical Garden, Vancouver, British Columbia. Grows 20 to 40 ft. high, half as wide. Zones 6 to 8, 9 and 10 on the West Coast. Have not observed in commerce on the East Coast.
CULTIVARS AND VARIETIES
'Camelliifolia', with lustrous black-green leaves, to 5 in. long, 3 in. wide, and dark red fruit, is one of the most popular forms.

'James G. Esson', with beautiful, undulating, spiny, dark green leaves and lustrous red fruit, is smaller than 'Camelliifolia', and habit is more open.

Ilex aquifolium
English holly
The plant of hedgerows, shady woods, and roadsides throughout England.

Long planted by the birds, and untended soil is often home to wayward seedlings. Has escaped from cultivation in the Pacific Northwest. Typically a dense pyramidal tree with spiny-margined, lustrous dark green leaves. Four-petaled, off-white, fragrant flowers in May give rise to ¼- to ⅞-in.-wide, rounded, red fruit. Grows in acid and higher pH soils, in sun or shade; displays great salt tolerance and is readily pruned. Some of the great hedges in English gardens are built of this biological material. Amazing number of cultivars, most best suited to the West Coast, although I have observed plants from Cape Cod to Pine Mountain, Georgia. Grows 30 to 50 ft. high with beautiful gray bark. Zones 6 and 7, 8 to 10 on the West Coast. Europe, northern Africa, and western Asia.
CULTIVARS AND VARIETIES
'Argenteomarginata' with white-

MORE ▶

Ilex aquifolium, English holly

Ilex ×*altaclerensis* 'Camelliifolia'

Ilex aquifolium

Ilex aquifolium 'Argenteomarginata'

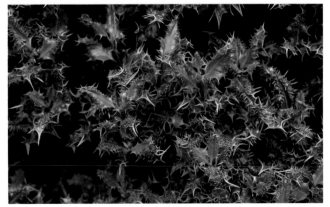
Ilex aquifolium 'Ferox', hedgehog holly

Ilex aquifolium CONTINUED

margined leaves and 'Aureomarginata' with gold-margined leaves are available.

'Balkans', 'Boulder Creek', Siberia™, and 'Zero' are more cold hardy forms with red fruit.

'Ferox', hedgehog holly, has small leaves with marginal and upper surface spines; several variegated selections of 'Ferox' are in cultivation.

Ilex ×aquipernyi

This group includes crosses between *Ilex aquifolium* and *I. pernyi*. Habit is distinctly pyramidal-conical. Plants respond well to pruning. Use for a handsome hedge or screen. Grows 20 to 30 ft. high. Zones 6 to 8.
CULTIVARS AND VARIETIES
'Aquipern' is a male clone; 'Brilliant' a female, red-berried form.

'San Jose' is the best form; it has lustrous dark green foliage and ⅜-in.-

wide, bright red fruit, which are borne in abundance even on young plants.

Ilex ×attenuata

This group of hybrids between *Ilex cassine* and *I. opaca* has produced many superior broadleaf evergreens for contemporary landscape use. Since no single type is representative of the group, only the cultivars are presented. Zones 6 to 9.
CULTIVARS AND VARIETIES
'East Palatka', 'Hume #2', and 'Savannah' are more popular in the South and are hardy into zone 6.

'Foster's #2', the most cold hardy of the group, has survived −20°F. The 1½- to 3-in.-long, lustrous dark green leaves may be entire or they may possess one to four spiny teeth on each side. Brilliant, almost fluorescent red fruit, ¼ in. in diameter, are borne in abundance and persist into winter. Habit is conical-pyramidal. Good in

Ilex ×attenuata 'Savannah'

Ilex ×attenuata 'East Palatka'

Ilex ×aquipernyi

Ilex ×aquipernyi

groupings, against walls in narrow planting areas where other hollies would grow too wide. Grows 20 to 30 ft. high.

Ilex cassine
dahoon

A southeastern native evergreen species that grows in moist woods of the southern Coastal Plain into the Bahamas and Texas. Typically a small tree or large shrub, open and somewhat scraggly, with light green leaves, 2 to 4 (to 6) in. long, toothed (at apex) to entire. Leaves assume varied manifestations, with small ½- to 1-in.-long leaves constituting var. *myrtifolia* and a longer narrow leaf form representing var. *angustifolia*. Both the species and the two varieties grew in Athens, and *none* inspired the average gardener. Most notably, the species hybridizes with *Ilex opaca* to form *I. ×attenuata* (which see). Fruit, ¼ in. in diameter,

globose, commonly red, to yellow on occasion, are borne on elongated pedicels (stalks). Fruit almost fluoresce and persist into winter in the South. Moist, well-drained, acidic soil suits it best. Terrifically susceptible to spittle-bug damage. Prune to maintain a dense habit. Grows 20 to 30 ft. high, 8 to 15 ft. wide. Zones 7 to 9.
CULTIVARS AND VARIETIES
'Autumn Cascade' is a heavily red-fruited, semi-pendent selection of var. *myrtifolia*. Selection by the author.

'Escatawba', 'Perdido', and 'Tensaw' are superior red-fruited selections from Tom Dodd III, Semmes, Alabama.

Ilex cornuta
Chinese holly

For the hot, dry areas of the country, this evergreen large shrub/small tree would rank in the top five safe choices. Typically a multi-stemmed shrub, occasionally a small tree, with five to seven (occasionally nine) sharp-spined, credit card–textured leaves. Indestructible—large plants pruned to within 6 to 12 in. of the soil line resprout and reform. Leaves, lustrous dark green, are 1½ to 4 in. long and maintain good coloration year-round. Flowers, four-petaled, dull white, fragrant, ¼ in. wide, are produced in

MORE ▶

Ilex cornuta 'Burfordii'

Ilex ×attenuata 'Foster's #2'

Ilex cassine, dahoon

Ilex cassine var. *myrtifolia* 'Autumn Cascade'

Ilex cornuta CONTINUED

prodigious quantities in the leaf axils. Bees hover about and consider these March flowers their first banquet of the season. If pollination is complete, fruit set is spectacular, with ¼- to ⅓-in.-wide, bright red fruit ripening in September and October and persisting into and often through winter. Full sun, moderate shade, heat, drought, and miserable soils, as long as they are well-drained, are adequate for successful culture. Can be pruned and maintained at any height. The cultivars discussed here are ideal for many landscape uses. Grows 8 to 10 (to 15) ft. high, often wider at maturity. Zones (6)7 to 9, 10 on the West Coast. China, Korea.

CULTIVARS AND VARIETIES

'Burfordii' is a spineless leaf form (except for the terminal spine) with large red fruit. Grows 20 ft. high and wide.

'Carissa' is a 3- to 4-ft.-high, 4- to 6-ft.-wide, compact form with an entire leaf margin. Occasionally reverts to 'Rotunda', its parental type. Occasionally sets fruit.

'D'Or' is a yellow-fruited sport of 'Burfordii' that, when laden with fruit, is formidable; 18-ft.-high plant at the JC Raulston Arboretum.

'Dwarf Burford' ('Burfordii Nana') is the smaller version of 'Burfordii', usually 5 to 6 (to 8) ft. high and wide but grows larger. Leaves are 1½ to 2 in. long, lustrous dark green, and unevenly surfaced. A plant on the Georgia campus is over 15 ft. high.

'Fineline' ('Fine Line') grows 12 ft. high, 8 to 10 ft. wide, with 1½- to 2½-in.-long, essentially spineless leaves and red fruit. Slower growing than 'Burfordii'; observed plants about 10 ft. by 8 ft.

'Needlepoint' is a Dirr favorite with narrow leaves, spineless leaf margins, and lustrous dark green color on a bulbous-conical framework. Grows 15 ft. high, 10 ft. wide, red fruit.

'O'Spring' is an upright, irregular shrub with cream-yellow leaf margins; leaf shape like the species. Relatively stable variegation pattern. About 10 ft. high. Male.

'Rotunda' is the porcupine of the group, 3 to 4 ft. high, 6 to 8 ft. across. Leaves are seven-spined and dangerous, making it a good "no cut-through," i.e., barrier planting. Occasionally sets fruit.

'Sunrise' is a yellow-foliage form with the Burford holly leaf shape; older leaves become green as do those in shade/interior of the plant.

Ilex crenata
Japanese holly

At its best, a functional broadleaf evergreen shrub that has been widely

MORE ▶

Ilex cornuta 'Burfordii'

Ilex cornuta 'Carissa'

Ilex cornuta 'D'Or'

Ilex cornuta 'Needlepoint'

Ilex cornuta 'Rotunda'

Ilex cornuta 'O'Spring'

Ilex cornuta 'Dwarf Burford'

Ilex cornuta 'Sunrise'

Ilex crenata CONTINUED

used for foundation planting, massing, and hedges. The habit is extremely variable, ranging from a dense, many-branched shrub to a small, upright tree. The dark green leaves, often lustrous, are ½ to 1¼ in. in length and have small, blackish glands on the undersides. Leaves may be either flat or cupped (convex). The ¼-in.-wide, blackish fruit occur under the foliage, hidden to all but the most observant. Easy to transplant and grow. Provide well-drained soils. As with most hollies, full sun is ideal, though *Ilex crenata* performs quite well in half shade. Susceptible to black knot fungus (*Thielaviopsis*) and nematodes. Grows 5 to 10 ft. high and wide; can reach 20 ft. high. Zones 5 to 8. Japan, Korea.

CULTIVARS AND VARIETIES

'Beehive' is a dense, compact-mounded form with lustrous dark green, ½-in.-long and ¼-in.-wide leaves. Originated as a cross of 'Convexa' × 'Stokes'. Possibly the most cold hardy of the *Ilex crenata* cultivars.

'Compacta', a globose form, has obovate, flat, ¾-in.-long, lustrous dark green leaves. Young stems are purple. Unfortunately, many different forms of 'Compacta' are in the trade, so you cannot always be sure of what you will get. Grows 6 ft. high.

'Convexa' is an old standby, with ½-in.-long, lustrous dark green, convex leaves. Although considered compact, plants can become quite large if not pruned. This is a female form that produces abundant black fruit. One of the more cold hardy cultivars. Grows 3 to 5 ft. high, slightly greater in spread.

'Drops of Gold' has brilliant yellow-gold leaves that held their color in full sun in zone 7. Will develop reversion shoots, and plants in shade turn yellow-green to green. A sport of

Ilex crenata, Japanese holly

Ilex crenata 'Drops of Gold'

Ilex crenata 'Convexa'

Ilex crenata 'Glory'

'Hetzii'; estimate 3 to 4 ft. high and wide.

'Glory' is among the most cold hardy of all *Ilex crenata* cultivars, and has survived –23°F with minimal injury. The flat, lustrous dark green leaves are ¼ to 1 in. long and ⅛ to ⅜ in. wide. Grows 5 ft. high and 8 ft. wide after 12 growing seasons.

'Green Luster' has flat, lustrous dark green leaves. It grows about twice as wide as it does tall. An 11-year-old plant measures 3 ft. high by 6 ft. wide.

'Helleri' is a dwarf, broad-mounded, compact form with flat, dark green, ½-in.-long leaves. A 26-year-old plant is 4 ft. high by 5 ft. wide.

'Hetzii' is a large, robust shrub with ½- to 1-in.-long, lustrous dark green, cupped leaves. It is a female, and not as cold hardy as 'Convexa'. Grows 6 to 8 ft. high and wide.

'Hoogendorn' has excellent dark green, ¾- to 1-in.-long, flat-surfaced leaves. Grows 2 to 2½ ft. high and wider; superior to 'Helleri'. As green meatballs go, this is one of the best *Ilex crenata* selections.

'Rotundifolia' is a larger-leaved form, but it is somewhat confused in

MORE ▶

Ilex crenata 'Sky Pencil'

Ilex crenata 'Green Luster'

Ilex crenata 'Hetzii'

Ilex crenata 'Helleri'

Ilex crenata 'Hoogendorn'

Ilex crenata CONTINUED

commerce. Not as cold hardy as some cultivars; −18°F caused complete defoliation. Grows 8 to 12 ft. high and wide.

'Sky Pencil' (Sky Sentry™) develops a totem-pole habit in youth, splaying as it hits the 8- to 12-ft. height range. Slightly convex, lustrous dark green leaves, black fruit.

'Soft Touch' is a 'Helleri' alternative with more lustrous dark green leaves and soft, flexible branches. About 2 ft. high and 3 ft. wide.

'Stokes' is an old cultivar with a rounded-mounded habit and flat, lustrous dark green leaves. Somewhat similar to 'Helleri'. Withstood −18°F without injury. Grows 2 to 3 ft. high by 3 to 4 ft. wide.

Ilex decidua
possumhaw

At one time, I thought this species would become a popular landscape plant because of its showy red fruit, rich silver-gray stems, and tolerance to dry, high pH (alkaline) soils. Unfortunately, the lack of extreme cold hardiness and the fact that the fruit may drop or discolor, plus the immense size and suckering habit of the plant, limit landscape uses. The large specimens that I have observed in Oklahoma, Missouri, Georgia, North Carolina, and Washington, D.C.—all 20 to 30 ft. high and wide, strongly suckering, and untidy—are what stick in my mind for this deciduous species. The ¼- to ⅓-in.-wide, rounded, red fruit, which color while the leaves are still green, ripen in September and persist until the following April, although they may look ragged. The 1½- to 3-in.-long, lustrous dark green leaves hold late, into November, and often mask the fruit effect. Possumhaw withstands moist soils as well as dry, alkaline soils. Observed in sunny fencerows and flooded flat woods in heavy shade with respectable fruit abundance. Requires full sun for best fruit set. Use only in large areas. Might be a good plant for naturalizing or for use along highways. Grows 7 to 15 ft. high, 5 to 10 ft. wide in cultivation. National champion is 44 ft. by 49 ft. Zones (5)6 to 9. Virginia to Florida, west to Texas.

CULTIVARS AND VARIETIES
Several, including 'Byers Golden' (yel-

Ilex crenata 'Soft Touch'

Ilex decidua

Ilex decidua, possumhaw

low fruit), 'Council Fire' (persistent, orange fruit), 'Pocahontas' (red fruit), and 'Sundance' (orange-red fruit).

'Finch's Gold' ('Gold Finch') is a beautiful yellow-fruited selection that holds the color into spring. I observed plants with the brightly colored fruit in early April at the Bartlett Arboretum, Charlotte, North Carolina.

'Warren's Red', possibly the best-known cultivar, has glossy dark green foliage and ¼-in.-wide, glossy, bright red fruit. May grow 25 ft. high, 20 ft. wide.

Ilex 'Emily Bruner'

A stately, dense, broad pyramid of leathery lustrous dark green leaves

that is now common in modern landscapes. This hybrid between *Ilex cornuta* 'Burfordii' and *I. latifolia* was brought to Don Shadow's (Shadow Nursery, Winchester, Tennessee) attention when he was a student at the University of Tennessee; he subsequently named and introduced it into cultivation. The 2- to 4- (to 5-) in.-long leaves have jagged, spiny margins, which several students described as rolling, white-capped seas. Leaves hold their color through the seasons, with slight discoloration in winter. Beautiful, ¼- to ⅓-in.-wide, rounded, red fruit ripen in September and October and persist into winter. Intensity of red color diminishes with age. Sun

or partial shade in well-drained soil. Suitable for use as a specimen plant and in groupings and screens. 'James Swan' is the male pollinator. Grows 20 to 25 ft. high, 10 to 15 ft. wide. Zones 7 to 9.

Ilex glabra
inkberry

Horticulturists have spent so much time making selections of *Ilex crenata* that they forgot to assess the landscape worth of *I. glabra*, a native and most aesthetic species. *Ilex glabra*, in its wildest form, is a spreading, suckering, colonizing broadleaf evergreen shrub of rather billowy constitution.

MORE ▶

Ilex decidua 'Warren's Red'

Ilex 'Emily Bruner'

Ilex decidua 'Finch's Gold'

Ilex 'Emily Bruner'

Ilex glabra CONTINUED

The flat, ¾- to 2-in.-long, lustrous dark green leaves may assume a bronzy purple cast in cold climates. Fruit are normally black, but several white-fruited forms are known. Inkberry grows in wet or drier soils, under acid or higher pH conditions, in full sun to moderate shade. One of the great plants for massing—trouble-free and beautiful. Certainly not used enough in modern landscaping. Grows 6 to 8 ft. high, 8 to 10 ft. wide. Zones 4 to 9. Nova Scotia to Florida, west to Mississippi.

CULTIVARS AND VARIETIES
Many of the newer cultivars offer great promise. A 2010 Longwood Gardens' report, evaluating 13 cultivars from 1999 to 2007, listed 'Densa', 'Bright Green', 'Shamrock', and 'Nigra' (in that order) as the best.

'Bright Green' has tiny, boxwood-like, brighter deep green leaves and upright-oval shape. Found in the New Jersey Pine Barrens.

'Compacta' is a somewhat oval-rounded, densely branched female form. It is a fine plant, but it tends to drop its lower foliage and becomes leggy at the base. Grows 4 to 6 (to 10) ft. high. Princeton Nursery introduction.

'Densa' has broad-mounded habit and deep green foliage. Observed a 10-ft.-high, leggy specimen with sparse fruit at the Arnold Arboretum.

Gold Mine™ is a gold-margined leaf sport of 'Shamrock'. "Wow" was my initial reaction; subsequent observa-

Ilex glabra, inkberry

Ilex glabra Gold Mine™

Ilex glabra 'Nigra'

Ilex glabra

Ilex glabra 'Densa'

tions indicated severe reversion tendencies to gold and green.

'Nigra' offers thick-textured, lustrous dark green leaves. Four-year-old plants are 2½ ft. high and 3 ft. wide, and leaves are retained on the lower branches. It is a female and produces lustrous black fruit.

Nordic® ('Chamzin') is a compact, more rounded form, and it, too, will drop its lower leaves. Grows 3 to 4 ft. high and wide.

'Shamrock' has lustrous dark green leaves and is denser in habit than 'Compacta' and 'Nordic'. Older plants exhibit a degree of legginess. Grows 5 ft. high and more.

Ilex ×koehneana
Koehne holly

I have introduced many visitors to *Ilex ×koehneana* in my Georgia trials, where it grows cheek-by-jowl with *I. opaca*. Numerous comments concern the former: "How beautiful compared to *I. opaca*!" and "Why is it not in commerce?" No easy response, except with thousands of hollies worldwide, there is little room for another species or cultivar in the marketplace. Interestingly, in ten years, *I. ×koehneana* outgrew the *I. opaca* cultivars by 50 percent

and was more dense, well shaped, and aesthetically pleasing: compact pyramid, densely branched, with bronze-purple new growth and lustrous dark green mature leaves. Leaves are 2 to 3½ (to 5) in. long with eight to 12, 1/16-in.-long, spiny teeth on each margin. Brilliant red, 1/3-in.-wide fruit ripen in early fall and persist. Any well-drained, acidic soil is suitable, full sun to partial shade. Displays high heat and drought resistance. Fast-growing, about 1½ to 2 ft. per year in average soil. Grows 20 to 25 ft. high, 10 to 15 ft. wide. Zones 7 to 9. Hybrid between *I. aquifolium* and *I. latifolia*. Not as cold hardy as 'Nellie R. Stevens'.
CULTIVARS AND VARIETIES
Many constituted through the years, with 'Hohman', 'Martha Berry', 'San Jose', and 'Wirt L. Winn' among the best.

'Agena' (female) and 'Ajax' (male), two vigorous U.S. National Arboretum releases, grow about 30 ft. high in 25 years.

Ilex latifolia
lusterleaf holly

Serves as a *Magnolia grandiflora* substitute by virtue of the large, 4- to 6½- (to 8-) in.-long leaves; several large

plants in Athens have been mistaken for southern magnolia. Matures into a broad pyramidal-oval shape with densely borne leaves, allowing for screening use. The thickish, lustrous dark green leaves are set with short, coarse, blackish gland-tipped teeth. The deep dull red, 1/3-in.-wide, globose fruit ripen in fall and hold into February and March, eventually becoming a duller, washed-out red. Extremely durable plant, tolerating full sun, mod-

MORE ▶

Ilex ×koehneana 'Wirt L. Winn'

Ilex glabra 'Shamrock'

Ilex ×koehneana, Koehne holly

Ilex latifolia CONTINUED

erate shade, drought, and heat. Amenable to pruning, like all hollies, and can be effectively espaliered against a wall. Makes a noble specimen or accent, screening, or grouping plant. Typically 20 to 25 ft. high, half as wide. Have observed 40-ft.-high specimens in Greenville, South Carolina, and on the University of North Carolina campus, Chapel Hill. Zones 7 to 9. Not as cold hardy as 'Nellie R. Stevens'. Japan, China.

CULTIVARS AND VARIETIES
'Mary Nell', named after the wife of J. C. McDaniel, University of Illinois, is a complex hybrid with *Ilex latifolia* as one part of the genetic puzzle. Has become more popular in southern nursery production because of glossy dark green leaves, red fruit, and pyramidal habit to around 20 ft. The only negative is the propensity to form multiple leaders; plants require considerable pruning during production.

Ilex ×meserveae
Meserve holly

This group of broadleaf evergreen hybrids has provided excellent choices for northern gardens. The Blue series cultivars, hybrids of *Ilex aquifolium* × *I. rugosa*, are shrubby in habit and offer leathery, lustrous dark green, almost blue-green leaves and excellent red fruit on the female forms. Grows 10 to 15 ft. high; can be pruned to maintain desired size and shape.

Several hybrids with *Ilex cornuta* × *I. rugosa* parentage have been introduced, and they are also quite worthy plants for northern gardens. These hybrids are more rounded, and the fruit can be spectacular. Several of these cultivars display greater heat tolerance than the Blue series cultivars. Grows 10 ft. high and wide; can be pruned to maintain any height. Zones (4)5 to 7.

CULTIVARS AND VARIETIES
'Blue Girl' and Blue Princess®

('Conapry') are the best females of the Blue series; 'Blue Boy' and Blue Prince® ('Conablu'), the best males. Hardy to −10 to −20°F, even lower with protection.

China Boy® ('Mesdob') and China Girl® ('Mesog'), introduced in 1979, are *Ilex cornuta* × *I. rugosa* hybrids. The ⅓-in.-wide, red fruit of China Girl® are outstanding. Hardy to about −20°F. Both range 10 ft. high and wide at maturity.

Dragon Lady® ('Meschick') is more correctly listed as an *Ilex ×aquipernyi* form (*I. pernyi* × *I. aquifolium*). Habit is distinctly pyramidal-columnar with lustrous dark green, spiny-margined leaves and large red fruit. Probably matures at 15 to 20 ft. by 4 to 6 ft.

Golden Girl® ('Mesgolg') is a golden-fruited hybrid (*Ilex cornuta* × *I. rugosa*); 12 to 15 ft. by 10 to 12 ft.

Red Beauty® ('Rutzan') is a narrow pyramidal-conical form that grew 7 ft. by 4 ft. in ten years. Produces abun-

Ilex 'Mary Nell'

Ilex latifolia, lusterleaf holly

Ilex ×meserveae 'Blue Girl'

dant, sparkling red fruit, and spiny, glossy dark green leaves. Meserve × *Ilex pernyi* hybrid.

Ilex mucronata
mountain holly

The name has changed, the plant is still the same. Previously, *Nemopanthus mucronatus*, a deciduous northern shrub with dark blue-green leaves, burgundy fall color, and fluorescent, vermilion-red fruit on 1-in.-long pedicels. Fruit ripen in August and September (Maine). Grows in moist to wet areas, in thickets, often in association with *Ilex verticillata* and *Viburnum cassinoides*. Nifty plant for naturalizing. Cannot remember "seeing" it in garden center commerce. An opportunity! Grows 6 to 10 ft. high and wide. Zones 4 to 6. Nova Scotia to Ontario, Wisconsin, and Virginia.

Ilex 'Nellie R. Stevens'

The grande dame of landscape hollies in the Southeast: common, overused, but beautifully functional to a pragmatic fault. Dense, broad-pyramidal outline, almost self-sustaining in maturity. The leaves, 2 to 3 (to 4) in. long, have two or three spines per margin. The long axis of the leaf is twisted, each leaf leathery lustrous dark green—the standard for other tree-type hollies. Flowers open in late March and April, and the ¼- to ⅓-in.-wide, bright red fruit ripen in fall and are less persistent

MORE ▶

Ilex ×*meserveae* Blue Princess®

Ilex mucronata, mountain holly

Ilex ×*meserveae* China Girl®

Ilex mucronata

Ilex mucronata fall color

Ilex 'Nellie R. Stevens' CONTINUED
than those of 'Emily Bruner'. Sun- and shade-tolerant, adaptable to any soils except wet. Keep fertilized for best leaf color. Eminently prunable; great hedge or screen. From Washington, D.C., to Florida, the first choice. Hybrid between *Ilex cornuta* 'Burfordii' and *I. aquifolium*. In our garden, even in deep shade, the habit without pruning was sufficiently dense to effect a solid

screen. Grows 15 to 25 ft. high, two-thirds as wide. Zones 6 to 9.
CULTIVARS AND VARIETIES
Discovered a yellow-leaf branch sport many years past, propagated and watched it develop into a rather pretty, 20-ft.-high, yellow-gold pyramid. Produces red fruit. I named it 'Golden Nellie'; Tony Avent called it 'Whoa Nellie'.

Ilex opaca
American holly
Considered by many gardeners the finest tree-type evergreen holly. The best forms have a densely pyramidal growth habit, dark green foliage, and abundant red fruit. Leaves are 1½ to 3½ in. in length, with widely spaced, spine-tipped teeth. Leaf miner, which causes serpentine tunnels, can be a problem. The dull red, ⅓-in.-wide fruit ripen in October and persist into winter. For optimal growth, provide moist, organic-laden, acid, well-drained soils, in sun or partial shade. Protect plants from desiccating winter sun and winds. Unfortunately for the grower, American holly is slow-growing; work in Ohio with 48 cultivars showed average growth of 6 in. per year. Use as a specimen or in groupings. Grows 40 to 50 ft. high, 18 to 40 ft. wide. Zones 5 to 9. Massachusetts to Florida, west to Missouri and Texas.
CULTIVARS AND VARIETIES
Cultivars are somewhat region-

Ilex 'Nellie R. Stevens'

Ilex opaca, American holly

Ilex 'Golden Nellie'

Ilex opaca 'Jersey Princess'

specific; over the years, more than 1,000 have been named. 'Carolina #2', 'Croonenburg' (one of the best), 'Dan Fenton', 'Jersey Princess', 'Judy Evans', 'Miss Helen', and 'Satyr Hill' are worth considering.

Dwarf spreading types include 'Clarendon Spreading' and 'Maryland Dwarf'; 'Canary', 'Goldie', and forma *xanthocarpa* with yellow fruit; and 'Christmas Snow' and 'Steward's Silver Crown' with cream-margined leaves.

Ilex pedunculosa
longstalk holly

An evergreen holly that looks like mountainlaurel (*Kalmia*), with long-stalked, bright red fruit and excellent cold hardiness—should be a sure thing in commerce, right? Wrong! Very few gardeners have heard of this plant. In its finest form, *Ilex pedunculosa* develops into a broad shrub or small tree, with 1- to 3-in.-long, lustrous dark green, entire-margined leaves. The ¼-in.-wide fruit occur on

1- to 2-in.-long stalks in October and November. Appears to be more tolerant of adverse conditions, particularly wind and cold, than many other hollies. Use in groupings, in borders, or as a specimen. Grows 20 to 30 ft. high, slightly less in spread. Zones 5 to 7. Japan, China.

Ilex Red Hollies

A series embracing several named introductions. The "red" refers to the color of the new growth, which is variable and not showstopping. All are females and produce ¼- to ⅓-in.-wide, red fruit. All are small, pyramidal trees with lustrous dark green leaves. Arose (supposedly) as open-pollinated seedlings of 'Mary Nell' in the 1980s. All are patented. Certainly they offer new foliage textures but it will be tough to supersede 'Nellie R. Stevens'. Southeastern nurserymen have grown the series, but whether they will continue to do so is question-

MORE ▶

Ilex opaca 'Maryland Dwarf'

Ilex opaca f. *xanthocarpa*

Ilex pedunculosa, longstalk holly

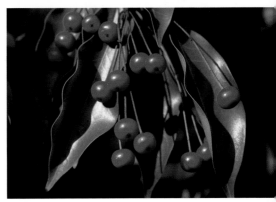

Ilex pedunculosa

able. Grows 10 to 15 (to 20) ft. high, half as wide, although size varies. Zones 7 to 9.

CULTIVARS AND VARIETIES
Cardinal™ ('Conal'), Festive™ ('Conive'), Little Red™ ('Coned'), Oak Leaf™ ('Conaf'), and Robin™ ('Conin') were the first introductions. Oak Leaf™ and Robin™ grow the fastest; Little Red™ and Festive™ the slowest.

Newer introductions include Arcadiana™ ('Magiana'), Liberty™ ('Conty'), Oakland™ ('Magland'), and Patriot™ ('Conot'). Liberty™ sports large, lustrous dark green, spiny leaves, abundant orange-red fruit, and upright pyramidal habit, 14 ft. by 8 ft. It is the best of the later introductions for aesthetics.

Ilex rotunda
Lord's holly

A rare species in cultivation but, based on my observation, one of the more heat-tolerant hollies. Reasonable specimens about 20 ft. high grow in the Coastal Plain of Georgia. Habit trends toward rounded-broad-spreading, forming a graceful canopy. The dark green leaves are entire and provide no clue as to holly affinity. The ¼-in.-wide fruit are borne in umbels on ¼-in.-long stalks from the leaf axils. In full fruit, the effect resembles a fireworks display. I remember a large specimen at the Coastal Garden in Savannah that would change anyone into a believer. Difficult to propagate via cuttings and nowhere common in trade. Appears to have uses for breeding. A collector's plant for zones 8 and 9(10). Japan and Korea.

Ilex serrata
finetooth holly

This broad-rounded, finely branched shrub plays second fiddle to the showier native *Ilex verticillata*, common winterberry. The 2- to 3-in.-long leaves emerge reddish purple and mature to dull dark green. The ¼-in.-wide, red fruit are smaller than and not as persistent as those of *I. verticillata*, and they will bleach (sun-scald) on the side exposed to full sun. Fruit occur in great numbers. I have observed many beautiful fruiting specimens and believe the species is worthy of consideration. It is one of the parents of the newer holly hybrids (*I. serrata* × *I. verticillata*). Grows 4 to 8 ft. high and wide; can reach 12 to 15 ft. Zones 5 to 8. Japan, China.

CULTIVARS AND VARIETIES
'Leucocarpa' produces creamy white fruit in great numbers.

Ilex serrata × *I. verticillata* Hybrids

Another popular group of deciduous hollies. New growth displays the rich plum-purple of *Ilex serrata*. The red fruit are larger and more persistent than those of *I. serrata*; and though

Ilex Oak Leaf™

Ilex Liberty™

Ilex rotunda, Lord's holly

they too will discolor (bleach) on sides exposed to sun, they remain unaffected longer. Zones 5 to 8.
CULTIVARS AND VARIETIES
'Autumn Glow', 'Bonfire', 'Harvest Red', and 'Sparkleberry' are the most common female forms, 'Harvest Red' and 'Bonfire' being the best of the bunch. These are vigorous, large shrubs in the 10-ft. range; their fruit color early and will bleach on the side facing the sun. 'Apollo' is a male for 'Sparkleberry'; 'Raritan Chief' is a male for 'Autumn Glow' and 'Harvest Red'.

Ilex verticillata
common winterberry
Like *Ilex decidua*, this is a deciduous species with bright red fruit, but it has a more compact habit and is better adapted to contemporary landscapes. The habit is distinctly oval to rounded, with a dense complement of fine, twiggy branches. Mature stems are dark gray to brown. The 1½- to 3-in.-long, dark green leaves may develop yellow- to purple-tinged fall color. The ¼-in.-wide, rounded, bright red fruit ripen in September and persist into December and January. A few cultivars, like 'Winter Red', may hold the fruit into March and April. For best landscape performance, site in full sun and provide moist, acid, reasonably fertile, well-drained soils. In the wild, it often grows in moist to wet soils. Great plant for color in the winter landscape. Use in groupings or masses for maximum effect. Needs a male for pollination. Grows 6 to 10 ft. high and wide. Zones 3 to 9. Eastern North America.
CULTIVARS AND VARIETIES
'Cacapon' is an upright-rounded form with large, true red fruit and glossy dark green, crinkled leaves. Grew 10

MORE ▶

Ilex serrata, finetooth holly

Ilex serrata 'Leucocarpa'

Ilex 'Sparkleberry'

Ilex verticillata CONTINUED

to 12 ft. in Georgia trials, where it was second to Winter Red® for fruit retention.

'La Have' is the most compact form I have observed, growing 3 ft. by 3½ ft. in 16 years in Georgia trials, densely branched with leathery, lustrous dark green foliage. Fruit ripen in September, persisting into winter. A good choice for smaller landscapes. Collected by Ray Fielding in Nova Scotia.

'Red Sprite' has lustrous dark green leaves and large, ⅜-in.-wide fruit. Grows 3 to 5 ft. high and wide.

'Winter Gold' bears ⅜-in.-wide fruit, yellowish, tinged pinkish orange, in great profusion. Rounded, multistemmed shrub, 7 ft. by 7 ft. Introduced by Robert Simpson, Vincennes, Indiana. Discovered as a branch sport of Winter Red®.

Winter Red® is the best selection for quantity and quality of bright red fruit. Fruit average ⅜ in. in diameter, and they do not discolor to the degree of other cultivars. Foliage is leathery, lustrous dark green. Grew 9 ft. high, 8 ft. wide in 30 years. Another Robert Simpson introduction.

Ilex vomitoria
yaupon

The quintessential southern holly—native, used with impunity, prospering everywhere, multi-functional, and attractive. My plane touches down

Ilex verticillata

Ilex verticillata, common winterberry

Ilex verticillata 'Red Sprite'

Ilex verticillata 'Winter Gold'

Ilex verticillata Winter Red®

at Houston's Intercontinental, and I peek out the window at fields of *Ilex vomitoria*. Bonnie and I visit Georgia's barrier islands, and I can barely contain myself before taking another photo of *I. vomitoria*. Variation is remarkable and has been exploited to select numerous cultivars. Typically a multi-stemmed, large, evergreen shrub, forming thickets. Bark, as on most hollies, is silver-gray to gray-brown. Finely serrated leaves, purplish tinged at emergence, eventually lustrous dark green, average ½ to 1½ in. long. The four-petaled, greenish white, ¼-in.-wide flowers open in mid to late April. The translucent, ¼-in.-wide fruit are produced in abundance and literally mask the branches. Fruit persist, often through winter, to the next year's flowering cycle. Grows in wet and dry, acid to alkaline soils, in sun and shade, withstanding salt spray and interminable pruning. Many uses including topiaries, hedges, freeforms, espaliers, loose screens, and groupings. Choice no-brainer selection, especially the compact cultivars, for green meatballs, gobs-of-green, and innocuous spinach. Grows 10 to 20 ft. high and wide. Zones 7 to 10. Southeastern Virginia to central Florida, west to Texas, southeastern Arkansas, and Oklahoma.

CULTIVARS AND VARIETIES
Bordeaux™ ('Condeaux') is a branch sport of 'Schillings' with more compact habit, smaller leaves, and wine-red winter leaf color; winter color is more green than purple on plants I observed. Will grow 5 ft. by 5 ft.

'Carolina Ruby' is a more compact selection with lustrous dark green leaves and abundant, shiny, ⅓-in.-wide, red fruit; 4 ft. and larger.

Hoskin Shadow™ ('Shadow's Female') has large, lustrous dark green leaves and abundant bright red fruit. More restrained and compact than the species. Estimate 10 to 15 ft. high.

MORE ▶

Ilex vomitoria, yaupon

Ilex vomitoria 'Nana'

Ilex vomitoria

Ilex vomitoria 'Pendula'

Ilex vomitoria CONTINUED

'Nana' is a female dwarf form, 5 ft. high, wider at maturity, with larger leaves than 'Schillings'. Ancient specimen on the Georgia campus was 10 ft. by 12 ft; cut to almost ground level, it has regenerated new shoots that cover the naked stems.

'Pendula' is a large (to 20 ft.) weeping form with red fruit; both male and female forms are offered. 'Folsom's Weeping', a female selection, is included here.

'Schillings' ('Stokes Dwarf'), one of the best compact forms, is 3 to 4 ft. high and wide, male, with purplish new shoot extensions.

'Will Fleming' is a fastigiate male form that is tight in youth but opens and splays to the point of no redemption with time. For all the hype about uprightness, a plant in the Georgia trials was 13 ft. by 12 ft. in nine years.

Illicium anisatum
Japanese anise-tree

Striking lustrous dark green leaves serve as the perfect contrast to the 1-in.-wide, 20- to 30-petaled, white, essentially nonfragrant flowers that open in March. Habit is pyramidal-columnar, often with a central leader. The wavy-surfaced leaves are 2 to 4 in. in length and are borne perpendicular to the stems. Requires shade and well-drained soil. It is not as hardy as *Illicium floridanum* or *I. parviflorum*, but in the Dirr garden, it does not flag in drought like these two species. Certainly a wonderful filler in the shady border. Always discernible because of the sheeny leaves. Grows 6 to 10 (to 15) ft. high, half as wide. A 25-ft.-high plant resides at the Atlanta Botanical Garden. Zones 7 to 9. Reported to have withstood −10°F on West Coast. China, Japan.

CULTIVARS AND VARIETIES
Several exciting new forms from Japan, with bronze-purple leaves and apricot-orange flowers, are now being evaluated and/or produced in commerce.

'Deep Purple' has rich lustrous purple new growth that matures lustrous dark green; subsequent growth flushes are also purple.

'Pink Stars' has pink-budded flowers that open pinkish white, new leaves reddish tinged fading to green. Introduced by JC Raulston Arboretum, Raleigh, North Carolina.

'Purple Haze' has intense rich purple new growth, maturing to yellow-green with green margins.

Variegated selections. An unnamed cream-margined, green-centered form of great beauty is listed from Hawksridge Nursery, Hickory, North Carolina.

Ilex vomitoria 'Schillings'

Illicium floridanum
Florida anise-tree

Almost unknown in the Southeast until the devastating freezes of the early 1980s, when this species surfaced as a possible alternative to redtip photinia and evergreen privets. Variable in habit from a relatively dense to a large, open, loose shrub. Easily restrained by tip pruning. Leaves are 2 to 6 in. long, entire, wavy-surfaced, and dull dark green. Several students described the bruised leaf odor as resembling a gin and tonic. How would they know? Flowers, 1 to 2 in. in diameter, maroon-purple, composed of 20 to 30 strap-shaped petals, open in April for four to six weeks. Fragrance is *stinky*! The 1- to 1½-in.-wide fruit are composed of 11 to 15 follicles in a star-like configuration. Grows in moist to wet soils. Shows drought stress. Requires shade in our Georgia garden to maintain dark green leaves. Wonderful in large groupings and masses. Grows 6 to 10 ft. high, wider at maturity. Zones 6 to 9. Florida, Georgia, Alabama, Mississippi, and Louisiana. Observed in the wild in north Florida, where it grew in a seepy habitat in dense shade.

CULTIVARS AND VARIETIES

'Cardinal' is a compact, mounded, green-leaf selection with red flowers; have observed only once. Estimate 3 to 4 ft. high at maturity.

'Halley's Comet' offers abundant flowers in spring and sporadically into fall; the deep red flowers are larger than the typical species. Grows 8 to 10 ft. high and wide.

'Pink Frost' is an upright, vigorous grower with good cold hardiness. Its marginal cream-swooshed, normal-sized leaves turn pink-rose in cold weather. Beautiful addition to a shady area of the new Dirr garden.

'Semmes' produces white flowers on a compact, 6 ft. by 6 ft. shrub growing by our front door, where it looks like a rhododendron. 'Alba' is similar but larger.

Shady Lady® ('Thayer') has wavy, gray-green leaves with gray-white marginal variegation and pink flowers. Potent variegation on a broad-mounded plant; not the fastest growing. Dodd & Dodd introduction.

MORE ▶

Illicium floridanum, Florida anise-tree

Illicium anisatum 'Purple Haze'

Illicium anisatum variegated form

Illicium anisatum, Japanese anise-tree

Illicium floridanum CONTINUED

'Southern Star' is a cream-margined leaf selection, the leaves somewhat distorted. Severely damaged at 13°F growing next to 'Pink Frost', which was unscathed.

Variegated selections. There are other, unremarkable, variegated types, as well as other compact ('Pebblebrook') and pink-flowered forms.

Illicium henryi
Henry anise-tree
Among the anise-trees, this is possibly the most aesthetic but least grown. Kalmia-like leaves, rigidly held, on an oval-rounded to pyramidal framework. The fragrant (when bruised) leaves, 4 to 5 (to 6) in. long, are lustrous dark green and maintain this color year-round. The rose-pink, ½- to 1-in.-wide flowers open in April and May. Requires shade for best growth but has succeeded in full sun better than *Illicium anisatum* or *I. floridanum*. More drought-tolerant than *I. floridanum*. In the Dirr garden, visitors frequently asked the identity of this species, which resided in an understory planting of eight other *Illicium* taxa. Superb textural element in the border, excellent screening evergreen under pines, the aristocrat of *Illicium* species. Grows 6 to 8 (to 15) ft. high, usually not quite as wide. Zones 7 to 9. China.

Illicium lanceolatum is similar in habit, leaf, and flower. I grew it and *I. henryi* side by side in Athens and saw minimal differences between the two.

Illicium mexicanum
Mexican anise-tree
Try as I might, I am unable to bond with this species because of the sprawling growth and mediocre performance. The leaves are similar to *Illicium floridanum* except more lustrous, with an elongated apex. Flowers (reddish) open in March and April in Athens, each 1½ to 2 in. across. Does not appear as prosperous under cultivation as other species discussed. Provide moist, well-drained soil in partial to moderate shade. For the collector only. Grows 5 ft. high and wide (the biggest I have observed). Zones 7 to 10. Mexico.

CULTIVARS AND VARIETIES
'Aztec Fire' has 2-in.-wide dark red-maroon flowers on long pedicels in May and June.

'Woodland Ruby' is a hybrid between *Illicium mexicanum* and *I. floridanum* with greater vigor; flowers are reddish pink and open in April and May.

Illicium parviflorum
small anise-tree
The true everyday garden plant among the anise-trees, with sun and shade

Illicium floridanum

Illicium floridanum 'Pink Frost'

Illicium floridanum 'Alba'

Illicium floridanum Shady Lady®

Illicium henryi, Henry anise-tree

resiliency, ease of culture, and beautiful olive-green foliage that distinguishes it from its taxonomic colleagues. Small, ½-in.-wide yellowish flowers are borne in the leaf axils from May through October. Fluffy, billowy masses of evergreen foliage drift through the understory, providing color, texture, and aromatic amenities. The 2- to 4-in.-long leaves are rich with safrole, the same oil that imparts fragrance to sassafras leaves. In the

MORE ▶

Illicium lanceolatum

Illicium mexicanum, Mexican anise-tree

Illicium parviflorum, small anise-tree

Illicium mexicanum

Illicium parviflorum CONTINUED
evening, the sweet odor is evident.
A former graduate student, Andrea
Southworth, determined that the
insect resistance of *Illicium* species
was related to the oil content of the
leaves. Nurserymen do not spray
Illicium for insects and diseases in the
production process. Prefers moist soil
in sun or shade. Requires pruning to
keep it in bounds. Grows 8 to 10 ft.
high, wider at maturity. Zones 6 to 9.
Found in wet areas in southern Georgia and Florida.

CULTIVARS AND VARIETIES
'Florida Sunshine', a yellow-leaf selection, is slower than the species but
commercially realistic. Found as a seedling by Tony Avent at Superior Trees
in Lee, Florida. Requires some shade
in the South. Beautiful color element
in shady areas of the garden. Plant
Introductions, Inc., may be releasing a
yellow-leaf selection with red-suffused
new yellow leaves, maturing to yellow.

'Forest Green' was the name I gave,
many years past, to a shiny dark
green, more oval-rounded leaf form.
Branches more fully and is decidedly
darker green than the species.

Variegated Form has white-green-
splashed, milky-wavy-patterned leaves;
not completely stable, but a few southeastern nurseries are growing.

Indigofera amblyantha
Save room for the indigoferas in the
garden: they are trouble-free and
aesthetically pleasing. Seeds of this
species, collected at the Hillier Arboretum in late January, produced flowering plants by June in Athens. The
leaves, composed of seven to 11,
½- to 1-in.-long, gray-green to bright
green leaflets, bring a low-key color
contrast to the dark green leaves of

other *Indigofera* species. Flowers are
unique, developing from each leaf axil
and held upright in a slender, elongated, conical raceme, 2 to 5 in. long,
that continues to lengthen as flowers
open. Buds are deeper rose-pink,
close to shrimp-pink, opening lighter,
and effective from April into fall. Like
the other indigoferas treated herein,
this species flowers on new growth,
so pruning promotes increased flower
development. Culture and use as for
Indigofera heterantha. Fits into herbaceous borders, for it functions as
a cut-back shrub that when pruned in
late winter will be glorious by summer. I may have scaled the heights
of hyperbole: the plant can also look
like a tall ragamuffin. Grows 4 to 6 (to
10) ft. high and wide. Zones 6 to 8.
China.

Indigofera amblyantha

Illicium parviflorum

Illicium parviflorum 'Florida Sunshine'

Indigofera decora 'Rosea'

Indigofera decora
Chinese indigo

What a wonderful chance discovery, years past at an antebellum home across from the Georgia campus, where a low subshrub with pink wisteria-like flowers was growing in the shade of pecan trees. Another key-out quest was performed, with this species surfacing as the leading candidate. A suckering, spreading shrub with seven to 13, 1- to 2½-in.-long, dark almost blue-green leaflets per leaf. Flowers, each ¾ in. long, pink, in 4- to 8-in.-long, 20- to 40-flowered racemes, explode in May (Athens) and continue sporadically into August and September on new growth. Have yet to observe fruit set. I hoped to breed this species with the others for improved floral characteristics. Prefers moist, moderately fertile, acid soil in partial shade (best) to full sun. Some foliage lightening in full sun but no diminution in floral production. Displays excellent heat and drought tolerance. Use as a groundcover in shade, at the front of a border, and in bank plantings. One of Bonnie's favorite plants. Our fine colony prospered under the shade of a southern red oak, *Quercus falcata*. Grows 12 to 18 in. high, spreads indefinitely. Zones 6 and 7(8). China, Japan.

CULTIVARS AND VARIETIES
'Alba', with white flowers, is in cultivation.

'Rosea' has deeper rose-pink flowers with a hint of lavender.

Indigofera heterantha
syn. *Indigofera gerardiana*
Himalayan indigo

A perpetual motion, i.e., flowering machine, initiating in June (April, May, June in Athens) and continuing through September on the new growth. I tested the plant for ten years at the University of Georgia, and its resilience in heat and drought was borderline miraculous. A rounded shrub, loose and refined, requiring some pruning to keep it tidy and presentable. The leaves are composed of 13 to 21 leaflets, each about ½ in. long and blue-green. The rose-purple, ½-in.-long flowers occur in a 3- to 5-in.-long raceme with 24 or more clustered along the axis of the raceme. Moderate moisture and fertility produce active growth, and as long as new growth emerges, new flowers are formed. Requires full sun, and moist, well-drained soils; pH adaptable. Excellent border plant. Functions as a "big" herbaceous perennial. Can be cut back in winter and will explode with new growth and flowers in summer. Grows 4 to 6 ft. high and wide; 4 ft. by 6 ft. in Georgia trials. Zones 6 to 8. Himalayas.

Indigofera decora, Chinese indigo

Indigofera heterantha, Himalayan indigo

Indigofera kirilowii
Kirilow indigo

A little-known but rather pretty shrub, this species forms great swaths of bright green spring foliage, followed in May, June, and July by rose-colored flowers borne in 4- to 5-in.-long, erect inflorescences. The leaves are composed of seven to 11 leaflets, each leaflet ½ to 1½ in. long. Extremely adaptable, well suited to acid and calcareous soils. Requires full sun for best growth. Tip prune to encourage new growth and thus new flowers. The plant may respond like a herbaceous perennial in extremely cold climates, but it comes back to normal by the summer. Use as a large groundcover on banks, parking lot islands, and other dry sites. Forms colonies 3 to 6 ft. high and wide. Zones 4 to 7(8). China, Korea, southern Japan.
CULTIVARS AND VARIETIES
'Alba' (var. *alba*), a white-flowered form, has lighter green foliage.

Indigofera kirilowii, Kirilow indigo

Itea virginica, Virginia sweetspire

Itea virginica
Virginia sweetspire

Ask American gardeners if they've ever heard of *Itea*, and most would probably answer no. With the selection of new forms, however, the species has become more popular. *Itea virginica* is found along shady stream banks throughout its native range. The roots dip their apices into the water, and the long, arching shoots playfully tickle the water's surface. The habit is strongly suckering and multi-stemmed, forming a rounded-mounded colony. The lustrous rich to dark green, 1½- to 4-in.-long leaves turn shades of yellow-orange, reddish purple, scarlet, and crimson in fall. In mild winters, the leaves persist into December and beyond. Fragrant white flowers occur in 2- to 6-in.-long, ⅝-in.-wide racemes in May (Athens), June, and July, and they are borne in sufficient numbers to be quite effective. One of the easiest shrubs to grow. It

Indigofera kirilowii

Itea virginica fall color

390

withstands heavy shade and full sun, in moist, wet to drier soils. Excessive drought causes leaf necrosis. Great plant for massing, along waterways, on banks, or in a border. One of my favorite shrubs. Grows 3 to 5 ft. high, generally greater in spread. Zones 5 to 9. New Jersey to Florida, west to Missouri and Louisiana.

CULTIVARS AND VARIETIES
Exciting breeding work for pink-flowered selections by Dr. Josh Kardos, Plant Introductions, Inc. Seedlings from controlled crosses flowered in the second year with spectacular red-purple fall color.

'Beppu' ('Nana') was originally described as an *Itea japonica* clone but was misidentified and belongs to *I. virginica*. Thought to be compact, it reached 4 to 5 ft. high in the University's Botanical Garden, where fall color varied from bright red to red-purple.

'Henry's Garnet' is a choice selection from the campus of Swarthmore College in Pennsylvania. It produces inflorescences up to 6 in. long and has consistent, brilliant reddish purple fall color. Grows 4 to 5 ft. high, about 6 ft. wide. Still the best of the many introductions.

Little Henry™ ('Sprich') is more compact, typically 3 to 4 ft. high, but I have observed 6-ft.-high plants. Flowers 3 to 4 in. long; red-purple fall color.

'Theodore Klein' is more upright, with smaller, 3- to 3½-in.-long inflorescences. Fall color is respectable red-purple; holds leaves later than 'Henry's Garnet'.

Ixora coccinea
ixora, flame of the woods

Handsome broadleaf evergreen shrub with beautiful red to orange-red summer flowers. Densely branched and foliated with dark green, leathery, opposite to whorled leaves up to 4 in. long. Young leaves are bronze-colored. Flowers, borne in axillary corymbs dur-

MORE ▶

Itea virginica 'Henry's Garnet'

Itea virginica 'Henry's Garnet' fall color

Ixora coccinea, ixora

Itea virginica 'Theodore Klein' fall color

ing summer, are effective for a long period; the tubular corolla is divided into four lobes at the end, each 1½ to 2 in. long. The fruit, rounded, about ½ in. in diameter, purplish black, ripen in fall. Prefers moderate to high fertility, acid soils, and partial shade. Foliage becomes chlorotic in high pH soils. Use in groupings, foundations, hedges, and masses. Grows 4 to 6 ft. high and wide. Zones 9 to 11. Southeast Asia, India.

Jasminum floridum
showy jasmine

Unusual among the more than 200 *Jasminum* species in that the leaves are alternately arranged. The masses of slender, arching, angular, glabrous green stems merge into an irregular haystack. Appears a degree more "messy" than *Jasminum nudiflorum*. The smallish dark green leaves are semi-evergreen to evergreen, depending on the degree of cold. Yellow flow-

ers appear on new growth from late April through June and flickeringly into fall. Have not observed fruit on campus plants. Makes a good massing plant. Prefers sun to partial shade in moist, well-drained soil. Grows 3 to 5 ft. high and wide. Zones (7)8 to 10. China.

Jasminum humile
Italian yellow jasmine

Slightly different from the other jasmine species, more upright, in the 5- to 7-ft.-high range, with three to seven leaflets per alternate leaf. The dark green leaves are semi-evergreen to evergreen. The minimally fragrant yellow flowers open in June and do not overwhelm. Glossy black, rounded berries were evident on cultivated plants in England. Best sited in partial shade in well-drained soil. Has displayed good heat and drought tolerance in Athens. More of a novelty plant, nowhere common. Frequently brought to me for identification, as it does not fit the typical jasmine profile. Noted a 12-ft.-high plant in England. Zones 7 to 9. Middle East, Myanmar, China.
CULTIVARS AND VARIETIES
'Revolutum' is larger, more cold hardy, and often with more leaflets.

Jasminum mesnyi
primrose jasmine

The first time I spied the species, the primrose-yellow, semi-double flowers were sparkling in the March sun. Flowering continues sporadically into April in Athens. Great billowy masses are forged when plants are sited in close proximity. Individually, the plant develops a mounded, broad-spreading habit with trailing branches. The lustrous dark green evergreen leaves are comprised of three leaflets, each 1 to 3 in. long. The 1½-in.-wide, semi-double flower is composed of six to ten divisions. Wonderfully adaptable and tolerates sun and moderate shade. Terrific in bank plantings, mass groupings, or as a *tall* groundcover. Beautiful in flower and well suited to gardens in the Coastal Plain of the Southeast. Grows 5 to 6 (to 9) ft. high, wider at maturity. Several massive plants on the Georgia campus that survived −3°F (but were defoliated and beaten back) rejuvenated and were feistily extant with all foliage present in late February 2010 after a cold winter. Zones (7)8 and 9. China.

Ixora coccinea

Jasminum floridum

Jasminum floridum, showy jasmine

Jasminum nudiflorum
winter jasmine

Waxy maroon-red buds explode to brilliant forsythia-yellow flowers from January through March. The flowers, each 1½ to 2 in. long, ¾ to 1 in. across, with five or six wavy corolla lobes, appear on naked stems. The four-angled, olive-green stems are attractive and provide both winter interest and background for the flowers. Leaves, oppositely arranged, are composed of three leaflets, lustrous deep green, each ½ to 1¼ in. long. For

MORE ▶

Jasminum humile, Italian yellow jasmine

Jasminum humile

Jasminum mesnyi

Jasminum mesnyi, primrose jasmine

Jasminum nudiflorum, winter jasmine

Jasminum nudiflorum CONTINUED
erodable slopes, banks, unmanageable areas, and groundcover use, this is the plant of choice. The branches root in contact with the soil, producing an interwoven fabric that is impenetrable. No special soil requirement; full sun to moderate shade permit ease of culture. Grows 3 to 4 ft. high, 4 to 7 ft. wide. Zones 6 to 10. China. CULTIVARS AND VARIETIES 'Variegatum' ('Argenteum', 'Mystique') is similar to the species but less vigorous, with whitish leaf margins and gray-green centers.

Jasminum officinale
common white jasmine
A delightfully fragrant twining vine, deciduous to semi-evergreen, producing flowers throughout summer. The oppositely arranged leaves, rich green, are composed of five to nine leaflets, each ½ to 2½ in. long and ⅙ to 1 in. wide. The ¾- to 1-in.-long and -wide, four- to five-lobed white flowers open from June through October. Partial shade and moist, well-drained soil prove beneficial. Great plant for trellises, walls, fences. One of the most cherished plants in English gardens. Grows 10 to 20 (to 30) ft. on about any climbing structure. Zones 8 to 10. Caucasus, northern Iran, Afghanistan, Himalayas, China.

Jasminum beesianum is a vining species that has been root hardy to 5°F. Pretty pink-rose flowers open in May in zone 7.

Jasminum officinale, common white jasmine

Jasminum nudiflorum

Jasminum officinale 'Inverleith'

Jasminum beesianum

Jasminum officinale 'Aureovariegatum'

CULTIVARS AND VARIETIES
'Affine' has pink-tinged flowers opening white.

'Aureovariegatum' ('Aureum') has yellow-blotched leaves.

Fiona Sunrise™ ('Frojas') has yellow emerging leaves that fade to green.

'Inverleith' has red flower buds and backs of the outer petals that contrast with the pure white inner surface.

Jasminum parkeri
dwarf jasmine

A wonderful, cute, diminutive evergreen shrub, mounded and spreading, that could serve as an effective groundcover. The alternate leaves, compound pinnate, composed of three to five, ⅛- to ⅜-in.-long, dark green leaflets, serve as a perfect contrast to the ½- to ¾-in.-long, ½-in.-wide, six-lobed, yellow flowers. Flowers appear in May and June and may be followed by greenish white, translucent, globose, ⅙-in.-wide berries. Requires good drainage, wind protection. Useful rock garden or container plant, or as a filler at the front of a border. Grows 12 (to 24) in. high, 30 in. wide. Zones (8)9 and 10. Northwest India.

Juglans nigra
black walnut

Like the hickories of the genus *Carya*, *Juglans* species are seldom planted in the everyday landscape. If native, however, they are certainly worth saving, and on large properties, a grouping of black walnut serves an aesthetically pleasing as well as functional purpose (the nuts are edible). This is a massive, upright-spreading tree that dwarfs the average home. The dark yellow-green, pinnately compound leaves drop sporadically through the growing season, especially on trees stressed by drought. The leaflets

MORE ▶

Jasminum parkeri, dwarf jasmine

Juglans nigra

Juglans nigra, black walnut

Juglans nigra

Juglans nigra CONTINUED

average 2 to 5 in. long and are strongly aromatic. The green, 1½- to 2-in.-wide, rounded fruit cascade to the ground, seemingly continually, in late summer and fall—one needs to wear a hard hat in the garden. Black walnut makes its best growth in deep, alluvial, moist, well-drained soils. Certainly not a plant for every landscape. Grows 50 to 75 ft. high. Zones 4 to 9. Massachusetts to Florida, west to Minnesota and Texas.

CULTIVARS AND VARIETIES
'Laciniata' has finely divided leaflets that impart a fern-like texture.

Juglans regia
Persian or English walnut

This species produces the thin-shelled nuts that are so common in mixes around the holidays. (Commercial nut production is centered in California.) The habit is distinctly rounded, with large, spreading branches forming a rather open crown. The deep green, compound pinnate leaves are composed of five to nine, 2- to 5-in.-long leaflets and do not develop appreciable fall color. Soils should be deep and loamy. Grows 40 to 60 ft. high and wide. Zones 4 to 9. Southeastern Europe to China and the Himalayas.

Juglans nigra 'Laciniata'

Juglans regia

Juglans regia, Persian walnut

Juniperus

juniper

Junipers have lost favor; in the 1970s and '80s, numerous new juniper introductions were being promoted; in the past ten years, perhaps ten or less. Nurseries have reduced production accordingly, by some 50 to 70 percent; the gardening public is now looking for colorful flowering shrubs and broadleaf evergreens. But without question junipers remain the most ubiquitous of all needle evergreens for general landscape use: they inhabit the most adverse cultural niches in nature, and they bring this durability to the altered landscape. Highly variable in habit, junipers exist as 60-ft.-tall trees and sprawling, 2- to 4-in.-high groundcovers. All have small, needle or scale-like foliage ranging in color from green to blue. They are readily transplanted and will prosper in anything but wet soils. Full sun is necessary for maximum growth. Mites, bagworms, and juniper blight (fungus) are the principal problems. Junipers are used for screens, groupings, masses, hedges, single specimens, groundcovers, and topiary. The following species and cultivars represent the more common types available for American landscapes.

Juniperus chinensis

Chinese juniper

The variation in this species has caused many good taxonomists to lose their minds. Some authorities have proposed that the shrubby types be included with *Juniperus* ×*media* (*J. chinensis* × *J. sabina*). The species has green to blue-green, needle-like foliage. The fleshy, rounded, silvery to blue cones, which range in size from 1/3 to 1/2 in. in diameter, are often the largest of the cultivated junipers. Grows 50 to 60 ft. high. Zones 3 to 9. China, Japan, Korea, Myanmar.

CULTIVARS AND VARIETIES

'Ames' initially grows as a dwarf spreading shrub but with time develops a broad-pyramidal shape, 8 to 10 ft. high. Steel-blue, needle-like foliage initially, turning green when mature; does not appear to cone heavily.

'Blue Alps' has blue, needle-type foliage on a full, dense plant with no disease problems. A pretty specimen, 12 ft. by 8 ft., grows at JC Raulston Arboretum.

Gold Coast® ('Aurea Improved') is a graceful, compact, spreading form with golden yellow new growth that persists and deepens in cold weather.

'Hetzii' is a large, upright-spreading female form with distinct bluish green needles. Landscape size, 5 to 10 ft. high and wide.

'Hetzii Columnaris' is a good plant for screens or vertical accents because of its uniform, columnar-pyramidal outline. This female cultivar has blue-green needles and sets abundant cones. Grows 15 to 20 ft. high.

'Kaizuka' ('Torulosa') is a softly textured, rich green form with tight, bunchy growth. The pyramidal growth habit is artistic and sculptural. Female with silver cones. Grows 20 ft. high or more. A cream-white splashed variegated form is available.

'Keteleeri', commonly used in Midwest landscapes, has scale-like, grass-green foliage and a distinct broad-pyramidal outline. Sets

MORE ▶

Juniperus chinensis 'Blue Alps'

Juniperus chinensis Gold Coast®

Juniperus chinensis 'Hetzii'

Juniperus chinensis CONTINUED

abundant crops of silvery cones. Grows 15 to 20 ft. high.

'Pfitzeriana' ('Wilhelm Pfitzer') is the granddaddy of juniper cultivars and still one of the most popular. A male cultivar, Pfitzer (as it is commonly known) forms a large, 5- to 10-ft.-high shrub. The branches diverge from the central axis at a 45° angle, with the outer tips somewhat pendulous. The foliage is sage-green. Use as a foundation shrub, in masses, on banks, or as an accent. Many cultivars, including the next three, have been selected from branch sports of 'Pfitzeriana'.

Juniperus chinensis 'Kaizuka'

Juniperus chinensis 'Pfitzeriana'

Juniperus chinensis 'Pfitzeriana Aurea'

Juniperus chinensis 'Robusta Green'

Juniperus chinensis 'San Jose'

'Pfitzeriana Aurea' has golden new growth that matures to green.

'Pfitzeriana Compacta' is a compact form, with the typical Pfitzer foliage. Grows 4 ft. high, 4 to 6 ft. wide at maturity.

'Pfitzeriana Glauca' has soft, bluish gray-green foliage and a habit similar to that of 'Pfitzeriana'. More wide spreading than 'Hetzii', although it is often confused with that cultivar.

'Robusta Green' has a certain artistic bent, displaying heavy tufts of gray-green foliage on an upright, open framework. Sets abundant cones. Makes a good accent or container plant. I have seen 15-ft.-high plants.

'San Jose', a popular cultivar for massing or groundcovers, has sage-green foliage that is both needled and scale-like. Grows 1 to 2 ft. high, 7 to 9 ft. wide.

Variety *sargentii* is truly one of the best groundcover types because of its handsome blue-green (more green than blue), scale-like foliage. 'Glauca' is a selection of var. *sargentii* with bluer needle color. Both grow 1½ to 2 ft. high, 6 to 8 ft. wide.

'Sea Green' is a compact spreader with fountain-like, arching branches and rich, dark minty green foliage. Grows 4 to 6 ft. high, 6 to 8 ft. wide.

Juniperus chinensis 'Parsonii'

syn. *Juniperus davurica* 'Parsonii' ('Expansa')

'Parsonii', the major representative of so-called Dahurian juniper in the trade, has primarily soft-textured, gray-green, scale-like needles, with an occasional shoot of prickly, needle-like foliage. This cultivar is

MORE ▶

Juniperus chinensis 'Keteleeri'

Juniperus chinensis 'Parsonii'

Juniperus chinensis 'Expansa Aureospicata'

Juniperus chinensis var. *sargentii*

Juniperus chinensis 'Sea Green'

Juniperus chinensis 'Parsonii' CONTINUED often confused with *Juniperus chinensis* 'San Jose', but it differs in its foliage characteristics and in the presence of cones. Growth habit is a dome-shaped mound. 'Expansa Variegata', with creamy white splotches, and 'Expansa Aureospicata', with golden splashes, are also known. Displays high heat adaptability and is one of the most successful groundcover junipers in the Southeast. Grows 2 to 3 ft. high, 8 to 9 ft. wide. Zones (5)6 to 9. Japan.

Juniperus chinensis var. *procumbens*

syn. *Juniperus procumbens*

Japanese garden juniper

I have always considered this dwarf, procumbent form one of the best groundcover junipers. It has long, wide-spreading, stiff branches and rich, shiny blue-green needles. Grows 2 ft. high, 10 to 12 ft. wide; plants over 3 ft. high and 22 ft. wide are known. Zones 4 to 9. Japan.
CULTIVARS AND VARIETIES
'Greenmound' (probably the same as 'Nana Californica') is lower growing with greener needles. It does not "hump up" in the middle like 'Nana' and has a soft, flat, rug-like texture. Grows 8 in. high, 4 to 6 ft. wide.

'Nana' is a groundcover juniper that can be used as a great accent or draped over a wall or structure. The needles are smaller and more closely spaced than those of the species. By no means compact, it can grow 2 to 2½ ft. high and 10 to 12 ft. wide.

Juniperus communis

common juniper

A fantastically varied species. I reflect on abandoned pastures in New England, where this species was domi-

Juniperus chinensis var. *procumbens*, Japanese garden juniper

Juniperus chinensis var. *procumbens* 'Nana'

Juniperus communis, common juniper

Juniperus communis Blueberry Delight™

nant and where I found variation from large, columnar tree types to low groundcovers. The spine-tipped, ½- to ¾-in.-long needles are usually dark green to bluish green below with a broad, silvery white band above. Prefers colder climates than the *Juniperus chinensis* types. Grows 5 to 10 (to 15) ft. high, 8 to 12 ft. wide; can

reach 40 ft. high. Zones 2 to 5(6). Worldwide.

CULTIVARS AND VARIETIES
Blueberry Delight™ ('AmiDak') has dark green needles, silver-blue on upper surface, and ascending branches, tips slightly arching. A worthy selection for Midwest and Plains states; 1 ft. by 4 to 5 ft.

'Depressa' is a low, broad, vase-shaped shrub, rarely growing taller than 4 ft. It spreads to form large circular masses. Many plants in the wild look like this form.

'Depressa Aurea' has strong, yellow-variegated shoots that fade with time.

'Hibernica' is a tall, columnar form with bluish green, prickly needles. It was common in older landscapes but has lost favor and is now seldom available in commerce. Called Irish juniper. Grows 10 to 15 ft. high or more.

'Saxatilis' (var. *saxatilis*) is typically low-growing to semi-prostrate with short blue-green needles. Have

observed enough discrepancies to know that one 'Saxatilis' is not the same as another.

'Suecica', Swedish juniper, is quite similar to 'Hibernica', except the tips of its branchlets droop.

Juniperus horizontalis
creeping juniper

A true spreading groundcover type with blue-green, plume-like, soft-textured foliage. Grows 1 to 4 ft. high, spread is variable. Zones 3 to 9. Nova Scotia to British Columbia, south in the higher elevations. Hiked Monhegan Island, Maine, where hanging from the cliffs above the Atlantic was the species in numerous foliage color manifestations, facing the full force of the maritime conditions.

CULTIVARS AND VARIETIES
Excessive selections, 69 described in the *Manual* (2009). All consistently develop mauve to deep purple colors

MORE ▶

Juniperus communis 'Depressa Aurea'

Juniperus communis 'Hibernica'

Juniperus communis 'Saxatilis'

Juniperus horizontalis, creeping juniper

Juniperus horizontalis 'Bar Harbor' winter color

Juniperus horizontalis 'Blue Chip'

Juniperus horizontalis 'Blue Horizon'

Juniperus horizontalis 'Plumosa'

Juniperus horizontalis 'Wiltonii'

in cold weather—a good way to distinguish creeping junipers from other groundcover junipers. Phomopsis blight can be more troublesome on this group.

'Bar Harbor' has bluish green summer foliage that turns reddish purple in winter. It is a male. Grows 8 to 12 in. high, 6 to 8 ft. wide.

'Blue Chip' is a true blue-needled form. Appears better suited to cooler climates. Susceptible to phomopsis blight. Grows 8 to 12 in. high, 8 to 10 ft. wide.

'Blue Horizon' is a genuine pancake, never mounding in the center. It has blue-green foliage that turns bronze-green in winter.

'Golden Carpet', 'Gold Strike', 'Maiden Gold', and 'Mother Lode' are yellow to gold sports of 'Wiltonii'. May develop yellow-orange, tinged with plum coloration in winter.

'Lime Glow' has chartreuse veering to yellow needle color that darkens to burnt orange in winter. Sport of 'Plumosa'?

'Plumosa', long the dominant creeping juniper cultivar, was once found in virtually every retail outlet in the United States. Blue-green summer foliage turns a rather ugly purple-bronze in winter. Grows 2 ft. high, up to 10 ft. wide. 'Plumosa Compacta', a male, tends to be smaller in habit and fuller in the center, and its foliage is light purple in winter.

'Wiltonii' ('Blue Rug') is an almost carpet-like form, with rich blue foliage that turns slight mauve in winter. Possibly the most popular groundcover juniper; this plant is "everywhere," judging by my travels around the United States. Female with small silver-blue cones. Grows 4 to 6 in. high, 6 to 8 ft. wide.

Juniperus rigida subsp. *conferta*

syn. *Juniperus conferta*
shore juniper
Truly a superb groundcover for dry, sandy soils and areas where salinity poses a problem. The rich blue-green, prickly, ¼- to ⅝-in.-long needles lose some of their sheen in cold weather. The silvery, ⅓- to ½-in.-wide cones are attractive throughout the year. Grows 1 to 1½ ft. high, 6 to 9 ft. wide. Zones

MORE ▶

Juniperus horizontalis 'Mother Lode'

Juniperus rigida subsp. *conferta* 'Blue Pacific'

Juniperus rigida subsp. *conferta*, shore juniper

Juniperus rigida subsp. *conferta* 'All Gold'

403

Juniperus rigida subsp. *conferta* CONTINUED
(5)6 to 9. Japan, Sakhalin, where it grows on sandy seashores.
CULTIVARS AND VARIETIES
'All Gold' has soft yellow needles and compact, low-spreading habit. Observed in high summer and winter with foliage color somewhat reduced. In production in the Southeast.

'Blue Pacific' has superseded the species in many areas of the United States because of its more compact habit and superior foliage. The rich, ocean blue-green needles are shorter and more densely borne than those of the species, and they do not discolor in cold weather to the degree of those of the species. Usually grows less than 1 ft. high.

'Emerald Sea' is somewhat similar to 'Blue Pacific', but with looser blue-green foliage and a taller habit. Considered hardier than either the typical species or 'Blue Pacific'.

'Silver Mist', with more compact habit and a distinct silvery cast to its blue-green needles, is a delightful addition to the stable of *Juniperus rigida* subsp. *conferta* cultivars.

Juniperus sabina
Savin juniper
Another variable species that exists as a groundcover as well as a columnar-pyramidal tree. Chiefly represented by the cultivars. The foliage is soft and scale-like, varying in color from green to blue. Bruised foliage has the strong odor of the oil of juniper, a characteristic that can be used to separate this from other species and cultivars. Zones 3 to 7. Mountains of central and southern Europe, the Caucasus, western Asia, Siberia.

Juniperus rigida subsp. *conferta* 'Silver Mist'

Juniperus sabina 'Broadmoor'

Juniperus sabina 'Tamariscifolia'

Juniperus scopulorum 'Blue Heaven'

'Broadmoor' is an excellent low-spreading male form with green foliage. Has performed well in the Midwest. Resistant to juniper blight. Grows 2 to 3 ft. high, up to 10 ft. wide.

'Tamariscifolia' (var. *tamariscifolia*) has been around forever. At times it appears world-class and at other times worn-out, tired, and bedraggled. Typical habit is broad-mounded with rich green foliage. Grows 1½ to 2 ft. high, 10 to 15 ft. wide. A blue-needled form is also in cultivation.

Juniperus scopulorum
Rocky Mountain juniper

This species is the western counterpart to the eastern redcedar, *Juniperus virginiana*, and the distinguishing characteristics between the two are minimal. This species is softly pyramidal in habit, with needle color varying from light green or gray-green to dark green, blue-green, and almost silver-blue. Numerous selections have been made, primarily for foliage color. In general, these plants are better suited to the northern and western states. Phomopsis blight, seiridium canker, and cedar apple rust are problematic. Have not observed a mature specimen in zone 7. Grows 30 to 40 ft. high, 3 to 15 ft. wide. Zones 3 to 6(7). Western North America.

CULTIVARS AND VARIETIES
'Blue Heaven' is a uniform, pyramidal form with striking blue foliage in

MORE ▶

Juniperus scopulorum 'Tolleson's Weeping'

Juniperus scopulorum, Rocky Mountain juniper

Juniperus scopulorum 'Skyrocket'

Juniperus scopulorum CONTINUED

all seasons. Also bears heavy cone crops.

'Skyrocket' is probably the most narrowly columnar of all junipers, and a 15-ft.-high plant may be only 2 ft. wide at the base. Foliage is primarily needle-like and bluish green. In winter, it often develops a slight purple tinge.

'Tolleson's Weeping' has silver-blue foliage that hangs string-like from arching branches. Rather interesting accent or container plant. A green-foliaged form, 'Tolleson's Green Weeping', is also available; both 20 ft. by 8 to 12 ft.

'Welchii' is another narrow, compact form, with silvery blue new growth that matures to bluish green. Have only seen 8-ft.-high plants but suspect larger at maturity.

'Wichita Blue' has brilliant, bright blue foliage and a pyramidal habit. Grows 18 ft. high or more, 5 to 8 ft. wide.

Juniperus scopulorum 'Wichita Blue'

Juniperus squamata
single-seed juniper

The cultivars are the only representatives of this species in cultivation. Supposedly quite variable in growth habit over its native range. Generally not as adaptable, North or South, as the other types presented here. Cultivars like 'Blue Star' are extensively planted but seldom persist for long periods in the South. Requires well-drained soils for consistent, long-term

Juniperus squamata 'Blue Carpet'

Juniperus squamata 'Blue Spider'

performance. Zones 4 to 7. Afghanistan, the Himalayas, western China.
CULTIVARS AND VARIETIES
'Blue Carpet' is a handsome groundcover form with rich blue-green foliage. Grows 8 to 12 in. high, 4 to 5 ft. wide.

'Blue Spider', akin to 'Blue Carpet', with perhaps more elongated, silver-blue shoots, becoming higher mounded in the center.

'Blue Star' is a much-ballyhooed cultivar, with rich silver-blue foliage that assumes a dirty tinge in winter. A low, rounded, squat plant, as broad as it is high. Grows 3 ft. high, 3 to 4 ft. wide.

'Meyeri' is the tried-and-true standard of this group, commonly found in older landscapes in the United States.

It has rich silvery blue-green foliage. Called fish-tail juniper because the branches resemble a fish's tail. Can become worn and ragged with age. Grows 5 ft. high, 4 ft. wide; plants to 20 ft. high are known. Many branch sports have arisen from this cultivar, including 'Blue Star' and 'Blue Carpet'.

Juniperus virginiana
eastern redcedar

A tough, irrepressible green soldier that can prosper where few other plants even survive. Found over a wide range in the midwestern, eastern, and southeastern United States. Densely columnar to broad-pyramidal in outline, it is a great screening, grouping, or naturalizing type of plant. Habit more open and artistic with age. The rich green summer foliage assumes a ruddy, yellow-green to brown-green color in winter. Male trees produce thousands of tiny brown cones that yield clouds of yellowish pollen in March and April. The female trees are often covered with frosty, rich blue, $\frac{1}{5}$- to $\frac{1}{4}$-in.-wide cones that provide good bird browse. Recently walked the Highland Light area, Truro, Cape Cod, Massachusetts, as well as the Outer

Banks of North Carolina, and there, in pure sand, grew quite contentedly thousands of *Juniperus virginiana* in the nutrient-deficient, windswept, salt-laden habitat. Grows 40 to 50 ft. high, 8 to 20 ft. wide. Zones 3 to 9. Eastern and central North America.

CULTIVARS AND VARIETIES
The many reliable selections raise the species to a higher level of landscape suitability.

'Burkii' has glaucous gray-green foliage that remains in juvenile form, prickly and needle-like, developing a light purple cast in cold weather. Its habit is pyramidal, maturing to a more open, loose pyramid around 20 ft. high. Handsome 25-ft.-high plant in the University's Botanical Garden.

MORE ▶

Juniperus squamata 'Meyeri'

Juniperus squamata 'Blue Star'

Juniperus virginiana, eastern redcedar

Juniperus virginiana CONTINUED

'Canaertii' is quite common in the Midwest. Its dark green, soft-textured, scale-like foliage appears tufted, particularly at the ends of the branches. Heavily pruned plants can be quite dense, but left unpruned, they become open and artistic. A female clone, setting large quantities of blue-green cones. Grows 20 to 30 ft. high.

'Emerald Sentinel' develops a pyramidal-columnar shape with dark green foliage and silver cones. Reaches 15 to 20 (to 30) ft. by 6 to 10 ft.; grew 30 ft. by 8 to 10 ft. in 15 years at Milliken Arboretum, Spartanburg, South Carolina. One of the best.

'Grey Owl' is an interesting spreading form with soft, silvery gray-green foliage. Grows 3 ft. high, 6 ft. wide, and produces abundant glaucous cones. Among the best of the shrubby, spreading junipers. Possibly a hybrid (*Juniperus virginiana* 'Glauca' × 'Pfitzeriana').

'High Shoals' with upright pyramidal habit has rich green foliage suffused with gray and maintains this color in winter. Estimate 25 ft. by 10 ft. A female. Selected from a native Georgia population by Ray Tate, Angel Creek Nursery, Bishop, Georgia.

'Pendula' covers any arching, weeping type, and I have encountered many: some large and irregular, others barely rising above ground level.

'Taylor' is an upright conical-columnar form that has gained traction in the Plains states; possibly the most

Juniperus virginiana 'Canaertii'

Juniperus virginiana 'Burkii'

Juniperus virginiana male cones

Juniperus virginiana female cones

upright eastern redcedar selection; observed in January in Wichita, Kansas, and needles were brownish.

Juniperus virginiana var. silicicola

syn. *Juniperus silicicola*
southern redcedar

In terms of taxonomic minutiae, possibly nothing more than the southern extension of *Juniperus virginiana*. However, extensive travels through central Florida and the Gulf Coast support horticultural differences. Typically a broad dense pyramid, finer in texture than its northern relative, with smaller bright green needles and cones. Trees in the Orlando area are 30 to 40 ft. high; the national champion in Alachua County, Florida, is 77 ft. high, 55 ft. wide. Grows on the sand dunes and coastal marsh edges in full sun. Use for screens, windbreaks, and hedges. Small, 1/5-in.-wide, blue-green cones provide feed

MORE ▶

Juniperus virginiana 'Emerald Sentinel'

Juniperus virginiana 'Grey Owl'

Juniperus virginiana var. *silicicola*, southern redcedar

Juniperus virginiana var. *silicicola* 'Brodie'

409

Juniperus virginiana var. *silicicola* CONTINUED
for birds. Zones 7 to 9(10). Southeastern United States.
CULTIVARS AND VARIETIES
'Brodie' is an upright form, 20 to 25
ft. high, 4 to 6 ft. wide, with scale-
like, grass-green foliage in summer
becoming more sage-green in winter.
A female with small silvery cones. One
of the best upright screening evergreens for the South.

'Glauca Compacta' is a broad-
columnar form with rich blue foliage,
slightly tinted purple-blue in winter;
grows 5 to 10 ft. high, 3 to 7 ft. wide,
female; one of the most beautiful
junipers.

Kadsura japonica

If only it were hardier, the commercial demand for this vigorous twining
vine would exceed supply. Its young
stems are delicate and reddish, with
2- to 4-in.-long, dark green leaves
that recall *Hoya carnosa*, a common
houseplant. Fragrant cream-ivory flowers emerge from the leaf axils and are
followed by 1-in.-long, fleshy, scarlet
berries. Place in partial to moderate shade in deep, moist soil high in
organic matter. Not as wild as *Campsis radicans* and *Wisteria* species.
Grows 12 to 15 ft.; requires a structure for support. Zones (7)8 and 9.
Leaves decimated in Athens at 13°F

on a south-facing brick wall. Japan,
China.
CULTIVARS AND VARIETIES
'Chirimen' has cream-white marbling
and streaking throughout the leaf.
Somewhat unstable and may revert to
green.

'Fukurin' offers leaves edged to various degrees with cream and yellow;
these same areas are rose-tinged in
winter.

Kalmia angustifolia
lambkill, sheep laurel

Restrained, diminutive, rounded evergreen shrub in its best presentation.
Leaves 1 to 1½ in. long, ¼ to ¾ in.
wide, are oblong to elliptic, rather
delicate and a pretty, soft blue-green.
Foliage is listed as poisonous. Flowers are rose-pink to purplish crimson,
½ in. across in 2-in.-wide corymbs,
opening in June and July. Quite pretty
and restrained in full flower. In nature,
grows on rocky, barren, old pastures,
wet sterile soils, often in semi-shade.
Not the easiest plant to culture.
Observed in New England gardens
and in the wild; never in Southeast,
although it is native to high elevations
in Georgia. Grows 1 to 3 ft. high and
wide. Zones 1 to 6. Newfoundland and
Hudson Bay to Michigan and Georgia.
CULTIVARS AND VARIETIES
White- ('Candida') and deep pink- to
rose- ('Rosea' and 'Rubra') flowered
forms are known.

Juniperus virginiana var. *silicicola* 'Glauca Compacta'

Kadsura japonica 'Chirimen'

Kadsura japonica 'Fukurin'

Kalmia latifolia
mountainlaurel

Many gardeners wax poetic over the wonderful floral display of this species. Without question, it is one of the handsomest flowering broadleaf evergreens, surpassing even the rhododendrons in its finest forms. The flowers, each ¾ to 1 in. across, are massed in 4- to 6-in.-wide inflorescences. The individual flowers offer intricate beauty, opening in May and June to a broad bell shape showing ten stamens with flexed filaments. The typical species ranges in color from white to pink; the habit is dense and rounded in full sun, more open and artistic when grown in shade. The 2- to 5-in.-long leaves emerge bronze, changing to lustrous dark green at maturity. Easily transplanted from containers or as balled-and-burlapped specimens. Plants prefer excellent drainage, acid soils, and winter shade, especially in the Midwest and Southeast. My success with mountainlaurel has been less than laudatory. As a mass or grouping in a shady border, *Kalmia latifolia* has few equals. Grows 7 to 15 ft. high and wide; newer cultivars are smaller. National champion is 20 ft. high. Zones 4 to 9. New

MORE ▶

Kalmia angustifolia, lambkill

Kalmia latifolia, mountainlaurel

Kalmia angustifolia

Kalmia latifolia 'Freckles'

Kalmia latifolia 'Fuscata'

Kalmia latifolia CONTINUED

Brunswick to Florida, west to Ohio and Tennessee.

CULTIVARS AND VARIETIES

At least 75 are known, and any attempt to describe them is beyond the scope of this book. Richard Jaynes is the author of *Kalmia: Mountain Laurel and Related Species* (1997), an excellent resource on the wide variety of mountainlaurel cultivars. His great breeding work, combined with the efforts of several West Coast horticulturists, has widened the range of flower colors, from pure white to almost red, with banding and flecking of the corolla.

'Carousel', with intricate starburst pattern of bright purplish cinnamon pigmentation inside the corolla, is striking.

'Freckles' has light pink buds, opening creamy white, with purple spots above the ten anther pouches.

'Fuscata' (f. *fuscata*) has a broad brownish, purple, or cinnamon band inside the corolla.

'Nipmuck', with intense red buds, opens light pink to creamy white.

'Ostbo Red', an excellent red-budded form with pink flowers, remains readily available in the trade.

'Raspberry Glow' has deep burgundy buds that open to deep raspberry-pink flowers; foliage is dark green.

'Sarah' is a beauty, with vivid red buds opening to bright pink-red flowers. Excellent foliage and compact habit, 3 to 4 ft. high.

Kalopanax septemlobus

syn. *Kalopanax pictus*

castor-aralia

In July and August, the entire canopy of this tree is covered with a creamy veil of flowers. The flowers are borne in immense, 10- to 14-in.-wide, umbellose panicles at the ends of the branches. In youth the habit is upright-oval, coarse, gaunt, and not particularly attractive; with age, rounded, massive, and impressive. The large, clubby, coarse stems are armed with stout, broad-based prickles. Old trunks become gray-black and deeply ridged and furrowed. The five- to seven-lobed, glossy dark green leaves are often 10 to 14 in. long and wide, lending an almost tropical appearance to the landscape. Fall color is sporadic; occasional yellow is about the optimum. Prefers moist, well-drained soils but is adaptable. Foliage and floral characteristics make this an interesting tree for large-scale use. Tends toward weediness as stray seedlings pop up on occasion. Grows 40 to 60 ft. high and wide. Zones 4 to 7. Japan, Korea, China, Russian Far East.

CULTIVARS AND VARIETIES

Variety *maximowiczii* has deeply cut lobes, each leaf reminiscent of the foot of a fine-toed dinosaur.

Kalmia latifolia 'Ostbo Red'

Kalmia latifolia 'Sarah'

Kalopanax septemlobus, castor-aralia

Kerria japonica
Japanese kerria

This fine heirloom shrub pops up in the most unusual places. Its tenacious constitution allows it to thrive where other plants disappear. The typical form is broad-mounded with a twiggy framework of bright green stems, spreading by stolons and consuming significant real estate. The bright green, 1½- to 4-in.-long leaves may develop lemon-yellow fall color. Bright yellow, five-petaled flowers, 1¼ to 1¾ in. in diameter, open during April and into May and are effective for two to three weeks. Flowers also develop sporadically through summer. Provide reasonable drainage in virtually any soil, from acid to high pH. For best flower effect, site in partial shade, because the yellow tends to bleach in full sun. Makes a great plant for the shady shrub or perennial border. Also useful in large masses. When the shrub becomes overgrown or unkempt, simply cut it to the ground after flowering. Grows 3 to 6 ft. high, slightly greater in spread. Zones 4 to 9. China.

CULTIVARS AND VARIETIES
'Albescens' is an off-white (cream-yellow) form that grew in the Dirr garden for many years. Not as vigorous as the species.

'Golden Guinea' and 'Shannon' produce larger golden yellow flowers than the typical species.

'Picta' is a dapper selection, smaller in stature, with gray-green leaves edged in white. Will revert to green and these shoots should be removed. Flowers are yellow but not as profuse or well-formed as those of the species. Site in some shade.

'Pleniflora' is quite common in southern gardens, less so in northern.

MORE ▶

Kalopanax septemlobus

Kalopanax septemlobus

Kerria japonica, Japanese kerria

Kalopanax septemlobus var. *maximowiczii*

Kerria japonica

413

Kerria japonica CONTINUED

It bears double, 1- to 2-in.-wide, almost ball-shaped, golden yellow flowers. Extremely vigorous and suckers with a vengeance. The looser the soil, the wider its reach. Magnificent in flower. Its bloom coincides with that of dame's rocket (*Hesperis*) and columbine (*Aquilegia*). Grows 6 to 8 ft. high or more.

Variegated selections. Several second-rate forms like 'Chiba Gold', 'Fubuki Nishiki', and 'Geisha' show up in commerce. All show reversionist tendencies.

Koelreuteria bipinnata
bougainvillea goldenraintree, Chinese flametree

Medium-sized tree on the ascension in southern gardens because of the late summer yellow flowers and pink capsules. Habit is beanpole-like in youth, becoming vase-shaped to rounded with age. The bipinnately compound, lustrous rich green leaves produce a tropical aura. In our garden, two trees literally stopped traffic in late August and early September when the

Kerria japonica 'Albescens'

Koelreuteria bipinnata, bougainvillea goldenraintree

Kerria japonica 'Picta'

Koelreuteria bipinnata

Kerria japonica 'Pleniflora'

Koelreuteria bipinnata

immense panicles, 12 to 24 (to 30) in. long, 8 to 18 in. wide, were slathered with bright yellow flowers. Flowers occur at the end of the shoots, the entire tree an orb of floral sunshine. The papery, three-valved capsules, 1 to 2 in. long, pink to rose, color soon after flowering and hold for three to five weeks. Capsules collected at peak color can be dried and will hold their color. Withstands drought, full sun, and miserable soils. Use as specimen or work into a border and underplant with shade-tolerant shrubs. Is weed-like and produces numerous

seedlings; Bonnie and I hoed 1,001 per garden year. Grows 20 to 30 (to 40) ft. high, about two-thirds as wide. Flowers on new growth, and even one- to two-year-old trees will flower. Zones 6 to 8(9). China.

Koelreuteria elegans, Chinese raintree, flamegold, is closely allied to *K. bipinnata* but less cold hardy, smaller, and densely round-headed in habit. Flowers and fruit are similar in color. Generally 20 to 30 ft. high and wide. Utilized in Florida, Gulf Coast and Louisiana. Zones 9 and 10(11). Taiwan, Fiji.

Koelreuteria paniculata
panicled goldenraintree

This species never receives its due, but it offers amazing climatic and cultural adaptability as well as stunning flowers and handsome fruit. In youth the habit is irregular, but with age it assumes a uniform, rounded outline. The seven to 15 leaflets of the rich green, compound pinnate leaves may turn a respectable golden yellow in fall, but more often than not fall color is disappointing. Rich yellow flowers appear at the ends of the branches in

MORE ▶

Koelreuteria paniculata, panicled goldenraintree

Koelreuteria paniculata

Koelreuteria paniculata 'Coral Sun'

415

Koelreuteria paniculata CONTINUED

June and July. Each flower is only ½ in. wide, but they occur in prodigious quantities, forming 12- to 15-in.-long and -wide, airy panicles. The papery, lantern-like, 1½- to 2-in.-long capsules pass from rich green to yellow to brown. The brown fruit persist for a time and become rather ragged. The species withstands drought, heat, and wind, and tolerates high pH or acid soils. Extremely fast-growing in moist, well-drained soils. Three- to four-year-old trees will flower. Excellent small lawn specimen. Use for shading a patio, as a street tree, in groupings, or in planters. Grows 30 to 40 ft. high and wide. Zones 5 to 9. China, Japan, Korea.

CULTIVARS AND VARIETIES

Selections are being made for superior habit, foliage, flower, and fruit.

'Coral Sun' has orange-red new growth that fades to green; the petioles remain reddish. Appears to be a weak grower.

'Fastigiata' is a distinct columnar form that seldom flowers. Older trees are rather ragged and unkempt. Grows 25 ft. high with a 4- to 6-ft. spread.

Golden Candle™ is a new introduction that looks suspiciously like 'Fastigiata' although listed as growing 35 ft. by 4 ft.

'September' has a broad-rounded habit and produces masses of yellow flowers in late August and September. Slightly less cold-tolerant than the species, it is hardy to zone (5)6. Reproduces true to type from seed.

'Sunleaf' has superior leaf gloss that gives the plant a healthy persona.

Koelreuteria paniculata fall color

Koelreuteria paniculata 'September'

Koelreuteria paniculata 'Fastigiata'

Kolkwitzia amabilis
beautybush

I have tried to love this species because it was one of Ernest H. Wilson's favorites, but I still cannot embrace it fully for general garden use. Beautybush bears lovely pinkish flowers in May and June that, at their best, smother the dull, dark blue-green foliage. Unfortunately, the rest of the year it offers little to excite even a passionate gardener. Fruit are bristly, ovoid capsules with "chicken feet" appendages: a tell-tale identification feature. The habit is upright-arching and vase-shaped with a fountain-like outline. Bark is light grayish brown and exfoliating on older stems. Tends toward openness at the base. Easy to grow, and perhaps worthy of inclu-sion in the shrub border. I have seen too many freestanding specimens that beg for help. Grows 6 to 10 (to 15) ft. high, slightly less in spread. Zones 4 to 8. China.

CULTIVARS AND VARIETIES
Dream Catcher™ ('Maradco') is a disastrous yellow-leaf calamity, perhaps worse, as Paul Cappiello and I gazed on a forlorn plant at Yew Dell Gardens in Kentucky, in June, with leaves that were toast or soon to be.

'Pink Cloud' and 'Rosea' offer deeper pink flowers than those of the species.

+Laburnocytisus adamii

A curious anomaly of great botanical interest and considerable collector's

MORE ▶

+Laburnocytisus adamii

Kolkwitzia amabilis, beautybush

Kolkwitzia amabilis Dream Catcher™

Kolkwitzia amabilis

Kolkwitzia amabilis

417

value. It is a graft-hybrid between *Cytisus* (now *Chamaecytisus*) *purpureus* and *Laburnum anagyroides*. A shoot that developed at the graft union contained cells of both parents. Forms a small tree, somewhat graceful in stature. Flowers, yellow, pinkish purple, and combination-colored, appear willy-nilly throughout the tree. Leaves display intermediate characteristics. A tree grew quite successfully at the Arnold Arboretum, so hardiness is a zone 6. Grows 15 to 25 ft. high. Arose in 1825.

Laburnum ×watereri

Waterer laburnum, goldenchain tree

Where plants are happy, golden chains of flowers cascade from the branches like yellow water over rocks, producing a spectacular landscape effect. Unfortunately, over most of the United States the flowering performance of this hybrid species does not measure up to that of specimens growing in cooler, more even climates, like that of England, where there is greater bud set and flowering. The habit is stiffly upright-spreading, usually with a flat-topped crown at maturity. The bark on younger branches is a pronounced olive-green. The bright green to almost blue-green, trifoliate foliage does not develop good fall color. Slightly fragrant, yellow, pea-shaped flowers appear in May and June in 6- to 10-in.-long, pendulous racemes. In cool weather, flowers last ten to 14 days. Tolerant of a variety of soils, but not long-lived, particularly in the Midwest and East. Prefers cooler summer temperatures. Grows 15 to 20 ft. high and wide. Zones 5 to 7.

The parent species, *Laburnum anagyroides* and *L. alpinum*, each have cultivars named 'Pendulum' that offer slender, weeping branches and reasonable flower production, as does 'Alford's Weeping', a selection of the latter.
CULTIVARS AND VARIETIES
'Vossii' is a superior form of Waterer

laburnum, with a denser habit and racemes up to 2 ft. long.

Lagerstroemia

crapemyrtle

To travel the South from June through August is to understand why crapemyrtles are the best flowering shrubs/trees for gardens large and small. Without question, they are premier flowering woody landscape plants for

zones 7 to 10, the Southeast, Southwest, and into California. Significant new introductions in the past decade have reenergized and excited gardeners. Requires significant summer heat to ripen the wood. Remarkably, flowering specimens grow in Philadelphia, St. Louis, Cincinnati, Boston, and on Martha's Vineyard, Massachusetts. In zone 7 (Athens), flowers develop on early cultivars in mid June

Laburnum ×watereri, Waterer laburnum

Lagerstroemia Cherry Dazzle®

with July and August peak, and lingering flowers in September; in Birmingham, Alabama, I noticed 'Natchez' in flower in late May. Cultivars flower on new growth of the season and should always be pruned lightly in the dormant season, never stubbed back to large-diameter trunks and limbs. For all, full sun, good air movement, and well-drained, acid soil are ideal. Crapemyrtles are not fussy but may require

fertilizer applications in late winter to keep the foliage rich green and spur strong shoot growth and flower development. The spectacular bark is often overlooked (flowers first), but the rich gray, cream, brown, rust, and sheathing combinations are equally beautiful. In our garden, a multi-stemmed allée of 'Natchez' was remarkable for the beauty of the cinnamon-colored bark. At 25 ft. high, the flowers were not

even noticeable until petals fell. Food for landscape thought.

Emerging spring foliage varies from fresh green to bronze, red, and purple combinations. The tender foliage is sensitive to late spring frosts, and 28 to 32°F will cause damage. Fall color depends on climatic conditions with long, cool (no freezes) autumns ideal for the yellow, orange, and red displays. Some cultivars like 'Sioux' have excellent fall color. Mildew, cercospora leaf spot, flea beetle, Japanese beetle (flowers and leaves), and Asian ambrosia beetle may cause problems. Ideally, plant the most disease-resistant cultivars and keep them actively growing. Easily propagated from softwood, hardwood cuttings, and seeds. Seedlings will flower in a single season from seed planted in the greenhouse in January in zone 7.

True genetic dwarfs 2 to 3 ft. high

MORE ▶

Lagerstroemia Diamond Dazzle®

Lagerstroemia Sweetheart Dazzle®

Lagerstroemia Berry Dazzle®

Lagerstroemia Strawberry Dazzle®

Lagerstroemia CONTINUED

(such as 'Pocomoke', bred by Dr. Don Egolf, U.S. National Arboretum) to 50-ft. tree-like *Lagerstroemia subcostata* var. *fauriei* 'Fantasy' reflect the great variation. Dr. Egolf introduced 27 cultivars over his remarkable career. Newer introductions are still emerging from his work. All are discussed in this treatment.

Dr. Carl Whitcomb, Lacebark Farms, Stillwater, Oklahoma, has bred crapemyrtles for about 30 years with early introductions like 'Prairie Lace' and 'Centennial Spirit' now outdistanced by Dynamite® ('Whit II'), Pink Velour® ('Whit III'), Red Rocket® ('Whit IV'), and five additional. His true reds Dynamite® and Red Rocket®, especially the latter, are outstanding.

Exuberance invaded every fiber of my body when I learned about the Fleming Filigree® series, described as cold hardy to −30°F. Skepticism too,

as I fully understand the cold hardiness limitations of the genus to about −10°F (at best). Finally obtained 'Coral Filli', 'Red Filli', and 'Violet Filli' for testing. Actually, colors are muted, habits weak and open, cercospora leaf spot susceptibility high, and commerical appeal minimal compared to Dr. Whitcomb's, Dr. Egolf's, and my own introductions.

Since 1997, my Georgia crapemyrtle breeding program has focused on compactness (ideally less than 5 ft.), clean foliage, and profuse, colorful flowers, with a true red-flowered form a major objective. Several early introductions were stinkbombs, but persistence and patience have lined the garden path with Berry Dazzle® (fuchsia-purple), Cherry Dazzle® (red), Diamond Dazzle® (white), Strawberry Dazzle® (near strawberry-rose), and Sweetheart Dazzle® (pink). Additionally, Cherry Dazzle® breeding work led

to Red Rooster®, a mid-size, true and brilliantly clean red-flowered selection. All are licensed to McCorkle Nursery, Dearing, Georgia, by the University of Georgia and Plant Introductions, Inc. PII continues to breed intermediate types, 5 to 10 ft. high, with colorful, disease-resistant foliage and vivid flower colors. 'Coral Magic', 'Plum Magic', 'Purple Magic', and 'Red Magic' are the 2011 introductions. Visit www.plantintroductions.com for information.

The Early Bird™ series from the Southern Living Plant Collection offers selections with lavender, purple, or white flowers that open as early as Mother's Day.

Lagerstroemia indica

The true "summer lilac" of southern gardens, with fluffy 6- to 12-in.-long, 3- to 6-in.-wide panicles of white, pink, lavender, watermelon-red, red,

Lagerstroemia Red Rooster®

Lagerstroemia 'Plum Magic'

Lagerstroemia 'Red Magic'

Lagerstroemia indica fall color

and purple. Foliage, given little press, when free of mildew and leaf spot, is dark green, eventually reinventing itself in autumnal yellows, oranges, and reds. Early fall freezes render foliage hay brown and as dry. Bark is exfoliating, exposing smooth inner bark, with snakeskin-like molting in summer. Ancient trunks are sinewy, smooth, artistic, and sculptural. Colors are cream, light brown to brown, usually not as colorful as *Lagerstroemia subcostata* var. *fauriei* or many of the hybrids. Full sun, moist, well-drained soil are requisites. Once established, will withstand considerable drought. Choice plant for specimen use, groupings, containers, urban settings, large shrub/small street tree. Height range is extreme: typically 15 to 25 ft. high, but plants can be 3 to 45 ft. high. Zones (6)7 to 9. China, Korea.

CULTIVARS AND VARIETIES

'Byers Wonderful White' produces dense white flowers. Upright habit to 20 ft.

'Carolina Beauty' is the time-honored common red-flowered form. Abundant yellow stamens; high susceptibility to mildew. Grows 20 ft. high.

'Catawba' (Egolf hybrid) has lustrous dark green, leathery leaves, excellent orange-red fall color, dark purple flowers; good mildew resistance. Grows 10 to 15 ft. high. One of the best purple-flowered cultivars.

'Cedar Red' is a smaller shrub form, 6 to 10 ft. high, with reddish purple new growth and red flowers with yellow stamens.

MORE ▶

Lagerstroemia indica

Lagerstroemia indica 'Carolina Beauty'

Lagerstroemia indica 'Catawba'

Lagerstroemia indica CONTINUED

'Centennial' is a compact form with bright lavender flowers. Grew this for a time, but flowers never measured up. Grows 3 to 5 ft. high.

'Cherokee' (Egolf hybrid), a red-flowered form with high mildew susceptibility, never found commercial acceptance. Grows about 10 ft. high.

'Comanche' (Egolf hybrid) is a loose, spreading form with coral-pink flowers. Grows 10 to 15 ft. high.

'Conestoga' (Egolf hybrid) has lavender-pink flowers on long splaying shoots. Open habit, grows 10 to 15 ft. high.

'Crescent Moon' is a remarkable white-flowering form with rich green, disease-resistant leaves. Habit is compact rounded, 3 to 4 ft. high and wide. The best white in Georgia trials. Flowered three times in 2010 when spent flowers were removed.

'Dallas Red' is a "red" flowered selection that displayed excellent winter hardiness at the JC Raulston Arboretum. Grows 20 ft. high or more.

Delta Jazz™ ('Chocolate Mocha'), with unique dark burgundy cupped leaves and brilliant pink flowers, grows 6 to 10 ft. high, 4 to 5 ft. wide. Foliage color persists in the heat of zone 7. Flower production is sparse. Displays high foliar disease resistance.

Lagerstroemia indica 'Byers Wonderful White'

Lagerstroemia indica 'Cedar Red'

Lagerstroemia indica 'Centennial'

Lagerstroemia indica Dynamite®

Lagerstroemia indica Pink Velour®

422

Dynamite® ('Whit II') is just that, with explosive red flowers smothering the foliage. I first witnessed it in early September in full flower and could not fully comprehend the intensity of the red. Vigorous upright habit to 20 ft. high; good mildew resistance. More susceptible to cercospora leaf spot than Red Rocket®. From Dr. Carl Whitcomb's breeding program.

'Hardy Lavender' is an old-time selection with medium lavender flowers. An upright grower to 20 ft.

'Near East' produces soft pink flowers on enormous, broad, billowy panicles on a framework of 10 ft. or more; moderate mildew resistance.

'Ocmulgee' is a compact shrub with dark green leaves, red-maroon buds, red flowers. Grows 3 to 4 ft. high and wide; aphids and sooty mold are problematic.

Pink Velour® ('Whit III') has crimson buds, opening fluorescent deep pink; beautiful burgundy new growth turns purple-green to dark green. Grows 10 to 12 ft. high; mildew-resistant. Potent in flower. High cercospora leaf spot susceptibility.

'Potomac' (Egolf introduction) develops clear medium pink flowers. Upright habit, 10 to 15 ft. high, half as wide; mildew susceptible.

MORE ▶

Lagerstroemia indica 'Near East'

Lagerstroemia indica 'Potomac'

Lagerstroemia indica Raspberry Sundae®

Lagerstroemia indica Red Rocket®

Lagerstroemia indica Rhapsody in Pink®

423

Lagerstroemia indica 'Seminole'

Lagerstroemia indica 'Crescent Moon'

Lagerstroemia indica 'Velma's Royal Delight'

Lagerstroemia indica Delta Jazz™

Lagerstroemia indica 'Watermelon Red'

'Powhatan' (Egolf introduction) flowers are medium purple, on a 10- to 12-ft.-high and -wide shrub; mildew-resistant.

Raspberry Sundae® ('Whit I') has crimson buds that open cardinal-red to pink, similar to red raspberries. Upright habit to 15 ft. high; slight susceptibility to mildew.

Red Rocket® ('Whit IV'), with beautiful pure red flowers, dark green leaves, upright habit 10 to 15 ft. high, and cercospora leaf spot resistance, has been a standout in Georgia trials.

Rhapsody in Pink® has merlot-tinted young leaves and soft pink flowers and produces little fruit. Upright habit to 12 ft.

'Seminole' was a favorite pink in the Dirr garden, rich, vibrant, and clear. The 10- to 15-ft.-high framework is smothered in July and August; mildew-resistant.

'Velma's Royal Delight' was the most cold hardy form in Dr. John Pair's evaluations at Wichita, Kansas; small in stature, 5 ft. high, 4 ft. wide, it produces abundant magenta flowers in summer.

'Victor' is much like 'Ocmulgee' with dark red flowers on a 3- to 5-ft.-high and -wide shrub. Good mildew resistance; susceptible to aphids and sooty mold.

'Watermelon Red' is appropriately named, with flowers of this color on a 15-ft.-and-higher upright shrub; mildew susceptible.

Lagerstroemia limii

Rare species with thickish, large, blue-green leaves that suggest little affinity with the genus. Rather unkempt shrub that itself deserves minimal garden space; however, it has been used for breeding purposes by the U.S. National Arboretum, with 'Arapaho' and 'Cheyenne' two of the latest red to blood-red releases from Dr. Egolf's program. Flowers are lavender-purple in a compact inflorescence. Exfoliating light cinnamon-brown bark is attractive. Cultural requirements are similar to those discussed in the introduction. Possibly a collector's plant. Grows 10 to 15 ft. high. Best specimen I ever observed resides at the JC Raulston Arboretum. Zones 6 to 9. China.

Lagerstroemia subcostata var. fauriei

syn. *Lagerstroemia fauriei*
Introduced in the 1950s from Japan by the U.S. National Arboretum, this became a most important source of mildew resistance and rich cinnamon bark in Dr. Egolf's breeding program. Early seedlings were sent

MORE ▶

Lagerstroemia limii

Lagerstroemia limii

Lagerstroemia subcostata var. *fauriei*

Lagerstroemia subcostata var. *fauriei*

425

to cooperating institutions, including North Carolina State University, where trees over 50 ft. high still exist. Habit is vase-shaped, similar to American elm, with a cloud of medium green, almost peach leaf-like foliage that turns yellow in autumn. Cinnamon-brown, chestnut-brown to dark red-brown bark is the primary ornamental calling card. This wonderful trait has been transmitted to many of Dr. Egolf's hybrids. Flowers lack the pizzazz of *Lagerstroemia indica* and the hybrids. In Athens, moderately fragrant, white flowers in 2- to 4- (to 6-) in.-long, upright pyramidal panicles open in early June. Reflowering does not occur, a trait that is inherent in *L. indica*. Fruit on the species are six-valved, dehiscent capsules with wafer-like brown seeds. Transplant as container-grown plants. Growth is maximized in moist, well-drained soils and full sun. Useful as a specimen plant, perhaps as a street tree if properly pruned. Almost always low-branched and multi-stemmed, so single stems must be trained from youth. Grows 30 ft. high or more, half as wide. Zones (6)7 to 9. Japan.

CULTIVARS AND VARIETIES

'Fantasy' is a tight vase-shaped selection with beautiful cinnamon-brown bark, white flowers, and yellow fall color. Extremely fast-growing, will grow 40 to 50 ft. high; mildew-resistant. Introduced by Dr. J. C. Raulston.

'Kiowa' grew 30 ft. high, 25 ft. wide, at the U.S. National Arboretum. White flowers and cinnamon-brown bark; mildew-resistant. This was one of Dr. Egolf's favorite forms. Somewhat difficult to propagate and never made commercial inroads.

'Sarah's Favorite' is similar to and may be a hybrid like 'Natchez', but its growth habit is not as floppy, and it is more cold hardy and flowers over a longer period. Fall color, on occasion, is a potent orange to red. Grows 20 ft. high or more; mildew-resistant.

'Townhouse', from the JC Raulston Arboretum, has darker red-brown bark. Probably will grow 20 to 30 ft. high, almost as wide; mildew-resistant.

Lagerstroemia Hybrids

These hybrids, all Egolf introductions, resulted from crosses of *Lagerstroemia indica*, *L. limii*, and *L. subcostata* var. *fauriei*, the latter parent providing mildew resistance and cinnamon-brown bark (on some selections). They are preferred for modern gardens because of mildew resistance. Cercospora leaf spot can be a problem.

CULTIVARS AND VARIETIES

'Acoma' is a white-flowered, broad-spreading shrub, 10 to 12 ft. high and wide, with light gray-brown bark.

'Apalachee', with lavender flowers, glossy dark green leaves, upright habit to 15 ft. high, and cinnamon to chestnut-brown bark, is among the best for cercospora leaf spot resistance.

'Arapaho' has red flowers with purple overtones, lustrous dark green leaves, rich brown bark; 15 to 20 ft. high. More cold susceptible, particularly to late spring freezes.

'Biloxi' is distinctly upright, 20 ft. high by 12 ft. wide, with pale pink flowers and dark brown bark.

'Caddo', relatively compact, 8 to 10 ft. high and wide, has bright pink flowers and light cinnamon-brown bark.

'Cheyenne' is akin to 'Arapaho' with similar parentage and red flower color but with bushier habit, 8 to 10 ft. high and wide, and more susceptible to cercospora leaf spot.

'Choctaw' offers bright pink panicles in loose structures, appearing on a vase-shaped, 20-ft.-high shrub/small tree, with light to dark cinnamon-brown bark.

'Hopi', rich pink, profuse, and long-flowering, is a dense oval-rounded shrub, 10 ft. high, 8 ft. wide, with gray-brown bark.

'Lipan' is wide vase-shaped, 15 ft. high and wide at maturity; lavender-pink flowers, near white to beige bark.

'Miami' carries flaming dark pink flowers on an upright large shrub/small tree. Grows 20 ft. high or more, dark chestnut-brown bark.

Lagerstroemia subcostata var. fauriei 'Fantasy'

MORE ▶

Lagerstroemia 'Acoma'

Lagerstroemia 'Hopi'

Lagerstroemia 'Natchez' Dirr garden

Lagerstroemia 'Arapaho'

Lagerstroemia 'Choctaw'

Lagerstroemia 'Lipan'

Lagerstroemia 'Miami'

427

Lagerstroemia Hybrids CONTINUED

'Muskogee', a 1981 introduction, is still coveted in the 21st century for its large shrub/small tree status (grows 20 ft. high or more), prolific lavender-pink flowers, and light gray-brown bark.

'Natchez' is the most common large-growing (to 25 ft.), white-flowered form, with rich cinnamon-brown bark. An allée in the Dirr garden was beautiful throughout the seasons.

'Osage', with light pink flowers

and chestnut-brown bark, has never attracted significant attention from gardeners. Grows 15 ft. high; shows considerable cold damage in Georgia trials.

'Pecos' opens medium pink, grows 10 to 15 ft. high, and develops dark

Lagerstroemia 'Muskogee'

Lagerstroemia 'Natchez' fall color

Lagerstroemia 'Sioux' fall color

Lagerstroemia 'Tonto'

Lagerstroemia 'Tuscarora'

Lagerstroemia 'Yuma'

brown bark; like 'Osage'; it is not common in commerce.

'Sioux', a Dirr favorite, is upright in habit, 12 to 15 ft. high, with rich pink flowers and lustrous dark green leaves that turn red in fall; gray-brown bark.

'Tonto', the best "red" from Dr. Egolf's program, may contract slight mildew. Grew 10 ft. high, 8 ft. wide in five years in Georgia trials; gray-brown bark. Not true red like Whitcomb's Red Rocket®.

'Tuscarora' is a large upright tree type, 20 ft. or more in height, 10 ft. wide. Dark coral-pink flowers, light brown bark.

'Tuskegee' has deep coral-pink flowers, not too different from 'Tuscarora'. A wide-spreading shrub, over 20 ft. high and wide at maturity, with light brown bark.

'Wichita' offers light lavender flowers and russet-brown bark on a large upright shrub, over 20 ft. high at maturity. Difficult to propagate.

'Yuma', with abundant bicolored lavender flowers and light gray bark, is remarkable in flower. Grows 12 to 15 ft. high and wide.

'Zuni' is as close to purple as possible in the hybrid group; the flowers are shaded with lavender, reducing intensity somewhat; gray-brown bark; grows 10 to 12 ft. high.

TRUE GENETIC DWARFS
For approximately 20 years, Dr. Egolf crossed, crossed, and crossed again, developing a core of true compact types, including 'Chickasaw' with mounded habit, 2 ft. high, 3 to 3½ ft. wide, rose-lavender flowers, small,

glossy dark green leaves; and 'Pocomoke', slightly larger in size, 3 ft. high and wide after ten years, better and bigger foliage than 'Chickasaw', flowers rose-pink. Many are still being tested and may be released. 'Chickasaw' is disappointing and has lost commercial favor; 'Pokomoke', the best selection, was used by the author to breed the Razzle Dazzle® series.

Lantana camara
lantana
Among the top five flowering plants for summer color, North, South, and West. In zone 7 (0 to 10°F), several cultivars are dieback shrubs but regenerate new shoots from the base. In zones 9 to 11, they become more

MORE ▶

Lagerstroemia 'Pocomoke'

Lagerstroemia 'Zuni'

Lantana camara 'Chapel Hill Yellow'

Lantana camara 'Chapel Hill Gold'

Lantana camara CONTINUED

perennial, woody, and evergreen. Along the Georgia coast, zone 8, plants become quite woody, semi-evergreen to evergreen, and are often still flowering in December. Typically a rounded-arching shrub. The medium to dark green leaves, (1) 2 to 3 (4) in. long, are scabrous (sandpapery) above and aromatic when crushed. Flowers initiate on new growth from (May) June through October (November) in Athens. Foliage is killed at 26 to 28°F. Each flower, four- to five-lobed, ¼ in. across, is held in a 1- to 2-in.-wide inflorescence. The flowers, like the leaves, have a slight odor, and their colors follow the rainbow. Favorite butterfly plant! Fruit are ⅓-in.-wide, berry-like drupes that turn metallic blue-purple-black. Well-drained soil, slightly acid, moderate moisture and fertility, along with full sun, suit it best. Displays good salt tolerance. Resistant to deer feeding. Hot weather accelerates flowering. Once in the garden, trouble-free and maintenance-free except for pruning to keep plants in check. Has become weed-like in the deeper South; I witnessed, north of Orlando, freeze-damaged orange grove acreage chock-ablock with lantana. Use in sunny borders, containers, and combined with annuals. Grows 1 to 5 ft. high, wider at maturity. Zones 9 to 11 for above-ground hardiness, otherwise treat as a subshrub. West Indies. Has naturalized in many warm temperate countries.

CULTIVARS AND VARIETIES

The number is beyond anyone's ability to remember. In many, the habit is sprawling and groundcover-like. Check www.uspto.gov for patented lantanas, too many!

'Chapel Hill Yellow' was discovered as a bird-planted seedling in our daughter Susy's Chapel Hill garden. Beautiful pure yellow, floriferous to infinity, smaller lustrous dark green, lemon-scented leaf, spreading habit, 15 to 18 in. high, 2 to 3 ft. wide, tender perennial. 'Chapel Hill Gold' is a gold-flowered branch sport found and named by my PII partner Mark Griffith. Both patented, with 30 percent of royalties given to the Sweet Melissa Fund to assist lung transplant patients and families.

BREEDING STRATEGIES

Controlled crosses utilizing the 'Chapel Hill' genes and any overwintering lantanas we could collect in Georgia have yielded remarkable hybrids. Pink, salmon, apricot, orange, and other unique colors are in the mix.

'Apricot Sunrise' opens yellow, transitioning to pinkish apricot. Small lustrous dark green leaves and trailing groundcover habit; a Chapel Hill hybrid.

'Miss Huff' is a spectacular performer with orange-yellow flowers; perennial in our garden, regrowing to a 5- to 6-ft.-high and -wide shrub in a single season. Root hardy in zone 7. In 2007, grew 800 seedlings of 'Miss Huff', with 'Miss Tara' (orange-red), 'Orange Crush' (orange-red), and 'Pink Crush' (pink) the resultant introductions. The three are perennial in zone 7.

'New Gold' is a Georgia Gold Medal Winner, less cold hardy than 'Miss Huff' but a wonderful carpet of yellow-gold all summer long. Grows 1 to 1½ ft. high, 3 to 4 ft. wide. Fruit development is minimal.

'Sunny Side Up' opens yellow, then outer florets turn white, inner yellow; eventually the entire flower is white. Foliage and habit like 'Chapel Hill Yellow'.

Lantana camara 'Sunny Side Up'

Lantana camara 'Sunset Orange'

Lantana camara 'New Gold' and 'Miss Huff'

'Sunset Orange' is a brilliant orange-flowered 'Chapel Hill Gold' hybrid with small shining dark green leaves and trailing habit.

Larix decidua
European larch

A deciduous conifer seldom seen in modern landscapes and most effectively used on larger properties. Pyramidal in habit, with horizontal branches and drooping branchlets, the tree is slender and supple in youth. Unfortunately, it becomes irregular and lacking in dignity with age, when the cones and dead branchlets persist, giving it a ratty appearance. The scaly, brown bark on larger branches is handsome. The bright green, 1-in.-long needles develop yellow to amber-yellow fall color. The cone scales are tightly overlapping, not reflexed like those of *Larix kaempferi*. Tolerant of moist and dry soils as well as wind-swept locations. In the Northeast, the larch casebearer eats the interior of the needles, resulting in a brownish cast. Grows 70 to 75 ft. high, 25 to 30 ft. wide. Zones 2 to 6. Northern and central Europe.

CULTIVARS AND VARIETIES
Several dwarf bun-types reside strictly in the domain of collectors.

'Pendula' is an interesting weeping form with a mop-like head of long, trailing branches.

Larix decidua, European larch

Larix decidua

Larix decidua fall color

Larix decidua 'Pendula'

Larix kaempferi
Japanese larch

In most respects, this species is quite similar to *Larix decidua*, differing primarily in its more open pyramidal habit and its slender, pendulous branchlets. The easiest and perhaps only reliable way to distinguish the two is by cone structure. The cones of *L. kaempferi* have reflexed scales, which give a rosette appearance, almost like the petals of a hybrid tea rose. Same cultural requirements as *L. decidua*. Grows 50 to 70 ft. high, 25 to 40 ft. wide. Zones 4 to 7. Japan.
CULTIVARS AND VARIETIES
Remarkable that over 30 cultivars have been described, among them 'Nana', a slow-growing, globose form.

Larix laricina
tamarack

A native North American species, tamarack is lovely in fall, when its golden color lights up the autumn landscape. Open and pyramidal in habit, with a slender trunk and a narrow crown formed by horizontal branches and drooping branchlets. The rich bluish green, ¾- to 1-in.-long needles turn handsome yellow to gold in October. The ½-in.-long cones are the smallest of the *Larix* species included here. Excellent plant for moist soils and cold climates; abhors heat. Common in Maine, where I observe it in low boggy

Larix kaempferi 'Nana'

Larix kaempferi, Japanese larch

Larix kaempferi

Larix laricina, tamarack

432

areas in relative abundance. Grows 30 to 50 ft. high. Zones 1 to 4(5). Northern North America.

CULTIVARS AND VARIETIES
Again, as with *Larix kaempferi*, many compact, weeping, and blue-needled forms have been introduced. No one has been able to sustain a livelihood from their commercialization.

Laurus nobilis
true laurel

The bay leaves of the culinary arts are derived from this evergreen species. Its presence in gardens is rooted in antiquity. Densely pyramidal-oval to haystack-shaped with 2- to 4-in.-long, wavy-margined, lustrous dark green leaves. The yellow-green flowers open in spring and do little to stir the aesthetic senses. Fruit are lustrous black, ½-in.-wide berries. Best in semi-shade (grows acceptably in full sun) and moisture-retentive soils under culti-

vation. Displays high degree of salt tolerance. Serves as a great container plant. Useful for topiary and hedges; also a natural in the herb garden. Grows 8 to 12 ft. high in the South, larger on the West Coast. Zones 8 and 9, 10 on the West Coast. Mediterranean region.

CULTIVARS AND VARIETIES
'Angustifolia', with long, narrow, lustrous dark green leaves, is considered more cold hardy than the species.

'Aurea' sports yellow-gold new growth that loses much of the color in the heat of summer.

Lavandula angustifolia
common lavender

Long established in herb gardens for oil of lavender (from flowers) and as a woody subshrub in Mediterranean climates. Beautiful, compact, broad-rounded habit with gray to blue-green evergreen leaves. Flowers rise above the foliage in elongated spires in shades of white, pink, blue, violet to lilac, and beyond. Flowers are profuse, and the best blue and purple cultivars are beautiful in their summer garb. Bonnie and I have grown lavenders

MORE ▶

Laurus nobilis

Larix laricina

Laurus nobilis, true laurel

Laurus nobilis 'Aurea'

Lavandula angustifolia CONTINUED

Lavandula angustifolia 'Hidcote'

Leiophyllum buxifolium, box sandmyrtle

Leiophyllum buxifolium

our entire gardening life. In Illinois and Georgia, long-term presence is not guaranteed. Sun and well-drained, sandy soil, on the dry side, with neutral to alkaline reaction, are best. Quite salt-tolerant. Use for foliage color, texture, and fragrance. Excellent in containers, groupings, low borders, and hedges. Remove spent flowers to keep plant tidy. Grows 1 to 2 ft. high and wide, or wider. Zones (5)6 to 8(9). Southern Europe, northern Africa. CULTIVARS AND VARIETIES Numerous, but the time-honored 'Hidcote', with compact habit and rich purple-blue flowers on 10- to 15-in.-long stalks, is still one of the best.

Leiophyllum buxifolium
box sandmyrtle

This small broadleaf evergreen shrub remains scarce in commerce, but it might be considered for nooks and crannies of the garden. Greatly variable, box sandmyrtle can be erect, prostrate, or decumbent, depend-

Leiophyllum buxifolium

Leitneria floridana

434

ing on its location. The lustrous dark green leaves are ⅛ to ½ in. long; leaves become bronze-green in winter. Flowers nearly cover the foliage in May and June. Pink in bud, opening white, each flower is about ¼ in. in diameter, composed of five petals and ten stamens. Requires acid, well-drained soils, in sun or partial shade. Somewhat finicky; requires extra care in the early period of establishment. May be a 5-in. groundcover or a 1½- to 3-ft.-high shrub. Zones 5 to 7. Encountered many times at about 5,000 ft. elevation on Whiteside Mountain, North Carolina, where it edges out on bare granite from organic duff. Its natural habitat is a clear barometer that heat is not its best ally. New Jersey to higher elevations of the Southeast.

Leitneria floridana
Florida corkwood
One of the lightest woods in the world, with a specific gravity less than cork, ornamentally useful in wet soils and

along stream banks for its tropical effect. Observed large, exotic plantings at the Arnold Arboretum and the Brooklyn Botanic Garden. Tends to sucker, neither a tree nor a shrub but simply a rover, forming lush colonies. Flowers are dioecious (male and female on separate plants), with the male in fuzzy willow-like catkins in late winter. Fruit is an oblong, ½- to ¾-in.-long, ¼-in.-wide, light olive-brown drupe. Best suited to moist and wet soils in sun to partial shade. A bamboo-like alternative without the rambunctiousness. Use for "naturalistic" effect in wet soil and stream bank areas. Grew for a time in our Georgia

garden and can't remember any visitor asking its identity. Grows 6 to 12 (to 20) ft. high, spreading to infinity. Zones 5 to 9. Southern Missouri to Texas and Florida.

Leptodermis oblonga
This shrub seldom shows on commercial radar, and through six editions of the Dirr *Manual* it is absent. I first experienced it over 30 years ago at Bernheim Arboretum, in Clermont, Kentucky, where the small lavender-violet-purple flowers reminded me of lilac blossoms. Had no idea of its identity until finding the label.

MORE ▶

Leitneria floridana

Leptodermis oblonga

Leptodermis oblonga

Leitneria floridana, Florida corkwood

Leptodermis oblonga CONTINUED
What? Several run-ins since provided assurances that this dainty, rounded shrub with ½- to ¾-in.-long, blue-green leaves was indeed worthy. The tubular flowers, five-lobed at the mouth, ½ to ¾ in. long, open over an extended period from June and July into autumn. Observed in flower in May, again in November, same plant, at JC Raulston Arboretum. Flowers are described as fragrant, yet I haven't noted much scent; they are formed on the new growth of the season. Fruit is a small, five-valved, dehiscent capsule. Adaptable to full sun and partial shade in well-drained soil. Observed on Martha's Vineyard, where it was quite prosperous. Utilize in perennial and shrub borders and groupings, and possibly for massing. Plants I witnessed were in the 2- to 3-ft.-high and -wide range. Zones 6 and 7, 8 and 9 on West Coast; Connecticut (zone 6) reports of plants killed to the ground but regrowing. Northern China.

Leptospermum scoparium
broom teatree

Remarkable evergreen shrub or tree with sharp-pointed, needle-like foliage and beautiful white, pink, and red flowers in May and June. Typically a compact-rounded, densely branched shrub, although I have observed large, bordering on tree-like specimens in southwest coastal England. The dark green, ½- to ¾-in.-long leaves develop bronzy purple hues in cold weather. Flowers, approximately ½ in. in diameter, are produced singly from the leaf axils. Single- (the norm) and double-flowered forms are available. Colors vary from white to pink, rose, and red. Transplant from a container into moist, fertile, acid to neutral, well-drained soil in full sun to partial shade. In San Francisco, a great garden plant; in Athens, a container plant that needs overwintering in a cool greenhouse. Grows 6 to 10 (to 15) ft. high and wide. Zones (8)9 and 10. New Zealand, Australia, Tasmania.
CULTIVARS AND VARIETIES
'Ruby Glow', an old standard with deep red, fully double, ½-in.-wide flowers, bronzy foliage, and red stems, is among the best. Grows 6 to 8 ft. high.

'Snow White', with double white flowers, is compact-spreading, 2 to 4 ft. high.

Leptospermum scoparium, broom teatree

Leptospermum scoparium 'Ruby Glow'

Leptospermum scoparium

Leptospermum scoparium

Lespedeza bicolor

shrub bushclover

Gangly shrub of loose-arching demeanor that, if pruned each winter, reinvents itself in fine style during late spring and summer with rosy purple flowers. The rich blue-green trifoliate leaves, each leaflet 1 to 2 (to 3) in. long, show no propensity toward fall coloration. The pea-shaped, ½-in.-long flowers are produced on 2- to 5-in.- long racemes on current season's growth from the leaf axils of the uppermost two feet of the shoot. Full sun, well-drained soil, pH adaptable—actually hard to kill. For the shrub border only, or as a cut-back shrub in perennial borders. Grows 6 to 10 ft. high and wide. Zones 5 to 9. North China to Manchuria, Korea, and Japan.
CULTIVARS AND VARIETIES
'Li'l Buddy' is a compact form, with narrow leaflets, graceful arching habit, and rose-purple flowers. Potential to 6 ft. high and wide.

Lespedeza thunbergii

Thunberg lespedeza

Technically not woody but a dieback (to the ground) shrub that rejuvenates itself annually into a mound of delicate cascading branches. The leaflets

MORE ▶

Lespedeza bicolor, shrub bushclover

Lespedeza thunbergii, Thunberg lespedeza

Lespedeza bicolor

Lespedeza bicolor

Lespedeza thunbergii 'Alba'

Lespedeza thunbergii CONTINUED

are rich bluish green, in threes, each 1 to 2 in. long, ½ to 1 in. wide. Foliage color is a pleasing contrast to the bright and dark greens of neighboring shrubs. The flowers are amazing, with abundant displays showing in June and again in August and September in Athens. Rosy purple, pea-shaped flowers appear in 6-in.-long racemes from the upper portions of the shoot, the whole constituting a 2- to 2½-ft.-long panicle. Flowers are effective for two to four weeks. Easily grown and ideally transplanted from containers. The richer and moister the soil, the more rapid the growth. Tolerates drier soils also. Full sun to light shade. Excellent plant to combine with "soft" herbaceous perennials. Lends a light, airy touch to the garden. Tidy up by removing old stems to within 6 in. of the soil line. Grows 3 to 6 ft. high and wide. Zones 5 to 8. China, Japan.

CULTIVARS AND VARIETIES
'Alba' is a white-flowered selection that has brighter green leaves and grows taller and more upright than the species.

'Gibraltar' produces deep rose-purple flowers and is a vigorous grower.

'Pink Cascade' is pink-flowered and not quite as rambunctious as the species, although in our garden it reached a height of 4 to 5 ft.

Spring Grove® is a selection from Spring Grove Cemetery and Arboretum, Cincinnati, Ohio, with rich deep rose-purple flowers. Introduced by the author.

'Variegata' has white-streaked leaflets, rose-purple flowers.

Leucophyllum frutescens
Texas sage
Enlightening how plants are promoted! This southwestern species was labeled as the next great "shrub" for East Coast gardens. Unfortunately, the plant did not read the hype and is simply not accustomed to the high humidity, heavy wet soils, and vagaries of temperatures. Beautiful when at peace, forming a rounded, dense, evergreen shrub, with ½- to 1-in.-long, silvery leaves. The entire shrub is similar to a gray-leaf artemisia. Almost totally defoliated after 10°F in Athens. Flowers, rose-purple, 1 in. wide, bell-shaped, appear in summer. Delicate and elegant when in flower. Use container-grown plants; place in perfectly drained, acid to higher pH soil in full sun. Avoid excessive fertility and root zone moisture. Have tried to grow the species in our garden, unfortunately with no success. University's Botanical Garden and Atlanta Botanical Garden have been successful with ideal siting of the plants. Beautiful in groupings and in shrub and perennial borders. The silver foliage is a real

Lespedeza thunbergii 'Pink Cascade'

Leucophyllum frutescens

Lespedeza thunbergii Spring Grove®

Leucothoe axillaris new growth

438

showstopper. Grows 5 to 8 ft. high, 4 to 6 ft. wide. Zones 8 and 9, 10 on the West Coast. Texas and Mexico.

CULTIVARS AND VARIETIES

Many are hybrids with related species.

'Alba' has white flowers.

'Compactum' is smaller in stature, with orchid-pink flowers.

'Rain Cloud' is a hybrid with violet-blue flowers, grows 5 ft. high, 3 ft. wide, in five years.

'Silver Cloud' is a dense, rounded form, 3 ft. high and wide, with silver-white leaves and violet-purple flowers.

'White Cloud' produces gray foliage and white flowers on a shrub 6 to 12 in. high by 4 to 6 ft. wide.

Leucothoe axillaris
coastal leucothoe

The church-mouse cousin of the more common *Leucothoe fontanesiana* but

achieving increased attention because of more compact habit, better garden adaptability, and the infusion of new cultivars. A broadleaf evergreen shrub, densely branched, forming a broad mound. The emerging leaves are bronze-red, maturing to lustrous dark green, turning bronze-green to reddish purple in winter. The small, urn-shaped, white flowers are borne

MORE ▶

Leucophyllum frutescens, Texas sage

Leucothoe axillaris, coastal leucothoe

Leucothoe axillaris

Leucothoe axillaris fall and winter color

Leucothoe axillaris Dodd form

Leucothoe axillaris CONTINUED

in 1- to 2½-in.-long racemes in April and May. Fruit are five-valved, brown capsules with no significant ornamental value. Site in moist, well-drained, acidic soils in partial to heavy shade. Detests winter sun, wind, and exposed locations. Great massing plant, combining seamlessly with its rhododendron brethren. Probably more resistant to the fungal leaf spot that devastates *L. fontanesiana*, but still susceptible. I challenge my own statement, for I have observed plants blanketed with diseases. Grows 2 to 4 ft. high, 3 to 6 ft. wide. Zones 5 to 9. Virginia to Florida and Mississippi in lowland areas.

CULTIVARS AND VARIETIES
At least ten in literature, none common. Have also observed several bronze- and copper- to cream-splashed leaf forms in my travels; the Dodd form, Semmes, Alabama, is perhaps the best to date.

Carinella™ ('Zebekot') is low-growing with arching shoots; 3- to 4-in.-long bright green leaves have reddish margins when emerging, maturing dark green tinted red-purple in winter. *Leucothoe fontanesiana* × *L. axillaris* hybrid. Pleasing compact habit as viewed by the author in the Hillier Arboretum.

'Curly Red' has twisted, bullate, dark bronze-green leaves that emerge orange-red to red-purple, turning deep red in winter. Leaf texture and shape are unique. Grows 18 in. by 24 in. Horrible mildew susceptibility.

'Greensprite' has year-round green leaves. Grows 5 to 6 ft. high, 10 ft. wide. From Mt. Cuba Center, Hockessin, Delaware.

'Jenkins' has lustrous dark green leaves; oval-rounded, distinctly differ-

ent shape. Better leaf spot resistance but still susceptible. Grows 2 to 3 ft. high and wide. From Margie Jenkins, Amite, Louisiana.

'Redsprite' has refined, twiggy growth, reddish new shoots, and coppery bronze winter leaf color; leaves are flat and arranged in a herringbone pattern. Grows 4 ft. high, 5 to 6 ft. wide.

Leucothoe fontanesiana
drooping leucothoe

One of the finest broadleaf evergreens for naturalizing, it develops into a graceful, fountain-like shrub with long, arching branches. However, it is so fragile in exposed sites that extreme caution must be exercised, avoiding drying winds and hot sun. *Leucothoe fontanesiana* has leathery, lustrous

Leucothoe fontanesiana, drooping leucothoe

Leucothoe axillaris 'Curly Red'

Leucothoe axillaris 'Jenkins'

Leucothoe fontanesiana

dark green, 2- to 5-in.-long leaves that often turn bronze to purplish in winter. Urn-shaped, ¼-in.-long, white, off-scented flowers develop from the leaf axils in 2- to 3-in. long, somewhat pendulous racemes. Their effect is masked by the foliage. Drooping leucothoe absolutely insists upon moist, acid, well-drained soils in a shady location. Any undue stress predisposes the plant to leaf spot, which disfigures and defoliates the shrub. Plants under ideal cultural conditions still contract the leaf diseases. Use in combination with other ericaceous plants or with other species that require acid soils. Grows 3 to 6 ft. high and wide. Zones 5 to 8. Virginia to Georgia and Tennessee. At 4,000 ft. elevation near Highlands, North Carolina, the species formed large masses, literally draped over a stream, over-storied by *Kalmia latifolia* and *Rhododendron maximum*.

CULTIVARS AND VARIETIES
'Girard's Rainbow' offers a stunning mixture of white, pink, and copper, in various combinations, on new foliage. Leaf color subsides with maturity to a creamy green variegation. Other characteristics are the same as for the species. High leaf-spot susceptibility.

'Nana' is a compact form with slightly smaller, lustrous dark green leaves. Grows 2 ft. high, 6 ft. wide.

'Royal Ruby', with ruby-red new shoots, leaves maturing dark green, then ruby-red in winter, appeared a shoo-in for gardeners; however, mildew, in production nurseries and the Dirr garden, pounded it into obsolescence.

'Scarletta' offers glossy scarlet new growth with a hint of purple. Foliage matures to dark green and develops rich burgundy hues in fall.

Whitewater® ('HOWW') has cream-white thin margins with pink-tinged to white areas in winter. Contracts leaf spot. Appears closer to *Leucothoe axillaris*, perhaps a hybrid.

Leycesteria formosa
pheasant-eye
Our first meeting occurred in a garden in Kent, England, and I had no idea of the plant's identity. Now it is one never to be forgotten because of its unique features. The typical habit is an upright-spreading shrub that requires tidying after winter's anguish because of dead branches. The new shoots are deep purplish red, the leaves maturing to deep green. The sessile, white, five-lobed, tubular flowers develop from the leaf axils in 3- to 4-in.-long, pendulous racemes. Each ¾ in. by ¾ in. flower is subtended by an ovate, claret-colored, 1- to 1¾-in.-long, persistent bract. The bead-like, berry fruit ripen from glossy sea-green

MORE ▶

Leucothoe fontanesiana winter color

Leucothoe fontanesiana 'Girard's Rainbow'

Leucothoe fontanesiana 'Scarletta'

Leycesteria formosa, pheasant-eye

Leycesteria formosa CONTINUED

to maroon then purple-black. Provide partial shade and moist, well-drained soils. Observed performing quite well in full sun. Often, in Europe, integrated

Leycesteria formosa

into shrub borders, occasionally herbaceous borders. Grows 3 to 5 ft. high, less in spread. Zones 7 to 9, 10 on the West Coast. Himalayas.

Leycesteria crocothyrsos, golden pheasant-eye, produces yellow flowers in whorls of six in arching terminal racemes to 7 in. long. Grows 3 ft. high. A hybrid between the two species is known. Zone 9. Himalayas. CULTIVARS AND VARIETIES Golden Lanterns® ('Notbruce') has emerging yellow foliage, tinted red, yellow-green at maturity, with dark red bracts subtending white flowers. Grows 3 to 5 ft. high.

Ligustrum amurense
Amur privet

In the Midwest and Northeast, this species was as common as grass. Entire city blocks where every house had a hedge in front and in back and shared one on either side with the

neighbor were the rule. The species develops into a dense, multi-stemmed shrub with a weak pyramidal outline. The dull medium to dark green foliage shows minimal propensity toward fall color. Creamy white flowers occur in 1- to 2-in.-long, pyramidal panicles in May and June. Their curious fragrance is that mystifying privet odor—heavy and objectionable. Flowers are seldom seen, because the plant is usually pruned to excess. The dusty, gray-black, ¼-in.-long fruit ripen in September and October and often persist. Neither flowers nor fruit overwhelm. All privets thrive with neglect. In dirty, sooty, air-polluted, or salt-laden environments and in impossible soils, the privets will grow. Hedging is the time-honored use, but many better plants are suited to that purpose, and the species is now almost nonexistent in commerce. Grows 12 to 15 ft. high, 8 to 10 ft. wide. Zones 3 to 7. China.

Leycesteria formosa

Leycesteria crocothyrsos, golden pheasant-eye

Leycesteria formosa Golden Lanterns®

442

Ligustrum amurense, Amur privet

Ligustrum amurense

Ligustrum japonicum

Ligustrum japonicum
Japanese privet

An absolute building block of southern and West Coast landscapes, with versatility and adaptability making it a decathlon species. A large, evergreen shrub, steely in framework, rounded in outline, that when limbed up makes a respectable, small, artistic tree or large shrub. Bark is gray, smooth, covered with large bumpy lenticels. Leaves, 2 to 4 in. long, are leathery in texture, black-green, with a mirror-like upper surface. The heavy-scented, cream-colored flowers occur in dense, 2- to 6-in.-long and -wide panicles at the end of the shoots in May and June. The ¼-in.-wide, oval-rounded, dull grayish, matte-black drupes ripen in September and October, persist into winter, and are latently scavenged by the birds. Remarkable durable plant in all but permanently wet soils. Adapt-

MORE ▶

Ligustrum japonicum

Ligustrum japonicum, Japanese privet

443

Ligustrum japonicum CONTINUED

able from full sun to heavy shade. Can be pruned into any shape and often is, to the limits of demented imaginations. One of the best hedging, screening, and massing plants. Grown by the millions in southern and West Coast nurseries. Grows 6 to 12 ft. high and wide. Potential to 15 to 18 ft. high. Zones (6)7 to 10. Japan, Korea.

CULTIVARS AND VARIETIES

Many selected through the garden ages. The following are available in commerce.

'Eastbay' is more compact than the species but still reaches 5 to 6 ft. by 6 to 8 ft., and larger: 7 ft. by 10 ft. specimen at the Raulston.

'Howard' ('Frazieri') has yellow new leaves that fade in heat to greenish; pretty strong color element, not for the faint of heart.

'Jack Frost', 'Silver Star', and 'Variegatum' have leaves that are deep green in center with gray-green mottling, cream-silver edges. Compact, grow 6 to 8 ft. high, 4 to 6 ft. wide, although 10 to 12 ft. high is attainable.

'Lake Tresca' is the most compact form I observed; grows 3 to 4 ft. by 5 to 6 ft. Abundant flowers. Performed well in Georgia trials; 3 ft. by 4 ft. in five years.

'Nobilis' is possibly the best large-leaved form; the leaves are waxy, glis-

Ligustrum japonicum 'Howard'

Ligustrum japonicum 'Jack Frost'

Ligustrum japonicum 'Lake Tresca'

Ligustrum japonicum 'Nobilis'

Ligustrum japonicum 'Recurvifolium'

Ligustrum japonicum 'Rotundifolium'

tening, dark green. Upright habit and grows faster than 'Recurvifolium'. To 10 ft. and greater.

'Recurvifolium' has been a standard forever in southern gardens. Lustrous dark green leaves with undulating, recurved margins are narrower than 'Nobilis'; habit is more compact and growth slower. Attractive form. Grows 8 to 10 ft. high.

'Rotundifolium' ('Coriaceum') is a stiff, upright, confused-looking plant, akin to the person in shorts at a black-tie shindig. The rounded, 1- to 2½-in.-long leaves are curiously twisted and closely spaced along the stems. Has flowered and fruited. Grows 4 to 6 ft. high. Less hardy than the species

and was defoliated at –3°F. A cream-margined leaf selection is now in commerce.

Ligustrum lucidum
waxleaf, glossy, or Chinese privet

For most garden situations, not preferable to *Ligustrum japonicum* because of large size, lack of hardiness (0°F to –5°F defoliates/kills), and weed-like nature. A broadleaf evergreen tree, upright vase-shaped, with rounded canopy and smooth gray bark. Leaves are larger than *L. japonicum*, 3 to 6 in. long, thinner, and often with a reddish rim. The cream flowers in 5- to 8- (to 12-) in.-long and -wide panicles open about two to three weeks later

than *L. japonicum*. The blue-black fruit are dusted with gray wax. Fruit persist through winter and, because of their weight, cause the branches to become semi-pendulous. Grows with ardor in almost any soil; weed-like as birds move the seeds to and fro. Utilize as a large shrub/small tree. Grows 20 to 25 (to 50) ft. high. Zones (7)8 to 10. China, Korea, Japan.

CULTIVARS AND VARIETIES
'Excelsum Superbum' is a strong-growing form with cream-yellow leaf margins.

'Tricolor' has mixed copper to purplish new leaves that settle down to irregular cream margins and green

MORE ▶

Ligustrum lucidum, waxleaf privet

Ligustrum lucidum

Ligustrum lucidum 'Excelsum Superbum'

Ligustrum lucidum 'Tricolor'

centers. Sean Hogan, Cistus Nursery, Oregon, selected a more intensely variegated margined-leaf type with 50 to 60 percent of surface in white.

Ligustrum obtusifolium
border privet

As privets go, this is respectable because of its handsome wide-spreading habit and more refined appearance. The medium to dark green foliage sometimes develops russet to purplish fall color. Flowers and fruit are similar to those of *Ligustrum amurense*. Makes a good screen, background, or hedge plant. Grows 10 to 12 ft. high, 12 to 15 ft. wide. Zones 3 to 7. Japan.

CULTIVARS AND VARIETIES
Variety *regelianum* has horizontally spreading branches with leaves regularly spaced in planar fashion. Grows 4 to 5 ft. high. I consider this one of the best deciduous privets.

Ligustrum ovalifolium
California privet

Another hedge plant, once a popular choice because its foliage is evergreen in zones 7 and 8 and semi-evergreen as far north as Boston (zone 6), before dropping most of the leaves by spring. The 1- to 2½-in.-long, lustrous dark green leaves are perhaps the most attractive of the small-leaf privets discussed here. The heavy-scented flowers are dull white and occur in 2- to 4-in.-long and -wide terminal panicles in May, June, and July. Fruit are globose, ¼ in. wide, usually shining black. Habit is oval-rounded and strongly multi-stemmed with erect branches. Without pruning, the species makes a good screen or barrier. Adaptable to extremes of climate. Seldom available in everyday commerce. Grows 10 to 15 ft. high. Supposedly the national champion is 30 ft. by 38 ft., but I have serious doubts about correct identification. Zones (5)6 to 8(9). Japan.

Ligustrum obtusifolium, border privet

Ligustrum obtusifolium var. *regelianum*

Ligustrum ovalifolium, California privet

CULTIVARS AND VARIETIES
'Aureum' has leaves strongly bordered in golden yellow with a green spot in the center. Remove any all-green and -yellow shoot reversions.

Ligustrum sinense
Chinese privet

Take note—a terrible and devastating escapee that terrorizes floodplains, fencerows, and even open fields, reducing native vegetation to rubble. This species, as I view it, is a large, thickly multi-stemmed, rounded shrub with dull dark green, 1- to 3-in.-long leaves. In northern climates (zone 6) it is deciduous, becoming more evergreen in the lower South. Leaves emerge early, often by March in Athens, and have a competitive advantage, particularly in woodland situations, since the native broadleaf canopy is not full until late April or early May (Athens). Cream-white flowers in 2- to 3-in.-long axillary panicles open in May. The dull waxy black fruit are produced in abundance and persist through winter. Eventually the birds eat the fruit and spread the seeds. Tenaciously adaptable, growing in dry soils and floodplain conditions, in sun or shade. A few of the cultivars might

MORE ▶

Ligustrum ovalifolium 'Aureum'

Ligustrum sinense

Ligustrum sinense 'Sunshine'

Ligustrum sinense, Chinese privet

Ligustrum sinense 'Variegatum'

447

Ligustrum sinense CONTINUED

be considered. As for the species, I urge abstinence. One of the most frequently pulled weeds in our garden. Grows 10 to 15 ft. high and wide. Co-national champions are 32 ft. by 36 ft. and 29 ft. by 39 ft. Zones (6)7 to 10. China.

CULTIVARS AND VARIETIES
'Green Cascade' and 'Emerald Mop' have arching-weeping branches and green leaves. Don Shadow discovered the first; the author, the latter. Original 'Emerald Mop' is 10 ft. by 12 ft.

'Sunshine' is a yellow-leaf form that maintains color although diminishes somewhat in heat. Introduced by Pat McCracken, Zebulon, North Carolina.

'Variegatum' with cream- to white-margined leaves is common. Not as rampant as the species, typically 6 to 8 ft. high; however, I have observed 15-ft.-high plants. Will revert to green. Flowers, fruits, and invades. 'Swift Creek' is more compact with more pronounced white marginal variegation.

'Wimbei' ('Wimbish') has ¼-in.-long, dark green leaves and closely spaced nodes. Looks more like a boxwood. Grows 6 to 8 ft. high, with upright ascending branches.

Ligustrum 'Vicaryi'

syn. *Ligustrum* ×*vicaryi*
golden Vicary privet
A hybrid between *Ligustrum ovalifolium* 'Aureum' and *L. vulgare*, this plant develops into a large, oval-rounded shrub. It displays golden yellow leaves for most of the summer. My observations indicate that the cooler the summer weather, the better the color. Use with discretion in any garden situation. Grows 10 to 12 ft. high and wide. Zones 5 to 7. Best utilized in the North and perhaps not even there.

Ligustrum vulgare
European privet
This species has essentially gone the way of the dodo bird. Once a favored privet, now seldom available in U.S. commerce. It develops into a large, cumbersome, upright-spreading shrub. White flowers occur in 1- to 3-in.-long racemes and are followed by lustrous jet black, ⅓-in.-wide fruit. The dark green leaves average 1 to 2½ in. long. This species has no advantage over the others, and a twig blight can prove

Ligustrum sinense 'Wimbei'

Ligustrum 'Vicaryi', golden Vicary privet

Ligustrum sinense 'Swift Creek'

Ligustrum vulgare, European privet

quite troublesome. Like *Ligustrum ovalifolium*, belongs in the has-been category. Grows 12 to 15 ft. high, similar spread. Zones (4)5 to 7. Europe, northern Africa.

Lindera

spicebush

A genus of some 80 species, although little known in gardens south, north, and west. The following places display and/or market many described herein: Arnold Arboretum; Atlanta Botanical Garden; Sarah P. Duke Gardens; JC Raulston Arboretum; Woodlanders, Aiken, South Carolina; Forestfarm, Williams, Oregon; and Nurseries Caroliniana, North Augusta, South Carolina. Most species adapt to full sun, partial shade and moist, acid soil, although they tolerate drier conditions. Traditionally difficult to propagate via cuttings, so seeds—thus variability—are the principal means. Dioecious yellow flowers, with only female plants producing red to black fruit.

Lindera aggregata

syn. *Lindera strychnifolia*

Japanese evergreen spicebush

A beautiful plant for shady borders. Sports 2-in.-long, 1-in.-wide, prominently three-veined, evergreen leaves on a 6- to 10-ft.-high, pyramidal shrub. Yellow flowers in spring. Fruit are ¼- to ½-in.-long, rounded black drupes. Zones 7 and 8. China, Japan, Philippines.

Lindera benzoin

spicebush

To my mind, this species has never been utilized enough in American gardens. A most appropriately named shrub, because its bruised stems emit a potent, spicy-sweet fragrance. Imagine an early April day in the North

(mid March, Athens) after a particularly difficult winter, the branches of spicebush studded with small, greenish yellow flowers—a harbinger that all will be well in the world. *Lindera benzoin* grows in moist soils throughout its range, often forming large colonies/thickets. It develops into a large, multi-stemmed, rounded shrub, growing dense in sun, rather artistically open in shade. The 3- to 5-in.-long, bright green leaves turn a respectable to outstanding shade of yellow in fall. The oval, ⅓- to ½-in.-long, bright red fruit ripen in September and October. Provide acid, moist soils, in full sun to partial shade. Plants appear ragged in extremely dry soils. Fine choice for naturalizing, but unfortunately, it has

MORE ▶

Lindera aggregata, Japanese evergreen spicebush

Ligustrum vulgare

Ligustrum vulgare

Lindera aggregata

449

Lindera benzoin CONTINUED

never found its way into commerce. For many years, a plant bumped along in our Georgia garden but was never at home. Needed more moisture than I could provide. Grows 6 to 12 ft. high and wide. Zones 4 to 9. Maine to Ontario and Kansas, south to Florida and Texas.

Lindera erythrocarpa

With dark green, 2½- to 5-in.-long, oblong leaves, this is a plant begging for scrutiny in autumn, when the leaves turn stunning yellow. Yellow flowers open in March and April, followed by red fruit. Tolerates dryness better than *Lindera benzoin*. A plant in the University's Botanical Garden was 18 ft. high, 20 ft. wide. Zones 6 to 8. China.

Lindera glauca

syn. *Lindera angustifolia*
oriental spicebush

This species has 3- to 4-in.-long, narrow-elliptical leaves, glossy green above, bluish green to silvery below, that turn yellow-orange-red in fall and die off gray-brown, persisting into winter. Yellow flowers and black, rounded fruit. Full sun to moderate shade, any well-drained soil. Grows 6 to 8 (to 15) ft. high; develops colonies. Have only observed in arboreta, where the fall color was typically spectacular orangered. Have never noticed any insect

or disease problems. Zones 6 to 8. Japan, China, Korea, Taiwan.

Lindera obtusiloba

Japanese spicebush

First met at the Arnold Arboretum during sabbatical. Thirty plus years later, I am still smitten but forlorn as the plant has escaped my clutches. The brilliant golden yellow fall color remains effective for two weeks or longer. Habit is multi-stemmed, broad-spreading, clothed in variably shaped, three-veined, unlobed or lobed, dark green leaves. The yellow flowers appear in early March (zone 7), one to two weeks earlier than *Lindera benzoin*. Fruit are globose, ¼ in. in diameter, red to shining black. Tolerates drier soils, sun, and shade. Would make a great woods' edge, understory, shrub border addition. To see is to believe, and I hope this brief passage spurs a few gardeners to pursue.

Lindera benzoin

Lindera benzoin, spicebush

Lindera erythrocarpa fall color

Usually in the lower range of 10 to 20 ft. high and wide. Zones 5 to 7. Japan, Korea, China.

Liquidambar formosana
Formosan sweetgum

An excellent tree for southern and West Coast gardens, unique for its three-lobed leaves and soft bristly fruit. A 100-year-old tree on the Georgia campus, now 50 ft. high and wide, produces soft butter-yellow fall color every November. In youth the habit is distinctly pyramidal, becoming rounded at maturity. The 2- to 5-in.-long, 3- to 6-in.-wide leaves, lustrous dark green in summer, turn yellow to red in fall. The 1-in.-wide, rounded fruit, each composed of 24 to 43 capsules, are not as spinily offensive as those of *Liquidambar styraciflua*. Tolerates drought and heat once established; I observed healthy trees in Tampa, Florida, and Mobile, Alabama.

Selection work needs to be undertaken for improved growth habit and fall color. Might prove an excellent tree for large areas, streets, and parks in warm climates. A seedling in my trials formed a 20 ft. by 14 ft. oval-rounded tree in six years, the dark green leaves turning deep maroon in fall! Grows 40 to 60 ft. high and wide. Zones 6 to 9. Taiwan, southern and central China.

Liquidambar acalycina is similar

MORE ▶

Lindera glauca, oriental spicebush, fall color

Lindera obtusiloba, Japanese spicebush, fall color

Lindera glauca

Lindera obtusiloba

Liquidambar formosana, Formosan sweetgum

Liquidambar formosana CONTINUED
to *L. formosana* and now offered by
several nurseries. Sports rich reddish
maroon new growth that matures dark
green, turning burgundy in autumn.
Has softer fruit, composed of 15 to 26
capsules. Displays excellent vigor and
is cold hardy to –10°F. Its selection

'Burgundy Flush' has bronze-purple
new leaves that unfortunately die off
brown in autumn, holding into December in Athens. Tested in Georgia and,
growing next to the seedling *L. formosana* tree just described, it is vastly
inferior, the leaves peppered with fungal lesions while *L. formosana* is lus-

trous dark green and spotless. Zones
6 to 8. China.

Liquidambar styraciflua
sweetgum

This lovely tree would be on every
gardener's wishlist were it not for the
woody, spiny, capsular, 1- to 1½-in.-
wide fruit, which abscise through fall
and winter. Nevertheless, sweetgum
is still widely planted throughout the
country for its excellent fall color. The
star-shaped, five- to seven-lobed, 4-

Liquidambar formosana fall color

Liquidambar acalycina new growth

Liquidambar styraciflua, sweetgum, fall color

Liquidambar styraciflua

Liquidambar styraciflua

to 7½-in.-wide, lustrous dark green leaves turn gorgeous shades of yellow, orange, red, and purple and persist late into fall. Decidedly pyramidal habit in youth, the tree develops an oblong to rounded crown at maturity. Excellent plant for moist soil areas along streams and watercourses; it also performs well in drier soils. Almost qualifies as invasive, as it seeds in with a fury and will conquer abandoned land, moist ditches, and wet bottomlands. Can develop chloro-sis in high pH soils. Grows 60 to 75 ft. high, 40 to 50 ft. wide. Zones 5 to 9. New York to Illinois, south to Florida, Texas, and Mexico.

CULTIVARS AND VARIETIES
'Burgundy', 'Festival', and 'Palo Alto' were selected in California for good fall color.

Emerald Sentinel® ('Clydesform') develops a uniform pyramidal outline, 30 ft. by 12 ft. Substantive, lustrous dark green foliage, yellow-orange in fall.

'Gumball' and 'Oconee' are compact forms, the latter with excellent red-purple fall color in Georgia.

'Moraine' offers glossy dark green foliage, burgundy-red fall color, and better cold hardiness.

'Rotundiloba' has rounded lobes and displays deep reddish purple to burgundy fall color; in zone 7, fall color is typically yellow. Reportedly sets fruit, although described as fruitless. It is also weak-wooded; I witnessed significant damage from ice storms.

MORE ▶

Liquidambar styraciflua 'Palo Alto' fall color

Liquidambar styraciflua 'Gumball'

Liquidambar styraciflua 'Moraine' fall color

Liquidambar styraciflua 'Slender Silhouette' fall color

Liquidambar styraciflua 'Rotundiloba' fall color

453

Liquidambar styraciflua CONTINUED

'Slender Silhouette' is columnar-conical, forming a totem pole of lustrous dark green leaves, which turn yellow with a hint of red in fall; will set fruit. Parent tree was 70 ft. high. Introduced by Don Shadow.

'Variegata' has leaves blotched and streaked with yellow. Gold Dust®, 'Golden Treasure', Jubilee™, 'Moonbeam', 'Silver King', and others sport various variegated leaf permutations. In most cases, save your garden cash.

Liriodendron tulipifera

tuliptree

Easily recognized because of its unique leaf, this native species enjoys near cosmopolitan distribution. It is hard not to bump into a tuliptree in the course of one's horticultural travels. The tree is found in many of the great gardens of the world. An extant tree dated 1785 was planted by George Washington at Mt. Vernon. Vanderbilt used it to frame Biltmore House in Asheville, North Carolina, as Jefferson had done at Monticello, where in 2008 a tree with a trunk 9 ft. in diameter was removed. My thoughts as I witnessed the stump? "If trees could only talk." The only significant drawbacks of this tree are its behemoth size and susceptibility to drought. Under severe drought, the interior leaves turn color prematurely and abscise as early as July or August, with only the outer leaves remaining. These minor flaws, however, do not diminish the plant's numerous landscape assets. Even in youth, when the habit is pyramidal, the uniformly spaced branches make the tree appear full and dense. With age the outline becomes oval-rounded, with several large, sinuous branches constituting the framework around an unusually long, slender bole. It is a magnificent and grand tree in its sunset years. The glossy bright green, 3- to 8-in.-long and -wide leaves turn golden yellow in fall. The interesting tulip-shaped flowers of yellow, orange, and green, 2 to 3 in. long and wide, appear after the leaves in May and June; late April in Athens. Borne high on the tree, the flowers are often missed by the unsuspecting. The cone-like fruit provide winter interest and a good identifying characteristic. Splendid for large-area use. Provide deep, moist soils or supplemental water in drought periods, if possible. Grows 70 to 90 ft. high, 35 to 50 ft. wide. Zones 4 to 9. Massachusetts to Wisconsin, south to Florida and Mississippi.

CULTIVARS AND VARIETIES

'Ardis' is a small-statured version of the species with leaves about one-third the size, flowers 1 to 1½ in. long and wide, and ultimate size about 30 ft. high.

'Aureomarginatum' has leaves margined with yellow or greenish yellow. The effect is quite striking.

Emerald City™ ('JFS-Oz') develops more upright-oval outline in youth with central leader and uniform branching.

MORE ▶

Liquidambar styraciflua 'Golden Treasure'

Liriodendron tulipifera 'Aureomarginatum'

Liriodendron tulipifera

Liriodendron tulipifera 'Tennessee Gold'

Liriodendron tulipifera fall color

Liriodendron tulipifera

Liriodendron tulipifera, tuliptree

Liriodendron tulipifera 'Fastigiatum'

455

Liriodendron tulipifera CONTINUED

Leaves are glossy dark green, yellow fall color. I am impressed.

'Fastigiatum' ('Arnold') is an upright form not unlike *Populus nigra* 'Italica', the Lombardy poplar, but wider at maturity. It makes a good screen, or it can be used in groupings for a strong vertical accent. Grows 50 to 60 ft. high by 15 to 20 ft. wide.

'Little Volunteer' is a mid-size tree, between 'Ardis' and the species; estimate 30 to 40 ft. high. Harald Neu-bauer, Hidden Hollow Nursery, Tennessee, introduction.

'Tennessee Gold' is another discovery by Don Shadow. Don showed Coach Vince Dooley and me the branch sport, about halfway to heaven in an immense tuliptree. Never deterred, he retrieved scion wood and now has one of the most beautiful yellow-gold leaf forms with a splash of green in the center. Excellent heat tolerance and good vigor. "Wow," as I witnessed the tree in April.

Lithocarpus henryi
Henry tanbark oak

I held great hope that this species and other *Lithocarpus* taxa would become major players in urban and suburban settings in the South. Alas, this has not come to pass because of the vast superiority of native *Quercus* species. This species is the most cold hardy and common, forming a rounded habit. The evergreen leaves, 4 to 8 (to 10) in. long, are leathery, lustrous, and entire along the margin. In cold

Lithocarpus henryi

Lithocarpus densiflorus

Lithocarpus edulis 'Starburst'

Liriodendron tulipifera 'Little Volunteer'

Lithocarpus henryi, Henry tanbark oak

weather the leaves become yellow-green. Bark is smooth and gray, similar to beech. The reproductive structure is an acorn, borne on an 8-in.-long spike at the end of the shoot. Usually sold in containers and easy to transplant. Adaptable; plants in coastal Georgia are thriving in sandy soils. Probably will always be a collector's plant. Grows 25 to 30 ft. high and wide. Zones 6 to 9. Central China.

The related species *Lithocarpus densiflorus* has the most beautiful, toothed, dark green leaves, silvery on the underside, on a large shrub/small tree framework. Quite susceptible to *Phytophthora ramorum*. The tree in our garden was killed by sapsucker feeding and subsequent canker. Grows 15 to 25 ft. high and wide. The national champion is 135 ft. high, 63 ft. wide. Zones 7 to 9. Southwestern Oregon, California.

Lithocarpus edulis, Japanese tanbark oak, has entire-margined, lustrous dark green leaves. Tends toward a shrubby habit with white flowers of sickeningly sweet odor. Small trees grow in Savannah, Georgia, 20 to 25 ft. high. Zones 7 and 8(9). Japan. Its selection 'Starburst' ('Variegata') has a cream-yellow center with shiny green margin; I have observed reversions on the only specimen I know, which resides in the shade house at the JC Raulston Arboretum.

Lonicera
honeysuckle

Honeysuckles are like sheep: there are too many of them (about 240 species), most stink, they all look alike, and they are rather pedestrian. People may argue the validity of this statement, and to be sure, honeysuckles are durable, adaptable, and quite serviceable shrubs. But like privet, they offer a sameness that does not inspire. Honeysuckles are on the move, bullying their way into understory and open areas, especially *Lonicera tatarica*, *L. japonica*, *L. morrowi*, and *L. maackii*. Flowers, largely unexceptional, fruit showy in certain species, fragrance wonderful in a few. Let's take a honeysuckle journey . . .

Lonicera alpigena
Alps honeysuckle

This species is an oval-rounded shrub with yellow-green flowers and dull red fruit. The 2- to 4-in.-long leaves are dark green and somewhat leathery. Withstands high-stress conditions. Might be used for groupings, in rock gardens, and as a facer plant. Grows 4 to 8 ft. high. Zones 5 to 7. Mountains of central and southern Europe.
CULTIVARS AND VARIETIES
'Nana' is a slow-growing form with large leaves and a dense, rounded-mounded outline. Grows 3 ft. high.

Lonicera ×*brownii*
Brown's honeysuckle

This hybrid species is a cross between
MORE ▶

Lonicera alpigena 'Nana'

Lonicera alpigena 'Nana'

Lonicera ×*brownii* 'Dropmore Scarlet'

457

Lonicera ×brownii CONTINUED

Lonicera sempervirens, trumpet honeysuckle, and _L. hirsuta_. In general characteristics, it resembles _L. sempervirens_, even to displaying that species' susceptibility to aphids. Zones (4)5 to 7.

CULTIVARS AND VARIETIES
'Dropmore Scarlet' is a red-flowered, cold hardy form, and 'Fuchsioides' has orange-red flowers. Neither measure up to _Lonicera sempervirens_, however.

Lonicera caprifolium
Italian honeysuckle

A vining honeysuckle, not well known in the United States, but with fragrant, pretty, 1¾- to 2-in.-long, tubular, yellowish white, purple-tinged flowers in four- to ten-flowered whorls from the axils of the terminal three pairs of leaves. The 2- to 4-in.-long leaves are dark green above, glaucous blue-green below, the upper leaf bases fused into a disk shape, subtending the flowers. Fruit are orange-red, rounded, about ¼ in. in diameter. Best in a cooler climate or the West Coast. Grows 10 to 20 ft. high. Zones 5 to 7(8). Europe, western Asia.

Lonicera flava
yellow honeysuckle

A beautiful, twining, restrained species that is found only in collectors' gardens and even then infrequently. The upper leaves are fused at their bases and subtend the flowers.

Lonicera ×brownii 'Dropmore Scarlet'

Lonicera caprifolium, Italian honeysuckle

Lonicera caprifolium

Lonicera flava, yellow honeysuckle

458

Leaves are rich green above, bluish green beneath. The orange-yellow flowers occur in whorls of one to three at the end of the shoot. Each flower is 1 to 1½ in. long, nonfragrant, with colors ranging from yellow to yellow-orange stained red in bud. The ¼-in.-wide, orange-red fruit are seldom produced, at least on plants I observed. Requires shade and a cool, moist root run. Unusual vine for trellises, arbors, and fences. Grows 6 to 10 ft. Zones 5 to 8. North Carolina to Missouri, Arkansas to Oklahoma.

Lonicera fragrantissima
winter honeysuckle

The small, cream-colored flowers of winter honeysuckle seldom attract attention, but their powerful fragrance perfumes an entire garden. Truly one of the best plants for late-winter and early-spring fragrance. The species develops a wide-spreading, irregularly rounded outline and consumes exten-

sive real estate. The dull blue-green to dark green leaves, 1 to 3 in. long and almost as wide, are leathery textured for a honeysuckle. The sweet, lemon-scented flowers open in March and April over a three- to four-week period. In Athens, I recorded flowers in January and still present in mid March. Dark red berries (two ovaries fused) develop under the foliage and are seldom noticed. Extremely tough and adaptable, this species survives sand, clay, and high pH soils, in sun or shade. Its large size restricts use to borders, groupings, or masses. Grows 6 to 10 (to 15) ft. high and wide. Zones 4 to 8(9). China.

Lonicera standishii, Standish honeysuckle, also bears fragrant flowers; it has larger dark green leaves than *L. fragrantissima*, 2 to 4½ in. long, ¾ to 2 in. wide, and has hybridized with *L. fragrantissima* to produce *L. ×purpusii*, which retains the fine fragrance of the parent species. 'Winter Beauty',

a backcross of *L. ×purpusii* and *L. standishii*, has extremely fragrant, creamy white flowers and a spreading habit. 'Spring Romance', a backcross using *L. standishii* var. *lancifolia*, has fragrant flowers and a more upright habit, but it is less evergreen and tolerant of frost than 'Winter Beauty'.

Lonicera ×heckrottii
goldflame honeysuckle

This is the most common vining honeysuckle in U.S. commerce. In most respects, it resembles *Lonicera sempervirens*, one of its parents (the other is *L. ×americana*), but it differs in its waxier blue-green foliage and the carmine flowers with yellowish interiors. Additionally, the flowers are fragrant. I used the species to cover an old stump, where it flowers heavily in April and May and then sporadically into fall. I have never observed the fruit on cultivated plants. Leaves are extremely

MORE ▶

Lonicera fragrantissima, winter honeysuckle

Lonicera standishii, Standish honeysuckle

Lonicera ×purpusii

Lonicera 'Winter Beauty'

Lonicera ×heckrottii CONTINUED
frost-tolerant and will survive 15 to 20°F. Grows 10 to 20 ft. high. Has been renamed a time or two; Mardi Gras™ and Pink Lemonade™ are those I know. Zones (4)5 to 8.

Lonicera japonica
Japanese honeysuckle

This Asian species has become a pernicious pest throughout the eastern, southeastern, and midwestern United States. In many places, it dominates the understory, outcompeting native wildflowers. The 1- to 3-in.-long, dark green leaves are evergreen, semi-evergreen, or deciduous, depending on winter temperatures. The 1½-in.-long, white flowers, which age to yellow, open from May to frost. Their fragrance is exceptional, and the air on a warm spring or summer day is heavy with the sweet scent. The ¼-in.-wide, black berries ripen in August through October and are disseminated by birds. In landscape situations, it should be used only for inhospitable sites and unmanageable areas. Grows 15 to 30 ft. high if provided a structure, 1 to 2 ft. high if used as a groundcover. Zones 4 to 9. Japan, China, Korea.

CULTIVARS AND VARIETIES
'Aureo-reticulata' has leaves with a yellow-netted veinal pattern. This is not a plant for the weak at heart.

Variety *chinensis* (var. *repens*) is less rampant and lower growing than the species, with pretty flowers tinged reddish purple and a similar coloration on new leaves and stems. It makes a better garden plant than the species.

Variegated selections. Several others, with minimal worth.

Lonicera korolkowii
blueleaf honeysuckle

This is actually one of the prettiest—and from a textural perspective, possibly the finest—of the shrub honeysuckles, but it is just not readily available in commerce, or often misidentified when it is. Forms a billowy, arching mound of pale bluish green leaves, each ¾ to 1¼ in. long, on rather willowy stems. Rose-colored flowers, about ⅔ in. long, occur in May. The flowers are not overwhelming but are attractive on close inspection. The fruit is a bright red berry that matures in July and August. I have seen the true species only a few times; it was growing in partial shade and appeared quite prosperous. Plants grew 6 ft. high and wide, nowhere close to the 12- to 15-ft. height mentioned in the literature. Zones 4 to 7. Southern Russia to south central Asia.

Lonicera maackii
Amur honeysuckle

A monstrous honeysuckle with few redeeming characteristics, this species deserves a minimal place in modern landscapes. Habit is upright-

Lonicera ×heckrottii, goldflame honeysuckle, on left, *L. japonica*, on right

Lonicera ×heckrottii

Lonicera japonica, Japanese honeysuckle

Lonicera japonica

Lonicera japonica 'Aureo-reticulata'

spreading and arching, becoming leggy at the base. Bark becomes ridged and furrowed, with ridges eventually scaly, and develops a pleasing gray-brown color. The 2- to 3-in.-long, dark green leaves hold late in fall. White, 1-in.-long flowers open in May and June and offer minimal to no fragrance. The ¼-in.-wide, bright red fruit are rather pretty and provide food for the birds. Unfortunately, Amur honeysuckle is so adaptable that it has become a weed. Like *Lonicera*

MORE ▶

Lonicera korolkowii, blueleaf honeysuckle

Lonicera korolkowii

Lonicera maackii, Amur honeysuckle

Lonicera maackii

Lonicera maackii

461

Lonicera maackii CONTINUED

tatarica, it will seed into a woodland area and outcompete the native material. Think twice before using this species. Grows 12 to 15 ft. high and wide. Zones 2 to 8. Northeastern China, Korea.

Lonicera nitida
boxleaf honeysuckle

Try as I might to successfully grow this evergreen species, results were abysmal. In Europe, the western United States, and occasionally the South, plants are successful. Typically, a dense, haystack-shaped mass of close-knit stems and leaves. The leaves, about ½ in. long, are glossy dark green. Creamy yellow flowers, ¼ to ½ in. long, are produced in axillary, short-stalked pairs. Fruit are ¼-in.-wide, translucent, amethyst-colored berries. Used extensively for hedges and masses in European gardens. Often confused with *Cotoneaster* species, but that genus has alternate leaves (those of *Lonicera* are opposite). Full sun to partial shade in any well-drained soil. Grows 6 to 8 ft. high and wide. Zones 7 to 9. China.
CULTIVARS AND VARIETIES
Many, with 'Baggesen's Gold' probably the most common: golden leaves and mounded habit; leaf color fades, but not completely, with time; better color under cool conditions. Bigger than advertised, reaching 4 to 6 ft. high and wide.

Edmée Gold™ ('Briloni') is a yellow-gold leaf selection that photo-bleaches (white) in sun and heat. Observed many times with similar second-rate performance. A sport of 'Maigrün'.

'Maigrün' ('Maygreen') has small, rounded, boxwood-like, lustrous dark green leaves and graceful, fountain-like habit.

Lonicera periclymenum
woodbine

After following this vine throughout Europe (or was it the reciprocal?), I could not resist bringing the cultivars to Georgia for evaluation. A vigorous twining species with beautiful blue-green foliage, the new growth often tinged with purple-red. Flowers are fragrant, 1½ to 2 in. long, and appear in peduncled spikes in three to five whorls at the end of the shoots. Typical flower color is yellowish white with a purplish pink tinge. Flowers open in May and June. Fruit are often abundant, red, ¼ in. in diameter, and showy. Adaptable to varied soils, full sun to partial shade. The cultivars

Lonicera nitida, boxleaf honeysuckle

Lonicera nitida 'Baggesen's Gold'

Lonicera nitida Edmée Gold™

are superior to the species for garden use. Grows 10 to 20 ft. Zones 4 to 8. Europe, North Africa, Asia Minor.

CULTIVARS AND VARIETIES

Many, and I recommend the Dirr *Manual* (2009) for a more complete treatment of the 15 or so cultivars.

'Belgica' is a common selection with whitish to yellowish (inside the corolla) tinged purplish red flowers in great profusion.

'Graham Thomas' is soft cream-yellow, with no trace of purple. The name honors the late great British plantsman.

'Honey Baby' is a more compact scandent shrub, 5 to 6 ft. high with dark green leaves. Red-purple buds open to fragrant, cream-yellow flowers, aging orange-yellow.

'Serotina' (Late Dutch) has dark purple-red flowers (outside), yellowish inside. Flowers open later and over a longer period than the species.

Lonicera pileata
privet honeysuckle

Often confused with *Lonicera nitida* but with longer leaves shaped like those of *Ligustrum vulgare*, European privet. Also, consistently more cold hardy. Broad-spreading, evergreen shrub, with branches layered, building on each other, resulting in an elegant cotoneaster-like habit. Leaves, ½ to 1 in. long, are lustrous dark green and remain so through winter. Flowers and fruit are similar to *Lonicera nitida*.

MORE ▶

Lonicera periclymenum 'Graham Thomas'

Lonicera periclymenum, woodbine

Lonicera periclymenum 'Belgica'

Lonicera periclymenum 'Serotina'

Lonicera pileata CONTINUED

Well adapted to sun, partial shade, well-drained soil. I thought this evergreen honeysuckle would prove the answer for broad swaths of green but attempts to use it on the Georgia campus have met with minimal success. Grows 2 to 3 ft. high, 3 to 6 ft. wide. Zones 6 to 8. China.

CULTIVARS AND VARIETIES

'Moss Green' is a low-spreading, compact form with thickish dark green leaves; looks like a reduced-in-stature 'Otto Luyken' cherrylaurel.

Lonicera sempervirens

trumpet honeysuckle

Trumpet honeysuckle is one of our most common native twining vines. The species is found in shady woods throughout its native range. In full sun, it develops into a dense-foliaged vine. The 1- to 3-in.-long, blue-green leaves serve as a great background for the narrow, trumpet-shaped, 1½- to 2-in.-long, orange-red to red flowers, which occur in terminal panicles during April (Athens), May, and June, sporadically thereafter, and have no fragrance. The ¼-in.-wide, red berries ripen from September to November. Prefers moist, well-drained, acid to near neutral soils. Leaf drop caused by a *Pseudomonas* bacterium results in a less-than-satisfactory appearance toward the end of summer. The leaves abscise, but this does no permanent damage. Aphids occur on succulent new growth. Utilize on fences, trellises, downspouts, rock piles, or even as a groundcover. Grows 10 to 20 ft. high. Zones 4 to 9. Connecticut to Florida, west to Nebraska and Texas.

A most spectacular flowering honeysuckle is *Lonicera* ×*tellmanniana*, Tellmann honeysuckle. The parentage is *L. tragophylla* × *L. sempervirens* 'Superba'. It has almost fluorescent yellow-orange flowers that are blushed with red in the bud stage. Each flower averages 2 in. long and 1 in. across at the mouth of the corolla. This species

Lonicera pileata, privet honeysuckle

Lonicera pileata 'Moss Green'

Lonicera sempervirens, trumpet honeysuckle

has the same landscape uses as *L. sempervirens* and is adaptable from zones 5 to 7(8).

Another unique hybrid is 'Mandarin' (*Lonicera tragophylla* × *L.* ×*brownii* 'Dropmore Scarlet'), the new leaves coppery brown, maturing glossy dark green, fruit red, 20 ft. high. The flowers, mandarin-orange with yellow centers, open in May and June. One of the most beautiful vining honeysuckles I have observed.

CULTIVARS AND VARIETIES
Many, all yellow, or orange-red to red; have yet to witness any totally resistant to the leaf disease caused by *Pseudomonas syringae*.

'John Clayton' is a compact, repeat yellow-flowering form with good red fruit production.

'Magnifica' is the form I most often observe. Orange-red flowers with perhaps the best repeat flowering trait.

'Sulphurea', a beautiful yellow-flowered form, produces a shower of flowers and bright green foliage.

Lonicera tatarica
Tatarian honeysuckle
Typically an upright-oval to rounded, multi-stemmed shrub, with 1½- to 2½-in.-long, blue-green leaves and white to pink, ¾- to 1-in.-long flowers in May. Like most honeysuckles, it leafs out extremely early in spring.

MORE ▶

Lonicera sempervirens

Lonicera ×*tellmanniana*, Tellmann honeysuckle

Lonicera 'Mandarin'

Lonicera sempervirens 'Magnifica'

Lonicera sempervirens 'Sulphurea'

Lonicera tatarica, Tatarian honeysuckle

Lonicera tatarica CONTINUED
Bright red berries ripen from late June to August. Unfortunately, like *L. maackii*, it has become a weed, particularly in the East and Midwest, where it was once a common screen and hedge plant. In recent years, the Russian aphid has decimated this species in eastern and midwestern gardens; infestation causes the growth to become distorted and bunchy, with smallish leaves and stems. This essentially eliminates the species and most cultivars from garden consideration. Grows 10 to 12 ft. high, 10 ft. wide. Zones 3 to 8. Central Asia to southern Russia.
CULTIVARS AND VARIETIES
Many cultivars offer different flower and fruit colors. 'Arnold Red' (red

flowers), 'Freedom' (white tinged pink flowers), and 'Honey Rose' (rose-red flowers) are aphid-resistant cultivars.

Lonicera xylosteum
European fly honeysuckle
Arguably, this species and a few selected cultivars may be the most acceptable choices for the conditions of the Midwest and Plains states. *Lonicera xylosteum* is a rounded-mounded shrub with spreading, arching branches. The grayish green, 1- to 2½-in.-long leaves are the most pubescent of the species presented here. The white to yellowish white, ⅝-in.-long flowers produce minimal effect when they open in May. The dark red berries offer some color in

July and August. A tough, durable honeysuckle for difficult environments. Grows 8 to 10 ft. high, 10 to 12 ft. wide. Zones 4 to 6. Europe to the Altai Mountains of Asia.
CULTIVARS AND VARIETIES
'Emerald Mound' ('Nana') is a fine selection, with rich bluish green foliage and a low-growing, mounded habit. Prefers colder climates. Grows 3 to 4 ft. high, 4½ to 6 ft. wide.

'Miniglobe' is more compact and has greater cold hardiness than 'Emerald Mound'. It displays dense, dark green foliage. Grows 3 to 4 ft. high and wide.

Loropetalum chinense
Chinese loropetalum, Chinese fringe-flower
If prescriptions could be written for perfect garden plants, this species would come close to filling the order. Upright, dense, evergreen shrub or

Lonicera tatarica

Lonicera xylosteum

Lonicera tatarica

Lonicera tatarica 'Arnold Red'

Lonicera xylosteum, European fly honeysuckle

Lonicera xylosteum 'Emerald Mound'

Loropetalum chinense, Chinese loropetalum

small tree, typically vase-shaped in large specimens. Foliage is densely borne in almost planar disposition along the stems. The ovate-roundish, 1- to 2½-in.-long leaves are dark green and rough above, gray pubescent below. Four-petaled, fleecy flowers occur in the axils of the leaves, producing a mottle of cream and green. Flowers open in late March and April (Athens) with an effective period of three to four weeks. Bark, on large specimens, is rich brown and exfoliating. Remarkably adaptable and drought-tolerant, full sun to moderate shade, best in well-drained, acid soil. Responds to pruning; a loose screen in our garden was 4 ft. high through selective feather pruning. Superb screening evergreen; useful in groupings and masses; makes a good hedge; lovely touch in the shrub border. In my biased opinion, this

MORE ▶

Loropetalum chinense

Loropetalum chinense

467

Loropetalum chinense CONTINUED
shrub and the cultivars with red-purple leaves can be blended into any southern or West Coast garden. Grows 6 to 10 (to 15) ft. high, similar spread. A 30-ft.-high plant resides in the Keith Arboretum, Chapel Hill, North Carolina. Zones 7 to 9, 10 on the West Coast. China.

CULTIVARS AND VARIETIES
Carolina Moonlight® ('NCI 002') is a more compact green-leaf form that produces abundant white flowers on a 4- to 5-ft.-high and -wide plant; will develop stray shoots and may outgrow this size estimate. Full flower in the Dirr garden in April.

Emerald Snow™ produces white flowers in spring, sporadically in fall, lime-green new growth, dark green at maturity, 3 to 4 ft. high and wide.

Snow Dance™ is more compact in habit with smaller green leaves; white flowers are profuse. A worthy choice and easily pruned to maintain small stature. Grows 6 to 8 ft. high, wider at maturity. A plant in the Georgia trials was 10 ft. by 10 ft. in six years.

Loropetalum chinense var. *rubrum*
redleaf Chinese loropetalum

A star on the rise, introduced from China about 1990, initially represented by two cultivars: 'Blush' with bronze-purple new growth and hot pink flowers, and 'Burgundy' with reddish purple new growth and hot pink flowers. With rabbit-like reproduction, these two became staples in southern nurseries and currently are among the most popular broadleaf evergreens in southern gardens. Foliage color is reduced in summer to green, green-red-purple, depending on the cultivar. Reddish purple leaf color is most pronounced with high fertility and moisture. Color is almost equally good in sun and shade. Bonnie and I have liberally sprinkled them about the garden. Easy to manage, unbelievably drought-tolerant, and pest-free. I consider this variety one of the top introductions in southern garden history. Grows 6 to 10 (to 15) ft. high and wide. Zones 7 to 9, 10 on the West Coast. China.

CULTIVARS AND VARIETIES
Cultivars are the garden essence of this remarkable plant. Counted 39 red-leaf cultivars in the *Manual* (2009). Worth noting that 'Blush', Razzleberri™, Piroche Form, and 'Daybreak's Flame' are the same plant.

'Crimson Fire' has rich ruby-red persistent foliage, neon-pink flowers, compact mounded, spreading habit, 1½ to 2 ft. high, 2 to 3 ft. wide, increased cold hardiness compared to Purple Pixie®, 2011 introduction from Plant Introductions, Inc.

'Daruma' is a more compact form, full and dense in youth. Foliage is rich reddish purple and holds the color better than many cultivars. Flowers hot pink. Matures 6 to 8 ft. high.

Loropetalum chinense Carolina Moonlight®

Loropetalum chinense Snow Dance™

Ever Red® ('Chang Nian Hong') has beautiful deep, dark red-purple foliage that keeps the color in sun, shade, heat, and drought; the best foliage form of all. More noteworthy: the red, yes red, flowers, in profusion. Possibly 4 ft. high by 6 ft. wide. Introduced by Mark Griffith.

Fire Dance®, with reddish purple leaves and hot pink flowers, was introduced by Piroche Plants, British Columbia. Grows 8 to 10 ft. high and wide.

Little Rose Dawn® ('Griff CRL') is a sport of 'Ruby' that does not develop the splaying shoots; flowers deeper pink than 'Ruby'. Original plant 10 to 12 ft. high and wide. Mark Griffith introduction.

Plum Delight® (Pizzazz™) maintains excellent reddish purple foliage and hot pink flowers on a shrub of smaller stature; in the Dirr garden, not as vigorous as 'Zhuzhou Fuchsia'; still 10 ft. by 8 ft. in Georgia trials. 'Hines Purple-

leaf' and 'Hines Burgundy' are the same plant.

Purple Diamond® ('Shang-hi') is a compact, rounded selection with spreading, arching, layered branches and intense dark red-maroon foliage that holds reasonably well in the heat of zone 7. Vibrant pink flowers. Possibly 4 to 5 ft. high and slightly wider at maturity. In Georgia trials, this suffered foliar injury in the cold winter

MORE ▶

Loropetalum chinense var. *rubrum*, redleaf Chinese loropetalum

Loropetalum chinense var. *rubrum* 'Blush'

Loropetalum chinense var. *rubrum* 'Burgundy'

Loropetalum chinense var. *rubrum* 'Daruma'

Loropetalum chinense var. *rubrum* Ever Red®

Loropetalum chinense var. *rubrum* Little Rose Dawn®

Loropetalum chinense var. *rubrum* CONTINUED of 2009–10, when temperatures dropped to 13°F.

Purple Pixie® ('Shang-lo') is a dwarf groundcover form, 1 to 2 ft. by 4 to 5 ft., with intense smallish dark red-purple foliage and hot pink flowers. Excellent foliage color that persists in the heat but extremely cold sensitive. I witnessed dead plants in Athens landscapes after the 2009–10 winter.

'Ruby' matures 6 to 10 ft. high and wide, leaves more rounded, deep reddish purple; pink flowers; foliage color diminishes in heat.

'Sizzlin' Pink' is another wide-spreading form, branches layered upon branches; reddish purple foliage and hot pink flowers. Grows 4 to 6 ft. high and wide.

'Zhuzhou Fuchsia' is distinctly upright in habit, with narrower reddish purple to deep black-purple leaves and hot pink-red flowers. The most cold hardy red-purple leaf form, about 15 to 20 ft. high at maturity. 'Pipa's Red' is the same plant.

Lyonia lucida
fetterbush lyonia

Could not wait to bring the species into the Dirr garden but less than stellar performance and abundant leaf spot resulted in early plant retirement. Occasionally, I experience healthy plants and, in their finest forms, they

Loropetalum chinense var. *rubrum* Plum Delight®

Loropetalum chinense var. *rubrum* Fire Dance®

Loropetalum chinense var. *rubrum* 'Sizzlin' Pink'

Loropetalum chinense var. *rubrum* 'Ruby'

Loropetalum chinense var. *rubrum* 'Zhuzhou Fuchsia'

tempt me to try again. Suckering, spreading, broadleaf evergreen, branches arching and loose. Leaves, 1 to 3 in. long, leathery, and a lustrous dark green, are the principal reason for growing the plant. Red, pink to pinkish white to white flowers emerge from the leaf axils in April and May. Requires moisture, light shade, and no stress under cultivation. Suitable for wet areas; respectable colonies crossed my path in such situations. Grows 3 to 5 ft. high, wider at maturity. Zones 5 to 9. Virginia to Florida to Louisiana.

Maackia amurensis
Amur maackia
Unheralded and unknown except in the gardens of the fortunate few. No singular quality sets this small tree apart, but the sum of its features contributes to a pleasing landscape presence. A dapper, round-headed tree of uniform proportions in youth and at maturity. New foliage is dusted with grayish pubescence that yields to rich green. The leaves are composed of five to seven leaflets, each 1½ to 3½ in. long. Fall color is virtually nonexistent, and the leaves die off green. Dull white, pea-like flowers appear in 4- to 6-in.-long racemose panicles in June or July. Their fragrance could be likened to that of new-mown alfalfa. Fruit are 2- to 3-in.-long, ⅓- to ½-in.-wide, flat brown pods. The shiny,

MORE ▶

Maackia amurensis

Lyonia lucida, fetterbush lyonia

Maackia amurensis

Maackia amurensis, Amur maackia

Maackia amurensis

Maackia amurensis CONTINUED

amber-colored bark peels with age into loose flakes and curls. When backlit by the setting sun, the bark has the color of a rich brown ale. Performs best in loose, acid or high pH, well-drained soils. An excellent small tree for streets, planters, lawns, and patios. Grows 20 to 30 ft. high and wide. Zones 4 to 7. Not as vigorous in zone 7 as in more northern zones. Northeastern China.

Maclura pomifera

osage-orange

Not many gardeners or nursery people become overly excited about this species. For the drier parts of the Midwest and Great Plains, however, it has merit, not only withstanding but thriving in the harshest conditions. It

Maclura pomifera, osage-oranges

Maclura pomifera 'White Shield'

is rounded in youth and old age, with a low trunk; the crown is composed of stiff, spiny, interlacing branches. The glossy, medium to dark green, 2- to 5-in.-long leaves turn a pleasing yellow in fall. Fruit on female trees are green, round, and 4 to 6 in. in diameter. As projectiles they are dangerous, as well as messy. Newton's Law of Gravity had nothing to do with falling apples; falling osage-oranges prompted the theory. The wood is rot-resistant and can be used for stepping rounds, and the use of osage-orange in the Midwest for hedgerows and fence lines is evident even today. Grows 20 to 40 ft. high, similar spread; can grow to 60 ft. high. Zones 4 to 9. Arkansas to Oklahoma and Texas.

CULTIVARS AND VARIETIES
Selection for thornless and fruitless forms, which could lead to greater usage, is ongoing. 'Wichita' and 'White Shield' are the two most thorn-free cultivars, the latter least thorny. Discovered in Kansas and Oklahoma, respectively.

Magnolia

With the merging of *Michelia* and *Manglietia* into *Magnolia*, the number of species in the genus has increased to 224, according to the International Magnolia Society. Truly a nightmare to sensibly discuss, because of the now even more numerous cultivars, each claiming to be "best." In research and garden evaluations, many were tested, but the "best of show" are tainted by the fact that there was never a complete collection of, for example, all the "yellows." Pat McCracken, McCracken's Nursery, North Carolina, told me over 100 yellow-flowered magnolias exist. I am always asked the best yellow. I don't know the answer, but in the pages that follow share my experiences and observations. Many garden tours to the southwest of England afforded me the opportunity to experience the Sino-Himalayan magnolias in magnificent flower—trees fully 60 ft. high, clothed in white, pink, rose, cyclamen-pink flowers. Heaven on earth, to be sure. Let's travel . . .

Maclura pomifera fall color

472

Magnolia acuminata
cucumbertree magnolia

Seldom seen in North American gardens for want of flashy flowers. It is a large native tree with dark green, 4- to 10-in.-long leaves. Yellow-green flowers appear after the leaves and are followed by small, irregular, eventually cucumber-shaped red fruit. Cucumbertree magnolia will never rival a saucer magnolia or star magnolia for flower effect, but as a shade tree it deserves consideration. Distinctly pyramidal when young, it becomes round-headed with age, bearing massive, wide-spreading branches. Transplant young specimens into deep, moist, acid or high pH soils. Superb specimens are found in the calcareous soils of the Midwest. For large properties only. Grows 50 to 80 ft. high, similar spread. Zones 4 to 8.

New York to Illinois, south to Georgia and Arkansas.

CULTIVARS AND VARIETIES
Numerous yellow-flowered, often with various tinges of pink, rose, purple.

'Butterflies' has deep yellow flowers, 3 to 4 (to 5) in. across, six to nine tepals. Precocious. At its best appears like yellow canaries have

MORE ▶

Magnolia acuminata, cucumbertree magnolia

Magnolia acuminata var. *subcordata*

Magnolia acuminata

473

Magnolia acuminata CONTINUED
perched on naked stems. Upright pyramidal grower, 18 to 20 ft. high.

'Coral Lake' is a pretty, coral-peach-pink-cream-green form with nine upright tepals. Fragrant flowers later than many, mid April at the JC Raulston Arboretum, leaves just emerging.

'Daybreak' has bright rose-pink flowers that open with the leaves and remind me of tutti-frutti ice cream; flowers over a long period. Mature height is 30 to 40 ft. by 20 ft.

'Elizabeth' is the result of a cross between *Magnolia acuminata* and *M. denudata* by the Brooklyn Botanic Garden. Habit is neat and pyramidal, but the genuine beauty resides in the finely tapering buds that open to display fragrant flowers of the clearest primrose-yellow, maturing to transpar-ent yellow. In heat, the flowers fade to cream. Extremely vigorous, probably to between 30 to 50 ft. high, 20 to 35 ft. wide.

'Hot Flash' produces soft cream-yellow flowers with streaky rose-purple stainings at base, six to nine tepals, before or with the leaves on a vigor-ous, upright to 30-ft.-high plant. Better each year in Georgia trials, with peak flowering in early to mid April.

Magnolia 'Butterflies'

Magnolia 'Daybreak'

Magnolia 'Elizabeth'

Magnolia 'Hot Flash'

Magnolia 'Sunsation'

Magnolia campbellii, Campbell magnolia

'Lois' has fragrant yellow flowers, almost primrose-yellow, darker than 'Elizabeth' and opening later but before leaves emerge. Flower form is almost chalice-like, with nine to 12 tepals. Vigorous, rounded tree to 20 ft. and greater.

Variety *subcordata* is smaller, 20 to 30 ft., with more consistent yellow flowers than the type. Restricted to North Carolina and Georgia but cold hardy to at least –25°F. The national champion is 84 ft. high. Had a small plant, about 15 ft. high, in the Dirr garden that flowered profusely.

'Sunsation' produces individual flowers 6 to 7 in. across with yellow to cream-yellow tepals, blushed rose-pink at base; flowers open before leaves and sporadically thereafter. Dark green, wavy foliage. Matures 20 to 30 ft. by 20 to 25 ft.

'Yellow Bird' holds its six tepals upright, each tepal 3 to 4 in. long, about 2 in. wide. Flower are essentially nonfragrant, yellow with slight greenish tinge at base of outer tepals. Leaves 4 to 8 in. long and akin to the species. Fast-growing to 40 ft.

Magnolia campbellii
Campbell magnolia

Without question, in flower, this species inflames the passion for plants unlike any other. Trees—with un-magnolia-like size and crowns that scrape the heavens with their cup-and-saucer flowers—infuse the soul. Allan Armit-

age and I, on our initial visit to the southwest of England, when first viewing the Sino-Himalayan magnolias, thought we had ascended to Heaven. Pretty heady plants! Flowers are fashioned from 12 to 15 tepals, the outer splaying to form a saucer, the inner a cup, in entirety 10 in. across. Flowers open in March and April on naked branches. Leaves are 6 in. long, dark green, and oval in outline. The bark

is gray, relatively smooth, becoming platy-scaly with age. For western North America only, in a belt from San Francisco to Vancouver Island, British Columbia. Specimen tree with no other use acceptable. Grows 50 to 60 ft. high. Zones 9 and 10 on the West Coast. Himalayas.

Magnolia dawsoniana and *M. sargentiana* var. *robusta* are other

MORE ▶

Magnolia campbellii subsp. *mollicomata*

Magnolia campbellii 'Lanarth'

Magnolia campbellii subsp. *mollicomata*

Magnolia campbellii CONTINUED
large-flowered species akin to *M. campbellii*.

CULTIVARS AND VARIETIES
Numerous selections for flower colors are known. The most beautiful is 'Lanarth' with cyclamen-purple buds that open to dark reddish purple.

Subspecies *mollicomata* is considered hardier than *Magnolia campbellii*, but there is minimal morphological difference. Supposedly the peduncle is hairy; that of *M. campbellii* not.

Magnolia cylindrica

A tough taxonomic nut to crack; I have seen many labeled as such but was never sure. Wide-spreading shrub-tree habit, 15 to 20 ft. high, typically wider, with 4- to 6-in.-long, 2- to 2½-in.-wide, dark green leaves. White, fragrant, nine-tepaled flowers, their backsides with a pinkish triangular blotch, open in March and April. Several plants, purchased from Piroche Plants, have

consistently flowered in late April in Athens. Zones 5 to 7. China.

Magnolia denudata

syn. *Magnolia heptapeta*
Yulan magnolia
More famous as a parent of *Magnolia ×soulangeana*, saucer magnolia, than in its own right. The nine-tepaled, 5- to 6-in.-wide, creamy white, fragrant flowers open early and, unfortunately, are often injured by spring freezes. When undamaged by weather, the floral display is a beautiful sight in March and April. The dark green leaves average 4 to 6 in. long. It is a rounded tree and has smooth gray bark. Excellent specimen magnolia, but often frustrating to grow because of its vulnerability to spring frosts. In hybridization work, it has served as a parent of many fine crosses, including, with *M. acuminata*, the creamy yellow-flowered 'Elizabeth'. Grows 20 to 30 (to 40) ft. high. Zones (4)5 to 8. China.

CULTIVARS AND VARIETIES
'Pristine' is, unfortunately, unknown to most gardeners, but it is certainly worthy of acquisition. A hybrid between *Magnolia denudata* and *M. stellata*, this cultivar bears ivory-white, lily-shaped, fragrant flowers, each with 15 to 18 tepals, which open in April. The habit is pyramidal, and the foliage is a handsome dark green. Grows 15 to 25 ft. high, slightly less in spread. Zones 5 to 9.

Magnolia figo

syn. *Michelia figo*
banana shrub
Appropriate common name for this broadleaf evergreen shrub of upright-oval to rounded habit. The floral fragrance, reminiscent of banana oil, is a pleasing olfactory addition to the spring garden. The newly emerging leaves are covered with silky brownish pubescence, at maturity glabrous, lustrous dark green, 1½ to 4 in. long.

Magnolia cylindrica

Magnolia denudata

Magnolia denudata, Yulan magnolia

Foliage alone is reason to grow the plant. The 1- to 1½-in.-long and -wide, six- to nine-tepaled, yellowish green, tinged purple, cup-shaped flowers are borne on a ½-in.-long brown pubescent peduncle from April through June. Their rich fragrance, particularly on still, warm days, trails one through the garden. Prefers rich, moist, well-drained acidic soils in some degree of shade, although plants succeed in sun. A plant in our former garden was shrouded by several southern red oaks and *always* held up in the heat and drought better than the next-door native azaleas, Japanese kerrias, and oakleaf hydrangeas. Excellent for shady areas of the garden. Withstands heavy pruning and still looks good. Grows 6 to 10 (to 15) ft. high. Zones 7 to 9, 10 on the West Coast. China.

GEORGIA EXPERIENCES

As mentioned in the *Magnolia* introduction, *Michelia* and *Manglietia* are now included in *Magnolia*. Over my 30 plus years in Athens, I have tested *Michelia* and *Manglietia* species with less-than-great success. Early flowering (late winter) on many former *Michelia* species dooms them to cold injury; but for West Coast gardens, many of the species are well adapted, and Sean Hogan's *Trees for All Seasons* (2008) provides excellent descriptions and actual experiences. The following brief notes reflect my Georgia experiences.

Magnolia doltsopa, a large tree with

MORE ▶

Magnolia figo, banana shrub

Magnolia 'Pristine'

Magnolia figo

Magnolia insignis

Magnolia yuyuanensis

Magnolia figo CONTINUED

multi-tepaled, fragrant, white flowers, is reserved only for zone 9 and 10 West Coast gardens.

Magnolia ×*foggii*, a hybrid between *M. doltsopa* and *M. figo*, with beautiful dark green leaves, fuzzy brown buds, and white to cream flowers often with pink edges, never flowered in the Georgia trials: flower buds were injured every winter. 'Allspice' and 'Jack Fogg' are the most common representatives.

Magnolia insignis (*Manglietia insignis*) with slightly fragrant, rose- to red-stained upright tepals, has flowered in April, May, June, and September; *Magnolia maudiae*, with eight or nine white tepals, in January, February, and March. Others (*M. crassipes, M. chapensis, M. foveolata*) planted in 2003 and 2004 did not inspire.

What I planted as *Michelia yunnanensis* became *Magnolia dianica* and is now known to be *M. yuyua-*

nensis. The cultivar was 'Michelle', with abundant white flowers, which unfortunately was irretrievably injured by the 2009–10 winter. The plant has been successfully cultured at the JC Raulston Arboretum for many years.

Magnolia platypetala (by some *M. cavaleriei* var. *platypetala*), aside from *M. figo*, has been, by significant measures, the best performer in Georgia. In 2009–10, a long, consistently cold winter delayed flowering, but one seedling of *M. platypetala* proved exceptional, smothered with slightly fragrant, 15-tepaled white flowers in mid March, while others singed, browned, or turned mushy. *Magnolia platypetala* has also flowered in January, February, September, and November. The habit is conical-pyramidal, and the plant grew 11 ft. 5 in. by 7 ft. 7 in. in seven years.

Magnolia skinneriana is closely related to *M. figo* but considered more cold hardy. In Georgia trials, it

has been a vigorous grower, but I see minimal differences between it and *M. figo*. In *New Trees* (2010), John Grimshaw and Ross Bayton place it in the Skinneriana Group; the flowers are paler than the deep cream of *M. figo* and lack reddish staining. Plants withstood −4°F.

In the end, the hardiest and most evergreen in Georgia trials was *Magnolia figo*, which grew 9 ft. 5 in. by 7 ft. in nine years. Did not lose a leaf in the 2009–10 winter.

CULTIVARS AND VARIETIES

'Port Wine' and 'Stubbs Purple', the flowers with more purple coloration, are probably one and the same selection of *Magnolia figo*.

Magnolia grandiflora
southern magnolia

The symbol of southern gardens, loved and cherished, accorded privilege and prestige, truly the broadleaf evergreen tree of noble lineage. Numerous

Magnolia platypetala in Georgia trials

Magnolia platypetala

Magnolia grandiflora

selections in the past 30 years have provided a variety of habits, sizes, and leaf shapes that better serve the small landscape. Strong, dense pyramid, usually with central leader, occasionally almost rounded in outline. Leaves with the consistency of a credit card, waxy-surfaced and dark green above, green to fuzzy brown below. Bark, smooth, gray, somewhat beech-like, is attractive. The true religious experience comes from the nirvanishly fragrant flowers, 8 to 12 in. wide, composed of six to 15 tepals (petals and sepals look the same), each thick, concave, broad-ovate. In Athens the floral parade begins in May, with cultivars like 'Little Gem' still flowering in October and November. Fruit, composed of follicles, develop in 3- to 5-in.-long, cone-like aggregates. The individual seeds, orange-red, emerge from a single suture and dangle from a white, thread-like stalk. Transplant small trees from containers, larger balled-and-burlapped material in August and later. Grows in acid soils, sun and shade, wet and dry. Once established, a drought- and heat-tolerant plant. Noble tree for grouping, street tree, hedge, and large screen use. Old leaves fall and accumulate; when tread upon, they sound like a loud bowl of Rice Krispies. Grows 60 to 80 ft. high, 30 to 50 ft. wide. Zones (6)7 to 9, 10 on the West Coast. North Carolina to Florida, Arkansas, and Texas.

CULTIVARS AND VARIETIES
Over 150 named, 30 to 40 extant, fewer available in commerce. Ray Bracken, Piedmont, South Carolina, started the introduction bandwagon in the Southeast with 'Bracken's Brown Beauty', patented in 1985. I estimate 15 to 18 new cultivars in the last 25 years.

Alta® ('TMGH'), upright-columnar to narrow-pyramidal form, like 'Hasse', with dark green foliage, slightly brown below. Good root system, easy to transplant; terrific dense foliage and branches, will make a great screen. Grows 21 ft. by 8 ft. Becomes wider with age, at least based on my observation of the original tree.

'Bracken's Brown Beauty' is compact in youth, with foliage extremely lustrous dark green above, rusty brown below, 6 in. long with undulating surface. Possibly mature at 30 to 50 ft. high, 15 to 30 ft. wide. One of the more cold hardy forms. Zone 6.

'Claudia Wannamaker' is still one of the best, and it becomes better with age, not as flashy in youth. Grows 50 ft. or more with maturity; a large, old specimen in Atlanta Botanical Garden reflects stateliness over time.

'Edith Bogue', possibly the most cold hardy selection, is an ideal choice for the Mid-Atlantic states; West Coast nurserymen reported branches less susceptible to breakage in heavy wet

MORE ▶

Magnolia grandiflora, southern magnolia

Magnolia grandiflora CONTINUED

snows. Opens with time in deeper South, 30 to 40 ft. high, 15 to 20 ft. wide

Greenback™ ('Mgtig') is unique: polished dark green convex leaves reflect the sun in all directions, leaf undersides have slight brown pubescence, finally green. Original plant was 30 ft. high, 12 ft. wide. Probably 50 ft. by 20 ft. at landscape maturity.

Magnolia grandiflora

'Hasse' is a tight pyramidal-columnar form with lustrous dark green leaves, rusty pubescence below. Parent tree was 45 to 50 ft. high, 15 to 18 ft. wide; one of the best for screening. Somewhat difficult to propagate and transplant, but worth the effort.

'Kay Parris' is a larger version of 'Little Gem', probably a hybrid of that and 'Bracken's Brown Beauty', with lustrous dark green leaves, wavy leaf surface, rusty brown below. Typical flowers and more restrained habit. A plant in my trials looks promising.

'Little Gem' is possibly the most popular selection because of precociousness to flower and smaller size. Small (to 4 in. long) lustrous dark green leaves are covered with bronze-brown pubescence below. The cream-white flowers, 3 to 4 (to 6) in. in diameter, initiate in May (Athens) and are still developing in October and November. Requires pruning to keep

it dense. Grows 20 ft. high or more at maturity; excellent for screening and hedging.

'Saint Mary' ('Glen St. Mary'), introduced about 1905, has beautiful lustrous foliage, bronze pubescence below, and large and copious flowers on young plants. Pyramidal habit, grows probably 30 ft. or more.

Teddy Bear® ('Southern Charm') is a beautiful, dense, compact, upright pyramidal form with wavy, lustrous dark green, 3 to 6 in. long, 2 to 4 in. wide leaves that are brown below. Grows 20 to 25 ft. by 10 ft. Excellent choice for the small property.

'Victoria', another cold hardy form, has lustrous dark green leaves with brown undersides. More open-growing than the types presented here; used in the Pacific Northwest. Supposedly hardy to –12°F. Does not compete aesthetically with the upper echelon southern magnolia.

Magnolia grandiflora 'Bracken's Brown Beauty'

Magnolia grandiflora Greenback™

Magnolia grandiflora 'Kay Parris'

Magnolia grandiflora 'Little Gem'

Magnolia grandiflora Alta®

Magnolia grandiflora 'Claudia Wannamaker'

Magnolia grandiflora 'Hasse'

Magnolia grandiflora Teddy Bear®

481

Magnolia kobus

Kobus magnolia

Seldom available and/or used in contemporary landscapes because of the time it takes for it to flower from seed; some take as long as 30 years to reach full flower. The six- to nine-tepaled, slightly fragrant flowers, white with a faint purple line at the base of the tepals, 3 to 4 in. in diameter, appear before the leaves in March and April. Beautiful when right. In youth the habit is pyramidal, becoming rounded at maturity. The dark green, 3- to 6-in.-long leaves develop appreciable yellow-brown fall color. The silver-gray bark is a lovely addition to the winter landscape. Very adaptable species. Grows 30 to 40 ft. high. Noted a 60-ft.-high tree in South Amherst, Massachusetts, that flowered in mid April. Zones 5 to 7(8). Japan.
CULTIVARS AND VARIETIES
Variety *borealis* is more cold hardy

Magnolia kobus fall color

Magnolia kobus, Kobus magnolia

Magnolia kobus

Magnolia kobus

(zone 4) and more tree-like in habit than the species. A plantsman in Maine noted that seedling trees of var. *borealis* did not flower until their 18th year. I grew seedling populations in Georgia that did not flower until the first week of March of their 14th year.

Magnolia liliiflora
lily magnolia

One of the parents of *Magnolia* ×*sou-langeana*, the Little Girl Hybrids,

'Galaxy' and 'Spectrum', and the Jury Hybrids. Never given credence in gardens, it is nevertheless one of the most beautiful shrub types thanks to its deep vinous purple flowers. Leaves are 4 to 7 in. long and resemble those of *M.* ×*soulangeana*. Unfortunately, mildew is a problem, and foliage may appear tatty by summer's curtain call. The flowers, the deepest red-purple in bud of any species, remain upright when opening, finally relaxing and

exposing lighter inner color. In Georgia, flowers open in late March and continue into April, before the leaves emerge. Reblooming is common, even into summer, a trait passed to *M.* ×*soulangeana*. Moist, acid, well-drained soil, full sun are ideal. Out of favor but attractive in flower, it often grows around old homesteads in the South. Grows 8 to 12 ft. high, similar spread. Zones 5 to 8. China.

MORE ▶

Magnolia liliiflora, lily magnolia

Magnolia liliiflora 'Nigra'

Magnolia 'Ann'

Magnolia liliiflora CONTINUED

CULTIVARS AND VARIETIES

Several rich, deep reddish purple forms have been introduced with 'Nigra' the best: deep lustrous green foliage, compact habit, dark reddish purple flowers. During sabbatical at Hillier Arboretum, England, I observed this cultivar blooming in April on naked stems and still flowering in July, with a full complement of leaves.

The Little Girl Hybrids from the U.S. National Arboretum combine *Magnolia liliiflora* 'Nigra' and *M. stellata* 'Rosea' to produce shrubby, later-flowering cultivars that avoid the spring frosts. All flower on naked stems and continue flowering as the leaves develop. Still, flower too early in the South to avoid occasional late frost damage. Foliage is often mildew-ridden in Boston and Athens. The Little Girls develop water sprouts, need occasional pruning, and grow 10 to 20 ft. high and wide. 'Ann' (deep purple-red), 'Betty' (deep pur-

ple-red), 'Jane' (reddish purple), 'Judy' (deep red-purple), 'Pinkie' (pale red-purple fading to pink), 'Randy' (purple), 'Ricki' (deep purple), and 'Susan' (red-purple) constitute the Little Girls.

'Galaxy' and 'Spectrum' are sister seedlings from crosses between *Mag-*

nolia liliiflora and *M. sprengeri* 'Diva'. They are upright pyramidal trees in youth, becoming more rounded with age, and have smooth grayish bark. The tepals, backed with rich reddish purple, open in late March (Athens) and April to expose 6-in.-wide pink-

Magnolia 'Galaxy'

Magnolia 'Pinkie'

Magnolia 'Susan'

Magnolia 'Galaxy'

Magnolia 'Spectrum'

ish centers. Mildew can be a problem in moist, humid climates. 'Galaxy' develops water sprouts, a legacy from its *M. liliiflora* parentage. Both make great specimen plants and are possible street trees in suburban areas. Grow 25 to 30 ft. high, slightly less in spread. Zones 5 to 8(9).

Magnolia ×*loebneri*
Loebner magnolia

A hybrid between *Magnolia kobus* and *M. stellata*, this small tree embodies the best characteristics of each of its parents. Normally forms a round-headed crown of dense branches. The flowers are white, blushed pink, fragrant, and have 12 to 15 tepals; they open in April, about seven to ten days ahead of those of *M.* ×*soulangeana*. In Athens, full flower is typically mid February to mid March. Leaves are dark green, 3 to 5 in. long, and turn mellow yellow-brown in fall. Grows 20 to 30 ft. high. Zones (4)5 to 8.

MORE ▶

Magnolia ×*loebneri*

Magnolia ×*loebneri* 'Ballerina'

Magnolia ×*loebneri* 'Leonard Messel'

Magnolia ×*loebneri* 'Spring Snow'

Magnolia ×*loebneri*, 'Leonard Messel'

Magnolia ×*loebneri* 'Merrill'

Magnolia ×*loebneri* CONTINUED
CULTIVARS AND VARIETIES
'Ballerina' has flowers with 30 tepals, pure white and pinkish in the center. It is pyramidal-oval in habit. Grows to 25 ft. high.

'Leonard Messel' produces 12- to 15-tepaled flowers, flushed purple-pink on the outside. Habit is smaller than that of other cultivars mentioned here. Grows 15 to 20 ft. high. Grew hundreds of 'Leonard Messel' seedlings, none better than the species. Flowers more frost-tolerant, typically opening early to mid March in the Dirr garden.

'Merrill' has 3- to 3½-in.-wide flowers with 15 tepals, borne profusely on a densely branched plant. Easily 25 to 30 ft. high and wide, often wider. Flowered after −45°F in Presque Isle, Maine.

'Spring Snow' has 12-tepaled, creamy white flowers. Grows 25 ft. high and wide.

Magnolia macrophylla
bigleaf magnolia

Although seldom available in commerce other than from specialty nurseries, this large, coarse species makes an interesting novelty specimen for parks, campuses, and large open spaces. At maturity, it is a cumbersome giant, seemingly too tired to lift its leafy arms skyward. And with good reason: its dark green, silver-undersided leaves are 12 to 32 in. long, truly almost too heavy to lift. The leaf litter from this tree, with some leaves facing up and others showing

Magnolia fraseri, Fraser magnolia

Magnolia tripetala, umbrellatree magnolia

Magnolia macrophylla, bigleaf magnolia

Magnolia macrophylla

Magnolia fraseri subsp. *pyramidata*, pyramid magnolia

their silver undersides, makes a great autumn sight. No rake is large enough! Six-tepaled, creamy white, fragrant flowers, 8 to 10 (to 14) in. in diameter, open in June at the ends of the branches. The 3-in.-long, roundish, egg-shaped, rose-colored fruit ripen in September. Plant in moist, deep, organic-laden, slightly acid soils for best growth. Will grow in sun or partial shade. Very difficult to use in the average residential landscape; it requires space to flex its muscles. Grows 30 to 40 ft. high and wide. Zones 5 to 8. Ohio to Florida, west to Arkansas and Louisiana.

Several closely related taxa include *Magnolia fraseri*, Fraser magnolia; *M. fraseri* subsp. *pyramidata*, pyramid magnolia; and *M. tripetala*, umbrellatree magnolia. These vary in their mature size, the shape of the leaf base, and the degree of bud pubescence. All have quite large leaves. All have crossed paths with the author in the wild, and I have grown all in the Georgia garden. Certainly *M. macrophylla* and its subsp. *ashei* (which see) have outperformed these, subsp. *ashei* flowering as a small plant.

Magnolia macrophylla subsp. *ashei*
syn. *Magnolia ashei*
Ashe magnolia
A wonderful textural element in gardens because of the large bold-textured leaves, clubby stems, and 12-in.-wide flowers in late May and June (Athens). More or less shrubby in habit, with dark green, 24- to 30-in.-long leaves, silvery on their lower surfaces. Fragrant flowers consist of six immense tepals often stained purple at the base. A three-year-old plant was 30 in. high in our garden when it first flowered. Almost a heavenly experience to witness such magnificent beauty. Requires moist, well-drained, acidic soils in partial to heavy shade. Much more heat- and drought-tolerant than hydrangeas. Utilize as a textural element in the shade garden. A Dirr favorite for its precociousness and stunning foliage. Grows 10 to 20 ft. high and wide. Zones 6 to 9. Florida to Texas along the Gulf Coast.

Magnolia salicifolia
anise magnolia
One of the least available magnolias in commerce, I surmise, but a rather pretty species, forming a narrow to broad pyramid, 20 to 30 (to 50) ft. high. The smooth silver-gray bark is striking. Flowers, white, fragrant, 3 to 4 in. across, are composed of six tepals, opening in late March (Athens) to April. Flowers are not overwhelming, a fact that has reduced the species' movement into garden commerce. When bruised or cut, young stems are highly aromatic, emitting a lemon-

MORE ▶

Magnolia macrophylla subsp. *ashei*, Ashe magnolia

Magnolia macrophylla subsp. *ashei*

Magnolia macrophylla subsp. *ashei*

Magnolia salicifolia CONTINUED
anise scent. Easy to grow; seedlings flowered in five to six years in my Georgia trials. Leaves emerge bronze, turning dull dark green, slight yellow in fall. Native in rocky, granite soil by the side of forest streams. Zone (3)4 to 7. Leaves appear tired/tatty in the heat of zone 7 by summer's close. Japan.
CULTIVARS AND VARIETIES
'Wada's Memory' is densely pyramidal-conical with larger flowers, to 6 in. in diameter, and soft yellow fall color. Considered a *Magnolia kobus* × *M. salicifolia* hybrid.

Magnolia sieboldii
Oyama magnolia
Nowhere common, safe to state, but forms a refined 10- to 15-ft.-high, wider-spreading shrub with 3- to 6-in.-long, 3- to 4-in.-wide, medium green leaves, quite pubescent on the lower surface. Fragrant flowers are borne horizontally or nodding on a 1- to 2½-in.-long pedicel. Egg-shaped buds open white, nine to 12 tepals, with maroon-crimson center (stamens). Flowers after the leaves in May (Athens) to June (Boston). Requires shade in the South, moist, well-drained soils. Worthy choice for a shady border or in a grouping at wood's edge. Zones 4 to 7. Japan and Korea.

Magnolia sieboldii subsp. *sinensis*

MORE ▶

Magnolia salicifolia, anise magnolia

Magnolia salicifolia

Magnolia salicifolia

Magnolia 'Wada's Memory'

Magnolia sieboldii, Oyama magnolia

Magnolia sieboldii

Magnolia sieboldii

Magnolia sieboldii subsp. *sinensis*

Magnolia wilsonii

Magnolia sieboldii CONTINUED

and *M. wilsonii* have more open white flowers, 3 to 4 in. across, with crimson-purple stamens. Certainly beautiful in flower but less cold hardy than *M. sieboldii*, to about –10°F.
CULTIVARS AND VARIETIES
'Colossus', an 18-tepaled tetraploid, performed well in Georgia trials.

Magnolia ×soulangeana
saucer magnolia

This quintessential hybrid magnolia is as common as fertilizer at every garden center. It is a precocious, small-size, flowering tree, reliable year in and year out. A specimen in full flower is one of spring's greatest spectacles. The cup-shaped, pinkish purple, nine-tepaled, fragrant flowers, 5 to 10 in. in diameter, open in April (March 1 to 15 in Athens) on bare stems. Unfortunately, like the flowers of *Magnolia denudata*, they are subject to the vagaries of spring weather. The habit is generally low-branched, with upright-arching branches forming a rounded outline. The dark green, 3- to 6-in.-long leaves are handsome into fall, but they seldom produce anything but a muddied yellow fall color. The smooth gray bark is a pleasant addition to the winter landscape. Extremely adaptable to a wide range of soils, and an excellent specimen plant. The hybrid was first made in France. Grows 20 to 30 ft. high, variable spread. Zones 5 to 9.
CULTIVARS AND VARIETIES
Many and confused. Wise to purchase in flower if trueness to cultivar name is desired.

Magnolia wilsonii

Magnolia ×soulangeana

Magnolia ×soulangeana, saucer magnolia

Magnolia ×soulangeana

Magnolia ×soulangeana 'Alexandrina'

'Alexandrina' produces tepals that are flushed light rose-purple outside, pure white inside. It is one of the larger- and earlier-flowering cultivars. There are at least three clones masquerading as 'Alexandrina' in the nursery trade, one with darker rose-purple flowers. Grows 20 to 30 ft. high.

'Big Pink' is a vigorous, upright, almost tree form that is more common in southern nurseries. Nine tepals with bar on back, flowers deep rose, flowers slightly larger than typical.

'Brozzonii' offers white tepals tinged pale purplish rose at the base. Each flower is fully 10 in. across when open. This large cultivar is about the last to flower. Grows 25 to 30 ft. high.

'Lennei' bears dark purplish magenta flowers fashioned in an almost goblet shape. Leaves are darker green than those of the species, and the growth habit is that of a stiff, broad shrub. Grows 15 to 20 ft. high and wide. 'Lennei Alba' offers beautiful, pure white flowers on a similar framework.

'Lilliputian' is a slow grower with a tight upright habit, probably one-half the size of the species at maturity. Smaller, light pink flowers. Have observed small plants just loaded with flower buds and flowers.

Pickard Hybrids are seedlings of *Magnolia ×soulangeana* 'Picture' raised by Amos Pickard of Canterbury, England. All are fast-growing and do not set heavy flower buds in youth as does *M. ×soulangeana*. Well-shaped vase to goblet flowers with intense colors. In my opinion, they do not

MORE ▶

Magnolia ×soulangeana 'Big Pink'

Magnolia ×soulangeana 'Brozzonii'

Magnolia ×soulangeana 'Lennei'

Magnolia ×soulangeana 'Lennei Alba'

Magnolia ×soulangeana 'Lilliputian'

Magnolia ×soulangeana 'Pickard's Firefly'

Magnolia ×soulangeana CONTINUED measure up to the older *M. ×soulangeana* cultivars.

'Picture' produces red-purple buds that open to pink-white inside, heavy red-purple staining outside; flowers larger than typical *Magnolia ×soulangeana*, up to 10 to 12 in. across, tepals 6 to 7 in. long. Vigorous, upright grower.

'Rustica Rubra' ('Rubra') has rose-red, 5½-in.-wide flowers. Forms a large, looser growing shrub.

'Verbanica' is a late-flowering cultivar, with rose tepals that grade to white at their tips. It bears abundant buds as a young plant. Habit is large and rounded, 20 to 25 ft. high and wide.

Magnolia stellata
star magnolia

Typically a dense, oval to rounded, twiggy shrub, but this species can attain a good size, and when the basal branches are removed to expose the smooth gray bark, the result is a handsome large shrub or small tree. The 2- to 4-in.-long, dark green leaves turn handsome yellow to bronze-yellow in autumn. Fragrant, 12- to 18-tepaled, 3- to 4- (to 5-) in.-wide flowers open in March and April, usually before those of *Magnolia ×soulangeana*. Flowering may last for ten to 20 days, because not all buds open at the same time. The leaves may even reach full size with some flowers still present. This is possibly the most cold- and heat-tolerant species for general ornamental use. Displays excellent adaptability to varied soils, and prospers from Maine to Georgia to Minnesota and to the West Coast. Grows 15 to 20 ft. high, 10 to 15 ft. wide. Zones 4 to 8. Japan.
CULTIVARS AND VARIETIES
Many excellent choices are available —I have never observed a bad one.

'Centennial' is a beautiful selection that commemorates the 100th anniversary of the Arnold Arboretum. Its flowers have 28 to 32 tepals, with each open flower up to 5½ in. wide. This form has a strong central leader and is the most vigorous of all *Magnolia stellata* types. It is also cold hardy to at least −30°F. Will reach 25 to 30 ft. in height.

'Centennial Blush' is a seedling of 'Centennial' with 5- to 6-in.-wide, white flowers, with an average of 56 tepals per flower. Pink in bud, opening white, fragrant, early to mid March (Athens). Habit is pyramidal-conical, 12 to 15 ft. by 4 to 6 ft. Flower buds are formed at almost every node, even on small plants; introduced by the author.

'Chrysanthemiflora' ('Chrysanthemumiflora') is a beautiful pink-flowered form with approximately 40 tepals; tepals are more frost-resistant than

MORE ▶

Magnolia ×soulangeana 'Picture'

Magnolia ×soulangeana 'Rustica Rubra'

Magnolia ×soulangeana 'Verbanica'

Magnolia stellata

Magnolia stellata, star magnolia

Magnolia stellata 'Centennial'

Magnolia stellata 'Centennial Blush'

Magnolia stellata 'Chrysanthemiflora'

Magnolia stellata 'Pink Stardust'

Magnolia stellata CONTINUED

'Waterlily'. Relatively compact and dense branching, 10 to 15 ft. high and wide. Have always considered this among the best of the *Magnolia stellata* selections.

'Pink Stardust' is an excellent pink-flowered cultivar. Flowers 4 to 5 in. wide, composed of 40 to 50 tepals. Grows 12 to 15 ft. high and wide.

'Royal Star' is a dense, oval to rounded, shrubby form. It has 25 to 30 nearly pure white tepals that open to 3- to 4-in.-wide flowers. Reports have indicated hardiness to –35°F. Slower growing than 'Centennial' and consistently one of the earliest to flower; West Coast literature states it flowers at the same time as 'Waterlily'. Matures around 10 to 12 ft. high.

'Waterlily' has rich pink buds that open to 14 to 25 tepals (on one occasion I counted 33). Flowers are highly fragrant; habit is upright-bushy. Probably more than one clone in cultivation. Grows 15 ft. high and larger. In my top three, with 'Centennial Blush' and 'Chrysanthemiflora'.

Magnolia virginiana
sweetbay magnolia

Although common in wet areas throughout the Coastal Plain of the southeastern United States, this native species occurs as far north as Massachusetts. Always a favorite

Magnolia stellata 'Royal Star'

Magnolia stellata 'Waterlily'

Magnolia virginiana, sweetbay magnolia

Magnolia virginiana

Magnolia virginiana

Magnolia virginiana 'Mardigras'

of mine, sweetbay magnolia is at its best on a June day, when the silvery-backed leaves are tousled by the wind and sparkle like diamonds and the lemony sweet floral fragrance rides on every current of air. The habit varies from a single-stemmed tree to a large, multi-stemmed, round-headed shrub. The dark green, 3- to 5-in.-long leaves are silvery on their undersides, and the bark is a silvery gray. The leaves are deciduous in northern latitudes, evergreen in the Deep South. Creamy white, 2- to 3-in.-wide, sweetly fragrant

MORE ▶

Magnolia virginiana

Magnolia virginiana Moonglow®

Magnolia virginiana 'Green Shadow'

Magnolia virginiana 'Henry Hicks'

Magnolia virginiana CONTINUED
flowers, each with nine to 12 tepals, appear in May and June. Use the species in outdoor living areas by patios, pools, and decks. Grows 10 to 20 ft. high and wide in the North; 60 ft. high in coastal Georgia and north Florida. Zones 5 to 9. Massachusetts to Florida and Texas.

CULTIVARS AND VARIETIES
'Green Shadow' is an upright pyramidal-oval form with evergreen foliage. Foliage remained evergreen after −20°F. Selected by Don Shadow, Winchester, Tennessee. This and 'Henry Hicks' are the two best cold hardy, evergreen cultivars; the latter quite difficult to propagate.

'Mardigras' ('Mattie Mae Smith') is a striking yellow-margined, green-centered leaf selection. Observed on enough occasions to know it is semi-evergreen (at best) in zone 7, and winter leaves are quite tatty.

Moonglow® ('Wilson') is a dark green-foliaged, semi-evergreen selection that withstood −28°F without injury. Matures 35 to 40 ft. by 15 to 18 ft. The silver-backed leaf undersides are prominent.

Magnolia zenii 'Pink Parchment'

My first exposure to *Magnolia zenii*, a rare Chinese species introduced into the United States around 1980, was at the Arnold Arboretum, where I collected seed; and one of the resulting seedlings became 'Pink Parchment'. Leaves emerge bronze, turn medium green in summer, variable yellow in fall. Beautiful silver-gray bark, reminiscent of American beech. Sets prodigious flower buds and, if not wrecked by cold, is spectacular in flower. I showed the plant to Bonnie and asked for a name; without hesitation she said, "Pink Parchment." Grew 35 ft. by 15 ft. in 18 years with 5-in.-wide, nine-tepaled, extremely fragrant flowers, pink-purple on outside, white inside, in February and March. Great example of the absolute folly of citing a specific flowering time, since I recorded peak flowering in late January 1997; February 14, 1998; February 28, 2000; February 19, 2001; and March 10, 2010 (a late spring). Estimate zones 5 to 7. China.

Mahonia aquifolium
Oregon grapeholly

One of the more cold hardy and functional broadleaf evergreens, this species offers pretty golden yellow flowers and blue fruit, as well as excellent shade tolerance. Several growth habits are evident, from a compact-mounded, suckering type to a taller, upright, irregular, and open form. The foliage is certainly spectacular, especially the newly emerging leaves, which range from lustrous, bright apple-green to bronzy orange. The leaves mature to lustrous dark green and assume bronze-purple tints in winter. The fragrant flowers open in

Magnolia zenii 'Pink Parchment'

Magnolia zenii 'Pink Parchment'

Magnolia zenii 'Pink Parchment'

496

March and April in 2- to 3-in.-long and -wide terminal inflorescences. The ½-in.-long, grape-like fruit ripen in summer. It prefers moist, acid, well-drained soils and a shady environment, sheltered from winter sun and wind. Plants often appear ragged in exposed locations. Use as a mass, in groupings, or as a specimen. Grows 3 to 6 ft. high and wide. Zones (4)5 to 8. British Columbia to Oregon.

CULTIVARS AND VARIETIES
Many, but only a few are commonly available.

'Compactum' is a beautiful mounded form with extremely glossy dark green leaves and bronze winter color. Grows 2 to 3 ft. high.

'Emerald' ('Smaragd'), with handsome, glossy emerald-green leaves, is worthy.

'King's Ransom' is upright in habit, with blue-green foliage that turns red-purple in winter.

Mahonia aquifolium

Mahonia aquifolium

Mahonia aquifolium winter color

Mahonia aquifolium, Oregon grapeholly

Mahonia aquifolium 'Compactum'

Mahonia aquifolium 'Emerald'

497

Mahonia bealei

leatherleaf mahonia

Functional broadleaf evergreen with leathery, spiny leaflets useful for shady areas of the garden. Stiff, almost clumsy growth habit, with strong upright stems and leaves borne at right angles, results in a bumpy cloud of foliage at the top. Leaves are composed of nine to 13 (occasionally 15), leathery, blue-green leaflets, each 1 to 4 in. long, 1 to 2 in. wide, with five to seven prominent spines. Leaves maintain consistent foliage color through the seasons. Lemon-yellow flowers, in 3- to 6-in.-long, 6- to 12-in.-wide terminal inflorescences, open in winter, February to March in Athens, remaining effective for four to six weeks. Flowers are wonderfully fragrant and attract all manner of bees for an early nectar harvest. Robin's-egg-blue fruit, each ⅓ to ½ in. long, ripen in late April and May. The color is beautiful, and birds quickly harvest the bounty. Tougher than rawhide and adaptable to any well-drained soil. Requires some shade for best appearance. Excellent in the woodland garden, in groupings and masses. Somewhat weedy; birds plant the seeds willy-nilly. Obviously, the birds do not have landscape architecture degrees. Grows 6 to 10 ft. high. Zones 7 to 9. China.

Mahonia japonica, Japanese mahonia, is similar and often confused with *M. bealei*. Leaflets are glossy green and are not strongly veined; and flowers are larger and brighter yellow. Grows 6 to 7 ft. high. Zones 6 to 8. Japan. Recent taxonomy retains *M. japonica* and places *M. bealei* in its Bealei Group.

Mahonia bealei

Mahonia bealei, leatherleaf mahonia

Mahonia japonica

Mahonia bealei

Mahonia japonica, Japanese mahonia

Mahonia fortunei

Chinese mahonia

At first glance, difficult to associate with *Mahonia*, for the leaflets are narrow and soft to the touch, and the flowers appear in late summer to early fall. Almost fern-like in leaf texture, leaves are densely borne, producing a full-foliaged evergreen shrub. The dark green leaflets, 2 to 5 in. long, ½ to ¾ in. wide, lightly serrated, range from five to nine (occasionally 13) per leaf. The bright yellow flowers, in 2- to 3-in.-long, erect racemes, are melded into the foliage. Although fruit are described as purple-black, I have yet to encounter them on cultivated plants. Adaptable like all *Mahonia* species; requires shade. Mildew occurs occasionally. Use in groupings and masses. Prospering in Savannah, killed to the ground in Athens at −3°F. Grows 5 to 6 ft. high and wide. Zones (7)8 and 9. China.

Mahonia eurybracteata also has narrow, soft-to-the-touch, feathery leaflets, dark blue-green, among the finest textured of any mahonia. Yellow flowers and small ovoid, bloomy blue-black fruit. Estimate 4 ft. by 4 ft. Observed seedling populations that looked exactly like Soft Caress™, a selection that is gaining landscape traction in the Southeast. Observed slight foliar injury at 12°F.

Mahonia ×media

The more this evergreen shrub (*Mahonia japonica* × *M. lomariifolia*) crosses my path, the greater my appreciation for its textural and floral attributes. A large, coarse evergreen with gray-brown checkered bark and foliage in the upper one-half. The dark green, somewhat glossy leaves are composed of 17 to 21 leaflets, each 2½ to 4½ in. long, 1 to 1½ in. wide. The lemon to bright yellow flowers occur at the end of branches in 10- to 14-in.-long

MORE ▶

Mahonia fortunei, Chinese mahonia

Mahonia fortunei

Mahonia ×media

Mahonia ×media

499

Mahonia ×media CONTINUED
and -wide, racemose panicles. Flowers are variably fragrant and open over an extended period in winter. Fruit are robin's-egg blue, oval-round, and provide great bird food. Adaptable, but best in some shade. Great winter-flowering shrubs for the border, combining beautifully with *Hamamelis ×intermedia* cultivars. Grows 8 to 15 ft. high. Zones (6)7 to 9.

CULTIVARS AND VARIETIES
'Buckland' (pale yellow), 'Charity' (yellow), 'Faith' (soft yellow), 'Hope' (bright yellow), 'Lionel Fortescue' (yellow), 'Underway' (yellow), and 'Winter Sun' (bright yellow, opening in December in Athens, lustrous dark green leaves) are the best known. The latter is show-

ing up at more retail outlets, particularly in the Southeast.

Malus
flowering crabapple

Without question, the flowering crabapples are the dominant spring-flowering trees in the northern tier of states, where cherries, dogwoods, and magnolias are often relegated to second-class status. A 2010 speaking engagement in Michigan reconfirmed this fact as *Cercis*, *Prunus*, *Halesia*, *Koelreuteria*, *Cornus* were few to absent; *Malus* everywhere! As a source of small- to medium-sized, cold hardy trees, *Malus* has few competitors. Many flowering crabapples are susceptible to foliar diseases and

fireblight and should be discarded. The newer selections have been chosen for disease resistance, annual flowering, and persistent fruit. Those presented here are selected on the basis of my observations and those of researchers at The Ohio State University, the University of Wisconsin, and the Morton Arboretum in Lisle, Illinois. Several older but commercially available cultivars are also discussed. These crabapple species and cultivars represent a range of habits, sizes, and flower and fruit colors. All should be adaptable in zones 4 to 7(8). Crabapples are not perfectly suited to warmer climates.

Malus angustifolia
southern crabapple

Malus angustifolia is a rounded, 20- to 25-ft.-high and -wide tree, with dense, spinescent branches. Finely toothed, rich green leaves, 2 to 4 in. long, turn yellow in fall. Fragrant, pink, five-petaled, 1- to 1½-in.-wide flowers appear in April (Athens) among the leaves. The yellowish green, rounded, ¾-in.-wide fruit ripen in late summer and fall. Serves as a great source of food for wildlife. Leaves are susceptible to rust. Not common, but a worthy native tree for woodland edges, open fields, and remote areas. Not for the manicured landscape. Zones 7 to 9. Southeastern United States.

Mahonia ×media 'Winter Sun'

Mahonia ×media 'Charity'

Mahonia ×media 'Winter Sun'

Malus floribunda

Japanese flowering crabapple

This species is an old favorite. It has carmine buds and 1- to 1½-in.-wide, white flowers. The ⅜-in.-wide fruit are yellow to red. Broad-rounded habit. Good disease resistance. Grows 15 to 25 ft. high. Performed well at Milliken Arboretum (zone 7), Spartanburg, South Carolina.

Malus hupehensis

tea crabapple

This species has the most elegant vase-shaped growth habit of any crabapple. Unfortunately, it is susceptible to fireblight. Dark pink buds open to 1½-in.-wide, white flowers. It bears ⅜-in.-wide, yellow to red fruit. Grows 20 to 25 ft. high and wide.

Malus floribunda

Malus angustifolia, southern crabapple

Malus floribunda, Japanese flowering crabapple

Malus hupehensis, tea crabapple

501

Malus sargentii

Sargent crabapple

A mounded, densely branched, shrubby species. Red buds open to ¾- to 1-in.-wide, white flowers. It bears ⅜-in.-wide, bright red fruit. Good disease resistance. Grows 6 to 10 ft. high.

CULTIVARS AND VARIETIES

'Tina' is a compact form of the species, with the same desirable features. Grows 5 ft. high.

Malus sieboldii var. zumi 'Calocarpa'

This crabapple has deep red buds, 1⅓-in.-wide white flowers, and ½-in.-wide bright red fruit. Dense and rounded in habit. Resistant to scab, but susceptible to fireblight. Grows 25 ft. high and wide.

Malus Hybrids

Numerous, with new selections added yearly; one wholesale producer on the West Coast alone offered 50 cultivars. 'Adams', 'Callaway', Harvest Gold®, 'Jewelberry', 'Liset', 'Prairifire', Red Jewel®, and Sugar Tyme® have performed well at Milliken Arboretum (zone 7), Spartanburg, South Carolina.

'Adams' offers 1½-in.-wide, rose-colored flowers and ⅝-in.-wide, red fruit. The habit is rounded. This hybrid exhibits high resistance to scab. Grows 24 ft. high.

'Amberina' has deep red buds that open to white flowers. Fruit is brilliant orange-red and persistent. Upright, semi-dwarf habit. High scab resistance. Grows 10 ft. high.

Centurion® ('Centzam') produces red buds that open to rose-red flowers. Glossy cherry-red fruit are ⅝ in. in diameter. Habit is upright in youth, rounded at maturity. Highly resistant to diseases. Grows 25 ft. high, 15 to 20 ft. wide.

Christmas Holly® ('Chrishozam') has red-budded, 1½-in.-wide, white

Malus sargentii, Sargent crabapple

Malus sargentii

Malus sieboldii var. zumi 'Calocarpa'

Malus sieboldii var. zumi 'Calocarpa'

flowers and bright red, ½-in.-wide fruit that persist into December. It has a small, spreading stature. Disease-resistant. Grows 10 to 15 ft. high.

'Donald Wyman' offers rich red buds that unfurl to 1¾-in.-wide, white flowers. Glossy bright red, ½-in.-wide fruit persist into winter. Large, rounded habit. Highly resistant to diseases. It tends toward alternating cycles of heavy and light flowering. Grows 25 ft. high.

Harvest Gold® ('Hargozam') is pink in bud, white in flower. Golden, ⅗-in.-wide fruit persist in good condition into December or later. Upright-spreading habit. Highly disease-resistant. Grows 25 ft. high and wide.

'Indian Summer' has rose-red flowers and long-persistent, bright red fruit, ⅝ to ¾ in. in diameter. Habit is a broad globe shape. Good disease resistance. Grows 18 ft. high, 19 ft. wide.

'Jewelberry' is a small but impressive tree with pink buds that open to white flowers. The ½-in.-wide, glossy red fruit persist into fall. Good disease resistance. Grows 8 to 12 ft. high.

'Liset' has dark crimson buds that produce 1½-in.-wide, rose-red to light crimson flowers. The maroon-red fruit average ½ in. in diameter. Rounded and dense in habit. Resistant to scab. Grows 15 to 20 ft. high.

MORE ▶

Malus 'Callaway'

Malus 'Callaway'

Malus Red Jewel®

Malus 'Adams'

Malus 'Adams'

Malus Centurion®

Malus Hybrids CONTINUED

'Mary Potter' is one of my favorites, but this cultivar may suffer from disease problems. Pink-red buds produce prodigious 1-in.-wide, white flowers. Fruit are bright red and ½ in. in diameter. Broad-mounded habit. Grows 10 to 15 ft. high, 15 to 20 ft. wide.

'Narragansett' is a National Arboretum release that prospers in heat. Northern reports indicate good disease resistance. Red buds open to white flowers with pink tinges. Cherry-red fruit are ½ in. in diameter. A broad-crowned small tree with wide crotch angles and leathery, dark green leaves. Grows 13 ft. high.

'Prairifire' is red-budded, with dark pinkish red flowers and ⅜- to ½-in.-wide, red-purple fruit. Rounded growth habit. Highly disease-resistant. Grows 20 ft. high and wide. About the closest to red flowers but *still not* red.

'Profusion' has red buds that open purplish red and fade to purplish pink on 1½-in.-wide flowers. The oxblood-red, ½-in.-wide fruit are persistent. Good disease resistance. Small tree. Grows 20 ft. high and wide.

'Red Jade' is an older, weeping cultivar with deep pink to red buds and 1½-in.-wide flowers. It tends toward alternate-year flowering. It offers glossy red, ½-in.-wide fruit. Rounded to broad-rounded, graceful, pendulous

MORE ▶

Malus Centurion®

Malus Christmas Holly®

Malus Christmas Holly®

Malus 'Donald Wyman'

Malus Harvest Gold®

Malus 'Mary Potter'

Malus 'Prairifire'

Malus 'Profusion'

Malus 'Donald Wyman'

Malus 'Indian Summer'

Malus 'Jewelberry'

Malus 'Mary Potter'

Malus **Hybrids** CONTINUED

habit. Moderately susceptible to scab. Grows 15 ft. high.

Royal Raindrops® ('JFS-KW5') produces single pink flowers and bright red, ¼-in.-wide, persistent fruit on an upright spreading tree, 20 ft. by 15 ft. Cutleaf foliage is deep purple, orange-red in autumn.

'Snowdrift' offers pink buds and 1¼-in.-wide, white flowers. Orange-red fruit are ⅜ in. in diameter. It is dense and rounded in habit and has lustrous dark green foliage. Slight susceptibility to scab, severe susceptibility to fireblight. Grows 15 to 20 ft. high and wide.

Sugar Tyme® ('Sutyzam') has pale pink buds that open to sugar-white flowers. The ½-in.-wide, red fruit are persistent. Oval-rounded in habit. Very disease-resistant. Grows 18 ft. high, 15 ft. wide.

Weeping Candied Apple® ('Candied Apple') produces red buds and white flowers. The persistent, cherry-red fruit are ⅝ in. in diameter. It has broad, pendulous branches. Slight to moderate scab susceptibility. Grows 10 to 15 ft. high.

White Angel™ ('Inglis') is pink in bud, opening to 1-in.-wide, pure white flowers. It has glossy red, ½- to ⅝-in.-wide fruit and an irregular, rounded habit. Disease-resistant. Grows 20 ft. high.

Malus 'Narragansett'

Malus 'Prairifire'

Malus 'Red Jade'

Malus Sugar Tyme®

Malus Sugar Tyme®

Malus Weeping Candied Apple®

Malus 'Snowdrift'

Malvaviscus arboreus var. *drummondii*

Turk's cap, Turk's turban

A subshrub to herbaceous perennial, moving South to North, with beautiful, twisted red flowers with prominent stamens, summer into fall. Develops a loose, shrubby outline, with 2- to 3-in.-wide, coarse-textured, yellow-green leaves on long petioles. The 1½- to 2-in.-long flowers, which develop on new growth, are hummingbird magnets. The flower effect is not overwhelming like *Hibiscus*. Requires full sun, well-drained soils; pH adaptable and drought-tolerant. Fills a niche in the border or mixed annual planting. Grows 3 to 5 ft. high. Zones 8 and 9. Mexico to Brazil.

Malus White Angel™

Malus White Angel™

Malvaviscus arboreus var. drummondii, Turk's cap

Malvaviscus arboreus var. drummondii

507

Mandevilla splendens
pink allamanda

Evergreen vine that finds a home on mailboxes, fences, walls, and trellises. Bonnie and I grew the plant in containers, and every autumn the fleshy roots and part of the top were removed to a cool greenhouse. The opposite, 3- to 8-in.-long, oval, deeply veined, lustrous dark green leaves are leathery, insect- and disease-resistant. The 2- to 4-in.-long and -wide, rich pink flowers open in summer and continue into fall. The five-lobed flower has a wide tubular base, flaring to flat-faced. Best in full sun and moderate fertility and moisture. Flowers develop on new shoots, so keep plants in active growth. Certainly one of the best summer-flowering vines, overwintering only in the Deep South, Southwest, and West Coast. Grows 10 to 20 ft.; more restrained in containers and where climbing space is limited. Zones 10 and 11. Brazil.

CULTIVARS AND VARIETIES
'Alice du Pont', a large-flowered (to 4 in. wide) selection with deep pink buds, opening pink, is one of the most common selections.

'Red Riding Hood' has deeper rose-red flowers that are smaller than 'Alice du Pont'.

Melia azedarach
chinaberry

A scourge over much of the South, consuming fencerows and open spaces. On the flip side, a pretty round-headed tree with glossy dark green leaves, 1 to 2 ft. long, with 1½- to 2-in.-long toothed or lobed leaflets. Leaves die off yellow-green, not spectacular, but noticeable. In May, fragrant, lavender-lilac flowers, each ¾ in. across, appear in loose, 8- to 16-in.-long panicles. Leaves are present, so floral effect is dampened. Beautiful on close examination, the petals glistening bicolored lavender-lilac. Fruit, scary in their abundance, are ½-in.-wide, rounded, yellow to yellow-brown drupes. Fruit persist through winter, providing ample forage for wildlife. Adaptable and weedy, prospers in heat and drought. A fruitless selection would prove a worthy small street tree. Grows 30 to 40 ft. high and wide. Zones 7 to 10. India, China.

CULTIVARS AND VARIETIES
'Jade Snowflake', with cream-speckled leaves and loose, lax, vase-shaped habit, and 'Umbraculiformis', Texas umbrella-tree, multi-stemmed with umbrella-like crown, 20 to 25 ft. high, are occasionally available. Both come true-to-type from seed.

Menispermum canadense
common moonseed

This twining, large-leaved vine maintains a permanent woody super-structure above ground and, like *Aristolochia durior*, Dutchman's pipe, makes a

Mandevilla splendens 'Alice du Pont'

Mandevilla splendens 'Red Riding Hood'

Mandevilla splendens, pink allamanda

508

Melia azedarach, chinaberry

reasonable cover or screen if provided support upon which to climb. The dark green leaves are 4 to 10 in. long and 4 to 7 in. wide. Flowers and fruit are inconspicuous. It is adaptable to any well-drained soil, in partial to heavy shade. Observed in the North Georgia mountains and along the Blue Ridge Parkway, often in shady locations. Grows 10 to 20 ft. high. Zones 4 to 8. Quebec to Manitoba, south to Georgia and Arkansas.

Melia azedarach

Melia azedarach

Melia azedarach 'Jade Snowflake'

Menispermum canadense, common moonseed

Menispermum canadense

Mespilus germanica

medlar, showy mespilus

Gosh, who knows? Who grows? And who cares? I have no answers except to admonish the reader to pay attention. A picturesque tree, broad-crowned, with tightly woven branches, and 2- to 5-in.-long, dull green leaves forming a dense canopy. Leaves develop golden orange to russet-red tints in fall. The white to lightly blushed pink, 1- to 2-in.-wide, five-petaled flowers occur at the end of short, leafy branches in May and June. The edible fruit is a brown, hard, 1- to 2-in.-wide, apple- to slightly pear-shaped (more top-shaped) pome. Fruit require softening before being palatable. Jelly tastes somewhat like that of mayhaw (*Crataegus*). Any well-drained soil, slightly acid to neutral, suits it. Successfully cultured at Morton Arboretum, Lisle, Illinois, and Missouri Botanical Garden, St. Louis. Grows 15 to 20 ft. and wider at landscape maturity. Zones 5 to 8. Southeastern Europe to Iran.

CULTIVARS AND VARIETIES
Many selections for fruiting properties. 'Breda Giant', 'Dutch', 'Large Russian', and 'Monstrous' bear large fruit.

Metasequoia glyptostroboides

dawn redwood

Dawn redwood was resurrected from near-extinction when a Chinese botanist discovered the plant in 1941. The Arnold Arboretum organized an expedition to collect seeds, and gardeners the world over have benefitted. In youth and old age, the habit is pyramidal and feathery. The bark is reddish brown in youth, becoming darker and fissured with age and exfoliating in narrow strips. The trunk becomes buttressed with maturity. The ½-in.-long, bright green needles are borne on small branchlets. In fall, the needles turn orangish brown to reddish brown. Once established, the species withstands dry soils, although it will also grow in wet soils. Plant in a sunny location. A single specimen is an imposing sight, but groupings and groves are also effective. Allow ample room for growth. Under ideal cultural conditions, 2 to 3 ft. of vertical growth per year is common. Many trees planted in the late 1940s are now over 100 ft. tall. Grows 70 to 100 ft. high, 25 ft. wide. Zones 5 to 8. China.

CULTIVARS AND VARIETIES
'Ogon' ('Gold Rush') with yellow leaves is attractive. Maintain even moisture, as heat, drought allow for photo-bleaching (whitening) and browning of needles. Relatively fast-growing under good cultural conditions, about two feet a year. Nice color addition against green backgrounds like pines and hollies.

Shaw's Legacy® ('Raven') is an elegant, uniformly branched, tight-conical selection with dark sage-green

Mespilus germanica

Mespilus germanica

Mespilus germanica, medlar

Metasequoia glyptostroboides, dawn redwood

Metasequoia glyptostroboides 'Ogon'

needles. Selected from the original Chinese-collected trees, planted in 1952, at the Missouri Botanical Garden and named in honor of Henry Shaw, founder, and Dr. Peter Raven, the remarkable director.

'Snow Flurry' with white spotted needles on a compact plant is quite attractive. Other cream-splotched and -spotted forms include 'Nitschke Cream', 'Spring Cream', and 'White Spot'.

MORE ▶

Metasequoia glyptostroboides

Metasequoia glyptostroboides fall color

Metasequoia glyptostroboides 'Snow Flurry'

Metasequoia glyptostroboides CONTINUED

Metasequoia glyptostroboides Shaw's Legacy®

Microbiota decussata, Russian arborvitae

Microbiota decussata winter color

Microbiota decussata
Russian arborvitae, Siberian cypress

The species had the plant world on its toes as the next great needle ever-green groundcover. Certainly beautiful when well grown: bright green sprays, soft-textured, turning bronze- to plum-purple in winter. Plants in the Dirr garden and Georgia campus succumbed to heavy soils, humidity, and heat. Best in northern latitudes in acid, well-drained, almost gritty soils. A great groundcover for full sun environments. Grows 12 to 28 in. high, spreading indefinitely. A report cited a 14-year-old plant that was 12 in. high and 15 ft. in diameter. Zones 3 to 6. Russia.

Millettia reticulata
evergreen red wisteria

The Atlanta Botanical Garden and JC Raulston Arboretum have successfully grown this species for many years, but coming out of winter this twining vine often assumes the appearance of an alley cat after a brawl. When right, the leathery, lustrous dark green leaves, composed of seven to 13 leaflets, each 1 to 2 in. long, provide a beautiful fence, trellis, and arbor cover. The dark purple-red, weakly (musky) fragrant flowers, in 6- to 10-in.-long inflorescences, develop from July and August into fall. The fruit are elongated, fat, bony pods, constricted between the seeds that mature in late fall. Fast-growing in moist, acid, fertile, well-drained soil and full sun. Requires support. Grows 10 to 20 ft. Zones 7 to 11, a true evergreen only in zones 10 and 11. China.

Mitchella repens
partridgeberry

Too often left behind in the dust of bigger, better, newer plants, this ever-green groundcover makes a wonder-ful woodland blanket. I remember teaching this in a wildflower course at the University of Illinois and then on a field trip showing the plant to students as we hiked Turkey Run State Park, Marshallville, Indiana. Sometimes the little things take center stage—such was the case with partridgeberry. Almost pancake-like in habit, the dark green, whitish-veined leaves, ¼ to 1 in. long and wide, are oppositely arranged along the stems. The fragrant, ½-in.-long, pink to white flower with four-lobed corolla opens over a long period in spring and summer. The red, berry-like, ¼- to ⅓-in.-wide fruit ripen in summer and fall and persist.

Requires moist, woodsy, acid soil and shade. For that small segment of the woodland garden! To appreciate this small woodland citizen is a signal that all biological entities, great and small, are important. Grows 1 to 2 in. high, spreads indefinitely. Zones 4 to 9. Canada to Florida, Arkansas, and Texas.

Morus alba
common or white mulberry
Mention "mulberry" to a gardener and

be prepared to listen to horror stories about the mess created by fruiting specimens. In the early years of my career, a mulberry had as much net worth as my bank account. With the advent of several fruitless (sterile) selections, the tree deserves a second glance. The typical species is a round-headed, twiggy, often unkempt tree. The 2- to 7-in.-long, lustrous dark green leaves may be lobed or undivided. Foliage may turn a pleasing

MORE ▶

Millettia reticulata, evergreen red wisteria

Morus alba, common mulberry

Mitchella repens, partridgeberry

Mitchella repens

Morus alba

513

Morus alba CONTINUED

yellow in fall. The April flowers are not showy, but the ½- to 1-in.-long, ellipsoidal, purplish black fruit can be used for pies or to feed the birds. Common mulberry is adaptable to any soil, in full sun to partial shade. The species grows in dry, high salt, acid, and high pH soils and is frequently seen in the Southwest. Can become a weed tree, as fruit are distributed by birds and other wildlife. Grows 30 to 50 ft. high and wide. Zones 4 to 8(9). China.

CULTIVARS AND VARIETIES

The following (with the exception of 'Paper Dolls') make effective short-term, urban-tolerant trees or accent plants.

'Chaparral' and 'Urbana'—both sterile, weeping trees with lustrous dark green foliage—are often grafted on a standard to produce a fast-growing, small, weeping tree.

'Ho-O' is a shrubby form with dark green crumpled leaves with the texture of crepe paper, female, 10 to 12 ft. high and wide in five years in Georgia trials.

'Issai' is a mini-shrub that produces supra-abundant fruit as a young plant. A 12- to 18-in.-tall plant has hundreds of fruit. Easy to culture.

'Mapleleaf' and 'Stribling' are fruitless, fast-growing tree types. The first has large, lobed, maple-like leaves; the second has the typical mulberry foliage and excellent yellow fall color. I have observed a plant of 'Stribling' that was 40 ft. high and 30 ft. wide.

'Paper Dolls' is a boondoggle: white, yellow, green variegated leaves are attractive, but the chimera is totally unstable and reverts to green. Grew in Georgia trials and was eliminated for greenness.

'Pendula' is a fruiting, weeping form.

Variety *tatarica* is considered the most cold hardy of the various forms. It is available from specialty nurseries.

Morus australis 'Unryu'

syn. *Morus bombycis* 'Tortuosa'

This nomenclatural anomaly has gained a small measure of popularity in the United States. It is a vigorous large shrub or small tree, with coarse, twisted, contorted branches. The lustrous dark green, 6- to 7-in.-long leaves turn rich bronzy yellow in autumn. A 12-in. plant in our garden was 20 ft. high and wide in 12 years. Will prove cold hardy to −10°F and below; I witnessed plants in Vassalboro, Maine, where −25°F is common. Late spring frosts severely damage

Morus alba 'Ho-O'

Morus alba 'Pendula' fall color

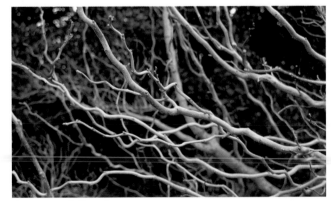

Morus australis 'Unryu'

Morus australis 'Unryu'

the leaves but regrowth ensues. Plant is extremely fast-growing and eats precious garden real estate. Zones (4)5 to 8. China.

Morus rubra
red mulberry

This native tree species is seldom available in commerce but deserves mention because of its wide range. The habit is upright-spreading. The dark green, 3- to 8-in.-long leaves hang from the branches like large green paper napkins. The edible red fruit turn to dark purple. For best growth, the species requires rich, moist, deep soils. It is often found as an understory or wood's-edge plant in the wild. I believe that with selection for desirable traits—clean foliage, maleness, uniform habit—this would make a good shade tree; its wide adaptability range gives it a cultural advantage over many native species. Grows 40 to 70 ft. high, 40 to 50 ft.

wide. Zones 5 to 9. Massachusetts to Michigan, south to Florida and Texas.

Musa
banana

These large-leaved tropical plants have become the focal points of container and annual color gardening in much of the United States. In zone 7, plants have overwintered, although die-back occurs. Develops soft, thickish stems, often clumping from offsets, with large 4- to 8-ft.-long, slightly arching to drooping leaves. Texture is bold, brash, and attention-grabbing. Yellow flowers with red to purple bracts develop in summer. Fruit set may occur in hottest parts of the South. Requires fertile, well-drained soils high in organic matter. Full sun to partial shade. Remove tattered leaves. In cooler areas of the South, cut off the top of the plant, dig roots (corms), and move to a protected

MORE ▶

Musa ornata, rose banana

Morus rubra, red mulberry

Morus rubra

Morus rubra

Musa CONTINUED

(nonfreezing) site. Always exciting to drive through central Georgia (zone 7) and experience a lush banana in a garden setting. The most common are *Musa acuminata* 'Dwarf Cavendish', 6 to 8 ft. high; *M. basjoo*, 10 to 15 ft. high; *M. coccinea*, red banana, 4 to 5 ft. high; *M. ornata*, rose banana, 8 to 10 ft. high; and *M. ×paradisiaca*, 15 to 20 ft. high. The most hardy is

M. basjoo, with cream-yellow flowers, inedible green fruit, and reasonable cold tolerance; a recent article traces nativity to China, not Japan as previously cited.

Myrica cerifera
syn. *Morella cerifera*
southern waxmyrtle

A walk along the beaches from southern New Jersey to the Florida Keys reveals this amazing evergreen species in myriad shapes and sizes. Prospers in pure sand; frequent bicycle touring on the Outer Banks of North Carolina indicated that beach grass and this species are about the only vegetation holding the sand in place. A large spreading shrub, it reinvents itself from root suckers into impenetrable colonies. Beautiful grayish white bark develops on older branches and

Musa basjoo

Musa ×paradisiaca

Myrica cerifera, southern waxmyrtle

Myrica cerifera

trunks. Olive-green foliage is dotted with small glands that, when broken, release the bayberry fragrance. On warm evenings, you can pick up the scent simply by passing by. Leaves are 1½ to 3 in. long, ⅓ to ¾ in. wide, and usually serrate toward the apex. The gray, globose fruit, ⅛ in. in diameter, are massed in clusters of two to six on the previous season's growth and occur only on female plants. Transplant from containers into about any soil, dry to wet. Fixes atmospheric nitrogen, which assures survival in miserable soils. Full sun to moderate shade. Withstands the endless pruning required to keep it in check. Great seaside plant but also a large screening evergreen. Can be used for hedges. Snow and ice have resulted in broken branches in the Athens area. Grows 10 to 15 (to 20) ft. high and wide. Zones 7 to 11.

CULTIVARS AND VARIETIES
'Don's Dwarf', with deep olive-green leaves and bluish gray fruit, grows 3 ft. high and wide. Many "dwarf" forms have been introduced, including 'Club Med', 'Georgia Gem', 'King's Dwarf', 'Luray', 'Lynn's Dwarf', and 'Tom's Dwarf'.

'Fairfax' is a densely foliaged and branched selection that grows 6 to 8 ft. high and wide. An improvement on the species because of restrained growth.

'Hiwassee' is more cold hardy and has withstood −4°F with minor foliage burn. Vigorous and can become as large as the species.

Variety *pumila* is definitely lower growing than the species, perhaps 3 to 4 ft. high or less. The JC Raulston Arboretum has an excellent, compact, female form.

'Soleil', with new growth golden yellow, then yellow, finally yellow-green, is quite attractive. Male. Grows 5 to 6 ft. high and wide.

Myrica cerifera 'Fairfax'

Myrica cerifera

Myrica cerifera 'Don's Dwarf'

Myrica cerifera 'Soleil'

Myrica inodora

syn. *Morella inodora*

odorless bayberry

Difficult to imagine a bayberry without foliar fragrance, but such is *Myrica inodora*. A handsome, rounded, evergreen shrub that becomes open with age. Leaves, dark green, 1½ to 3 in. long, are entire. Although glands are present on leaf, no fragrance is detectable. The ¼-in.-wide, oblong-oval drupes, dark brown to black, are sometimes covered with white wax.

Adaptable to wet soils and grows in swamps, bogs, and ponds in its native habitat. The species is beautiful in foliage but has never caught on in gardens. Excellent wetland mitigation species. Grows 15 to 20 ft. high and wide. Zones 8 and 9. Panhandle of Florida, Alabama, and Mississippi.

Myrica pensylvanica

syn. *Morella pensylvanica*

northern bayberry

A most handsome plant, particularly in its native coastal habitat, where the dark green leaves stand out against the sandy soils. It is amazingly tolerant of salt and infertile soils. Forms great rounded colonies because of its suckering nature. The species is dioecious, bearing minimally showy, yellowish green flowers on male plants and gray, waxy-coated, ⅙- to ⅕-in.-wide drupes on female plants. The fruit ripen in September and may persist until the following April. Transplant from a container into well-drained, preferably acid soils. Withstands clay soils, but will develop chlorosis in high pH soils. Great plant for massing and grouping, in full sun or shade. I have observed it in combination with groundcover junipers, and the textural differences are quite striking. Variable in size. Grows 5 to 12 ft. high, equal or greater in spread. Zones (2)3 to 6. Newfoundland to western New York, south to North Carolina.

CULTIVARS AND VARIETIES

Bobbee™ ('Bobzam') is a compact,

Myrica inodora, odorless bayberry

Myrica inodora

Myrica pensylvanica, northern bayberry

Myrica pensylvanica

dense, mounded form with deep forest-green leaves and gray fruit. Observed only once; it's not too different from many in the wild.

Myrtus communis
common myrtle

The myrtle of antiquity, long a staple of garden-making throughout warm temperate regions. Handsome evergreen foliage and beautiful bark place it in the front ranks of broadleaf evergreens. In habit a dense, leafy shrub or small tree, upright in youth, more oval-rounded with age. Lustrous dark green leaves, 1 to 2 in. long, are oppositely arranged. In May and June, small pinkish buds open to ¾-in.-wide, five-petaled, fragrant, white flowers. Flowers are effective over a long period. The ovoid, ½-in.-long, purplish black berry is masked by the foliage. Bark is beautiful, brown, smooth, becoming scaly with age. Worthwhile to limb up lower branches to expose the bark. Full sun to partial shade; good drainage is essential. A superb hedge plant, quite common in European gardens. Lovely foliage accent in the border. Encountered a 5-ft.-high plant in an Athens garden, which indicates more cold hardiness than I thought possible. Observed an 8- to 10-ft.-high plant at Tryon Palace Gardens, New Bern, North Carolina. Grows 10 to 12 ft. high and wide. Zones (8)9 and 10. Iran and Afghanistan.

MORE ▶

Myrtus communis, common myrtle

Myrtus communis

Myrtus communis

Myrtus communis

Myrtus communis 'Variegata'

Myrtus communis CONTINUED
CULTIVARS AND VARIETIES
'Variegata', with cream margins to the leaves, is a pretty, dainty form.

Nageia nagi

syn. *Podocarpus nagi*
broadleaf podocarpus
If appearance is everything, then this distant relative of the genus *Podocarpus* needs shaping up. In fact, recent taxonomic treatment provided the new nomenclatural identity, *Nageia nagi*. The typical habit is softly pyramidal with lustrous dark green leaves, 1 to 3 in. long, ½ to 1¼ in. wide, with numerous veins running lengthwise. Could be mistaken for a *Eucalyptus* species or some member of the Liliaceae. Naked seeds are ½ in. wide, purplered with a waxy plum-like bloom. Adaptable but cold sensitive. Utilize as a specimen or accent plant. Grows 30 to 40 ft. high, usually smaller. Zones 9 and 10. Was killed on Georgia coast at 11°F. Southern Japan, Taiwan, and southern China.

Nandina domestica

nandina, heavenly bamboo
A bread-and-butter broadleaf evergreen shrub with alley-cat toughness and durability. Mature plants remain extant in old home sites in the South long after the home has crumbled and disappeared. A member of the barberry family; the only easily discernible shared characteristic is the yellow cambium. Usually an upright, strongly caned shrub, with the foliage concentrated in the upper one-half of the plant; however, suckers and colonizes,

Nandina domestica, heavenly bamboo

Nageia nagi, broadleaf podocarpus

Nageia nagi

Nandina domestica

thus forming densely foliated mounds. Tri-pinnately compound leaves, 1 to 2 (to 3) ft. long, are composed of ¾- to 3-in.-long, rich metallic bluish green leaflets. Selected seedlings and cultivars have plum-purple new growth. Low temperatures induce reddish pigmentation that varies from a blush to deep reddish purple to red, depending on seedling or cultivar. Pink buds are evident in May and June, in 8- to 15-in.-long terminal panicles, and open to six-petaled, ¼- to ⅓-in.-wide flowers, white with yellow anthers. The beautiful ⅓-in.-wide globular red fruit ripen in September and October, persisting into and through winter. Their color and persistence lend great aesthetics to the winter garden. Adaptable to sun, shade, and varied soils, except permanently wet. Bulletproof to insects and diseases. Utilize for foundation plantings, masses, groupings, slope stabilizers, in shady borders and understory plantings. Plants will become leggy; rejuvenation pruning in late winter induces basal shoot development and subsequently fuller plants. Although beyond common, it is one of the most serviceable broadleaf evergreens. Grows 6 to 8 (to 10) ft. high, usually less in spread, but with time becomes more wide than high. Zones 6 to 9, 10 on the West Coast. China.

CULTIVARS AND VARIETIES
Selections for foliage, fruit, and growth habit dominate the marketplace. About 40 are described in my *Manual* (2009), with new acquisitions arriving every year from Japan. The resulting genetic soup gives rise to numerous cultivars and seedlings, many of which I have grown. Southern Living Plant Collection has recently introduced Blush Pink™ ('AKA'), Flirt™ ('Murasaki'), and Obsession™ ('Seika'), all with pretty foliage colors.

'Alba' ('Aurea') has whitish to cream-yellow fruit and lighter green foliage. Grows 5 to 6 ft. high. Seedlings from 'Aurea' segregated 1:1 for yellow:red fruit. Interesting to note the yellow-fruited seedlings have no reddish pigment in the new leaves; red-fruited always with red pigmented new growth.

'Atropurpurea Nana' is a stiff meatball, light green in summer foliage, uniformly red with the advent of cold. Grows 2 ft. high, 2 to 3 ft. wide; no flowers. Leaves somewhat cupped and curled.

'Fire Power' ('Firepower') is virus-free and with the noncontorted leaves of 'Atropurpurea Nana'. Similar to 'Wood's Dwarf'.

'Gulf Stream' is among the most popular cultivars in nursery production. Grows 3 to 3½ (to 4½) ft. high, slightly less in spread, dense in habit and foliage. Somewhat leggy and open at the base with age. Winter coloration is variable, some years intense red,

MORE ▶

Nandina domestica

Nandina domestica

Nandina domestica 'Alba'

Nandina domestica 'Atropurpurea Nana' winter color

Nandina domestica 'Gulf Stream'

Nandina domestica 'Harbour Dwarf'

Nandina domestica Moon Bay™ winter color

Nandina domestica 'Fire Power' winter color

Nandina domestica 'Moyer's Red'

Nandina domestica 'San Gabriel' winter color

Nandina domestica 'Sasaba'

others red-green; inflorescences about 4 in. long with red fruit developing.

Harbour Belle™ ('Jaytee') forms a dense, suckering mound, 18 to 24 in. high, with blue-green summer foliage, deep burgundy or maroon in winter, flowers and fruit more abundant than 'Harbour Dwarf'. Have yet to be impressed with performance.

'Harbour Dwarf', with rich metallic blue-green foliage, reddish-tinged in winter, develops a spreading, suckering habit. Grows 2 to 3 ft. high, wider at maturity. Excellent for low masses, groupings; flowers and fruit develop. One of the more graceful cultivars for foliage.

Moon Bay™, a mounded grower, 1½ to 2½ ft. high and wide, has shinier, lighter green leaves that acquire red hues in winter. Good-looking selection but has not taken off like 'Gulf Stream'. Plants 4 to 4½ ft. high and wide grew in the University's Botanical Garden.

'Moyer's Red' is a large-growing form to 6 ft. or more, with typical species characteristics except winter foliage is glossy red. Reported to be slightly less cold hardy in the Atlanta area, compared to other cultivars. Flowers and fruit are produced.

'San Gabriel' ('Kurijusi', 'Orihime') is truly unique, with individual leaflets modified into narrow fern-like segments that are reddish when young, then blue-green, and finally reddish purple in winter. Grows 1 to 2 ft. high. My observations indicate less cold hardiness than the species.

'Sasaba' with rich blue-green, delicately cupped leaves presents an oriental aura. Recently introduced from Japan. Estimate 3 to 4 ft. high.

'Umpqua Warrior' is a 6- to 9-ft.-high form, not unlike the species, with large flowers and fruit. The JC Raulston Arboretum, Raleigh, North Carolina, holds the best collection of nandinas, including the Umpqua series, i.e., 'Chief' and 'Princess'; as I studied them, any good seedling is as notable.

'Wood's Dwarf', with rich green summer foliage and red winter leaf coloration, grows 2 to 2½ ft. high, not too different from 'Fire Power'; developed by Ed Wood, when he was a student at Oregon State University.

Neillia sinensis
Chinese neillia

In its best form, this species is a refined, delicately branched, rounded shrub that offers rich green foliage and pink flowers, which appear in 1- to 2½-in.-long racemes in May. The rich green leaves are 2 to 4 in. long, with small lobes. Glabrous shiny brown stems develop an exfoliating character with age. Soils should be moist, acid, and well drained. Use in the shrub border or in mass plantings, in light shade or full sun. Grows 5 to 6 ft. high and wide. Zones 5 to 7. China.

Neillia thibetica, Tibet neillia, and *N. affinis* have rose-pink flowers on

MORE ▶

Nandina domestica 'Umpqua Warrior'

Nandina domestica 'Wood's Dwarf' winter color

Neillia sinensis, Chinese neillia

Neillia sinensis CONTINUED

2- to 6-in.-long and 2-to 3-in.-long racemes, respectively. Both mature at about 6 ft. high. Zones 5 to 7, 6 and 7, respectively.

Neillia uekii is a compact, suckering, 3- to 4-ft.-high shrub with white flowers that open in May (Boston). Zones 6 and 7.

Nerium oleander
oleander

Superb shrub or small tree for the Deep South into the Florida Keys, Southwest, and West Coast. On a late March trip to Key West, Bonnie and I marveled at the beautiful flowers in singles and doubles, whites to reds. The flowers develop on new growth and are most vibrant in summer. A broadleaf evergreen, upright-branched, oval-rounded shrub, with 3- to 5- (to 8-) in.-long, ½- to ¾-in.-wide, leathery dark green leaves. The 1- to 2-in.-wide, five-petaled flowers are phenomenal in their variations. Colors alone range from white, cream, yellow, pink, lilac, salmon, apricot, and flesh to copper, orange, red, carmine, and purple, in singles and doubles. Fruit are elongated, pod-like structures, 5 to 7 in. long, containing small, fringed seeds. Tougher than a tick in terms of adaptability. Withstands sun, heat, wind, salt, drought, and pollution.

Neillia thibetica, Tibet neillia

Neillia sinensis

Nerium oleander

Neillia uekii

Nerium oleander

Easily transplanted from containers. Cut back overgrown or cold-damaged plants. Superb summer-flowering plant for groupings, containers, and masses. Bacterial leaf scorch is problematic in California and has spread to the South; it is carried by the glassy-winged sharpshooter; symptoms are yellowing and necrosis of leaves. All parts of the plant are poisonous.

MORE ▶

Nerium oleander 'Petite Pink'

Nerium oleander, oleander

Nerium oleander fruit

Nerium oleander 'Hardy Pink'

Nerium oleander CONTINUED

Grows 6 to 12 ft. high and wide; 20-ft.-high plants in Florida. Zones 8 to 11. Southern Asia, Mediterranean region.

CULTIVARS AND VARIETIES

Over 400 cultivars described. Several compact forms, like Carnival™ (salmon-pink) and 'Petite Pink' (shell pink), as well as larger-growing, hardier forms (zones 7 and 8), like 'Hardy Pink', 'Hardy White', and 'Sugarland Red', are available. None are truly cold hardy, and leaves are often killed; but shoots do regenerate from basal areas. In my Georgia trials, so-termed 'Hardy Yellow', a hose-in-hose, soft yellow, was killed to ground at 9.5°F in 2006–07 and 13.8°F in 2008–09. Grew seedlings of 'Hardy Red', hoping for increased cold hardiness. Nothing positive.

Neviusia alabamensis

Alabama snow-wreath

This shrub is more of a conversation piece than a first-rate, multi-dimensional landscape plant, although the flower effect can be striking. The quirky, creamy white flowers are apetalous; the stamens are the showy part. Flowers appear in three- to eight-flowered cymes from early April (Athens) through May, creating an effect akin to new-fallen snow covering the branches. The habit is somewhat scraggly, with arching branches and a propensity to sucker, eventually developing into a rounded outline. The 1½- to 3½-in.-long leaves are medium green and offer no fall color. In fact, the plant is so nondescript out of flower that few people recognize it. Requires moist soils for best growth, but this adaptable species appears to thrive under less-than-ideal conditions. Tolerant of sun or shade. A good choice for the shrub border, or for quizzing your friends to identify. Grows 3 to 6 ft. high and wide. Zones 4 to 8. Alabama.

Nyssa ogeche

Ogeechee tupelo, Ogeechee-lime

I'm always on the watch for potential "new" urban and stress-tolerant trees, and this swamp species, like many bottomland species, lends itself to more compacted soils. J. C. Raulston grew it in the west side of the Arboretum in Raleigh, North Carolina, in soil so hard that roots barely penetrated; yet the plant appeared remarkably robust. Habit in cultivation is rounded, branches coarse and covered with 4- to 6-in.-long, dark green leaves. Flowers serve as a major nectar source for bees. On female trees, ovoid fruit, ¾ to 1½ in. long, change to red or remain green with a red blush. Fruit are extremely sour, which suggested the name Ogeechee-lime. Unusual tree for naturalizing; found in wet soils in the wild and excellent for wet soil areas. Requires root pruning to facilitate easier transplanting. Two hundred trees were evaluated in a 13-year study at Auburn University, with *Nyssa ogeche* in the top eight. Grows 30 to 40 ft. high and wide. Zones 6 to 9. South Carolina, Georgia, and Florida.

Nyssa aquatica, water tupelo, is another swamp–wet soil native species with large, 4- to 7- (to 12-) in.-long, dark green leaves. Zones 6 to 9. Virginia to southern Illinois, Florida and Texas.

Nyssa sylvatica

black tupelo

A true harbinger of autumn. In September, before most trees acknowledge that summer has ended, a smattering of leaves on black tupelo trees start to twinkle yellow, orange, and red. The habit is distinctly pyramidal in youth and may maintain that form into old age or become rounded. The dark gray, almost black, bark is broken

MORE ▶

Neviusia alabamensis, Alabama snow-wreath

Neviusia alabamensis

Nyssa ogeche, Ogeechee tupelo

Nyssa ogeche

Nyssa ogeche

Nyssa sylvatica, black tupelo, fall color

Nyssa sylvatica

Nyssa sylvatica 'Autumn Cascades' fall color

Nyssa sylvatica CONTINUED

into thick ridges that are divided horizontally, producing a blocky configuration. The 3- to 6-in.-long, lustrous dark green leaves turn fluorescent yellow, orange, scarlet, and maroon in fall. Fall color is often fleeting, for the leaves do not persist like those of maples and oaks. A leaf spot, *Mycosphaerella nyssaecola*, induces black lesions and premature defoliation. Prospers in deep, moist, acid soils, but it is found in dry woods and in swamps throughout its native range. A single specimen is spectacular, but groupings of five to seven trees, each expressing a different fall color, provide pause for reflection. Grows 30 to 50 ft. high, 20 to 30 ft. wide, although size is highly variable. National champion is 92 ft. by 92 ft. Zones 4 to 9. Maine to Ontario and Michigan, south to Florida and Texas.

CULTIVARS AND VARIETIES

New cultivars with superior ornamental traits and disease resistance should help place this among the top five shade trees in contemporary landscapes. Many selections are being evaluated at J. Frank Schmidt & Son Nursery, Boring, Oregon.

'Autumn Cascades' is a semi-weeping form with shiny dark green leaves turning yellow-orange-red in fall. A female, and the blue-black fruit are attractive. Less susceptible to leaf spot than 'Lakeside Weeper'. Not truly weeping and, at times, kind of gruff, disheveled, and unruly.

Forum™ ('NXSXF') with a central leader, conical outline, dark green leaves, yellow-orange-red fall color, and fast growth was introduced by Tree Introductions, Inc., Athens, Georgia.

Green Gable™ ('NSUHH') is a new introduction with lustrous dark green leaves that turn beautiful red in fall. Foliage is more leaf spot resistant. Branches are upswept, creating a tighter, denser habit at a young age.

Red Rage® ('Hayman Red') with lustrous dark green leaves, superb red fall color, and high leaf-spot resistance, is one of the best new introductions.

'Sheri's Cloud' is a cream-margined, gray-green-centered leaf selection from Arkansas.

'Wildfire', with bronze-red to reddish purple new shoots, is attractive in spring and as new growth flushes develop. Fall color was reasonable yellow-orange-red in Dirr garden. Broad pyramidal growth habit.

'Zydeco Twist' with strongly twisting, spiraling, contorted stems is a nifty conversation piece. Leaves are sparkling dark green and less susceptible to leaf spot. A young plant in the new Dirr garden is a great conversation starter.

Olea europaea
olive

I failed to realize the beauty of this economically important fruit-produc-

Nyssa sylvatica 'Sheri's Cloud'

Nyssa sylvatica 'Wildfire'

Nyssa sylvatica 'Zydeco Twist'

Olea europaea

ing species, possibly because of its paucity in southeastern landscapes. However, sightings in California and its greater presence in containers in the Southeast have struck a chord. The gray-green, evergreen leaves, 2 to 3 in. long, one-third as wide or less, are beautiful through the seasons, their undersides dressed in pubescent silver. Habit is a large shrub to small tree in the 15- to 30-ft. range, architectural, bending, creaky in the knees, with pretty bark. Photos of mature olive trees in the Mediterranean countries provide the incentive to "try" one. Flowers, white, fragrant, appear in axillary racemes. Fruit is a drupe, the well-known olive, that comes in many sizes and shapes. Requires well-drained, drier soils and drier climate, full sun. Best in zones 9 and 10. Withstands 10 to 15°F. Mediterranean region with subspecies in Africa and China.

CULTIVARS AND VARIETIES
'Arbequina' is a self-fruitful, early-ripening cultivar that withstood 10°F in an above-ground container in Athens.

Orixa japonica

Potential uses include challenging guests to identify this member of the citrus family (Rutaceae) and checking their tolerances to one of the strongest odors in the leafy kingdom. The "curious" leaf odor recalls the oils of lemon, lime, orange, and feet. Back to horticulture—dense, mounded,

MORE ▶

Olea europaea, olive

Orixa japonica

Orixa japonica

Orixa japonica 'Variegata'

Orixa japonica CONTINUED

spreading shrub, almost like flowering-quince (*Chaenomeles*) in impenetrability. Lustrous bright green leaves, 2 to 5 in. long, become soft yellow in fall; dioecious greenish flowers in spring. The seldom-produced fruit offer little ornament. Prefers partial shade in moist, well-drained, acid soil high in organic matter. Have observed plants in substandard soils and full sun yet still prosperous. Novelty shrub for the collector. Listed as deer-resistant. Grows 6 to 8 ft. high, wider at maturity. Zones 6 and 7. Japan.

CULTIVARS AND VARIETIES

'Aurea', a yellow-foliage form, returns to green faster than I can turn off a light switch. Tested several times in Athens with green results.

'Variegata', with irregular cream-white-margined leaves, is striking when the shoots first emerge, settles down with maturity. Leaf shape is somewhat convex and puckered.

Osmanthus americanus
devilwood

Out of character for the genus, as the leaves are spineless; the only other *Osmanthus* species native to the U.S. Southeast is *Osmanthus megacarpus*, which is similar, except smaller in habit and larger of fruit. At times wispy and without great landscape appeal; occasionally robustly foliated. Bark is smooth gray on older trunks. Leaves, 2 to 5 in. long, are lustrous dark olive-green above, pale green beneath.

In March and April, the four-petaled, ¼-in.-wide, fragrant, cream-colored flowers appear in axillary terminal panicles. Sexes are separate, and the ½-in.-long, ovoid, dark blue-purple fruit develop on female plants. The female flower has a bowling pin–shaped pistil; male with two stamens. I have watched fruit persist into the following spring, then disappear in a day with the frenzied feeding of feathered flocks. Wonderful wet soil plant, growing naturally along swamp margins, hammocks, and borders of streams. Tolerates drier soils once established. Bonnie and I grew several plants; none will ever overwhelm, but they do possess a latent beauty. Good choice for naturalizing in moist soils. Prune to maintain density. Used in a grouping

behind the first green at the Augusta National Golf Club, home of the Master's. Grows 15 to 25 ft. high, variable spread. Zones 6 to 9(10). North Carolina to Florida and Mississippi.

Osmanthus armatus

Certainly not well known but adaptable to full sun and heavy shade conditions in Southeast and West Coast. Leaves cardboard-thick, leathery, dark green, 3 to 6 in. long, with stout, often hooked teeth, up to ten per margin, making a formidable barrier. Leaves become entire as plants age, and one questions if it is the same plant. Habit is rounded and impenetrable, so thick and dense that it serves as a barrier. White flowers are sweetly scented and occur in small clusters from the leaf

Osmanthus americanus, devilwood

Osmanthus americanus

Osmanthus americanus

axils in autumn (late October, Athens). Fruit are egg-shaped, dark violet, ¾-in.-long drupes. Any well-drained soil is suitable. In the wild, it grows on humus-clad cliffs and boulders, in both full sun and dense shade. Best in a border or in groupings and masses. Grows 6 to 10 ft. high and wide. Zones 6 and 7, 8 and 9 on West Coast. Western China.

Osmanthus decorus is somewhat similar, with 2- to 5-in.-long, ½- to 1¾ in.-wide, leathery, generally entire-margined, glossy dark green leaves. Fragrant white flowers, ⅓ in. in diameter, open in axillary clusters in spring (late March, Athens). The oval fruit, ½ in. long, reddish to purple-black, are borne on slender, ½-in.-long stalks in fall. Ironclad performance in eight years of Georgia trials. Large, wide-spreading, dense, mounded habit. Grows 5 to 10 ft. high. Noted an 18-ft.-high plant in England. Zones 7 to 9. Southeastern coast of the Black Sea.

Osmanthus ×burkwoodii

A taxonomic enigma, at one time given the name ×Osmarea burkwoodii, but now contained within Osmanthus. A hybrid of Osmanthus delavayi and O. decorus, the species develops into a compact broadleaf evergreen shrub of haystack to rounded outline. The oppositely arranged leaves are 1 to 2 in. long, serrated, a leathery, lustrous dark green. Flowers, fragrant, small, open in April and May. Profuse flowers

MORE ▶

Osmanthus armatus

Osmanthus ×burkwoodii

Osmanthus armatus

Osmanthus decorus

Osmanthus ×burkwoodii

531

Osmanthus ×burkwoodii CONTINUED

in our Chapel Hill garden. I have not observed fruit set. Another piece of the puzzle in the *Osmanthus* picture that makes our gardens more beautiful. Easy to grow; several prospering plants in the Athens and Chapel Hill, North Carolina, area indicate adaptability to southern heat and humidity. Place in moderate shade, well-drained soil. Useful as a filler in borders and the like. Grows 6 to 10 ft. high and wide. Zones 6 to 8, 9 and 10 on the West Coast.

Osmanthus delavayi
Delavay teaolive

My many trips to English gardens provided the introduction to this species, and the very first encounter, at Lanhydrock in Cornwall, had me doubting myself. It was a chilly (actually bone-chilling) late March day when this unknown 15-ft.-high, broadleaf evergreen shrub looked me in the eye, in full flower and fragrance, daring me to identify it. I simply could not put two and two together. The lustrous dark green leaves, ½ to 1 in. long, with strong teeth, are reminiscent of small holly leaves. The fragrant white flowers are produced in four- to eight-flowered cymes from each leaf axil, resulting in a swath of cream along the branches. Fruit are roundish, ½-in.-long, blue-black drupes. I have grown the plant in Athens, but it never lived up to Lanhydrock. Substitute *Osmanthus*

×*burkwoodii* for similar characteristics and improved performance. Wonderful plant for foliage and late winter to spring flowers. Grows 6 to 10 ft. high and wide. Zones 7 and 8, 9 and 10 on the West Coast. China.

Osmanthus ×fortunei
Fortune's teaolive

A hybrid of *Osmanthus heterophyllus* and *O. fragrans*, and among the most durable of plants for sun, shade, and dry soils in the Southeast and West. Introduced from Japan in 1856, the initial introduction was male. My monitoring of flowers indicates all in cultivation are males. Makes the most uniform, dense haystack of dark green. Occasionally limbed up to display the smooth gray bark. At the University of Georgia, two 20- to 25-ft.-high specimens attract the attention of the entire student body in mid to late October, when the perfume of the flowers lays a sweet, smog-like blanket across the campus. The small, four-petaled, white flowers appear in cymose clusters from the leaf axils and are effective for

two to three weeks. The spiny juvenile leaves, thick leathery dark green, 2 to 4 in. long, have ten to 12 triangular teeth per margin. As the plant ages, serrations disappear; the large plants just mentioned have almost no serrated leaves. Mature plants also flower more intensely than the juvenile delinquents. Container-grown and easily transplanted. Shade and sun adaptable. Requires well-drained soil. A great grouping, screen, or hedge plant. Grows 10 to 15 (to 20) ft. high, usually less in spread. Zones 7 to 9.
CULTIVARS AND VARIETIES
Both 'Fruitlandii' and 'San Jose' grow in our garden, with the former possibly the best overall and increasingly more common in the Southeast.

'Fruitlandii' is faster growing than typical *Osmanthus* ×*fortunei*. It has less stiff serrations and is more upright in habit, particularly in youth.

'San Jose', with more elongated, more uniformly serrated leaves than the species, is more open than 'Fruitlandii' in outline. Plants were damaged at –12°F but revegetated quickly.

Osmanthus delavayi

Osmanthus delavayi, Delavay teaolive

Osmanthus ×fortunei, Fortune's teaolive

Osmanthus fragrans
fragrant teaolive

For continuous floral fragrance, fragrant teaolive has no peers. Starting in September, it provides sweet perfume, with flowers still emerging in April (Athens) and appearing sporadically in late spring and summer. Most passersby do not see the flowers but remark about the pleasing aroma. Upright, broad-columnar, broadleaf evergreen shrub in youth, becoming tree-like at maturity. Leaves, 2 to 5 in. long, are finely toothed or entire and maintain the lustrous dark green color year-round. Bark, when exposed, is smooth, gray-brown, and attractive. The small, four-petaled, whitish flowers appear in small axillary clusters. Fruit are elongated, olive-like, purple-black drupes with a waxy coating and seldom develop on cultivated plants. Adaptable to varied soils, except per-

MORE ▶

Osmanthus ×fortunei

Osmanthus ×fortunei

Osmanthus ×fortunei 'Fruitlandii'

Osmanthus ×fortunei 'San Jose'

Osmanthus fragrans CONTINUED

manently wet. Sun and shade adaptable. Like all *Osmanthus* species, no serious insects or diseases. Utilize in combination with other broadleaf evergreens, in mixed borders, screens, and even hedges. Great in shady situations and a wonderful container plant. Bonnie and I have "spotted" the species and cultivars throughout our gardens for a continuum of floral fragrance. Cold is the prime enemy, and anything below 0°F will injure leaves. In Oregon, 0°F knocked the leaves off plants, and plants were killed, in some instances to the ground, at −3°F in the Athens area. Grows 10 to 15 ft. high (20 to 30 ft. high in zones 9 and 10). Zones 7 to 10. China, Japan.

CULTIVARS AND VARIETIES
Numerous, many selected over the centuries, but differences, except for a few, are minor. A Chinese reference listed 167 cultivars.

'Aurantiacus' (f. *aurantiacus*) produces pale to deep orange flowers in fall; typically does not repeat flower like the species. Leaves are more leathery and darker green, less serrated, and habit is dense, pyramidal-conical-oval. Gorgeous in flower and fragrance. Appears more cold hardy than the species. Grew for many years in the Dirr garden with great success.

'Nanjing's Beauty' ('Fudingzhu') produces more abundant, fragrant, cream-white flowers than the species. This, to date, is the most prolific flowering cultivar available in the United States. A plant in the Georgia trials has proven exceptional, and the abundant flowers literally camouflage the stems.

Osmanthus heterophyllus
holly teaolive

Appropriately named, for the spiny-margined leaves that, although smaller, otherwise resemble English holly leaves. Many people misidentify this species as holly, but the leaves are always opposite on *Osmanthus*,

Osmanthus fragrans, fragrant teaolive

Osmanthus fragrans

Osmanthus fragrans 'Aurantiacus'

Osmanthus fragrans 'Nanjing's Beauty'

Osmanthus heterophyllus, holly teaolive

alternate on *Ilex*. Dense upright-oval to rounded evergreen shrub that is virtually impenetrable. The 1- to 2½-in.-long, leathery lustrous dark green, spiny-margined leaves become, with age, entire. An ancient specimen is a thing of beauty and comes without the excruciatingly painful "sticky" leaves. White, four-petaled, ¼-in.-wide, fragrant flowers open from mid to late October into early November. The floral scent is heavenly and spices the entire garden. The fruit that occasionally develop, usually hidden among the leaves, are ⅜- to ½-in.-long, bluish purple-black drupes. Resilient and ironclad shrub that withstands sun, shade, heat, drought, pruning, and vandalism. Makes a superb hedge and barrier. Grows 8 to 10 ft. high; 20-ft. plants grow in Athens, Georgia, and Aiken, South Carolina. Zones 6 to 9. Japan.

MORE ▶

Osmanthus heterophyllus

Osmanthus heterophyllus 'Aureomarginatus'

Osmanthus heterophyllus 'Aureus'

Osmanthus heterophyllus 'Goshiki'

Osmanthus heterophyllus CONTINUED

Osmanthus heterophyllus 'Variegatus'

CULTIVARS AND VARIETIES
Certainly one of my favorite species for unusual cultivars; several offer greater breadth of landscape benefits, and many are great everyday garden plants.

'Aureomarginatus', with yellow-margined, green-centered leaves, forms a large haystack to 10 ft. or more.

'Aureus' ('Ogon', 'Allgold') has golden yellow leaves that fade to yellow-green and green. Leaves are strongly spiny in youth. Slower growing and smaller than the species. Requires some shade in hot climates as leaves bleach or become brown.

'Goshiki' is a spectral rainbow with new growth tinged pink and bronze, flecked with gold, maturing gold, cream, and green—all rather pretty when finally settled down. Grows 6 ft. high and wide; good choice in shady areas of the garden to provide a touch of color.

Osmanthus heterophyllus 'Purpureus'

Osmanthus heterophyllus 'Rotundifolius'

Osmanthus heterophyllus 'Sasaba'

Osmanthus heterophyllus 'Latifolius Variegatus'

'Gulftide', with extremely spiny young leaves, upright habit, white flowers, and fruit, is an excellent hedge or barrier plant. Leaves, with maturity, become entire. Male and bisexual flowers on same plant. Grows 10 ft. high or more.

'Purpureus' derives its name from the appearance of the new shoots, which look as if they were dipped in purple-black tar. Leaves are extremely beautiful and eventually become dark green; spiny-margined when young, finally entire. One of the most cold hardy cultivars, forming a dense rounded outline to 10 ft. high.

'Rotundifolius' offers 1½- to 2-in.-long, 1- to 1¼-in.-wide, leathery dark green leaves without spines, fragrant white flowers, and bluish purple fruit. Habit is more compact, 4 to 5 (to 8) ft. high and wide. A superb foundation, grouping, and massing shrub.

'Sasaba', with extremely spiny leaves and upright habit, 8 to 10 ft. high, is more of a collector's item. Fragrant white flowers open in early November in the Dirr garden. It is a

female, and I have observed abundant seedlings around a 15-ft.-high plant at Sarah P. Duke Gardens.

'Variegatus' is the most frequently available cultivar in commerce, with cream-white-margined leaves that are not as spiny as the species. Forms a pyramidal-oval to rounded outline, eventually reaching 8 to 10 ft. in height. About half a zone less hardy than the species. 'Kembu', with leaves splashed, streaked, and margined with cream, and 'Latifolius Variegatus', with broader leaves margined white, are included in this bucket.

Osmanthus serrulatus

One of the most beautiful teaolives for foliage, the 2- to 3½-in.-long, leathery, lustrous dark green leaves have 26 to 30, plastic, saw-like teeth per margin. As plants mature, the leaves become entire, and it is difficult to locate a single serrated leaf. Habit parallels a large, broad mound, truly impenetrable. Flowers, winter to spring, are white, fragrant, and produced in clusters of four to nine from the leaf axils.

Fragrance is not as overpowering as that of *Osmanthus fragrans*. Fruit are oblong, blue-black drupes. Have grown this in our Athens garden but not as successfully as *O. ×fortunei*, *O. heterophyllus*, and *O. fragrans*. Appears to be in suspended animation. At the Hillier Arboretum, England, I witnessed a 15-ft.-high and -wide specimen. Remarkably beautiful where it can be grown. Grows 6 to 12 ft. high and wide. Zones 7 to 10. China.

Ostrya virginiana
American hophornbeam

Although it is a handsome small tree, this American native has been relegated to the forest shadows and has never been embraced by the gardening or tree-planting public. Graceful and pyramidal in youth, it becomes more rounded with age. The grayish brown exfoliating bark is attractive in the winter months. The 2- to 5-in.-long, dark green, sharply serrated leaves develop yellow-brown color and drop early in fall. Worm-like, 1½-in.-long, yellow-brown male catkins open in April. Catkins occur in threes at the end of the branches and are a reliable identification characteristic. The fruit are enclosed in hop-like bracts with thin hairs. The hairs penetrate the skin and are difficult to remove, I know from personal experience. American hophornbeam tolerates dry, acid, and higher pH soils. It prospers in full sun

MORE ▶

Osmanthus serrulatus

Osmanthus serrulatus

537

Ostrya virginiana CONTINUED

and is also a good understory tree. The species has been used for street and campus plantings. Grows 25 to 40 ft. high, 20 to 40 ft. wide. Zones 4 to 9. Ontario to Minnesota, south to Florida and Texas.

Ostrya virginiana

Oxydendrum arboreum
sourwood

Northern gardeners would give their best trowel for a specimen sourwood, a tree that in its native habitat assumes almost blatant commonality. One of our best native trees and a well-grown specimen rivals even the best dogwoods. The habit is delicately pyramidal with finely textured, drooping branches. Young stems vary from olive-green to rich red, and the brown bark becomes blocky with age. Iridescent green young leaves, finely serrated, mature to lustrous dark green, 3 to 8 in. long. The foliage turns yellow, red, and maroon in fall. White, ¼-in.-long, urn-shaped, fragrant flowers are borne in 4- to 10-in.-long and -wide panicles in June and July. The flowers open over an extended period, perhaps three to four weeks. They are followed by small, ⅓-in.-long, brownish, dehiscent capsules that persist through winter. Sourwood is difficult to produce under typical nursery conditions and is

not the easiest plant to move. It is best to work with small, container-grown plants. A great choice for naturalizing in infertile, acid soils, in sun or partial shade. Grows 25 to 30 ft. high, 20 ft. wide; can grow larger. Trees in Athens area are 60 ft. high; national champion is 81 ft. by 50 ft. Zones 5 to 9. Southeastern United States.

Pachysandra procumbens
Allegheny pachysandra

Without equivocation one of the most beautiful native groundcovers, this broadleaf evergreen species forms a blanket of blue-green that complements and enhances the shrubs and trees above. The habit is stoloniferous-spreading, forming large mats of rich green (emerging) to dark blue-green leaves with grayish mottling at maturity. The 2- to 4-in.-long, almost rounded leaves are entire at the base with coarse teeth from the middle to the apex. Flowers occur at the base of the leaf stalk (petiole) in 2- to 4-in.-

Ostrya virginiana, American hophornbeam

Ostrya virginiana

Oxydendrum arboreum

long spikes in March and April. The pinkish white flowers are fragrant and often not visible, as they are buried in the crown of the plant. Requires moist, acid to higher pH, loose, friable soils, high in organic matter, and some degree of shade for best growth. In northern climates, snow tends to flatten the leaves, but with new growth in spring the sins of winter are absolved. Grows 6 to 10 in. high, spreading to infinity. Zones 5 to 9. Eastern Kentucky, West Virginia to Florida and Louisiana.

MORE ▶

Oxydendrum arboreum, sourwood

Oxydendrum arboreum

Oxydendrum arboreum

Pachysandra procumbens

Oxydendrum arboreum fall color

Pachysandra procumbens, Allegheny pachysandra

539

Pachysandra procumbens CONTINUED
CULTIVARS AND VARIETIES
'Eco Treasure' is a more highly variegated selection; 'Forest Green' is listed as darker green, although I see little difference between it and the species type.

'Pixie' is a low-growing selection, the leaves with prominent gray markings. Observed only once. Cute but stalled in biological time. A sure-fire, go-out-of-business plant.

Pachysandra terminalis
Japanese pachysandra
A standard in American landscapes along with ivy, vinca, and euonymus for evergreen groundcover use. One of the most beautiful in spring when the lovely light green leaves push forth, contrasting with the dark green, older leaves. Flowers in white, terminal, 1- to 2-in.-long spikes, open in March and April. Best performance in loose, acid, moist, organic-laden soils in shade. Observed under beech trees and performing admirably. Great groundcover. Grows 6 to 12 in. high, spreading by rhizomes to form a perfect carpet. Zones 4 to 7(8). Japan.
CULTIVARS AND VARIETIES
'Green Sheen', with high-gloss dark green leaves, is attractive but was not as vigorous as the species in the Dirr garden; slightly shorter in stature, too.

'Variegata' ('Silver Edge') has gray-green leaves, mottled and margined with cream; attractive in shady nooks. Does not grow as fast as the species.

Pachysandra procumbens

Pachysandra terminalis, Japanese pachysandra

Pachysandra terminalis

Pachysandra terminalis 'Green Sheen'

Pachysandra terminalis 'Variegata'

Palms

Approximately 200 genera and 2,600 species of palms grow in the far-flung subtropical and tropical climates of the earth. Palms make great container elements for patios, pools, and entrances, and a selected few are cold hardy to zone (6)7, in recent years becoming fashionable elements in landscapes. Over my gardening tenure in Georgia, six palm species have been grown, with only *Rhapidophyllum hystrix*, needle palm, the clear-cut survivor. Fifty to 100 miles south of Athens–Atlanta, palms increase in landscape commonality: *Butia capitata*, pindo palm, *Trachycarpus fortunei*, Chinese windmill palm, *Sabal palmetto*, cabbage palm, and *S. minor*, dwarf palmetto, dot the countryside, looking somewhat out of place among the pines and deciduous trees.

Palms are easily transplanted and often container-grown, making the planting process even easier. They have rope-like roots like a corn plant, and large trees are often moved with a small root ball. I witnessed *Sabal palmetto* lying on the ground in a garden center in Columbia, South Carolina, all parts exposed without protection. Plant in well-drained soil, provide adequate moisture and fertility. Palms will show micronutrient deficiencies in sandy soils, often from insufficient manganese. The addition of dolomitic lime, especially in extremely acid soils, at time of planting is helpful. About ¼ lb. of fertilizer (10-10-10 or palm special) per 2 ft. of linear trunk, once or twice during growing season is recommended. Palms require little care once established and from my observations withstand more abuse than most trees and shrubs. They are extremely wind-tolerant: even Hurricane Hugo was unable to significantly dislodge *S. palmetto* from the South Carolina coast.

Palms tolerate full sun and significant degrees of shade; indeed, palms like *Caryota*, *Chamaedorea*, *Howea*, *Phoenix*, *Livistona*, and others function as indoor plants because of shade tolerance. Mites, scale, and other sucking-type insects are occasional problems on indoor plants. The needle palm in the Dirr garden grew in the shade of a southern red oak and performed magnificently; the same species grows equally well in full sun.

Propagation is typically via seeds, and I have myself germinated numerous *Sabal minor* and *Rhapidophyllum hystrix* seeds. Germination times can be long. Clean fleshy outer covering, soak seeds for about 24 hours, sow, and wait.

Palms elongate from the terminal meristem and increase in diameter via the primary thickening meristem. Take care not to injure the growing point in transplanting. I have observed larger transplanted trees where the two or three leaves above the meristem are all that remain, and these are tied into a bundle for protection.

Cold is the major limiting factor to successful culture; and leaf edges, entire leaves, and often the growing point are injured by repeated low temperatures. Leaves may be killed outright, with growth renewed from the undamaged meristem; if cold damage occurs, wait until early summer for new growth before removing the plant. Typically, younger plants are more susceptible to severe cold damage than older, established plants.

Landscape uses are abundant: single specimen use, groupings, containers, and foundation planting are the most common. Be adventurous, for palms offer foliage texture and form nowhere else available in the woody plant world. Ask yourself how many resort hotels utilize palms in lobbies and outdoor settings to evoke the aura of elegance, hospitality, and warmth.

Palms are in vogue, hence more readily available in commerce and with significant new literature for interested readers. *An Encyclopedia of Cultivated Palms* (2003) by Robert Lee Riffle and Paul Craft discusses approximately 890 species. *Palms Won't Grow Here and Other Myths* (2003) treats cold hardy species; author David A. Francko is a faculty member at Miami University, Oxford, Ohio, my wife's alma mater. We visited to study the cold hardy collection. In brief, there was not much. *Hardy Palms for the Southeast* (2007) by Tom McClendon, Will Roberds, and Joe LeVert is an excellent reference based on significant testing; across zone 7, cold hardy species listed in it include *Rhapidophyllum hystrix*, *Sabal* 'Birmingham', *S.* 'Brazoria', *S. etonia*, *S. minor*, *S. minor* 'Louisiana', *S.* 'Tamaulipas', *Trachycarpus fortunei*, *T. nanus*, *T. takil*, and *T. wagnerianus*. Betrock Information Systems (www.betrock.com) publishes at least three palm references, with *Cold Hardy Palms* (2005) by Alan M. Meerow most pertinent to my presentation.

Butia capitata
pindo or jelly palm

Butia capitata is a beautiful small tree species with stout trunk and 3- to 6- (to 10-) ft.-long, pinnately compound, grayish to bluish green leaves. The slender leaflets, up to 2½ ft. long,

MORE ▶

Butia capitata

Butia capitata CONTINUED

Butia capitata, pindo palm

ascend from the spiny leaf stalk to form a V-shape. The leaves arch gracefully creating a semi-pendent to weeping effect. The crown is relatively dense and full. Older, declining leaves should be removed by cutting the large woody petiole base as close to the trunk as possible. Flowers are small, cream-yellow to reddish, in inflorescences to 3 ft. long. Fruit is an orange-yellow drupe, about 1 in. wide, sweet, edible, and with a pineapple flavor. Species displays high salt tolerance and is often planted on the ocean side of houses and resort complexes. Used in parking lot islands, which attests to its high heat and drought tolerances. Grows 12 to 18 (to 25) ft. high, about half this in spread. Zones 8 to 11. In the early 1980s, I was involved with assessing cold damage at a resort on the Georgia coast. Low temperature was 11°F, and this species was largely uninjured. Southern Brazil, northern Uruguay.

Chamaerops humilis, Mediterranean fan palm

Chamaerops humilis
Mediterranean, European, or dwarf fan palm

This handsome, small, clumping species develops a rounded outline with 18- to 24- (to 36-) in.-long leaves, each divided into narrow, stiff segments. Foliage color ranges from green to blue-green. Petiole is covered with sharp, spiny teeth that point toward the leaf blade. Leaf stalks may extend to 5 ft. in length. Yellow flowers are followed by small, round, yellow-orange to brown fruit. Provide well-drained soil in full sun to heavy shade. Slow-growing in more northern areas. Useful in a container, foundation plantings and groupings. Utilized extensively along coastal Southeast. Heat- and salt-tolerant. Grows 3 to 6 ft. high, often wider; potential in warmest areas to 15 to 20 ft. high. Zones 9 to 11, although suitable for zone 8. Listed as surviving 10 to 15°F; one reference noted 6°F. Grows on mountainsides in coastal areas of southwestern Europe and northern Africa.

Livistona chinensis
Chinese fan palm, Chinese fountain palm

Handsome species with large, coarse-textured, palmate leaves and smooth trunks resulting from the clean abscission of the leaf bases. Often described as single-stemmed, but specimens I observed were full and dense, as wide as they were high. The emerald-green leaves are 3 to 6 ft. across, the segments cut one-third to one-half the diameter, and the lobes arching at their extremities like a cupped hand facing the ground. The petiole is about as long as the blade with brown, ¾- to 1-in.-long spines from the base to the middle. Flowers (cream) occur on up to 6-ft.-long inflorescences obscured by the large leaves. Fruit are oval to rounded, dark blue to gray-blue when mature. The trunk, about 1 ft. thick at maturity, is gray and marked with the scars of the fallen leaf bases. The plant in youth is trunkless and forms a large mound, eventually becoming tree-like. Grows best in well-drained, moist, fertile soil, in sun and partial shade. Protect in more northerly areas. Handsome accent and container plant. Have observed it massed in an understory planting. Grows 10 to 15 (20 to 30) ft. high. Can grow to 50 ft. in native range. Survived with leaf burn at 15°F and fully recovered. Zones (8)9 to 11. Temperatures in the low to mid 20s will injure foliage. Southern Japan, Ryukyu and Bonin Islands, southern Taiwan.

Phoenix canariensis
Canary Island date palm

A large, thickish, single-trunked palm, one of the most widely cultivated, with globular head of upright and arching fronds; its beautiful habit elicits accolades from those who know little about palms. Each lustrous dark green, compound pinnate leaf is up to 15 ft. long and divided into numerous leaflets. The thick, gray-brown trunk, 2 to 3 ft. in diameter on mature trees,

MORE ▶

Phoenix canariensis

Chamaerops humilis

Livistona chinensis, Chinese fan palm

543

has diamond-shaped leaf bases, wider than high, on the mature trunk, with old petiole bases persisting below the crown. Numerous cream-yellow flowers are borne in drooping inflorescences up to 3 ft. long. The yellow-red (pale orange), oblong-ellipsoid fruit, ¾ in. long, appear in large paniculate clusters during the warm months. A dioecious species, so a male is needed for pollination. Prefers full sun, fertile, well-drained soil. Used as a street tree, specimen palm, and accent plant. A specimen, now 60 ft. high, grows in Cairo, Georgia (zone 8), at Monrovia Growers. Stewart Chandler of Monrovia says it is reported to have been planted around the turn of the 19th century as one of the first groups of plants brought in from the Canary Islands. The lone palm has lost its fronds several times in its history, but the growing point (meristem) has

Phoenix reclinata, Senegal date palm

Phoenix canariensis, Canary Island date palm

Phoenix roebelenii, pygmy date palm

never been seriously injured. The tree survived even the 1985 freeze, when Cairo saw a low of 6°F with wind chill below zero, with only foliage burn. A large specimen on St. Simons Island, Georgia, was killed outright by 11°F; however, the plant had grown in the location for around 30 years. Grows 20 to 30 ft. high, 15 ft. wide. Zones 9 to 11. Temperatures below 20°F injure foliage. Canary Islands.

The related *Phoenix reclinata*, Senegal date palm, a low-branched, clumping species, is used as a specimen palm at the Disney complexes in Orlando. The branches recurve upward and are wide-spreading. The dark green, pinnate leaves range from 10 to 20 ft. long. The edible, reddish brown fruit are ½ in. long. Grows 15 to 25 ft. high, wider at maturity. Only for the warmest areas of zone 9, into 10 and 11. Below 28 to 30°F, leaf damage will occur. Tropical Africa.

Phoenix roebelenii, pygmy date palm, is a common container plant in northern gardens and conservatories. It is a fine-textured, lustrous green, graceful arching, pinnate-leaf species that grows 4 to 6 (to 10) ft. high, 5 ft. and greater in width, and, like the previous species, bears slender, needle-like spines along the petiole base. Light yellow to white flowers are fol-

lowed by first red then black, oblong, ½-in.-long fruit. Zones (9)10 and 11. Laos, China, southern Vietnam.

Rhapidophyllum hystrix
needle palm
Without debate the most cold hardy palm, with reports of its culture as far north as Cincinnati, Ohio. A rounded, dense-foliaged palm with the characteristic needle-like spines in the center of the clump, from which the leaf bases arise. The palmate leaves, lustrous dark green, are divided almost to the base into seven to 20 stiff segments. Individual leaf blades are up to 3 ft. across on 2- to 3-ft.-long, slender, unarmed petioles. Yellowish white flowers are followed by reddish brown to brown, ½-in.-wide fruit, dusted with white. Trunk is thick, short, and does not elongate; it is covered with the leaf bases, spines, and brown matting. The species is found in a variety of soils in the wild, from river bluffs and limestone hammocks to moist to wet floodplains and seepage areas, often in shade. Tolerates drought and heavy soils under cultivation. Probably the best "no brainer" for someone remotely interested in palms. Good evergreen shrub for containers, the shady border, as an accent plant. A winner in the Dirr garden. A large plant

at JC Raulston Arboretum has experienced negative Fahrenheit temperatures; another survived –20°F in 1985 in Knoxville, Tennessee. Observed great colonies in shady ravines and bluffs above the Apalachicola River in Torreya State Park, Bristol, Florida. Grows 6 to 8 ft. high and wide. Zones (6)7 to 11. South Carolina, Georgia, Florida, Alabama, and Mississippi.

Rhapis excelsa
lady palm
Handsome small palm with glossy, dark green, finger-like lobes and refined aesthetic habit. Forms clumps of cane-like stems covered with brown fibers toward the top, becoming smoother with maturity. The overall effect is reminiscent of bamboo, particularly *Sasa palmata*. The palmate leaves are divided into five to ten segments, cut almost to the base, with the petiole unarmed. Leaves are 10 to 20 in. across. Requires moderate to heavy shade, deep, moist, organic, well-drained soils. Useful as a foundation plant, in containers and shady borders, and as a textural accent. Common in conservatories and as a houseplant, as it tolerates low light. Grows 5 to 10 ft. high and wide. Several cream-white variegated forms

MORE ▶

Rhapidophyllum hystrix, needle palm

Rhapis excelsa, lady palm

Rhapis excelsa CONTINUED

are in cultivation. I have not observed them. Clumps can be divided. Zones 9 to 11, with protection in zone 8. Low-temperature tolerance is listed as 18°F. Southern China. No known native populations in the wild.

Sabal palmetto
cabbage palm

A wonderful hardy species for coastal South Carolina to Texas and the most common tree palm in the Coastal Plain of the Southeast, utilized as a single specimen, in groupings, along streets, and in groves. Single-trunked, with the old leaf bases attached or cleanly abscising below the crown. The crown is usually quite full, with the lower leaves gently arching. The leaves are costapalmate, somewhere between pinnate and palmate, to 6 ft. long and 3 ft. wide, divided one-third of the way to the base with many thread-like leaf pieces in the sinuses (indentations). Leaves vary from gray-green to green. Fragrant cream-white flowers occur in large panicles in summer. Fruit are rounded, brown-black, ¼- to ⅓-in.-wide drupes; I noticed fruiting specimens in Savannah, Georgia, that were dropping drupes all over the sidewalks and streets. Fruit described as edible; I have yet to sample. Adaptable species, tolerating everything from urban conditions to the best garden soils. Extremely salt- and wind-tolerant, and grows

Sabal palmetto, cabbage palm

Sabal minor

Sabal minor, dwarf palmetto

(happily) in coastal sands. Found wild in coastal forest, tidal flats, elevated areas in marshes. Have observed as far north as Ocean City, Maryland, where it was struggling. Grows 30 to 40 ft. high. National champion is 60 ft. by 14 ft. Lower zone 7 with protection. Typically, zones 8 to 11. Now being installed in increasing numbers in Athens landscapes, where it certainly appears out of place. This is the state tree of Florida and is displayed on the state flag of South Carolina, whose nickname is the "Palmetto State." Lower Coastal Plain of southeast Georgia and South Carolina into Florida.

I have tried a trio of smaller shrubby species—*Sabal etonia* (scrub palm, native to Florida, grows in dry, sunnier locations, Bahamas and Cuba), *S. louisiana* (considered slightly less hardy to zone 7, forms a slight trunk), and *S. mexicana* (*S. texana*)—with no success. The −3°F low temperature and back-to-back cold winters of 1984–85 and 1985–86 devastated marginal or borderline plants.

Sabal mexicana grows 20 to 50 ft. high; co-national champions are 48 ft. by 18 ft. and 50 ft. by 11 ft. Produces fragrant white flowers on 7- to 8-ft. panicles in spring and edible pulp on the one-seeded, dull black fruit. Only two native groves (less than 100 acres) remain in Texas of the original 40,000 acres of sabal palm forest.

Sabal minor, dwarf palmetto, grows 6 to 10 ft. high with large, fan-shaped leaves, up to 3 ft. across, each segment 1 to 3 ft. long, pointing forward and arching; petioles up to 5 ft. long. Co-national champions, 24 ft. by 12 ft. and 28 ft. by 13 ft. Leaves are deeply cut to the base, producing 30 to 40 dagger-like segments, varying from shiny dark green to blue-green in coloration. 'Glauca', a distinct blue-foliaged form, is in cultivation. Cream flowers in large panicles are followed by rounded, ⅓- to ½-in.-wide, dark brown to black fruit. Fruit production has been abundant in Athens. The stem usually is at or below ground level but with age may develop above ground. Forms suckering colonies in wet and poorly drained soils in the wild, often growing in heavy evergreen shade. Tolerates salt spray. Handsome foliage mass, textural accent, or foundation plant. Zones (6)7 to 11. Survived −5°F, leaf damage at 5°F. Native in moist forests, ravines, and bottomlands from North Carolina to Florida, Alabama, Texas, Oklahoma, and Arkansas.

CULTIVARS AND VARIETIES
Sabal 'Birmingham' is hardy to about 0°F and has survived subzero temperatures. Shrub-like in youth, forming a trunk with age. The lone parent tree was growing in Birmingham, Alabama; to my knowledge, offspring are seed-produced and may not be as cold hardy as the original.

Serenoa repens
saw palmetto

Almost a frightening experience in the wild, where the spreading trunks, covered with leaf bases and brown fiber, look like large snakes. Habit is dense, suckering, colonizing, forming large-spreading, impenetrable thickets. I walked the shoreline of the north end of Jekyll Island, Georgia, where the trunks are exposed by the pounding sea. Some are 9 to 12 in. thick, formidable antagonists to the ocean's eroding forces. The palmate leaves are 2 to 3 ft. wide, divided into 25 or 30 segments cut over halfway to the base. Each leaf segment is cleft and sharp to the touch. Additionally, the 3- to 4-ft.-long petioles have sharp saw-teeth on the basal portion. Leaf color is dark green, although bluish green to silver-green selections occur. Small, white flowers are followed by black, 1-in.-wide malodorous fruit. Grows in shade and sandy soils in the wild. Also found in wetter situations. I notice that coastal developments

MORE ▶

Serenoa repens, saw palmetto

Serenoa repens

Serenoa repens CONTINUED

are preserving the species by limiting construction and building boardwalks over established plantings. Grows 6 to 10 ft. high, spreading indefinitely. Conational champions 17 ft. by 4 ft. and 22 ft. by 7 ft. Zones 8 to 11. South Carolina to Florida and Louisiana.

Syagrus romanzoffianum

Syagrus romanzoffianum, queen palm

Syagrus romanzoffianum

syn. *Arecastrum romanzoffianum*
queen palm

I learned this species as *Arecastrum* and then was subjected to the *Syagrus* spelling bee. Nomenclature aside, queen palm is an elegant, large, single-trunked species with feathery, dark green (both surfaces) leaves. Leaves range from 8 to 15 ft. long, with the drooping leaflets up to 3 ft. long and the petiole entire. Flowers, cream, appear in large, drooping panicles, shaped like pampas-grass flowers or feather dusters. The 1-in.-long fruit mature yellow to rich orange. I first witnessed the species in H. P. Leu Gardens, Orlando, Florida, and from among their large collection, it was this aristocratic species that was forever imprinted upon my memory. The 1- to 2-ft.-wide trunk is gray and smooth with irregular bulges over its length. Best sited in well-drained soils in full sun. Displays moderate salt tolerance. Use for formal plantings, and as a specimen or street tree. Grows

×*Butyagrus nabonnandii*

40 ft. high and more. Zones 9 to 11. Expect some leaf damage at 25°F, but has recovered from temperatures in the mid teens. Argentina, Uruguay, Paraguay, southeast Brazil.

×*Butyagrus nabonnandii*, a hybrid between this and *Butia capitata*, offers the aesthetics of queen palm and the hardiness of *B. capitata*. Estimate zone 8 adaptability. Several observations indicate it is hardier than either parent.

Trachycarpus fortunei
Chinese windmill palm

'Tis difficult to reconcile that one is looking at a palm on the northwest coast of Scotland at the latitude of Newfoundland. But indeed, at Inverewe Garden this most hardy tree species grew with great resolve. The trunk, about 1 ft. in diameter, is usually smaller at the base, fattest toward the top and densely covered with brown, stringy fibers and old leaf bases. Identification is easy for this palm, especially if it is growing in zone

7 and upper zone 8, for there is nothing to confuse it with. The leaves are palmate, 2 to 3 ft. across, cut almost to the base with 40 to 50 segments arching near the tops, borne on 1½- to 2-ft. leaf stalks. Color is dark green, grayish below, the petiole rough and bumpy, but without teeth. The canopy is ovoid-globular with the lowest leaves often tatty. Needs tidying to keep it smiling. Small, yellow flowers borne in large panicles in early summer. Typically dioecious but sometimes both sexes on same tree. Fruit rounded, ⅓ in. wide, black covered with white bloom (wax). Has fruited abundantly in Georgia trials. Adaptable, full sun to partial shade, and grows in any soil except wet. Displays wind, drought, and salt tolerance. Grows slowly in colder climates so can be craftily engaged in foundation plantings. Good container plant or tropical look in annual/perennial plantings. Grows 10 to 20 ft. high, potential to 40 ft. Zones 8 and 9, with protection in 7; a 30-ft.-high plant grew in a protected corner of a churchyard in Athens, Georgia. Not a good doer in zone 9 and hotter. China, Taiwan, and Chusan Islands.

Several related species: *Trachycarpus takil*, Kumaon palm, 30 to 35 ft., and *T. wagnerianus*, windmill palm, to 20 ft., are listed as cold hardy to −5°F and −3°F, respectively. *Trachycarpus nanus*, a nearly groundcover-sized, trunkless palm, to 5 ft., is reasonably cold hardy to 0°F. *Trachycarpus martianus*, Khasia palm, is rated to 5°F.

Washingtonia robusta

Mexican fan or Washington palm

Common in Florida, this large-growing species has a slender trunk, rounded crown, and older leaves that persist, forming a dense skirt. The palmate leaves, divided halfway to the base, are bright green and 3 to 5 ft. across, with the tips slightly drooping and cottony threads. The 3- to 4-ft.-long petiole, reddish brown, is armed with prominent yellow-green spines.

MORE ▶

Trachycarpus fortunei

Trachycarpus fortunei

Trachycarpus fortunei, Chinese windmill palm

Trachycarpus fortunei

Washingtonia robusta CONTINUED

Slightly fragrant, white flowers are followed by black fruit. Prospers in dry, well-drained, sandy soils and full sun. The trunk is smooth toward the base, with leaf bases near the crown. Use as a specimen, in groupings, and for street plantings. Grows 40 to 80 ft. high. Zones 8 to 11; 20°F and below

Washingtonia robusta

result in leaf injury. Native to the Mexican state of Sonora.

In California, *Washingtonia filifera*, California or desert fan palm, is the preferred and native species. It is similar to *W. robusta* but with a thick trunk, and the long-petioled, 3- to 6-ft.-long leaves on a spine-edged leafstalk to 6 ft. long form a more open crown. Gray-green leaves are divided into numerous segments, which droop at the tips and are edged with white threads. Inflorescences, to 15 ft. long, are composed of white flowers and are followed by ¼ in.-wide, dark brown to black fruit. Grows to 60 ft. Tri-national champions are 68 ft. by 18 ft., 86 ft. by 21 ft., and 66 ft. by 19 ft. Slightly more cold hardy than *W. robusta*. Zones (7)8 to 11. Hardy to 15°F. Arizona, Baja California.

The principal characteristics that differentiate the two species follow.

In *Washingtonia robusta*, the petioles of young palms are brown and distinctly spiny; in *W. filifera*, petioles are green and relatively unarmed. In *W. robusta*, the basal sheath has a bright tawny-colored patch; *W. filifera* has no such patch. In *W. robusta*, the crown of mature specimens is dense and compact, whereas a mature *W. filifera* carries its leaves in a loose and open arrangement. The leaflets of *W. robusta* are stiff, and their cottony threads fall off with age; the leaflets of *W. filifera* are pendulous and swinging, and the white threads persist. Finally, the trunk of *W. robusta* is slender (slightly swollen at the base) and can get 100 ft. tall; the trunk of *W. filifera* is barrel-shaped, and the palm rarely exceeds 60 ft. in height. Hybrids are known between the two species, so intermediate characteristics are to be expected.

Washingtonia robusta, Mexican fan palm

Parkinsonia aculeata
Jerusalem thorn

Feathery, light, airy, small tree with bipinnately compound foliage composed of tiny, bright green leaflets. Habit is open-arching, broad-spreading, either single or multi-stemmed. The leaves range from 8 to 16 in. in length with ¼- to ½-in.-long, small, linear, rich green leaflets. The bark is green, becoming brown and fissured with age. Stems are armed with thorns at the nodes. The beautiful yellow flowers, with orange markings, ¾ to 1 in. wide, fragrant, open in spring and repeat in summer with new growth flushes. The fruit are gray-brown, 6-in.-long pods. On the Georgia Coastal Islands, the species performs magnificently in full sun and well-drained soil. Excellent drought and alkaline soil tolerance. Displays high degree of salt tolerance. Makes a small specimen tree; be careful in siting because of the thorns. Grows 15 to 20 ft. high and wide. Zones 8 to 11. Caribbean.

Parrotia persica
Persian parrotia

I love this tree: the clean summer foliage; the yellows, oranges, and reds of autumn; the cream, green, gray, and brown exfoliating bark; and the small, maroon-red flowers that glow on a late-winter day. Showy parts of the flowers are the stamens. Over the years, my travels have led me to many parrotias, no two alike. A 60-ft.-high specimen in the Jardin des Plantes in Paris and the 11-trunked national treasure, more than a century old, in the Arnold Arboretum are two of the finest specimens I have seen. The developing leaves are reddish purple to bronze, maturing to lustrous dark green, 2½ to 5 in. long,

MORE ▶

Parkinsonia aculeata

Parrotia persica

Parrotia persica

Parkinsonia aculeata, Jerusalem thorn

Parrotia persica CONTINUED

1 to 2½ in. wide. The foliage is seldom troubled by insects or diseases, although in recent years, Japanese beetle feeding has been pronounced. The species prefers moist, well-drained, acid to neutral soils in full sun to partial shade. Cooler climates are best, especially those with cooler night temperatures; however, several plants on the Georgia campus have performed spectacularly in the hottest and driest years on record. Utilize as a specimen plant, in the background of borders, or in groupings. Grows 20 to 40 ft. high, 15 to 30 ft. wide; many trees, especially in Europe, are wider than they are tall at maturity. Zones 4 to 8. Iran, Azerbaijan, Caspian Forest.

CULTIVARS AND VARIETIES

'Biltmore' is beautiful, venerable, low-branched, massively trunked, with rounded habit. Bark is striking.

'Jennifer Teates' is the best upright form (superior to 'Vanessa'), with tightly ascending branches, early leaf-

Parrotia persica fall color

Parrotia persica

Parrotia persica, Persian parrotia

ing, lustrous dark green, heat-tolerant foliage, prolific red-maroon flowers, 20 to 25 ft. by about 6 ft. Introduced by Alex Niemiera, Virginia Tech, and named after his wife.

'Pendula' is a confused entity in American horticulture. The true 'Pendula' has a stiff, umbrella-like, weeping habit that results in a dome-shaped configuration. What is commonly offered is a more or less horizontally branched shrub.

'Ruby Vase', with ruby-red young leaves, is a pretty selection.

'Vanessa' is more upright columnar-spreading than the species; not as dense or as upright as 'Jennifer Teates'. Fall color is a consistent vivid yellow.

Parrotia subaequalis

Chinese parrotia

I first observed this exciting Chinese species at the Arnold Arboretum and now have a 6-ft. cherished treasure in the new garden. Young trees are wide-spreading, splaying, if left to their own DNA devices. Staking to a central leader will be necessary under nursery production. The dull deep green, jagged-margined leaves, stellately pubescent (with star-shaped hairs), are 1½ to 3½ in. long, ¾ to 2 in. wide. Nary a leaf developed scorch symptoms in a full-sun setting with over 80 days at 90°F or above in Athens in 2010. Fall color proved spectacular as leaves turned deep maroon, then orange and red, with a few colorful leaves still present in late November. Leaves are frost tolerant: 28°F did not damage them. Plants in a 50-percent nursery shade structure developed superb orange-red fall coloration. Four to 15 red-purple stamens comprise each apetalous flower; fruit are two-valved, dehiscent, woody capsules with shiny brown seeds. Bark is similar to *Parrotia persica*, exfoliating to expose greenish white patches. In the wild, grows along streams, amid rocks, in an understory setting. Under cultiva-

MORE ▶

Parrotia persica 'Pendula'

Parrotia persica 'Vanessa'

Parrotia subaequalis CONTINUED

Parrotia subaequalis, Chinese parrotia, fall color

Parrotiopsis jacquemontiana

Parrotiopsis jacquemontiana

tion, appears adaptable to any well-drained, acid soil. Currently a collector's plant, but I envision robust garden acceptance with exposure. Roots readily from cuttings—an important asset for commercialization. Vigorous in zone 7, easily growing a foot or two per year with proper nutrition and water. Could be utilized for breeding with other Hamamelidaceae genera. Grows 20 to 30 ft. high in the wild with trunks 20 to 28 in. in diameter. Zones (5)6 to 7 are estimates. Critically endangered in the wild, where it grows in montane forests at about 2,000 ft. elevation. Eastern China.

Parrotiopsis jacquemontiana

A unique member of the witchhazel family (Hamamelidaceae) with coarsely toothed leaves that resemble those of *Hamamelis*, witchhazel. Rare in cultivation and probably reserved for the collector of biological antiquities. An upright, oval to rounded shrub with stiff branches and dense foliage—kind of unmistakable when confronted. The roundish dark green leaves, 2 to 3½ in. long and wide, seldom develop appreciable fall color. The true flowers are borne in small clusters (yellow stamens in groups of 15 to 24) in April and May, subtended by four to six, petal-like, ½- to 1-in.-long, white bracts. Flowered late March at JC Raulston Arboretum, Raleigh, North Carolina. Certainly the flowers do not overwhelm but are curiously interesting. Site in partial shade, although the plant will grow in full sun. Provide moist, acid, well-drained soil. Use for accent, for novelty, or to drive visitors loony. Grows 8 to 12 ft. high; observed a 20-ft.-high plant. Zones 5 to 7. Western Himalayas.

Parthenocissus henryana
silvervein creeper

For many years in Georgia, I observed this beautiful vine complete its seasonal cycles, yet have *never* seen it offered in southern commerce. Like *Parthenocissus quinquefolia* and *P. tricuspidata*, it is a true clinging vine, meaning small, cup-like holdfasts

MORE ▶

Parthenocissus henryana new growth

Parthenocissus henryana, silvervein creeper

Parthenocissus henryana CONTINUED
"glue" it to structures. The emerging leaves are bronze-purple, maturing to dark blue-green with silver veins above, purplish on the lower surface. In autumn, leaves become red to reddish purple. Best sited in some shade in moist, well-drained soil. Common in England and offers greater aesthetics than *P. quinquefolia* and *P. tricuspi-* *data*. Grows 15 ft. or more. Not as rampant as *P. quinquefolia* and *P. tricuspidata*. Zones (6)7 and 8. China.

Parthenocissus quinquefolia
Virginia creeper, woodbine

No vine is more evident in early fall than Virginia creeper, when the leaves develop flaming shades of orange and red. This species is a true clinging vine, with five to eight adhesive-tipped tendril branches that cling to any surface, including aluminum siding. The lustrous dark green leaves are composed of five (sometimes three) serrated leaflets, each 1½ to 4 (to 5) in. long. Yellowish green flowers occur under the leaves, followed by ¼-in.-wide, blue berries. Adaptable

Parthenocissus henryana fall color

Parthenocissus quinquefolia

Parthenocissus quinquefolia, Virginia creeper, on left

to sandy and heavy clay soils, in full sun or heavy shade. I have observed it growing in pure sand along the Atlantic Ocean. Japanese beetles relish the foliage. Requires considerable pruning to keep it tidy and in bounds. Can function as a groundcover or a high-climbing vine, 30 to 50 ft. high. Used, along with *Parthenocissus tricuspidata*, to cover campus buildings;

and climbs the tallest trees, sometimes draping itself over the high-rise branches and dangling as it descends. Zones 4 to 9. New England to Illinois, south to Florida and Mexico.
CULTIVARS AND VARIETIES
I observed a speckled, splashed cream-green leaf form that reverts to green. Star Showers® ('Monham') may be the same plant.

Parthenocissus tricuspidata

Boston ivy, Japanese creeper

This species is similar in most respects to *Parthenocissus quinquefolia*, except for the shape of its leaves, which are simple, generally three-lobed, and average 4 to 8 in. wide. Zones 4 to 8. Japan, central China.

MORE ▶

Parthenocissus quinquefolia

Parthenocissus quinquefolia fall color

Parthenocissus quinquefolia Star Showers®

Parthenocissus tricuspidata, Boston ivy

Parthenocissus tricuspidata fall color

Parthenocissus tricuspidata CONTINUED
CULTIVARS AND VARIETIES
'Beverley Brook' has large leaves that turn brilliant shades of red and scarlet in fall.

'Fenway Park', an Arnold Arboretum introduction, has brilliant yellow new growth that mellows to lime-green and turns orange and red in autumn.

'Ginza Lights' has leaves splashed pink and white, turning red in autumn.

Passiflora incarnata
wild passion vine, maypop
Native vine, almost invasive but with the most beautiful floral configuration of any flowering plant, which is best described as a complex of five petals, five sepals, a row (or two) of thread-like fringe above the petals, and five elevated anthers, each with a broad stigma that encircles three styles. Flowers, 2 to 3 in. wide, open from May through autumn, never in great numbers, the colors ranging from lavender to white. Leaves are three-lobed, dark green, 2 to 6 in. long and wide. Fruit are 1½- to 3-in.-wide, ovoid berries, green ripening to yellow, containing numerous dark brown seeds. Grows on moist to dry sites in nature, full sun to semi-shade. Overwinters as a rootstock. Climbs by tendrils, similar to grapes. Not utilized enough in modern gardens. Good on trellises, arbors, fences. Attracts butterflies. Grows 10 to 20 ft. but easily restrained by pruning. Zones 6 to 9. Pennsylvania to Illinois, Missouri, Oklahoma, south to Florida and Texas.

About 500 species worldwide, but only a few are in commerce. Considerable breeding for unique flower colors in England. *Passiflora caerulea*, blue passion flower, is semi-evergreen to evergreen in zones 9 to 11. Leaves are five-lobed. Flower colors vary from white to pale pink and blue. Fruit are orange. Brazil, Argentina.

Passiflora coccinea, red passion flower, is semi-evergreen to evergreen with brilliant scarlet flowers. Zones 10 and 11. Southern Venezuela, Peru, Bolivia, Brazil.

Paulownia tomentosa
royal paulownia
Royal paulownia is actually a weed species, much like *Morus alba*, common mulberry, and it has escaped from cultivation from New York to Georgia. In the standard frame of reference for shade trees, *Paulownia tomentosa* is a total loser. At Longwood Gardens in Kennett Square, Pennsylvania, however, there was the grandest allée imaginable of 70- to 80-ft. specimens. As part of the historical Longwood landscape, these

Parthenocissus tricuspidata 'Fenway Park'

Passiflora incarnata, wild passion vine

Passiflora incarnata

Passiflora caerulea, blue passion flower

558

aging (decrepit) trees were removed and replaced with . . . *Paulownia tomentosa*. The habit is rounded with large, stiff, coarse branches. The dark green leaves, significantly warm, fuzzy pubescent below, which average 5 to 10 in. long and wide, have the endearing characteristic of shedding in summer (variably) and fall. A single leaf gives the appearance of a small flying saucer on the lawn. Pale violet (lavender), 2-in.-long, foxglove-shaped flowers occur in 8- to 12-in.-long panicles before the leaves in April and May (late March to early April, Athens) and give off a vanilla fragrance. The 1- to 2-in.-long, ovoid, Pac-Man-shaped fruit

MORE ▶

Paulownia tomentosa

Paulownia tomentosa

Paulownia tomentosa, royal paulownia

Paulownia fortunei

are borne in uncountable quantities, and each fruit houses up to 2,000 small, winged seeds. Royal paulownia is exceedingly adaptable. It has been used to revegetate strip-mined land. For residential landscapes, the species has few redeeming qualities. Grows 30 to 40 ft. high and wide. Zones 5 to 9. China.

Paulownia fortunei produces cream, flushed with lilac, foxglove-like, 3- to 4-in. flowers, in immense panicles. Large trees in Aiken, South Carolina, are impressive in flower. Old fruit persist like bad company. Grows 50 to 70 ft. high. Zones 7 and 8. China, Taiwan.

Paxistima canbyi
Canby paxistima

Such a nifty, refined, evergreen, native groundcover, yet *nowhere* common. Not sure that I understand the reason for its paucity, but in the finest manifestations, it is both functional and beautiful. Small, linear- to narrow-oblong leaves, ¼ to 1 in. long, are lustrous dark green, usually finely serrate, with revolute margins. Leaves may develop slight bronzing in winter. Flowers, green or reddish, minimally exciting, are borne in ½-in.-wide cymes in May. Adaptable but requires well-drained, calcareous, higher pH

Paxistima canbyi, Canby paxistima

Paxistima canbyi

soils, in sun to partial shade. Attractive in combination with broadleaf evergreens. Grows 12 in. by 3 to 5 ft. Zones 3 to 6(7). Mountains of Virginia and West Virginia, chiefly in calcareous soils.

Persea borbonia
redbay

A broadleaf evergreen native shrub or tree that grows in standing water yet also withstands drier conditions. On the Outer Banks of North Carolina, plants were growing in water; on Georgia's Jekyll Island, a 40-ft.-high tree was prospering in sandy soil. Leaves are lustrous medium green, 2 to 6 in. long, becoming yellow-green in exposed (to wind or sun) locations. The ovoid-rounded, dark blue to black, ½-in.-long drupes ripen in October. Useful for naturalizing in difficult sites. Leaves are often infested with a gall and appear swollen, water-soaked, and ugly. Grows 20 to 30 ft. high, two-thirds to equal this in spread. A relatively new insect, redbay ambrosia beetle, is wreaking havoc on this and other members of the Lauraceae; it bores holes and carries a fungus into the stems and trunks, resulting in wilt-type symptoms and eventually death.

MORE ▶

Persea borbonia, redbay

Persea borbonia leaves with gall

Persea borbonia

561

Persea borbonia CONTINUED

Currently, reported in coastal South Carolina, Georgia, and Florida. Plants on the Georgia campus were defoliated or killed to the ground at −3°F. Zones (7)8 and 9. Southern Delaware to Florida, westward to southeastern Texas.

Phellodendron amurense
Amur corktree

Amur corktree is a boldly branched, broad-spreading tree with a short trunk. Its corky, gray-brown bark accounts for the common name. The dark green leaves are composed of five to 11 leaflets, each 2½ to 4½ in. long. Fall color is often bronzy yellow

Phellodendron amurense, Amur corktree, fall color

Phellodendron amurense

Phellodendron amurense

Phellodendron amurense

Phellodendron sachalinense, Sakhalin corktree

to rich yellow but is fleeting. The yellowish green flowers are inconspicuous, but the ⅓- to ½-in.-wide, black fruit are often borne in great profusion on female trees. Plants require moist, acid or near neutral, well-drained soils and full sun. Amur corktree has received plaudits for its urban tolerance, but my experiences indicate otherwise. I have seen great specimens of this species and its relatives in many arboreta and on campuses, but I do not remember a single quality plant in an urban situation. If the fine trees that I have seen at the Minnesota, Morton, and Arnold arboreta could be duplicated in the urban landscape, the nursery industry could not produce enough trees to meet the demand. Utilize the species in a broad expanse of lawn where stress is minimal. Grows 30 to 45 ft. high and wide. Zones 4 to 7. Northern and northeastern China, Japan.

Phellodendron lavalleei, Lavalle corktree, and *P. sachalinense*, Sakhalin corktree, grow larger, as much as 50 to 60 ft. high. So similar to *P. amurense*, some recent taxonomic thinking lumps these species with it.
CULTIVARS AND VARIETIES
His Majesty™, from my data collection, is the best of the male introductions. This, Eye Stopper™ ('Longenecker'), and 'Macho' grow in proximity at Milliken Arboretum, Spartanburg, South Carolina. His Majesty™ has the best form, upright spreading, broad vase-shaped, fastest growth and, to date, maleness. Also, it extends the northern adaptability, reportedly hardy in zone 3.

Philadelphus
mockorange
Philadelphus species, some 65 in number, thrive with neglect. They withstand heavy clay or lighter soils, acid or high pH. Require full sun for maximum flowering. Best in borders. Essentially a single-season flowering shrub, lacking grace, fall color, and fruit. Still, the legendary mockorange fragrance lends credence to at least the thought of planting *one*. The large number of hybrids are astronomically mixed in the trade, and my attempt to track 'Belle Étoile', for example, was an odyssey. Reading the Gosslers' *Best Hardy Shrubs* (2009), I learned about their frustration chasing the same plant. Happy Philadelphing!

Philadelphus coronarius
sweet mockorange
This species and its best cultivars offer 1- to 1½-in.-wide, four-petaled, fragrant, white flowers in May and June. The rest of the garden year, the plant fades into the background. Typically a large, rounded shrub, with stiff,

Philadelphus coronarius, sweet mockorange

Philadelphus coronarius 'Aureus'

MORE ▶

Philadelphus coronarius CONTINUED

straight, ascending branches that arch with age. Considerable garden space is required. The 1½- to 4-in.-long, dark green leaves are remotely serrated, with three to five main veins. Grows 10 to 12 ft. high and wide. Zones 4 to 8. Southeastern Europe, Asia Minor. CULTIVARS AND VARIETIES
'Aureus' offers yellow foliage and the typical fragrant white flowers. It is used extensively in Europe, where cooler temperatures keep the foliage more vibrant. More compact than the species. Grows 8 to 10 ft. high.

'Variegatus' has leaves irregularly bordered with creamy white. Somewhat weak growing, but a rather dainty shrub when well grown. Flowers are fragrant. Ultimately 4 to 6 ft. high and wide.

Philadelphus inodorus
mockorange

Native southeastern member of the *Philadelphus* clan that to most gardeners is represented only by *Philadelphus coronarius*. I first identified the plant 32 years past, growing in the shade garden area of the University's Botanical Garden. I kept smelling the flowers with no resultant odor detected, and the meaning behind the name *P. inodorus* was brought into nasal focus. Habit is upright-oval, multi-stemmed, with opposite, 2- to 4-in.-long, dark green, three-veined, serrate to entire leaves engulfing the upper one-third to one-half of the plant. The four-petaled, white flowers are 1 to 1½ in. in diameter and are borne in terminal axillary cymes

of three in mid May (Athens). Flowers are present from May into June and are followed by small, brown capsules. Tough plant that requires only sun, and moderately moist, well-drained soil for maximum effect; however, plants in half shade flower respectably. Good border plant, as a filler along woodland edges, and for a screen in partial shade. Grows 6 to 10 ft. high, 6 to 8 ft. wide. Zones (5)6 to 9. Pennsylvania to North Carolina to Georgia and Mississippi.

Philadelphus pubescens, hairy mockorange, has leaves gray pubescent on their undersides and flowers borne in racemes, otherwise similar to *P. inodorus*. Flowered in June at Hillier with ever-so-slight fragrance. Zones 6 to 9. Illinois, south to Tennessee and Arkansas.

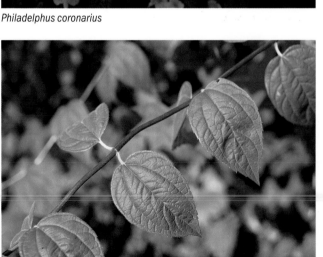

Philadelphus coronarius

Philadelphus coronarius 'Variegatus'

Philadelphus inodorus, mockorange

Philadelphus inodorus

Philadelphus Hybrids

Philadelphus hybrids offer a great variety of growth habits and floral characteristics, including a good selection of flower sizes and colors (many with a purplish blotch in the middle of the corolla), single or double flowers, and tremendous differences in fragrance. Among the more garden-worthy are *Philadelphus ×cymosus* (*P. ×lemoinei × P. grandiflorus*), *P. ×lemoinei*, and *P. ×virginalis* (*P. ×lemoinei × P. nivalis* 'Plena'). When I visited the Royal Botanic Garden Edinburgh in July, many mockoranges were flowering. In a fragrance test, I discovered some had delicious fragrance, others had none. Since fragrance is the main attribute of

MORE ▶

Philadelphus 'Belle Étoile'

Philadelphus 'Minnesota Snowflake'

Philadelphus 'Belle Étoile'

Philadelphus 'Silver Showers'

Philadelphus 'Sybille'

Philadelphus Hybrids CONTINUED

the plant, I would sniff before purchasing.

Hybrid cultivars with excellent cold hardiness include 'Frosty Morn', 'Minnesota Snowflake', 'Snowdwarf', and 'Snowgoose'. 'Natchez', an 8- to 10-ft.-high shrub, has 1½-in.-wide, slightly fragrant flowers that completely cover the foliage in May. One of the more popular in the Southeast. Susceptible to cercospora leaf spot.

'Belle Étoile', 'Beauclerk', 'Manteau d'Hermine', 'Silver Showers', and 'Sybille' are Dirr recommendations. All are fragrant. 'Belle Étoile', 'Beauclerk', and 'Sybille' have a pink to purple-stained eye. Intense heat reduces the potency of corolla color in the South.

Philadelphus 'Manteau d'Hermine'

Phillyrea angustifolia

Phillyrea angustifolia

Closely related to *Osmanthus* and often confused with that genus. The habit is dense and rounded with smallish, narrow, lustrous dark green, 1- to 1½-in.-long, essentially entire, leaves. Small, white, fragrant flowers open in spring, followed by blackish fruit. Like *Osmanthus* species, grows in sun to moderate shade in any well-drained soil. Useful for screens, hedges, and fillers. Grows 10 ft. high and wide. A striking specimen at RHS Garden, Wisley, was 8 to 10 ft. by 12 to 14

ft. Zones 7 to 9, 10 on West Coast. China, Japan.

Phillyrea latifolia has 1- to 2½-in.-long, ovate, sharply serrate, lustrous dark green leaves. Greenish white flowers in axillary clusters open in spring. A 20 ft. by 12 ft. plant has survived for over 40 years on the Georgia campus in a shade-laden habitat. Does not fit (exactly) the species profile, and I suspect it is f. *spinosa* with more narrow, serrate leaves. At −3°F, leaves were killed but no stem damage. Zones 7 and 8(9). Southern Europe, Asia Minor.

Phillyrea latifolia

Photinia davidiana

syn. *Stranvaesia davidiana*

Chinese stranvaesia

A name change from the generic *Stranvaesia* to *Photinia* has muddied the taxonomic waters, but the plant characteristics remain the same. Tends toward a wide-spreading, shrub-like habit but can be grown as a small tree. The 2- to 5-in.-long, ⅜- to 1¾-in.-wide, *entire* (the major *Photinia* species discussed herein all have serrated leaves), lustrous dark green, evergreen leaves turn a pretty red as the old foliage abscises. Flowers, white, are borne in 3-in.-wide, lax, hairy corymbs in May and June and are followed by globose, ¼- to ⅜-in.-wide, bright red, long-persistent fruit. Performs best in moist, slightly acid, organic, well-drained soil in full to moderate shade. May be susceptible to fireblight. Pretty in a shrub border or mixed with needle evergreens. Will never become mainstream. Have "run into" plants in the Northwest, England,

MORE ▶

Photinia davidiana

Photinia davidiana

Photinia davidiana, Chinese stranvaesia

567

Photinia davidiana CONTINUED
and Ireland. Potential to 30 ft. high, usually smaller. Zones (5)6 and 7. Western China.
CULTIVARS AND VARIETIES
Several, including 'Fructu Luteo' (yellow fruit), 'Palette' (pink, white, green variegated leaves), Salicifolia Group (narrow leaves), and Undulata Group

(wavy-margined leaves). The latter grew at the Arnold Arboretum, shrubby habit to 5 ft. by 10 ft.

Photinia ×*fraseri*
Fraser or redtip photinia
Both a blessing and a curse; at one time it was the premier hedging and screening plant in the Southeast,

where millions were planted. The beautiful ruby-red new growth has enticed gardeners worldwide to utilize the plant, and it remains common in California and the Southwest. The allure and economic power of an aesthetic hedging plant are phenomenal; one Georgia nursery's wholesale sales were $3 million in redtips out

Photinia ×*fraseri* new growth

Photinia ×*fraseri*

Photinia ×*fraseri*, Fraser photinia

568

of $20 million total sales. Unfortunately, a devastating fungal disease (caused by *Entomosporium maculatum*) has wreaked havoc. In its finest form, an upright, oval, broadleaf evergreen shrub becoming tree-like if left to itself. Often pruned into a block of red and green for screening purposes, it makes a pretty small tree when trained to a single stem. In fact, some southern cities have used the species for street tree plantings. The young leaves emerge ruby-red, mature to dark green, and subsequent growth is also reddish turning to green. White, malodorous flowers occur in 5- to 6-in.-wide, terminal corymbs in April. Red fruit mature in late summer. At its finest, one of the most adaptable plants, growing in hot, dry, miserable soils in sun to moderate shade but thriving where moisture and sunlight are available. Also quite salt-tolerant. Grows 10 to 15 (to 20) ft. high. Zones 7 to 9, 10 on the West Coast. Originated as a chance seedling at the Fraser Nurseries, Birmingham, Alabama, around 1940.

CULTIVARS AND VARIETIES
A redtip explosion of introductions, with Cracklin Red™ ('Parred'), Dynamo Bronze™ ('Parsub'), Dynamo Red™ ('Parsur'), and Fireball™ ('Parbri') the newest. Supposedly more disease-resistant; time will tell. Observed Cracklin Red™ and Fireball™ with minimal enthusiasm. As the hamburger lady said, "Where's the beef?"

'Red Robin', with darker ruby-red foliage and more rounded, spreading habit, is popular in Europe.

'Robusta' is larger growing, more tree-like, with coppery red leaves; a 25-ft.-high specimen grew in the Hillier Arboretum.

Photinia glabra
Japanese photinia
Quite a handsome broadleaf evergreen shrub with red new growth that settles to a life of green. One of the parents of *Photinia* ×*fraseri* and, unfortunately, the carrier of the genes for susceptibility to leaf spot. Several plants on the Georgia campus have formed dense oval-rounded outlines. The leaves are 1½ to 3½ in. long, emerge rich bronzy red, finally glossy dark green, and are without hairs (hence, *glabra*). Flowers and fruit are similar to *P.* ×*fraseri*, except smaller. The limiting factor is leaf spot, so

MORE ▶

Photinia ×*fraseri*

Photinia ×*fraseri* Cracklin Red™

Photinia ×*fraseri* 'Red Robin'

Photinia glabra 'Rubens'

Photinia glabra CONTINUED

Photinia glabra 'Variegata'

Photinia serratifolia

where annual rainfall is high, resist the temptation to plant. Grows 10 to 12 ft. high and wide. Zones (7)8 to 10. Plants were killed to the ground at −3°F in Athens. Japan, China.

CULTIVARS AND VARIETIES
Like the species, these prosper in European climates and the West Coast. 'Rubens', a bright, bronze-red leaf form, and 'Variegata', pink and bronze-red new leaves, maturing white and green, are reasonably common; 'Parfait', 'Pink Lady', and 'Roseomarginata' are other variegated forms.

Photinia serratifolia
Chinese or oriental photinia

Although uncommon, it is the most disease-resistant species and, in its own aesthetic matrix, a respectable broadleaf evergreen shrub or tree. Habit is upright in youth, gradually evolving into an oval-rounded form. Makes a respectable small tree and, if trained single-stemmed, could be utilized along streets. The new leaves are apple-green to bronze-tinted, maturing lustrous dark green. Immense clusters of stinky, white flowers appear in late March and early April. With the advent of autumn, the ¼-in.-wide fruit turn their characteristic red. Fruit persist into winter and are foraged by the birds. Stray seedlings pop up in fencerows and woodland habitats, the leaves strongly cut and incised like holly. As leaves mature, the serrations become less dramatic and uniform; actually difficult to believe the young leaves come from the same species. Prospers in any soil except wet, in full sun to moderate shade. Could prove useful for screens, hedges, and as a small tree. Does not have the calling-card red new growth of *Photinia ×fraseri* and *P. glabra* but is the preferred choice because of high disease resistance. Grows 20 to 25 (to 30) ft. high, about two-thirds to equal that in spread. Witnessed a 50-ft.-high specimen in England. Zones 6 to 9, 10 on the West Coast. China.

Photinia serratifolia new growth

Photinia serratifolia, Chinese photinia

CULTIVARS AND VARIETIES
'Green Giant' is an oval-rounded form, 30 to 45 ft. high, 20 to 30 ft. wide, with apple-green new growth, lustrous dark green at maturity; selected by the author from the University of Georgia campus.

Photinia villosa
oriental photinia

Not a well-known shrub, but certainly worthy of consideration, as long as fireblight is not a serious problem. Oriental photinia offers excellent red fruit and variable yellow, orange, and red fall color. The species is a large, multi-stemmed shrub with an irregular, obo-void crown. It can also be trained as a small tree. The dark green leaves are 1½ to 3½ in. long, finely and sharply serrated, densely pubescent below. White flowers appear in 1- to 2-in.-wide corymbs in April (Athens), May, and June, but they are not particularly effective. The bright red, ⅓-in.-long fruit ripen in October and persist into winter. Provide moist, acid, well-drained soils, in full sun. Best used in the shrub border, although I have seen full-grown specimen plants that were effective. Grows 10 to 15 ft. high, generally less in spread. Zones 4 to 7. Japan, Korea, China.

CULTIVARS AND VARIETIES
'Village Shade', with more tree-like, vase-shaped habit, dark green foliage, and abundant flower and fruit production, was introduced by the JC Raulston Arboretum.

Physocarpus opulifolius
common ninebark

Although native to the United States, this species is more common in European gardens, particularly the golden-foliaged forms. The advent of red-purple leaf introductions has increased enthusiasm for the species in American gardens. Common ninebark is a tough, durable shrub that becomes dense and rounded

MORE ▶

Physocarpus opulifolius

Physocarpus opulifolius

Photinia villosa

Photinia villosa

Photinia villosa, oriental photinia

571

Physocarpus opulifolius, common ninebark

with age. The brown bark exfoliates in shaggy sheets and offers winter interest. The medium green, 1- to 3-in.-long leaves, usually with three to five lobes, may develop yellowish to bronze fall color. White to slightly pink-tinged flowers are borne in 1- to 2-in.-wide corymbs along the length of the shoot in May (Athens) and June. The inflated fruit ripen in September and October and vary in color from green to red. The species is adaptable to all conditions, probably even nuclear attacks, and once established, requires a bulldozer for removal. For use as a large foliage mass, screen, or hedge, it has possibilities. Grows 5 to 10 ft. high, 6 to 10 ft. wide. Zones 2 to 7. Observed numerous plants in the

Physocarpus opulifolius Diabolo®

Physocarpus opulifolius Coppertina™

Physocarpus opulifolius Summer Wine™

Physocarpus opulifolius 'Dart's Gold'

wilds of Virginia and North Carolina, primarily along streams and based on locations, at times flooded. Quebec to Michigan, south to Virginia and Tennessee.

CULTIVARS AND VARIETIES
Absolutely phenomenal the number of purple-leaf cultivars since the introduction of Diabolo® ('Monlo'), an 8- to 10-ft.-high and -wide form patented in 2000. The availability of purple genes from this cultivar was the impetus

for continued breeding. I witnessed seedlings from Diabolo®, almost all red-purple. Too many similar types have been introduced, and it is now a commercial free-for-all. The compact types are potentially more serviceable in contemporary landscapes. Mildew has surfaced as a serious problem on Diabolo®.

Center Glow™, Burgundy Candy™ ('Podaras 1'), Caramel Candy™ ('Podaras 2'), Coppertina™ ('Mindia'),

Lady in Red™ (Ruby Spice™, 'Tuilad'), and Summer Wine™ ('Seward') are purple-leaf types. My take is the greater the heat, the less intense the purple, although a gardening colleague from the Memphis area sent photos of deep purple, almost purple-black leaf color on Summer Wine™.

'Dart's Gold' is smaller than 'Luteus' and has better yellow foliage color. With the heat of summer, however, the color diminishes or is lost completely. Worthwhile for spring and early summer foliage color. Specimens are often cut back to encourage new shoot extensions.

Lemon Candy™ ('Podaras 3') with chartreuse leaves grows 2 to 2½ ft. high, 2 to 3 ft. wide.

'Luteus', an old standby, has yellowish foliage that gradually changes to yellowish green and finally to almost green. Large shrub. Grows 8 to 10 ft. high and wide.

Picea abies
Norway spruce
The most common spruce for general landscape use, *Picea abies* has a pyramidal outline, with a strong central leader, horizontal secondary branches, and pendulous tertiary branches. It is an extremely dominant focal point in the average landscape. Needs ample space to spread

MORE ▶

Picea abies, Norway spruce

Picea abies

573

Picea abies 'Nidiformis'

Picea abies 'Pendula'

its limbs. The lustrous dark green needles average ½ to 1 in. long and maintain their color throughout the winter as well as any evergreen. The 4- to 6-in.-long cones are purple-violet to greenish purple in youth, finally light brown. Transplant balled-and-burlapped or container-grown material into moderately moist, acid, well-drained soils. Have read that pH 4 to 7.2 is a suitable range. This species is tremendously adaptable, except to high heat. Best used in groupings or perhaps as a specimen evergreen. Grows 40 to 60 ft. high, 25 to 30 ft. wide. Zones 2 to 7. Northern and central Europe.

CULTIVARS AND VARIETIES
These number in the hundreds, but only a selected few are available from the average nursery. (I did unearth one wholesale grower who listed 36 forms.)

'Nidiformis' is appropriately named bird's nest spruce because of the depression in the middle of its tight, compact, mounded habit. Makes a good rock garden or foundation plant. Not exactly dainty. Grows 3 to 6 ft. high and wide.

'Pendula' may be the generic name for a number of weeping types. No two are exactly alike, but all tend to splay their limbs in a wild, often awkward, weeping configuration. Certainly a great novelty plant and a conversation piece at parties.

'Pumila' is a dwarf—flattened, quite broad, 3 to 4 ft. high, wider at maturity. Much confusion under this name.

Picea breweriana
Brewer spruce

Among the most elegant of all cone-bearing evergreens because of the graceful, pendulous tertiary branches. Habit in most trees I observed is broad-pyramidal. Dark green, glossy needles, 1 to 1½ in. long, radiate equally around the stem. Cones cylindrical-oval, 3 to 6 in. long to 1½ in. wide, are purple when opening, red-brown at maturity. Appears to be climate-specific and not suited to hot, dry environments. If *Picea breweriana* was an easy garden companion, every gardener would opt for one. Estimate 30 to 50 ft. under cultivation. Have yet to witness any over 40 ft. Zone 5(6). Found at about 7,000 ft. elevation in Siskiyou Mountains of California and Oregon.

Picea glauca
white spruce

White spruce is quite popular in the Midwest, Northeast, and West. Side by side with the more popular Norway and Colorado spruces (*Picea abies* and *P. pungens*, respectively), however, it has no chance with the average consumer. Habit is densely pyramidal, compact, and symmetrical, with ascending branches. The ½- to ¾-in.-long needles are pale green to

MORE ▶

Picea glauca, white spruce

Picea breweriana, Brewer spruce

Picea glauca

Picea breweriana

glaucous green, inspiring little emotion. The cylindrical, pendulous, 1- to 2½-in.-long cones are the smallest of the cones of commonly cultivated spruces; they are green in youth, maturing to pale brown. Culture is essentially like that of *P. abies*, and it withstands wind, heat, cold, drought, and crowding. Useful as a specimen, in a mass planting, or as a hedge or windbreak. Grows 40 to 60 ft. high, 10 to 20 ft. wide. Zones 2 to 5(6). Common in Maine, where I have observed pretty blue-needled forms. Labrador to Alaska, south to New York, Minnesota, and Montana.

CULTIVARS AND VARIETIES
'Conica', often termed dwarf Alberta spruce or dwarf white spruce, is a broad-conical form, with light green, ¼- to ½-in.-long needles that radiate around the stem like a bottlebrush. It is probably the best known and most widely sold dwarf conifer in the United States. Numerous cultivars of 'Conica' with blue, variegated needles and more compact habits are known. Grows 10 to 12 ft. high in 25 to 30 years. Susceptible to spider mites.

Picea omorika
Serbian spruce
Perhaps my favorite spruce, although it is difficult to choose between this and *Picea orientalis*. Mature plants are elegant, and even small plants have character. Serbian spruce has a remarkably slender trunk and short, ascending or drooping branches on a narrow-pyramidal framework. Consid-

Picea glauca 'Conica', dwarf Alberta spruce

Picea omorika, Serbian spruce

Picea omorika

erable variation in habit is evident in any seed-grown population, however. The ½- to 1-in.-long needles are flattish, lustrous dark green, with two silver bands. The 1¼- to 2-in.-long, pendulous, violet-purple cones turn shiny cinnamon-brown at maturity. A formal evergreen best reserved for specimen use, but also quite good in groupings of threes or fives. Adaptable and deserving of wider use. Prospers in high pH soils. A good choice for eastern and midwestern gardens. Grows 50 to 60 ft. high, 20 to 25 ft. wide. Zones 4 to 7. Southeastern Europe.

Picea orientalis
oriental spruce

To see her is to love her. This species matures to a shining, black-green pyramid in an ocean of landscape. It develops a dense, compact, narrow-pyramidal habit, with horizontal or pendulous branches. The lustrous, almost black-green needles are ¼ to ½ in. long, the shortest of the needles of cultivated species. The males are attractive carmine-red, strawberry-shaped cones. Female cones are 2 to 4 in. long and 1 in. wide, reddish purple in youth, maturing to brown. Tolerates infertile, gravelly, or clay soils. Notable specimens occur in the Midwest. Makes a great specimen conifer but is extremely formal. Grows 50 to 60 ft. high, 10 to 15 ft. wide. Zones 4 to 7. Caucasus, Asia Minor.

Picea orientalis, oriental spruce

Picea orientalis young female cones

Picea orientalis mature female cones

Picea pungens

Colorado spruce

A most popular specimen tree, Colorado spruce is used throughout the northern states into the West. Stiffly conical-pyramidal in habit, with densely set, horizontal whorls of branches that skirt the ground. The plant is so thick and the needles so prickly that it would be impossible to lob a cat through it. The four-sided needles, ¾ to 1¼ in. long, range in color from green to gray-green, blue-green, or silver-blue. Female cones, green with violet bloom (wax), average 2 to 4 in. long, and the tips of the scales are wavy. Cones mature light to yellow-brown. Withstands virtually any soil, except those that are exceedingly moist. Not suitable for zone 7 in the Southeast, as the high night temperatures limit growth. Often used as a specimen plant, although it can detract from the total landscape. Grows 30 to

Picea pungens var. *glauca* 'Hoopsii'

Picea pungens var. *glauca*, blue spruce

Picea pungens var. *glauca* 'Glauca Pendula'

Picea pungens var. *glauca* 'Montgomery'

Picea pungens var. *glauca* 'Thompsenii'

60 ft. high, 10 to 20 ft. wide. Zones 2 to 7. Western United States.

CULTIVARS AND VARIETIES
Numerous blue-needled seedlings with various growth habits—most notably those of var. *glauca* (Glauca Group)—have inspired the common name "blue spruce."

'Fat Albert' is a cutting-produced clone with a wide, pyramidal habit and excellent, rich blue needle color.

'Glauca Pendula' is a blue-needled, sprawling, spreading form that, when staked, forms a weeping outline.

'Hoopsii' is an old standard. It has a dense, pyramidal form and extremely glaucous blue needles.

'Moerheimii' is another old cultivar. It too has rich blue foliage, but it tends to be more open in habit than some of the others.

'Montgomery' is silver-blue needled, relatively compact, 6 to 8 ft. by 3 to 4 ft.

MORE ▶

Picea pungens var. *glauca*

Picea pungens var. *glauca*

579

Picea pungens CONTINUED

'Thompsenii', with its glaucous silver-blue foliage and symmetrical, pyramidal habit, is one of the best.

Picea rubens

red spruce

A drive along 441 to Newfound Gap in Tennessee exposes one to numerous red spruces, each easily discernible for pyramidal habit and lustrous dark green needles. The needles are ½ to ⅝ in. long, borne on light reddish brown, first-year stems. Cones are 1¼ to 2 in. long, purplish green at first, maturing reddish brown. Requires ample moisture, acid, well-drained soil, and cool temperatures. Not an everyday spruce like Norway. Common along the Blue Ridge Parkway in the highest peaks of North Carolina and Virginia and increasing in abundance into Maine (where I bump into it in concert with *Picea glauca*) and Nova Scotia. Grows 60 to 70 ft. high in cultivation; national champion is 147 ft. high. Zones 3 to 5.

Picea sitchensis

Sitka spruce

Bonnie and I drove a million (seemed that way) miles to visit the Hoh Rain Forest on Washington's Olympic Peninsula. Was it worth it? Indeed, as we walked/stumbled through the magnificent Sitka spruce forest and saw seedlings germinating in the arms of their mothers—fallen trees, left in place, slowly decaying. This is a tall, sky-scraping timber tree, not an everyday landscape conifer. Needles are ¾ to 1 in. long, dark green, with prickly apices and two glaucous bands below. Cones, thick as mulch in the Hoh Rain Forest, are 2½ to 4 in. long, pale yellowish to reddish brown. Suited only for high moisture climates; observed in Scotland, where it is utilized for reforestation. National champion is 191 ft. high. Zones 6 and 7. Alaska to California.

Picrasma quassioides

Indian quassiawood

Rare. Worthy? I will allow the reader to decide. I have a plantsman's affinity for the species and am at a loss to explain its remoteness in cultivation (nor have I noted any recent nursery availability). It is a deciduous tree with

Picea sitchensis, Sitka spruce

Picea rubens, red spruce

Picea rubens

Picrasma quassioides, Indian quassiawood

a beautiful round-headed outline, its foliage rich green in summer, yellow, perhaps orange and red in fall. The compound-pinnate leaves, 10 to 14 in. long, are composed of nine to 15 leaflets. Flowers are yellow-green, fruit red; neither have I experienced. Adapted to acid and calcareous soils. Grows 20 to 40 ft. high and wide. Zones 6 and 7 (not totally known). Japan, Korea, Taiwan, China, India.

Pieris floribunda
mountain pieris

A diminutive broadleaf evergreen species with a broad-mounded outline and dark green leaves. White flowers occur in upright, 2- to 4-in.-long, racemose panicles in April. The floral effect is not as striking as that of *Pieris japonica*, and this

MORE ▶

Picrasma quassioides fall color

Pieris floribunda, mountain pieris

Pieris floribunda

Pieris floribunda CONTINUED

species is more difficult to propagate and not as readily available. Once established, however, it shows bulldog tenacity. Resistant to lace bugs. Useful in shady areas of the garden. Grows 2 to 6 ft. high, equal or greater in spread. Walked among 6-ft.-high colonies along the Blue Ridge Parkway in the Pisgah National Forest. Zones 4 to 6. Virginia to Georgia.

Pieris floribunda × *P. japonica* Hybrids

Although they are susceptible to lace bugs, the hybrids between *Pieris floribunda* and *P. japonica* share some of the resistance to lace bugs that is found in *P. floribunda*. Someone once commented to me that *P. floribunda* would consistently die out in the Atlanta area, but the hybrids would persist. Perhaps there is much greater heat tolerance in the hybrids.

CULTIVARS AND VARIETIES
'Brouwer's Beauty' offers the best features of both parents. It has yellow-green new foliage that matures to shiny dark green. Deep purplish red buds open to white flowers in horizontal, slightly arched panicles. Grows 6 ft. high and wide. Not as cold hardy as *Pieris floribunda*.

'Eco-Snowball', 'Karenoma', and 'Spring Snow' are other notable hybrids.

Pieris 'Karenoma'

Pieris formosa var. *forrestii* 'Forest Flame'

Pieris formosa var. *forrestii* 'Wakehurst'

Pieris 'Brouwer's Beauty'

Pieris formosa var. *forrestii* 'Wakehurst'

Pieris formosa var. *forrestii*

Himalayan pieris

One of the most beautiful of all *Pieris* species, with electric-red new growth that literally stops people in their tracks. During our English garden tours, this plant receives as much attention as any. The new growth transitions from red to cream then to green, and any subsequent new growth is similar in coloration. The habit is quite dense, eventually rounded in outline. The 2- to 4-in.-long evergreen leaves are larger than other *Pieris* species. Flowers, in large terminal panicles to 6 in. long, appear in late winter to spring, typically March. The urn-shaped, 1/3-in.-long, fragrant flowers are effective for four to six weeks. A great conversation piece and unbelievably colorful in a border, especially in a cool, moist environment akin to San Francisco and the Pacific Northwest. Provide well-drained soil. Grows 10 ft. high and wide. Zones 8 to 10 on the West Coast. Western China, Myanmar.

CULTIVARS AND VARIETIES
Two relatively common selections in Europe include 'Forest Flame', with brilliant red leaves, and 'Wakehurst', with similar foliage coloration.

Pieris japonica

Japanese pieris

A broadleaf evergreen of the first order that deserves consideration in any garden where shade and moist soil are available. It is one of the best ericaceous plants for the Midwest, particularly in calcareous soils. In its best forms, the habit is dense, almost haystack-shaped, with branches reaching to the ground. The 1½- to 3½-in.-long, lustrous dark green leaves are lovely through the seasons. The new growth displays shades of apple-green, bronze, and rich red, and several cultivars offer excellent red color on new foliage. Urn-shaped, fragrant, white flowers, ¼ to ⅜ in. long, are borne in 3- to 6-in.-long and -wide, racemose panicles in March and April, and are effective for two to three weeks. Remove spent flowers. Next year's flower buds are developed by July or August and evident through fall and winter. For maximum performance, provide moist, organic-laden soils, in partial shade. Lace bugs are serious pests

MORE ▶

Pieris japonica, Japanese pieris

Pieris japonica new growth

Pieris japonica 'Mountain Fire'

Pieris japonica 'Temple Bells'

Pieris japonica CONTINUED

Pieris japonica 'Valley Valentine'

Pieris japonica 'Variegata'

Pieris phillyreifolia, vine-wicky

that suck the sap from the leaves, often rendering the plant various shades of cream-yellow-green. Utilize the plant in foundation plantings, borders, groupings, or masses. Grows 8 to 12 ft. high, 6 to 8 ft. wide. Zones 5 to 8, 9 on West Coast. Japan.

CULTIVARS AND VARIETIES
Usually much smaller than the species. 'Cavatine' with leathery dark green leaves, abundant white flowers and compact habit, 2 to 3 ft. high and wide, is among the best of the many.

'Grayswood' is a mound of snow 4 to 5 ft. high when in bloom, with bronze-green new leaves, dark green at maturity, and white flowers in arching racemes, freely borne.

'Mountain Fire' offers exceptional fire-red new growth, white flowers, and a compact habit. It is widely available in commerce. Listed as growing as large as 9 to 12 ft. by 6 to 8 ft.

'Temple Bells' is a beautiful selection with lustrous dark green leaves, pristine white flowers, and a compact habit, 3 to 4 ft. high.

'Valley Valentine' has rich maroon flower buds that open to deep rose-pink flowers in abundance on a dense, upright plant; glossy deep green foliage; 6 to 8 ft. high at maturity.

'Variegata' has leaves edged with white. Makes a rather pretty accent in a shady nook of the garden.

Pieris phillyreifolia
vine-wicky

This humble broadleaf evergreen vine/shrub is found in swampy habitats in the Southeast. Typically a vine in nature, it develops into a small shrub when brought into garden culture. Beautiful leathery, lustrous dark green leaves, ¾ to 2½ in. long, are revolute (turned under) around the margins. Milk-white, ⅓-in.-long, urn-shaped flowers appear in three- to nine-flowered racemes in late winter to early spring. Beautiful plant for the collector. Would appear to have potential for breeding root-rot resistance and heat tolerance into *Pieris japonica*. Grows 1 to 2 ft. high as a shrub. Witnessed in the Okefenokee Swamp, Georgia, where it grew submerged in blackish waters, clinging to the trunks of baldcypress, *Taxodium distichum* and var. *imbricarium*; leaves were smaller, narrower than the terrestrial form, which has longer, more ovate leaves. Zones 7 to 9. South Carolina, Georgia, Florida, and Alabama.

Pieris phillyreifolia on pond cypress trunks

Pinckneya bracteata

syn. *Pinckneya pubens*

pinckneya, feverbark

One of the early (c. 1980) plants in the Dirr garden because of its beautiful flowers (bracts). Cold in the mid 1980s (−3°F) killed it to the ground, yet 120 or so miles south, in Little Ocmulgee State Park, McRae, Georgia, it grows naturally in abundance.

Large shrub to small tree, often loose and open. Needs to be integrated with other plants to look its best in a garden setting. Large leaves, up to 8 in. long, oppositely arranged and semi-dog-eared, emerge bronze-green, becoming medium to dark green. True flowers are yellowish green, mottled brown and purple, ½ to 1 in. long, with five reflexed corolla lobes resulting in a distinct trumpet-shaped flower. The large bracts, white to pink, subtend the flowers and provide the pizzazz. Flowers, which open in May and June in Athens, are effective for several weeks and beyond. Fruit are ¾-in.-wide, two-valved capsules that contain numerous flattish seeds. Seeds germinate immediately upon sowing. Provide moisture and soils rich in organic matter. Have observed plants in sun and partial shade; the plant in our garden was on the north side of the house. Unique and quite beautiful signature plant. Not common but worth pursuing. Grows 10 to 20 ft. high, less in spread. Zones (7)8 and 9. Found in low, wet woods in South Carolina to Florida.

Pinus

pine

About the only common denominator is the unique "pine" cone, but even then shape varies—rounded, conical, banana-shaped. Cones ripen in second year. Needles generally in fascicles of two, three, or five (singular in *Pinus monophylla*). Bark often quite showy. A genus of remarkably adaptable plants, and their uses in the advancement of civilization are legendary. The chance that pine bark constitutes a large part of the medium of any container-grown plant is great. Kudos to the pines.

Pinckneya bracteata, feverbark

Pinckneya bracteata

Pinus aristata

Pinus aristata
bristlecone pine

A wonderful novelty plant for that special garden niche; however, growth is extremely slow. Generally, this species is dwarf, shrubby, and picturesque in youth, characteristics that make it a first-rate accent plant, and it retains this habit into old age. The 1- to 1¾-in.-long, dark blue-green needles occur in fascicles of five and are covered with resinous exudations. Succeeds in infertile, dry, or rocky soils in a range of pH levels. Best transplanted from a container. One of the oldest trees on earth; specimens range from 4,000 to 5,000 years old. Expect to pay a tidy sum for a quality plant. Grows 8 to 20 ft. high, variable spread. National champion is 63 ft. high. Zones 4 to 7. Southwestern United States.

Pinus longaeva, western bristlecone pine, lacks the resinous exudations on the needles. Plants to 5,000 years old have been documented. Zones 4 to 6. California, Nevada, Utah.

Pinus banksiana
Jack pine

This species has few redeeming features other than its tremendous cold tolerance (to −40°F) and its adaptability to impoverished sandy or clay soils. The habit is pyramidal, open and spreading in youth, often flat-topped at maturity. The ¾- to 2-in.-long, olive-green needles occur in fascicles of two. In winter, needles

Pinus aristata, bristlecone pine

Pinus banksiana, Jack pine

become a sickly yellow-green. Adaptable for windbreaks, shelterbelts, and mass plantings, particularly in sandy soils. Many better pines are available for normal conditions. Grows 35 to 50 ft. high, spread variable but usually less than the height. Zones 2 to 6. Arctic regions, south to New York and Minnesota.

Pinus bungeana
lacebark pine

A biological specimen of great beauty. This tree has lustrous, rich green needles and exfoliating, sycamore-like bark. Usually multi-stemmed, though it may be single-stemmed. The branches reach to the ground; remove lower branches to expose the excellent bark. The bark actually starts to exfoliate on 1- to 2-in.-wide branches, with color varying from whitish, gray, and green to brownish. The 2- to 4-in.-long, stiff, sharp-pointed needles occur in bundles of three. Growth is quite slow, and consequently, the plant is not abundant in commerce. Transplant balled and burlapped into well-drained soils. Once established, tolerates drought, as well as acid and high pH soils. A fine specimen evergreen or accent plant. Grows 30 to 50 ft. high, 20 to 35 ft. wide. Zones 4 to 7. China.
CULTIVARS AND VARIETIES
'Great Wall' is a magnificent broad-columnar form with great density of branches and foliage. Stunning. From Don Shadow, Winchester, Tennessee.

Pinus bungeana, lacebark pine

Pinus bungeana

Pinus bungeana 'Great Wall'

Pinus cembra
Swiss stone pine

I have always considered this to be among the top five pines for landscape use because of its uniform, narrow, densely columnar habit. Mature trees in the wild are looser, more open, and pyramidal. The 2- to 3- (to 5-) in.-long, rich blue-green needles occur in bundles of five. They persist for four to five years, contributing to the overall fullness of the plant. Young stems are covered with a thick, orange-brown pubescence, a characteristic that separates this species from *Pinus flexilis*, *P. peuce*, and *P. strobus*. Provide well-drained, loamy, slightly acid soils, in full sun. Great specimen evergreen; ideal in multiples because of its rigid formality. Unlike a fastigiate *P. strobus*, this species will not outgrow its location. Grows 30 to 40 (to 70) ft. high, 15 to 25 ft. wide. Zones 4 to

Pinus cembra

Pinus clausa, sand pine

Pinus cembra, Swiss stone pine

Pinus contorta var. *latifolia*

7. Mountains of central Europe and southern Asia.
CULTIVARS AND VARIETIES
Prairie Statesman™ ('Herman') is an erect form with densely borne, emerald-green needles and zone 3 cold hardiness. Introduced by Dr. Dale Herman, North Dakota State University.

Pinus clausa
sand pine
A pine that is grown only in the Deep South, where I observed it functioning as a windbreak. A soft, pyramidal tree, short-statured compared to many pines. Bark is relatively smooth in youth, becoming reddish brown and scaly. Needles are rich green, in twos, sometimes threes, often twisted or bent, 1½ to 3 in. long. Cones are ovoid-oblong, 2 to 3 in. long, brown, with hard, inflexible scales, and a prickle on each scale back. Open and closed cones may be on the same tree. Strictly for use in deep, sandy soils, where it is found in the wild. Picturesque growth habit. Has been domesticated for Christmas tree use. Grows 30 to 40 ft. high, 20 ft. wide, although the national champion is over 70 ft. high. Zones 8 and 9. Florida, southwestern Alabama.

Pinus contorta
lodgepole pine
Pinus contorta and P. contorta var. latifolia are two-needle taxa of the western United States. The former performs best in moist, well-drained, sandy or gravelly soils, while the latter tends to establish in wet, boggy areas and is seldom found far from tidewater. Zones 7 and 8 of West Coast.
CULTIVARS AND VARIETIES
'Frisian Gold', 'Chief Joseph', and 'Taylor's Sunburst' are gold-needled selections.

Pinus densiflora
Japanese red pine
A mature Japanese red pine is indeed majestic, with its wide-spreading, slightly upward-arched branches and

MORE ▶

Pinus contorta, lodgepole pine

Pinus densiflora 'Burke's Red Pine'

589

Pinus densiflora CONTINUED

Pinus densiflora, Japanese red pine

Pinus densiflora 'Umbraculifera'

plumes of rich green needles. The orange bark develops an exfoliating character. Certainly one of the more picturesque pines. The 3- to 5-in.-long, bright green needles occur in twos. A well-drained soil is necessary, but otherwise the species is quite adaptable. Use as a specimen or in groupings. An open-grown tree qualifies as a botanical sculpture. Every seedling shows character and somewhat irregular growth, and even young plants show no propensity toward the widget mold. Grows 40 to 60 ft. high and wide. Zones (4)5 to 7. Japan, Korea, China.
CULTIVARS AND VARIETIES
'Burke's Red Pine' is a super-charged,

Pinus densiflora 'Oculus-draconis', dragon's-eye pine

Pinus densiflora 'Umbraculifera'

i.e., more colorful, compact version of 'Oculus-draconis' with more pronounced yellow banding.

'Jane Kluis' is a pancakey, flat-topped form with stiff needles. Grows 3 to 4 ft. high and wide. Hybrid between this and *Pinus thunbergii*.

'Oculus-draconis', commonly known as dragon's-eye pine, has two yellow bands on each needle. When viewed from above, the alternate rings of yellow and green create an "eyeball" effect, hence, the common name. More of a conversation piece or novelty item, but definitely unique.

'Pendula' is a rather effective weeping form that will tend to sprawl and act as a groundcover, unless grafted on a standard or staked to produce a small, weeping tree.

'Umbraculifera' is a beautiful upright, broad-spreading, umbrella-headed form. The branches are upright-spreading, and with time, the habit becomes vase-shaped. The orange bark develops the exfoliating character typical of the species and is superb on old specimens. Amazingly adaptable and heat-tolerant. Great accent plant but by no means small: although listed as a 10-ft. specimen, it can easily reach 20 ft. tall. A 42-year-old plant at the Secrest Arboretum, Wooster, Ohio, was 25 ft. high.

A compact form of 'Umbraculifera' grows 4 to 6 ft. high and wide.

Pinus echinata
shortleaf pine

Among the most beautiful southern pines in old age. Artistically assembled, with a long slender bole (trunk), a narrow pyramidal crown, contorted branches, and scale-like bark that is arranged in jigsaw puzzle pieces. I told my students the easiest way to distinguish this from *Pinus taeda*, loblolly pine, is by the puzzle-piece bark and sinuous branches, compared to the ridged and furrowed

MORE ▶

Pinus densiflora 'Pendula'

Pinus echinata

Pinus echinata, shortleaf pine

591

Pinus echinata

Pinus elliottii

bark and straight branches of *P. taeda*. Needles, dark bluish green, 2 to 4½ in. long, occur in fascicles of two, occasionally three. Cones are dark brown-black, 1½ to 2½ in. long and 1 to 1½ in. wide. Extremely tolerant of harsh sites, it grows naturally on dry, upland soils. Useful in groupings and groves. Towering mature specimens on the Georgia campus inspire and humble. Witnessed the first witch's-broom in the top of a 70-ft. tree at the University's Horticulture Farm. Grows 80 to 100 ft. high. Zones 6 to 9. New Jersey, south to Georgia, Texas, Oklahoma.

Pinus elliottii
slash pine
Another important southern timber species with a more coastal distribution. I frequently mistake this species for *Pinus taeda*. Slash pine is a tall slender-trunked tree with an ovoid crown. The 4- to 9- (to 12-) in.-long, glossy dark green needles appear in fascicles of two, occasionally three. The cones are ovoid, 3½ to 6 in. long, lustrous chestnut-brown, and armed with a short prickle at the end of each scale. With age, the red-brown to purple-brown bark is fractured into large, irregular blocks with scaly, flaking plates, similar to that of *P. echinata*. Excellent species for use in the Coastal Plain of the Southeast. Grows in wet soils, interdune hollows, and near coastal sands. Like *P. taeda* and *P. echinata*, excellent in groupings and groves. Grows 80 to 100 ft. high. Zones 8 to 10. South Carolina to Florida, west to southeastern Mississippi and Louisiana.

Pinus flexilis
limber pine
Limber pine is often mistaken for *Pinus strobus*, white pine, but it differs in its needles, which have entire, rather than serrated, margins. In youth it is often a dense pyramid of rich blue-green needles, becoming more open and picturesque with age. The

Pinus elliottii, slash pine

2½- to 3½-in.-long needles persist for five to six years. Easily transplanted, extremely adaptable, and certainly one of the most beautiful of the five-needled pines. Makes a fine specimen or grouping. Grows 30 to 50 ft. high, 15 to 35 ft. wide. Zones 4 to 7. Western North America.
CULTIVARS AND VARIETIES
'Glauca' has a blue-green needle color that is much more intense than that of the species.

'Glauca Pendula' is a wide-spreading, irregular shrub with rich blue-green foliage. Tends to sprawl and scamper rather than truly weep.

'Vanderwolf's Pyramid', an upright form with pretty blue-green needles, grew 17 ft. in eight years.

Pinus glabra
spruce pine

Unique two-needled pine that I envisioned as the next great Christmas tree and screening pine for the Southeast: a beautiful oval-rounded crown, dark green summer needles, and varied soil tolerances suggested landscape greatness. It was tested in

MORE ▶

Pinus flexilis 'Vanderwolf's Pyramid'

Pinus glabra

Pinus flexilis, limber pine

Pinus glabra, spruce pine

Pinus glabra CONTINUED

Athens and grown by a local nursery, but it became obvious that the winter yellowing of needles precluded whole-sale acceptance. Open-grown trees tend to hold their branches to the ground. The spirally twisted needles

are 2 to 4 in. long. Cones, 1¾ to 3¾ in. long, brown, the scales with minute prickles, often persist two to four years. Bark is dark gray, closely ridged and furrowed. Beautiful pine for naturalizing in the Deep South. Magnificent 80-ft.-high specimen in the Coker Arboretum, UNC Chapel Hill. Grows 40 to 60 ft. high. Zones 8 and 9(10). South Carolina to northern Florida to Louisiana.

Pinus heldreichii
Bosnian pine

Somewhat confusing species now encompassing *Pinus leucodermis*, with which I am more familiar. Conic-ovoid crown with ash-gray, ridged and furrowed bark. Needles, in twos, dark green, stiff, spine-tipped, 2 to 4 in. long, ¹⁄₁₂ in. wide, hold color year-round. Cones, ovoid, 4 to 5 in. long, are yellow-brown with a short acute umbo (point). Plants I experienced from New England to England were

dense, compact, and more appealing than *P. nigra*. Resistant to diplodia needle blight and quite salt-tolerant. Suitable for dry, chalky (high pH soils). Beautiful specimen or accent. No reliable size data, but a plant grew 31 ft. by 15 ft. in northern Illinois. Zones 5 and 6. Balkan Peninsula, southern Italy.
CULTIVARS AND VARIETIES
'Satellit' is a handsome selection, narrow-conical, with dark green needles, 10 to 12 ft. high.

Pinus koraiensis
Korean pine

Certainly not well known in landscape circles, but one of the most elegant of the five-needled pines. The habit is loosely pyramidal, with branches of densely set needles feathered to the ground. The blue-green (possibly gray-green) needles average 3½ to 4½ in. long and are heavier textured (thicker) and more coarsely serrated than other five-needled types. Stems

Pinus heldreichii, Bosnian pine

Pinus heldreichii 'Satellit'

Pinus koraiensis, Korean pine

are covered with a dense, reddish brown pubescence that becomes dirty brown with age. Quite adaptable, and one of the more cold hardy pines. Great as a specimen, in groupings, or for screening. Grows 30 to 40 ft. high, 15 to 20 ft. wide. Zones 4 to 7. Korea, Japan.

Pinus mugo
mugo or Swiss mountain pine

Somewhat of an anomaly in American gardening. The dwarf types of this pine are often sold as the typical species, even though the true species can grow to 75 ft. high and the forms in cultivation are generally 10 ft. or less and quite shrubby. In the native populations of the species that I have seen in the Swiss Alps, no two plants were exactly alike. The medium to dark green, 1- to 2- (to 3-) in.-long needles occur in fascicles of two. The species and its cultivars are extremely adaptable and will prosper in Maine,

Iowa, or Maryland. Quite adaptable to extremes of soil, pH, and climate. Use for massing and foundation plantings, or in rock gardens, perennial borders, and containers. To maintain a dwarfed condition, prune the new candles (shoots) when the needles are half their mature length. Grows 15 to 20 ft. high and wide; can grow 30 to 80 ft. Zones 2 to 7. Definitely not well adapted to zone 7 of the Southeast. Have tried many times with no success. Mountains of central and southern Europe.

CULTIVARS AND VARIETIES
Many named cultivars, but they are seldom available in the everyday trade.

Variety *mughus* and Pumilio Group (var. *pumilio*) are considered low-growing (less than 8 ft. high) natural variants.

'Ophir' is mounded, flat-topped, to 2 ft. high, green in summer with significant yellow needle color in winter.

Pinus mugo, mugo pine

Pinus mugo

Pinus nigra

Pinus nigra
Austrian pine

One of the most popular landscape pines in the Midwest and East because of its densely pyramidal habit, attractive needles, cold hardiness, and cultural adaptability. In old age the outline is umbelliform, and the bark becomes ridged and furrowed. The flat furrows are scaled in a mosaic of white, gray, and brown. The lustrous dark green, almost black-green needles, 3 to 5 (to 6) in. long, occur in bundles of two and are extremely stiff and sharp-pointed. Needles persist for four (occasionally eight) years, giving the branches a full mane of green. *Pinus nigra* is adaptable to high pH, heavy clay soils. It transplants readily and establishes quickly. Used extensively for groupings and screenings. This species has been troubled by *Diplodia pinea*, which causes tip dieback, and pine wilt, caused by the pinewood nematode. Pinewood nematodes, transmitted by beetles and borers, plug the vascular system of the plant and can kill an entire tree, or portions of it, often in a single season. Assess the prevalence of disease and pinewood nematodes in an area before planting. Grows 50 to 60 ft. high, 20 to 40 ft. wide. Zones 4 to 7. Europe.

Pinus palustris
longleaf pine

An important pine ecologically, surviving through fires that burn off the competing grasses and weedy vegetation. Great acreages have been lost because of development and lack of natural fires. In youth the grass stage is apparent, a single stem with long needles producing a drooping mane. Eventually, side branches develop, producing a saguaro cactus look-alike. With age, a narrow crown of loosely arching needles develops. The brown bark becomes platy-scaly with age. The dark green needles, in fascicles of three, are 6 to 12 (to 18) in. long. The brown, ovoid-oblong cones, 6 to 8 (to 10) in. long, up to 5 in. wide, open

Pinus palustris

Pinus palustris

Pinus nigra, Austrian pine

promptly and abscise over winter. Extremely adaptable and common in the sandy or clay-sand ridges of Georgia. Useful in coastal landscapes, as it adds texture and unique architecture to large-scale plantings. Grows 60 to 70 ft. high. Zones 7 to 10. Southeastern Virginia to Florida, east to Texas.

Pinus parviflora
Japanese white pine

A beautifully sculptured tree at maturity, with wide-spreading, artistically arranged branches. In youth it is often reasonably dense with 1- to 2½-in.-long, blue-green needles, which occur in bundles of five. Attractive 1½- to 4-in.-long

MORE ▶

Pinus parviflora, Japanese white pine

Pinus palustris, longleaf pine

Pinus palustris

Pinus parviflora CONTINUED

cones have thick, waxy, greenish scales that mature to brownish red and are borne even on young trees. Japanese white pine is easily grown and displays reasonable salt tolerance. Perfect tree for restricted spaces. A good accent or specimen conifer. Grows 20 to 50 ft. high, equal or greater in spread. Zones 4 to 7. Japan.

CULTIVARS AND VARIETIES
Glauca Group umbrellas any variation with blue needles, including 'Glauca', 'Glauca Brevifolia', 'Glauca Compacta', and 'Glauca Nana'.

Pinus peuce
Balkan pine
A rarity, to be sure, but this five-needled pine, with maturity, develops a statuesque and noble outline. In youth the habit is much like that of *Pinus cembra*, becoming more open with age. A mature specimen at Stourhead in England is easily confused with a giant *P. flexilis* or *P. strobus*. The needles are dark gray-green, 3 to 4 in. long, and have slightly toothed margins. They persist for up to three years. Adaptable to varied soils.

Pinus parviflora

Pinus pumila, Japanese stone pine

Pinus peuce, Balkan pine

Pinus resinosa, red pine

Another great specimen or accent plant. Grows 30 to 60 ft. high. Have tested in Georgia with no success. Zones 4 to 7. Balkans.

Pinus resinosa

Pinus pumila
Japanese stone pine, dwarf Siberian pine

Not very well known except in botanical garden circles, but deserving of consideration in virtually every garden. Plants I've observed were shrubby, none being taller than 15 ft. The rich bluish green, 1½- to 3- (to 4-) in.-long needles are densely set and occur in fascicles of five. Cones are quite small, averaging 1½ in. long and 1 in. wide. They are purplish when young, turning dull reddish or yellowish brown. Appears to be adaptable and easy to transplant. Great accent plant or addition to the shrub or perennial border. Grows 1 to 15 ft. high. Zones 5 and 6. Japan, China, Korea.

Pinus resinosa
red pine

In the past, red pine has been utilized throughout the East and Midwest, but this northern U.S. native is vastly inferior to most other landscape species. Although extolled for the quality of its foliage and growth habit, to find a noble specimen would prove a challenge. The habit is dense in youth and symmetrically oval in old age. The thin, medium green, 5- to 6-in.-long needles, two per fascicle, break or snap when bent. The bark is orange-red and scaly on young trees; on old trunks, it breaks into large, flat, reddish brown, superficially scaly plates. Probably best suited to exposed, dry, acid, sandy, or gravelly soils. Use for groves or windbreaks. Grows 50 to 80 ft. high, variable spread. Zones 2 to 5. Newfoundland to Manitoba, south to Michigan and the mountains of Pennsylvania.

Pinus rigida
pitch pine

Scruffy, forlorn, straggly, and rather disheveled in habit, especially in sandy, windswept, maritime habitats,

MORE ▶

Pinus rigida, pitch pine

Pinus rigida CONTINUED

but tenacious and adaptable when other species would perish. From Isle au Haut and Cadillac Mountain, Maine, Cape Cod, Massachusetts, and at 5,000 ft. on Whiteside Mountain, North Carolina, it has crossed my path. Best described as an irregular pyramid in youth, venturing forth wildly with age. Needles, yellow to dark green, in threes, slightly curved and twisted, 3 to 5 in. long, margins finely toothed, persist two to three years. Bark, dark, scaly in youth, brownish with flat plates separated by narrow, irregular fissures at maturity. Cones, 2 to 3 in. long, 1 to 1½ in. wide, ovoid-conical, remaining on trees for two or more years. One of the few pines that produces shoots from cut stumps. Also, tufts of shoots develop from the trunk. Remarkably resilient species. Seldom available in commerce but if present on a site, be appreciative. Great naturalizing species. Grows 40 to 60 ft. high, with a 30- to 50-ft. spread. Certainly variable in size over its native range. Zones 4 to 7. New Brunswick to Georgia, west to Ontario and Kentucky.

Pinus strobiformis
western white pine

I tested numerous *Pinus* species in Georgia, hoping to unearth an alternative for *Pinus strobus*, which struggles in the heat. For many years, this species has proven the best. Softly pyramidal habit, blue-green needles in fives, and no flinching in the hottest, driest years on record. Needles are 3 to 6 in. long and finely serrate along the margin, a feature that permits separation from *P. flexilis*. Cones are cylindrical, 7 to 14 in. long, yellow-brown to rich brown. Adaptable as long as soil is well drained. Makes a beautiful specimen; plants I observed in Kentucky and Massachusetts, along with the Georgia plants, provide pause for reflection as to scarcity. Interesting assertion: *P. flexilis*, *P. monticola*, *P. strobiformis*, and *P. ayacahuite* form a continuum from Pacific Northwest to Mexico with subtle differences. I have grown all, and there is a measure of wisdom to the assertion. Zones (5)6 and 7.

Pinus strobus
white pine

If I had to choose one pine for general landscape use, *Pinus strobus* would be it. The soft, plumy texture of the needles, the wide-spreading, horizontally disposed branches, and the hauntingly beautiful asymmetry of ancient trees will make believers out of doubters. Young trees, particularly when pruned, are often full

Pinus rigida

Pinus strobiformis, western white pine

and dense, but they never appear stiff and rigid like Scotch pine (*P. sylvestris*) or Austrian pine (*P. nigra*). Needles range in color from light green to medium green to blue-green and average 2 to 4 (to 5) in. in length. The needles, which occur in fascicles of five, persist for a year and a half before abscising in late summer and fall. White pine is easily transplanted and fast-growing. Seems to withstand pruning better than most pines. A great plant as a specimen, in groupings, or for screens and, possibly, hedges. In the Midwest, in high pH soils, iron chlorosis can be a problem. At times, trees die inexplicably. In the Northeast, tip moths destroy the terminal shoots, resulting in distorted growth. Still, the best species for general use. Grows 50 to 80 ft. high, 20 to 40 ft. wide. Zones 3 to 7.

MORE ▶

Pinus strobus 'Globosa'

Pinus strobus

Pinus strobus

Pinus strobus, white pine

Pinus strobus CONTINUED

Newfoundland to Manitoba, south to Georgia, Illinois, and Iowa.

CULTIVARS AND VARIETIES

'Angel Falls' is a striking form with lax, graceful, descending branches clothed with blue-green needles.

'Compacta', 'Globosa', 'Nana', 'Pumila', and other dwarfish forms are known. All are slower growing than the species and tend toward a rounded or broad-mounded outline. They make choice accent plants.

'Fastigiata' has always been a favorite of mine because of the softly vertical outline that opens somewhat with age. Branches ascend at a 45° angle to the central leader. Specimens over 70 ft. high are known.

'Golden Showers' is shrubby, quite dense, with cream-yellow needles.

'Pendula' is a flailing, arching, pendulous, irregular form that is often staked to provide a semblance of a leader. Use as an accent plant; one is acceptable, two represent bad taste, and three disgrace.

Pinus sylvestris
Scotch pine

Common as a Christmas tree in the northern United States. In youth the species forms an irregular pyramid with short, spreading branches, the lower soon dying. At maturity, trees are picturesque, open, wide-spreading, and flat- or round-topped, almost umbrella-shaped. Bark becomes orangish brown and flakes off in small plates and scales. The bluish green, 1- to 3- (to 4-) in.-long needles occur in twos. Each needle is rather flattish, with a slight spiral or twist to its long axis. Many variations of needle size and color, depending on the geographic origin of seeds. Scotch pine is easily transplanted and extremely

MORE ▶

Pinus strobus 'Golden Showers'

Pinus strobus 'Fastigiata'

Pinus strobus 'Pendula'

Pinus sylvestris

Pinus sylvestris, Scotch pine

Pinus sylvestris

603

Pinus sylvestris CONTINUED

adaptable to varied soils. Often used for screening and massing, particularly in the Midwest. Grows 30 to 60 ft. high, 30 to 40 ft. wide. Not suited to culture in zone 7, at least based on my 31 years in Athens. Zones 2 to 7. Europe, Asia.

CULTIVARS AND VARIETIES

Aurea Group includes the yellow-needle types with yellow-green new shoots, green in summer, then golden in winter. 'Aurea', 'Gold Coin', and 'Gold Medal' are housed herein.

'Fastigiata' is frequently listed as the "sentinel pine" because of its pronounced narrow-columnar habit. Sub-ject to snow and ice damage. Grows 25 ft. high or more.

'Watereri' is an old clone, densely pyramidal to flat-topped, with steel-blue needles and handsome orangish brown bark. Slow-growing, averaging about 10 ft. in height, although the original plant is 25 ft. high and wide.

Pinus sylvestris 'Aurea'

Pinus sylvestris 'Watereri'

Pinus taeda, loblolly pine

Pinus taeda
loblolly pine

In the Southeast the forester's primary timber species and the landscaper's most reliable, fast-growing, screening species. I have grown to admire its tenacity and persistence in colonizing highway cuts, banks, ditches, open grassy fields, abandoned agricultural land, and marsh edges along the coast. Pyramidal in youth, more open, with a slender trunk and wide-spreading, straight branches. Open-grown, large trees are enchanting. Bark is ridged and furrowed. The needles, 6 to 10 in. long, in fascicles of three, occasionally two, are dark green. The ovoid-cylindrical, buff to rust-brown cones, 3 to 6 in. long, have sharp, recurved prickles on the backs of the scales. Several trees in our garden appeared to "spit" cones on a daily basis. I have filled large garbage cans in a single cleanup. Easy to transplant from containers or when balled and burlapped. Settles in quickly, yielding 10 to 20 ft. of linear (height) growth in five to ten years. The best screening, massing, situational pine for the Southeast. It will establish where broadleaf trees cannot gain a toehold. Grows 60 to 90 ft. high. Zones 6 to 9. Southern New Jersey to Florida, west to eastern Texas and Oklahoma.

Pinus thunbergii
Japanese black pine

One of the most salt-tolerant needle evergreens, this species is used from Cape Cod to the Outer Banks of North Carolina. Unfortunately, it is not long-lived, and trees over 20 ft. tall are seldom seen. The habit is shrubby, artistic, and picturesque, usually with wide-spreading branches. The stiff, prickle-pointed, lustrous dark green needles occur two to a bundle. A distinguishing characteristic of the species is its elongated, silky white, candle-like buds. Plant in well-drained soils, in full sun. As a young plant, Japanese black pine makes for rather pretty groupings. In January, Bonnie and I walked the Highland Light area, Truro, Massachusetts, where smallish Japanese black pines, cones present in abundance, pretended to be an invasive species. Grows 15 to 25 ft. high, wider at maturity. Zones (5)6 to 8. Japan.

CULTIVARS AND VARIETIES
'Thunderhead' is a broad mounded form with prominent silky white buds set like candles on the dense dark green needles.

Pinus taeda

Pinus thunbergii

Pinus thunbergii, Japanese black pine

Pinus thunbergii 'Thunderhead'

Pinus virginiana
Virginia or scrub pine

Possibly the only redeeming quality of this species is its ability to withstand heat and adverse soil conditions. It will colonize heavy clay soils and is a good cover for such areas. The yellow-green to dark green needles occur in twos and usually turn sickly yellow-green in winter. *Pinus virginiana* develops a broad, open, pyramidal outline, becoming flat-topped with time. Old cones persist, and the tree carries this visual baggage throughout its life. Once a common Christmas tree in the South, but it required tremendous maintenance—including dyeing the needles—for successful production. Leyland cypress and other species have stolen some of its thunder. A fast-growing tree useful in screens, groupings, or for soil protection, but use with the knowledge that 20 years is probably a long life. Grows 15 to 40 ft. high, 10 to 30 ft. wide. Zones 4 to 8. New York to Alabama.

CULTIVARS AND VARIETIES
'Wate's Golden' offers golden needles in winter, green in summer, the golden-yellow color initiating in October and November.

Pinus wallichiana
Himalayan or Bhutan pine

An elegant pine, considered by some the most beautiful pine species. The habit is broad-pyramidal in youth and old age. The 5- to 8-in.-long, blue-green needles occur in bundles of five and often arch gracefully over their length, providing a fine-textured appearance. Move as a young plant into moist, acid, well-drained soils, and provide shelter from desiccating winds. Only use should be as a specimen. Grows 30 to 50 ft. high, generally equal in spread. Zones 5 to 7. Himalayas.

CULTIVARS AND VARIETIES
'Zebrina' is similar to *Pinus densiflora* 'Oculus-draconis', although the bands on the needles of this Himalayan pine cultivar tend to be more cream-colored.

Pistacia chinensis
Chinese pistache

An unheralded and largely unknown small to medium-sized tree that provides sugar maple–like fall color in the middle to Deep South into the Southwest and California. Oval-rounded to broad-rounded in outline, coarsely and

Pinus virginiana 'Wate's Golden'

Pinus virginiana, Virginia pine

Pinus wallichiana

Pinus wallichiana, Himalayan pine

irregularly branched in youth, becoming more uniform and dense with maturity. Bark becomes scaly, gray to gray-black, and as the scales flake off they expose salmon to orange inner bark. Compound pinnate leaves with

MORE ▶

Pinus wallichiana 'Zebrina'

Pistacia chinensis, Chinese pistache, fall color

Pistacia chinensis CONTINUED

Pistacia chinensis

Pittosporum heterophyllum

Pittosporum heterophyllum

Pittosporum tenuifolium, tawhiwhi

ten to 12 leaflets, each 2 to 4 in. long and lustrous dark green, turn brilliant yellow-orange and orange-red in fall. I have walked seedling populations in autumn displaying every color from yellow-green to fluorescent red in their plumage. Male and female flowers (dioecious) are greenish to purplish and open before the leaves in April. The robin's-egg-blue, ¼-in.-wide, rounded drupaceous fruit ripen in October. Prospers in a wide range of soils and pH levels, and amazingly drought-tolerant once established. Full sun for best growth and fall foliage. High insect and disease tolerance. Great lawn, street, and park tree for the South and West. When a selection for a male clone with excellent fall color that propagates easily is eventually made, the species will become the next, only better, Bradford pear. Grows 30 to 35 ft. high, 25 to 35 ft. wide. Zones 6 to 9, 10 on the West Coast. China, Taiwan, Philippines.

Pittosporum heterophyllum

What a pleasant surprise in the Georgia trials—a robust shrub with shiny green foliage and greater cold hardiness than *Pittosporum tobira*. The narrow-obovate to -lanceolate, 1- to 1½-in.-long leaves are densely set along the stems. Flowers, white aging yellow, fragrant, appear in the leaf axils in profusion in May. Use in groupings, as hedging, or in the background of a border. Adaptable to any well-drained soil. Withstands heavy pruning. Estimate 8 to 10 ft. high and wide at maturity. Zones 7 to 9. China. CULTIVARS AND VARIETIES 'Variegatus', with smaller, cream-margined leaves, is smaller, slower growing, and slightly less cold hardy than the species based on side-by-side comparisons. 'Winter Frost' may be the same plant with a more saleable name.

Pittosporum tenuifolium
tawhiwhi, kohuho

A unique broadleaf evergreen of tight pyramidal-conical habit, possibly reserved for the Mediterranean climate around San Francisco and other West Coast parts. Singularly beautiful foliage; each 2- to 3-in.-long leaf has rolled, undulating edges and lustrous dark green color. Numerous leaf selections have been introduced, including silver, yellow, purple, green maturing to purple, cream-edged, yellow-edged, and others. Flowers (purple) and fruit are inconspicuous. Tolerant of sun and shade. Best in well-drained soil. Useful for a color accent in mixed plantings, screens, groupings, and even hedges. Grows 10 to 20 (to 30)

Pittosporum tobira, Japanese pittosporum

ft. high. Zones 8 to 10 on the West Coast. New Zealand.

Pittosporum tobira
Japanese pittosporum

One of the most essential broadleaf evergreen shrubs for southern and West Coast landscapes, growing in sand, seaside conditions, full sun or shade, heat, and drought. Wonderful, robust, dense, compact shrub, usually broad-mounded at maturity. Have observed the species pruned to small tree status and, indeed, picturesque plants 20 to 25 ft. high are known. Tough-as-rawhide leaves, recurved at the margins, measure 1½ to 4 in. long, up to 1½ in. wide. The lustrous dark green foliage color persists year-round in sun and shade. Flowers appear in April and May, when not removed by the pruning shears, and are borne in 2- to 3-in.-wide, terminal umbels. Each ½- to 1-in.-wide, five-petaled flower opens white, finally yellow, and provides orange-blossom fragrance. The fruit are pear-shaped, three-valved, ½-in.-wide capsules. Easy to grow, withstands heavy pruning and salt spray. Used in foundation plantings; terrific under trees, in hedges, screens, buffers, and barrier plantings; effective in containers and raised planters. Seeds germinate readily; populations I grew for superior cold hardiness ended up on the compost pile. Grows 10 to 12 ft. high, one and a half to two times this in width. Zones (7)8 to 10. Japan, Korea, China.

CULTIVARS AND VARIETIES

'Mojo', with potent cream-white variegated leaves, compact habit, 18 to 22 in. by 36 to 48 in., was described as more cold hardy. The variegation is attractive, but a plant in our Chapel Hill garden suffered winter damage, and a planting in Wrightsville Beach, North Carolina, had bleached to uniform cream-brown on the previous season's leaves.

'Variegatum' is one of the more genteel cream-edged forms, with the center of the leaf gray-green. Reasonably vigorous to 6 ft. and higher, same sweet floral fragrance as the species. A common house and conservatory plant in the North.

'Wheeler's Dwarf' is perhaps the best compact form of the species, 3 to 4 ft. high, slightly wider, forming a dense mound of lustrous green leaves.

Planera aquatica
water elm

Certainly looks like an elm, especially the shiny medium green, 1¼- to 2½-in.-long, broad-ovate, serrate

MORE ▶

Pittosporum tobira

Pittosporum tobira

Pittosporum tobira 'Variegatum'

Planera aquatica

Pittosporum tobira 'Wheeler's Dwarf'

Planera aquatica CONTINUED

to doubly serrate leaves. Leaf base
is asymmetrical like an elm. Forms
a small, finely branched, spreading,
round-topped canopy. I have yet to witness a tree in cultivation that was anything but pristine. The fruit are ⅓-in.-
long, one-seeded, nut-like drupes with
irregularly crested, fleshy ribs. Bark
is gray to light brown and exfoliates
in flat scales. Native in wet, swampy
habitats but performs well in drier situations. Grows 20 to 30 ft. high and
wide. Might be a prospect for high-
stress, urban spaces. Certainly does
not carry the cachet of *Cornus florida*
but with selection could be a worthy
contributor to diversity. Zones 6 to
9. North Carolina to Florida, west to
southern Illinois, south to Oklahoma
and Texas.

Platanus ×acerifolia
London planetree

London planetree received its name
from extensive use in the city of London, where it was one of the few survi-
vors of the coal-polluted air. No other
shade tree has been more widely
planted in cities worldwide than *Platanus ×acerifolia* (a hybrid of *P. orientalis*
and *P. occidentalis*). It is a massive
tree with wide-spreading branches, a

fact belied by its tight-pyramidal youthful outline. The cream- to olive-colored
bark is one of the winter landscape's
bright beacons. The dark green
leaves, 6 to 7 in. long and 8 to 10 in.
wide, turn yellow-brown in autumn. I
have not seen a soil condition that
this tree will not tolerate—wet, dry,
acid, and alkaline are all acceptable.
Anthracnose kills young leaves, especially in moist weather. Stems also

Platanus ×acerifolia

Planera aquatica

Planera aquatica, water elm

Platanus ×acerifolia 'Bloodgood'

die back as a result of anthracnose, resulting in a "brooming" effect. *Platanus ×acerifolia* is certainly more resistant than *P. occidentalis*, however. Bacterial leaf scorch is serious and has manifested itself on 'Yarwood' in the Southeast. Use for street plantings, commercial sites, campuses, golf courses, or any large area. In finest form, it is a beautiful and imposing specimen tree. Grows 70 to 100 ft. high, 65 to 80 ft. wide. Zones 4 to 8(9).

CULTIVARS AND VARIETIES

Several anthracnose-resistant cultivars are available, including 'Bloodgood', which is one of the most common in commerce, 'Columbia', 'Liberty', Ovation™ ('Morton Euclid'), and 'Yarwood'.

Exclamation™ ('Morton Circle') is pyramidal, with a strong central leader and vigorous constitution. Dark green leaves are resistant to anthracnose, powdery mildew, and frost cracking. Grows 60 ft. by 45 ft., quite impressive as I viewed it in Oregon. Bred by Dr. George Ware, Morton Arboretum.

Platanus occidentalis
American sycamore

Along with *Liriodendron tulipifera*, tuliptree, this species is one of the tallest of the native eastern North American deciduous trees. In southern Ohio, where I grew up, American sycamore was a common fixture along every

MORE ▶

Platanus ×acerifolia

Platanus ×acerifolia, London planetree

Platanus ×acerifolia 'Yarwood' fall color

611

Platanus occidentalis CONTINUED
stream and river. In most respects, the habit is similar to that of London planetree, except the bark is more creamy and the 1½-in.-wide, rounded fruit occur singly (those of *Platanus ×acerifolia* occur in twos). Prefers deep, moist soils and requires abundant space. A great and noble tree.

Use for naturalized plantings along streams, in groves, or as a single specimen. Anthracnose is a serious malady in cool, rainy springs, disfiguring and killing developing leaves. Grows 75 to 100 ft. high, similar spread. National champion is 129 ft. high. Zones 4 to 9. Maine to Ontario, south to Florida and Texas.

Plumbago auriculata
syn. *Plumbago capensis*
plumbago
Strictly a conservatory plant or summer annual in zone 7 and north, but a fine evergreen vine to scandent shrub in lower zone 8 and south. Forever it has been a remembrance of my visits to Longwood Gardens, where in the

Platanus occidentalis

Platanus occidentalis

Plumbago auriculata

Platanus occidentalis, American sycamore

Platanus occidentalis

conservatory it grew across the aisle from the tropical Chinese hibiscus, *Hibiscus rosa-sinensis*. Longwood visitors photograph the beautiful pale blue flowers while shunning the bright yellow, orange, and red flowers of the hibiscus. In Orlando, Florida, at Leu Gardens, this grew in the parking lot island, next to *Callistemon* species.

In habit, shoots fall over each other, producing a shrub-like mass. Can also be trained on a trellis or similar structure. The light green leaves, ¾ to 3 in. long, are arranged alternately and clustered along the stem, providing a pleasing backdrop to the flowers. The azure-blue flowers, 1 to 1½ in. across, five-lobed, trumpet-shaped, occur on short racemes over much of the year. Heaviest flowering is from May through November, although flowers appear throughout the year. Well-drained, moderately fertile soils, and full sun are ideal. Flowers on new growth, so maintain active shoot production via pruning. Used as a groundcover and in bank and mass plantings; excellent spilling over the edges of large containers. Grows 2 to 3 ft. high, 5 ft. wide; to 10 ft. on a climbing structure. Zones (8)9 to 11. South Africa.

CULTIVARS AND VARIETIES
'Alba' (var. *alba*) produces white flowers but is otherwise similar to the species.

Podocarpus macrophyllus 'Maki'

syn. *Podocarpus macrophyllus* var. *maki*

shrubby Chinese podocarpus

The true species has largely yielded landscape space to 'Maki' (var. *maki*). The leaves of the species are 3 to 4 in. long; those of 'Maki' are ½ to 2¾ in. long and narrower. In youth an irregular columnar pyramid of

MORE ▶

Plumbago auriculata, plumbago

Podocarpus macrophyllus 'Maki'

Podocarpus macrophyllus 'Maki'

Podocarpus macrophyllus '**Maki**' CONTINUED

feathery branches and needles, easily sculpted into any shape. In fact, in Florida and California, this is often used for topiary. The lustrous waxy dark green needles have two glaucous (gray) bands below. Bark is similar to yew, *Taxus*, reddish brown and loosely affixed in strips. Fruit (actually naked seeds), red to red-purple, ½ in. long, are attached to a fleshy receptacle, generally the same color. The species is dioecious, and the seeds are produced only on female plants. Adaptable to most soils, full sun to heavy shade. Abhors wet soils and cold; anything below 5 to 10°F produces injury or death. One of the best hedge and topiary plants. Grows 20 to 35 ft. high. Zones 8 to 10. Japan, southern China.

I have tested other *Podocarpus* species in Georgia with limited resultant

Podocarpus macrophyllus 'Maki', shrubby Chinese podocarpus

Podocarpus nivalis, alpine totara

Podocarpus lawrencei, mountain plum pine

Podocarpus salignus, willowleaf podocarp

enthusiasm. *Podocarpus alpinus*, Tasmanian podocarp, *P. lawrencei*, mountain plum pine, and *P. nivalis*, alpine totara, are among the hardiest. In well-drained soil, i.e., raised beds, such as provided by the Atlanta Botanical Garden, they persevered. In Georgia red clay, full sun, and exposed conditions, they languished.

Podocarpus salignus, willowleaf podocarp, develops a graceful pyramidal-rounded habit with 3- to 5-in.-long, lustrous dark green, "willowy" leaves. A beautiful evergreen but cold hardy only in zones 9 and 10. Grows 20 to 30 ft. high. Southern Chile.
CULTIVARS AND VARIETIES
Several spreading-bushy types.

'Brodie' is 3 ft. high, 6 ft. wide.

'Golden Crown' produces bright yellow growth flushes, maturing to green.

'Nana' is rounded and compact.

'Royal Flush' has bright pink young shoots that age to green.

'Spreading' has a groundcover-like habit.

Poliothyrsis sinensis

For future generations to decide its garden merits, compelling facts are herein aggregated. My first exposure occurred in 1991 at the Arnold Arboretum, where

MORE ▶

Podocarpus macrophyllus 'Maki'

Podocarpus alpinus, Tasmanian podocarp

Poliothyrsis sinensis

Podocarpus salignus

Poliothyrsis sinensis

615

Poliothyrsis sinensis CONTINUED

in late July the white, aging to yellow, flowers were developing in 6- to 8-in.-long, loose, terminal panicles. The foliage, a rather nondescript medium green, turns yellow-burgundy in autumn. Emerging leaves are yellowish before maturing. Each leaf is 3 to 6 in. long with dentate margins and three prominent veins. Habit is shrub-like, vase-shaped, with arching branches. Prefers full sun, moist, well-drained soil. Once established, tolerates drought. Could be utilized as a large shrub or fashioned into a small tree. Possibly lacks the aesthetic "oomph" necessary for the smaller contemporary landscape. Seeds germinate without pretreatment. Grows 15 to 20 ft. high and wide. Zones 6 to 8. Central China.

Poncirus trifoliata
hardy-orange

The primary shortcoming of this extremely adaptable species is the 1- to 2-in.-long, stout spines, which are quite sharp, almost lethal. The rich glossy green, trifoliate leaves turn a reasonable yellow in fall. White, five-petaled flowers, 1½ to 2 in. in diameter, appear in April and May; I

Poncirus trifoliata

Poncirus trifoliata, hardy-orange

Poncirus trifoliata

Poncirus trifoliata

Poncirus trifoliata 'Flying Dragon'

detect no floral fragrance, although cheesy literature records its presence. Flowers are followed by 1½-in.-wide, rounded, yellowish fruit that ripen in September and October. Juice can be used to flavor adult beverages but is extremely sour (acid). The green stems are attractive in the winter months. Prospers in any well-drained soil and displays excellent drought tolerance. Could provide an artistic touch to the garden; I have observed it used thus at the Arnold Arboretum and in the Mediterranean garden at Longwood. Have also observed localized areas consumed by seedlings; at Jefferson's Monticello, it has seeded-in sporadically in the woods by the cemetery. Has been utilized for hedges and barriers. Take care to plant out of the way of traffic. Grows 8 to 20 ft. high, 5 to 15 ft. wide. Zones 6 to 9. China, Korea.

CULTIVARS AND VARIETIES

New dwarf and variegated leaf cultivars have been introduced in the last decade. Observed many of these at several undisclosable locations: the resident collectors appear to be amassing the smallest, most contorted, exuberantly spiny, disgustingly variegated forms to release on unsuspecting gardeners.

'Flying Dragon' has contorted, twisted stems; seedlings are true to type, with similar contortions.

Populus

poplar

In all my traveling and consulting work, I have *never* recommended, at least when conscious, a poplar. The species are susceptible to fungal leaf spots that virtually defoliate trees by late summer. Cankers can also cause injury or death. Poplars are dirty trees, dropping leaves, twigs, and branches with minimal provocation. The genus *Populus* does contain many cold-climate species and cultivars. A recent Michigan trip refreshed my memory about the commonality of *Populus* species in northern climates.

Populus alba

silver or white poplar

Silver poplar is a wide-spreading tree with an irregular, round-topped crown. The bark is cream-colored. The three- to five-lobed, 2- to 5-in.-long leaves are lustrous dark green above and covered with white, woolly pubescence on the undersides. Although adaptable to dry soils, this species is longer lived in moist situations. For cold climates, it is a possibility, but beware, because diseases can wreak havoc. Typically defoliated by September in the Athens area. The species also develops suckers that result in large colonies. Grows 40 to 70 ft. high and wide. Zones 3 to 9. Europe, Asia.

CULTIVARS AND VARIETIES

'Pyramidalis', the Bolleana poplar, is

MORE ▶

Populus alba, silver poplar

Populus alba

Populus alba 'Richardii'

Populus alba 'Pyramidalis', Bolleana poplar

Populus alba

Populus deltoides

Populus deltoides, eastern cottonwood

columnar in habit and maintains this trait into old age. Grows 70 ft. high, 12 to 18 ft. wide.

'Richardii' has yellow upper-surfaced leaves, white below. Ideally cut back to encourage more colorful new growth.

Populus deltoides
eastern cottonwood

As one travels west through Kansas, Wisconsin, and Minnesota, this species becomes the most common sight along watercourses. It has an upright-spreading, vase-shaped habit and an irregular, ragged branch structure. The ash-gray bark is divided into thick, flattened ridges, separated by deep fissures. The dark green, deltoid leaves, 3 to 5 in. long and wide, may turn a respectable yellow in fall. Where few other trees will grow and for quick cover, eastern cottonwood is justified. Grows 75 to 100 ft. high, 50 to 75 ft. wide. Zones 2 to 9. Quebec to North Dakota, south to Florida and Texas.
CULTIVARS AND VARIETIES
Several male selections or hybrids (usually with *Populus nigra* as the other parent) are available. In spring, these seedless forms do not produce

the cottony froth of the typical species; they grow 2 to 4 ft. per year.

'Noreaster' and 'Siouxland' are two male cultivars, although the latter tends to shed abundant leaves by late summer in the lower Midwest. In Cincinnati, Ohio, and Spartanburg, South Carolina, trees were essentially defoliated by late August to early September.

'Purple Tower' develops dark red to purple leaves in full sun; pyramidal habit, 30 to 35 ft. high.

Populus grandidentata
bigtooth aspen

Bonnie and I make the pilgrimage to Maine every fall, when the tourists have left, a heavenly calm blesses the landscape, and this species, singly but often in groves, is in sparkling yellow-gold fall color. Young leaves are silver-gray upon emergence, maturing mid-green and largely hairless. The strong serrations give rise to the common name. Habit is pyramidal in youth, usually with a central leader, developing an oval, open, irregular crown. Bark is gray-brown to greenish gray. Adaptable to dry, sandy, gravelly soils. Typically 50 to 70 ft. by 20 to 40 ft.; national champion in Appleton, Maine, is 93 ft. by 51 ft. Zones 3 to 5(6). Nova Scotia to Ontario, south to North Carolina, Tennessee, Illinois, and Iowa.

Populus grandidentata

Populus nigra 'Italica'
Lombardy poplar

Lombardy poplar is a common sight throughout the East, Midwest, Plains States, and West, where it postures like a Titan rocket ready for launching. To most horticulturists, this tree is taboo because of its susceptibility to a devastating canker. Interest-

MORE ▶

Populus grandidentata

Populus deltoides 'Siouxland'

Populus grandidentata, bigtooth aspen, fall color

619

Populus nigra 'Italica' CONTINUED
ingly, in Europe, 80-ft.-tall trees are common in the countryside, suggesting that specimens in Europe may not be as susceptible to the canker, the canker absent, or conditions unfavorable for its development. The distinctive columnar, telephone pole–like habit limits contemporary landscape use. The 2- to 4-in.-long, dark green leaves do not color to any degree in fall, although some yellow is possible. Grows 70 to 90 ft. high, 10 to 15 ft. wide in 20 to 30 years. Zones 3 to 9. The species is native to western Europe, North Africa, Russia. CULTIVARS AND VARIETIES 'Lombardy Gold' has yellow-gold leaves and a similar growth habit.

Populus nigra 'Italica'

Populus tremuloides
quaking aspen
Although usually short-lived as a cultivated landscape plant, quaking aspen has few rivals when it ripens to yellow in the autumn woods of the northern and western states. This species is softly pyramidal in habit, with greenish white to creamy tan bark. Forms large colonies due to its suckering nature. The 1½- to 3-in.-

Populus nigra 'Italica', Lombardy poplar

Populus nigra 'Lombardy Gold'

long and -wide, lustrous dark green leaves have slender, flattened petioles. The slightest breeze induces the "shakes," hence, the common name. Will grow in a range of soils, from moist, loamy sands to shallow, rocky soils and clay. Discovered a colony south of Athens, which indicates a measure of heat tolerance. If native, do not destroy, simply appreciate. Grows 40 to 50 ft. high, 20 to 30 ft. wide. Zones 1 to 6. Labrador to Alaska, south to the mountain regions of Pennsylvania, Missouri, Mexico, and California.

CULTIVARS AND VARIETIES
Mountain Sentinel™ ('JFS-Column') is narrow fastigiate, 35 ft. by 8 ft., with golden yellow fall color. Observed in Oregon, quite dramatic.

Prairie Gold® ('NE Arb') is an oval to pyramidal selection, 35 ft. by 15 ft., resistant to leaf spot, with golden fall color. Well-adapted to the heat, drought, and humidity of the Great Plains. Somewhat open habit as a young tree.

Potentilla fruticosa
shrubby cinquefoil

For northern gardens, the shrubby potentillas can be considered first-class shrubs because of their extended flowering period, from June until frost. Plants vary in habit from groundcover types to robust shrubs. The leaves are composed of three to seven leaflets and range in color, gray and gray-green to bright and dark green. Stems are rich brown and

MORE ▶

Populus tremuloides

Populus tremuloides

Populus tremuloides Mountain Sentinel™

Populus tremuloides, quaking aspen, fall color

621

Potentilla fruticosa 'Coronation Triumph'

Potentilla fruticosa 'Goldfinger'

Potentilla fruticosa, shrubby cinquefoil

Potentilla fruticosa 'Jackman's'

Potentilla fruticosa 'Katherine Dykes'

Potentilla fruticosa 'Princess'

Potentilla fruticosa CONTINUED

provide winter interest. The number one landscape attribute is the flowers, which are variable in size (usually about 1 in. in diameter) and color, ranging from white to yellow to almost red. Shrubby cinquefoil is extremely adaptable and withstands any soil condition, except permanently wet. Thrives in the dry, calcareous clay soils of the Plains and Midwest states. Requires full sun for maximum flower production, although in some forms, the flowers bleach in hot sun. Great versatility in the landscape, limited only by the creativity of the gardener. Groundcover types grow 1 to 1½ ft. high; shrub types grow 4 ft. high and wide. Zones 2 to 7. Northern hemisphere.
CULTIVARS AND VARIETIES
Available in confusing numbers.

Numerous cultivars have been introduced, some of parentage other than *Potentilla fruticosa* but embodying similar landscape attributes. The following are worth considering, with flower color indicated: 'Coronation Triumph', 'Dakota Sunrise', 'Goldfinger', 'Jackman's' (bright yellow); 'Elizabeth' (soft yellow); 'Goldstar' (deep yellow-gold, up to 2 in. in diameter); 'Katherine Dykes' (lemon-yellow); 'Princess' (delicate pink); 'Red Ace' (red-orange, fades in heat); 'Tangerine' (orange, fades to yellow in heat).

The results of a major evaluation at RHS Garden, Wisley, were published in 2002; those rated best are listed here, with size and/or flower color indicated: 'Chelsea Star' (small yellow); 'Jackman's', 'King Cup', 'Medicine Wheel Mountain', 'Summerflor'

(large yellow); 'Yellow Bird' (average yellow); 'Limelight', 'Primrose Beauty' (cream or pale yellow); 'Abbotswood', 'Groneland', 'Penny White' (white); 'Pink Beauty' (Lovely Pink™) (pink); 'Hopleys Orange' (orange); Marian Red Robin™ ('Marrob') (red).

Prinsepia sinensis
cherry prinsepia

Virtually unknown in gardens, but this is one of the first shrubs to leaf out in spring. It tends to become rather large and unkempt with time, developing a haystack to rounded outline and spiny branches. The bark peels in long, papery strips. The 2- to 3-in.-long, bright green leaves develop minimal yellow fall color. Creamy yellow, ⅗-in.-wide flowers occur in groups of one to

MORE ▶

Potentilla fruticosa 'Goldstar'

Potentilla fruticosa 'Hopleys Orange'

Potentilla fruticosa 'Red Ace'

Potentilla fruticosa 'Tangerine'

Potentilla fruticosa 'Abbotswood'

623

Prinsepia sinensis CONTINUED

five on previous year's wood in March and April. The ½-in.-long, ovoid, red fruit ripen in July, August, and September. Birds make quick snacks of the fruit. Easily grown. Requires full sun. Perhaps useful as a reminder that hope springs eternal. Grows 6 to 10 ft. high and wide. Zones 3 to 7. Northeastern China.

Prinsepia uniflora, hedge prinsepia, is much smaller, its habit a moderately dense aggregate of light gray, thorny branches and sparse foliage. It has lustrous dark green, 1- to 2-in.-long, distinctly toothed leaves, white flowers, and waxy, dark purplish red, ½-in.-long fruit. For the fanatical collector, this and *P. sinensis* might have a place. Grows 4 to 5 ft. high and wide. Zones 3 to 5(6). China.

Prunus

cherry, plum, et al.

In spring, the plums and cherries in white, pink, and rose colors elevate winter souls to the highest level. Unfortunately, countless insects and diseases contribute to the decline of many of these plants. In general, *Prunus* species prefer moist, well-drained, acid to near neutral soils in full sun. The sweet cherries, such

Prinsepia sinensis

Prinsepia sinensis

Prinsepia uniflora

Prinsepia sinensis, cherry prinsepia

Prinsepia uniflora, hedge prinsepia

624

as *Prunus avium* and others, require another clone for cross-pollination and fruit production.

Prunus americana
American red plum

My old jogging treks introduced me to this species, a handsome, small, oval-rounded tree or suckering thicket, not unlike sumac, in both the tree form and colonizing habit. The shiny dark green leaves, 2 to 4 in. long, sharply and doubly serrate, turn yellow to red in autumn. The pure white flowers, plum-fragrant, two to five together, open in March. Interestingly, the variation in flowering times is extensive, with one colony in full flower, another in tight bud. The yellow to red, 1-in.-long, yellow-fleshed fruit ripen in June and July. Tougher than cement and grows in comparable soils along roadsides, ditches, banks, and fence lines. Excellent wildlife plant, also useful for naturalizing. Appears to take care of itself with no grooming necessary. Grows 15 to 25 ft. high, 10 to 15 ft. wide. Zones 3 to 8. Massachusetts to Manitoba, south to Georgia, New Mexico, and Utah.

Prunus angustifolia, chickasaw plum, is similar and prevalent in comparable habitats. Flowers, ½ in. in diameter, white, plum-like fragrance, are evident by early March in Athens.

MORE ▶

Prunus americana

Prunus angustifolia, chickasaw plum

Prunus americana, American red plum, fall color

Prunus americana

Prunus angustifolia

Prunus americana CONTINUED

Fruit is a ½- to ¾-in.-wide, rounded, lustrous yellow to red drupe that ripens in June and July. More colonizing, not as tree-like, typically 5 to 10 (to 20) ft. high, developing wide-spreading thickets. Zones 5 to 9. Maryland and southern Delaware to Florida, west to Arkansas and Texas.

Prunus avium 'Plena'

Prunus avium
Mazzard cherry

Although used primarily as a rootstock for grafting the more ornamental oriental cherries, Mazzard cherry has much to offer in its own right. This large tree is conical to rounded in habit and has gray-brown bark that can develop reddish tones in winter. Leaves emerge bronze, mature to deep green, and turn yellow to bronzy red in fall. The

Prunus avium

1- to 1½-in.-wide, fragrant, white flowers are produced in profusion during April and May. Fruit are reddish black, 1-in.-wide, rounded, sweetish drupes. Grows 30 to 40 ft. high, similar spread. Zones 3 to 8. Europe, western Asia.

CULTIVARS AND VARIETIES

'Plena' is beautiful, with double white, 1½-in.-wide flowers composed of approximately 30 petals.

Prunus besseyi
western sand cherry

A pretty, diminutive shrub with 1- to 2½-in.-long, gray-green leaves and pure white, ½-in.-wide flowers in April and May. The sweet, purplish black, ¾-in.-long fruit ripen in July and August. Useful in inhospitable hot, dry conditions. Grows 4 to 6 ft. high and wide. Zones 3 to 6. Great Plains.

Prunus avium, Mazzard cherry

CULTIVARS AND VARIETIES
Many have been selected for fruit quality.

Pawnee Buttes® is a groundcovering selection, 15 to 18 in. by 4 to 6 ft., with lustrous green leaves that turn bright red and purple. Flowers are white followed by black fruit. This appears to represent var. *depressa*.

Prunus campanulata
bell-flowered or Taiwan cherry

The best flowering cherry for the Deep South, requiring minimal chilling hours to send its carmine-rose buds bursting forth. In the Dirr garden, it typically flowers in late February and early March, complementing the witchhazels. In fact, the two make a pretty bouquet. Small, graceful, rounded in outline with spreading branches, it was among the most admired plants in our garden. Typical cherry leaves: glands on the petiole, margins set with fine, slightly incurved teeth, lustrous dark green, occasionally yellow-bronze-red in autumn. The carmine-rose flowers, 1½ in. long, ¾ in. wide, five-petaled, open along the naked branches. If untainted by freezing temperatures, flowers may be expected to provide three weeks or more of color. When the petals fall, the calyx tube, a deep ruby-rose color, is exposed and extends the overall effect. The fruit are red, ½ in. long, ⅜ in. wide, appearing almost rounded. Adaptable to sand and clay soil, preferably acid and well drained. Full sun to partial shade (pine) in coastal areas. Wonderful small garden tree. Where it can be grown successfully, should be in every gardener's top ten. Grows 20 to 30 ft. high and wide. Zones 7 to 9, 10 on the West Coast. Taiwan, southern China, Ryukyu Islands of Japan.

MORE ▶

Prunus campanulata 'First Lady'

Prunus besseyi

Prunus campanulata

Prunus besseyi, western sand cherry

Prunus campanulata, bell-flowered cherry

627

Prunus campanulata CONTINUED
CULTIVARS AND VARIETIES
'First Lady' has single deep rose-pink flowers, oval-upright habit, dark green leaves, yellow-orange to red fall color, 28 ft. by 18 ft. A hybrid of *Prunus* 'Okame' and *P. campanulata*.

Prunus caroliniana

Prunus caroliniana
Carolina cherrylaurel

A weed in the Coastal Plain of the Southeast, prevalent in fencerows and planted with regularity by the birds. Large evergreen shrub or small pyramidal-oval tree, although becomes more rounded and open with age. I questioned the identity of a 40-ft.-high tree in Orlando, Florida, never having observed one that large. Bark is relatively smooth in youth, more irregular with time, dark gray to almost black. The scent of almond extract, inherent in the leaves and stems, is released when they are bruised; in fact, the odor equates with maraschino cherries. The 2- to 3- (to 4-) in.-long, lustrous dark green leaves are serrated in youth, entire on older plants. The sickeningly sweet, white flowers, each ¼ to ⅓ in. across, appear on 1½- to 3-in.-long racemes from the leaf axils in March and April. Flower effect is not potent but reliably effective for a long period. The top-shaped drupes, ⅜ to ½ in. in diameter, lustrous black, ripen in October and to some degree are present the next flowering cycle. Birds resist eating them until other, more palatable fruit are taken, but eat they do, and distribute with reckless abandon. Adaptable to well-drained sandy and clay soils in sun to partial shade. Utilize for screens and hedges and to soften harsh vertical lines. On the Georgia campus, hedges have been maintained for more than 30 years and are no less effective or aesthetic. Grows 20 to 30 (to 40) ft. high, 15 to 25 ft. wide. Zones 7 to 10. Coastal Virginia to northern Florida, west to Louisiana.
CULTIVARS AND VARIETIES
Bright 'N Tight™ is a compact, tightly

Prunus caroliniana Bright 'N Tight™

Prunus caroliniana, Carolina cherrylaurel

branched form, almost flame-shaped in outline, with lustrous dark green leaves. Grows 10 to 20 ft. high; makes a good hedge, screen, and barrier.

Prunus cerasifera
Myrobalan plum
This small, white-flowered tree has been used for rootstocks, but the real garden interest lies in the purple-leaf hybrids and cultivars presented herein. They usually flower in April (mid March, Athens), before the leaves emerge. The reddish purple foliage is eye-catching, but use with discretion, for a little travels a long way. Trees are not long-lived; 15 to 20 years would be considered a respectable span. Leaf spot, probably caused by *Ento-mosporium* species, can be unsightly.

MORE ▶

Prunus ×cistena, purpleleaf sand cherry

Prunus cerasifera 'Atropurpurea'

Prunus cerasifera CONTINUED

Grows 15 to 30 ft. high, 15 to 25 ft. wide. Zones (4)5 to 8. Western Asia, Caucasus.

Prunus ×blireana is a hybrid between *P. cerasifera* 'Atropurpurea' and *P. mume*, Japanese apricot. It has reddish purple foliage and fragrant, pink flowers. The ten- to 15-petaled, 1¼-in.-wide flowers open in March (Athens) and April, before the leaves. Leaves fade to green with maturity. Grows 20 ft. high and wide. 'Moseri' appears to have deeper red-purple leaves and a uniform vase-shaped habit. To my way of assessing: not much different from the species. Zones 5 to 8.

Another purple-leaf hybrid species is *Prunus ×cistena*, purpleleaf sand cherry, a cross of *P. cerasifera* 'Atropurpurea' and *P. pumila*. It is a shrub or small tree that displays ruby-purple to reddish purple foliage. Fragrant pinkish flowers open after the leaves have developed. Grows 10 ft. high, slightly less in spread. Zones 2 to 8.

CULTIVARS AND VARIETIES

'Atropurpurea', the oldest purple-leaf form, is often referred to as the Pissard plum: it was discovered before 1880 by a Monsieur Pissard, gardener to the Shah of Iran. Leaves are reddish purple. Pinkish, ⅓-in.-wide flowers usually arrive before the leaves. Grows 20 to 25 ft. high.

Crimson Pointe™ ('Cripoizam') is columnar-fastigiate to tight vase-shaped, 20 ft. by 5 to 6 ft., with merlot-purple leaves and white flowers. Leaves age bronze-green at Milliken Arboretum, Spartanburg, South Carolina.

'Krauter Vesuvius' has dark reddish purple foliage and whitish pink, ½- to ¾-in.-wide flowers. It is similar to 'Thundercloud', but the flowers arrive earlier and are a lighter pink. Grows 30 ft. high, 20 ft. wide. The differences between this and 'Thundercloud' are debatable.

'Newport' is a round-headed tree with bronze-purple new growth that matures to dark reddish purple. Foli-

Prunus ×blireana

Prunus cerasifera Crimson Pointe™

Prunus cerasifera 'Krauter Vesuvius'

Prunus cerasifera 'Newport'

Prunus cerasifera 'Thundercloud'

age color not as intense as 'Krauter Vesuvius' and 'Thundercloud'. The pale pink to near white flowers open before the leaves emerge. Produces dull purple, 1-in.-wide fruit. Grows 15 to 20 ft. high and wide. Zones (4)5 to 8. The most cold hardy of the purple-leaf plums.

'Thundercloud' has single, pink, fragrant flowers that appear before the leaves. It retains its deep purple foliage color throughout the growing season. Easily confused with 'Krauter Vesuvius'. Flowers may open later. Grows 20 ft. high and wide. The best performer and longest lived of Big Cis® ('Schmidtcis'), 'Krauter Vesuvius', and 'Mt. St. Helens' at Milliken Arbore-

tum, where it grew 20 to 25 ft. high and wide in 20 years. Zones 5 to 8.

Prunus glandulosa 'Rosea Plena'

syn. *Prunus glandulosa* 'Sinensis'
dwarf flowering almond
A small, wispy shrub with essentially no redeeming characteristics other than its double, rose-pink flowers that cover the naked branches in April and May. After flowering, the plant is so bland it practically disappears until the next flowering season. Leaves are bright to medium green. An amazingly durable and adaptable plant. It has somewhat of a suckering tendency and will sneak around the garden and

neighborhood, appearing in places it was never planted. Despite all my biases against the plant, I must admit that the floral display is quite pretty. Prune after flowering to rejuvenate the plant. Can be used effectively in a border. Grows 4 to 5 ft. high and wide. Zones 4 to 8. China, Japan.
CULTIVARS AND VARIETIES
'Alba Plena' ('Alboplena') has double white flowers.

Prunus 'Hally Jolivette'

Some specimens of this hybrid cultivar (*Prunus subhirtella* × *P.* ×*yedoensis* backcrossed to *P. subhirtella*) form a tree-like habit, but most are densely

MORE ▶

Prunus glandulosa 'Rosea Plena'

Prunus glandulosa 'Alba Plena'

Prunus glandulosa 'Rosea Plena', dwarf flowering almond

Prunus 'Hally Jolivette'

Prunus 'Hally Jolivette' CONTINUED
branched shrubs, often wider than
they are tall. The small leaves are
glossy green and may develop yellow-
bronze fall color. The double, 1¼-in.-
wide flowers are pink in bud, opening
to pinkish white, and are effective
over a ten- to 20-day period in April
and May. Fine-textured stems add to
the beauty of the plant throughout the
seasons. Quite adaptable and fast-
growing, to 15 to 20 ft. high and wide.
Zones 5 to 7.

Prunus 'Hally Jolivette'

Prunus incisa 'Kojo-no-mai'

Prunus incisa 'Snow Cloud'

Prunus incisa
Fuji cherry
Dainty, refined, elegant, and seldom
available in garden commerce. A
large shrub or small tree with spreading habit and medium to dark green
leaves, 1 to 2¾ in. long, ⅔ to 1¼ in.
wide, that turn yellow, bronze, and red
in autumn. Not bad for a start yet the
best feature is the flower, white to
pale pink, single, campanulate, ¾ to 1
in. across, opening before the leaves
in late March to early April (zone 7).
The fruit are ¼- to ⅓-in.-long, ovoid,
purple-black drupes. I grew several
cultivars, and all perished without
expressing the reasons. Full sun,
well-drained soil should be sufficient.
Observed in many English gardens,
where it thrives with neglect. Beautiful accent or shrub border element.
Grows 15 to 20 (to 30) ft. high and
wide. Zones 5 and 6(7). Japan.
CULTIVARS AND VARIETIES
'Fair Elaine' is quite vigorous, with
pale pink petals, dark pink sepals,
and reddish bark.

'Kojo-no-mai' is a smallish shrub/
tree with twisted branches and pale
pink-white flowers. Was in every gar-

den center in England when I was on
sabbatical. Nifty plant, 4 ft. by 3 ft.,
although size is listed as 5 to 6 ft.
high. I believe rebranded in the United
States as Little Twist®.

'Snow Cloud' is smaller-statured
than 'Fair Elaine' with white pendent
flowers aging pink. Flowered late
March in the Dirr garden.

Prunus laurocerasus
common cherrylaurel, English laurel
A serviceable broadleaf evergreen
shrub with cosmopolitan adaptability from Atlanta to Boston to the
Pacific Coast. 'Tis a favorite of the
landscape architect clan, appearing
on their plans with the regularity of
eraser marks. The numerous cultivars fill many landscape niches and
have superseded the species, which
is rarely planted. The species develops into a large evergreen shrub,
oval-rounded to broad-spreading, of
solid, dense constitution. Dark green,
almost black-green, lustrous leaves,
2 to 6 (to 10) in. long, rank with yew
for somber expression. To be sure,
no broadleaf evergreen matches it
leaf-to-leaf for effectiveness. Flowers,

Prunus incisa, Fuji cherry

much like those of *Prunus caroliniana*, occur in 2- to 5-in.-long racemes from the leaf axils in April and May. The fragrance is the haunting, never-to-be-forgotten, plum aroma. Fruit are conical-rounded, purple to black, ⅓- to ½-in.-long drupes; seldom set on plants in the Southeast, more so in the West and Europe. Adaptable to sun and shade, requires well-drained soil. Shot hole—a disease complex that produces buckshot-like holes in leaves which enlarge, rendering the plant "mad dog" ugly—can be trouble-some. Used for screens, groupings, hedges, foundations, and massing. Grows 10 to 18 ft. high and wide, or wider. A pleasant and solitary walk along the River Test in Hampshire, England, revealed 30-ft.-high *P. laurocerasus* with 10- to 12-in.-wide trunks. Wow! Zones 6 to 8. Southeastern Europe into Asia.

CULTIVARS AND VARIETIES
Many, over 40 described, with a handful of key players in North American horticulture.

MORE ▶

Prunus laurocerasus Etna™

Prunus laurocerasus

Prunus laurocerasus, common cherrylaurel

Prunus laurocerasus

Prunus laurocerasus 'Otto Luyken'

Prunus laurocerasus 'Marbled White'

Prunus laurocerasus CONTINUED

'Batumi Rubies' is a large-leaf, vigorous selection with abundant red to black fruit. Leaves were prodigiously infected by *Entomosporium* at the JC Raulston Arboretum. Estimate 10 to 15 ft. high, 6 to 10 ft. wide.

'Castlewellan', 'Marbled Dragon', and 'Marbled White' are probably the same. Leaves splotched and streaked cream and green; unstable, reverting to green. Grows upright vase-shaped, 6 to 10 ft. high.

Etna™ ('Anbri') with compact, broad-upright habit and lustrous dark green leaves that clothe the branches, grows 2 to 4 ft. by 3 to 5 ft. Among the most beautiful of cultivars.

'Magnoliifolia', with immense 10- to 12-in.-long, 3- to 4½-in.-wide, lustrous black-green leaves, grows 20 to 25 ft. high, 30 to 35 ft. wide with maturity. At a distance, could be mistaken for *Magnolia grandiflora*.

'Majestic Jade' is a seedling selection from 'Otto Luyken' that grows 12 ft. by 8 to 10 ft., upright-oval-rounded in habit, with lustrous dark green leaves. It is more resistant to shot hole than 'Otto Luyken'. Introduced by the author.

'Otto Luyken', the crown prince of cultivars, is small, 3 to 4 ft. high, 6 to 8 ft. wide, with 2- to 4-in.-long, lustrous black-green leaves. Upper leaves are borne at a 45° angle to stem; abundant flowers on mature plant.

'Schipkaensis' grows 4 to 5 (to 10) ft. high and wide, forming a dense mound of 2- to 4½-in.-long, lustrous dark green leaves, each leaf with a few serrations toward the apex. Several different forms masquerade under this name, with 'West Coast Schipkaensis' distinctly different—more upright with prominently serrated leaves.

'Zabeliana' has that dog-eared, gracefully arching, willow-like leaf appearance; lustrous dark green leaves are not toothed and are narrower than either 'Otto Luyken' or 'Schipkaensis'. Grows 5 ft. high and considerably greater in spread.

Prunus lusitanica
Portuguese cherrylaurel
A large, bushy, evergreen shrub or small tree with 2½- to 5-in.-long, dark green leaves on rhubarb-red petioles

Prunus laurocerasus 'Schipkaensis'

Prunus laurocerasus 'Majestic Jade'

Prunus laurocerasus 'Zabeliana'

which hold the color in winter. Not well known but in many aspects, superior to *Prunus laurocerasus* because of shot hole resistance. White, ⅓- to ½-in.-wide, plum-fragrant flowers are produced in 6- to 10-in.-long, 1- to 1¼-in.-wide racemes, May and June, from the ends of the previous season's growth and from the axils of the leaves. The ⅓-in.-long, cone- to top-shaped fruit are shiny red, maturing dark purple-black. Sun- and shade-tolerant. Any well-drained soil, acid to neutral. Excel-

lent for groupings or screens, and has for 20 years been maintained as a hedge at the Atlanta Botanical Garden. Grows 10 to 20 ft. high in Southeast; larger on West Coast. Zones (6)7 to 9. Spain, Portugal.

CULTIVARS AND VARIETIES

'Myrtifolia' has smaller, ovate leaves, 2 to 2½ in. long, and a neat, rounded to conical habit.

'Variegata', with leaves irregularly margined with cream, is common in English gardens.

Prunus lusitanica

Prunus lusitanica

Prunus lusitanica 'Variegata'

Prunus lusitanica, Portuguese cherrylaurel, topiary

Prunus maackii

Amur chokecherry

On a sunny winter day, Amur choke-cherry is identifiable from a mile away. The glossy, amber to reddish brown to cinnamon-brown bark provides spectacular color in winter. The bark of young trees often exfoliates in shaggy masses, but it loses this quality with age. The habit is distinctly pyramidal in youth, becoming more rounded at maturity. The 2- to 4-in.-long, medium green leaves turn, at best, yellow-green in fall. White flowers are borne in 2- to 3-in. racemes in May and are followed by red fruit that mature to black in August. Tolerates less than perfect soil conditions as long as well drained. This species does not tolerate excessive heat and should be used only in colder climates. Grows 35 to 45 ft. high and wide. Most trees I observed were smaller. Zones 2 to 6. Manchuria, China.

CULTIVARS AND VARIETIES

'Amber Beauty', with a narrow crown and amber-colored bark, is not that different from everyday seedlings based on the plant I witnessed.

Goldrush® ('Jeffree') has coppery orange bark that resists frost-cracking; 25 ft. by 20 ft.

Goldspur® ('Jefspur') is a more compact tree, 15 ft. by 10 ft.

Prunus maritima

beach plum

Beach plum is not utilized to any degree in contemporary landscapes, but along the Atlantic Coast this shrub provides a burst of white spring flowers. Edible, ½- to 1-in.-long, yellow-orange fruit ripen to dull purple or crimson in August and are relished for jams and jellies. The 1½- to 3-in.-long, dull dark green leaves may develop slight fall color. Appears to thrive with neglect in sandy, salt-laden environ-

Prunus maackii

Prunus maackii

Prunus maackii, Amur chokecherry

ments. Good naturalizing plant. An artistic garden element when the lower branches are removed; I have observed many plants treated this way on Cape Cod, Massachusetts. Can form rather large colonies. Grows 6 ft. high or more. Observed large, 15- to 18-ft.-high plants on Martha's Vineyard and Cape Cod. Zones 3 to 6. Maine to Virginia.

Prunus mume
Japanese apricot

A favorite tree of J. C. Raulston, North Carolina State University, who advocated its use in southern gardens with preacher-like zeal. Unique because it flowers in January and February, when gardening lies dormant in reality and in mind. But the explosion of fragrant white, pink, and red flowers on

dormant stems turns the tide in this species' favor. A small tree, upright vase-shaped, finally with a rounded head, stems glistening green, it blends into any garden niche. A rooted cutting planted in our garden was 15 ft. high and wide in eight years. Foliage is nondescript medium green in summer, yellow-green at best in fall.

MORE ▶

Prunus maritima, beach plum

Prunus maritima

Prunus maritima

Prunus mume

Prunus mume

Prunus mume CONTINUED

The five-petaled flowers, single and double, 1 to 1¼ in. in diameter, occur singly or in pairs on long stems of the previous season and on short spurs on larger branches. The delicate fragrance is an added bonus, along with the extended, four- to eight-week floral period. Fruit are largely inedible, yellowish, globose, 1- to 1½-in.-wide drupes. A well-drained, reasonably fertile, acid soil in full sun is ideal. Not the longest lived tree, with ten to 20 years a reasonable span. Many uses, with single specimen, groupings, and border use among the best. Handsome specimens from Washington, D.C., to Charleston, South Carolina, have crossed my path. Grows 15 to 20 ft. high and wide. Zones 6 to 9, 10 in California. Japan, China.

CULTIVARS AND VARIETIES

Over 250 named selections with unique growth habits and flower characteristics.

'Dawn' has large, ruffled, double pink flowers and is later flowering.

'Matsurabara Red' produces double, dark red flowers on an upright tree to 20 ft. high.

'Peggy Clarke' bears double, deep rose flowers with extremely long stamens and a red calyx.

'Rosemary Clarke' has large, double, fragrant white flowers with red calyces.

'W. B. Clarke' offers double pink flowers on a weeping framework.

Prunus mume, Japanese apricot

Prunus mume 'W. B. Clarke'

Prunus mume 'Dawn'

Prunus mume 'Matsurabara Red'

Prunus 'Okame'

Okame cherry

This upright, eventually arching, flowering cherry has received greater garden press than any other cherry. In youth the outline is distinctly upright and vase-shaped, almost broad-columnar, becoming more rounded with age; many trees on the Georgia campus have followed this script. The polished, reddish brown bark is covered with horizontal lenticels. Rich carmine-pink petals and the ruby-red calyx provide an extended period of color. The flowers appear before the leaves in March and April (February in Athens). The 1- to 2½-in.-long, dark green leaves turn bronzy red in autumn. Okame cherry is deservedly one of the most popular garden cherries, demonstrating excellent heat and cold tolerance. It makes a handsome specimen tree or can be used in groupings of three to five. Hybridized by Collingwood Ingram of England, using *Prunus incisa* and *P. campanulata*. Grows 20 to 30 ft. high. Zones 5 to 8.

CULTIVARS AND VARIETIES
'Dream Catcher', an open-pollinated seedling of 'Okame', produces bright pink flowers one week after 'Okame'; dark green leaves turn orange-red in fall. An introduction from the U.S. National Arboretum, it grows 25 ft. high, 20 ft. wide in 12 years. Early leafing by mid April in zone 7. Almost in full leaf when flower buds of Pink Flair® are just opening.

Prunus 'Okame'

Prunus 'Okame', Okame cherry

Prunus 'Okame'

Prunus 'Dream Catcher'

Prunus padus

European bird cherry

In early spring, this is one of the first trees to leaf out in the Midwest. The new leaves are combinations of bright and bronzy greens, and they mature to a dull dark green. Autumn foliage color ranges from yellow to bronze. The mature habit is rounded with ascending branches. Fragrant white flowers occur in drooping, loose racemes, 3 to 6 in. long, in April and May. Small, black fruit ripen in July and August. This species is susceptible to black knot, a fungal disease that causes grotesque blackish growths on the stems. At its best, European bird cherry has much to offer the northern landscape. Grows 30 to 40 ft. high and wide. Zones 3 to 6. Europe, northern Asia to Korea and Japan.

CULTIVARS AND VARIETIES
Several red- to burgundy-leaf selections including 'Berg', Merlot® ('Drietree'), and Summer Glow® ('DTR 117').

'Watereri', with 8-in.-long racemes, is quite effective in flower.

Prunus padus fall color

Prunus padus 'Watereri'

Prunus padus, European bird cherry

Prunus persica

peach

Beautiful in flower—an entire peach orchard in rich pink spring flower is a spectacular sight—but unfortunately, unreliable as a garden plant over the long haul. I cannot remember seeing any truly old trees in landscapes. Flowers appear in March and April before

Prunus persica, peach

the leaves, and even the worst forms are eye-catching. The habit of most trees is rounded. The lustrous dark green, 3- to 6-in.-long leaves die off yellow in fall. For maximum growth and landscape longevity, provide moist, acid, well-drained soils, in full sun. Borers and cankers are troublesome. Use and enjoy with the knowledge that the tree may not be present next year. Grows 15 to 25 ft. high and wide. Zones 5 to 9. China.

CULTIVARS AND VARIETIES
The number of flowering peach cultivars that have been named over the centuries is astronomical. Flower color varies, from white to pink to deep red or multi-colored, in singles and doubles. 'Bonanza', a dwarf pink-flowered form, and the columnar Corinthian™ series offer single and double, white- to pink-flowered selections with green or red-purple foliage. Double-flowered types like 'Peppermint Stick', red and white striped flowers, are especially numerous.

Prunus sargentii
Sargent cherry
Many gardeners consider this the crème de la crème of the flowering cherries. The habit is upright-spreading to rounded, with deep reddish brown, polished bark. The 1¼- to 1½-in.-wide, pink flowers open before the leaves in April and May and are followed by pea-sized fruit, ⅓ in. across, yellow to red ripening to a dark purple in June and July. The reddish tinged new leaves become shiny dark green in summer and bronze-red in autumn.

MORE ▶

Prunus sargentii, Sargent cherry

Prunus persica

Prunus persica Corinthian™ Pink

Prunus persica

Prunus sargentii CONTINUED

Prunus sargentii

Prunus sargentii

Prunus 'Accolade'

Prunus sargentii Pink Flair®

The flowers coincide with daffodils, and Sargent cherry trees underplanted with bulbs paint a springtime masterpiece. Once established, this species exhibits greater staying power than most *Prunus* species, and old specimens in New England attest to its persistence. Grows 20 to 30 ft. high and wide under landscape conditions. Zones 4 to 7. Japan.

CULTIVARS AND VARIETIES
'Accolade' is a rounded, spreading form with 1½-in.-wide, blush-pink flowers in April. Each flower is composed of 12 to 15 petals. Grows 20 to 25 ft. high. I have always considered this hybrid cultivar, the result of a cross between *Prunus sargentii* and *P. subhirtella*, one of the most beautiful flowering cherries.

'Columnaris' is somewhat of a misnomer, for the trees become vase-shaped rather than truly columnar. It possesses the same desirable attributes as *Prunus sargentii*. Grows 25 to 35 ft. high, 10 to 15 ft. wide.

Pink Flair® ('JFS-KW58') with single, clean pink flowers, late March to early April, dark green leaves, orange-red fall color, upright, narrow vase-shaped habit, grows 25 ft. by 15 ft. Cold hardy in North Dakota and considered zone 3 adaptable. Superior performance to 'Dream Catcher' and 'First Lady' in Spartanburg, South Carolina.

'Shosar' is a narrow-crowned, vase-shaped tree with single, rich vibrant pink, 1½-in.-wide flowers several weeks ahead of *Prunus sargentii*. Parentage is (*P. incisa* × *P. campanulata*) × *P. sargentii*. Matures in the 20- to 25-ft. height range.

Prunus sargentii 'Columnaris' fall color

Prunus serotina
black cherry

I do not remember ever seeing this native species listed in a nursery catalog, probably because it is almost weed-like over much of the eastern United States. The propensity of black cherry to produce thousands of stray seedlings has not endeared it to gardeners. The habit is pyramidal to conical in youth, becoming oval-headed with pendulous branches. New leaves are sparkling bronzy to bright green, turning dark green with maturity and developing reasonable yellow to red fall color. White flowers occur in 4- to 6-in.-long, ¾-in.-wide racemes in April, followed by prodigious quantities of ⅓-in.-wide, red to black fruit. Not a good tree for the average garden, but in a native setting it is certainly worth enjoying. Source of valuable timber for furniture. Grows 50 to 60 ft. high, 20 to 30 ft. wide. Zones 3 to 9. Ontario to North Dakota, south to Florida and Texas.

Prunus serrula
paperbark cherry

Spectacular bark—glistening, polished, reflective reddish brown with soft exfoliating paper sheets or fragments. Sounds great? Indeed, but the caveat is that it is somewhat touchy under cultivation. Lustrous dark green leaves, 2 to 4 in. long, ½ to 1¼ in. wide, offer little ornament, as do the white flowers produced in twos and threes with the foliage. My prototype specimen resided in Beth Chatto's garden in England, probably

MORE ▶

Prunus serrula

Prunus serotina

Prunus serotina, black cherry

Prunus serotina

643

Prunus serrula, paperbark cherry

Prunus serrula CONTINUED
30 ft. by 30 ft., with a trunk and branch structure that maximized bark color. Cankers and borers appear to minimize success in the United States; perhaps it is achieved in the Pacific Northwest, but I can't remember a single plant there. Grows 20 to 30 ft. high and wide. Zones 5 and 6. Central China.

Prunus serrulata
Japanese flowering or oriental cherry
This species, or at least its cultivars, epitomizes to most gardeners all that is sacred about cherries. In its finest forms, the habit is vase-shaped to rounded. Newly emerging leaves vary from fresh spring-green to bronze-green. The lustrous dark green, 2- to 5-in.-long summer leaves turn bronze to subdued red in fall. Flowers open in early to mid April on the majority of cultivars (Athens, zone 7). Fruit are seldom produced. *Prunus serrulata* is used for every imaginable landscape situation, from a single lawn specimen to a street tree to formal allées.

Prunus serrulata 'Amanogawa'

Prunus serrulata 'Kanzan'

Prunus serrulata, Japanese flowering cherry

Many cultivars are short-lived (ten to 15 years); in recent years, 'Kanzan' has suffered more than most. Viruses and cankers lead to gradual decline and, eventually, death. Species grows 50 to 75 ft. high, but the cultivars are 20 to 35 ft. high. Zones 5 to 8. Japan, Korea, China.

CULTIVARS AND VARIETIES

'Amanogawa' develops an upright-columnar habit and produces single to semi-double, pink flowers. Grows 20 ft. high, 4 to 5 ft. wide.

'Kanzan' ('Kwanzan', 'Sekiyama'), with deep pink, double flowers, is the most common garden representative of the species. May grow 30 to 40 ft. high and wide.

'Royal Burgundy' is a branch sport of 'Kanzan' with reddish purple leaves. Upright vase-shaped in youth, rounded with age, 20 to 25 ft. by 15 to 25 ft. Rather pretty in spring flowering mode.

Flowers deeper pink-rose-purple than 'Kanzan'.

'Shirofugen' is pink in bud, opening to white, and fading again to pink, with 30 petals per flower. New leaves are deep bronze. A vigorous grower that develops a wide-spreading, flat-topped crown. Grows 25 to 30 ft. high, 20 to 25 ft. wide.

'Shirotae' ('Mt. Fuji') is rich pink in bud, opening white. New leaves are pale green with a bronze tint. The growth habit is broad-spreading, rather flat-topped. Grows 15 to 20 ft. high and wide.

'Taihaku' produces single white, 2- to 2½-in.-wide flowers, reddish bronze leaves when unfurling, yellow-orange in fall. Broad, inverted cone-shaped habit, 20 to 25 (to 40) ft.

'Ukon' offers semi-double to double, 1¾-in.-wide, greenish yellow flowers; 20 ft. by 30 ft.

Prunus subhirtella

Higan cherry

Along with *Prunus sargentii*, this is one of the longest lived flowering cherries. The ½- to ¾-in.-wide, white to pinkish flowers arrive before the leaves in March and April. The habit is typically upright-spreading to rounded. The 1- to 4-in.-long, lustrous green leaves turn yellowish in fall. For the gardener who wants one cherry that will provide many years of enjoyment, this tree and its cultivars are possibly the best choices. Plants, once established, will grow in brick-hard clay. Tolerant of heat, more so than *P. sargentii*. Interestingly, I have observed this species surviving on the campus of the University of Maine at Orono, where most of the desirable flowering cherries are not sufficiently cold hardy. Grows 20 to 40 ft. high, 15 to

MORE ▶

Prunus serrulata 'Kanzan' fall color

Prunus serrulata 'Taihaku'

Prunus serrulata 'Shirotae'

Prunus serrulata 'Shirofugen'

Prunus subhirtella CONTINUED

30 ft. wide or more. Zones 4 to 8(9). Japan.

CULTIVARS AND VARIETIES
'Autumnalis' flowers in fall and spring, producing pinkish white, ten- to 15-petaled flowers, ½ to ¾ in. in diameter. The spring bloom is more potent than the fall bloom. Grows 20 to 30 ft. high and wide.

'Pendula' is greatly variable. It reproduces partially true to type from seed, so many forms are available in commerce. In youth it is a wild and woolly weeping tree, but it calms down with age, attaining a rather elegant, dap-

per, stately character. Flowers may be white but are usually pink. Buy the tree when it is in flower to be sure of flower color. Grows 40 ft. high and wide. There is also a double pink form, 'Pendula Plena Rosea'. Winter outline,

Prunus subhirtella 'Autumnalis'

Prunus subhirtella 'Pendula'

Prunus subhirtella 'Pendula'

Prunus subhirtella 'Autumnalis'

Prunus subhirtella 'Pendula'

stem and bark coloration are beautiful. In my travels, I see more weeping Higan than any other cherry, particularly in the Southeast.

Pink Snow Showers™ ('Pisnshzam') with clean, leaf-spot-resistant, lustrous dark green foliage and single pink flowers is touted as one of the best new weeping cherries. Witnessed in flower at Milliken Arboretum, where flowers had faded to almost white.

Prunus tenella
dwarf Russian almond

Certainly not very common in the United States, but the few I have seen in flower were extremely showy. It is a low, suckering shrub with 1½- to 3½-in.-long, dark green leaves. The rose-red, ½-in.-wide flowers occur singly or in clusters of two or three, from buds of the previous year's growth. Minimal information is available on

culture, but well-drained soils and full sun are imperative. Use in the border. Grows 2 to 5 ft. high and wide. Zones 2 to 6. Europe, Asia.
CULTIVARS AND VARIETIES
'Firehill' bears potent red flowers on naked stems. Weak habit but flowers are vivid.

Forma *georgica* has larger leaves and white flowers; 15 to 20 ft. high, the largest *Prunus tenella* I have witnessed.

Prunus tomentosa
Manchu or Nanking cherry

Manchu cherry is sold for its edible scarlet fruit, but in the northern states it is one of the first shrubs to flower and is worth using for that reason alone. By no means a small shrub, *Prunus tomentosa* is broad-spreading and densely twiggy, becoming more open and picturesque with age. It

MORE ▶

Prunus tenella 'Firehill'

Prunus tomentosa

Prunus tomentosa yellow-leaf form

Prunus tomentosa, Manchu cherry

Prunus tomentosa CONTINUED

is not a bad idea to prune the lower limbs to expose the exfoliating reddish brown bark. Fragrant white flowers, ¾ in. in diameter, appear on leafless branches in early to mid April. The fruit ripen in June and July. The 2- to 3-in.-long, dark green leaves are extremely hairy on their undersides. Very adaptable to soils. Provide full sun. Useful in mass plantings or in the shrub border. Grows 6 to 10 ft. high, may spread to 15 ft. Zones 2 to 6(7). China, Japan.

CULTIVARS AND VARIETIES

Witnessed a yellow-leaf form at Scott McMahan's Clermont, Georgia, nursery. Loses color in Georgia heat. Might prove more colorful in northern climes.

Prunus triloba var. multiplex

flowering almond, double flowering plum

For rich pink flower effect in April, this is a most magnificent choice. The 1- to 1½-in.-wide, double flowers clothe the naked branches in rich rose-pink.

The medium green leaves, 1 to 2½ in. long, turn yellow to bronze in fall. An adaptable shrub, but it requires full sun for best flowering. Looks a bit bedraggled in the winter months. Use in a border or mass. Grows 12 to 15 ft. high and wide. Zones 3 to 6. China.

Prunus virginiana

common chokecherry

This suckering small tree or large shrub is similar to *Prunus padus* in several respects, and the two species are quite difficult to accurately separate. Flowers, white, are borne in 3- to 6-in.-long, 1-in.-wide racemes in April and May. The fruit, red to dark purple, round, ⅓ in. in diameter, are used for making jams, jellies, pies, sauces, and wines. Suited only to the colder areas of North America. Tolerates high pH and clay soils. Have picnicked next

Prunus triloba var. *multiplex*, flowering almond

Prunus virginiana

Prunus triloba var. *multiplex*

Prunus triloba var. *multiplex* fall color

to the species growing along the rocky coast of Maine. Grows 20 to 35 ft. high, 18 to 25 ft. wide. Zones 2 to 5. Canada, northern United States.

CULTIVARS AND VARIETIES
'Schubert' ('Canada Red') is a selection with reddish purple foliage. New growth emerges green. It reproduces true to type from seed. Suitable only for northern climates, although a single plant in an Athens garden is defying my contention. Apparently black knot disease is serious in Plains States.

Prunus ×*yedoensis*
Yoshino cherry

This is the species that dominates the Tidal Basin in Washington, D.C. Several years past, I witnessed this rim of billowy white that surrounds the water—never have I seen more cameras aimed at the same subject. It's a shame that the allure and power of a cherry in flower cannot be transferred to the politicians. The habit of Yoshino cherry is rounded to broad-rounded. The 2½- to 4½-in.-long, dark green leaves develop a semblance of yellow to bronze fall color. The ½- to ⅝-in.-wide flowers are light pink in bud, opening to clouds of white. Although fleeting, the effect is spectacular. The falling petals are reminiscent of giant snowflakes. Blackish, ⅓- to ½-in.-wide fruit ripen in June and July. The species is used extensively for street plantings; in some cities, such as Macon, Georgia, it has become a monoculture, and festivals celebrate the tree's mystique. As a single specimen, Yoshino cherry provides great beauty in the early spring garden. It flowers reasonably well when used as an understory tree with pines overhead. Grows 40 to 50 ft. high and wide; usually smaller under cultivation. Zones 5 to 8. Japan.

CULTIVARS AND VARIETIES
'Akebono' ('Daybreak') has soft pink

MORE ▶

Prunus virginiana, common chokecherry

Prunus ×*yedoensis*

Prunus virginiana

Prunus virginiana 'Schubert'

Prunus ×yedoensis

Prunus ×yedoensis CONTINUED

flowers and a rounded, spreading growth habit. In youth it is extremely vigorous. A great cherry. The first in the new Dirr garden.

'Shidare Yoshino' is a weeping, white-flowered selection. Grows 15 ft. high and 20 to 25 ft. wide in ten years. Eighteen-year-old plant in the University's Botanical Garden was 20 ft. by 30 ft. with wildly arching-pendulous branches. Often treated as syn-onymous with f. *perpendens*, but there is no guarantee that plants labeled f. *perpendens* will grow like 'Shidare Yoshino'.

'Snow Fountains' ('White Fountain' by Wayside), a semi-weeping form with white flowers, is widely promoted but lacks grace. Foliage is dark green and turns gold and orange shades in fall. Grows 6 to 12 ft. high and wide. Often grafted on a standard to produce a tidy, small, weeping fountain.

Prunus ×yedoensis 'Snow Fountains'

Prunus ×yedoensis, Yoshino cherry

Prunus ×yedoensis 'Shidare Yoshino'

Prunus ×yedoensis 'Akebono'

Pseudocydonia sinensis

syn. *Cydonia sinensis*

Chinese quince

Perhaps the best feature of this large shrub or small tree is its exfoliating bark in colors of gray, green, orange, and brown. The trunks become fluted or corrugated with age. The leathery, lustrous dark green foliage is also handsome. Soft pink, self-fertile flowers, 1 to 1½ in. across, appear in April and May. The 5- to 7-in.-long, egg-shaped fruit are citron-yellow; they are exceptionally firm but can be utilized for jelly. Provide well-drained soils, in full sun to partial shade. Fireblight is a significant problem and may limit successful culture. Use as a specimen. Great and spectacular plants in Chapel Hill and Athens. I am tempted to plant a grouping in the garden. Grows 10 to 20 ft. high, 5 to 15 ft. wide. Zones (5)6 and 7. China.

Pseudocydonia sinensis

Pseudocydonia sinensis

Pseudocydonia sinensis, Chinese quince, fall color

Pseudolarix amabilis

syn. *Pseudolarix kaempferi*

golden larch

What a beauty! Especially in autumn when the needles turn clear golden yellow: during my sabbatical at the Arnold Arboretum, October 16 was the peak, essentially dissipated by October 24. Softly pyramidal in youth, more open with horizontal branches and a habit akin to that of cedar of Lebanon. The softest light green needles are borne singly on long shoots, in a radiating cluster, on spur-like branches. Cones,

MORE ▶

Pseudolarix amabilis male cones

Pseudocydonia sinensis

Pseudocydonia sinensis

Pseudolarix amabilis CONTINUED
magnificent, 2 to 3 in. long, 1½ to 2 in.
wide, soft lime-green to golden maize
brilliance, shattering at maturity, ripening in their first year. Adaptable to any
soil except wet but prefers light, moist,
acid, deep, well-drained soils. Wonderful specimen tree, in groupings, and
anywhere space exists. Every gardener
should at least consider the species.
I grew it in Athens and Chapel Hill.
Grows 30 to 50 ft. high, spreading 20
to 40 ft. A respectable 30-ft. specimen at the JC Raulston Arboretum.
Estimate trees at the Arnold Arboretum to be 60 ft. or greater. Zones (4)5
to 7. Eastern China.

Pseudotsuga menziesii
Douglas-fir

I had never seen this magnificent
needle evergreen in the wild until I
was able to experience it first-hand
during a trip along the West Coast.
Douglas-fir is a great tree for the
northern states and should be used
more often. It is a tall, airy, spire-like,
soft-textured tree. In youth the habit
is uniformly pyramidal with drooping
lower branches and ascending upper
branches; in old age the top remains
irregularly conical and the long, slender bole is branchless. The 1- to
1½-in.-long, flattish, blue-green needles are arranged in a spiral around
the stem, so that a small V-shaped

Pseudolarix amabilis, golden larch, fall color

Pseudolarix amabilis fall color

Pseudolarix amabilis female cones

groove is evident on the upper side of the branches. The 3- to 4-in.-long cones have extended bracts reminiscent of a horseshoe crab's tail. The species prefers moisture-retentive soils but is quite adaptable. Ideal as a specimen, in groupings, or as a screen. Also makes a fine Christmas tree, because the needles are retained better than those of spruce or fir under hot, dry conditions. Great variation in needle color. Opt for the best bluish green forms, which are considered more cold hardy. Grows 40 to 80 ft. high, 12 to 20 ft. wide. Co-national champions in the 300 ft. range. Zones 4 to 6. Not adapted to the heat of zone 7 and higher in the South. Western United States.

Ptelea trifoliata
hoptree

A wonderful native shrub or small tree with a wide geographical range. Found in the understory but nowhere very abundant. Leaves are trifoliate, each leaflet 2½ to 5 in. long, narrowed at ends, lustrous dark green and, when bruised, emit a potent citrus-oil aroma. Flowers, greenish white, in 2- to 3-in.-wide corymbs in May and June, blend with the foliage. Nifty samara, ¾ to 1 in. across, rounded, winged around the periphery, the seed in the middle. Prefers moist, well-drained, acid soil but in wild inhabits rocky woods, better drained lowlands, and moist woodlands. Adaptable to

MORE ▶

Pseudotsuga menziesii

Ptelea trifoliata

Pseudotsuga menziesii, Douglas-fir

Ptelea trifoliata 'Aurea'

Ptelea trifoliata CONTINUED
full sun and shade. Best use is in a naturalized situation. Not enough "socko" to excite weekend garden center customers. Grows 5 to 15 ft. high and wide. Witnessed a 20-ft. specimen on the New Hampshire campus. Zones 3 to 9. Ontario and New York to Florida, west to Minnesota, southern Colorado, Arizona, south to southern Mexico.
CULTIVARS AND VARIETIES
'Aurea' has soft yellow foliage that matures to green. Pretty effect in the spring landscape. Comes 90 percent true to type from seed.

Pterocarya fraxinifolia
Caucasian wingnut
One of the unknown Noble Trees reserved for the sanctuaries of arboreta and botanical gardens. Beautiful, bordering on majestic, and specimens at Vineland Station, Ontario, Canada, and Abbotsbury Garden, England, exceed the lofty accolades. Round-headed with massive limbs, the leaves bringing textural softness because of compound pinnate nature, with 11 to 25 leaflets, each 3 to 5 in. long, and shiny dark green. Have yet to experience fall color of any ilk. Greenish monoecious flowers in 5-in.-long catkins (male), to 20-in.-long (female). Fruit are reminiscent of a wing-nut, about ¾ in. in diameter, green to brown, attached along the length of the infructescence. Best performance in moist soils; the largest specimens witnessed were next to lakes and streams. Tendency to sucker. Speci-

Ptelea trifoliata

Ptelea trifoliata, hoptree

Pterocarya stenoptera

Pterocarya fraxinifolia

men use only. Seldom available in commerce. Grows 30 to 50 ft. high and wide. Genetics point to even larger trees. Witnessed a 160-year-old tree. Zones 5 to 8(9). Caucasus to northern Iran.

Pterocarya stenoptera, Chinese wingnut, is occasionally present in collections. Differs from *P. fraxinifolia* by the winged and toothed rachis of the leaf. Zones (5)6 to 8. China.

Pterostyrax hispida
fragrant epaulettetree

In flower, quite respectable as the fragrant, white flowers are borne in 5- to 10-in.-long, 2- to 3-in.-wide, pendulous, pubescent panicles in May and June after the leaves mature. Fruit are ½ in. long, ten-ribbed, cylindric, densely bristly dry drupes and persist into fall. Habit is round-headed with an open crown of slender, spreading branches.

MORE ▶

Pterocarya fraxinifolia, Caucasian wingnut

Pterostyrax hispida

Pterostyrax corymbosa, little epaulettetree

Pterostyrax hispida, fragrant epaulettetree

Pterostyrax hispida CONTINUED

Leaves, bright green, silver-green below, are 3 to 7½ in. long, 1½ to 4 in. wide, and develop at best yellow-green fall color. Best in moist, well-drained soil in sun to partial shade. Unusual accent or small specimen tree. Witnessed respectable plants in partial shade. Grows 20 to 30 ft. high and wide. Zones 5 to 8. Japan, China.

Pterostyrax corymbosa, little epaulettetree, is just that, smaller in all its parts, leaves 2 to 5 in. long with bristly teeth, 3- to 5-in.-long panicles, five-winged, ½-in.-long, woolly drupe, and perhaps a better garden plant. Seldom encountered in gardens but a worthy flowering shrub; 10 to 15 ft. high. Zones 5 to 7. Japan, China.

Punica granatum
pomegranate

Beautiful shrub that receives minimal press in southern and western garden literature yet produces beautiful five- to seven-petaled, orange flowers in June, lustrous rich green foliage, and edible, reddish fruit. In zone 7, plants are injured by low temperatures, and tender spring foliage may be killed by a

Pterostyrax corymbosa

Punica granatum 'Wonderful' fall color

Punica granatum, pomegranate

late freeze. These liabilities aside, the species develops into a large upright-oval to spreading rounded shrub composed of numerous slender branches. The "bundle-of-sticks" appearance in winter scares some gardeners. The 1- to 3-in.-long, oval-lanceolate, lustrous dark green leaves change to soft yellow-green, on occasion brilliant yellow, in fall. The 2-in.-long, 2-in.-wide flowers—petals like crepe paper, calyx cup rindy like an orange—open in May and June (Athens), with an occasional flower present into late summer. The 2- to 3½- (to 5-) in.-wide fruit, with thick leathery rind and edible fleshy-coated seeds, ripen in September and October. Site in full sun, well-drained soil; pH adaptable, tolerates sand and clay. Handsome shrub in flower and worthy of inclusion in the border. Tolerates partial shade and still flowers with moderate gusto. Spring frost damage has killed three different cultivars to the ground in our garden. Grows 12 to 15 ft. high and wide. Zones (7)8 to 10. Eastern Mediterranean to the Himalayas.

CULTIVARS AND VARIETIES
'Legrellei' produces double salmon-pink flowers on a large shrub.

Variety *nana* ('Nana') grows 3 to 4 (to 6) ft. high and wide, with red-orange single flowers and 2-in.-wide, orange-red fruit. Beautiful in mass plantings; one such on the Georgia campus persisted for 18 years. More cold hardy than the species.

'Orange Blossom Special' is a compact, var. *nana* type with unabated, relentless production of orange, 1½-in.-long flowers from May to November (Athens). Fruit are about 1 in. wide, rounded, green-blush-red, shiny. Grows 2 to 3 ft. high and wide. From Plant Introductions, Inc.

Purple Sunset™ ('PIIPG-I') is a more upright form of var. *nana* with 1½-in.-long, orange flowers, May to October, and ovoid-rounded, polished purple fruit about 1 in. long. Beautiful lustrous dark green, narrow lanceolate leaves, 1 to 1½ in. long, turn soft yellow in autumn. Estimate 3 to 4 ft. high and wide at maturity. Displayed elevated cold hardiness with no injury to uncovered container plants at 10°F. Not as prolific a flowerer as 'Orange Blossom Special', but the eggplant-shiny, purple-black fruit are beautiful into November. Developed by Plant Introductions, Inc.

'Wonderful,' a large shrub type with orange flowers, is among the most common of the numerous fruiting cultivars in commerce.

Punica granatum

Punica granatum

Punica granatum var. *nana*

Punica granatum 'Orange Blossom Special'

Punica granatum Purple Sunset™

Pyracantha coccinea
firethorn

For fruit display in the winter garden, few plants rival pyracanthas. Framed by the dark leaves, or nestled among them, the bright orange-red fruit provide spectacular fall and winter color. Typically, firethorn is a large, unkempt and splaying evergreen shrub with stiff, thorny branches. The 1- to 2½-in.-long, lustrous dark green

Pyracantha coccinea

Pyracantha coccinea

Pyracantha coccinea 'Navaho'

leaves may develop bronzy off-green colors in extremely cold weather. Slightly malodorous white flowers smother the plant in May and June. The fruit ripen in September and October and persist into winter. Transplant from a container into any well-drained soil. Pyracanthas are amazingly adaptable and make good choices for dry soils. They require full sun for best fruiting but will do well in partial shade. Many uses, including barrier, mass, hedge, and espalier. Select cold hardy cultivars for zone 6 and lower. Grows 6 to 18 ft. high and wide. Zones (5)6 to 8. Italy to Caucasus.

CULTIVARS AND VARIETIES
'Chadwickii' develops a more compact, spreading habit and orange-red fruit. Shows good hardiness. Grows 6 ft. high.

'Fiery Cascade' is an 8-ft.-high and 9-ft.-wide cultivar with small red fruit.

'Gnome', a compact (6 ft. by 8 ft.)

shrub with orange fruit, and 'Rutgers', a selection that grows 3 ft. by 9 ft. and bears orange-red fruit, are cold hardy to about −10°F or lower.

'Lalandei' is a large, shrubby form. It offers orange-red fruit and good cold hardiness. Grows 10 to 15 ft. high.

'Mohave' and 'Navaho' are scab-resistant, orange-red fruiting selections from Dr. Don Egolf, U.S. National Arboretum.

'Wyattii' is a vigorous form with orange-red fruit and good cold tolerance. Grows 9 to 12 ft. high and wide.

Pyracantha koidzumii
Formosa firethorn

This species picks up the landscape slack in the South, about where *Pyracantha coccinea* ends. A large, upright, wild, splaying, "thuggy," broadleaf evergreen shrub with sharp spines, it consumes large chunks of real estate. Lustrous dark green,

Pyracantha coccinea, firethorn

spatulate-shaped, 1- to 3-in.-long leaves, essentially without marginal teeth, permit separation from the toothed margins of *P. coccinea*. The white flowers smother the foliage in April and May, each five-petaled, ¼ in. in diameter, and with hawthorn-like odor. Fruit are spectacular, persistent into winter, and, along with *Nandina*, provide maximum effect for extended periods. The ¼-in.-wide, red pome colors in September and October. Full sun, hot, dry locations in well-drained soil suit it best. Transplant from a container and do not move once located. Best use is espaliered on south and west walls and fences. Reasonable barrier plant but a maintenance nightmare. Pyracanthas in general have descended from favor due to rampaging growth, spiny branches, and insect and disease problems. Grows 8 to 12 (to 20) ft. high and wide. Zones 8 to 10. Taiwan.

CULTIVARS AND VARIETIES
'Low-Dense' grows in a mounded form to 6 ft. high and produces orange-red fruit. Less cold hardy than the species.

'Santa Cruz' is a more prostrate form, almost groundcover-like, 2½ to 3 ft. high, 5 to 6 ft. wide, with beautiful dark green leaves and red fruit. Highly resistant to fruit scab.

Silver Lining™ ('Cadvar') has fewer thorns, orange-red fruit, and a silver variegation to the leaves, aging to green, then bronze and rose in winter. Listed at 3 ft. by 3 ft.; I witnessed a 6- to 7-ft.-high and -wide plant in north Florida. Flowers open in early May in Athens.

Pyrus calleryana
Callery pear

True *Pyrus calleryana* is a thorny, coarse, irregular tree, the only redeeming characteristic of which is the early spring white flowers, but even they are mildly disagreeable in their odor. The true species is generally used as an understock for budding the more desirable cultivars, the tree's main representatives in the landscape. The species was used as breeding stock in an attempt to incorporate fireblight resistance into *P. communis*, common pear; this experiment did not work, but gardeners have benefited (I am having doubts) from the ornamental attributes of the resulting cultivars. The most notable cultural aspect of *P. calleryana* is its tremendous tolerance to heat, drought, and compacted soils. Zones 5 to 8(9). Korea, China.

CULTIVARS AND VARIETIES
Pears have invaded the Southeast and are the biggest threat to any fallow/vacant fields/highway interchanges/

MORE ▶

Pyracantha koidzumii, Formosa firethorn

Pyracantha koidzumii

Pyracantha koidzumii Silver Lining™

Pyrus calleryana CONTINUED
fencerows; seedlings dominate the landscape along I-85 from Chapel Hill, North Carolina, to Atlanta. Observed runaway seedlings from Long Island to Birmingham. Of the many cultivars, the following are worth considering:

Pyrus calleryana 'Autumn Blaze' fall color

Pyrus calleryana, Callery pear

Pyrus calleryana 'Bradford'

Pyrus calleryana

Pyrus calleryana fall color

Pyrus calleryana

Pyrus calleryana 'Trinity'

'Autumn Blaze', one of the most cold hardy, −30 to −35°F; Edgewood® ('Edgedell'), a hybrid (*Pyrus calleryana × P. betulifolia*) that performed well in Spartanburg, South Carolina, with rounded, 30 ft. by 25 ft. outline, early white flowers, clean foliage; and 'Trinity', with rounded head and good cold hardiness. 'Capital' and 'Whitehouse' are to be avoided because of high disease susceptibility.

'Aristocrat' is a pyramidal to broad-pyramidal form, with coarse, horizontal branches. The lustrous dark green, wavy-margined leaves turn persim-

MORE ▶

Pyrus calleryana 'Aristocrat'

Pyrus Edgewood®

Pyrus calleryana 'Aristocrat'

661

Pyrus calleryana CONTINUED

mon-orange in fall. The white flowers are not as profuse as those of 'Bradford', but this cultivar is more structurally sound. Better suited to the North; fireblight has been problematic in the South. Grows 40 ft. high, 20 to 25 ft. wide. Does not grow old gracefully.

'Bradford', introduced in the early 1960s, is as common as mud in U.S. landscapes. It is densely branched and foliaged, broad-conical in habit in youth and maturity. A profusion of white flowers appear in March and April, and the leathery, 1½- to 3-in.-long and -wide, dark green leaves turn fluorescent orange and red in fall. Highly resistant to fireblight. Despite

Pyrus calleryana 'Bradford'

Pyrus calleryana 'Bradford' fall color

Pyrus calleryana 'Chanticleer'

Pyrus communis, common pear

662

all its desirable attributes, however, 'Bradford' suffers from a fatal genetic flaw that causes it to self-destruct, literally falling apart with time—the many branches will cause the tree to split in half after ten to 15 years. For short-term use, it may be acceptable, but to plant entire streets with this cultivar is playing biological Russian roulette. My current thinking is to not plant it.

'Chanticleer' (also 'Select', 'Cleveland Select', or 'Stone Hill') is an upright pyramidal form that shows no propensity to break apart with age.

It flowers heavily and displays good fireblight resistance, but its yellow-orange-apricot fall color does not measure up to that of 'Bradford'. Grows 35 ft. high and 16 ft. wide in 15 years.

Pyrus communis
common pear

Gardeners rarely utilize the fruiting pear for ornamental purposes, but many older residences and farmsteads have a tree or two. The 1- to 1½-in.-wide, white flowers open in

MORE ▶   *Pyrus communis*

Pyrus communis espalier

Pyrus communis

Pyrus communis fall color

Pyrus pyrifolia, Chinese sand pear

Pyrus pyrifolia fall color

April and are quite disagreeable to the olfactory sense. Habit is irregularly pyramidal, and the lustrous dark green leaves often turn rich red in fall. Fruit are 3- to 4-in.-long pomes. Grows 20 to 30 ft. high, generally less in spread. Zones 4 to 8(9). Europe, western Asia.

Pyrus pyrifolia
Chinese sand pear

Like *Pyrus ussuriensis*, this attractive species plays second (or, perhaps, third) fiddle to the *P. calleryana* selections. It develops into a dense, broad-pyramidal to rounded tree. The foliage is lustrous dark green in summer and yellow, orange, and red in fall. White flowers blanket the tree in April, and they are followed by hard, 1½-in.-wide, rounded fruit, which are quite messy. Because of the large fruit, it is doubtful that this species or *P. ussuriensis* will ever become popular in gardening circles. Grows 30 to 40 ft. high and wide. Zones 5 to 8. Central and western China.

Pyrus salicifolia
willowleaf pear

If fireblight were not so problematic, this gray-leaved species would be as common as *Pyrus calleryana* 'Bradford'. The graceful, fine-textured branches are clothed with 1½- to 3½-in.-long, woolly, gray-green leaves. Flowers and fruit are not spectacular. Grows 15 to 25 ft. high. Zones 4 to 7. Southeastern Europe, western Asia.

Pyrus pyrifolia

CULTIVARS AND VARIETIES
'Pendula', the most common form in cultivation, boasts elegant drooping branches and silvery gray foliage. Grows 15 ft. high.

Pyrus ussuriensis
Ussurian pear

Although seldom seen outside of arboreta, this round-headed, white-flowered species has merit, especially in northern gardens (zones 3 and 4), where the *Pyrus calleryana* types are not cold hardy. The 1⅓-in.-wide flowers open in April and May and are followed by 1- to 1½-in.-wide, greenish yellow fruit. The lustrous dark green leaves may turn respectable red to reddish purple in fall. Grows 40 to 50 ft. high. Zones 3 to 6. Northeastern Asia.

CULTIVARS AND VARIETIES
Prairie Gem® ('Mordak') from North Dakota State University has an oval to rounded habit and thick, glossy green leaves. A tree at Milliken Arboretum, Spartanburg, South Carolina, did not perform well: it was defoliated by leaf spot, and flowers were not as profuse as *Pyrus calleryana* types.

Pyrus salicifolia 'Pendula'

Pyrus ussuriensis Prairie Gem®

Pyrus salicifolia 'Pendula'

Pyrus ussuriensis, Ussurian pear

Quercus

oak

The purest of Noble Trees, with 500 species distributed worldwide. The umbrella of the genus spreads far, from deciduous types to diminutive, scrubby, shrubby, evergreen species with leaves similar to holly, and all permutations between. The fruit is an acorn, the nut covered by a cap of scales, or involucre. Leaves may be entire, serrated, lobed, spiny, but always alternate, buds imbricate, usually with a cluster of buds toward the stem end. Two great groups: red/black (with acorns ripening in two years) and white (in a single season). Hybrids occur only within red/black or white. Probably the best genus for general use across the United States. Traveling from Minnesota (red oak) to Florida (live oak), oaks will be shadowing your car. Sudden oak death, identified in California, killed over a million native oak and tanoak trees in that state; *Phytophthora ramorum* is the causal organism. Concerns about the disease's spread into the eastern/southern forests appear unfounded. Numerous host plants carry SOD. Abundant information is available on the web. Type "sudden oak death" and your computer will burp!

The International Oak Society, www.internationaloaksociety.org, offers annual meeting, publications, seed exchanges, taxonomic database, cultivar registration, et al. A membership fee is charged. The *Field Guide to Native Oak Species of Eastern North America* (2003), edited by John Stein, Denise Binion, and Robert Acciavatti, has great photos and knowledgeable text. I utilized the reference on many occasions.

Quercus acuta

Japanese evergreen oak

Often confused with and sold as *Quercus myrsinifolia* or *Q. glauca* because of similar evergreen leaf and growth habit; however, the leaves of *Q. acuta* are entire—those of the other two are serrated. Not as cold hardy in Athens, but a 20-ft.-high and -wide, low-branched, rounded tree grows in Aiken, South Carolina, about 140 miles south-

Quercus alba against a winter sky

east. The 2½- to 5½-in.-long leaves are leathery, lustrous dark green through the seasons. Bark is smooth and gray. Acorns are similar to those of *Q. myrsinifolia*, with the cap covering about one-third of the ¾-in.-long nut. Excellent for use in small spaces. Should be tested for container and street tree potential in the lower Southeast. Will grow in sandy soils with an acid reaction in full sun to moderate shade. Zones 8 and 9. Japan.

Quercus acutissima
sawtooth oak

This unsung species of the oak world offers great aesthetic benefits for garden and large-area use. The habit is distinctly pyramidal in youth, becoming rounded to broad-rounded with age. The lustrous dark green, prominently serrated leaves turn yellow to golden brown in autumn. They emerge early in spring, color late in fall, and may

MORE ▶

Quercus acutissima

Quercus acuta, Japanese evergreen oak

Quercus acutissima

Quercus acuta

Quercus acuta

667

Quercus acutissima CONTINUED

Quercus acutissima, sawtooth oak, fall color

persist into winter. The bark becomes deeply ridged and furrowed with age, appearing almost corky. The rich brown nuts are enclosed in a scaly cap to about two-thirds of their length. Sawtooth oak tolerates dry soils but prospers in moist, well-drained, acid soils. Transplants more readily than most oaks. A great choice for campuses, parks, or golf courses. Useful along streets or in medians, but can be a nuisance in autumn when the nuts roll about like marbles. Grows 40 to 60 ft. high and wide. A 52 ft. by 42 ft. specimen grew at the Morton Arboretum, Lisle, Illinois. Zones (4)5 to 8. Asia.

Quercus alba

white oak

White oak is the standard by which all other oaks are measured. The majesty of a mature tree warrants pause for reflection. Distinctly pyramidal in youth, the outline becomes oval-rounded to rounded with age.

Quercus acutissima

Quercus alba, white oak

Quercus alba

The dark green, almost blue-green leaves often turn a good russet-red to red in fall. Bark is light ash-brown and often breaks into various sized, vertically arranged, scaly plates. The rich brown, 1-in.-long acorn is one-quarter covered by the bumpy scaled cap. Grows best in deep, moist, acid, well-drained soils, but it is adaptable. Unfortunately, it is quite difficult to transplant and must be moved as a small tree, ideally of less than 2½-in. caliper, for best success. White oak is excellent as a specimen tree and also in groves. One of America's most handsome native species. Grows 50 to 80 ft. high and wide. Zones 3 to 8. Maine to Minnesota, south to Florida and Texas.

Quercus alba

Quercus alba fall color

Quercus bicolor

swamp white oak

A virtually unknown landscape species that should be utilized more frequently, particularly in areas with moist soils. In a sense, it plays second fiddle to white oak, but it is easier to transplant. The habit is stiffly pyramidal in youth, becoming irregular to rounded at maturity. The secondary branches develop small spur shoots

MORE ▶

Quercus bicolor

Quercus bicolor, swamp white oak

Quercus bicolor

Quercus bicolor CONTINUED

that give the tree a more coarse appearance than *Quercus alba*. The lustrous dark green leaves are often covered with a white pubescence beneath. Fall color is usually yellowish brown but occasionally russet-red. The brownish black bark is rough and scaly even on young trees, becoming deeply ridged and furrowed with age. Plant in moist, acid soils. Chlorosis may develop in high pH soils. A worthwhile plant for wet areas. Good for naturalizing or for use in parks, golf courses, and large areas. Significant enthusiasm for the species and is now more available in commerce. Grows 50 to 60 ft. high and wide. Zones 3 to 8. Quebec to Michigan, south to Georgia and Arkansas.

Quercus cerris

turkey oak

Noble Tree, to be sure. I gazed across a broad expanse of pasture in the sullen light of late March to a grouping of 70- to 80-ft.-high, massive-trunked trees in Knightshayes Garden, Devon, England, and questioned why they do not appear in more American landscapes. Leaves, 2½ to 5 in. long, 1 to 3 in. wide, coarsely dentate to pinnately lobed, lustrous dark green, are genteelly elegant. Acorn, 1 in. long,

is about one-half covered by a cap with fimbriated, reflexed scales. Well adapted to limestone soils and maritime conditions. Shade and specimen tree use, as superbly evidenced at the Morris and Spring Grove arboreta. Fast-growing, to 40 to 60 ft. high and wide. Zones 5 to 7. Southern Europe, western Asia.

CULTIVARS AND VARIETIES
'Argenteovariegata' is rather pretty, with creamy white blotches and margins reaching to the midrib.

Quercus cerris

Quercus cerris, turkey oak

Quercus cerris

Quercus cerris 'Argenteovariegata'

670

Quercus coccinea

scarlet oak

Certainly among the most handsome of the red/black oak group. Unfortunately, the species is seldom available in commerce because of its transplanting difficulty. Also, what is often sold as scarlet oak is actually *Quercus palustris* (pin oak), *Q. rubra* (red oak), or *Q. shumardii* (Shumard oak). The lustrous, almost reflective, dark green summer leaves yield to brilliant reds and scarlets in the fall. Fall coloration

may last three to four weeks. The habit is softly pyramidal in youth, becoming upright-spreading and open with age. The ½- to 1-in.-long acorns are covered to about one-half their length in a bowl-like cap. Scarlet oak is adaptable, but it prospers in moist, well-drained, acid soils. In the wild, it is often found on dry, sandy soils. Does not appear to be as sensitive to higher pH soils as *Q. palustris*. Ideally, move as a small, 6- to 10-ft.-high container plant or balled-and-burlapped specimen. Grows 70 to

75 ft. high, 40 to 50 ft. wide. Zones 4 to 8(9). Maine to Minnesota, south to Florida and Missouri.

Quercus ellipsoidalis

northern pin oak

Appears to fall between the landscape cracks and needs a jump start in commerce. I grew seedlings in Athens and could not separate them from *Quercus palustris*. Walked among a large native stand east of St. Paul, Minnesota; their habits were more open than pin oak, more rounded, with horizontal spreading branches. New leaves are silky tomentose upon emergence, lustrous dark green and respectable red in autumn. Leaves five- to nine-lobed, 4 to 9 in. long, 2 to 5 in. wide, sinuses rounded, lobes narrow. Acorn, ½ to ¾ in. long, enclosed one-third to one-

Quercus coccinea, scarlet oak, fall color

Quercus ellipsoidalis

Quercus coccinea fall color

Quercus coccinea

671

Quercus ellipsoidalis CONTINUED
half by the turbinate cup with closely appressed pale brown scales. Amenable to dry, calcareous, limestone soils. Should be the tree of choice in high pH soil regions. Specimens in Morton Arboretum are over 80 ft. high. Zones 4 to 6. Southern Michigan to Manitoba and Iowa.
CULTIVARS AND VARIETIES
Majestic Skies™ ('Bailskies') is broad-pyramidal to oval with excellent red fall color; 55 ft. by 40 ft.

Quercus falcata
southern red oak
The large oak growing in the most infertile, worn-out soil is, in most instances, *Quercus falcata*. Truly, a biologically tough *hombre*, bearing up and even thriving where other oaks would sputter. At maturity, rounded to broad-rounded, as a juvenile delinquent, pyramidal and without distinction. Massive, large, muscular branches lend credence to its tough-guy persona. Leaves appear in numerous manifestations, from three- to seven-lobed and 5 to 12 in. long, lustrous dark green above, grayish green below. Leaves may turn russet-red in autumn, but color is never spectacular. The leaf base is usually rounded, a distinction separating the species from other red/black oaks. Acorns, ½ in. long, with the cap sitting on top of the striated (alternating brown and black stripes) nut, are borne in abundance. Difficult to transplant in large sizes and has not gained commercial acceptance. Grows anywhere except swamps. Full sun to partial shade. Worthy tree for dif-

Quercus falcata

Quercus falcata

Quercus ellipsoidalis, northern pin oak, fall color

Quercus falcata var. *pagodifolia*, cherrybark oak

Quercus falcata var. *pagodifolia* fall color

672

ficult (impossible) sites. Drought and heat tolerances are legendary. Grows 70 to 80 ft. high and wide. National champion is 123 ft. high, 152 ft. wide. Zones (6)7 to 9. New Jersey to Florida, west to Missouri and Texas.

CULTIVARS AND VARIETIES
Variety *pagodifolia*, cherrybark oak, is found in bottomland habitats from Virginia to Florida, west to southern Illinois and Arkansas. The leaves are more uniformly five- to 11-lobed, sinuses not as deeply cut, and the bark is blackish and scaly. Trees I have grown maintain a central leader and more uniform habit. I believe this variety has landscape and street tree possibilities. Observed immense trees, 80 to 100 ft. high, in the floodplain of the Oconee River. Long slender boles stretched 40 to 50 ft. before the first branch. Zones 6 to 9.

Quercus georgiana
Georgia oak
An honor to have a tree named after the great state of Georgia, and this smallish round-headed species appears to have potential. A few southern growers have produced quality field-grown trees, but the ultimate test will be the degree of acceptance by the landscape profession, which, to date, has not been all-embracing. Small, dapper, broad-rounded in outline with 1½- to 4½-in.-long, three- to seven-lobed leaves, sinuses shallow, upper surface lustrous dark green, lower pale green with tufts of hairs in the vein axils. Fall color is red, reddish purple to burgundy in November. The ½-in.-long, dark brown nuts are covered about one-quarter by the cap. Grows on granite outcrops and thin soils. High degree of drought and heat tolerance. Easy to transplant. Choice small tree for planters, lawns, and streets. Grows 15 to 30 ft. high and wide. National champion is 59 ft. by 65 ft. Zones 6 to 8. South Carolina, Georgia, and Alabama.

Quercus falcata, southern red oak

Quercus georgiana, Georgia oak

Quercus georgiana fall color

673

Quercus glauca
blue Japanese oak

Probably the most commonly cultivated evergreen oak, with the exception of *Quercus virginiana*. Upright-oval habit with such a tight, dense canopy that the species can be utilized for large screen plantings. In Atlanta, I witnessed plants skirted to the ground with branches that served as handsome buffers. The 2½- to 5½-in.-long leaves are strongly toothed in their upper one-half, lustrous dark green, gray-green beneath. Upon emergence, leaves range from rich green, bronze, to purple-green. Acorn is similar to that of *Q. myrsinifolia*. Prospers in clay-based and sandy soils in full sun to partial shade. Handsome small specimen tree, useful as large screen; looks, as do many evergreen oaks, more like a holly. Grows 20 to 30 ft. high, spread one-half to three-quarters the height. Witnessed a 30-ft.-high, 40-ft.-wide specimen with low-slung, wide-spreading branches. Zones 7 to 9. Japan and China.

Quercus hemisphaerica
laurel oak

Although terribly confused and misidentified in commerce, this semi-evergreen species is a respectable tree for planting in infertile, sandy to clay-based upland soils. Plants on the Georgia campus have weathered the years and emerged as stately specimens. Distinctly pyramidal in youth, becoming more rounded with age. In fact, the national champion is 98 ft. high and 108 ft. wide, which reflects "roundability." Leaves may have a few teeth; they are almost entire on old trees. Each is about 1 to 4 in. long, ½ to 1½ in. wide, lustrous dark green above, lighter green below. New leaves emerge bright yellow-green before settling down. Acorn is striated, ½ in. long, enclosed ¼ to ⅓ in. by the saucer-shaped cap. Relatively easy to transplant. Tolerates substandard soils from sand to clay; pH adaptable. Utilize for residential, park, urban, and street tree. Leaves hold into February and March in zone 7. Densely branched in youth and makes a good early appearance. Does not grow old as gracefully as *Quercus phellos*, willow oak. In fact, in even-age plantings, *Q. hemisphaerica* is the first to decline. Grows 40 to 60 ft. high, 30 to

Quercus glauca, blue Japanese oak

Quercus glauca

Quercus hemisphaerica

Quercus hemisphaerica, laurel oak

Quercus imbricaria, shingle oak

60 ft. wide. Zones 6 to 9. Southeastern United States.

Quercus laurifolia, swamp laurel oak, is frequently confused with *Q. hemisphaerica* but is distinguished by diamond-shaped leaves and earlier leaf drop (late December and January). Grows in wetter habitats in the wild. Both grow on the Georgia campus and are easy to separate, especially in February and March when *Q. hemisphaerica* has leaves, *Q. laurifolia* none.

Quercus imbricaria
shingle oak

Shingle oak develops a pyramidal outline in youth, eventually becoming rounded to broad-rounded. The lustrous dark green, 2½- to 6-in.-long leaves are unlobed and, to the casual observer, represent anything but an oak. Leaves turn, at best, yellow-brown to russet-red in fall and often persist into winter. Many gardeners find the persistent leaves objectionable; others appreciate the rustling sound of the dried leaves. Shingle oak is relatively easy to transplant and is adaptable to a wide range of soil conditions, from acid to higher pH and moist to dry. Old trees are quite imposing because of the mammoth, spreading branches. Grows 50 to 60 ft. high and wide. Zones 4 to 7. Pennsylvania to Nebraska, south to Georgia and Arkansas.

Quercus imbricaria

Quercus lyrata
overcup oak

A hidden gem; overlooked and, by
some, scorned because of the large
acorns. Now receiving acceptance
by commercial nurseries because of
uniform growth habit, fast growth,
handsome foliage, and ease of transplanting. A Georgia producer told
me it was the most uniform oak he
ever grew. Pyramidal-oval in youth,
rounded at maturity. Branches are
upturned, translating to effective and
safe use along streets and trafficked
areas. The 6- to 8-in.-long, lustrous
dark green leaves, with three to five
lobe pairs, become yellow-brown in
autumn. Acorns are chunky, ¾ to 1 in.
long and wide, covered for the bulk of
their length by the acorn cap. Readily
transplanted; tolerates wet, dry, and
moist well-drained sites; pH adaptable. A great tree for urban use. Have

Quercus lyrata, overcup oak

Quercus lyrata

Quercus lyrata

Quercus macrocarpa

Quercus macrocarpa

observed large, 75-ft. specimens in Cincinnati, Ohio. Beautiful noble trees on the Georgia and UNC campuses. Grows 40 to 60 ft. high and wide. Zones 5 to 9. New Jersey to Florida, west to Missouri and Texas.
CULTIVARS AND VARIETIES
Highbeam® ('QLFTB'), with superior uniform habit, yellow, orange, and red fall color, and ease of rooting from cuttings, provides consistency of characteristics and performance. Introduced by Select Trees, Athens, Georgia.

Quercus macrocarpa, bur oak

Quercus marilandica, blackjack oak

Quercus macrocarpa
bur or mossycup oak
Certainly a most impressive species when viewed as an open-grown specimen in a grassy field in the Midwest, but it is perhaps too big, too messy, and too lacking in ornamental characteristics for the average landscape. In its finest form, *Quercus macrocarpa* is a behemoth, with a massive trunk and a broad crown of stout branches. The large (up to 10 to 12 in. long), dark green leaves turn yellow-brown in fall.

The gray-brown bark becomes deeply ridged and furrowed with age. Somewhat difficult to transplant and, for that reason, is not as available in commerce as pin oak; however, northern nurseries reported successful transplanting and increased sales. Ideally, transplant young balled-and-burlapped or container-grown plants to a permanent location. Adaptable to many soils. In nature, the tree is found on sandy plains and moist, alluvial bottoms, in limestone and dry clay soils. Grows 70 to 80 ft. high and wide. Zones 2 to 8. Nova Scotia to Manitoba, south to Texas.
CULTIVARS AND VARIETIES
Jordan Street® ('Atwood') is a beautiful, upright spreading clone (*Quercus macrocarpa* × *Q. alba*) with a rounded crown and dark green, mildew-resistant leaves. Parent tree, 90 ft. by 75 ft. Introduced by Earl Cully, Heritage Trees, Jacksonville, Illinois.

Urban Pinnacle™ ('JFS-KW3') with narrow-pyramidal habit, dominant central leader, anthracnose- and mildew-resistant, glossy dark green leaves, is a 2009 introduction from J. Frank Schmidt & Son Nursery, Oregon.

Quercus marilandica
blackjack oak
Ragged, the last oak standing in a street fight—rugged, the worse for wear, sap oozing from every lenticel, but a winner. What a way to characterize a wayward oak. I find it growing in sandy, acid, largely third-rate soils. Gothic, *Hound of the Baskervilles* habit, the stout branches forming an irregular outline. I reached an identification milestone and can now "spot" this species at 60 mph by its Addams Family, haunted-house habit and extremely lustrous, approximating black-green leaves. Black, cracked-and-fissured bark keeps the diabolical effect alive. Leaves, unlike most oaks, 4 to 8 in. long, broad obovate, with three- to five-lobed apex, die off

MORE ▶

Quercus marilandica CONTINUED

Quercus marilandica

Quercus michauxii

Quercus michauxii fall color

Quercus michauxii, swamp chestnut oak

yellow-brown to bronze-red. Acorns, ¾ to 1 in. long, about half as wide, are enclosed one-half by the yellow-brown cap. Variable size due to soils. National champion is 122 ft. by 49 ft. Zones 6 to 9. New York to Iowa, south to Florida and Texas.

Quercus michauxii
swamp chestnut oak
Acorns as big as golf balls, and I forage like a famished squirrel to collect every nut possible for propagation.

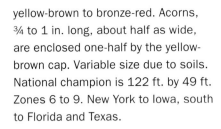

Yes, true, as I groveled under an 80- to 100-ft.-high behemoth at Brookgreen Gardens, Murrells Inlet, South Carolina, on a late November day. The species is taxonomically similar to *Quercus montana*, with the former growing in wetter soils. At Weeks Bay Reserve, near Mobile, Alabama, the tree was common in the swampy habitat. The leaves, similar to *Q. montana*, perhaps thicker-textured and more pubescent, were bronze-red. A mammoth tree, rounded in outline with 4- to 8-in.-long, dark green, scallop-margined leaves. Bark, even on young trees, is gray-brown and quite scaly; bark of *Q. montana* is ridged and furrowed, corky in texture, and non-scaly. Acorns are similar to *Q. montana*. Small trees on the Georgia campus were transplanted without difficulty and have grown exceedingly fast. I believe this is, like *Q. lyrata*, *Q. nuttallii*, and *Q. montana*, a noble tree for large-space landscapes. Grows 80 to 100 ft. high and wide. National champion is 106 ft. high, 103 ft. wide. Zones 5 to 9. New Jersey, Delaware to Florida, west to Indiana, Missouri, and Texas.

Quercus montana
syn. *Quercus prinus*
chestnut oak
An unheralded oak species but worthy of landscape respect; and, for little more than a walk in the woods, the hiker will be treated to one of nature's most important cafeterias. The species provides sweet acorns for the gray squirrel, black bear, white-tailed deer, and other wildlife. My son Matt, a Civil War history buff, and I toured battlefields, Revolutionary and otherwise, from Kings Mountain, South Carolina, to Gettysburg, Pennsylvania, and the species was a constant. As we ascended the dry ridge of Big Round Top, the blocky bark signaled the presence of the species, some trees clearly descending from the 1860s. It is certainly a tree

for the ages. Oval-rounded, eventually vase-shaped, with large spreading branches. Bark is brown to nearly black, appearing corky in texture, and on old trees, deeply and coarsely furrowed. The 4- to 6- (to 12-) in. long, 1½- to 4-in.-wide leaves, with ten to 14 pairs of roundish teeth, are dark green, changing to orange-yellow and yellow-red-brown in fall. Plump, rich brown acorns, 1 to 1¼ in. high, ¾ in. wide, are one-third to one-half enclosed by the cap. Moderately easy to transplant, with an affinity for rocky, dry, upland sites in the wild. An excellent large-area tree and even grows in parking lot islands in South Carolina. Truly a beautiful species that should be a greater part of southern and northern tree planting initiatives. Auburn University showed this to be a superior species in its 13-year evaluation. Grows 60 to 70 ft. high, about as wide. Zones 4 to 8. Southern Maine and Ontario to South Carolina and Alabama.

Quercus montana, chestnut oak, fall color

Quercus montana

Quercus montana

Quercus montana

Quercus muehlenbergii
chinkapin oak

Another worthy oak species but still relatively unknown in commerce because of transplanting difficulties. The habit is weakly rounded in youth, becoming open and rounded with maturity. The lustrous dark green leaves turn yellow to orangish yellow in fall. Massive trees occur in dry, limestone-based soils as well as in rich bottomlands. If native in the area, trees should be protected and enjoyed. As with many of the difficult-to-transplant species, small seedlings can be successfully established. Chinkapin oak is a fine park or large-area tree. Observed handsome trees in north Florida and central Illinois. A sleeper that needs a degree of promotion. Grows 40 to 50 ft. high and wide under landscape conditions; will reach 70 to 80 ft. high in the wild. Zones 4 to 7. Vermont to Nebraska, south to Virginia, Texas, and Mexico.

Quercus myrsinifolia
Chinese evergreen oak

Rare and unusual evergreen oak that grows in Savannah, Georgia, and Washington, D.C., with equal facility. Oval to rounded outline, small branches and leaves, result in refined texture, somewhat atypical for an oak. Newly emerging foliage is exquisite purple-bronze. Leaves mature lustrous medium green, gray-green below, with finely serrated margins from the basal third to the apex of the

Quercus muehlenbergii, chinkapin oak

Quercus myrsinifolia

Quercus myrsinifolia

Quercus muehlenbergii

Quercus myrsinifolia

leaf. The smooth gray bark is comparable to that of the beech. Nifty, ½- to 1-in.-long, brownish black, oval-oblong acorns are one-third to one-half covered by a cap with three to six concentric rings. Transplanting can be difficult unless trees are root-pruned. Tolerates extremes of soil (except wet). Sapsuckers, a type of woodpecker, drill rings of holes in concentric circles that may serve as avenues for fungal invasion. I lost two trees via these "critters." When well grown, a beautiful lawn, park, and street tree. Grows 20 to 30 (to 40 to 50) ft. high, slightly less in spread. Zones (6)7 to 9. Japan, China, Laos.

Quercus nigra
water oak

Ubiquitous tree in the Southeast to Missouri and Texas! Native but relentless in its pursuit of open ground, where it takes hold and acts like an obnoxious, exotic weed. With that said, it is remarkable in its ability to reach monumental sizes in miserable soils. Large, almost overwhelming in stature, it can quickly become the dominant tree if left to its reseeding devices. A tree survey of the Georgia campus taken in 2000 reflected its dominance over the 25 other oak species. Leaves are dull, dark bluish green to lustrous dark green, paler beneath. Shape is obovate, three-lobed at apex to entire, with each leaf 1½ to 4 in. long, ½ to 2 in. wide. Acorns rain in October and November, literally mulching the ground. Each is ½ in. long and wide, striated brown and black, enclosed one-quarter to one-third by the cap. Ironclad in tough soil from wet to stone dry, moderate shade to full sun; pH adaptable. Weaker wooded than other oaks but still more stable than the widely planted, weak-wooded *Acer saccharinum*, silver maple. Seldom avail-

MORE ▶

Quercus nigra

Quercus nigra

Quercus myrsinifolia, Chinese evergreen oak

Quercus nigra, water oak

681

Quercus nigra CONTINUED

able in nursery commerce. Pretty much the domain of "Squirrel Nursery Company." Grows 50 to 80 ft. high and wide. National champion is 118 ft. high, 108 ft. wide. Zones 6 to 9. Southern New Jersey, south to Florida, west to eastern Texas, and northward in the Mississippi Valley to southeastern Missouri and eastern Oklahoma.

Quercus nuttallii

Nuttall oak

One of those rare plants that excites the pragmatist and researcher because of aesthetics and cultural adaptability. A bottomland species that is closely allied to *Quercus coccinea*, *Q. palustris*, and *Q. shumardii*, the real differences reside in its development of a full canopy at an early age, its rapidity to caliper, its greater range of pH adaptability, its wet soil tolerance, and the ease with which it may be dug in early summer. I have walked nurs-

eries and observed this growing next to *Q. shumardii*: uniformity of crown, density of foliage, and consumer appeal are heavily weighted toward *Q. nuttallii*. In short, it is a nurserygrower's tree as well as a gardener's tree. Pyramidal in youth, more rounded with age. Leaves, five- to nine-lobed, 4 to 9 in. long, 2 to 5 in. wide, lustrous dark green, turn shades of red in fall, mostly followed by complete leaf drop. New growth ranges from green to rich red to reddish purple. Acorns are ¾ to

1¼ in. long, ovoid-oblong, and one-third to one-half covered by the cap. Most acorns I collected were on the small side of the range. Easy to transplant and grow. Use as a specimen and street tree, for parks, campuses, and golf courses. I asked a friend how to separate this from *Q. shumardii* with reliability; his answer: if there is standing water around the tree in the wild, then it is *Q. nuttallii*. Mr. Charles Webb, Superior Trees, Lee, Florida, showed me a reliable acorn feature:

Quercus nuttallii fall color

Quercus nuttallii Sangria® young leaves

Quercus nuttallii, Nuttall oak, fall color

Q. nuttallii has a turbinate cap with raised (bumpy) scales that covers more of the nut, while Q. shumardii is a broader, shallower, flat-topped cap with scales gently overlapping. Grows 40 to 60 ft. high. Zones 5 to 9. Western Alabama to east Texas and Oklahoma, north to southeastern Missouri and southern Illinois.

CULTIVARS AND VARIETIES
Tree Introductions, Inc., Athens, Georgia, introduced Arcade® ('QNST6') and Sangria® ('QNSTD'), both with

red to deep red new growth that holds into May. Subsequent growth flushes are reddish in color. Pretty trees as I viewed them on a late April day. Sangria® appears more dense and is slightly slower growing. These selections are own-root (clonal) and true-to-characteristics, i.e., not seed-grown.

Quercus palustris
pin oak

In a popularity poll by *American Nurseryman* magazine, this species was the most commonly planted shade and street tree. Pin oak has consumer recognition, and it is also one of the easiest oaks to grow and transplant, which contributes to its popularity. The habit is strongly pyramidal, usually with a central leader. The lower branches are descending (pendulous), the middle are horizontal; and the upper branches are upright. The lustrous dark green, 3- to 6-in.-long, five- to seven-lobed, leaves turn russet-red to red in fall. Pin oak requires acid soils for best performance. Chlorosis is common throughout the Midwest on plants in calcareous soils; noted on a recent trip to St. Louis both majestic dark green trees and some as yellow as a canary. Use for lawn and street plantings. Major maintenance is required for the latter use: the lower branches must be removed to facilitate vehicular and pedestrian traffic. Grows 60 to 70 ft. high, 25 to 40 ft. wide. Zones 4 to 7. Massachusetts to Wisconsin, south to Delaware and Arkansas.

CULTIVARS AND VARIETIES
'Crownright' and 'Sovereign' lack the weeping lower branches of the species, but these clones were grafted and subsequently developed incompatibility problems.

Green Pillar® ('Pringreen') is a columnar form with extremely glossy dark green leaves into late summer. Grows 50 ft. by 15 ft. I believe this selection has significant promise.

Quercus phellos
willow oak

The most popular tree in the Southeast for streets, parks, estates, and residential properties, willow oak is also grown as far north as Cape Cod with reasonable success. The fine-textured, oval to rounded habit with upswept branches makes this species one of the most desirable oaks for general use. The 2- to 5½-in.-long, narrow, willow-like leaves are lustrous dark

Quercus palustris, pin oak

Quercus palustris fall color

Quercus palustris

MORE ▶

Quercus phellos CONTINUED

Quercus phellos

green in summer, changing to brownish yellow and occasionally orangish yellow in fall. Acorns are ½ in. long or less, with thin, saucer-like cap, striated with alternating brown and blackish bands, and not as messy as those of *Quercus acutissima*, *Q. alba*, *Q. macrocarpa*, and *Q. rubra*. Transplant in late winter, when dormant, into moist, well-drained, acid soils. Once established, *Q. phellos* is extremely tolerant of heat, drought, and stress. Beautiful specimen oak and an excellent street tree. Grows 40 to 60 ft. high, 30 to 40 ft. wide or equal in spread. Zones 6 to 9. New York to Florida, west to Missouri and Texas.

CULTIVARS AND VARIETIES
Hightower® ('QPSTA'), with pyramidal outline, central leader, and lustrous dark green leaves, is a clonal, own-root oak, so uniformity is guaranteed. Demonstrates good mite resistance. Introduced by Tree Introductions, Inc., Athens, Georgia.

Additional clonal selections include Ascendor® ('QPSTJ'), Shiraz® ('QPSTB'), Upperton™ ('RT3'), and Wynstar® ('QPMTF').

Quercus phillyraeoides
Ubame oak

This evergreen species may be at the furthest end of the oak variation curve with its upright-oval, large shrub/small tree habit. The new growth emerges bronze-red, settling to shiny dark green and pale green beneath. Each leaf is 1 to 2½ in. long, almost as wide. I have yet to observe acorns on cultivated plants. Has prospered at the JC Raulston Arboretum, Raleigh, North Carolina. Best in the collector's garden. Grows 15 to 25 ft. high. Zones 7 and 8. China, Japan.

CULTIVARS AND VARIETIES
'Emerald Sentinel', distinguished for its upright habit, fast growth, and ease of propagation from cuttings, is a selection from the JC Raulston Arboretum.

Quercus phellos, willow oak

Quercus phellos Hightower®

Quercus phillyraeoides 'Emerald Sentinel'

Quercus robur
English oak

A trip through the English country-side will provide sufficient reason for bringing an English oak into the garden. The broad-rounded habit, the wide-spreading, ridged and furrowed branches, and the sturdy, imposing trunk provide architectural elegance. The three- to seven-lobed, 2- to 5-in.-long, rich blue-green leaves hold late in fall but seldom develop good color. English oak is easier to transplant than white oak or bur oak. Tolerates dry, high pH, limestone soils. It is quite adaptable and has been successful from North Dakota to Utah to Georgia. Mildew is often a problem. Great for large areas. Grows 40 to 60 ft. high and wide. Zones 3 to 7. Europe, northern Africa, western Asia.

CULTIVARS AND VARIETIES
Several forms with colored foliage are available, including 'Atropurpurea'

MORE ▶

Quercus phillyraeoides 'Emerald Sentinel'

Quercus robur

Quercus robur

Quercus phillyraeoides, Ubame oak

Quercus robur, English oak

Quercus robur CONTINUED
(purple leaves), 'Concordia' (yellow), and 'Variegata' (white-margined).

Crimson Spire™ ('Crimschmidt') is a hybrid (*Quercus alba* × *Q. robur* 'Fastigiata') that develops a columnar fastigiate outline, 45 ft. by 15 ft.

'Fastigiata' is upright-columnar in habit with dense ascending branches. Often seed-grown and therefore variable. Susceptible to mildew. Grows 60 ft. high, but only 10 to 15 ft. wide.

Fastigiata Group includes upright selections that can be used in more

Quercus robur 'Concordia'

Quercus robur

Quercus robur 'Variegata'

Quercus robur 'Fastigiata'

Quercus Regal Prince®

restricted spaces, such as 'Attention' (60 to 80 ft. by 15 ft.), Rose Hill® ('Asjes') (45 ft. by 18 ft.), and Skyrocket®; the latter two have mildew-resistant and more handsome foliage. Witnessed a 45 ft. by 20 ft. tree of Skyrocket® at J. Frank Schmidt Jr. Arboretum, Oregon. Rose Hill® becomes more open and wide with age.

Kindred Spirit® ('Nadler') is upright, slightly pyramidal, with glossy dark green, mildew-resistant leaves; 35 ft. by 7 ft. *Quercus robur* 'Fastigiata' × *Q. bicolor*.

Regal Prince® ('Long') has been terrific in zone 7 with upright-oval silhouette similar to the red maple *Acer rubrum* 'Bowhall'. Glossy dark green leaves, resistant to powdery mildew. *Quercus robur* 'Fastigiata' × *Q. bicolor*.

Quercus rubra
red oak

Unique among the landscape oaks for its rounded growth habit in both youth and maturity. The seven- to 11-lobed, lustrous dark green, 4½- to 8½-in.-long leaves change to russet-red and red in fall. New spring growth is a dusty bronze-red color, and the effect can be as handsome as the spring-

flowering trees. Its ¾- to 1-in.-long, medium brown acorns are among the first of the landscape oaks to ripen, providing an early harvest for animals. Adaptable to extremes of soil, but it prefers acid, well-drained sites. The root system is shallow compared to that of most oaks, and in extreme drought, trees may suffer. Rivals

MORE ▶

Quercus rubra new growth

Quercus rubra

Quercus rubra, red oak

Quercus rubra CONTINUED

pin oak for ease of transplanting. A superb large-area tree, it has also been used effectively as a street tree, particularly along the VFW Parkway and the Arborway in Boston. Our fall trips to Maine reflect its dominant position, particularly evident along the coast. Grows 60 to 75 ft. high and wide. Zones 4 to 7. Nova Scotia to Pennsylvania, west to Minnesota and Iowa.

CULTIVARS AND VARIETIES
'Aurea' is a yellow-leaf form, the leaves maturing to green.

Quercus shumardii
Shumard oak

Long a staple in the southeastern and southwestern landscapes but natively growing into Michigan and southwestern Ontario. The first large (80-ft.) tree I experienced was at the Missouri Botanical Garden, on an October day; the memory of its yellowish bronze fall color has followed me throughout my career. A 2010 visit reaffirmed the magnificence of this specimen. On the Georgia campus, the species has been planted in spades with great success. Pyramidal when young,

rounded with maturity. Seven- to nine-lobed, lustrous dark green leaves, 4 to 8 in. long, 3 to 4 in. wide, turn yellow-bronze to reddish in autumn; I have rarely experienced outstanding pure red fall color. Acorns are ¾ to 1½ in. long, striated with brown-black lines, covered only at the base by the cap. Relatively easy to transplant; pH adaptable, tolerant of dry and moist soils. Rated superior in 13-year shade-tree evaluations at Auburn University. Tremendously drought-tolerant shade, street, or large-area tree. Good growth and survival on pH 7.8 to

Quercus rubra 'Aurea'

Quercus shumardii, Shumard oak

Quercus rubra fall color

Quercus shumardii

8 alluvial soils along the Mississippi River. Grows 40 to 60 ft. high and wide. National champion is 96 ft. high, 96 ft. wide. Zones 5 to 9. Kansas to southern Michigan to North Carolina, Florida to Texas.

CULTIVARS AND VARIETIES Panache® ('QSFTC'), with glossy dark green foliage, consistent orange-red fall color, and Prominence® ('QSSTH'), with dense habit, ascending branches, consistent red fall color, and fast growth, are own-root, clonal selections from Tree Introductions, Inc., Athens, Georgia.

Quercus stellata
post oak

A mid June day on Martha's Vineyard, studying the native vegetation—and what jumps in the way but a beautiful, 40- to 50-ft.-high and -wide post oak. In my beloved Georgia, I have jogged by the species on numerous occasions. While visiting Oklahoma, I saw a lone wind-modulated specimen standing in a grassy field. Pretty adaptable tree! Pyramidal initially, becoming round-topped with spreading, muscular branches. The 4- to 8-in.-long leaves, tough as rawhide, reflective dark green above, grayish to brownish below, develop, on occasion, a golden brown fall patina. The egg-shaped, ¾- to 1-in.-long acorns are one-third to one-half covered by the top-shaped cap. Considered difficult to transplant. Grows on dry, gravelly or sandy soils and rocky ridges but is extremely adaptable. Not as long-lived as Quercus alba in trafficked landscape situations. Trees on Georgia and North Carolina campuses support this contention. Grows 60 to 70 ft. high and wide. Zones 5 to 9. Southern Massachusetts to Florida, west to Iowa and Texas.

Quercus velutina
black oak

Just when . . . you think . . . the oak . . . in question . . . is black . . . you have doubts. Listen carefully . . . Discovered a tree in my Georgia garden. *Buds* confirmed identity: they are *large*, to ½ in. long, five-sided, covered with pale yellowish gray to dirty gray pubescence. Leaves seven- to nine-lobed, 4 to 10 in. long, lustrous

MORE ▶

Quercus stellata, post oak

Quercus shumardii fall color

Quercus stellata

Quercus velutina CONTINUED

Quercus velutina

dark green, yellow-brown fall color . . . the identity is locked. Variable but typically large, rounded habit, with somewhat blocky, black bark. Adaptable and grows on poor, dry, sandy and heavy clay soils in the wild. Difficult to transplant, so largely uncommon in landscape but, if native, leave it be. Grows 50 to 60 ft. high and wide. Zones 3 to 9. Maine to Florida, west to Minnesota and Texas.

Quercus virginiana
live oak

This crown jewel of evergreen oaks consumes large swaths of real estate from coastal Virginia to Texas. In cities from Savannah, Georgia, to Houston, Texas, and in between, it is the dominant landscape tree for streets, parks, and residential areas. Truly excessive in size but without equal for majesty. Rounded in youth, wide-spreading with time, the low-slung branches stretch great distances from the trunk. Bark is blackish and cross-checked into well-defined blocks. The 1- to 3- (to 5-) in.-long, leathery leaves are convex-surfaced, lustrous dark green, with recurved margins. The gray-green, pubescent lower surface allows separation from *Quercus hemisphaerica* (which see). The acorns, ¾ to 1 in. long, dark brown to black, enclosed

Quercus velutina, black oak

Quercus virginiana

Quercus velutina

Quercus virginiana

one-third by the cap, are held on a ½- to 3-in.-long stalk. Finicky during transplanting; most tree growers root-prune field-grown trees to ensure successful establishment. Often container-grown and, thus, more easily transplanted. Adaptable to about any soil type in full sun to partial shade. A climax species in the coastal Southeast. Tolerant of salt, drought, and wind. A magnificent large-area tree. Grows 40 to 80 ft. high, 60 to 100 ft. wide. Zones (7)8 to 10. Virginia to Florida, west to Oklahoma and Texas into Mexico.

CULTIVARS AND VARIETIES
Highrise™ ('QVTIA'), a fastigiate to upright-oval form, was the first live oak produced on a large scale via cutting propagation; will prove effective as a street tree and in sites where lateral space is limited. Estimated ultimate size: about twice as high as wide. Additional own-root (i.e., cutting-propagated) live oaks with unique growth characteristics are Boardwalk® ('FBQV22'), Cathedral® ('SDLN'), Millennium® ('CLTF2'), and Park Side® ('FBQV1').

Quercus virginiana, live oak

Quercus virginiana

Quercus virginiana

Rhamnus cathartica
common buckthorn

A terribly invasive species, simply out of control in the Chicago area, Midwest in general, and East. A large shrub or low-branched tree with a rounded, bushy network of short, stoutish, pseudo-spinescent stems. Glossy dark green leaves, 1½ to 3 in. long, have three to five pairs of impressed veins. Small yellow-green flowers yield glossy black, ¼-in. rounded fruit that birds disseminate far afield. Adaptable—sun, shade, wet, dry, acid, alkaline. It plants itself and has created ecological havoc. I see no real use for it. Be leery and forearmed. Grows 18 to 25 ft. high and wide. Zones 3 to 7. Europe, western and northern Asia.

Rhamnus alaternus, Italian buckthorn, is a 10- to 12-ft.-high, evergreen shrub with glossy green leaves and pretty red-to-black fruit. Observed on several occasions in Europe. 'Argenteovariegata' is an attractive, creamy white-margined leaf form that grows 6 to 8 (to 10) ft. high. Zones 8 and 9 on West Coast. Mediterranean region. Considered invasive.

Rhamnella franguloides was promoted for a short time in the Southeast but dead-ended when the word "invasive" was invoked. Leaf shape

Rhamnus cathartica

Rhamnus alaternus 'Argenteovariegata'

Rhamnus cathartica, common buckthorn

Rhamnus alaternus 'Argenteovariegata'

Rhamnella franguloides

692

reminiscent of *Frangula caroliniana* and turns pure yellow in fall. Abundant orange-colored, ¼-in.-wide, ovoid fruit ripen in late summer. Large, straggly shrub or small tree. The largest I observed was 20 ft. high. Zones 6 and 7. China.

Rhaphiolepis umbellata
Indian hawthorn

An essential element of warm-climate landscapes from the sea coast to Atlanta, Birmingham, Little Rock, the Southwest, and the West. I am amazed at the numbers used for mass effect in residential and commercial settings. Mounded in habit and thickly set with heavy foliage, plants meld together into dark green to blue-green fabrics. Leaves are extremely variable in shape, 1 to 3

MORE ▶

Rhaphiolepis umbellata, Indian hawthorn

Rhaphiolepis umbellata

Rhaphiolepis umbellata

Rhaphiolepis umbellata 'Bonfire'

Rhaphiolepis umbellata Calisto®

Rhaphiolepis umbellata CONTINUED
in. long, almost as wide, toothed to entire. New growth emerges gray-green and extremely pubescent in March and April; in winter, foliage often assumes a purplish tinge. White to pink flowers in 2- to 3-in.-high and -wide inflorescences open in April and May. The fruit, ⅜- to ½-in.-wide, purple-black to bluish black, one- to two-seeded berries, ripen in fall and persist attractively through winter. Easily cultivated in sun and shade but suffers from fungal leaf spot and deer browsing; in fact, it is occasionally referred to as "deer candy." When grown to optimum, a worthy plant for numerous landscape niches. Grows 4 to 6 ft. high and wide. Zones 7 to 10. Japan, Korea.

The related hybrid species *Rhaphiolepis ×delacourii* (*R. umbellata × R. indica*), with pretty pink flowers, grows 4 to 5 ft. high and wide.

×*Rhaphiobotrya* Majestic Beauty™

Rhaphiolepis umbellata Eleanor Taber™

Rhaphiolepis ×delacourii Snowcap® winter color

694

CULTIVARS AND VARIETIES

Forms both smaller (2 to 3 ft. high) and larger (to 15 ft. high) than the species are known. Retired Georgia researcher Will Corley tested numerous cultivars for leaf spot resistance and found little.

'Bonfire' is a pretty selection from Japan introduced by Rick Crowder and named by Bonnie Dirr. It sports red to red-purple new growth, the color holding and eventually turning green; each new-growth flush is reddish. Foliage has been clean. Vigorous grower, expect 3 to 5 ft. high and wide. Pink flowers fade to pinkish white. Appears to have potential for breeding superior traits into the same-old, same-old cultivars.

Calisto® produces beautiful, vibrant dark pink flowers; fully open mid April, Dearing, Georgia. Foliage is dark green, shiny, with a twist (spiral) to long axis; burgundy winter color. If resistant to leaf spot, it will become the classic pink by which all others are judged. Dense, compact habit, 2½ to 3 ft. by 4 ft.

Eleanor Taber™ ('Conor') is a vigorous mounded form, 3 ft. by 4 ft., with large dark green leaves and pinkish flowers; good leaf spot resistance; performed well in Georgia trials.

Majestic Beauty™ ('Montic') is a large form, 8 to 10 (to 15) ft., often trained into a small tree. Leaves up to 4 in. long, bronze turning deep green; has shown good resistance to leaf spot. Flowers are pinkish and fragrant. Killed at −3°F; this is the most robust of the common cultivars. Now considered a hybrid between *Eriobotrya* and *Rhaphiolepis* with the intergeneric name, ×*Rhaphiobotrya*.

Snowcap® ('Corleyscourii') has an excellent rounded-mounded, almost dome-shaped habit. Extremely dense foliage, dark green with a slight luster, turning burgundy-merlot in cold weather; extremely resistant to *Entomosporium*. White flowers; blue-black fruit. Derived from Will Corley's cold hardy material and appears more cold-resistant than most; listed as a *Rhaphiolepis* ×*delacourii* selection.

Southern Moon™ ('Rutrhaph'), with dark green leaves and white flowers, is compact, self-mounding, and disease-resistant, growing 3 to 4 ft. by 5 to 6 ft. A selection from *Rhaphiolepis umbellata* 'Minor'. Introduced by Dr. John Ruter, University of Georgia.

Rhododendron
rhododendron, azalea

Among the most common evergreen and deciduous woody flowering shrubs in the United States, with myriad shapes, sizes, and flower colors. Most flower in the spring months. Too often the gardener is confronted with iron-clad rhododendrons and the standard evergreen azaleas like 'Hino-Red', 'Delaware Valley White', 'Fashion', and 'Coral Bells'; but amateur breeders have expanded the horizons of this great genus, and enterprising nurserymen have tied their wagons to the newer introductions. They are discussed herein as species and hybrid groups (the Encore® evergreen azaleas, for example), along with some of the cultivars.

Rhododendron and azalea species thrive in well-drained, organic-laden, acid, moist soils. Provide as much light as possible to foster maximum growth and flower bud set. Many insects and diseases, particularly root rot or wilt-type diseases, wreak havoc on rhododendrons and azaleas. Drought and lace bugs are serious maladies, the former because of the shallow root system. One of the keys to successful culture is excellent drainage. I know gardeners who break up the ground, set the plant on top, and cover its roots with an organic substrate, like pine bark. Most flower on old wood, so pruning and removal of developing seed heads are best accomplished after flowering. Rhodo-

MORE ▶

Rhaphiolepis ×*delacourii* Snowcap®

Rhaphiolepis umbellata Southern Moon™

695

Rhododendron CONTINUED

dendrons and azaleas can be renewed by cutting/pruning large naked stems to within 6 to 18 in. of the ground in the dormant seasons.

My experiences with evergreen and deciduous azaleas point toward excellent drainage, even moisture, mulch, shade, and monitoring for lace bugs! Millions are sold annually, and millions die annually. In flower the azaleas are "wow" plants; the rest of the year they beg for attention. Proceed with the knowledge that azaleas have a place in landscapes, but many other plants offer beauty of flower, fruit, and foliage and long-term performance.

Rhododendron alabamense
Alabama azalea

A favorite in the Dirr garden. Enticingly sweet white flowers, often with a yellow blotch, open in mid April. Foliage (deciduous) and flowers develop at the same time, so the floral show is somewhat diminished. Flowers are borne in six- to ten-flowered clusters.

Usually a refined, rounded shrub with dark green leaves. Utilize under pines, mixed with broadleaf evergreens, and in groupings. Every visitor to the Dirr garden is enthralled with this species. Grows 5 to 6 (to 8) ft. high and wide. Zones (6)7 and 8. Found in dry open woodlands and rocky hill sites in north central Alabama and isolated areas of west central Georgia.

Rhododendron atlanticum
coast azalea

A delightful small, suckering, deciduous shrub with glaucous, blue-green leaves and fragrant, white to light pink flowers. Flowers occur with or slightly before the leaves in May. Makes a lovely addition to the shrub border. Grows 6 to 8 ft. high and wide. Zones 5 to 8. Delaware to South Carolina.

Rhododendron austrinum
Florida azalea

Another native, deciduous azalea with sweet fragrance and vivid pale yellow to orange flowers. Flowers open before the leaves and are often still effective as the leaves emerge. Many seedlings grew in our garden, and all were different in flower color. An upright shrub, loose, arching, almost rounded at maturity. Dark green leaves may develop yellow to bronze-orange fall coloration. Flowers open in mid April, anywhere from eight to 15 per cluster. The effect is tremendous, especially

Rhododendron alabamense, Alabama azalea

Rhododendron alabamense

Rhododendron atlanticum, coast azalea

en masse. A planting on the Georgia campus of eight to ten large plants generates abundant questions when in flower. Same uses as *Rhododendron alabamense* and even easier to grow. Grows 8 to 10 ft. high and wide. Zones (6)7 to 9. Northern and eastern Florida to southwest Georgia, southern Alabama, and southeastern Mississippi.

Rhododendron calendulaceum

flame azalea

This species bears yellow to orange to red, nonfragrant flowers in May and June. One of the finest deciduous native azaleas, it is abundant in north Georgia, where entire hillsides are covered with every color mentioned

and a wealth of in-betweens. Medium green summer foliage develops yellow to bronze to reddish fall color. Grows 4 to 8 ft. high and wide; can grow 12 to 15 ft. Better in cooler climates. Zones 5 to 7. Mountains of Pennsylvania, south to Georgia.

Rhododendron canescens

Piedmont azalea

The most common and widely distributed deciduous native azalea. In many respects, a white to pink counterpart of *Rhododendron austrinum* and, in fact, hybridizes freely with that species to produce a range of intermediates. One of the taller growing species, often 10 to 15 ft. high, particularly in shady habitats; more

"compact" when open-grown. Plants in full sun set liberal quantities of flower buds. The dark green leaves develop reddish hues when environmental

MORE ▶

Rhododendron canescens, Piedmont azalea

Rhododendron austrinum, Florida azalea

Rhododendron calendulaceum, flame azalea

Rhododendron austrinum

Rhododendron calendulaceum

Rhododendron canescens CONTINUED
conditions in the fall are perfect. Fragrant flowers, white, pink to rose, in nine- to 14-flowered clusters open in late March and early April on naked stems. Their delicate color and texture blend with any landscape situation. As understory plants, they are at home. Grows 6 to 10 (to 15) ft. high and wide. Zones 5 to 9. North Carolina, Tennessee to north Florida, Georgia, Alabama, and Texas.

CULTIVARS AND VARIETIES
'Varnadoe's Phlox Pink' has fragrant, vivid pink flowers in April; this is a beauty.

'White Canescens' ('Album') has pretty, pure white flowers.

Rhododendron canescens 'Varnadoe's Phlox Pink'

Rhododendron canescens 'White Canescens'

Rhododendron catawbiense 'Album'

Rhododendron catawbiense

Catawba rhododendron

A large, bold, broadleaf evergreen with a dense, oval-rounded to rounded outline. Considered the most durable and easy-to-grow rhododendron for everyday gardening purposes. The typical species flower is lilac-purple

Rhododendron catawbiense, Catawba rhododendron

Rhododendron catawbiense 'America'

and occurs in 5- to 6-in.-wide inflorescences in May and June. At the edges of woodlands, in naturalized situations, or in the shrub border, this species makes a stunning show. Numerous cultivars in a variety of flower colors are available; check with the local nursery for those best adapted to the area. Grows 6 to 10 ft. high and wide. Zones 4 to 8. Hiked under a particularly large flowering specimen in late June at about 4,000 ft. elevation on Georgia's Rabun Bald. Southern Appalachians.

CULTIVARS AND VARIETIES
Astoundingly numerous; a few I have grown.

'Album', with flushed lilac buds opening to pure white flowers with greenish yellow spotting, is hardy to –25°F.

'America' has brilliant deep red flowers and is hardy to –20°F.

'Anah Kruschke' forms a dense plant with glossy foliage and deep purple flowers. Hardy to –15°F.

MORE ▶

Rhododendron catawbiense 'Roseum Elegans'

Rhododendron catawbiense 'Anah Kruschke'

Rhododendron catawbiense 'Blue Ensign'

Rhododendron catawbiense 'English Roseum'

Rhododendron catawbiense 'Nova Zembla'

Rhododendron catawbiense CONTINUED

'Blue Ensign' has flowers that are lavender-blue with a prominent dark blotch held in a rounded truss. Hardy to −15°F.

'English Roseum' with light rose flowers is heat-tolerant and hardy to −25°F.

'Nova Zembla' has red flowers, perhaps not as intense and with more lavender than 'America'. It is quite heat- and cold-tolerant (to −25°F), probably one of the best for the Midwest and does well in the South.

'Roseum Elegans', the old standby with lavender-pink (rosy purple) flowers, withstands temperature extremes without injury. Hardy to −25°F with excellent heat tolerance.

Rhododendron degronianum subsp. yakushimanum

syn. *Rhododendron yakushimanum*
Yakushima rhododendron

A slow-growing, dense, mounded, compact evergreen shrub. The dark green leaves with recurved margins are covered with a light gray-brown, woolly pubescence on their undersides. Flow-

Rhododendron degronianum subsp. *yakushimanum*

Rhododendron flammeum, Oconee azalea

Rhododendron degronianum subsp. *yakushimanum*, Yakushima rhododendron

ers are spectacular, varying from bright rose to red in bud and opening to white in full flower; inflorescences average 3 to 6 in. in diameter. Used extensively in breeding. Grows 3 ft. high and wide after 20 years; the Gosslers mentioned 2 ft. by 3 ft. and 12 ft. by 12 ft. plants after 40 years in their Oregon garden. Hardy to –15°F, probably lower. Zones 5 and 6(7). Windswept mountains of Yakushima Island, Japan.

CULTIVARS AND VARIETIES
Numerous. I have visited gardens with collections of cultivars, and most plants, at least in habit and leaf, appeared similar. Classic collection at Mt. Congreve in Ireland with all manner of bumps, humps, mounds, and rounds.

Rhododendron flammeum

syn. *Rhododendron speciosum*
Oconee azalea

Another excellent deciduous native azalea and one of the more easily identified because the flowers are slightly later than *Rhododendron*

canescens and have no fragrance. A rounded shrub, relatively dense and full, with dark green leaves. Unbelievable range of flower colors from yellow to pink, salmon, orange-red, and red. Flowers mid to late April in Athens. Lives in harmony with other garden shrubs. Grows 6 to 8 ft. high and wide. Zones 6 and 7(8). Georgia to South Carolina.

Rhododendron hyperythrum

This sleeper has been utilized to breed heat-tolerant, large-leaved, evergreen rhododendrons, particularly for the South. Forms a dense, 3- to 5-ft. mound of leathery dark green foliage, the leaf undersides dotted with reddish markings. Flowers in large trusses, April (zone 7); buds rich pink, opening to white, quite spectacular. Somewhat reminiscent of *Rhododendron degronianum* subsp. *yakushimanum*, particularly the flowers. During my 31 years in Georgia, I observed more large-leaf rhododendrons that

languished or died than grew into respectable garden plants. Based on several robust plants at Sarah P. Duke Gardens and the JC Raulston Arboretum, this species is worth the effort in zones 7 and 8. Taiwan.

CULTIVARS AND VARIETIES
Southgate™ series of hybrids from Southern Living Plant Collection incorporates the heat- and disease-resistant genes of this species.

Rhododendron hyperythrum

Rhododendron hyperythrum

Rhododendron maximum, rosebay rhododendron

Rhododendron maximum

Rhododendron minus

Rhododendron minus var. chapmanii, Chapman rhododendron

Rhododendron maximum
rosebay rhododendron

Although seldom available in commerce, this large-leaved (4 to 8 in. long) evergreen rhododendron offers possibly the greatest cold hardiness of any native species. It develops into a massive, rounded shrub. The pink-budded flowers open white, with an olive-green spot in the center. Flowers occur in 4- to 6-in.-wide inflorescences in June and July. Use for naturalizing purposes. Grows 15 to 20 ft. high and wide in the wild. Tri-national champions average 30 ft. in height. So abundant in north Georgia that thickets prevent anyone from navigating through. Zones 3 to 7. Nova Scotia to Ontario, south to Georgia and Alabama.

Rhododendron minus
syn. *Rhododendron carolinianum*
Piedmont rhododendron

A rounded evergreen shrub of gentle proportions. The 3-in.-wide inflorescences vary in color from pale rose to rose and lilac-rose. Not used a great deal in modern landscapes, but beautiful in a woodland setting. One of the parents of *Rhododendron* 'PJM'. Grows 3 to 6 ft. high and wide. Observed large colonies at about 1,500 ft. elevation in Georgia's Panther Creek wildlife area, and at 5,000 ft. on Whiteside Mountain, North Carolina. Almost always some shade of pink. Zones (4)5 to 8. Georgia, North and South Carolina, Tennessee.

Rhododendron minus var. chapmanii
syn. *Rhododendron chapmanii*
Chapman rhododendron

Unique because of its northwest Florida nativity, it would appear the perfect species to increase heat tolerance in rhododendrons. By itself, unremarkable but intriguing, with 1- to 2-in.-long, dark green, evergreen leaves, often with rolled, curled, undulating margins. The habit is loose, open, and spreading, and selections would have to be made to bring it to commerce. The rose-pink-lavender flowers open in late spring, although in north Florida, I observed plants in flower during October. Worthy candidate for the adventuresome warm-season garden. A collector's and possibly breeder's plant. Grows 6 to 10 ft. high and wide. Zones (6)7 to 9.

Rhododendron minus, Piedmont rhododendron

Rhododendron mucronu-latum

Korean rhododendron

Korean rhododendron is a deciduous shrub that offers bright rose-purple, 1½-in.-long and -wide flowers on naked stems from March to early April. It was a welcome sight in the Dirr Illinois garden after the hostilities of the midwestern winter. Use in a shrub border or grouping framed by an evergreen background. Grows 4 to 8 ft. high and wide. Zones 4 to 7. Northern and northeastern China, Korea, northern Japan.

CULTIVARS AND VARIETIES

'Cornell Pink' has phlox-pink flowers.

Rhododendron mucronulatum, Korean rhododendron

Rhododendron 'PJM'

Rhododendron pericly-menoides

syn. *Rhododendron nudiflorum*

pinxterbloom azalea

A deciduous, fragrant-flowered species that forms a many-branched, rounded to spreading shrub. The 1½-in.-wide, variably fragrant flowers occur in May in clusters of six to 12, before the leaves. Colors range from near white to pale pink to violet. Grows 4 to 6 (to 10) ft. high. Observed at higher elevations in Georgia and Virginia. Zones 4 to 8. Massachusetts to North Carolina and Ohio.

Rhododendron 'PJM'

Since its origination in about 1943, 'PJM' has become the standard by which all small, broadleaved, cold hardy rhododendrons are judged. I am told it is the only evergreen rhododendron that flowers in the Minnesota

MORE ▶

Rhododendron mucronulatum 'Cornell Pink'

Rhododendron periclymenoides, pinxterbloom azalea

Rhododendron '**PJM**' CONTINUED
Landscape Arboretum. The habit is dense and rounded. Vivid lavender-pink flowers occur in mid to late April. The dark green leaves turn reddish purple in winter. This hybrid, a result of crosses involving *Rhododendron minus* and *R. dauricum* var. *sempervirens*, was introduced by Weston Nurseries, Hopkinton, Massachusetts. Grows 3 to 6 ft. high and wide. Grew

Rhododendron 'PJM'

Rhododendron prinophyllum

Rhododendron prunifolium, plumleaf azalea

successfully in our Illinois garden, where it flowered after −20°F. Recent trip to Dow Gardens, Michigan, confirmed the importance of 'PJM' and related types to successful rhododendron culture in cold climates. Zones 4 to 7.

CULTIVARS AND VARIETIES
Weston Nurseries has introduced other hybrids with excellent cold hardiness and varying foliage and flower colors. Consult my *Manual of Woody Landscape Plants* (2009) for cultivar specifics.

Rhododendron prinophyllum

syn. *Rhododendron roseum*
roseshell azalea
A wonderfully fragrant, pink-flowered, deciduous shrub. Five to nine flowers are borne on each inflorescence in

Rhododendron prinophyllum, roseshell azalea

May. Summer foliage is bright green; fall foliage is bronze-red. The habit is tremendously variable, but plants in full sun are dense and rounded. Grows 2 to 8 (to 15) ft. high and wide. Zones 4 to 8. Southern Quebec to Virginia, west to Missouri.

Rhododendron prunifolium
plumleaf azalea
At the distant end of the flowering spectrum lies this most beautiful orange-red to red-flowered deciduous native azalea. In July and August, nonfragrant flowers snap to attention yet are so far embedded in the foliage that their powerful colors are somewhat masked. Terrific plant for attracting hummingbirds; in August, I watch the remarkable creatures work their magic on the flowers. A large shrub, 10 to 15 ft. high; the few plants

in the Dirr garden are 6 ft. high after six years. Has been used for hybridizing to extend flowering season. Worthwhile garden plant for woodland edges, borders, and irregular groupings. Zones 5 to 8. Southwestern Georgia and eastern Alabama.

Rhododendron schlippenbachii

royal azalea

Possibly the most handsome of all the deciduous azaleas when the soft pink, fragrant flowers cover the shrub in May. Three to six flowers are present in each 2½- to 3-in.-wide inflorescence. Foliage is dark green in summer, developing subdued yellow, orange, and red tints in autumn. Grows 6 to 8 ft. high and wide. Zones 4 to 7. Korea, northeastern China.

Rhododendron vaseyi

pinkshell azalea

This deciduous species offers abundant 1½-in.-wide, pink flowers before the leaves in May. The medium to dark

MORE ▶

Rhododendron vaseyi

Rhododendron schlippenbachii, royal azalea

Rhododendron schlippenbachii

Rhododendron schlippenbachii fall color

Rhododendron vaseyi, pinkshell azalea

Rhododendron yedoense var. *poukhanense*, Korean azalea

green leaves develop excellent reddish fall color. Grows 5 to 10 ft. high. Zones 4 to 8. North Carolina.
CULTIVARS AND VARIETIES
Several white-flowered selections are available, including 'Alba' and 'White Find'.

Rhododendron viscosum
swamp azalea

This is a wonderful deciduous native species that has been used by hybridizers to produce summer-blooming azaleas. The white, rarely pink, flowers have a clove-like fragrance. They occur in four- to nine-flowered inflorescences after the leaves have fully matured. The flowers are not particularly striking, but the fragrance more than compensates for the lack of show. The lustrous dark green leaves have a glaucous cast on their undersides. A rather open shrub. Grows 5 to 8 ft. high, wider at maturity. Zones 3 to 9. Maine to South Carolina, Georgia, and Alabama, in swamps. Observed it growing along the edges of freshwater ponds on Cape Cod.

Rhododendron yedoense var. poukhanense
Korean azalea

Korean azalea displays excellent flower bud hardiness (−20 to −25°F). It is a compact shrub with a mounded-rounded outline. The 2-in.-wide, rose to lilac-purple, slightly fragrant flowers

Rhododendron viscosum, swamp azalea

Rhododendron yedoense, Yodogawa azalea

appear in May. The dark green foliage often develops orange to red-purple fall color. Performed well in Illinois and Georgia. Grows 3 to 6 ft. high and wide. Zones 4 to 8. Korea.

Rhododendron yedoense, Yodogawa azalea, has double flowers of a similar color.

Rhododendron Hybrids
Exbury, Ghent, Ilam, Knap Hill, Mollis, Northern Lights, Windsor

These hybrid groups are spectacular deciduous shrubs that are covered with flowers in white, yellow, orange, red, and every shade in between, during May and June. Flowers generally occur before the leaves emerge, although this is variable. The medium green leaves may develop yellow, orange, and red fall color. Best in cooler climates. Many selections offer flower bud hardiness to about –20°F or even the low –30s Fahrenheit (Northern Lights azaleas). Habit is shrubby, to 8 to 12 ft. high and wide. Zones 4 to 7.

'Gibraltar', an Exbury azalea with bright orange flowers, is still the clear leader in American commerce.

Confederate Hybrids

A relatively new group of heat-tolerant azaleas, meshing the floral characteristics of the Exbury Hybrids ('Hotspur Yellow') and *Rhododendron austrinum*, Florida azalea. This work was carried by Alabama plantsmen Bob Schwalt, Tom Dodd Jr., and Tom Dodd III. The selections have terrific flowers, before and with the leaves. The dark green, deciduous leaves, to date, are mildew-free. Flowers are knockouts, appearing in 3- to 4- (to 5-) in.-wide trusses in mid April in the Dirr garden. Great potential for southern gardens, where Exbury and Knap Hill types turn to rot, ruin, and mildew. Grows 6 to 10 ft. high. Zones 6 to 9.

'Admiral Semmes' has fragrant yellow flowers and is one of the most reliable for abundant flower production.

MORE ▶

Rhododendron 'Stonewall Jackson'

Exbury azalea collection

Knap Hill azalea

Rhododendron 'Admiral Semmes'

707

Rhododendron Hybrids CONTINUED

'Colonel Mosby' is a personal favorite, with beautiful foliage and fragrant, deep rose flowers, each with a yellow blotch, that fade to pink.

'Robert E. Lee' produces fragrant, ruffled red flowers.

'Stonewall Jackson' is a southern 'Gibraltar', with fragrant, large, solid, rich orange flowers. A vigorous grower and happy garden camper.

Encore® Hybrids

A novel concept indeed: extend the flowering season from spring, with a summer gap, to resume in late summer to fall. Such is the case with this well-crafted and -marketed group of evergreen azaleas, the introductions of which carry the prefix "autumn" to distinguish them from spring azaleas. All are spreading to rounded shrubs, 1 to 2 (to 3) ft. high, 3 ft. wide and more. Now up to 25 introductions: white, pink, rose to purple, single and double. Bonnie loves the colors and the fact that flowers open in fall and spring. Not as blowsy as the Kurume and Southern Indica hybrids. Some lace bug damage but not as heavy as the Kurumes. Truly beautiful at their best but absolute cold hardiness is suspect, since *Rhododendron old-hamii* is one parent. Probably best in zones 7 to 9. Bred by Robert E. (Buddy) Lee.

The best performers of the early introductions in the Dirr garden were Autumn Amethyst™ ('Conlee') (rosy purple), Autumn Coral™ ('Conled')

Rhododendron Autumn Coral™

Rhododendron Autumn Royalty™

Rhododendron Autumn Ruby™

Rhododendron 'Hot Shot'

Rhododendron 'Pleasant White'

Rhododendron 'Renee Michelle'

(salmon-pink), Autumn Embers™ ('Con-leb') (orange-red), Autumn Rouge™ ('Conlea') (pink-red), Autumn Royalty™ ('Conlec') (rich purple), and Autumn Ruby™ ('Conler') (salmon-red).

Girard Hybrids

The skilled plantsmanship of Ohio's Girard Nursery, through the generations, resulted in these improved evergreen azaleas, which I first grew over 30 years ago in our Illinois garden. Most have excellent, lustrous foliage, large flowers, and –5 to –15°F flower bud hardiness. Size varies, 3 to 6 ft. in height. The nursery industry is replacing many of the smaller-flowered Kurume Hybrids with the Girards. I counted over 50 cultivars, both evergreen and deciduous, released by Girard Nursery. Based on observations and performance in the Dirr garden, I recommend 'Hot Shot' (deep orange-red to scarlet flowers), 'Pleasant White' (large white flowers), 'Renee Michelle' (clear pink flowers), 'Rose' (rose flowers, glossy deep green leaves, deep red in winter), and 'Scarlet' (strong red). Newer cultivars may have superseded these stellar performers, but I have yet to test them. Zones (5)6 to 8.

Glenn Dale Hybrids

Tell me it's not true . . . 70,000 azalea seedlings: tested, screened, selected, and reduced to a *mere* 454 named cultivars. Insanity? Absolutely! And I'll bet dollars to doughnuts, the reader could not name a single one. This government initiative was the brain-child of Benjamin Y. Morrison, U.S. National Arboretum, and carried out at the Plant Introduction Station, Glenn Dale, Maryland. Concept: hardiness to –10°F, unique colors, evergreen foliage.

'Glacier' has 3-in.-wide, white flowers, with a faint green spot/hue in the throat, and lustrous dark green foliage. Erect to spreading habit, 4 to 6 ft. high. About the best and still in circulation.

Where are the other 453?

Kurume Hybrids

Although often associated with northern gardens, particularly the coastal Northeast into the Mid-Atlantic states, this hybrid Japanese group is more commonly grown and utilized in the Southeast. At their best, 4- to 6-ft.-high and -wide, broadleaf evergreen shrubs with smallish, 1-in.-long leaves

MORE ▶

Rhododendron 'Mother's Day'

Rhododendron 'Glacier'

Rhododendron 'Coral Bells'

Rhododendron Hybrids CONTINUED

and 1- to 2-in.-wide flowers. In Pine Mountain, Georgia, Callaway Garden's famous azalea bowl was largely planted with Kurume Hybrids. Petal blight and susceptibility to lace bugs necessitate abundant maintenance. In my opinion, they could be replaced by the Girard and Robin Hill hybrids. Zones 6 to 8(9).

'Coral Bells', with coral-pink, ½-in.-wide, hose-in-hose (double) flowers, on a 3- to 4-ft.-high and -wide shrub, remains one of the most popular.

'Hershey's Red' has 2-in.-wide, bright red flowers.

'Hinodegiri' produces vivid red, 1½-in.-wide flowers and dark green summer foliage that turns wine-red in fall.

'Mother's Day' has large, red flowers on a wide-spreading plant.

Robin Hill Hybrids

A group of delicate-hued, large-flowered, evergreen azaleas with the lateness and large flowers of the Satsuki Hybrids. Flowers are large, 2½ to 4 in. across.

Habit is spreading, and, for selected cultivars, size in ten years ranges from 15 in. high, 34 in. wide, to 25 in. high, 28 in. wide. Starting to make inroads in southern gardens. Zones 7 and 8(9).

Rhododendron 'Pink Ruffles'

Rhododendron 'Hershey's Red'

Rhododendron 'Red Ruffles'

Rhododendron 'Nancy of Robin Hill'

Rhododendron 'Gumpo Pink'

'Hilda Niblett' produces large pink and white flowers on a compact mounded plant.

'Nancy of Robin Hill' is a beautiful light pink, hose-in-hose (double), low-growing form.

Rutherfordiana Hybrids
Beautiful, ruffled flowers, evergreen foliage, and compact habit, 2 to 4 ft. high and wide, make these azaleas common in the Coastal Plain of the Southeast. The forms most often encountered in cultivation are 'Pink Ruffles', with pink-violet, semi-double, 2-in.-wide flowers, and 'Red Ruffles', with large, 3-in.-wide, deep red, ruffled flowers. Zones 8 and 9.

Satsuki Hybrids
Called "fifth-month azaleas" because they flower in May. About the latest of the commonly grown evergreen azaleas in southern gardens (with exception of Encore® Hybrids). Spreading branches clothed with evergreen leaves, less than 1 in. long, serve as the perfect framework for the 2- to 4-in.-wide flowers, which open in mid to late May into June in Athens. Require shade for best performance. Excellent massing plants under pines and broadleaf trees. Numerous cultivars boggle the aesthetic senses. Grow 1 to 2 (to 3) ft. high, wider at maturity. Zones 7 to 9, 10 on the West Coast. Japan.

'Gumpo Pink' (pink) and 'Gumpo White' (white) are extremely popular.

Southern Indica Hybrids
These amazing large-flowered evergreen azaleas are a staple in coastal Georgia landscapes and the dominant understory shrub at resort hotels. Habit is broad-mounded, with 1- to 3-in.-long, dark green leaves. Flowers appear in late March and April in clusters, each flower 2½ to 3 in. across, sometimes greater. Rich color range, from white to deepest purple. From my observations, among the most adaptable evergreen azaleas, with an ability to tolerate full sun to live oak shade. Grow 5 to 10 ft. high and wide. Zones (7)8 to 10.

Time-tested and time-honored, with greater cold hardiness, the most common cultivars are 'Formosa' (magenta with deep blotch), 'G. G. Gerbing' (pure white), and 'George L. Taber' (orchid-pink). Grew these last two in our Athens garden, and from year to year flowering was variable due to cold. In fact, from 2003 to 2008, there was only one great flowering exposition, in 2008, and the lowest temperature over those years was 9.5°F.

Rhodotypos scandens
black jetbead
An old-fashioned shrub, black jetbead is seldom available in commerce, but it is receiving increasing attention because of its tremendous urban tolerance and its adaptability to shady habitats. In the best form, it develops into a mounded, loosely branched shrub with ascending and arching branches. The bright green, 2¼- to 4-in.-long leaves look like raspberry foliage. The leaves are among

MORE ▶

Rhodotypos scandens, black jetbead

Rhodotypos scandens

Rhododendron 'G. G. Gerbing'

Rhododendron 'George L. Taber'

Rhodotypos scandens CONTINUED

the first to emerge in spring, and they hold late into fall. Four-petaled, white, 1- to 2-in.-wide flowers open in mid to late April (Athens), May, and June, with scattered flowers often into the summer. The ⅓-in.-long, ovoid fruit are shining black, hard as a rock, and persistent through winter. Extremely adaptable; in fact, it is almost impossible to kill once established. Use as a foliage filler in shady borders, on banks, or in hostile soil areas. Never sensational, but certainly functional. Grows 3 to 6 ft. high, 4 to 9 ft. wide. Zones 4 to 8. Japan, central China.

Rhus aromatica
fragrant sumac

Fragrant sumac is a useful shrub for groundcover and massing situations. It is adapted to the hottest, driest conditions and has proven a great plant for midwestern landscapes. Habit varies from a low groundcover to an irregular, spreading shrub with lower branches that turn up at the tips. Produces suckers and will create a tangled, almost impenetrable mass of stems and leaves. The trifoliate, near blue-green leaves are often glossy on the upper surface. They develop orange to red to reddish purple fall

Rhodotypos scandens

Rhus aromatica

Rhus aromatica

Rhodotypos scandens

Rhus aromatica, fragrant sumac

712

color. Yellowish catkins open on naked stems of male plants in March and April. Red, hairy, ¼-in.-wide fruit ripen on female plants in August and September. Extremely adaptable to varied soils. Withstands sun or shade. Nice shrub for naturalizing, groundcover, or border use. Has not performed well on Georgia campus, and I suspect heavy, wet soils were the culprit. Grows 2 to 6 ft. high, 6 to 10 ft. wide. Zones 3 to 9. Vermont to Ontario and Minnesota, south to Florida and Louisiana. CULTIVARS AND VARIETIES 'Gro-low' is a wide-spreading form with excellent glossy green foliage and orange-red fall color. A female, it bears yellow flowers and hairy red fruit. Grows 2 ft. high, 6 to 8 ft. wide.

Rhus chinensis

Chinese sumac

This species ranges from a large, multi-stemmed shrub to a small tree. In northern latitudes, it is often shrubby. The bright green leaves are composed of seven to 13 leaflets, each 2 to 5 in. long, and develop respectable yellow, orange, and red fall color. The real show occurs in August and September, when 8- to 16-in.-long and -wide, fleecy, white panicles smother the foliage. Flowers last for two to three weeks or longer. Chinese sumac is ideal for dry, infertile soils. Requires full sun for maximum flower-

MORE ▶

Rhus aromatica 'Gro-low'

Rhus chinensis 'September Beauty'

Rhus aromatica fall color

Rhus chinensis, Chinese sumac, fall color

Rhus chinensis CONTINUED

ing. Suckers do develop; to keep the plant in bounds, simply mow them off. A good choice for use where walls, walks, and roads will limit its spread. Grows 20 to 25 ft. high, spreads indefinitely. Zones 5 to 7(8). China, Japan.
CULTIVARS AND VARIETIES
'September Beauty' was selected by Dr. Elwin Orton of Rutgers University for its larger flowers and tree-type habit. It is stunning in flower. Aggressive and will sucker, engulfing considerable real estate. Easily 20 ft. high and 25 ft. wide unless restrained.

Rhus copallina
flameleaf or shining sumac
At one time, I considered this species the best of the large-growing, suckering native sumacs, but now I defer to *Rhus typhina* 'Laciniata', primarily because of availability. The flameleaf

sumac is a large, suckering, colonizing shrub with invasive qualities similar to that of the other sumacs. The leaves are composed of nine to 21 lustrous dark green leaflets, each 1¾ to 4 in. long. Foliage changes to rich red, crimson, scarlet, and maroon in autumn. Greenish yellow flowers are borne in 4- to 8-in.-long, 3- to 4-in.-wide, feathery panicles in July and August. The crimson fruit ripen in September and October, but they are not as showy as those of *R. glabra* or *R. typhina*. As with the other species, flameleaf sumac will grow in any soil except one that is permanently moist. Grows 20 to 30 ft. high and wide. Zones 4 to 9. Maine to Ontario

and Minnesota, south to Florida and Texas.
CULTIVARS AND VARIETIES
Prairie Flame™ ('Morton') is a compact, 4- to 6-ft.-high form, spreading by suckers, with lustrous dark green leaves, flaming orange-red to red in autumn. A male. Observed in full flower in late July, JC Raulston Arboretum; just opening late August, J. Frank Schmidt Jr. Arboretum, Oregon.

Rhus glabra
smooth sumac
Perhaps no native plant is as flamboyant as smooth sumac in autumn, when large colonies create blankets of fluorescent yellows and reds along

Rhus copallina Prairie Flame™

Rhus copallina, flameleaf sumac, fall color

Rhus glabra

Rhus copallina

the highways and byways of America. Most gardeners consider this species a pernicious weed, however, and would not give it a second thought for general landscape use. The habit is colonizing, suckering, rampant, spreading. The deep green leaves consist of 11 to 31 leaflets, each 2 to 5 in. long, with evenly serrated margins. Flowers are yellowish green and appear in June and July. The fruit, which occur on female plants, are small, hairy, red drupes arranged in a conical, 6- to 10-in.-long panicle. Culture is abysmally easy. Once invited into the garden, the plant immediately becomes like an unwanted guest—difficult to get rid of. Even root pieces will regenerate quickly.

Use for naturalizing, on difficult slopes and banks, or in large areas. Seems to outcompete other woody vegetation. Grows 10 to 15 ft. high, considerably greater in spread; I have observed 20-ft.-tall tree forms that were quite attractive. Zones 2 to 9. Most of the United States, parts of Canada.

CULTIVARS AND VARIETIES

'Laciniata' is a pretty form, with deeply cut leaflets reminiscent of a fern frond. It is a female and carries the same handsome fruit as the species. A confused entity, sometimes listed as *Rhus* ×*pulvinata* 'Red Autumn Lace', a hybrid of *R. glabra* and *R. typhina*, with intermediate pubescence on leaves and stems.

Rhus michauxii
Michaux's sumac

Rare but worthy endangered species that is definitively more restrained than *Rhus copallina*, *R. glabra*, and *R. typhina*. The habit is low-growing, suckering, the end result large colonies. Leaves are composed of nine to 15 leaflets, each 2 to 4 in. long, dark green, and coarsely toothed. Fall

MORE ▶

Rhus michauxii fall color

Rhus michauxii, Michaux's sumac

Rhus glabra, smooth sumac, fall color

Rhus glabra

Rhus glabra 'Laciniata'

715

Rhus michauxii CONTINUED
color is beautiful and long persisting, an excellent deep reddish purple. The yellow-green flowers occur in 6- to 8-in.-long panicles in June and July, followed on female plants by pubescent, compressed red drupes. Like all *Rhus* species, extremely adaptable; plants I witnessed were prospering in low-fertility, rocky soils. A collector's plant as well as a good candidate for naturalizing. Grows 2 to 3 ft. high, spreading indefinitely. Zones 5 to 7. North Carolina to Georgia.

Rhus typhina
staghorn sumac
Staghorn sumac is very similar to *Rhus glabra* in both appearance and habit. The principal difference is that its stems are hairy, whereas those of *R. glabra* are non-hairy (glabrous). Not as widespread in nature, but this species appears as adaptable as smooth sumac under cultivation. Mature

size is larger, generally 15 to 25 ft. high, although it can grow 30 to 40 ft. National champion is 57 ft. by 41 ft. Zones 3 to 8. Quebec to Ontario, south to Georgia and Iowa.
CULTIVARS AND VARIETIES
'Laciniata' offers divided leaflets that create a fine-textured, ferny appearance. It is a female.

Tiger Eyes® ('Bailtiger') has bronze-yellow new growth, settling to yellow, then yellow-green in July and August, finally orange-red in fall; foliage is dissected. Held up well in Georgia trials, slower growing than 'Laciniata' but will sucker; 5 to 10 ft. high.

Rhus typhina, staghorn sumac

Rhus typhina fall color

Rhus typhina Tiger Eyes®

Rhus typhina 'Laciniata'

Ribes alpinum
alpine currant

Alpine currant is a choice shrub for colder climates, where it is often used for masses, hedges, and groupings. The habit is densely twiggy and rounded with stiffly upright stems and spreading branches. The three- to (rarely) five-lobed, bright green leaves, 1 to 2 in. long and wide, develop minimal yellow fall color. The leaves emerge early in spring.

Flowers are rather inconspicuous greenish yellow catkins. Fruit are ¼- to ⅓-in.-wide, scarlet berries that ripen in June and July; they occur on female plants only. Their effect is masked by the foliage, and the fruit are eaten by birds. *Ribes alpinum* is readily transplanted. It is adaptable to virtually any well-drained soil and withstands sun or shade. Does not perform well in high heat. Great plant for northern landscapes. Grows 3 to 6 (to 10) ft. high and wide. Zones 2 to 7. Europe.

CULTIVARS AND VARIETIES
'Green Mound' is a dense, dwarf form that is used frequently in the Midwest. Grows 2 to 3 (to 4) ft. high and wide. Good resistance to leaf diseases. Green Jeans™ ('Spreg'), 'Nanum', 'Pumilum', and 'Compactum' are also listed.

Ribes aureum var. villosum

syn. *Ribes odoratum*
clove currant

A rare gem in the shrub world, this species offers wonderfully fragrant, golden yellow flowers in early to mid April. The habit is upright-arching, usually prolifically suckering. The 1- to 3-in.-wide, three- to five-lobed, rich blue-green leaves turn yellowish to reddish in fall. The flowers have the

MORE ▶

Ribes alpinum, alpine currant

Ribes aureum var. *villosum*, clove currant

Ribes alpinum

Ribes aureum var. *villosum*

Ribes aureum var. *villosum* CONTINUED fragrance of cloves. Quite adaptable to varied soils, in full sun or partial shade. Use in a shrub border or combine with bulbs and wildflowers. Rare in cultivation but worthy. Serves as alternate host for white pine blister rust. Grows 6 to 8 ft. high, greater in spread. Zones 4 to 6(7). Minnesota and South Dakota, south to Arkansas and Texas.

Ribes sanguineum
winter currant

A West Coast native, observed on many occasions during my visits to the Portland environs. Consistently buried in the understory. Leaves, three- to five-lobed, 2 to 4 in. wide, are dark green. Habit is upright-arching, relatively loose and open in shade, more dense in sun. Common in English gardens, where it flowers in March and

April. Flowers, white, pink to red, occur in 3-in.-long, pendulous racemes, along the length of the naked stems. Fruit are bloomy, bluish black, slightly glandular, ⅓-in.-wide berries. Prefers moist, well-drained soil in full sun to partial shade and tolerates summer drought, which is common in its native habitat. Excellent for shrub border, edges of woodlands, naturalizing. Grows 6 to 10 (to 15) ft. high and

Ribes aureum var. *villosum* fall color

Ribes speciosum

Ribes sanguineum, winter currant

Ribes sanguineum

Ribes sanguineum 'Pulborough Scarlet'

wide. Zones 5 and 6, 7 to 10 on West Coast. British Columbia to northern California.

Ribes speciosum is a semi-evergreen shrub, usually sited against a wall in English gardens, with beautiful, rich red, slender fuchsia-shaped flowers in pendent inflorescences in April and May. The leaves are lustrous green; stems and fruit with bristly appendages. Grows 6 to 10 ft.

high. Zones 8 to 10 on West Coast. California.

CULTIVARS AND VARIETIES
'Brocklebankii' has yellow leaves and pink flowers.

'King Edward VII' produces rose-red flowers on a compact habit. This is the sole winter currant I have observed on the East Coast, only once, in the Boston area, where it was in rich red flower, 5 to 6 ft. high.

'Pulborough Scarlet' has deep red flowers.

White Icicle™ has white flowers.

Robinia hispida
bristly or roseacacia locust

For landscape purposes, the effect of this suckering shrub and that of *Robinia fertilis* (var. *fertilis*) are very similar, and their characteristics are almost identical. The one major difference is that *R. hispida* does not set fruit. For both, the branches, petioles, and floral stalks are covered with brown, bristly pubescence. The dark blue-green leaves are composed of nine to 15 leaflets, each 1 to 2 in. long. Rose to rose-lavender, nonfra-

MORE ▶

Robinia hispida, bristly locust

Robinia hispida

Ribes sanguineum 'Brocklebankii'

Ribes sanguineum White Icicle™

719

Robinia hispida CONTINUED

grant flowers occur in 2- to 4-in.-long racemes in May and June. Fruit of *R. fertilis* are 2- to 4-in.-long, bristly pods. Extremely adaptable, even in infertile, dry soils. Fixes atmospheric nitrogen. A good plant to reclaim waste soil areas. Grows 6 to 10 ft. high, spreads indefinitely. I often chance upon random colonies in Georgia; only noticeable in flower, in late April and early May. Zones 5 to 8. Southeastern United States.

Robinia pseudoacacia
black locust

Its ability to seed and establish quickly on infertile soils qualifies black locust

as a weed tree in many sections of the United States. Growth habit varies from a suckering shrub to an upright tree with a narrow, oblong crown. The bluish green, 6- to 14-in.-long leaves, composed of seven to 19, 1- to 2-in.-long, oval leaflets, seldom change color in fall and die off yellowish brown, at best. The greenish to reddish brown stems are often armed with sharp paired stipular prickles at the nodes. The grayish to brownish black bark becomes deeply ridged and furrowed with age. Creamy white, fragrant flowers occur in 4- to 8-in.-long racemes in May and June. Virtually any soil is suitable, but the plant requires full sun for best growth. Black locust is a respectable choice for

sandy, infertile soils, and is somewhat salt-tolerant. Borers and leaf miner are serious, the latter rendering the leaves brown in summer. Grows 30 to 50 ft. high. Zones 3 to 8. Pennsylvania to Iowa, south to Georgia and Oklahoma.
CULTIVARS AND VARIETIES
'Frisia' offers golden yellow leaves that become green with the heat of summer in the East. Still yellow in late August in Portland, Oregon, area. Larger than often cited, reaching 40 to 50 ft. high, 20 to 30 ft. wide at maturity.

'Purple Robe' has dark rose-pink flowers on a compact rounded tree, probably in the 20- to 30-ft. range. I believe 'Rouge Cascade', 'Casque

Robinia pseudoacacia

Robinia pseudoacacia 'Umbraculifera'

Robinia pseudoacacia, black locust

Rouge', and 'Pink Cascade' are the same.

'Pyramidalis' ('Fastigiata') is a slender columnar tree with closely set, essentially spineless branches; two 40- to 50-ft.-high trees at Milliken Arboretum have flowered quite profusely and maintained the tight columnar habit.

Twisty Baby™ ('Lace Lady') is an artistic, twisted stem/branch selection with more refined foliage than the species. Not small as marketed; I've witnessed 20- to 30-ft.-high trees.

'Umbraculifera' forms a dense, globe-headed outline. Grows 20 ft. high and wide.

Rosa
rose

With hundreds of species and thousands of cultivars of roses in the world, providing literary and photographic justice to the genus *Rosa* is nearly impossible. For the purposes of this book, I focused on several adapt-

MORE ▶

Robinia pseudoacacia

Rosa Coral Drift®

Robinia pseudoacacia 'Frisia'

Rosa Explorer series 'Alexander MacKenzie'

Robinia pseudoacacia 'Purple Robe'

Rosa Explorer series 'William Baffin'

Rosa CONTINUED

able shrub species and hybrid groups that make excellent additions to borders and are effective in masses or groupings. Some shrub roses are useful as soil-stabilizing agents. Many species-type roses are more resistant to the problems that typically beset the hybrids, but even these shrub species are not without their problems—diseases and pests can take their toll. I remember vividly the excitement of planting *Rosa chinensis* 'Mutabilis', *R. roxburghii*, *R. rubrifolia*, and *R. rugosa* in my Georgia garden. Unfortunately, only 'Mutabilis' was retained, and it was defoliated by black spot in the warm, humid summers. A new wave of "carefree" roses has been introduced that offer greater disease resistance, but these lower-maintenance roses are still far from perfect. The Meidiland series received the most early press and indeed are worthy garden

subjects. Do not be misled, however, for some disease will develop if climatic conditions are optimal. Use roses with the knowledge that at certain times of the gardening cycle they appear less than pristine. Several series are available in U.S. commerce.

DRIFT® SERIES

First witnessed at the 2008 Farwest Show in August, then at Hawksridge Nursery in September. Naturally dwarf hybrids of groundcover/shrub and miniature roses, they have glossy dark green foliage; good resistance to rust, powdery mildew, and black spot; and

cold hardiness to zone 5. Witnessed Coral Drift® and Pink Drift® with flowers only at end of shoots; certainly not overwhelming; relatively clean foliage for September in zone 7. Prune back in late winter to encourage vigorous growth and flowers; deadhead during growing season. Coral Drift® and Red Drift® have performed magnificently in Athens; in 2010, flowering was profuse in May then shut down completely in June; a small amount of black spot was present on lower (older) leaves by mid June. None of the three mentioned appear to have

Rosa Pink Knock Out®

Rosa Pink Flower Carpet®

Rosa Scarlet Meidiland™

Rosa Oso Easy™ Cherry Pie

the reblooming propensity of Knock Out® roses. Bred in France by Meidiland; marketed in the United States by Conard-Pyle.

EASY ELEGANCE® SERIES

Bred by Ping Lim for Bailey Nurseries, St. Paul, Minnesota, incorporating great flower colors, foliage, disease resistance, and cold hardiness. I observed them at Bailey's as well as at McCorkle's in Dearing, Georgia, but do not have a good handle on their overall performance. Suggest interested readers visit www.easy elegancerose.com. I checked the site in October 2010 and found 20 listed with photos and information. I was told that Knock Out® is not hardy in Minnesota (zone 4) and several of the Easy Elegance® are. The 2010 Bailey catalog lists 12 of 20 with zone 4 designations.

EXPLORER SERIES

For years Agricultural Canada has introduced cold hardy, disease-free roses for Canada and the northern United States. As long as I can remember Dr. Felicitas Svejda had her name attached to many (perhaps all?) of the new introductions, which were tested at several locations in Canada and the northern United States over a number of years to assess floriferousness, hardiness, and disease resistance. They are called the Explorer series and are named accordingly. Many have *Rosa rugosa* in their parentage. May experience stem dieback in extremely cold winters, –25 to –35°F, but will flower on regrowth of season. Although these roses were bred for cold hardiness and disease resistance for the harsh climates of Canada and the northern United States, they did not prove particularly worthy in Jeff Epping and Ed Hasselkus's trials in Madison, Wisconsin.

FLOWER CARPET® SERIES

Flower Carpet® and the series resulted from 35 years of breeding by Dr. Noack Rosen and are marketed by Anthony Tesselaar. They are described as possessing "natural strength against rose diseases." I have not been impressed with everyday performance, especially compared to Knock Out® roses. Have grown some of each in Georgia trials and my personal gardens. I have no vested interest in either group: good garden performance is the overriding criteria. Might mention that one of our Chapel Hill neighbors had Double Knock Out® and Pink Flower Carpet® in the front garden. Mid September found the Knock Out® loaded with flowers and buds, the foliage clean; the Flower Carpet® with minimalist flowers at the end of long, spreading shoots, about one-half the basal foliage absent.

KNOCK OUT® SERIES

The greatest rose success story in the United States is the Knock Out® series bred by Bill Radler, Wisconsin.

MORE ▶

Rosa Knock Out®

The original Knock Out® ('Radrazz', red, single) energized gardeners who simply did not want to nuke (chemical atomization) roses to keep them in good working order. I am an advocate for *no* chemical input on plants and am thankful for Mr. Radler's contributions. Knock Out® series are the largest selling roses in the United States from zones 5 to 9(10). Double Knock Out® ('Radtko'), double cherry-red; Pink Double Knock Out® ('Radtkopink'), double bright pink; and Pink Knock Out® ('Radcon'), single bright pink, are my favorites of the current eight introductions.

MEIDILAND SERIES

The jury is still out on the absolute carefree nature of these landscape shrub roses, but to date the reports have been favorable. They are definitely resistant to black spot and mildew. However, early spring and mid summer fungicide applications are recommended. In my Georgia trials, Scarlet Meidiland™ and White Meidiland™ fared the best. All contracted some black spot. Bred in France by Meidiland; intoduced in the United States by Conard-Pyle.

OSO EASY™ ROSES

Oso Easy™ roses are offered by Spring Meadow Nursery. Described as disease-resistant. All carry the Oso Easy™ trademark and are patented or in process. They include Cherry Pie (red), Fragrant Spreader (pink), Honey Bun (blush pink, butter yellow to white; highest disease resistance), Paprika (red-orange with yellow eye), Peachy Cream (peach to cream), and Strawberry Crush (strawberry pink to cream). Most were hybridized in Europe, so long-term performance is unknown, especially in zones 7 to 9, where long growing season, heat, drought, and humidity stress roses like nowhere else. Tested Paprika and Cherry Pie at Plant Introductions; by September, Paprika was heavily infested with black spot, Cherry Pie infested but not

as severe in 2009; reverse in 2010. All are shrubby, 1 to 2 ft. high, twice as wide. Listed to zone 5.

PARKLAND SERIES

Hybrids of native prairie roses from Morden Research Station, Canada. Introductions do freeze back, but they flower on new growth of the season.

Rosa banksiae 'Lutea'
Lady Banks' rose

A mainstay in southern landscapes, often used for entryways and espal-

iers and along fences. Almost a scandent, evergreen shrub, exhibiting vine-like tendencies if trained to a structure. Left alone, it forms an arching, rounded shrub. The evergreen leaves consist of three to five (occasionally seven), 1- to 2½-in.-long, lustrous dark green leaflets. Stems are shiny grass-green and without prickles. In late March and April, the double, soft primrose-yellow, delicately fragrant flowers appear. A profusion of yellow engulfs the shoots and makes for a

Rosa banksiae 'Lutea', Lady Banks' rose

spectacular and lovely effect. I have observed considerable mildew but, to date, black spot has not been a problem. One of the easiest roses to culture, with numerous garden uses. At Powis Castle, Wales, a 30-ft. specimen climbs the castle wall. Grows 15 to 20 ft. high. Zones 7 and 8(9). China.

CULTIVARS AND VARIETIES
'Normalis' ('Alba') might be considered the species type with 1-in.-wide, slightly fragrant, single white flowers.

Rosa carolina
Carolina or pasture rose
This rather lax, erect-arching species offers lustrous, rich green summer foli-age that turns dull red in fall. The 2- to 2½-in.-wide, single pink flowers appear in June and July. Red, pear-shaped, glandular-hairy fruit, ⅓ in. in diameter, ripen in fall and may persist into winter. Grows 6 to 7 ft. high. Zones 4 to 9. Common in low, wet grounds and borders of swamps and streams. Maine to Wisconsin, south to Florida and Texas.

Rosa banksiae 'Lutea'

Rosa carolina

Rosa carolina, Carolina rose

Rosa glauca

syn. *Rosa rubrifolia*

redleaf rose

One of my favorites because of its leaves: glaucous bluish green overcast with reddish purple. New leaves are reddish purple upon emergence. Pink, 1½-in.-wide flowers bloom in June and are not particularly potent. Flowers on seed-grown plants vary from light to deep pink. The ½-in.-long fruit mature to dark red. Habit is upright-spreading, eventually rounded. Great choice for a colorful addition to a shrub or perennial border. Susceptible to foliar disease but, interestingly, West Coast gardeners reported no problems after 20 years in the garden. Grows 5 to 7 (to 10) ft. high. Zones 2 to 8. Mountains of central and southern Europe.

Rosa laevigata

Cherokee rose

For some unusual reason, this species was chosen as the state flower of Georgia. An unruly, evergreen to semi-evergreen, scandent shrub, forming wide-spreading, impenetrable tangles of sharply prickled stems. Great place for rabbits and vermin to establish residency. The three to five leaflets, thick-textured, lustrous dark green, are 1½ to 4 in. long. The thickish canes are armed with red-brown prickles that cut to the quick. Be careful! Five-petaled, fragrant, solitary, pure white, 3- to 4-in.-wide flowers open in April and May. The pear-shaped fruit, densely set with bristles, mature reddish brown to red, each 1½ to 1¾ in. long, ¾ in. wide. Tougher than a nail.

Have observed excellent flowering in sun and moderate shade. Difficult to keep in bounds and has no place in the small landscape. Grows 8 to 10 ft. high, 15 to 18 ft. wide; canes as long as 30 ft. occur. Zones 7 to 9. China, Taiwan, Myanmar.

Rosa laevigata

Rosa glauca, redleaf rose

Rosa laevigata, Cherokee rose

Rosa glauca

Rosa moyesii, Moyes rose

CULTIVARS AND VARIETIES
'Anemone' is a pink-flowered form that has hybrid blood. A member of the Dirr garden until it outgrew the boundaries of hospitality.

Rosa moyesii
Moyes rose
A beautiful large, rounded shrub with lustrous dark green leaves and 2- to 2½-in.-wide, blood-red flowers in June and July. Common in European gardens, this is one of the most beautiful of all shrub species in flower. The bright orange-red fruit are 1½ in. long, shaped like bottles. Grows 6 to 10 ft. high. Zones 5 to 7. Western China.
CULTIVARS AND VARIETIES
'Geranium' produces 3-in.-wide, geranium-red flowers and is showier than the typical species. For red flower effect, this is one of the most beautiful.

Rosa rugosa
rugosa or saltspray rose
Perhaps the best known and loved of all shrub roses because of its tenacious constitution, deliciously fragrant flowers, and large, orange-red fruit. Develops into a rounded, suckering shrub that colonizes large areas if not restrained. The leathery, lustrous dark green, prominently veined leaves turn yellow to bronze to orange and red in

MORE ▶

Rosa moyesii

Rosa moyesii 'Geranium'

Rosa rugosa, rugosa rose

Rosa rugosa

Rosa rugosa

Rosa rugosa 'Frau Dagmar Hastrup'

Rosa rugosa 'Hansa'

Rosa rugosa CONTINUED

autumn. White to rose-purple flowers, 2½ to 3½ in. in diameter, open from June through August, and sporadically into September and October. The 1-in.-wide, tomato-like fruit ripen from August through fall. The species has been utilized in breeding because of its disease resistance. Not as vigorous in zone 7 as further north. Many single- and double-flowered forms are known. Grows 4 to 6 ft. high. Zones 2 to 7. Russia, northern China, Korea, Japan.

CULTIVARS AND VARIETIES

Some of the better cultivars include 'Albo-plena' (double, fragrant, pure white), 'Belle Poitevine' (semi-double, slightly fragrant, light mauve-pink with showy yellow stamens), 'Blanc Double de Coubert' (double, fragrant, pure white), 'Frau Dagmar Hastrup' (prolific bloomer, fragrant, light pink flowers, large red fruit), and 'Hansa' (semi-double, very fragrant, purplish red flowers, orange-red fruit).

Rosa spinosissima
syn. *Rosa pimpinellifolia*
Scotch rose

The overwhelming variation in this species contributes to taxonomic nightmares but also serves as a gardener's

Rosa spinosissima

Rosa spinosissima 'Petite Pink'

Rosa spinosissima, Scotch rose

delight. The only common feature I can find is the bright green leaves that are composed of five to 11 rounded, delicate leaflets, each ½ to 1 in. long. The plant varies in habit from ground-cover-like to 3- to 4-ft.-high, mounded shrubs. White, yellow, or pink, 1- to 2-in.-wide, single flowers are borne in profusion on short branches along the stems in May and June. Blackish to dark brown fruit are ½ to ¾ in. in diameter. One of the most widely distributed rose species in its native range. Zones 4 to 8. Europe, western Asia.
CULTIVARS AND VARIETIES
'Petite Pink', with double pink, 1½-in.-wide flowers and shiny green foliage, gained a measure of fame, but mites and inconsistent flowering mitigated grandeur.

Rosa virginiana
Virginia rose
A lovely native species, Virginia rose bears 2- to 2½-in.-wide, pink flowers. The glossy dark green foliage develops excellent yellow to red fall color. Bright red, ½-in.-wide fruit persist into winter, and the reddish canes also provide winter interest. Very adaptable and at home by the sea or inland. I have never observed black spot on this species. Grows 4 to 6 ft. high. Zones 3 to 7(8). Newfoundland to Virginia, Alabama, and Missouri.

Rosmarinus officinalis
rosemary
"Woody shrub?" you ask. Actually one of the best evergreen woody plants if sited in sun and well-drained soil. A plant in our garden was over 15 years old and still prosperous. Each time I visit Sissinghurst Garden, England, I marvel at the large rosemary plants by the tower. Rounded, spreading, they form billowy, cloud-like masses. The evergreen leaves are ¾ to 2 in. in length and are gray-green to dark green. Close inspection reveals a green upper surface, gray to white-tomentose lower. The leaves emit a potent, unmistakable aromatic odor;

MORE ▶

Rosmarinus officinalis 'Prostratus'

Rosa virginiana, Virginia rose

Rosa virginiana

Rosmarinus officinalis, rosemary

729

Rosmarinus officinalis CONTINUED
simply brushing the hand across the foliage is sufficient to release the sweet pungency. The pale to dark blue, ½-in.-long flowers are borne in the leaf axils from fall to spring. In our garden, flowers are most pronounced in December, January, and February. Easily cultured, requiring well-drained soils. Best in full sun, but partial shade is acceptable. Handsome foliage color and texture contrast with other shrubs. Easily pruned and maintained, even for hedging use. My observations indicate it is highly deer-resistant. Grows 2 to 4 ft. high and wide. Zones (6)7 and 8(9). Southern Europe, Asia Minor.

CULTIVARS AND VARIETIES
Numerous and confused; the following have crossed my path.

'Benenden Blue' ('Collingwood Ingram') has a semi-erect habit, dark green narrow leaves, and vivid, almost gentian-blue flowers.

'Lockwood de Forest' and 'Prostratus' are similar, with lighter green foliage and blue flowers. Grow 2 ft. high, 4 to 8 ft. wide.

'Severn Sea' has fine blue flowers on a free-flowering, arching-spreading shrub.

Rostrinucula dependens
weeping rostrinucula
No great shakes but worth sharing what I learned about this species. When first introduced, it was placed with *Buddleia*; then it flowered and became *Rostrinucula*. Grew the plant in Athens, where it is well adapted. Forms a broad-mounding, gracefully arching outline of 4- to 6-in.-long, ¾- to 1-in.-wide, elliptic, mid-green leaves, gray-green below. Flowers, pink with long exserted pink stamens and styles, are produced in 8- to 10-in.-long, indeterminate spikes in late summer, extending into fall. Well-drained

Rosmarinus officinalis

Rostrinucula dependens, weeping rostrinucula

Rubus biflorus

Rubus lasiostylus var. *hubeiensis*

soil, full sun, suit it best. Reasonably heat- and drought-tolerant. Probably best in a border as a half-hardy woody shrub. Grows 3 to 5 ft. high, wider at maturity. Zones 7 to 9. China.

Rubus
bramble

The story goes that Liberty Hyde Bailey, the father of American horticulture and one of the world's great taxonomists, tried to organize the genus *Rubus* and gave up in frustration. I applaud the efforts of the fruit industry to produce easy-to-grow and more palatable blackberries, dewberries, raspberries, boysenberries, tayberries, and loganberries; and on the aesthetic side of the equation, several forms with colorful foliage and stems are offered. Be forewarned: most carry a prickly chip on their stems and are aggressive to the degree of being combative. All require well-drained soil and full sun for best foliage and stem coloration.

Rubus biflorus and its variety *quinqueflorus*, *R. cockburnianus*, *R. coreanus*, *R. koehneanus*, *R. lasiostylus* and its variety *hubeiensis*—all have silvery white stems. *Rubus idaeus* 'Aureus' produces bright yellow foliage. *Rubus thibetanus* 'Silver Fern' has silver-gray, attractively dissected leaves and waxy, silver-white stems. Zones 6 to 9. All are Asiatic in origin.

Rubus odoratus, flowering raspberry, offers rich pink-purple, fragrant, 1- to 2-in.-wide flowers in June and July. Large, ovoid, edible, orange-yellow fruit. Abundant in southern Appalachians into New England. Forms large colonies, about 5 ft. high. Zone 5.

MORE ▶

Rubus odoratus, flowering raspberry

Rubus spectabilis 'Olympic Double'

Rubus thibetanus 'Silver Fern'

Rubus cockburnianus

Rubus idaeus 'Aureus'

Rubus CONTINUED

Rubus spectabilis, salmonberry, was abundant in the Hoh Rain Forest, Washington. Bright rose, 1- to 1¾-in.-wide, fragrant flowers open in April. 'Olympic Double' bears beautiful double rose-red flowers. Grows 3 to 5 ft. high. Zones 7 to 9 on West Coast.

Rubus pentalobus

syn. *Rubus calycinoides*
I never envisioned this species making inroads into the commercial groundcover sector, but it has done so on the West Coast and its use has increased in some parts of the South. A broadleaf evergreen groundcover with bristly, brown, pubescent stems and three- to five-lobed, wrinkled, leathery, lustrous dark green leaves. Flowers are white, the fruit orange to red and described as edible; I have yet to sample. Witnessed abundant

orange fruit developing in late June on plants at the Sarah P. Duke Gardens. Requires well-drained soil in partial shade, although colonies in full sun have prospered. I question long-term performance in heavy, wet soils. Have observed die-back in a planting on the Georgia campus. Excellent groundcover with beautiful foliage. Grows 3 to 9 in. high, spreading indefinitely. Zones 7 to 9. Taiwan.

CULTIVARS AND VARIETIES
'Emerald Carpet' is a more compact clone with smaller leaves that turn burgundy in autumn.

'Golden Quilt' is a yellow-leaf selection, the leaves maturing green, burgundy in fall.

Ruscus aculeatus

butcher's broom
Neat, tidy, smallish broadleaf evergreen shrub that prospers in heat and drought. One of the great nook-and-cranny plants, for it survives in the most shade-laden, forsaken spots in the garden. Develops into a neat mound of erect, rigid stems, suckering and colonizing as it matures. Dull gray-white flowers appear in the middle of the cladophyll (modified stem); on female plants, these are followed by ⅓- to ½-in.-wide, rounded, glossy bright red fruit, ripening in September and October, and persisting through winter. Requires shade and dryish, well-drained soil. Makes a good bor-

Ruscus aculeatus, butcher's broom

Rubus pentalobus

Rubus pentalobus

Ruscus aculeatus

der or mass planting. Foliage holds up forever and is often dried and dyed for Christmas decorations; it's quite prickly, so handle with care. Grows 1½ to 3 ft. high, wider at maturity. Zones 7 to 9. Europe, northern Africa, Middle East.

CULTIVARS AND VARIETIES
Several bisexual forms are in commerce, including 'Christmas Berry' and 'John Redmond'. My first introduction to the hermaphrodite- (perfect-) flowered form was at Kew Gardens, where the gardener was dividing the plant and offered me a piece; in the backpack it traveled, jabbing me senseless but making it to the Dirr garden. Beautiful—fruit like small red cherries cover the branches without the need for pollination.

'Wheeler's Variety' grows 2 ft. high and wide; produces brilliant scarlet berries without the presence of a male.

Salix

willow
A genus of 250 to 300 species, with perhaps 75 in North America. Whether dwarf shrubs or large noble trees, willows are usually at their best with ample moisture (the exception being the alpines). Flowers are dioecious in most cases, the male in fuzzy catkins and quite attractive, the fruit a capsule, with a number of cottony or silky, hairy seeds. These are carried on air currents, and it is common for seedlings to pop up inside greenhouses. Moisture is required for germination. Willows have preformed root initials, meaning that pieces of dormant stems, simply placed in soil, will regenerate.

Interest in colorful-stemmed species for winter gardens is considerable. These types as well as those used to weave fences/baskets should be hard-pruned in winter to encourage long, supple growth. Trees are messy, and many diseases, particularly cankers, affect them.

Salix alba 'Tristis'

syn. *Salix* ×*sepulcralis* 'Chrysocoma'
weeping-gold white willow
This is one of the best loved and most hated trees in landscape history. The graceful weeping habit and the long, trailing, supple stems, golden in the winter sun, have inspired poets and artists along with gardeners. This cultivar develops a rounded outline with age, and it can overtake portions of real estate thought to be uninhabitable. The lustrous rich green, 1½- to 4-in.-long summer leaves may turn shimmering yellow in fall. Interest-

ingly, it is one of the first trees to leaf out and one of the last to shed its leaves. Bark on mature trunks is yellowish brown to brown in color and corky in texture. Plant in moist soils alongside a stream or lake, where the long branches can brush the surface of the water. Susceptible to canker. Can be a messy tree, as the small branches and twigs constantly litter the ground. Grows 50 to 70 ft. high and wide. Zones 4 to 9. Southern Europe to western Siberia, central Asia, China.

MORE ▶

Salix alba var. *sericea*

Salix alba 'Tristis' CONTINUED
CULTIVARS AND VARIETIES
'Britzensis' has reddish to orange-red
stems; in Georgia trials, stems were
yellow-orange, suffused red. Grew 10
ft. in a single season.

'Golden Ness' has brassy yellow
stems. Could not see much difference
between this and var. *vitellina*.

Variety *sericea*, with silver-gray
leaves, is particularly attractive con-
trasted with green foliage. Observed
large trees in the Netherlands.

Variety *vitellina* ('Vitellina') has
bright egg-yoke-yellow stems.

'Yelverton' has orange-red stems
grading to orange-yellow at the bases.

Salix babylonica
Babylon weeping willow
Although many weeping willows are
sold under this name, very few, if any,
are the real thing. The true form is
a graceful, refined tree with a short,
stout trunk and a broad-rounded crown

Salix alba 'Tristis', weeping-gold white willow, fall color

Salix alba 'Britzensis'

Salix alba var. vitellina

Salix alba 'Yelverton'

of weeping branches that sweep the ground. The supple stems are reddish brown in winter, never yellow like those of *Salix alba* 'Tristis'. Grows 30 to 40 ft. high and wide. Zones 6 to 8. China.
CULTIVARS AND VARIETIES
'Crispa' ('Annularis') is an unusual form, with spirally curled leaves.

Salix caprea
pussy or goat willow
When winter has lulled many people into a blue-gray funk, this species offers hope that, yes, spring is just around the corner. In Washington, D.C., I have seen pussy willow in flower as early as late February. The habit is distinctly upright, almost oval in outline. Although considered a shrub, more often the species has the habit of a small tree. The 2- to 4-in.-long, dark green leaves have slightly crisped and crimped margins. Yellowish brown to dark brown stems are studded with ¼- to ⅓-in.-long, purple-brown buds that open to expose soft, furry, 1- to 2-in.-long, grayish male catkins in March and April. The branches can be cut and forced earlier for use in arrangements. The species grows in virtually any soil, particularly those that are moist, and prefers full sun. In most cases, it is short-lived because of insect and disease problems. Use in moist or wet areas of the landscape. Could be used in a shrub border. Grows 15 to 25 ft. high, 12 to 15 ft. wide. Zones 4 to 8. Europe to Japan.

Salix chaenomeloides, Japanese pussy willow, is similar in most respects to *S. caprea*. It is a large shrub with

MORE ▶

Salix babylonica, Babylon weeping willow

Salix caprea, pussy willow

Salix babylonica 'Crispa'

Salix caprea

Salix caprea CONTINUED

Salix chaenomeloides, Japanese pussy willow

Salix discolor

Salix caprea 'Pendula'

stout, reddish purple stems and fat, ½-in.-long, red buds that open to pink to rose-tinted, silver-gray catkins. Grew 12 ft. by 12 ft. in two seasons in Georgia trials. Zones 6 to 8. Japan.

Salix discolor is the American equivalent of *S. caprea*.

Salix elaeagnos, rosemary willow

Salix exigua, coyote willow

CULTIVARS AND VARIETIES
'Pendula', a male weeping form of *Salix caprea*, is often grafted on a standard and makes a handsome accent for the small garden. 'Weeping Sally' is the female weeping form.

Salix elaeagnos

syn. *Salix rosmarinifolia*

rosemary willow

A virtual unknown among shrubby willows, but an ideal plant for foliage effect in the border or along streams and other moist areas. Rosemary willow develops a strongly multistemmed, oval-rounded habit. The 3- to 4-in.-long leaves are only ⅛ to ⅞ in. wide. They are dark green above and covered with white, woolly pubescence below. From a distance, the effect is a pleasing gray-green color. Like all willows, *Salix elaeagnos* is easy to grow and thrives in moist areas. Longwood

Gardens prunes the plant to within 6 to 12 in. of the ground each spring to force long shoots during the growing season. Grows 6 to 10 ft. high and wide. Zones 4 to 7. Mountains of central and southern Europe, Asia Minor.

Salix exigua, coyote willow, has intense silver-gray, narrow leaves. Will grow 10 (to 30) ft. high. Alaska to Mexico.

Salix gracilistyla

rosegold pussy willow

Another pussy willow type, this species offers 1¼-in.-long, grayish catkins tinged with pink that open in

March and April. The pinkish character seems to be variable from plant to plant. The 2- to 4-in.-long, grayish green leaves provide a diversion from the typical green. A mounded, wide-spreading shrub. Grows 6 to 10 ft. high. Zones 5 to 7. Japan, Korea, Manchuria, China.

CULTIVARS AND VARIETIES
'Melanostachys' is often referred to as black pussy willow because of its deep purple-black male catkins. The stems also assume a rich purple-black color in winter. The catkins are smaller than those of typical *Salix gracilistyla*. Sometimes listed as *S.* 'Melanostachys' or *S. melanostachys*, it is most likely a hybrid or cultivar of *S. gracilistyla*.

Salix matsudana

Hankow willow

The species is seldom seen in cultivation, but it is represented by several

MORE ▶

Salix gracilistyla, rosegold pussy willow

Salix gracilistyla 'Melanostachys'

Salix elaeagnos

Salix 'Golden Curls'

737

Salix matsudana CONTINUED

cultivars, of which 'Tortuosa' is the most common. Grows 40 to 50 ft. high. Zones 5 to 8. China.

CULTIVARS AND VARIETIES

'Golden Curls' is a hybrid between *Salix alba* 'Tristis' and *S. matsudana* 'Tortuosa'. It has slightly contorted, golden stems and somewhat

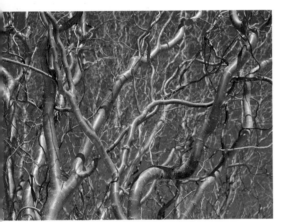

Salix 'Scarlet Curls'

Salix matsudana 'Tortuosa', contorted Hankow willow

Salix pentandra

curled leaves. Growth habit is semi-pendulous.

'Scarlet Curls' has curled leaves and contorted stems that are reddish in winter. Popular for a time in the Southeast but canker ate its lunch. Listed as a *Salix ×erythroflexuosa* selection in the past. 'Erythroflexuosa' is a designated cultivar that may, in fact, be 'Scarlet Curls'.

'Tortuosa', contorted Hankow willow, is the most commonly encountered Hankow willow in the United States. Habit is upright-oval to rounded, with slender, yellow-brown, gnarled and contorted branches. The more vigorous the growth, the more contorted the stems. Leaves are similar to those of *Salix alba*. In many parts of the United States, this is a short-lived

tree. Use as a short-time investment or cut back heavily (pollard) to encourage vigorous shoots. Provide moist soil. Grows 30 to 40 ft. high.

Salix pentandra
laurel willow

Scarcely recognizable as a deciduous willow, more akin to a broadleaf evergreen: the 1½- to 5-in.-long, ¾- to 2-in.-wide, lustrous, polished, shimmering dark green leaves are the handsomest of the genus. The cylindric catkins, 1 to 2 in. long, ½ in. wide, appear with the leaves. Unfortunately, at least in the Midwest, diseases can leave trees utterly defoliated by August. Habit is compact-oval, spreading with time. Probably best reserved for drier climates, assuming

Salix pentandra, laurel willow

the root zone is moist. Grows 30 to 35 ft. high. Zones 2 to 5. Europe, naturalized in the United States.

CULTIVARS AND VARIETIES

Prairie Reflection™ ('Silver Lake') is a handsome, round-headed selection with glossy dark green leaves. Introduced by Dr. Dale Herman, North Dakota State University.

Salix purpurea
purpleosier willow

This is a good choice for stabilizing stream banks and covering large, moist areas. *Salix purpurea* is a rounded, dense, finely branched shrub that becomes unsightly if not occasionally pruned back to the ground. The dark blue-green leaves are 2 to 4 in. long, ⅛ to ⅓ in. wide, and hold late in fall. Grows 8 to 10 (to 18) ft. high and wide. Zones 3 to 6(7). Europe, northern Africa, Asia.

CULTIVARS AND VARIETIES

'Hakuro-nishiki' produces white, pink, green new shoot growth that matures to green. Observed large plants, 15 ft. by 15 ft. More correctly a *Salix integra* cultivar. Ideally, cut to ground to stimulate vigorous shoot growth and more potent foliage color.

'Nana' is a compact form with dark blue-green leaves. Grows 5 ft. high and wide.

'Pendula' is a more or less wide-spreading, weeping form that is often grafted on a standard.

Salix udensis 'Sekka'
syn. *Salix sachalinensis* 'Sekka'
Japanese fantail willow

This interesting male clone has fasciated, flat, and twisted branches, which can be utilized in floral arrangements. To maximize this defining characteristic, prune severely in late winter. The lustrous dark green leaves are 4 to 6 in. long and ¾ in. wide. Pretty, ½- to ¾-in.-long, grayish catkins occur in March. Definitely not a choice for the small property: it develops into a broad-rounded shrub, 10 to 15 ft. high and wide. Zones 4 to 7. Japan.

MORE ▶

Salix purpurea, purpleosier willow

Salix udensis 'Sekka'

Salix purpurea

Salix integra 'Hakuro-nishiki'

Salix udensis 'Sekka' CONTINUED
CULTIVARS AND VARIETIES
'Golden Sunshine' has rich golden yellow leaves throughout the growing season. Have observed only via photos and have doubts about color retention in heat.

Sambucus canadensis
American elder, elderberry
Perhaps no shrub is more common than *Sambucus canadensis* along roadways, where it often inhabits moist ditches. Large and scruffy, usually broad-rounded in outline, it is suitable only for rough areas of the garden. The bright green leaves are composed of seven, 2- to 6-in.-long leaflets. The chief merits are the 6- to 10-in.-wide, creamy cymes of flowers in June and July and the ¼-in.-wide, purple-black fruit in August and September, which can be used for jellies and wine. Prefers moist soils and full sun. Grows 5 to 12 ft. high and wide. Zones 3 to 9. Nova Scotia and Manitoba, south to Florida and Texas.
CULTIVARS AND VARIETIES
'Acutiloba' ('Laciniata') has finely divided leaflets.

'Maxima' develops immense inflorescences 10 to 18 in. across. A plant in Georgia trials "developed" a weeping habit, the inflorescences were so weighty.

Salix udensis 'Sekka'

Sambucus canadensis

Sambucus canadensis 'Acutiloba'

Salix udensis 'Sekka', Japanese fantail willow

Sambucus canadensis, American elder

Sambucus nigra

common or European elder

This species does not appear to be as well adapted to the heat of North America as *Sambucus canadensis*. The general characteristics of the two shrubs are similar, except the inflorescences of European elder are smaller, about 5 to 8 in. in diameter, and the leaves are composed of three to seven (usually five) leaflets. Like *S. canadensis* in America, *S. nigra* is a weed species in Europe, inhabiting moist or wet areas and flowering in June and July. Grows 10 to 20 ft. high; may develop into a small tree, and 30-ft.-tall plants are known. Zones 5 and 6(7). Europe, northern Africa, western Asia.

CULTIVARS AND VARIETIES

Black Beauty® ('Gerda') with purple-

MORE ▶

Sambucus nigra, common elder

Sambucus nigra Black Beauty®

Sambucus nigra Black Lace®

Sambucus nigra 'Laciniata'

Sambucus nigra 'Pulverulenta'

Sambucus nigra CONTINUED

black leaves and Black Lace® ('Eva') with purple-black, finely dissected leaves are better suited to colder climates. In Georgia trials, leaf color on both faded to green with slight purple. Excellent performance in cooler, more even climate of the Pacific Northwest. Black Beauty® grows 10 ft. and larger; Black Lace® is more arching in habit, to 5 ft.

'Laciniata', which has finely dissected leaflets, is attractive.

Sambucus racemosa, European red elder

Sambucus racemosa

Variegated selections. 'Madonna', 'Marginata', and 'Pulverulenta' are available.

Sambucus racemosa
European red elder

Another dubious species for culture in the heat of North America; best where summers are cool. White flowers occur in pyramidal panicles and are followed by red fruit. Grows 8 to 12 ft. high and wide. Zones 3 to 6(7). Europe, western Asia.
CULTIVARS AND VARIETIES
'Plumosa' is a green-leaf, dissected form.

'Plumosa Aurea' is a handsome form with finely cut leaflets and bright yellow new leaves that mature

to green. 'Goldenlocks' and 'Goldfinch' also have deeply divided yellow foliage.

'Sutherland Golden' is similar to 'Plumosa Aurea', but it is probably more cold hardy.

Santolina chamaecyparissus
lavender cotton

From Cape Cod to Georgia, this small, evergreen member of the daisy family performs with remarkable resilience. A tight, dense, silver-gray mound in its best incarnation; however, with heat and humidity, it tends to open up and splay. The evergreen leaves are ½ to 1½ in. long, ⅛ in. wide, whitish tomentose, with strong aromatic odor.

Santolina rosmarinifolia, green santolina

Sambucus racemosa 'Plumosa Aurea'

Santolina chamaecyparissus, lavender cotton

I love the flowers, which look like yellow Tootsie Pops: no petals, just fertile flowers in a ball-like head, arising 4 to 6 in. above the foliage from June through August. Flowers are set on new growth of the season; after flowering, remove spent inflorescences and tidy the plant. Prefers relatively dry, low-fertility soils in full sun. Will grow in sand. Displays salt tolerance. Use for foliage contrast and in borders, low edges, and herb garden–type hedges.

Does not last "forever," and some replacements are necessary. Grows 1 to 2 ft. high, twice as wide. Zones 6 to 9. In our Illinois garden I grew this and *Santolina rosmarinifolia*, and *S. chamaecyparissus* was more cold hardy. Southern Europe.

Santolina rosmarinifolia (*S. virens*), green santolina, is a dead ringer for *S. chamaecyparissus* except for the deep green, glabrous foliage and more compact growth habit.

CULTIVARS AND VARIETIES
'Lemon Queen' produces pale lemon flowers on a compact mound of gray foliage. Grows 2 ft. high and wide.

Sapindus drummondii
western soapberry

Quite exciting to encounter this species in the wild in western Oklahoma, where it was growing in dry soils. In Athens, Georgia, a lone specimen, 30 to 35 ft. high, 40 ft. wide, thrives in the heat, humidity, and drought, yet nowhere in cultivation is the tree common. Broad-oval to rounded crown of stiff branches with a scaly patchwork of gray-brown, orange-brown to reddish brown bark. The pinnate leaves, 10 to 15 in. long, are composed of eight to 18 leaflets, each 1½ to 3 in. long, to 1 in. wide, lustrous medium green. The leaves turn beautiful yellow-orange in autumn. The yellowish white flowers, each ⅕ in. across, are produced in 6- to 10-in.-long, loose, pyramidal, terminal panicles in May and June. The ½-in.-wide, round, yellow-orange drupe ripens in October and remains on the tree through winter and into spring; in the later stages, it may turn black. Adaptable species that should be utilized for urban sites. Only drawback is the fruit, which can be untidy. Grows 40 to 50 ft. high and wide. National champion is 59 ft. high, 39 ft. wide. Zones 6 to 9. Southern

MORE ▶

Sapindus drummondii, western soapberry, fall color

Sapindus drummondii

Sapindus drummondii

Missouri, Kansas, New Mexico, and Arizona to Louisiana, Texas, and northern Mexico.

Sarcandra glabra

A visit to the health food store finds *Sarcandra* berries, an important plant in traditional Chinese medicine. This species is a rounded-mounded, broadleaf evergreen with 4- to 6-in.-long, 1½- to 2-in.-wide, sharply and coarsely serrated leaves that maintain their lustrous dark green color year-round. Although minimally cold hardy in our garden, it picks up steam 100 miles southeast, near Augusta. Flowers are yellowish and inconspicuous; however, the ¼-in.-wide, rounded, orange-scarlet drupes are showy, ripening in September and October and persisting into the following year. Prefers moist, acid, woodsy soil in partial to heavy shade. In the wild it grows as an understory plant, often near streams. Grows 1 to 3 ft. high and wide. Zones 8 and 9. Japan, Korea, Taiwan, China, India, and Malaysia.

CULTIVARS AND VARIETIES
'Golden Treasure' has bright golden orange-yellow fruit in terminal panicles.

A new purple-bronze-green leaf selection was recently introduced from Japan. Foliage is beautiful in spring, but color fades in the heat of summer.

Sarcococca confusa

The name says it all: the taxonomy is confused; however, the unique leaf shape permits separation from all cultivated taxa. Long a staple in the Dirr garden, it often shows up in older southern gardens. In youth somewhat loose, with age more dense and rounded, with dark olive-green, splaying stems and lustrous black-green leaves. Each leaf is 1 to 2½ in. long with an undulating surface and margin. From the leaf axils, in February and March, small, white, fragrant, apetalous flowers emerge and maintain their effectiveness for four or more weeks. The fruit, red changing to black, mature in fall and persist into spring. On numerous occasions I have grown seedling populations (clean pulp from seed and sow) and have observed essentially no variation in leaf or habit. A great plant for shade (requires such) in moist, woodsy soils; however, once established it tolerates drought. Superb in mass plantings and as a single specimen mixed with other broadleaf evergreens. No insects or diseases plague it, making it a great choice for environmentally conscious gardeners. Grows 3 to 5 ft. high and wide. Zones 6 to 8. China.

Sarcococca hookeriana
Himalayan sarcococca, sweetbox
A wonderful plant for a shady environment, this shrub offers lustrous dark green evergreen foliage and small, cream-colored, sweetly fragrant flowers in February (Athens), March, and April. The habit is variable; generally a multi-stemmed, suckering shrub. Fruit are ⅓-in.-wide, shiny black drupes, normally not produced in great quantities. Prefers organic, moist, well-drained soils, but I have observed it looking rather prosperous under severe water stress. Possibly more stress-tolerant than it is generally given credit for. Use in combination with ericaceous and other shade-loving plants. Grows 4 to 6 ft. high, greater in spread. Zones (5)6 to 8. Western Himalayas, Afghanistan.

Sarcandra glabra

Sarcococca confusa

Sarcococca confusa

CULTIVARS AND VARIETIES

Variety *digyna* 'Purple Stem' has purple-tinted stems with 1¾- to 3-in.-long leaves that are not as dark green as the species.

Variety *humilis* is the most common form of Himalayan sarcococca in the commercial sector. The habit is more uniform and compact than that of the species. For groundcover use in shade, it is a first-rate plant. Grows 1½ to 2 ft. high. A 20-year-old planting was 1 ft. high and 10 to 12 ft. across. Zones 5 to 8.

Sarcococca orientalis

A relatively new species to modern cultivation, but one that, I believe, will become a staple where it can be grown. Tough and durable like *Sarcococca confusa*, yet more rounded, compact, and actually "better looking" in youth. Leaves are closely spaced along the stems, each 1½ to 3 in. long, lustrous dark green and flat-surfaced, without the wavy margins of *S. confusa*. Flowers, fragrant, enticingly so, have opened as early as late December in the Dirr garden and still perfume the atmosphere in April. Two to five buds on a short, crooked stalk open white, the males with pink-blushed anthers and sepals. The shin-ing black fruit are similar to those of *S. confusa* but do not initiate red before turning black. Tremendous plant in our garden, surviving under a southern red oak, *Quercus falcata*, while *Hydrangea quercifolia* 'Snowflake' gasps for moisture. Requires shade and forms large masses if planted 2 ft. apart. My belief is the garden boat was missed by not utilizing *Sarcococca* species to greater advantage. This species, introduced from China by the great British plantsman Roy Lancaster, is among the five most beautiful broadleaf evergreens ever to grace our garden. Grows 2 to 4 ft. high, slightly wider. Zones 6 to 8(9). China.

Sarcococca ruscifolia
fragrant sarcococca

Often confused with and sold as *Sarcococca confusa* but, in my opinion, not as garden-worthy or beautiful. The habit is more irregular than those of other *Sarcococca* species, with branches developing willy-nilly from the crown. Habit is eventually rounded, with the arching branches touching the ground. Leaves at their best are lustrous dark green, flat in disposition, with an elongated apex. The milk-white, fragrant flowers open

MORE ▶

Sarcococca ruscifolia var. *chinensis*

Sarcococca ruscifolia var. *chinensis* 'Dragon's Gate'

Sarcococca orientalis

Sarcococca hookeriana, Himalayan sarcococca

Sarcococca hookeriana var. *humilis*

Sarcococca ruscifolia CONTINUED

in the axils of the terminal leaves in January and February. Fruit are red, rounded, ¼ in. in diameter, and persist into winter. Culture and uses similar to other species. Not as cold hardy as *S. confusa* and *S. orientalis*; leaf browning occurred at 7°F in our garden. Grows 3 ft. high and wide. Zones (7)8 and 9. China.

CULTIVARS AND VARIETIES
Variety *chinensis* has longer, narrower leaves, but what I see in cultivation is similar to the species.

'Dragon's Gate', a var. *chinensis* selection introduced by Roy Lancaster, is more compact, with smaller, narrower, shiny green leaves. Based on evaluations in Georgia, it has significant landscape merit. Estimate 2 to 3 ft. high and wide at maturity.

Sarcococca saligna

The largest-leaved species, looking minimally like a member of the genus. The habit is rhizomatous-spreading, dense, but with gracefully arching branches. The evergreen leaves are 3 to 5 in. long, less than ¾ in. wide, and reminiscent of willow leaves in shape. The flowers, green with yellow stamens, nonfragrant, open in March and look nothing like other *Sarcococca* species. Fruit are dark purple to black. In our zone 7 garden, the plant is injured or dies to the ground every winter. Useful grouping and groundcover plant, where adaptable. Grows 2 to 4 ft. high, wider at maturity. Zones 8 and 9. Himalayas.

Sarcococca wallichii has 2- to 3-in.-long, ¾- to 1¼-in.-wide, leathery, lustrous dark green, three-veined leaves. Sets abundant flower buds as a young plant. Grows about 5 ft. high. Tested in Georgia, and hardiness is shaky. Zones 8 and 9 on West Coast. Nepal.

Sarcococca ruscifolia var. *chinensis*

Sarcococca saligna

Sarcococca saligna

Sassafras albidum

common sassafras

If a third-grader had to pick but one tree to include in his or her leaf collection, this would be it. The leaves are entire, three-lobed, or mitten-shaped. The "mittens" come in left- and right-hand versions. The bright green foliage turns brilliant shades of yellow, orange, and red in autumn. Next to *Nyssa sylvatica*, black tupelo, this may be the best native tree for fall color. The growth habit varies from pyramidal to highly irregular. Many short, stout, contorted branches spread to form a flat-topped, irregular, round-oblong head at maturity. The dark cinnamon to reddish brown bark is deeply ridged and furrowed. Yellow flowers

MORE ▶

Sassafras albidum fall color

Sassafras albidum, common sassafras, fall color

Sassafras albidum

Sassafras albidum

Sassafras tzumu, Chinese sassafras

Sassafras albidum

747

Sassafras albidum CONTINUED

appear in April before the leaves. Female plants produce ½-in.-long, oblong, dark blue fruit. Unfortunately, common sassafras is almost impossible to transplant and must be moved as a container-grown plant. Adaptable to varied soils with low to slightly acidic pH. Great tree for naturalistic plantings. Grows 30 to 60 ft. high, 25 to 40 ft. wide. Zones 4 to 8. Maine to Ontario and Michigan, south to Florida and Texas.

Sassafras tzumu, Chinese sassafras, is larger in all its parts. Develops wide-spreading, horizontally stratified branches. Phenomenal growth rate, about three feet a year. Yellow flowers in February and March. Young leaves are sensitive to late frosts. Fall color is a mottle of yellow, orange, and red. Zones 7 and 8, 9 on the West Coast. China.

Schizophragma hydrangeoides

Japanese hydrangea vine

For gardeners, this species has achieved cult status, particularly as represented by the silvery leaved 'Moonlight'. A true clinging vine, similar to *Hydrangea anomala* subsp. *petiolaris* (climbing hydrangea), Japanese hydrangea vine offers lovely lustrous dark green, 2- to 4-in.-long, coarsely serrated leaves and 8- to 10-in.-wide, flattish inflorescences in May (Athens), June, and July. One major difference between this and climbing hydrangea is the shape of the sepals: the sepals of *Schizophragma hydrangeoides* are single and ovate; those of climbing hydrangea are three- to five-parted. Uses and culture are similar to those of *H. anomala* subsp. *petiolaris*. Grows to 30 ft. Zones 5 to 7(8). Japan.

CULTIVARS AND VARIETIES

'Moonlight' has light gray-silver shading/mottling over the upper leaf surface.

'Roseum' has rich pink to rose-colored, showy sepals. When the color is fully developed, the effect is striking.

'Silver Slipper' has silver-green leaves with white margins.

Schizophragma hydrangeoides, Japanese hydrangea vine

Sciadopitys verticillata, Japanese umbrellapine

Schizophragma hydrangeoides 'Moonlight'

Schizophragma hydrangeoides 'Roseum'

Sciadopitys verticillata

Sciadopitys verticillata
Japanese umbrellapine

An oddly textured needle evergreen, like a relic from the past. Certainly a unique and artistic specimen plant where it can be grown. Habit is variable, from spire-like to broadly pyramidal. The 2- to 5-in.-long, dark green needles spread in whorls from the ends of the branches. The bark on old specimens is orangish to reddish brown and exfoliates in plates and strips. Not a fast-growing evergreen; expect about 6 in. per year. Plant in moist, well-drained soils, in full sun to partial shade. Magnificent specimens are found in New England. Great as a specimen or perhaps in a border. Patience is the key. Grows 20 to 30 ft. high, 15 to 20 ft. wide. Zones 4 to 8. Japan.

Sequoia sempervirens
California or coastal redwood

The quiet giant of the West Coast from southern Oregon to California, easily reaching 300 ft. high along the fog-shrouded coast. In the East, the species will grow 30 to 60 ft. high, and a 40-ft.-high specimen grows in Atlanta, Georgia. Imposing conifer, densely

MORE ▶

Sequoia sempervirens 'Adpressa'

Sequoia sempervirens, California redwood

Sequoia sempervirens 'Cantab'

Sequoia sempervirens CONTINUED
branched and gracefully pyramidal
in youth, with age losing the lower
branches yet maintaining a relatively
narrow pyramidal crown. I walked
among the redwoods at Muir Woods
and wondered how anyone could ever
cut one. They are sacred, noble trees.
The needles, ¼ to 1 in. long, are dark

Sequoia sempervirens

blue-green above, with two, top-of-
the-exclamation-point, whitish bands
below. The rich red-brown bark, fibrous
on the surface, develops deep ridges
and furrows. Cones are ¾ to 1¼ in.
long, ½ to ¾ in. wide, somewhat
egg-shaped and dark brown. Plant
container-grown trees in deep, moist,
organic, acid soils; shelter from wind
and extreme winter sun. Use for specimen and novelty. Grows 40 to 60 ft.
high on East Coast; over 300 ft. high
in native habitat. Zones 7 to 9.
CULTIVARS AND VARIETIES
'Adpressa' ('Prostrata') has shorter
needles and compact habit: grows
4 ft. high and wide in ten years. The
tips of young shoots are dull cream-
colored. Apparently more cold hardy
than the species; survived –9°F at
the JC Raulston Arboretum, Raleigh,
North Carolina, while the species
died. Will revert and produce upright

shoots that, if not pruned, result
in a tree.
   'Cantab' is a reversion shoot of
'Adpressa', with tight pyramidal-conical habit and shorter dark green needles. Grows 30 to 40 ft. high. A 50-ft.
specimen at Hillier Arboretum, growing
in significant shade, was still full to
the base.

Sequoiadendron giganteum
giant sequoia, big tree
Related to and often confused with
Sequoia sempervirens. The needles
are awl-shaped, triangular in cross
section, slightly appressed, and pointing forward to the apex. The Europeans planted the species in parks and
botanical and private gardens. The
100-ft.-high, garden variety *Sequoiadendron giganteum* is as common in
Europe as the meatball broadleaf ever-

Sequoiadendron giganteum, giant sequoia

green shrubs that serve as foundation plants in the United States. Beautiful, dense, broad-pyramidal in youth, maintaining a similar outline in old age yet devoid of lower branches. The spongy bark, somewhat cork-like in texture, is rich reddish brown, ridged and furrowed. Needles, ⅛ to ½ in. long, broad at the base tapering to a sharp point, are bluish green through the seasons. Cones are larger than those of *Sequoia*, similar in shape, 1½ to 3 in. long, 1 to 2 in. wide, and reddish brown. In the eastern United States, this species is better adapted than *Sequoia sempervirens*, although moving further south to zone 7, *Sequoia* picks up steam. Soil requirements are similar to *Sequoia*. I knew of a 100-ft.-high specimen at Tyler Arboretum, Lima, Pennsylvania. Strictly a specimen plant. Grows 60 ft. high in eastern and southern United States.

National champion is 274 ft. high, 107 ft. wide. Zones 6 to 8. California in the Sierra Nevada at elevations of 4,500 to 8,000 ft.

Sequoiadendron giganteum

CULTIVARS AND VARIETIES

'Glaucum' is more narrow-conical in habit with glaucous needles.

'Hazel Smith' is a strong-growing, upright tree with bluish needles and greater hardiness. Did not perform well in the Georgia trials.

'Pendulum' has an erratic leading

MORE ▶

Sequoiadendron giganteum

Sequoiadendron giganteum 'Pendulum'

Sequoiadendron giganteum CONTINUED
stem that zigs, zags, dips, dives,
arches, and bends to form living sculpture; the secondary branches hang
mop- (mane-) like. If staked, grows
30 ft. or so, more often simply gliding
above ground level.

Serissa japonica
syn. *Serissa foetida*
yellow-rim
A much-loved bonsai plant that transitions to a semi-evergreen to deciduous shrub in zones (6)7 to 9. A grouping on the Georgia campus, 3 to 4
ft. high, grows in the shade and root
competition of live oak, *Quercus vir-*

giniana, and flowers with abandon.
A rounded shrub, densely branched,
but fine-textured and airy in character. The deep green, 1- to 1½-in.-long
leaves have a marginal yellow rim.
The four- to six-lobed, ⅓-in.-wide flowers twinkle like Christmas lights for
four weeks or more in May and June.
Never overwhelming in flower but with
enough allure to entice even the sedentary gardener. Site in partial shade;
full sun is acceptable, with adequate
moisture. Nifty in small hedges, groupings, masses, and containers, and for
bonsai. No insects or diseases afflict.
Grows 3 to 4 ft. high and wide. Zones
(6)7 to 9. Southeastern Asia.

CULTIVARS AND VARIETIES
'Rosea' includes single and double
pink-flowered forms.

'Variegata' is used here in a universal sense to umbrella the more prominently cream- and white-margined
forms; in general these are less hardy
than the species.

Sesbania punicea
syn. *Daubentonia punicea*
rattlebox
Superb orange-red, yellow-spotted
flowers, in wisteria-like racemes,
droop from the branches in summer
and fall. This South American native
has become rather widespread in
zones 9 and 10 and self-seeds freely.
Forms an irregular shrub with spreading canopy and pinnately compound
leaves, composed of 12 to 14 leaflets,
each ½ to 1 in. long and rich green.
Flowers are formidable, and the long
flowering season invites use in the

Serissa japonica, yellow-rim

Sesbania punicea, rattlebox

Serissa japonica

Serissa japonica 'Variegata'

garden. Requires sun and well-drained soil, although on St. Simons Island, Georgia, it grows along ditch banks. Grows 4 to 6 ft. high and wide. Zones 9 and 10. Southern Brazil, Uruguay, northeast Argentina.

Shepherdia argentea
silver buffaloberry

Many people express excitement about this species, but I have yet to see one that stimulates my gardening juices. The plant is typically an open shrub, with leafy branches terminating in 1- to 2-in.-long spines. The slender, 1- to 2-in.-long leaves are covered with silvery scales on both surfaces. Small,

yellowish flowers are followed by orange to red fruit. Utilize in infertile, dry, alkaline and high pH soils. Prefers sunny, open areas. Most plants growing on the East Coast are smaller than the typical Midwest and Plains States' versions. Grows 6 to 10 (to 18) ft. high. Zones 2 to 6. Minnesota and Manitoba to Saskatchewan, Kansas, and Nevada.

Shepherdia canadensis, russet buffaloberry, is essentially like *S. argentea* in flower and fruit. Variable in habit, generally loosely branched and rounded in outline, with ½- to 2-in.-long leaves that are dark green above and silver below. No great redeem-

ing characteristics, however. Grows 6 to 8 ft. high, 3 to 9 ft. wide. Zones 2 to 6. Newfoundland to Alaska, south to Maine, Ohio, northern Mexico and Oregon.

Sinojackia rehderiana
jacktree

A mysterious and clandestine member of the silverbell family (Styracaceae). The species has gained snail-like momentum in gardens, and growers are having a difficult time marketing it. Its virtues are many, however, particularly the spectacular, lustrous dark green foliage that remains green into October in zone 7. Leaves emerge early, often in March in zone 7. On occasion, yellow to bronze fall color in November (Athens). Habit is several degrees irregular and, without staking, becomes arching and unkempt. Also, displays a shrub-like propensity if left

MORE ▶

Shepherdia argentea, silver buffaloberry

Sinojackia rehderiana, jacktree

Shepherdia argentea undersides of foliage

Sinojackia rehderiana

Sinojackia rehderiana CONTINUED

alone. Each 1- to 3- (to 4-) in.-long leaf is leathery, lustrous dark green with fine, marginal teeth. The five- to seven-petaled, white flowers, 1 in. wide, appear in three- to five-flowered cymes at the ends of lateral shoots in April (Athens) and May (Boston). Flowers are suspended like spiders on webs. The woody drupe is ¾ in. long, ½ in. wide, with a broad conical apex. Pleasantly surprised by the species' heat and drought (as well as full sun to heavy shade) tolerances. I have yet to observe insect and disease problems. Small specimen tree or large shrub for about any location. Grows 15 to 20 (to 30) ft. high and wide. Zones 6 to 8. China.

CULTIVARS AND VARIETIES

'La Grima' is a more or less broad fastigiate form with the attributes of the species.

'Linda Carol' is a stiff, semi-arching form. I witnessed this and 'La Grima' at the JC Raulston Arboretum without doing back-flips.

Skimmia japonica
Japanese skimmia

An absolutely magnificent plant in its finest forms. Unfortunately, this shrub is better adapted to the cool, moist climate of Europe than to the vagaries of midwestern and eastern North America. Perfectly well adapted to cooler areas of West Coast. Habit is rounded to haystack-shaped, and it is clothed with dark green, 2½- to 5-in.-long evergreen leaves that are potently aromatic when bruised. Creamy white flowers occur in 2- to 3-in.-long, 1- to 2-in.-wide, upright terminal panicles in April. Globose, ⅓-in.-wide, bright red fruit occur only on female plants and may persist through winter. If the plant is under drought stress, mite infestations are problematic. Transplant from a container into organic-laden, moist, well-drained soils, in shady environments. A great plant for shady nooks of the garden. Use in combination with rhododendrons and azaleas. Only respectable plants I remember on the East Coast were on Cape Cod and at the Keith Arboretum, Chapel Hill. Grows 3 to 4 ft. high and wide. Zones 6 and 7, 8 and 9 on West Coast. Japan.

CULTIVARS AND VARIETIES

'Rubella' (male) and several other cultivars have deep maroon-red flower buds that are actually more attractive than the open white flowers.

Skimmia japonica subsp. *reevesiana*
syn. *Skimmia reevesiana*
Reeves skimmia

This subspecies is lower growing, more loose and open, and perhaps less attractive a shrub than the typical

Skimmia japonica, Japanese skimmia

Skimmia japonica 'Rubella'

Skimmia japonica subsp. *reevesiana*, Reeves skimmia

species, but it does have the advantage of being perfect-flowered. The 1- to 4-in.-long, dark green evergreen leaves are narrower than those of *Skimmia japonica*. The white, fragrant flowers are followed by oval to pear-shaped, ⅓-in.-long, crimson fruit that persist into winter. Culture is similar to that of the type; there is no hard evidence to support that this is more

Smilax smallii, bamboo vine

cold hardy. Grows 1½ to 3 ft. high, 2 to 3 ft. wide. Zones 6 and 7. China.
CULTIVARS AND VARIETIES
'Temptation' is self-pollinating, producing abundant scarlet fruit on a compact plant. A cross of subsp. *reevesiana* and *Skimmia japonica*.

Smilax
green-brier
A large genus with 200 species of deciduous or evergreen, woody or herbaceous climbers, the stems often lethally prickly. The real beauty resides in the evergreen foliage and blue-black to red fruit. My arms ran red from the attacks of *Smilax rotundifolia* during early efforts to clean the one-and-three-quarter acres lovingly termed the Dirr garden. The only species cultivated to any degree in the South is *S. smallii*, bamboo or Jackson vine; this

essentially thornless, evergreen form offers the most beautiful, waxy, lustrous dark green foliage, which is utilized for Christmas decorations. *Smilax walteri*, coral green-brier, produces red fruit and grows in wet soil areas. Utilize sparingly for foliage effect and naturalized plantings. Zones 7 to 9. Southeastern United States.

Sorbaria kirilowii
syn. *Sorbaria arborea*
tree falsespirea
Sorbaria tomentosa
syn. *Sorbaria aitchisonii*
Kashmir falsespirea
I have great difficulty distinguishing between these two species. Both shrubs bear immense, fleecy panicles, 12 to 15 (to 18) in. long and

MORE ▶

Smilax rotundifolia

Sorbaria kirilowii

Sorbaria kirilowii, tree falsespirea

Sorbaria tomentosa, Kashmir falsespirea

755

Sorbaria kirilowii CONTINUED

8 to 14 in. wide, of creamy white flowers in June, July, and August. The flowers are spectacular, but they mature to a rather dirty brown and should be removed. The leaves of *Sorbaria tomentosa* are composed of 11 to 23 leaflets, each 2 to 4 in. long and ¼ to ⅝ in. wide; those of *S. kirilowii*, composed 13 to 17 leaflets, are generally wider. Both require well-drained soils, full sun, and plenty of real estate. The best specimens I have observed were on Cape Cod, growing in essentially pure sand. Like *S. sorbifolia*, they appear to be quite heat- and drought-tolerant. Both grow 10 to 15 ft. high and wide. Zones 5 to 7. Asia.

Sorbaria sorbifolia
Ural falsespirea

This rather obscure plant offers a gorgeous display of creamy white flowers on a suckering, multi-stemmed shrub. The 8- to 12-in.-long leaves are composed of 13 to 25 deep green leaflets, each 2 to 4 in. long. New growth has a reddish tinge before maturing. Flowers occur in 4- to 10-in.-long, fleecy terminal panicles in June and July. As flowers senesce, the petals turn brown, the entire inflorescence appearing the worse for wear. Plant in well-drained soils, in full sun. Appears to be a good choice for dry soils, especially where mass-type cover is required. One of the first shrubs to leaf out in spring. Can become somewhat invasive because of its spreading, suckering nature. Observed in Minnesota in large masses in roadside embankment plantings. Grows 5 to 10 ft. high, wider at maturity. Zones 2 to 7. Northern Asia to Japan.

CULTIVARS AND VARIETIES
'Sem' is more compact, with copper-pink-bronze emerging leaves. Supposedly grows only 3 ft. high; I have doubts, but the foliage is rather pretty.

Sorbus
mountainash

A genus of about 100 species, mountainash has lost significant favor in commerce; Canada, the northern United States, and the Pacific Northwest are its domain. Mountainashes are in general among the most beautiful trees for fruit effect, but they are beset with borer and canker problems, which limit their use in hostile environments. All species discussed here prefer cool climates for best growth.

Sorbus alnifolia
Korean mountainash

At its best, this species has perhaps the most magnificent fruit display of all the *Sorbus* species. The habit is

Sorbaria sorbifolia, Ural falsespirea

Sorbus alnifolia

Sorbaria sorbifolia 'Sem'

Sorbus alnifolia

softly pyramidal in youth, becoming pyramidal-oval to rounded with age. The simple, beech-like foliage is atypical for a mountainash. Leaves emerge a bright, fresh spring green, turn lustrous dark green, and then mellow to yellow, golden brown, and orange in fall—truly inspirational! Young stems develop diamond-shaped lenticels; older branches become smooth and gray, resembling beech bark. White flowers occur in 2- to 3-in.-wide corymbs in May, alternating somewhat in abundance from year to year. Fruit can be spectacular, ripening with the fall foliage in September and October, in colors ranging from waxy pinkish red to orangish red and scarlet. Generally more adaptable than other mountainashes, it is easily grown in well-drained soils and full sun. The species is not borer-resistant, and excessive stress, such as those encountered in urban settings, will induce problems. Use against an evergreen background to maximize ornamental effects. A respectable tree is growing at the Keith Arboretum, Chapel Hill; great trees at the Arnold Arboretum, Boston. Grows 40 to 50 ft. high, 20 to 30 (to 50) ft. wide. Zones 3 to 6(7). Central China, Korea, Japan.

Sorbus americana
American mountainash

This native species is seldom available in commerce, so if it is present on a site, be appreciative. It is certainly handsome in fruit. Variable in habit, growing as a shrub or as a small tree with a short trunk and spreading, slender branches that form a rounded crown. Foliage, flowers, and fruit are similar to those of *Sorbus aucuparia* (although the fruit may be redder). Fall color ranges from orange-yellow to reddish purple to red. Grows along the borders of cold swamps and bogs, as well as on the sides of mountaintops in relatively dry soils. Grows 10 to 30 ft. high and wide. Zones 2 to 5. Newfoundland to Manitoba, south to Michigan and in the southern Appalachians to Georgia. Observed on Brasstown Bald and Rabun Bald, Georgia's two highest mountains, above 4,500 ft. elevation.

Sorbus aria
whitebeam mountainash

Although rarely utilized in the United States, this species enjoys popularity

MORE ▶

Sorbus alnifolia, Korean mountainash, fall color

Sorbus americana, American mountainash

Sorbus americana fall color

757

Sorbus aria CONTINUED

Sorbus aria

in European gardens. It has many of the same requirements and difficulties as *Sorbus aucuparia*, European mountainash, and using whitebeam mountainash in the average landscape is like a roll of the dice. However, the silvery-backed, simple leaves and the large, orange-red to scarlet fruit have tempted more than one gardener to take that chance. The habit is oval to broad-pyramidal. The foliage effect is beautiful, especially on windy days when the leaves are buffeted about. A

worthwhile tree in the Pacific Northwest, perhaps in the Northeast and Canada as well. Grows 35 to 45 ft. high. Zones 4 and 5. Europe.

Sorbus aucuparia
European mountainash

This is the most widely available mountainash species in the United States, and the brilliant display of orange-red fruit justifies any attempt to grow it. The habit is erect and oval in youth, becoming ovate or spherical with age. The leaves are composed of nine to 15, uniformly serrated, dark green leaflets, each ¾ to 2½ in. long. Foliage changes to yellow, red, and reddish purple in fall. Bark is shiny gray-brown and smooth, becoming slightly roughened on old trunks. White, rather malodorous flowers occur in 3- to 5-in.-wide corymbs in May. The fruit ripen in

Sorbus aria, whitebeam mountainash

Sorbus aucuparia Cardinal Royal®

Sorbus aucuparia

Sorbus aucuparia 'Beissneri'

late August and September, but they make palatable bird food and seldom last very long. Provide acid or high pH, moist, well-drained soils; keep stress to a minimum. When right, it makes a very pretty fruiting tree. Grows 20 to 40 (to 60) ft. high, 15 to 25 (to 40) ft. wide. Zones 3 to 6(7). Europe, western Asia, Siberia.

CULTIVARS AND VARIETIES
'Beissneri' displays rich copper-brown bark.

Cardinal Royal® ('Michred') has dark green leaves, silvery beneath, rust-red in fall with brilliant red fruit. Witnessed this in fruit in mid August at J. Frank Schmidt Jr. Arboretum, Oregon; appears vigorous and perhaps more resilient than the straight species.

'Pendula', a weeping form, bears orange fruit.

Spiraea
spirea

Spireas grow best in well-drained, preferably acid soils, in full sun. These plants are not seriously troubled by insects or diseases, although aphids are an occasional problem. Most are quite cold hardy and adaptable. Unless otherwise indicated, *Spiraea* species discussed here should be pruned after flowering, since flowers are formed on the previous year's growth.

Spiraea alba var. *latifolia*
broad-leaved meadowsweet

Spiraea tomentosa
steeplebush

Spiraea alba var. *latifolia* and *S. tomentosa* are suckering, 2- to 4-ft.-high shrubs common along roadsides and in fields. The white to pink to deep rose flowers appear on new growth of

MORE ▶

Sorbus aucuparia, European mountainash

Spiraea alba var. *latifolia*, broad-leaved meadowsweet

Spiraea alba var. *latifolia* fall color

Spiraea tomentosa, steeplebush

Spiraea alba var. *latifolia* CONTINUED

Spiraea betulifolia var. *aemiliana*, birchleaf spirea

Spiraea betulifolia var. *aemiliana* 'Tor'

Spiraea cantoniensis 'Lanceata', double Reeves spirea

Spiraea fritschiana, Korean spirea

the season in summer, and so can be pruned either before or after flowering (late winter is safe). Adaptable to moist and dry soils. The former has glabrous leaves; the latter, leaves that are tomentose on the lower surface. Northern latitudes. Zones 4 to 6.

Spiraea betulifolia var. *aemiliana*
birchleaf spirea

Compact, mounded shrub, 2 to 2½ ft. high, with ¾- to 1½-in.-long, broad-ovate to rounded, strongly toothed leaves. White flowers in flattish corymbs in early May. Not content in the heat of the South. Zones 4 to 6. Japan, Kuril Islands, Kamchatka.
CULTIVARS AND VARIETIES
'Tor' is a clone with white flowers, deep green summer foliage, yellow-gold, bronze, and red fall color. Grows 2 to 3 ft. high.

Spiraea cantoniensis 'Lanceata'
double Reeves spirea

At its best, this plant provides excellent early spring foliage and a profusion of white, button-like, double flowers. Unfortunately, the leaves and flower buds, which emerge in March and April, are compromised by low temperatures. The habit is gracefully arching, forming a mounded outline. The 1- to 2½-in.-long, bluish green leaves are handsome throughout the seasons and hold into late fall. The ½-in.-wide flowers appear in terminal corymbs in April and are effective for two to three weeks. Utilize in a border or in groupings. Among the most durable and persistent spireas in the Dirr garden, never fazed by drought, insects, or disaster. The species produces five-petaled, single, white flowers. Grows 4 to 6 ft. high and wide. Zones 6 to 9. China, Japan.

Spiraea fritschiana
Korean spirea

Never accepted in commerce but a rather pretty, compact-mounded shrub with dark green leaves, white flowers in flat-topped corymbs in May and June, on a 2- to 3-ft.-high, 4- to 5-ft.-wide outline. Fall color is often a pleasant yellow. Grew in my Illinois trials with good success. Zones (3)4 to 6. Central China to Korea.

Spiraea cantoniensis 'Lanceata'

Spiraea japonica
Japanese spirea

Japanese spirea forms an upright, mounded habit. The leaves are 1 to 3 in. long and have distinct sharp serrations. Flowers—white, pink, rose, carmine, close to red—are borne in flat-topped corymbs in May and June on new growth, so if necessary, prune this species and its cultivars in late winter. Remove spent flowers to induce another wave of flowering. Grows 4 to 5 ft. high. Zones 4 to 8. Japan, China, Korea.

CULTIVARS AND VARIETIES
The remarkable variation of the species is reflected in its numerous (too many) cultivars. The yellow- and gold-leaf selections are utilized in abundance in the Midwest and East.

Over 30 yellow-foliage cultivars in my *Manual* (2009); a total of 79 cultivars are described, and new ones are still being introduced.

'Albiflora' is a low, mounded, densely branched shrub with 2½-in.-long, almost blue-green leaves topped with 2- to 3-in.-wide, white, flattish inflorescences in June. As with many

MORE ▶

Spiraea japonica var. *alpina*

Spiraea japonica 'Anthony Waterer'

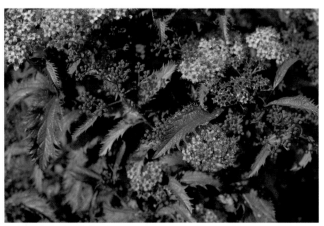
Spiraea japonica 'Crispa'

Spiraea japonica CONTINUED

compact spireas, a great filler in a perennial or shrub border, wonderful in groupings, and excellent massed as a large groundcover. Grows 2 to 3 ft. high and wide.

Variety *alpina* ('Alpina') is a dainty, fine-textured, low-growing, wide-spreading form with pink flowers and blue-green foliage. Grows 1 to 2½ ft. high.

'Anthony Waterer', the old standard, has 4- to 6-in.-wide, carmine-pink inflorescences and often produces yellow to cream branch reversions. Be careful when buying this cultivar; several forms are sold under this name. Grows 3 to 4 ft. high, 5 to 6 ft. wide.

'Crispa' and 'Dolchica' are cut-leaf forms that are, in most other respects, similar to 'Anthony Waterer', including tendency to develop cream to yellow branch reversions. Both are subject to aphids and chlorosis.

'Froebelii' is supposedly smaller than 'Anthony Waterer' and has deeper carmine-pink flowers. Most 'Froebelii' I have seen in cultivation, however, have lighter pink flowers. I have not observed branch reversions.

'Genpei' ('Shibori', 'Shirobana') offers deep rose, pink, and white flowers on the same plant. It is a recurrent flowerer; after a time, the pink flowers seem to dominate. A vigorous, rounded cultivar with lustrous dark green leaves. Leafs out earlier than other cultivars. Grows 3½ to 4 ft. high and wide.

'Goldflame' is an older cultivar with russet-orange to bronze-red new growth that changes to soft yellow, yellow-green, and finally green. The cooler the temperatures, the more intense the yellow coloration. The pink flowers are a little difficult to digest next to the yellow foliage. Produces green and gold shoots. May produce excellent bronze-red to red fall color.

'Gold Mound' has rich golden yel-

Spiraea japonica 'Albiflora'

Spiraea japonica 'Gold Mound'

Spiraea japonica 'Genpei'

Spiraea japonica 'Golden Princess'

low leaves, and the foliage color holds much better than that of 'Goldflame' in the heat. Flowers are pink. Grows 2½ to 3½ ft. high. 'Candlelight', Dakota Goldcharm® ('Mertyann'), 'Firelight', 'Golden Elf', 'Golden Princess', and Limemound® ('Monhub') are similar golden-foliaged cultivars.

'Little Princess' is a large version of var. *alpina*, with pink flowers and a more rounded habit. Grows 2½ ft. high or more. Still one of the best, uniform, compact, blue-green foliage selections.

Magic Carpet™ ('Walbuma') has reddish to pinkish flowers and orange-red to reddish purple young shoots, yellow-gold at maturity. In the Dirr garden, foliage color is significantly reduced in heat of summer. Have watched this selection emerge as a legitimate successor to and more restrained version of 'Goldflame'; no

shoot reversions have been observed. Listed as 10 to 18 in. high, now 2½ ft. by 3½ ft. in U.S. gardens.

'Neon Flash' is an 'Anthony Waterer' type with rich red flowers, reddish new growth, dark green at maturity, and no branch reversions. Matures about 3 ft. high.

'White Gold' has clean white flowers. Foliage initiates yellow, then greenish, and yellow again in fall; has photobleached (turned white) in heat of zones 7 and 8.

Spiraea nipponica 'Snowmound'
Snowmound Nippon spirea

For some strange reason, this selection is commonly used in the Midwest but seldom in great quantities elsewhere. The tight-knit branches are covered with 1- to 1½-in.-long, dark blue-green leaves. White flowers cover the

branches in April (Athens), May, and June. It is a respectable plant for use on banks, in masses, or in groupings. With time, it develops into a shapely, rounded shrub. Grows 3 to 5 ft. high and wide. Zones 4 to 8. Japan.

Spiraea nipponica 'Snowmound'

Spiraea japonica 'Little Princess'

Spiraea japonica 'White Gold'

Spiraea nipponica 'Snowmound'

Spiraea japonica Magic Carpet™

Spiraea japonica 'Neon Flash'

763

Spiraea prunifolia

bridalwreath spirea

Along with *Spiraea* ×*vanhouttei*, this is the *Spiraea* species with which the general gardening public is familiar. To my mind, it does not measure up to the newer, more compact spireas (such as the *S. japonica* types), but it has withstood the test of time around farmsteads and residences for more than a century. The habit is open, straggly, and leggy, with the bulk of the foliage on the upper half of the plant. The 1- to 2-in.-long, lustrous dark green leaves turn yellow-orange to purplish brown in fall. Double, white, 1/3-in.-wide flowers occur three to six together along the naked stems in March (Athens) and April. Probably of little value in modern gardens compared to some of the other spireas. Grows 4 to 9 ft. high, 6 to 8 ft. wide. Zones 4 to 8. Korea, China, Taiwan.

Spiraea prunifolia

Spiraea thunbergii

Spiraea thunbergii

Thunberg spirea

I take great delight in this wispy, fine-textured shrub. It offers willow-like leaves and five-petaled, single white flowers, together with a bulldog's tenacity that allows it to prosper in virtually any environment. The ultimate form is gracefully arching with a rounded-mounded outline. The light green leaves are 1 to 1½

Spiraea thunbergii 'Fujino Pink'

Spiraea prunifolia, bridalwreath spirea

Spiraea thunbergii, Thunberg spirea

in. long, ⅛ to ¼ in. wide, and turn orange and bronze in autumn. The ⅓- to ½-in.-wide flowers appear on naked branches in March and April, well ahead of the majority of flowering shrubs. Makes a great mass effect, or it can be used for color and textural purposes in the shrub border. Grows 3 to 5 ft. high and wide. Zones 4 to 8. Japan, China.

Spiraea ×*arguta*, garland spirea, is closely related, but it flowers later and grows slightly larger. The leaves are entire at the base, while those of *S. thunbergii* are serrated to the base.
CULTIVARS AND VARIETIES
'Fujino Pink', with pink-red buds, opens pink to white. Pink effect is short-lived in the heat of zone 7.

'Ogon' ('Mellow Yellow') sports beautiful soft yellow leaves, the color persisting even in the heat of zone 7.

One of the better yellow-leaf shrubs for the South. Grows 4 to 5 ft. high and wide.

Spiraea ×*vanhouttei*
Vanhoutte spirea

The granddaddy of all spireas. The habit is distinctly arching and fountain-like. The ¾- to 1¾-in.-long leaves are often three-lobed and have a distinct

MORE ▶

Spiraea thunbergii 'Ogon'

Spiraea ×*vanhouttei* 'Pink Ice'

Spiraea ×*vanhouttei*, Vanhoutte spirea

Spiraea ×vanhouttei CONTINUED
blue-green color. White flowers, which
appear in April (Athens) and May after
the leaves, are raised above the foliage in 1- to 2-in.-wide inflorescences.
In flower, the shrub is extremely
showy, one of the main reasons for its
continued popularity. Extremely durable, and in some respects it can be
like even a welcome guest—unwanted
after a period of time. Grows 6 to 8 (to
10) ft. high, 10 to 12 ft. wide. Zones
3 to 8(9).
CULTIVARS AND VARIETIES
Firegold™ ('Levgold') and 'Gold
Fountain' have yellow-gold leaves.
Observed both and was not
impressed. Noticed green reversion
shoots on the latter.

'Pink Ice' is a mottle of pink, white,
and green leaves that are unstable
and revert.

Spiraea virginiana

I have adopted this native species and
hope to see it in wider use. Loose,
open, spreading, rounded shrub, with
beautiful blue-green, 1- to 2½-in.-
long leaves that die off with a hint of
yellow in fall. Flowers, white, in 3- to
6-in.-wide corymbs, open in May and
June. Grows in moist to wet soils in
its native range and successfully in
full sun and Georgia red clay. Have
observed plants in standing water.
Described as sterile yet . . . I hybridized this with *Spiraea japonica*, and
the progeny show promise. Grows 8
to 10 ft. high and wide. Zones 5 to 7.
Virginia, North Carolina, Georgia, and
Tennessee.

Stachyurus praecox

I have always waffled about the merits
of this coarse, almost cumbersome
shrub, but after observing a number
of specimens in respectable flower, I
believe it deserves consideration. It
forms a broad-mounded outline and
bears 3- to 7-in.-long, lustrous dark
green leaves. Typically fall color is

Spiraea virginiana

Spiraea ×vanhouttei

Spiraea virginiana

Stachyurus praecox

negligible, although yellow to pink has been reported on the West Coast. Small, pale yellow (yellow-brown) flowers appear in 2- to 3-in.-long, pendulous racemes from each axil in April. The flowers occur on naked stems and resemble long beaded chains; the U.S. National Arboretum has a particularly long-flowered form (6-in. racemes) that is definitely superior to the typical species. Site in moist, acid, organic, well-drained soils, in partial shade; plants in hot, dry sites and full sun will never prosper. This is not a shrub for every garden, but in a woodland or naturalized setting, it might prove a good fit. Grows 4 to 6 (to 8) ft. high, possibly wider at maturity. Observed 14 ft. by 20 ft. and 16 ft. by 20 ft. plants. Zones 6 to 8. Japan.

CULTIVARS AND VARIETIES
‘Aureus Variegatus’, ‘Joy Forever’, ‘Magpie’, and ‘Sterling Silver’ have yellow- to silver-margined leaves.

‘Rubriflorus’ has red buds, opening to light pink, soon fading.

Staphylea trifolia
American bladdernut

I stumbled upon this species, growing contentedly in an alluvial plain above the Oconee River, during a hike through a local woodland. Not an unworthy plant, upright-spreading; a small side shoot was extricated and moved to the Dirr garden. Years later, root pieces were still throwing up suckers. The genetic propensity to sucker soon renders the small tree a large, rounded shrub. Bark is striated, greenish gray with vertical white fissures, reminiscent of *Acer pensylvanicum*, one of the snakebarks. The trifoliate leaves, each leaflet 2 to 4 in. long and dark green, turn green-yellow in autumn. The greenish white, bell-shaped, 1/3-in.-long flowers are borne in 1½- to 2-in.-long, nodding panicles

MORE ▶

Stachyurus praecox

Staphylea holocarpa ‘Rosea’

Stachyurus praecox ‘Magpie’

Staphylea trifolia

767

Staphylea trifolia CONTINUED

Staphylea trifolia, American bladdernut

Stephanandra incisa, cutleaf stephanandra

Staphylea trifolia

Stephanandra tanakae

in April and May. Not overwhelming but noticeable and daintily pretty. The inflated capsule, 1 to 1½ in. long, is three-lobed, green to brown, with yellowish brown seeds. Prefers moist soil and shade, although I observed plants in full sun. Good naturalizing species that suckers and colonizes. Grows 10 to 15 ft. high, wider at maturity. Zones 4 to 8. Quebec to Ontario and Minnesota south to Georgia and Missouri.

Other *Staphylea* species and cultivars reside in arboreta and botanical gardens but are seldom, if ever, available in commerce. I observed all described herein, but the similarity of characteristics precludes individual discussion. All have three to five, occasionally seven (in *Staphylea pinnata*) leaflets, shrub-type habits (except for *S. holocarpa*), and white flowers in panicles of various lengths. All flower in April and May. *Staphylea bumalda*, Bumald bladdernut, grows 6 to 10 ft. high. *Staphylea holocarpa* is a tree to 30 ft.; 'Rosea' is a pink-flowered form. *Staphylea colchica*, Colchis bladdernut, reaches 10 ft. high, and I witnessed a 20 ft. by 18 ft. plant. *Staphylea pinnata*, European bladdernut, may grow to 20 ft. high; witnessed such a plant in England that had the appearance of a brush pile.

Stephanandra incisa
syn. *Neillia incisa*
cutleaf stephanandra

This shrub forms a graceful mass of

spreading, arching branches, and it suckers freely from the base. Yellowish white flowers appear in May and June and are not showy. Prefers acid, well-drained soils, in full sun or partial shade. The species is seldom used in contemporary landscaping, having been replaced by the cultivar 'Crispa'. Grows 4 to 7 ft. high, equal or greater in spread. In the wild, it grows in thickets on moist slopes, along streams at 1,600 to 3,300 ft. elevation. Zones 4 to 7. China, Japan, Korea.

Stephanandra tanakae (*Neillia tanakae*) is more vigorous than *S. incisa* with three- to five-lobed leaves. Fall color is warm golden yellow. Routinely achieves 6 ft. Zones 5 to 7. Japan.

CULTIVARS AND VARIETIES
'Crispa' has 1- to 2-in.-long, bright green, deeply cut leaves that produce a fine texture. It forms a thick tangle of branches that root along their length, resulting in a wide-spreading groundcover. Grows 1½ to 3 ft. high.

Stewartia koreana
Korean stewartia
Many people insist that Korean stewartia is distinctly different from Japa-

nese stewartia (*Stewartia pseudocamellia*, which see), but from all landscape standpoints, they are similar. I have looked at enough plants of each species, and I simply cannot reliably distinguish them. Current thinking places them in the Koreana Group. No matter where the taxonomists place it, I would not want my life to rest on absolute identification. On selected specimens of this species, more vivid red fall color and perhaps greater exfoliation of the bark are evident. Forms a pyramidal outline. Several nursery professionals have advised me that this species is considerably more heat-tolerant than *S. pseudocamellia*. E. H. Wilson introduced the species

Stewartia koreana, Korean stewartia

from Korea in 1917. Grows 20 to 30 ft. high. Zones 5 to 7. Korea.

Stewartia malacodendron
silky stewartia
Every gardener's dream plant but, unfortunately, difficult to culture. Four times, I tried and failed. The great Hillier Arboretum, England, has a perfect, 18-ft.-high specimen that flowers in June. A bushy shrub or small tree, low-branched and densely foliaged with 2- to 4-in.-long, dark green leaves. Bark is gray-brown, lightly ridged and furrowed, similar to that of *Stewartia ovata*. The five-petaled, 2½- to 3½- (to 4-) in.-wide, white, purple-filamented, blue-

MORE ▶

Stewartia koreana fall color

Stewartia koreana

Stephanandra incisa 'Crispa'

Stewartia malacodendron CONTINUED anthered flowers appear singly from the leaf axils in June and July. The base of each petal may be streaked or stained with vinous purple coloration. To my way of thinking, few flowers are more beautiful. Flowers open over a long time frame, and I have stood in place for minutes simply appreciating their beauty. Fruit are woody, egg-shaped, ½-in.-wide, five-valved, dehiscent, beaked capsules containing wingless, lustrous brown seeds. Plant high for maximum drainage, mulch for even moisture, and site in partial shade. A real gardener's collector plant, like the finest piece of art or sculpture. Those who grow this species with success have climbed the ladder of garden achievement. I am still on the bottom rung. Have observed a wonderful plant at the Polly Hill Arboretum, on Martha's Vineyard, Massachusetts. Taxonomy professor Wilbur Duncan grew a superb plant in his Athens, Georgia, garden. Had it sited in shallow organic soil on granite rocks near a stream in partial shade. Grows 10 to 15 (to 18) ft. high, not quite as wide. Zones (6)7 to 9. Virginia and Arkansas to Florida, Louisiana, and Texas.

Stewartia monadelpha
tall stewartia

In terms of culture, tall stewartia is possibly the easiest of the genus. It is also one of the most heat-tolerant species, and it withstands dry soils better than *Stewartia koreana* or *S. pseudocamellia*. The habit is shrubby and multi-stemmed, although some specimens may develop a single trunk and oval-

Stewartia monadelpha fall color

Stewartia monadelpha

Stewartia malacodendron, silky stewartia

Stewartia malacodendron

Stewartia monadelpha

rounded outline. In shade, the habit is open with wide-spreading branches. The 1½- to 3-in.-long, dark green leaves develop excellent deep reddish fall color. Leaves hold late, and severe cold may reduce or eliminate fall color expression. White, 1- to 1½-in.-wide flowers open from June into July and are almost lost among the leaves. The bark is a rich mosaic of gray, brown, and cinnamon flakes that expose a rich brown underbark. Although not as spectacular as the best forms of Japanese stewartia or Korean stewartia, it is still a choice ornamental for the discriminating gardener. Grew this successfully in the Dirr garden. Grows 20 to 30 ft. high and wide after 30 years. Literature lists size in the wild as 75 to 80 ft. high. Remarkable specimens with ancient, architectural trunks at Trewithen in Cornwall, England. Zones 5 to 8. Japan.

Stewartia ovata
mountain stewartia

This, along with *Stewartia malacodendron*, represents the southeastern contribution to the genus. Mountain stewartia typically grows as an understory shrub on slopes above streams, often in moist soils. Spreading, bushy habit, vase-shaped in outline, although most garden plants are rounded and without great character. Bark, unlike its Asiatic relatives, is gray-brown and slightly ridged and furrowed. The dark green summer leaves offer a promise of orange to scarlet fall color that seldom materializes. Exquisite, glistening white, five- to six-petaled flowers with yellow-white stamens, each 2½ to 3 (to 4) in. in diameter, open in June and July. Flowers are not simply beautiful but romantic. Fruit, as for all *Stewartia* species, are five-valved, dehiscent capsules,

containing flattish, brown seeds. Culture is ripe with landmines, and I continue to agonize over my inability to successfully grow this and *S. malacodendron*. Provide moist, acid, woodsy, well-drained soil under high shade. Combine with ericaceous plants,

MORE ▶

Stewartia ovata var. *grandiflora*

Stewartia monadelpha, tall stewartia

Stewartia ovata CONTINUED

which have similar garden habitat
requirements. To successfully flower
the species is a great feeling. I'm still
patiently waiting for the day when I
will experience that feeling. Grows 10
to 15 ft. high and wide. Zones 5 to
8. North Carolina to Tennessee and
Florida. Found in rich soils under broadleaf trees, sometimes in moist soils,
steep slopes, and bluffs.

CULTIVARS AND VARIETIES
Variety *grandiflora* has larger flowers,
to 4 in. in diameter, and blue-purple
stamens; the validity of this taxonomic
unit is truly doubtful, since the purple-
stamened types occur in wild populations of the true species. Grandiflora
Group recognizes seed-grown plants
with purple stamens and larger flowers.

'Scarlet Sentinel' is a hybrid (*Stewartia ovata* var. *grandiflora* × *S. pseudocamellia*) with dense, upright habit,
21½ ft. by 8¼ ft. in 12 years, white
flowers with red-pink stamens; gray-
brown bark exfoliates in thin strips.
Arnold Arboretum introduction.

Stewartia pseudocamellia
Japanese stewartia

I suspect that there is not a gardener
who, upon seeing this species, would
not opt for one in the garden. Flowers
and fall foliage can be memorable,
but the exquisite lightning-bolt pattern of the exfoliating bark is the real
show, bringing pizzazz to the winter

Stewartia pseudocamellia, Japanese stewartia, fall color

Stewartia pseudocamellia

Stewartia pseudocamellia

garden. Generally pyramidal-oval in youth, the habit becomes more open and rounded with maturity. The character of the bark is not particularly dazzling until the branches reach 2 to 3 in. in diameter, at which time the bark exfoliates in striking patterns of gray, orange, and red-brown. The 2- to 3½-in.-long, medium to dark green leaves have serrated margins. Leaves emerge bronzy purple and, in fall,

may develop excellent orange to red to bronze-red color. The five-petaled, white flowers, 2 to 3 in. in diameter, have a central golden orange mass of anthers. Flowers open in June and July. The fruit is a five-valved, brownish capsule that splits at maturity to expose the brown seeds. Ideally soils should be moist, well drained, and on the acid side. Plants prefer full sun but also perform well in partial shade. High summer heat and dry soil conditions limit the growth of the species. Japanese stewartia is ideal as an accent or focal point. Several trees in a grove-like setting are terrific. Expect, at best, 6 to 12 in. of growth per year until well established. Grows 20 to 40 ft. high and wide at mature landscape size. I have failed miserably with this species in Athens but have observed superb specimens in other Athens gardens and in Atlanta. Zones (4)5 to 7. Japan.

Stewartia sinensis
Chinese stewartia
A truly magnificent species, described by W. J. Bean as having bark "as smooth as polished alabaster and the color of weathered sandstone." In my travels, I have come across many specimens that give little credence to this description; however, gigantic old trees at Trewithen, Cornwall, and 25- to 30-ft.-high specimens at Wakehurst Place, Sussex, and Rowallane,

Northern Ireland, made a believer out of me. The medium green leaves are 1½ to 4 in. long and seldom develop appreciable fall color. The white, fragrant flowers, 1½ to 2 in. across, are not overwhelming, opening over a long period. Culture is similar to that of *Stewartia pseudocamellia*; in more northerly locations, plants should be protected from harsh weather. Had a small plant in the Georgia garden that grew contentedly but did not flower. Fall color was orange-red. Grows 15 to 25 ft. high. Zones 5 to 7. China.

Styphnolobium japonicum
syn. *Sophora japonica*
Japanese pagodatree, scholar-tree
In the scheme of great trees, the Japanese pagodatree ranks in the first order. A full-grown tree is an impressive sight, with branches that seem to stretch to infinity, rich green leaves without a care in the world, and fragrant, cream-colored flowers that create a frothy mass over the canopy. Even young trees, particularly the better cultivars, display a dense, rounded, full crown and make their presence known. With age the tree assumes an upright-spreading to broadly rounded crown. The lustrous green leaves do not develop significant fall color. In July and August, the creamy panicles, 6 to 12 in. high and wide, cover the foliage in a lacy veil.

MORE ▶

Stewartia pseudocamellia

Stewartia sinensis, Chinese stewartia

Stewartia sinensis

Styphnolobium japonicum CONTINUED

The fruit are 3- to 8-in.-long pods, with constrictions between seeds, that change from pea-green to yellow and brown. They can be somewhat messy when they abscise. Soils should be well drained; otherwise, the species is quite adaptable. Canker can prove troublesome. Japanese pagodatree requires tremendous space and is best reserved for large-area use. Grows 50 to 70 ft. high and wide. Zones 4 to 7. Not well adapted to zone 7—trees simply do not prosper. Many planted on Georgia campus, none thriving. China, Korea.

CULTIVARS AND VARIETIES

'Pendula' is a weeping type that should not be used by the faint of heart—the branches are rather frightening, particularly in the winter landscape. Have grown seedlings, which segregate 1:1 (normal:weeping).

'Regent' has excellent vigor and a handsome oval-rounded form. It flowers at an early age.

Styrax americanus
American snowbell

Abundant number of *Styrax* species, hovering around 100, with most better suited to garden culture in cooler climates. The two southeastern species, *Styrax americanus* and *S. grandifolius*, are worthy garden choices if correctly sited. American snowbell is an underappreciated, underutilized native shrub (could be trained as a small tree) with delicate leaves and white, bell-shaped flowers with highly reflexed petals. The habit is oval-rounded to rounded. The bright green, 1½- to 3½-in.-long leaves do not develop appreciable fall color. Flowers occur in great abundance from the leaf axils in April and May (Athens). Prefers moist soils and partial shade. A good shrub for naturalizing; in the

Styphnolobium japonicum 'Pendula'

Styphnolobium japonicum, Japanese pagodatree

Styphnolobium japonicum

Styphnolobium japonicum

wild, it occurs in lowlands bordering streams. Grows 6 to 8 (to 10) ft. high; a specimen in the Arnold Arboretum is 15 ft. high. Zones (5)6 to 9. Virginia to Florida, west to Missouri and Louisiana.

Styrax grandifolius
bigleaf snowbell

Styrax grandifolius is a large shrub or small tree with 2½- to 7-in.-long, 1½- to 3¾-in.-wide, dark green, denticulate to almost entire leaves. Leaves resemble those of *S. obassia*. In May and June, the fragrant, white, ¾- to 1-in.-wide flowers open in seven- to 12- (occasionally 20-) flowered, 4- to 8-in.-long, nodding racemes. In nature, where I observed it mixed with mountainlaurel, it occurs as an understory tree. Typically found along the banks of streams, although it grows in drier woods. Has been difficult to root from cuttings and is seldom available in commerce. Certainly a most beautiful native woody plant for woodland edges and naturalizing. Not as easy to culture as *S. obassia*. Grows 8 to 12 (to 15) ft. high. The national champion is 17 ft. by 26 ft. Zones 7 to 9. Virginia to Georgia.

Styrax japonicus
Japanese snowbell

For years I chased this plant, until I was finally able to secure one for my Illinois garden. A 25-ft.-high tree sited next to a wall at Longwood Gardens, Pennsylvania, provided my first introduction to the consistently superb flower display. A delicate beauty, Japanese snowbell

MORE ▶

Styrax japonicus 'Pink Chimes'

Styrax grandifolius

Styrax americanus, American snowbell

Styrax americanus

Styrax grandifolius, bigleaf snowbell

775

Styrax japonicus CONTINUED

is best viewed from below so that one can most appreciate the medium to dark green leaves perched like butterflies above the white, bell-shaped flowers. The five-lobed, slightly fragrant flowers occur three to six together on short lateral shoots and appear in May and June. Leaves, medium to dark green, are 1 to 3½ in. long. The smooth gray bark is quite pleasing when framed by evergreens or another dark background. Full sun to partial shade is suitable. Prefers moist, acid, well-drained soils abundantly supplied with organic matter. It does not tolerate high heat or extremely dry conditions. At −20°F, young trees die back to the snowline, while on older plants the stems die back and the flower buds perish. Great in the shrub border or as an understory or hillside plant, where flowers can be viewed by passersby. Grows 20 to 30 ft. high and wide. Zones 5 to 8. China, Japan.

CULTIVARS AND VARIETIES

Dr. Sandy Reed has selected several hybrids, the best a tight pyramidal-conical tree with leathery, lustrous dark green leaves and abundant white flowers. This selection (71587) is more heat-tolerant based on performance in the Georgia trials.

'Emerald Pagoda' ('Sohuksan'), an introduction from Korea by J. C. Raulston and the U.S. National Arboretum, has dark green leaves, larger and more leathery than the those of the species, and heavy-textured, waxy, 1-in.-wide flowers. Beautiful plant when healthy—upright-oval, full, and dense; but there are some problems with culture, and trees decline and die.

'Fragrant Fountains' is a more graceful, tree-like form than 'Pendula' with abundant white flowers. Listed as 10 ft. by 7 ft. but potentially larger.

'Pendula' ('Carilon') has a compact, stiff, weeping habit. Leaves and flowers are similar to those of the species.

'Pink Chimes' offers pink flowers on a small, graceful tree. High heat reduces the intensity of the pink coloration. Grown for ten years in Georgia trials with showy pink flowers on a consistent basis. Seedlings have yielded pink and white flowering forms; none deeper than 'Pink Chimes'.

Styrax japonicus, Japanese snowbell

Styrax japonicus

Styrax japonicus 'Fragrant Fountains'

Styrax obassia
fragrant snowbell

My wife Bonnie and I have always admired this large-leaved, white-flowered tree, which occupies a place of prominence in our garden. In winter, fragrant snowbell has a certain sculptural quality because of its architecturally elegant smooth gray branches. The dark green leaves, to 8 in. long, provide a bold textural effect. Occasionally leaves develop good yellow fall color. Leaves may be injured by spring frosts. The fragrant, 4- to 8- (to 10-) in.-long flowers open as the leaves mature, generally in May and June (mid April, Athens). Moist, well-drained, acid soils are best, in full sun to partial shade. Use for specimen effect only; an isolated plant makes a striking landscape element. It is hardier than *Styrax japonicus*, with an estimated cold hardiness of −25°F. Appears slightly more heat-tolerant as well. Grows 20 to 30 ft. high, slightly less in spread. Zones (4)5 to 8. Japan, Korea, northeastern China.

Sycopsis sinensis
Chinese fighazel

My crazy affinity for this species runs tangential to my great love for the witchhazel family (Hamamelidaceae). Loose, oval-rounded, shrubby forms exist as well as rather narrow, small tree forms with smooth, gray bark. The evergreen leaves, 2 to 4 in. long, are essentially entire, lustrous dark green, and hold their color year-round. In winter, typically February and March, the small, yellowish flowers with red anthers and dark reddish brown tomentose bracts appear. Never over-

MORE ▶

Styrax obassia

Styrax obassia, fragrant snowbell

Styrax obassia fall color

Styrax obassia

Sycopsis sinensis CONTINUED

whelming but, like *Parrotia persica*, with color sufficient to perk up the winter garden. Tolerates sun and shade (best) in acid, well-drained soils. Has possibilities for screening and hedge use. Observed thriving specimens in Portland, Oregon, Washington, D.C., and Athens and Savannah, Georgia. Grows 10 to 15 ft. high and wide. A clone at the U.S. National Arboretum

has survived –10°F. Zones 7 to 9. Central and western China.

×*Sycoparrotia semidecidua*, an intergeneric hybrid between *Parrotia* and *Sycopsis*, is a botanical curiosity and potentially worthy small street tree. In 15 years in our garden, it never exhibited heat or drought stress, and large robust plants in Aiken, South Carolina, and Chapel Hill, North Carolina, corroborate these tolerances. Leaves

look like those of *Parrotia*, flowers like *Sycopsis*. Foliage is semi-evergreen, senescing to yellow-green to yellow. Flowers are reddish brown, eventually yellow as the stamens develop in February. Bark remains smooth, gray into old age and displays none of the exfoliating traits of *Parrotia*. Grows 10 to 15 (to 20) ft. high. Zones 7 to 9. Originated around 1950 in Basel, Switzerland.

Sycopsis sinensis

×*Sycoparrotia semidecidua*

Symphoricarpos albus, common snowberry

Sycopsis sinensis, Chinese fighazel

Symphoricarpos albus

Symphoricarpos albus
common snowberry

A native species with attractive white fruit in autumn and excellent shade tolerance. Common snowberry is a rounded to broad-rounded shrub, with numerous ascending, fine, twiggy shoots. It suckers profusely and can develop large colonies. The ¾- to 2-in.-long, dark, almost blue-green leaves remain into fall. Flowers are pinkish, May and June, and not particularly showy. The white, ½-in.-wide, pop-corn-like fruit ripen in September and persist into November. Very adaptable plant that prospers in limestone, clay soils. Provide a shady environment. Good as a filler or in mass plantings. Can become rather unkempt; prune it in late winter to bring it back to summer respectability. Grows 3 to 6 ft. high and wide. Zones 3 to 7. Nova Scotia to Alberta, south to Virginia and Minnesota.

Symphoricarpos ×chenaultii
Chenault coralberry

This hybrid has a low, spreading, arching habit, insignificant flowers, and pink fruit. Grows 3 to 6 ft. high and wide. Zones 4 to 7.

CULTIVARS AND VARIETIES
'Hancock' is a beautiful low-growing type with small, blue-green leaves. A 12-year-old plant may be 2 ft. high and 12 ft. wide.

Symphoricarpos orbiculatus
Indiancurrant coralberry, buckbrush

I have seen fields of this plant in Virginia, where it qualifies for weed status. Attractive purplish red, ⅙- to ¼-in.-wide fruit mature in October and persist into winter. The yellow-ish white flowers are flushed with pink and are borne in short axillary clusters on terminal spikes. Unfortunately, the species is quite susceptible to mildew. Similar to *Symphoricarpos albus* in growth habit. It is an inherently durable shrub for difficult areas of the garden. Grows 2 to 5 ft. high, 4 to 8 ft. wide. Zones 2 to 7. New Jersey

MORE ▶

Symphoricarpos ×chenaultii 'Hancock'

Symphoricarpos orbiculatus, Indiancurrant coralberry

Symphoricarpos ×chenaultii, Chenault coralberry

Symphoricarpos orbiculatus 'Pink Magic'

Symphoricarpos orbiculatus CONTINUED
to South Dakota, south to Georgia and
Texas.
CULTIVARS AND VARIETIES
Doorenbos Group represents hybrids
of the previous three species with
names like 'Magic Berry' (rose-pink
fruit), 'Mother of Pearl' (white, pink-
cheeked fruit), 'Pink Magic' (polished
ivory-blushed-pink fruit), and numerous other fruiting selections with
"fantasy" or "magical" as part of the
name.

Symplocos paniculata
sapphireberry
Sapphireberry is a large, rounded
to broad-rounded shrub that could
easily be grown as a small tree. The
gray bark is quite appealing, having
a ridged and furrowed character. The
1½- to 3½-in.-long, dark green leaves
offer no appreciable fall color. White,
½-in.-wide flowers are borne in 2- to
3-in.-long panicles in May and June
(late April to early May, Athens); they
are slightly fragrant and occur in great
profusion. The real treasure is the
⅓-in.-long, ellipsoidal, turquoise-blue
fruit; they generally ripen in September and persist into October, if the
birds do not eat them earlier. When
this shrub is in fruit, one questions
why it is not more abundant in commerce. Provide well-drained soils and
full sun for best growth; will tolerate
light shade. An excellent plant for

Symphoricarpos orbiculatus

Symplocos paniculata, sapphireberry

Symplocos paniculata

Symplocos paniculata

attracting birds. Use as a single specimen, in the shrub border, or in groupings. Grows 10 to 20 ft. high, similar spread. Zones 4 to 8. Himalaya, China, Japan, Taiwan.

Symplocos tinctoria
horse-sugar

Related to the more garden-worthy *Symplocos paniculata*, but several attributes might endear this species to southern gardeners. The biggest problem is nondescriptness in

Symplocos tinctoria, horse-sugar

Symplocos tinctoria

Syringa ×*chinensis*, Chinese lilac

habit and foliage, for few people can ever identify the plant. In the woodsy understory from the Piedmont to the Coastal Plain of the Southeast, it is either a loose, upright, broadleaf shrub of no distinction or a suckering, colonizing shrub that one could grow to love. The 3- to 6-in.-long leaves, thickish, lustrous dark green, are entire or obscurely serrate toward the apex. Leaves range from semi-evergreen to deciduous, depending on low temperatures. I love the fragrant cream-yellow flowers, which occur in dense, axillary clusters from the previous season's growth in March, April, and May. Fruit are orange to brown, 1/3- to 1/2-in.-long, ellipsoidal drupes. Tolerates a wide range of soils, from drier woods to bottomlands and swamps. Strictly a naturalizing plant. Called horse-sugar because the leaves are sweet. Grows 15 to 25 ft. high. Zones 7 to 9. Delaware to Florida to Louisiana.

Syringa
lilac

A genus of about 20 species, none in North America, which have spawned thousands of cultivars. Lilacs can be

magnificent flowering shrubs or trees, but they are not without their shortcomings. The fragrant flowers are certainly delightful additions to any garden; after flowering, however, most lilacs offer limited interest. Transplant lilacs from a container or as a balled-and-burlapped specimen in late winter or early spring. Provide well-drained, near neutral soils, although plants perform well in acid soils. Site in full sun to maximize flowering. The oldest branches should be pruned out on a regular basis to ensure vigorous, flower-producing shoots. Remove spent flowers to prevent seed set. Lilacs make great border shrubs and should not be isolated in an expanse of lawn. Mildew, scale, borers, leafroll necrosis, pseudomonas blight, and other maladies affect the plants. Heat precludes great success except for a few species like *Syringa* ×*laciniata*, *S. meyeri*, *S. oblata*, and *S. pubescens*.

Syringa ×chinensis
Chinese lilac

A large, broad-spreading, relatively fine-textured shrub, *Syringa* ×*chinensis* is a common inhabitant of midwestern

MORE ▶

Syringa ×*chinensis* 'Saugeana'

Syringa ×chinensis CONTINUED

and eastern landscapes. Its 1½- to 3-in.-long, dark green leaves are less susceptible to mildew than those of *S. vulgaris*, common lilac. Fragrant purple-lilac flowers are borne in 4- to 6-in.-long panicles in May. Grows 8 to 15 ft. high and wide. Zones 3 to 7.

CULTIVARS AND VARIETIES

'Lilac Sunday' is a fine-textured, 10- to 12-ft.-high and -wide shrub with

Syringa ×*hyacinthiflora* 'Asessippi'

Syringa ×*laciniata*, cutleaf lilac

Syringa Tinkerbelle®

lavender-pink flowers the length of the stems. From the Arnold Arboretum, where I experienced the plant before it was named. Bred by Jack Alexander.

'Saugeana', with lilac-red flowers, is more colorful than the species.

Syringa ×hyacinthiflora
hyacinth lilac

These early-flowering hybrids between *Syringa oblata* and *S. vulgaris*, first raised by Lemoine in France in 1876, are vigorous shrubs, upright in youth, fattening with age, reaching 10 to 12 ft. high and wide. Considerable resistance to leafroll necrosis. Best in cold climates. Zones 3 to 6(7).

CULTIVARS AND VARIETIES

Several Canadian and U.S. breeders have added to the palette. 'Asessippi' (single lavender), 'Evangeline' (light purple, fragrant), 'Maiden's Blush' (single pink), 'Pocahontas' (single, deep violet), and 'Sister Justena' (single white) have crossed my path in Northeast gardens and nurseries.

Syringa ×laciniata
cutleaf lilac

Comparable to *Syringa ×persica*, Persian lilac, in most characteristics, except for the leaves, which are gener-

ally three- to nine-lobed and not susceptible to mildew. Fragrant, pale lilac flowers are borne in 3-in.-long, loose panicles all along the stems in late March to early April (Athens). Produces reasonable flowers in partial shade. Forms a graceful, rounded-mounded outline. *Syringa ×laciniata* is the most heat-tolerant lilac, and literature mentions its successful culture in north Florida. Grows 6 to 8 ft. high and wide. Zones 4 to 8. Turkestan, China.

Syringa meyeri
Meyer lilac

A midwestern favorite. Although many dismiss this species as inferior to *Syringa vulgaris*, I consider it a superior choice because of its reliably heavy bloom, clean foliage, and compact but spreading habit. The plant is not small, and it develops a dense, broad-rounded outline and excellent branch structure. The ¾- to 1¾-in.-long, dark green leaves are almost rounded in outline. The purplish pink, fragrant flowers generally occur before the leaves are fully developed, in 4-in.-long and 2½-in.-wide panicles in April and May; they literally cover the entire shrub from top to bottom and remain effective for ten to 14 days. A great

Syringa meyeri, Meyer lilac

choice for the border, especially if backed by evergreens. Also works well in groupings and masses. Grows 4 to 8 ft. high, 6 to 12 ft. wide. Zones 3 to 7. Northern China.

CULTIVARS AND VARIETIES
Bloomerang® ('Penda') produces fragrant purple-pink flowers in spring, again in mid summer to fall; grows 5 ft. by 4 ft.; observed weak reblooming; open-pollinated seedling selection from Josee™ ('Morjos 060F').

Fairytale® series, hybrids of 'Palibin' and *Syringa pubescens* subsp. *microphylla,* are all compact, 5 to 6 ft. high, with pink, rose, lavender flowers. Several, including Tinkerbelle® ('Bailbelle'), show remontant flowering activities.

'Palibin' is a compact form with reddish purple buds that open to icy pink flowers. Grows 4 to 5 ft. high, 5 to 7 ft. wide. Often grafted on a standard to produce a "lollipop" tree.

Syringa oblata var. dilatata

early lilac

The common name for *Syringa oblata* is appropriate, for this is the first species to flower in the Arnold Arboretum's extensive collection. Flowered in late March at the JC Raulston Arboretum. Variety *dilatata* is shrubbier than the type and has longer leaves and a longer, more slender corolla tube. Plants in cultivation appear to be this variety rather than the species. The fragrant, pale lilac to purple-lilac flowers occur in broad, 2- to 5-in.-long panicles from the uppermost nodes of the previous year's wood. The dark blue-green leaves, 2 to 4 in. long and wide, are free from mildew. Foliage turns muted reddish to reddish purple in fall. Forms an oval-rounded shrub or small tree. Like all lilacs, requires well-drained soils and full sun. Displays more heat tolerance than *S. vulgaris,* common lilac, and is probably a better choice where heat stress is prevalent. The floral fragrance is not as sweet as that of *S. vulgaris* but still very pleasant. Grows 10 to 12 ft. high. Zones 3 to 6(7). Korea.

CULTIVARS AND VARIETIES
Alba Group encompasses white-flowered forms. I observed and/or grew both 'Betsy Ross' and 'Frank Meyer', the better of the two, with early white, fragrant flowers in loose panicles and robust habit, 10 ft. high and wide.

'Betsy Ross' flowers early April in Athens, the pristine white flowers

quite fragrant. Leaves become a bit tattered by late summer. Original plant was 9 ft. 9 in. by 13 ft. in 16 years. Result of a cross between *Syringa oblata* and an unidentified lilac from Highland Park, Rochester, New York.

'Declaration' produces fragrant, striking dark reddish purple inflorescences on an upright rounded shrub. Original plant was 8 ft. 6 in. by 6 ft.

MORE ▶

Syringa oblata var. *dilatata,* early lilac

Syringa oblata var. *dilatata* fall color

Syringa meyeri 'Palibin'

Syringa oblata var. *dilatata* 'Frank Meyer'

Syringa oblata var. *dilatata* CONTINUED
9 in. after 25 years. Result of cross between 'Sweet Charity' and 'Poca-hontas'. Considered more heat-tolerant.

'Old Glory', with fragrant bluish purple flowers, is from the same cross as 'Declaration'. Grew 11 ft. 6 in. by 13 ft. 6 in. in 25 years. The three ('Betsy Ross', 'Declaration', and 'Old Glory') resulted from the breeding genius of Dr. Don Egolf, U.S. National Arboretum.

Syringa ×persica
Persian lilac
Another shrub that was planted exten-sively in older gardens of the East and Midwest. Persian lilac develops into a graceful, rounded shrub. It has 1- to 2½-in.-long, dark blue-green leaves and fragrant, pale lilac flow-ers. The flowers occur in May in 2- to

Syringa pubescens subsp. *microphylla*, littleleaf lilac

3-in.-long and -wide panicles from the upper nodes of the previous season's growth. The leaves are often infected by mildew. Grows 4 to 8 ft. high, 5 to 10 ft. wide. Zones 3 to 7.

Syringa pubescens subsp. microphylla
syn. *Syringa microphylla*
littleleaf lilac
Littleleaf lilac is a handsome broad-spreading shrub. It has grayish green, ½- to 2-in.-long leaves and fragrant, rosy lilac flowers. The flowers are

borne in 2- to 4-in.-long, 1½- to 2-in.-wide panicles in May and June. Often flowers sporadically in late summer and early fall. A versatile, adaptable, heat-tolerant, mildew-resistant spe-cies that is worthy of greater use. Uti-lized in breeding to develop reflower-ing lilacs. Grows 6 ft. high, 9 to 12 ft. wide. Zones 4 to 7(8). Northern and western China.
CULTIVARS AND VARIETIES
'Superba' has single, deep pink flow-ers and is more colorful than the species.

Syringa ×persica, Persian lilac

Syringa pubescens subsp. *microphylla* 'Superba'

Syringa pubescens subsp. *patula* 'Miss Kim'

Syringa pubescens subsp. patula

syn. *Syringa patula*

Manchurian lilac

This species is frequently confused with *Syringa meyeri* and *S. pubescens* subsp. *microphylla*, but it has larger (2 to 5 in. long), leathery, dull dark green leaves. The habit is oval-rounded. Lilac-purple, fragrant flowers open in May and June. Grows 8 to 10 ft. high. Zones 3 to 7. Northern China, Korea.

CULTIVARS AND VARIETIES

'Miss Kim' is a lovely oval-rounded selection with purple flower buds and icy pink flowers. It is extremely dense in habit. The leaves often turn a respectable reddish purple fall color. Grows 10 ft. high. Worthy for flower production in Georgia trials, but foliage pretty miserable by August or September.

Syringa pubescens subsp. *patula*, Manchurian lilac

Syringa reticulata, Japanese tree lilac

Syringa reticulata

Japanese tree lilac

Possibly the most adaptable lilac for difficult sites, this species develops into a large shrub or small tree with an oval to rounded crown. The bark is lustrous brown, with horizontal lenticels reminiscent of cherry bark. The dark green, 2- to 5½-in.-long leaves develop no appreciable fall color. White flowers are borne in May and June in panicles 6 to 12 in. long and 6 to 10 in. wide; the fragrance is almost privet-like. This species is highly resistant to mildew and scale. Attractive as a small landscape tree or large shrub. Use as a specimen. Common in upper Midwest and Northeast as a street, park, and garden tree. Not amenable to greatness in the heat of zones 7 and 8. Grows 20 to 30 ft. high, 15 to 25 ft. wide. Zones 3 to 7. Japan.

CULTIVARS AND VARIETIES

'Ivory Silk', 'Regent', and 'Summer Snow' should be used, if available, instead of the species because of superior flower production, more uniform habit, and superior foliage. Newer cultivars, at least five, may prove better than these, but I have yet to experience or test them.

Syringa reticulata 'Ivory Silk'

Syringa reticulata subsp. pekinensis
Pekin lilac

At times confused with *Syringa reticulata* but differing in smaller, narrower, finer-textured leaves; often exfoliating cherry-like (*Prunus serrula*) bark; and from my observations, greater heat tolerance. Considered smaller in stature than *S. reticulata*, 15 to 20 ft. high, but trees 30 ft. high were observed. Creamy flowers occur in 6- to 12-in.-long and -wide (and larger) panicles

Syringa reticulata subsp. *pekinensis* China Snow®

in late May to early June (zone 7). Flowers are somewhat fragrant, with privet-like odor. Adaptable to any well-drained soil, acid to neutral, full sun to partial shade. Observed single-stemmed and multi-stemmed trees/shrubs. Bark is rich reddish brown and peels, flakes and sheets, providing great winter beauty. Beautiful specimen tree and quite forceful in groupings. Zones 3 to 7. Northern China.
CULTIVARS AND VARIETIES
Many in recent years, with China Snow® ('Morton')— dark green summer foliage, cream-white flowers, outstanding early exfoliating copper-amber bark—one of the best. Grows 20 ft. by 20 ft.

Syringa villosa
late lilac

Certainly not a force in the world of landscape lilacs, but this species has been utilized in breeding because of its late flowering period. Typically a large, bushy shrub with erect or ascending,

stout, stiff branches; most older specimens become leggy and open at the base. The medium green leaves are 2 to 7 in. long and have deeply impressed veins, resulting in a pleated appearance. The rosy lilac to white flowers occur in 3- to 7-in.-long panicles at the end of the shoots of new growth of the season in May and June. The fragrance is somewhat similar to that of the privet, definitely not the sweet perfume associated with *Syringa vulgaris*. Grows 6 to 10 ft. high, 4 to 10 ft. wide. Zones 2 to 7. China.

Syringa vulgaris
common lilac

It is unfortunate that such a treasured shrub with such wonderfully fragrant flowers should have so many flaws. Common lilac is a large, cumbersome shrub of irregular outline, often becoming leggy at the base. The 2- to 5-in.-long, dark green to blue-green leaves may contract significant mildew

MORE ▶

Syringa villosa, late lilac

Syringa vulgaris 'Charles Joly'

Syringa vulgaris 'Jeanne d'Arc'

Syringa vulgaris var. *alba*

Syringa vulgaris, common lilac

Syringa vulgaris 'De Miribel'

Syringa vulgaris 'Katherine Havemeyer'

Syringa vulgaris 'Krasavitsa Moskvy'

Syringa vulgaris CONTINUED

by summer. Undeniably, the deliciously fragrant lilac flowers make all the other liabilities seem tolerable. Flowers occur at the ends of the shoots in 4- to 8-in.-long panicles in May, before or as the leaves mature. They make wonderful cut flowers for the home. Plant in the border or even in the vegetable garden, wherever the fragrance can be enjoyed. Grows 8 to 15 (to 20) ft. high, 6 to 12 (to 15) ft. wide. Zones 3 to 7. Southern Europe.

CULTIVARS AND VARIETIES
It's anybody's guess as to their number, but 2,000 is a current estimate. Variety *alba* ('Alba'), with white flowers, is common throughout the northern states. Others to look for: 'Charles Joly' (double magenta), 'De Miribel'

(single violet), 'Henri Robert' (double violet), 'Jeanne d'Arc' (double white), 'Katherine Havemeyer' (double pink, mildew-resistant foliage), 'Krasavitsa Moskvy' (double white, pink in bud), 'Paul Hariot' (double purple), 'President Roosevelt' (single purple, highly fragrant), 'Primrose' (single yellow), and 'Sensation' (single purple, edged white).

Taiwania cryptomerioides
taiwania

Not sure what to think about this needle evergreen anomaly. Softly elegant pyramidal growth habit with a central leader, radiating secondary branches, and gracefully arching foliage. Blue-green needles, ⅓ to ½ in. long, sickle-shaped, extremely sharp-

pointed, are spirally borne and fully clothe the stem. The female cones are cylindrical and about ½ in. long. Moist, well-drained, acid soil and protection from wind are the best options. Utilize as an accent, specimen, or in groupings. Certainly nowhere common in commerce, but I recently witnessed this and *Taiwania flousiana* side by side; the former as described but more open in habit, the latter with green needles and more compact habit but quite graceful and refined. Ultimate size unknown but estimate 30 to 40 ft. high. Wild-collected *T. cryptomerioides* from Taiwan was 30 to 40 ft. high after 20 years at UBC Botanical Garden, Vancouver. Zone 7, 8 and 9 on West Coast. China, Myanmar for *T. cryptomerioides*; Taiwan for *T. flousiana*.

Syringa vulgaris 'President Roosevelt'

Taiwania cryptomerioides, taiwania

Syringa vulgaris 'Sensation'

Taiwania cryptomerioides

Tamarix ramosissima, five-stamen tamarix

Tamarix ramosissima
five-stamen tamarix

This species is often used in coastal landscapes or alkaline soil areas because of its excellent salt tolerance. I have encountered plants growing on the beaches of Georgia and the Carolinas, in the heavy clays of Michigan, and in the deserts of Arizona. Amazingly, all were prospering. It is a large, irregular shrub or small tree. The foliage is scale-like, almost like that of junipers, and usually light green to gray-green in color. Rose-pink flowers occur in large panicles in June and July on new growth of the season. Full flower by early to mid April in Athens. The flowers persist for four to six weeks, but they show their age toward the end of the cycle. It is probably best to prune the plant back in late winter to induce long, feathery growth and summer flowers. Transplant from a container; the root system is sparse. Provide full sun for best flowering. Grows 10 to 15 ft. high; I have observed 20- to 25-ft.-high forms. Zones 2 to 8. Southeastern Europe to central Asia.

CULTIVARS AND VARIETIES
'Summer Glow' has dense, feathery, blue-tinged foliage on a rangy, splaying, irregular habit. Bright rose-pink flowers in early June, Cincinnati, Ohio; mid July, Chanhassen, Minnesota.

Taxodium distichum
common baldcypress

Europeans consider the common baldcypress one of the finest North American trees, and its use in Europe, particularly in German gardens, borders on the fanatical. This deciduous conifer is a tall, airy spire, columnar to uniformly pyramidal in habit; the western populations are more open and tree-like, although I witness many trees in the Southeast with spreading canopies. The rich green foliage appears on feather-like branches and turns rusty orange to brown in

Tamarix ramosissima 'Summer Glow'

MORE ▶

Taxodium distichum CONTINUED

autumn. The fibrous, reddish brown to gray-brown bark sparks winter interest. Use container-grown or small balled-and-burlapped plants. Found in swamps and moist areas throughout its native range, this species performs admirably in drier soils and is adaptable to a variety of soil conditions, except high pH, which causes chlorosis of foliage. Knees generally develop around trees that grow in or near water. Ideal for use near water or in moist areas where few other trees will prosper. Makes its greatest statement in groupings or groves. Also good as a street tree. Grows 50 to 70 ft. high, 20 to 30 ft. wide; can grow to 100 ft. or more. Zones 4 to 9. Delaware to Illinois, south to Florida and Texas.

CULTIVARS AND VARIETIES

Autumn Gold™ ('Sofine') is a relatively compact-pyramidal selection with sage-green new leaves and rust-orange fall color. A good doer, according to southern growers. Grows about anywhere except calcareous soils.

'Cascade Falls' is an irregular but artistic weeping form that requires staking in early days to develop a leader and then builds upon itself. Witnessed 20-ft.-high plant in Coach Vince Dooley's Athens garden; the photo included herein is taken there.

'Fallingwater' has more of a central leader, with secondary branches uniformly weeping.

'Peve Minaret' is columnar-pyramidal with closely spaced dark green needles

Taxodium distichum

Taxodium distichum 'Cascade Falls'

Taxodium distichum, common baldcypress, fall color

along the stems; large fattened trunk; 10 ft. by 3 ft. Planted as a grove the effect is akin to a pygmy forest.

Shawnee Brave® ('Michelson') is a narrow-pyramidal form with blue-green foliage. It is resistant to gall mite. Parent tree was 75 ft. high and 18 ft. wide when the selection was made. Introduced by Earl Cully, Heritage Trees, Jacksonville, Illinois.

Taxodium distichum var. *imbricarium*

syn. *Taxodium ascendens*
pond cypress

Taxonomically, this species has been juggled over the years. From a landscape standpoint, it is more columnar than *Taxodium distichum*. Secondary branches originate at right angles to the central leader, and the soft, appressed, rich green needles produce a foliage effect similar to that of

MORE ▶

Taxodium distichum var. *imbricarium* 'Prairie Sentinel'

Taxodium distichum var. *imbricarium*

Taxodium distichum Shawnee Brave®

Taxodium distichum var. *imbricarium*, pond cypress

Taxus baccata

Cryptomeria japonica or juniper. Uses are similar to that of *T. distichum*. Grows 70 to 80 ft. high, 15 to 20 ft. wide. Zones (5)6 to 9. Virginia to Florida and Alabama.

CULTIVARS AND VARIETIES
'Prairie Sentinel' is a narrow, columnar-conical selection with almost grass-green needles and mellow soft orange-brown fall color; great in groupings; grows 60 ft. high and 10 ft. wide.

Taxus
yew

The genus is one of the most essential components of cold temperate gardens but sputters about zone 7 in the South. Too often mutilated by the pruning shears, yews may assume a disgusting regularity. Left to their own genetic devices, however, *Taxus* species make splendid, artistic trees and shrubs. Not so much in this country, but in England, where the large native trees have not been pruned, the stately, dark green, somber yew trees with a broad pyramidal habit grow 40 to 60 ft. high. Yews are fantastically adaptable to acid and limestone, high pH soils. They thrive in sun or shade, in moist or dry soils. Good drainage is essential for successful culture.

Transplant balled and burlapped. For function and aesthetics, yews rank in the first order of needle evergreens. The abundant uses for these plants include foundation plantings, screens, hedges, masses, and accents. Yews are generally free of significant insects and diseases, although they are favored by deer.

Taxus baccata
English yew

Typical English yew is an immense plant, but the cultivars are more in scale with contemporary landscapes. The height of all forms is easily controlled by pruning. The ½- to 1¼-in.-long, dark green needles maintain their color through the seasons, although some discoloration is common in cold, windy climates. The reddish brown, furrowed, scaly, flaky bark is beautiful, particularly on mature trees. The ¼- to ⅜-in.-long, football-shaped seeds have a fleshy red covering called an aril. Seeds occur on female plants. Grows 30 to 60 ft. high, 15 to 25 ft. wide. Zones (5)6 and 7. Not well adapted to zone 7 (there, the various cultivars of *Cephalotaxus harringtonia* are great alternatives). Europe, northern Africa, western Asia.

MORE ▶

Taxus baccata

Taxus baccata, English yew

Taxus baccata 'Fastigiata'

Taxus baccata 'Repandens'

Taxus baccata

Taxus baccata 'Aurea'

Taxus baccata CONTINUED
CULTIVARS AND VARIETIES
'Adpressa' has short, ¼- to ½-in.-long, dark green needles densely set along the stems. Makes a large shrub or small tree. Plants as large as 30 ft. tall are known. 'Adpressa Fowle' is more compact and smaller in stature.

'Aurea' ('Aurescens') is a golden-needled form. Similar types exist under this name. The ones I have observed display rich golden yellow new growth that gradually fades to green.

'Fastigiata' is commonly known as the Irish yew, although other upright forms masquerade with this title. Decidedly columnar in habit with strongly vertical branches. Grows 15 to 30 ft. high, 4 to 8 ft. wide.

'Repandens' is frequently used in North American gardens because of its greater cold hardiness. A superb wide-spreading form. The tips of the branches are slightly pendulous. Grows 2 to 4 (to 6) ft. high, 12 to 15 ft. wide.

Taxus canadensis
Canadian yew
Similar to *Taxus baccata* except for its size and winter color. This species is not used to any degree because its needles turn an inferior reddish brown in winter. Plants in the wild are often prostrate, loose, and straggling. For heavy shade situations in a natural-istic garden, it is worthy of consider-ation. Observed in the wild in Turkey Run State Park, Indiana, where it grew in deep shady ravines. Grows 3 to 6 ft. high, 6 to 8 ft. wide. Zones 2 to 6. Newfoundland to Manitoba, south to Virginia and Iowa.

Taxus canadensis, Canadian yew

Taxus canadensis

Taxus chinensis, Chinese yew

Taxus chinensis

Chinese yew

J. C. Raulston championed this species because it performed so magnificently in the Arboretum at Raleigh, North Carolina, where it is still growing in full sun next to the lath area. Its habit is pyramidal-conical, almost like *Taxus cuspidata* 'Capitata' but with slightly longer needles and much faster growth. The dark green needles, 1 to 1½ in. long, have two bands on their lower surface. Since J. C.'s initial introduction, I observed other forms of the species that are more shrubby and wide-spreading. Grew these for over 15 years in Georgia trials; all plants were spreading types and discolored in winter, never living up to the promise of the JC Raulston Arboretum plant. Easy to root from cuttings; takes pruning; tolerant of heat and drought, sun and shade. Susceptible to deer browsing. Potential use in zones 7 and 8 for screens, hedges, and foundation plantings but has not yet been embraced by commerce. Grows 5 to 10 ft. high, spread variable. Zones (6)7 and 8. Morton Arboretum, Lisle, Illinois, mentioned growing the plant. China.

The related *Taxus floridana*, Florida yew, grows naturally in a narrow area along the Apalachicola River in northwestern Florida. Typically shrubby in cultivation, plants are tree-like in the wild; the national champion is 22 ft. high, 23 ft. wide. Some discoloration of needles in exposed situations in winter. I thought it might serve as a breeding partner for introducing heat tolerance into the genus. Noted respectable specimens at the Biltmore Estate, Asheville, North Carolina, and the Atlanta Botanical Garden. Zones (6)7 to 9.

Taxus cuspidata

Japanese yew

In most respects, this species could be considered the Japanese equivalent of *Taxus baccata*, English yew (which see). Size is variable. Zones 4 to 7. Japan, northeastern China.
CULTIVARS AND VARIETIES
The numerous cultivars are better choices for colder climates.

'Capitata' is a tree form often used for screening and hedging in the East

MORE ▶

Taxus floridana, Florida yew

Taxus chinensis

Taxus cuspidata, Japanese yew

Taxus cuspidata CONTINUED

and Midwest. The habit is pleasingly pyramidal. Unless pruned, it grows 40 to 50 ft. high.

'Densa' makes a broad mound, almost twice as wide as it is high, and is clothed with extremely dark green needles. Grows 4 ft. high, 8 ft. wide.

'Nana' is another compact form with dark green needles. Grows 3 ft. high, 6 ft. wide.

Taxus ×media
English-Japanese yew

Plants included in this group, hybrids between the English and Japanese species, are better choices for modern landscapes. In Midwest and Northeast landscapes, *Taxus ×media* selections predominate. Zones (4)5 to 7.

CULTIVARS AND VARIETIES

Many selections have been made; most are shrubby, but there are several distinctly upright types.

'Brownii' is an old clone with a dense, rounded outline and dark green needles. Grows 9 ft. high, 12 ft. wide in 15 to 20 years.

'Densiformis' is one of the more popular forms. Grows 3 to 4 ft. high and twice as wide.

'Hatfieldii' is a male form with dark green needles. Dense and broadly pyramidal-columnar in habit. A 20-year-old plant may be 12 ft. high and 10 ft. wide.

'Hicksii' might be considered a replacement for *Taxus baccata* 'Fastigiata', Irish yew, in colder climates. Makes a good hedge or screening plant. Grows 15 to 20 ft. high, 5 to 8 ft. wide.

'Wardii' is a wide-spreading, flat-topped, densely branched cultivar with dark green needles. Usually grows about two to three times as wide as it is tall. A 20-year-old plant was 6 ft. high by 19 ft. wide.

Taxus ×media 'Brownii'

Taxus cuspidata 'Capitata'

Taxus ×media 'Hicksii'

Tecoma capensis

syn. *Tecomaria capensis*

cape honeysuckle

Much like *Campsis radicans* in appearance but more refined and less aggressive. My original introduction to the species occurred in a garden in Orlando, where I agonized over the identity of this bright orange-red flowered vine. The compound pin-nate leaves are composed of five to nine, lustrous dark green, ½- to 1½-in.-long, sharply serrate leaflets. The 2- to 3-in.-long, tubular flowers, orange to orange-red, develop in terminal racemes from fall into winter, with sporadic flowering at other times. Requires no special care, other than well-drained soil and full sun. Like *C. radicans*, displays reasonable salt tolerance. Has a self-clinging nature and will attach itself to structures, so provide fence, trellis, post, or some other suitable surface. I have also observed it pruned into a freestanding shrub. Useful for covering banks, slopes, hard-to-maintain areas. Grows 10 to 15 ft. or more. Zones 9 to 11. South Africa.

Taxus ×media 'Densiformis'

Tecoma capensis, cape honeysuckle

Taxus ×media, English-Japanese yew

Ternstroemia gymnanthera new growth

Ternstroemia gymnanthera

Ternstroemia gymnanthera

Japanese ternstroemia

With its colorful new growth, wide soil adaptability, and sun and shade tolerances, this species has shouldered some of the garden responsibilities of redtip photinia, *Photinia ×fraseri*. The young foliage varies from apple-green to bronze, red, reddish purple, and almost blackish purple. With maturity, leaves turn lustrous dark green and in winter often assume rich reddish bronze coloration. Leaves are obovate, entire, somewhat spatulate in shape, 2½ to 4 in. long with a blunt apex, usually with an indentation. The five-petaled, white, ½-in.-wide flowers are borne on reflexed stalks from the previous season's growth in May and June. Their effect is masked by the current season's foliage. Fruit are cute, 1-in.-long, ½-in.-wide, egg-shaped, green to red, speckled berries that ripen in September. Primarily seed-grown; easily transplanted and grown in all but heavy, wet soils. Responds to pruning and can be kept in check. Excellent foundation, hedge, screen, or massing plant. No serious insects. Cercospora leaf spot can be troublesome. Grows 8 to 10 ft. high, 5 to 6 ft. wide. Have observed 20-ft.-high specimens in South Carolina. Zones 7 to 9(10). Japan, Korea, Taiwan, China, India, Borneo.

CULTIVARS AND VARIETIES

Newer introductions for foliage color

Ternstroemia gymnanthera, Japanese ternstroemia

Ternstroemia gymnanthera 'Burnished Gold'

Ternstroemia gymnanthera 'Variegata'

and growth habit include Bigfoot™ ('Sotall') at 15 to 20 ft. by 5 to 6 ft., Bronze Beauty™ ('Conthery'), Copper Crown® ('Grewad'), Jade Tiara® ('Grevan'), LeAnn™ ('Contherann'), Regal™ ('Conthera'), and Sovereign® ('Greyou').

'Burnished Gold' has yellow-gold-bronze foliage that diminishes with the heat of summer.

'Variegata' has a cream-white to yellow-white margin that turns rose-pink in winter; one of the more colorful variegated plants for shade, and does not revert.

Tetradium daniellii

syn. *Evodia daniellii*

Korean evodia

Never popular in American gardens, but several assets make this species worthy of consideration. In its finest form, it is a uniform, round-headed tree with lustrous dark green, compound pinnate foliage. The leaves are composed of five to 11 leaflets, each 2 to 5 in. long. Creamy white flowers are borne in 4- to 6-in.-wide, flattish corymbs in June and July and provide excellent bee pasture. The fruit capsule changes from red to black and splits to expose shiny, brownish black seeds. Even the bark is handsome, becoming smooth and gray with maturity. This species has no serious flaws. Not finicky as to soil types, it makes a good choice for difficult sites. Grows 25 to 30 (to 50) ft. high and wide. Not well adapted to intense heat, but a tree has persisted on the Georgia campus for more than 30 years. Zones 4 to 8. Northern China, Korea.

Tetradium hupehensis is now merged with *T. daniellii*. European taxonomy uses the Hupehense Group as the taxonomic umbrella.

Tetradium daniellii, Korean evodia

Tetradium daniellii

Tetradium daniellii Hupehense Group

Tetradium daniellii

Teucrium chamaedrys

wall germander

A broadleaf evergreen subshrub that is utilized for hedges and masses. The smallish, rounded-mounded habit, ¼- to 1-in.-long, dark green leaves, and rose-purple, summer flowers have endeared it to gardeners worldwide. Often used in formal gardens, it is time-honored for knot and herb gardens. Prefers well-drained, sandy soil, slightly on the dry side, in full sun. Prune to reinvigorate the plant and maintain dense branching. Grows 12 to 15 in. high and wide. Zones 6 to 8(9). Europe, northern Africa, western Asia.

Teucrium fruticans, shrubby germander, has silver-white leaves and stems owing to the heavy pubescence. Pale blue flowers in terminal racemes open in summer. Requires sun and well-

Teucrium chamaedrys

Teucrium fruticans, shrubby germander

Teucrium chamaedrys, wall germander

drained soil. Keep the fertility minimal. Performed well in Athens; 3 to 5 ft. high and wide. Zone 7, 8 to 10 on West Coast. Southern Europe, North Africa.

Thuja occidentalis
American arborvitae

In northern landscapes, this species and its cultivars are as common as grass. Plants are used around foundations, in groupings, as screens or hedges, and occasionally as free-standing specimens. The rather stiff, narrow- to broad-pyramidal habit makes the plant useful for hedging. The foliage is rich green in summer, often yellowish green to brownish green in winter, especially on plants exposed to winter sun and wind. Amazingly durable and can be grown in virtually any soil, acid to limestone, high pH. In the wild, it is found in rocky and

MORE ▶

Thuja occidentalis 'Ellwangeriana Aurea'

Thuja occidentalis, American arborvitae

Thuja occidentalis 'Pendula'

Thuja occidentalis 'Rheingold'

Thuja occidentalis CONTINUED
marshy soils. Takes pruning with grace and dignity, and makes, as hedges go, a fine green wall. Highly susceptible to deer browsing. Grows 40 to 60 ft. high, 10 to 15 (to 25) ft. wide. Zones 2 to 7. Eastern North America. Observed growing abundantly from Maine's Cadillac Mountain to deep ravines in the Natural Bridge, Virginia.

CULTIVARS AND VARIETIES
Numerous cultivars confound and confuse, but several are good for general landscape use.

'Degroot's Spire' is a narrow-columnar form with rich green, twisted foliage like 'Spiralis'; bronzes in cold weather; 6 to 12 ft. by 3 to 5 ft.

'Hetz Midget' produces rich green foliage and is quite an attractive selection—dense, globe-shaped, and doubtfully will ever grow more than 3 to 4 ft. high.

'Nigra' has good dark green foliage throughout the seasons. Grows 20 to 30 ft. high.

'Pendula' is an attractive small pyramidal form with rather open ascending-arching branches and pendulous branchlets. A first-class plant for accent use; about 15 ft. high; requires staking. Held green color into February at Sarah P. Duke Gardens, Durham, North Carolina. Developed before 1862 in the Standish Nursery, England.

'Pumila Sudworth' forms an irregular outline with green, gold-tipped foliage. Has performed well in zone 7 for over 20 years. Holds color in heat better than most other *Thuja occidentalis* types. Grows 6 to 10 ft. high, 4 to 5 ft. wide.

'Rheingold', a slow-growing, ovoid or conical shrub, 4 to 5 ft. high by 3 to 4 ft. wide, is quite similar to 'Ellwangeriana Aurea' except smaller in stature; no doubt propagated from the juvenile shoots of that form. The foliage primarily adult and rich deep gold turns copper to brownish yellow in winter.

Thuja occidentalis 'Smaragd'

Thuja occidentalis 'Techny'

Thuja occidentalis 'Woodwardii'

'Smaragd' ('Emerald') is a compact pyramid of lustrous emerald-green foliage. Does not discolor in winter. Displays excellent heat tolerance and is described as hardy to −40°F. Slower growing than the species. Grows 10 to 15 ft. high, 3 to 5 ft. wide.

Technito® ('BailJohn') is a compact pyramidal form, more dense than 'Techny', appears slower growing, retains dark green color. Grows 6 ft. by 2½ ft.

'Techny' ('Mission') is a broad-based pyramidal form with dark green foliage throughout the seasons. Grows slowly, to 15 ft. or more.

'Wintergreen' ('Hetz Wintergreen') is a columnar pyramidal form holding good green winter color; coarser than other selections and faster-growing than most; 20 to 30 ft. high, 5 to 10 ft. wide. May display better shade tolerance.

'Woodwardii' is a common sight in midwestern landscapes. It has a broad-rounded habit. The dark green summer foliage may turn ugly brown in winter. Grows 8 to 10 ft. high, 16 to 20 ft. wide.

Thuja orientalis

syn. *Platycladus orientalis*

oriental arborvitae

An amazing plant with reasonable cold tolerance (zone 5, Maine) and even greater heat tolerance (to Key West, Florida, zone 11). The habit is densely pyramidal with a rotund base and vertically arranged sprays of foliage. The rich grass-green leaves will discolor in cold weather. Cones, roundish egg-shaped, ¾ in. long, fleshy, bluish green, have hook-like projection on back of cone scales. Like *Thuja occidentalis*, it is ideal for miserable soils and can be utilized for a wide range of landscape needs. Not as susceptible to deer browsing. Grows 18 to 25 ft. high, 10 to 15 ft. wide. Zones (5)6 to 10(11). Korea, northern and north-eastern China. Nomenclature currently embraces *Platycladus* as correct genus. For comparative gardening purposes, I have kept it with *Thuja*.

CULTIVARS AND VARIETIES

'Aurea Nana', Berckman's golden arborvitae, represents the most common form in cultivation. It is dense, compact, and ovoid-pyramidal in habit. The rich golden yellow new

MORE ▶

Thuja orientalis, oriental arborvitae

Thuja orientalis 'Aurea Nana', Berckman's golden arborvitae

Thuja plicata

Thuja koraiensis, Korean arborvitae, undersides of needles

Thuja standishii, Japanese arborvitae

Thuja plicata Golden Spire™

Thuja orientalis CONTINUED

foliage fades to a lighter yellow-green. Although considered smallish, it grows 10 ft. high and more. Easily kept under control with pruning.

'Baker', 'Blue Cone', and 'Fruitlandii' are quality green-foliaged forms that are preferable to the typical species.

Thuja plicata

western redcedar, giant arborvitae

Over the years, I pushed and promoted the better forms of *Thuja occidentalis*, American arborvitae, and missed the truly noble member of the genus. Typically, the habit of *T. plicata* is narrow- to broad-pyramidal. The lustrous, rich dark green foliage is the most beautiful of all the arborvitaes, elegantly postured, like a lady's hand outstretched for a kiss. The foliage does not discolor in winter to the degree of that of *T. occidentalis* or *T. orientalis*. Moist, acid, well-drained soils are preferred, but plants prosper in heavy clays in the Midwest as well. Although native to the Pacific Northwest, where it grows 180 to 200 ft. high, this species thrives from Chicago to Boston to Cincinnati to Raleigh. On the Isle of Mainau in Germany and at Stourhead, England, reside the most magnificent 80-ft.-high trees, with layered lower branches that provide

Thuja plicata, western redcedar

a density belied by the aging specimens. Grows 50 to 75 ft. high, 15 to 25 ft. wide. Zones 5 to 7. Alaska to California.

Additional species with garden merit include *Thuja koraiensis*, Korean arborvitae, with blue-green upper surface and distinct whitish markings below. Plants I grew in Georgia were broad, irregular shrubs of no great beauty except for foliage. Might add the foliage did not discolor significantly in winter. In England, witnessed graceful pyramidal forms that would translate well to American commerce and gardens. Estimate 20 to 30 ft. high and gracefully pyramidal in the tree type. Zones 5 to 7. Northeast China, Korea.

Thuja standishii, Japanese arborvitae, develops a broad conical crown with arching branch sprays, almost resulting in a semi-weeping, somewhat shaggy appearance. The foliage is light to dark green and when bruised emits a lemon verbena fragrance. Needles, based on Georgia evaluations, turn yellow-brown-green in winter. Probably 20 to 30 ft. high, although described as reaching 100 ft. in Japan. Zones 5 and 6(7).
CULTIVARS AND VARIETIES
'Atrovirens' is a large pyramidal form. Superb, shining dark green foliage.

Discolors to yellow-brown in winter in the South.

Golden Spire™ ('Daniellow') is a yellow-foliage selection that holds the color in the heat of zone 7; upright, conical habit.

'Green Giant' is one of the most popular screening and hedging needle evergreens, a standard for that purpose from the Midwest to the Southeast. Dark green summer foliage color; some bronzing in winter. Plant in Georgia trials was 35 ft. tall in 13 years; suspected hybrid of *Thuja standishii* and *T. plicata*.

'Zebrina' seldom appears in garden centers, but its yellowish striped foliage sprays (flattened fronds) provide a less-than-offensive golden hue. Color is diminished in heat of the South. Broad-pyramidal habit. Grows 30 ft. high.

Thujopsis dolabrata
Hiba arborvitae
The species makes a good garden plant and a great conversation piece, since few people have any idea of its identity. The broad-pyramidal habit is reminiscent of that of typical *Thuja*, but the individual segments of the foliage are thicker, wider and more lustrous, darker green above, with distinct silvery white markings below. Quite adaptable, requiring only well-drained soils. Withstands full sun and

MORE ▶

Thuja 'Green Giant'

Thuja plicata 'Zebrina'

Thujopsis dolabrata 'Variegata'

Thujopsis dolabrata CONTINUED

partial shade. Generally does not discolor in winter. Cuttings root readily, and I see no reason for its paucity in commerce. Use as a specimen evergreen, for it is too beautiful to mutilate with pruning shears. Grows 30 to 50 ft. high, 10 to 20 ft. wide. Zones 5 to 7. Not well adapted to high heat, although a plant was thriving in Wilmington, North Carolina. Japan.

CULTIVARS AND VARIETIES

Variety *hondae* is more compact in habit with densely arranged branchlets clothed with thickish dark green needles.

'Nana' is a great evergreen plant for the rock garden or shrub border, or as an accent. It has a rounded-mounded outline. Grows 3 ft. high and wide.

'Variegata' has sprays marked with creamy white.

Tilia americana
American linden, basswood

Not utilized to any great degree in American landscapes but still one of America's most beautiful trees, found in the wild over much of eastern, midwestern, and southeastern United States. The habit is sturdy and imposing—pyramidal in youth, oval-rounded with arched and spreading branches at maturity. The gray to brown bark

Thujopsis dolabrata undersides of needles

Thujopsis dolabrata 'Nana'

Thujopsis dolabrata, Hiba arborvitae

Tilia 'Redmond'

is smooth and shiny on young trees, developing a flat, scaly, ridged and furrowed character with age. The 4- to 8-in.-long, lustrous dark green leaves turn, at best, yellow-green in fall. Cream-yellow, fragrant flowers appear in June and are followed by rather inconspicuous hard-shelled nutlets. Provide moist, deep, well-drained soils, in full sun. If native in an area, make every effort to keep the plant. Grows 60 to 80 ft. high, 20 to 40 ft. wide. Zones 2 to 8(9). Maine to Florida, west to North Dakota, south to Oklahoma and Louisiana.

Tilia caroliniana, *T. floridana*, *T. georgiana*, *T. glabra*, *T. heterophylla*, *T. michauxii*, *T. monticola*, and *T. neglecta* represent slight taxonomic variations of *T. americana*, and the identification of these species can be confused. From the pragmatic per-spective, all have been folded into *T. americana*.

CULTIVARS AND VARIETIES
'Redmond', a hybrid between *Tilia americana* and *T. ×euchlora*, resembles the former in most respects. It has a distinctly pyramidal outline and is more densely branched than *T. americana*. Common in commerce, especially in the Midwest. Beautiful allée lines the entrance drive to the Missouri Botanical Garden.

Tilia cordata
littleleaf linden
This smaller-leaved linden is more suited to traditional landscapes than the previous species. Popular and fashionable because of the many reliable selections that represent it, littleleaf linden is without question a first-rate cool-climate lawn, street, or shade tree, a staple from Maine to the Midwest and south to just below the Mason-Dixon line; plants in the

MORE ▶

Tilia cordata, littleleaf linden

Tilia americana

Tilia americana, American linden

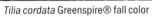
Tilia cordata Greenspire® fall color

Tilia cordata Summer Sprite®

Tilia cordata pleached

Southeast simply languish or never reach their full genetic potential. Distinctly pyramidal in youth, becoming pyramidal-rounded with age. Densely branched and foliaged, it makes an ideal landscape tree. The 1½- to 3-in.-long, dark green leaves may turn a reasonable yellow in fall. Yellowish, fragrant flowers occur in June. Relatively easy to transplant. Its tolerance of harsh soil conditions is legendary. The species thrives in heavy clays and acid to higher pH soils; tolerates drier soils better than many trees. Japanese beetles (which plague all lindens), aphids, and sooty mold (a fungus that feeds on aphid residue) are serious problems. Site with care, because the abundant flowers often attract bees. Grows 60 to 70 ft. high, 30 to 45 ft. wide. Witnessed a pair of 80-ft.-tall trees on an old Maine homestead. Zones 3 to 7. Europe.

CULTIVARS AND VARIETIES
Numerous and superior to the species. Based on sustained evaluations at the Milliken and Schmidt arboreta, my top choices for habit and foliage are Chancellor® ('Chancole') with beautiful dark green leaves, Corinthian® ('Corzam') with more compact habit, smaller, lustrous dark green leaves, and 'Olympic' with uniform branching and lustrous dark green leaves.

'Glenleven' (*Tilia ×flavescens*) and Greenspire® are good selections. Greenspire® is the most popular because of its central leader, uniform branching habit, and time-tested performance.

Summer Sprite® ('Halka') is a cute, diminutive form, a dense, plump pyramid, 20 ft. by 18 ft. Good heat tolerance.

Tilia ×euchlora
Crimean linden

Little used in commercial landscaping because of competition from *Tilia cordata*, but this hybrid between *T. cordata* and *T. dasystyla* is still a handsome tree. Habit is softly pyramidal, with branches that skirt the ground. The 2- to 4-in.-long leaves are lustrous, polished dark green. The leaf margins have elongated, mucronate serrations, almost like bristles, a trait that separates this species from littleleaf linden. Tends to sucker from the base, producing unwanted shoots that need to be removed. Supposedly more resistant to aphids than *T. cordata*. A fine tree for parks, campuses, and large areas. Do not limb up the lower branches, since they add much to the character of a mature tree. Originated about 1860. Grows 40 to 60 ft. high, 20 to 30 ft. wide. Zones 3 to 7.

Tilia ×euchlora, Crimean linden

Tilia ×euchlora

Tilia kiusiana

There are times when one knows that the "plant" is potentially the next great landscape tree. Such is the situation with *Tilia kiusiana*, a unique linden, the leaves not fitting the typical profile. The dark green leaves are 1½ to 2½ in. long, oblong-ovate, obliquely rounded or subcordate at base. The habit is gently conical-pyramidal with elegant, refined, arching branches that skirt the ground. Bark exfoliates in elongated strips and plates. Appears adaptable. Have seen the tree only at the Arnold Arboretum. Estimate 20 to 30 ft. by 8 to 15 ft., possibly larger. Zones 6 and 7. Southern Japan.

Tilia 'Petiolaris'

syn. *Tilia petiolaris*
pendent silver linden

A noble tree of weeping habit, with all the fine attributes of *Tilia tomentosa*, silver linden. In my opinion, this pyramidal-oval to oval-rounded, weeping form is probably nothing more than a selection of *T. tomentosa* and, more

Tilia kiusiana

Tilia 'Petiolaris', pendent silver linden

Tilia kiusiana

Tilia 'Petiolaris'

and more, taxonomic thinking treats it thusly. The fall color is often striking yellow. Great specimen tree, deserving of space in every park, campus, or golf course. Large trees on Illinois and Swarthmore campuses. Certainly one of the most beautiful of all the lindens. Grows 60 to 80 ft. high, 30 to 40 ft. wide. Zones 5 to 7.

Tilia platyphyllos
bigleaf linden

The common name does not really reflect the actual leaf size of this species. Averaging 2 to 5 in. in length, the leaves of bigleaf linden are not a great deal larger than those of littleleaf linden. This species is occasionally grown in the United States, most often in the Midwest and Northeast, but in Europe, it is common, particularly in formal allées and along streets. The stems are covered with long pubescence, a characteristic that separates the species from the others presented here. The habit is densely broad-pyramidal. Dark green leaves and yellowish white flowers make this a tree of great beauty. Grows 60 to 80 ft. high, 20 to 40 ft. wide. Zones 2 to 6. Europe.
CULTIVARS AND VARIETIES
'Rubra' has subdued reddish stems in winter.

'Tortuosa' is an anomaly, with curiously curled and twisted leaves and stems.

Tilia tomentosa
silver linden

In the world of lindens, this species deserves the beauty-queen title. Stunning, lustrous dark green, 2- to 5-in.-long, silver-backed leaves reflect like silver dollars in the summer sun. Fall color is a respectable yellow. This has always been one of my favorite lindens, but unfortunately, it is not widely available in commerce. The habit is distinctly pyramidal in youth, tightly broad-pyramidal with a uniform branching structure in old age. The smooth, light gray bark borders on silver-gray, carrying the plant's common name into the winter months. Generally the last of the cultivated lindens to bloom, with yellowish white flowers opening in late June and early July. Requires ample moisture in the early years of establishment. Less troubled by Japanese beetles and insects in general, and overall less prone to the untidiness of the other species. Use as a lawn, street, or specimen tree. Grows 50 to 70 ft. high, 25 to 45 ft. wide. Zones 4 to 7. Southeastern Europe, western Asia.

MORE ▶

Tilia platyphyllos

Tilia tomentosa underside of foliage

Tilia platyphyllos, bigleaf linden

Tilia tomentosa CONTINUED

Tilia tomentosa, silver linden

CULTIVARS AND VARIETIES
'Sterling' is an impressive selection. It has a sculptured, broad pyramidal crown, with the fine foliage and bark features of the species. The parent tree was 45 ft. high and 24 ft. wide after 30 years.

Toona sinensis
syn. *Cedrela sinensis*

Chinese toon

This tree-of-heaven (*Ailanthus altissima*) look-alike is not meant for the everyday gardener, but its environmental adaptability might keep it in good standing with urban planners. At maturity, it develops a rather coarse, upright-spreading outline. The species also suckers, meaning that one tree may, like a sumac, become a grove. The dark green leaves are composed of 10 to 22 leaflets, each 3 to 6 in. long, that emerge bronzy red in spring. Bruised foliage has an onion-like odor. The brown bark peels

Toona sinensis

Toona sinensis

Toona sinensis, Chinese toon

off in long strips. Fruit are 1- to 1½-in.-long, woody capsules that look like roses when mature. The species tolerates extremes of soil and climate and might prove beneficial on infertile, eroded, or abused soils. Grows 30 to 40 ft. high, variable spread. Noble 80-ft.-high giant at Jefferson's Monticello. Zones 5 to 8. Northern and eastern China.

Toona sinensis 'Flamingo'

Torreya taxifolia

Torreya taxifolia

CULTIVARS AND VARIETIES

'Flamingo' is an interesting form with rose- or pink- to cream-colored new foliage that matures to green. Cut back in late winter to induce long, colorful spring shoot extensions.

Torreya taxifolia

stinking cedar, Florida torreya

The first inclination is to identify this species as yew, *Taxus*, but a clasp of the foliage indicates something else. The stiff and prickly pointed needles literally penetrate the skin, compared to the soft, flexible needles of yew. A handsome needle evergreen, usually loosely pyramidal in outline. A dense, broad-pyramidal specimen in

Torreya taxifolia, stinking cedar

Monticello, Florida, is, at 30 to 35 ft. high, the largest I have observed. The gray-brown bark, ridged and furrowed, forms a woven pattern. Each 1- to 1¾-in.-long needle is flat, lustrous dark green with gray-green bands below. When bruised, a stinky odor is evident, hence, one of the common names. The olive-like, naked seed, dark green with purplish stripes, 1 to 1¼ in. long, ½ to ¾ in. wide, develops on female plants. Listed federally as an endangered species; the Atlanta Botanical Garden and Arnold Arboretum have contributed greatly to propagation and preservation. Not for the everyday garden, but for the gardener

MORE ▶

Torreya nucifera, Japanese torreya

to know, appreciate, and preserve at all its worth. Most plants I observed are 10 to 20 ft. in height. Zones 6 to 9. Found on wooded slopes and bluffs east of the Apalachicola River and northward into Georgia.

Torreya nucifera, Japanese torreya, with ¾- to 1¼-in.-long, lustrous dark green needles with sharp apices, is a superior ornamental. A great and noble specimen, 40 ft. high, is ensconced on the Swarthmore campus outside Philadelphia. Zones 6 to 8. Japan.

Trachelospermum asiaticum

Japanese star or Asiatic jasmine

I first experienced this species over 35 years ago, used as a groundcover on the Louisiana State University campus at Baton Rouge, and thought it one of the most beautiful plants. Calmer, cooler, more even-tempered and "together" than *Trachelospermum jasminoides*, it provides the uniform lustrous dark green effect that remains the domain of "true" groundcovers. The evergreen leaves are ¾ to 2 in. long, elliptic to ovate, and glossy dark green with darker veins. I have yet to experience flowers on the species in a groundcover planting but have observed the yellowish white, ¾-in.-wide, fragrant flowers on climbing specimens. Occasionally, *T. jasminoides* is mixed with *T. asiaticum* in groundcover plantings; the former

Trachelospermum asiaticum, Japanese star jasmine

Trachelospermum asiaticum

grows taller and flowers. *Trachelospermum asiaticum* is utilized more frequently in zone 7, and new cultivars have heightened landscape interest. Tolerates full sun and shade. Drought-tolerant compared to *Vinca* species. Plantings are often damaged by late winter to early spring freezes, which render the foliage brown. I suspect the plant dehardens in response to the first warm weather (about 60°F), and the leaves become sensitive to low temperatures that follow. By June, foliage has regenerated. Excellent groundcover and in zones 8 and 9 has few peers. Grows 6 to 12 in. high, spreading and rooting laterally. Grows 15 to 20 ft. high on a structure. Zones 7 to 9. Japan, Korea.

CULTIVARS AND VARIETIES
Extremely dark green, smaller leaf forms like 'Elegant' and 'Nortex' are in cultivation. Variegated leaf forms, usu-ally cream-splotched or -margined, are available.

'Ogon-nishiki' (Salsa™) with bright red-orange leaves, yellow-gold centers, slowly becoming green but maintaining variegation, is a real traffic-stopper. Has become more common in Southeast.

Snow-N-Summer™ ('HOSNS') develops pink new shoots, then white, then green spots/specks/blotches on white background, eventually turning dark green with white veins (some leaves).

Trachelospermum jasminoides
Confederate or star jasmine
Multi-talented, broadleaf evergreen groundcover or vine, with sweetly scented flowers in spring to summer and terrific cultural adaptability. Used as a groundcover on the Georgia campus to stabilize slopes, it has outcom-peted English ivy and blanketed entire areas. As a groundcover, the stems twine around each other, producing a carrot-top effect. It grows no more than 18 in. high but does not provide the carpet-like effect of *Vinca* and *Pachysandra*. A climbing structure like a trellis, coarse tree trunk, or wire is required if it is to be utilized as a vine. I had lunch in Augusta, Georgia, where a woven fence surrounding the eating area was covered with this species. Never did a cheeseburger taste (and smell) so delectable. The 1½- to 3½-in.-long leaves emerge bronze-purple and mature lustrous dark green with pronounced darker green veins. Flowers, shaped like boat propellers, five-petaled, cream to yellow, and fragrant, appear in April and May in Athens and sporadically thereafter. Easy to culture, requiring only good drainage. Best in

MORE ▶

Trachelospermum asiaticum 'Ogon-nishiki'

Trachelospermum jasminoides

Trachelospermum asiaticum Snow-N-Summer™

Trachelospermum jasminoides 'Variegatum'

Trachelospermum jasminoides CONTINUED
some shade, but plants in full sun grow well. Winter sun and wind may cause some degree of discoloration. Uses as aforementioned—but it is worth the space to reiterate the garden excellence of this twining vine. Grows 10 to 12 (to 20) ft. high as a vine. Zones (7)8 to 10. Japan, China.
CULTIVARS AND VARIETIES
'Madison' is a more cold hardy selection with heavy pubescence on the underside of the leaf.

'Pink Showers' was touted as having rich pink flowers. I flowered it in the greenhouse, and the pink disappeared almost before my eyes. Perhaps better outside.

'Variegatum' is bordered and blotched with cream, the interior of the leaf is gray-green; in winter, creamy areas turn pinkish red to carmine. Several forms with comparable variegation patterns are in commerce.

Triadica sebifera
syn. *Sapium sebiferum*
Chinese tallow tree
Entertaining and educational how one person's weed is another's garden treasure. This species is just such a double-edged sword, with rampageous, self-seeding, noxious weed status in the coastal South and respectable small tree status in zone 7. Habit is pyramidal to rounded with a thin, airy canopy. The poplar-like leaves are bright to medium green, 1½ to 3 in. long and wide, turning yellow to reddish purple in fall. The inner leaves color first, with the outer following along; the effect is never overwhelming in zone 7. Flowers, greenish yellow, appear in the same structure, the males at the apex, females at base. The eventual fruit are three-valved capsules containing white, wax-coated seeds. I have seen it in south Georgia, Alabama, and northern Florida, where it has wreaked havoc upon the native vegetation. Grows 30 to 40 ft. high and wide. Zones (7)8 to 10. China.

Sapium japonicum has longer, darker blue-green leaves that turn

Trachelospermum jasminoides, Confederate jasmine

Triadica sebifera

Triadica sebifera fall color

Triadica sebifera

handsome reddish purple in fall. Each leaf is 3 to 5 in. long, 2 to 4 in. wide, and broad-ovate rather than deltoid, as in *Triadica sebifera*. Flowers in slender, axillary, catkin-like, greenish yellow racemes in May. Trees I observed were small, 20 to 30 ft. high. Zones (7)8 and 9. May actually be more cold hardy than *T. sebifera*. China, Korea, Japan.

Trochodendron aralioides
wheel tree

Rare broadleaf evergreen tree, primarily relegated to the sanctuaries of arbo-reta and botanical gardens. At Hillier Arboretum, there are so many that, in cleaning and thinning an area, I was afforded the privilege of cutting down a 20-ft.-high tree. My hands trembled, the blade quivered, the wheel tree groaned. Never again will I be coerced into such a heinous act. Develops a pyramidal outline with tiered branches. Foliage is lustrous dark green, each leaf 3 to 6 in. long, with prominent crenate serrations toward the apex. Flowers are bright green, ¾ in. in diameter, with a spoke-like arrangement of 40 to 70 stamens. Locate in moist, acid, woodsy, well-drained soil in shade. Protect from wind to keep foliage from discoloring. Strictly a conversation piece, but the unique habit and foliage combine favorably with other evergreens. Grows 10 to 20 ft. high, one-half this in spread. Zones 6 and 7. Japan, Korea, and Taiwan, where it grows in mountain forests. *Hillier Manual* (2007) mentioned this species was unharmed and quite outstanding when most evergreens looked bedraggled

MORE ▶

Trochodendron aralioides

Triadica sebifera, Chinese tallow tree

Trochodendron aralioides, wheel tree

817

Trochodendron aralioides CONTINUED
after the severe winter of 1962–63. Respectable trees at Longwood Gardens and Coker, Raulston, and Keith arboreta.

Tsuga canadensis
Canadian or eastern hemlock

What a grand needle evergreen— softly pyramidal in outline, deep green needles, good tolerance of shade or sun, and many landscape uses. I have never met a specimen I did not appreciate. The ½- to ¾-in.-long needles have two silver bands on their undersides. The ½- to ¾-in.-long, ovoid, brown cones look like dangling ornaments. The rich brown bark is ridged and deeply furrowed on old trees. Transplant balled and burlapped or from a container into cool, moist, acid, well-drained soils. Protect from desiccating winter winds. Does not display great tolerance to heat or urban stress. Use as a specimen or in screens and groupings; can also be fashioned into a magnificent hedge. Grows 40 to 70 ft. high, 25 to 35 ft. wide. National champion is 156 ft. by 53 ft. Zones 3 to 7. Nova Scotia to Minnesota, south in the mountains to Alabama and Georgia. Unfortunately, on the East Coast *Tsuga canaden-*

Tsuga mertensiana

Tsuga canadensis, Canadian hemlock

Tsuga mertensiana, mountain hemlock

sis has suffered from attacks of the woolly adelgid, which has taken the wind out of the sails (and sales) of this great, native conifer. I have witnessed the devastation caused by the adelgid to native trees in the southern Appalachians. Ecologically frightening what an introduced pest can do.

Tsuga mertensiana, mountain hemlock, and *T. heterophylla*, western hemlock, are western species of great beauty, the former with narrower habit and green-gray-blue needles, the latter looser in outline, perhaps more graceful, with dark green needles. Both are large trees, with national champions over 150 ft. high.

CULTIVARS AND VARIETIES
Astronomical in number; only specialized treatises can do justice to the broad range. One of the most notable cultivars is mentioned here.

'Sargentii' (var. *sargentii*) is one of the best weeping evergreens for general use. It is commercially common and reasonably priced. As a freestanding specimen in a lawn, by the edge of a stream, or cascading over rocks, or as a container plant, it has great worth. The broadly weeping habit can be controlled with judicious pruning. Grows 10 to 15 ft. high, 20 to 30 ft.

MORE ▶

Tsuga canadensis

Tsuga heterophylla

Tsuga heterophylla, western hemlock

Tsuga canadensis CONTINUED

wide; an old specimen at the Biltmore Estate in Asheville, North Carolina, is 25 to 30 ft. high.

Tsuga caroliniana
Carolina hemlock

Many gardeners rave about this species, but to my mind, it is inferior to *Tsuga canadensis*. I have observed several young and mature specimens, and my heart never missed a beat. The habit is supposedly more compact and more narrowly pyramidal than that of *T. canadensis*, but trees I have observed are more open-foliaged. The ¼- to ¾-in.-long, dark green needles have two white bands on their undersides, and they are entire along the margin, a detail that separates this species from *T. canadensis*. Also, the 1- to 1½-in.-long, 1-in.-wide cones have scales that radiate from the central axis, as opposed to overlapping like those of *T. canadensis*. Supposedly more tolerant of urban conditions, but I know of no quantitative data that supports this. Susceptible to woolly adelgid feeding. Makes a respectable specimen plant. Not common in commerce. Grows 45 to 60 ft. high, 20 to 25 ft. wide. Zones 4 to 7. Southeastern United States. Observed many times in northeast Georgia, growing from the sides of rocky cliffs, ravines, and gorges.

Tsuga chinensis
Chinese hemlock

Chinese hemlock is touted for its resistance to woolly adelgid feeding and the potential for breeding with *Tsuga canadensis*. I tested the species in Athens and it simply sat there, never growing with any enthusiasm. Needles are ½ to 1 in. long, $\frac{1}{12}$ to ⅛ in. wide, glossy dark green with broad whitish bands beneath. Grows more than 100 ft. in China. Hybrids have been consummated, are elegant and more *T. canadensis*–like in habit. Am hopeful they are resistant to the adelgid. Breeding was initiated by USDA-U.S. National Arboretum. Zones 5 and 6.

Tsuga caroliniana

Tsuga chinensis

Tsuga caroliniana, Carolina hemlock

Tsuga chinensis, Chinese hemlock

Tsuga diversifolia
northern Japanese hemlock

This species is a real beauty with gracefully arching, pyramidal habit and lustrous dark green needles, each only ¼ to ⅝ in. long, and densely borne with two clearly defined, chalk-white bands below. Grows in Maine and North Carolina. Observed three magnificent 40-ft.-high trees at Mount Congreve Gardens in Ireland. The Maine tree was designated 'Emerald Ice'. Zones (4)5 and 6. Japan.

Ulmus
elm

In the 1940s and '50s, elms were absolutely hammered by Dutch elm disease (DED) and phloem necrosis, especially American and European species (the Asiatic taxa were resistant). Significant breeding in the Netherlands and North America has produced a panoply of resistant elms with a range of growth characteristics. I have observed most of the new wave and herein provide encapsulated thoughts of aesthetics and degrees of resistance.

In my finite time on this green Earth, entire cities and towns have been ravaged by DED, with few to no trees surviving. What to do? Diversify! Consider *Ulmus japonica* and *U. parvifolia*, taxa that offer significant resistance. In fact, a venerable specimen of *U. japonica* by South College Building, now more than a century old, along with an ancient grove behind the chancellor's residence, University

MORE ▶

Tsuga diversifolia

Tsuga diversifolia, northern Japanese hemlock

Ulmus alata

Ulmus CONTINUED

of Massachusetts, Amherst, have observed most American elms retire to the woodpile in the sky. Hybrids by Dr. George Ware, Morton Arboretum, using *U. japonica* (as well as *U. minor*, *U. pumila*, and *U. wilsoniana*) are significantly resistant, and hopefully his work with 12 Chinese species will be continued. But even the newer resistant cultivars of *U. americana*, American elm, should be viewed (and planted) with caution: the fungus has previously mutated to a more virulent strain and may do so again.

Ulmus alata, winged elm, fall color

Ulmus alata 'Lace Parasol'

Ulmus alata
winged elm

Afforded not even casual glances by the woody cognoscenti because of commonality, perceived miserable habit, and mildew-laden leaves. Hold the negatives! I too was disrespectful, having seen many trees overrun with mildew that turned the entire tree ghostly gray in late summer and fall. However, selected trees appear resistant. The habit can be scruffy, but large, 70-ft.-high trees, like *Ulmus americana*, American elm, in outline, are reasonably common. Leaves are smaller versions of American elm leaves, 1 to 2½ in. long, dark green, turning yellow in autumn. Flowers, greenish red, appear in February and are followed by oval, ⅓-in.-long, hairy samaras. Tends to seed everywhere and becomes weed-like. Grows in the most miserable soils. With selection for desirable traits, it has the potential for restrained use in urban settings. Grows 50 to 60 ft. high, two-thirds this in spread. Zones 6 to 9. Virginia to Florida, west to Illinois, Oklahoma, and Texas.

CULTIVARS AND VARIETIES
'Lace Parasol' was discovered by Dr. Charles Keith in Chapel Hill, North Carolina, and given to the JC Raulston Arboretum. The plant is stiffly weeping with prominently two-winged stems that resemble a weeping *Euonymus alatus*. Leaves contract mildew in summer and fall. A beautiful accent plant, particularly in the winter garden. The original plant is now 20 ft. high, 30 ft. wide, kind of like a giant multi-legged spider.

Ulmus americana
American elm

A fantastic, majestic, almost-perfect native tree that once permeated the consciousness of every American. Unfortunately, Dutch elm disease stripped our cities, towns, and gardens of this green beauty. Majestic in habit, American elm has an upright-spreading outline and semi-pendent outer

branches. Trees planted along boule-
vards meet to form cathedral ceiling–
like archways. The 3- to 6-in.-long,
leathery, dark green leaves turn butter-
yellow to rich yellow in autumn. This
elm species and, to my knowledge, all
elms are very easy to transplant and
withstand extremes of soil conditions
and pH. From a pragmatic viewpoint, it
is difficult to recommend this species
because of the disease problem. If the
newer, resistant selections prove successful, then I would consider planting,
but still in a cautious vein. Grows 60 to
80 ft. high, 30 to 50 ft. wide. Zones 2
to 9. Newfoundland to Florida, west to
the Rockies.

CULTIVARS AND VARIETIES
Considerable effort has been made to
breed and/or select clones that are
resistant to DED. The U.S. National
Arboretum has released 'Valley Forge'
and 'New Harmony'. These two, along
with 'Creole Queen', 'Jefferson', Prairie
Expedition™ ('Lewis and Clark'), and

MORE ▶

Ulmus americana 'Princeton' fall color

Ulmus americana, American elm

Ulmus crassifolia, cedar elm

Ulmus glabra 'Horizontalis'

'Princeton', are the best of the resistant types. 'Princeton' and 'Valley Forge' are the most available in commerce.

Ulmus crassifolia
cedar elm

Like *Ulmus alata*, left behind in the commercial world but used with some regularity in the Southwest. I remember seeing numerous specimens in San Antonio, Texas. A large tree, oval-rounded, with dense branches and 1- to 2-in.-long, dark green leaves, stiff and rough to the touch, like sandpaper. Flowers and fruit are unremarkable. Withstands drought and heavy, infertile soils; pH adaptable. A reasonable street and lawn tree for drier areas of the South and Southwest. Not superior to *U. parvifolia*. Grows 50 to 70 ft. high, 40 to 60 ft. wide. Zones 7 to 9. Mississippi to Arkansas and Texas.

Ulmus glabra
Scotch elm

Because of Dutch elm disease, elm leaf beetle, and general scruffiness, this species does not deserve planting, at least not in the United States. Zones 4 to 6(7). Northern and central Europe, western Asia.

CULTIVARS AND VARIETIES
Two cultivars, although not without their foibles, deserve mention. Both are susceptible to DED and elm leaf beetle but, based on the number of extant specimens, are more resistant than the species.

Ulmus crassifolia

'Camperdownii' is a strong weeping form. The dark green, sandpapery leaves seem to hover in the summer landscape. The leaves abscise to expose a handsome silhouette of weeping branches that sweep the ground. It bears few to no fruit. Effective as a character or accent plant. Usually grafted 6 to 7 ft. high on a standard, it grows 20 to 25 ft. high.

'Horizontalis' is often sold as 'Camperdownii' and in many arboreta is labeled as such, but it has smoother leaves, abundant fruit, and branches that are semi-pendent, never really touching the ground. Grows 15 ft. high, 33 ft. wide.

Ulmus minor
syn. *Ulmus carpinifolia*
smoothleaf elm
Probably, if one took the time and searched every nursery catalog in the

MORE ▶

Ulmus glabra 'Camperdownii'

Ulmus minor, smoothleaf elm

Ulmus minor 'Sarniensis'

Ulmus minor CONTINUED

United States, this elm or one of its cultivars might be offered in one or two. At one time, smoothleaf elm was widely planted, particularly in the Midwest and Northeast, where it is found on campuses. This species is susceptible to Dutch elm disease, but not to the degree of *Ulmus americana*. The habit is weakly pyramidal-oval, with a straight trunk and slender, ascending branches. The 1½- to 4-in.-long, lustrous dark green leaves develop limited yellow fall color. Damage from the elm leaf beetle (browning of leaves) is also often evident. Several magnificent trees behind the director's home at the Missouri Botanical Garden ascend to 80 ft. in height. Grows 70 to 90 ft. high. Zones 5 to 7. Europe.
CULTIVARS AND VARIETIES
'Sarniensis' is narrowly upright conical in habit with glossy dark green, 1¾- to 2½-in.-long leaves. Grows 60 to 70 ft. high. I see occasionally in Mid-Atlantic and New England states. Susceptible to DED.

Ulmus parvifolia
Chinese or lacebark elm

Without question, the dominant elm shade and street tree of the 21st century. In the past, this species suffered in popularity, because it was often confused with the woeful *Ulmus pumila*, Siberian elm, and simply because it was an elm, which to many people connotes susceptibility to disease. But *U. parvifolia* has proven highly resistant to Dutch elm disease and the elm leaf beetle, facts that have been borne out by scientific research. The habit is generally rounded with a finely textured, uniform branching structure. The ¾- to 2½-in.-long, leathery, dark green leaves may turn yellow to burgundy in fall. The most endearing ornamental characteristic of this species is the splendid exfoliating bark, which shows shades of gray, green, brown, and orange. The bark brings welcome color to the winter landscape, and the tree is worth incorporating into the garden for that reason alone. Unbelievably adaptable to extremes of soil and climate, it thrives from Iowa to Florida and from the Atlantic Coast

Ulmus parvifolia Athena® Classic

Ulmus parvifolia Allée®

Ulmus parvifolia Allée®

Ulmus parvifolia 'Milliken'

to the Pacific. A great lawn, street, park, or grove tree. Its greatest days are ahead. Grows 40 to 50 ft. high and wide; the variation in size, however, is phenomenal. Seedlings of *U. parvifolia* are so variable that the gardener may end up with a bonsai specimen or a 70-ft. tree. Zones 5 to 9. China, Korea, Japan, Taiwan.

CULTIVARS AND VARIETIES
Many superior new selections are now being produced in commerce. The following offer great hope for the 21st-century landscape.

Allée® ('Emer II') is perhaps the finest introduction because of its resemblance to American elm. It has an upright-spreading outline, dark green leaves, and astounding gray to orange-brown exfoliating bark. The original tree's 3-ft.-wide trunk is fluted (corrugated), and the bark's brilliant mosaic extends from the 2-in.-wide branches to the exposed surface roots. The parent tree was 70 ft. high and 60 ft. wide.

Athena® Classic ('Emer I') is a broad-spreading-rounded tree with fine-textured branches. The leathery, extremely lustrous dark green leaves abscise early in autumn with a hint of yellow-bronze coloration. The bark develops the typical puzzle-piece pattern of gray, gray-green, and orangish

MORE ▶

Ulmus parvifolia 'Golden Rey'

Ulmus parvifolia 'Drake'

Ulmus parvifolia Everclear®

Ulmus parvifolia CONTINUED

brown. The parent tree was 30 to 35 ft. high, 55 ft. wide.

'Drake' is common in the Deep South and West. Habit is more rounded-spreading, 20 to 30 ft. high, wider at maturity. Develops exfoliating, richly colored bark. Not particularly cold hardy; −5 to −10°F will cause injury.

Everclear® ('BSNUPF') is an upright, columnar selection with lustrous dark green foliage. Original tree was 40 ft. by 15 ft. Introduced by Bold Spring Nursery, Hawkinsville, Georgia.

'Frontier' is a vase-shaped hybrid (*Ulmus minor* × *U. parvifolia*) with dark green foliage that supposedly turns red in fall (15 years in Georgia trials produced *no* fall color); grew 27 ft. by 16 ft. in 19 years. Gray-brown, moderately ridged and furrowed bark.

'Golden Rey' ('Golden Ray', 'Aurea') develops a broad-spreading outline with yellow foliage. Excellent gray-orange-brown exfoliating bark. About 30 ft. high.

'Milliken' is an oval-rounded form with rich green foliage and prominent exfoliating bark. Develops a white oak–like outline at maturity. Parent tree was 50 ft. high, 40 ft. wide.

'Small Frye' is a "perfect" mushroom-headed small tree with uniform dense branching and thickish, lustrous dark green leaves. Potential for use under power lines and where vertical space is limited. Bark exfoliates in gray, orange, brown patchwork. Parent tree 18 ft. by 25 ft.; selected by the author.

Ulmus pumila
Siberian elm

What a disastrous tree—unfortunately, it is still sold and planted. Many arborists made their fortunes from the limb breakage and general decline of this species. Usually I can find a bright light in every tree's closet—not so here. Although highly

Ulmus pumila, Siberian elm

Ulmus parvifolia 'Small Frye'

Ulmus parvifolia 'Milliken' fall color

resistant to Dutch elm disease, the leaves of Siberian elm are unbelievably susceptible to elm leaf beetle. In fact, the tree often looks like a brown bag in summer because of the incessant beetle feeding. The dark green leaves are ¾ to 3 in. long and have no appreciable fall color. Admittedly, the species will tolerate miserable climates and soils, and it has been used for hybridizing purposes to impart resistance to DED. With the resistance, however, came the susceptibility to the elm leaf beetle, and the introductions, such as 'Urban', 'Homestead', and 'Pioneer', are less than satisfactory. Grows 50 to 70 ft. high, 40 to 50 ft. wide. Zones 4 to 9.

Eastern Siberia, northern and northeastern China, Korea

Ulmus Cultivars

Several elms, often of complex hybrid parentage, were selected for their resistance to Dutch elm disease, but they do not always embody other quality elm traits. 'Cathedral', 'Frontier', 'Jacan', 'New Horizon', 'Prospector', 'Regal', and 'Sapporo Autumn Gold' represent a few of the selections that gardeners and horticulturists might consider.

Emerald Sunshine® ('JFS-Bieberich') has thick-textured, lustrous dark green leaves, densely pubescent below, resistant to beetle feeding.

Excited about this DED-resistant, American elm–shaped, *Ulmus japonica* selection.

Ware Hybrids: Accolade® ('Morton), Commendation™ ('Morton Stalwart'), Danada Charm™ ('Morton Red Tip'), Triumph™ ('Morton Glossy'), and Vanguard™ ('Morton Plainsman'). Accolade® has exceedingly glossy dark green leaves, rich golden yellow fall color, and high DED resistance; witnessed a wild and splaying Accolade®, the leaves covered with galls, at Missouri Botanical Garden. Triumph™, with better habit than the former, dark green foliage, and DED resistance, is the best in my opinion; it outperforms the others in zone 7 and in youth is more uniform and dense—i.e., it has the appearance of a tree the gardener would want to plant.

Ungnadia speciosa
Mexican buckeye

Shrubby, often multi-stemmed, it develops a rounded outline. Leaves are compound pinnate with three to 13 leaflets, lustrous dark green, turning golden yellow in fall. Showstopping beauty is provided by the rich rosy pink, redbud-like flowers that, in Georgia, open on naked stems in March and April and continue as the leaves develop. Each fragrant flower is up to 1 in. wide and composed of four or five petals with prominent stamens. The

MORE ▶

Ulmus Triumph™

Ulmus japonica Emerald Sunshine®

Ungnadia speciosa CONTINUED

capsular, brown fruit, with three cells, resemble buckeye and dehisce to release the black, ½-in.-wide, rounded seeds. Durable species that grows in sandy, limestone soils in the wild but has performed well in the heavier soils of Georgia. Useful as a specimen plant and in borders and groupings.

Ungnadia speciosa

Although adaptable in the Southeast, the species has not made a dent in commerce. Grows 10 to 15 ft. high and wide. Zones (7)8 to 10. Texas, New Mexico, and northern Mexico.

Vaccinium angustifolium
lowbush blueberry

Lowbush blueberry is the most economically productive native fruit crop in the state of Maine, and native stands of the plant are simply managed to prevent excessive weed growth. The species is rarely planted in cultivation, but the white to delicate pink and rose flowers and sweet, bluish black berries are justification for use. It is a spreading, stoloniferous shrub, with lustrous dark green to blue-green foliage that turns brilliant yellow to scarlet and crimson in fall. Requires nothing but acid, low-fertility soils, in full sun or partial shade. Makes a fine groundcover mass and needs minimal maintenance. One of Maine's natural wonders and, on many occasions, Bonnie and I have photographed glowing red swaths of low-

bush blueberry, interrupted only by a menagerie of granite boulders. Grows 6 to 24 in. high. Zones 2 to 5. Newfoundland to Saskatchewan, south to the mountains of New Hampshire and New York.

Vaccinium arboreum
sparkleberry, farkleberry

Absolutely beautiful, native, large shrub/small tree that offers the garden an aesthetic attribute in every season. Native on our property—I love to watch it sing and dance. Spring brings small, white flowers in profusion; summer the leathery, glossiest foliage imaginable; fall provides rich red to crimson leaves and shiny black fruit; and winter the exposed bark in grays, rich browns, oranges, and reddish browns. Sound worthy? It knows how to dress for the seasons, but even better is its street (cultural) toughness. Found as an understory plant, often in drier woods, with hickories, oaks, tupelos, and beeches. With all the hype, the truth must be told: it is difficult to find in

Vaccinium angustifolium, lowbush blueberry

Vaccinium angustifolium

Ungnadia speciosa, Mexican buckeye

commerce. Virtually impossible to root from shoot cuttings, so seed propagation is necessary. Root cuttings would probably work. Great understory filler. A stunning native that has resisted commercialization. Grows 15 to 20 ft. high. Zones 7 to 9. Virginia to North Carolina to Florida, southern Illinois and Texas.

Vaccinium ashei
rabbiteye blueberry

Many botanists consider this species little more than the southern extension of *Vaccinium corymbosum*. Taxonomically, perhaps—horticulturally, no! The large, upright-spreading habit with coarse, gray-brown stems

MORE ▶

Vaccinium ashei, rabbiteye blueberry

Vaccinium arboreum fall color

Vaccinium arboreum

Vaccinium arboreum, sparkleberry

Vaccinium arboreum

Vaccinium angustifolium fall color

Vaccinium ashei CONTINUED

makes it a poor fit for smaller landscapes. The 1- to 2½-in.-long, blue-green leaves turn shades of red in autumn. Fall color can be spectacular and is often long persistent, up to four weeks. The ¼-in.-long, urn-shaped, white flowers appear on naked stems in March and April. The fruit mature in June and July (Athens) and are the most beautiful powder blue to purplish

Vaccinium ashei

Vaccinium ashei Blue Suede® fall color

Vaccinium ashei Blue Suede®

blue. Fruit are rounded, ⅜ to ½ in. across, sweet and scrumptious. Provide moist, acid soil and full sun, and let them be. Excellent for use along the side of the vegetable garden. Also blends well in the shrub border. Grows 8 to 10 (to 12) ft. high. Zones 7 to 9. Southeastern United States.
CULTIVARS AND VARIETIES
Rabbiteye blueberry, like its northern relative, has been hybridized, and numerous fruit-producing cultivars have been introduced, each with its own rich blue patina. Wise to plant two different cultivars to ensure cross-pollination and heavy fruit set. 'Climax', 'Tifblue', and 'Woodard' are among the best of the approximately 20 cultivars for home-garden fruit production. The University of Georgia has long been the leader in breeding rabbiteye selections, and Dr. Scott NeSmith continues the tradition with 'Alapaha', 'Camellia', 'Ochlockonee', 'Palmetto', 'Rebel', and 'Vernon'.

Blue Suede® is a new, self-pollinating (self-fertile) selection from Dr. NeSmith, with white flowers, large powder-blue sweet fruit, glaucous rich blue summer foliage, orange-red fall color, and compact habit, 3 to 5 ft. high and wide. Will prove a great home garden plant.

'Sunshine Blue' (aka 'Blue Pearl') is a self-fertile cultivar with red buds, pink flowers, medium-size, sweet blue fruit, blue-green leaves, and rich red fall color. Grows 4 to 5 ft. high and wide.

Vaccinium corymbosum
highbush blueberry

For years, I have touted this most handsome shrub as a fine ornamental that also produces sufficient blueberries for cereal, jams, and pies. It is an excellent choice for incorporating in the border or the back of the vegetable garden. A strong, multi-stemmed shrub, its spreading branches form a rounded, dense, compact outline, especially when grown in full sun. The winter stems vary from yellow-green to deep red. The 1- to 3½-in.-long, dark green to blue-green leaves may turn yellow, bronze, orange, or red in fall. White or pink-tinged, ⅓-in.-long, urn-shaped flowers are borne in axillary racemes in April and May. The blue-black, waxy-coated, ¼- to ½-in.-wide fruit ripen in July and August. Fruit are not as sweet as those of *Vaccinium angustifolium*. Provide acid soils. Most blueberry plants are container-grown and present no transplanting problem. Grows 6 to 12 ft. high, 8 to 12 ft.

Vaccinium corymbosum, highbush blueberry

wide. Zones 3 to 7. Maine to Minnesota, south to Florida and Louisiana.

Vaccinium crassifolium
creeping blueberry

Unusual evergreen groundcover blueberry with lustrous dark green, finely serrate, ⅓- to ¾-in.-long, ⅛- to ⅜-in.-wide, oval leaves. Rose-red, ¼-in.-wide flowers occur in short lateral and terminal racemes in May. Requires sandy, acid, well-drained soil in partial shade. Beautiful in the right situation, simply not an adaptable groundcover. Grows 6 in. high (as I witnessed the plant), although 24 in. is mentioned in the literature; continuously spreading and rooting. Zones 7 and 8. North Carolina to Georgia.

CULTIVARS AND VARIETIES
Creeping blueberry was part of the breeding program at North Carolina State University; the several cultivars selected have had a difficult time in commerce because of susceptibility to phytophthora root rot and stem anthracnose.

'Bloodstone' is a subsp. *sempervirens* form with reddish new growth that matures to lustrous dark green. Grows 6 to 8 in. high and makes a rather pretty groundcover.

'Wells Delight' offers lustrous dark green elliptic leaves.

Vaccinium elliottii

What a beauty, especially in November and December, when the leaves become rich red to purplish red. Exists as an understory shrub, finely branched, gently upright-spreading, and finally arching. Stems are green in summer, becoming red in autumn. The mirror-surfaced, rich green leaves, ½ to 1¼ in. long, finely serrate, turn rich red and reddish purple and persist into December (Athens). White to pink flowers occur in two- to six-flowered fascicles from buds of the previous season's wood before the leaves in March and April. The ⅓-in.-wide, black fruit ripen in summer. The berries are sweet and edible. Prospers in well-drained, acid, moist soils. Appears to tolerate considerable drought. Terrific naturalizing shrub for the shade. Common around Athens, where it grows at woodland edges and in deep shade. Over its range occurs in lowlands to drier upland habitats. Grows 6 to 12 ft. high and wide. Zones 6 to 9. Southeastern Virginia to north Florida, westward to east Texas and Arkansas.

Vaccinium stamineum
deerberry

Variable shrub with green to glaucous blue-green foliage, often wispy and arching habit, but capable of growing to 15 ft. high. The ¾- to 3-in.-long

MORE ▶

Vaccinium corymbosum

Vaccinium corymbosum

Vaccinium corymbosum fall color

Vaccinium elliottii fall color

Vaccinium stamineum CONTINUED

Vaccinium stamineum, deerberry

leaves are either entire or slightly toothed. The small, white flowers resemble miniature bells with the pistil-stamen complex about twice as long as the corollas. Flowers hang from the leaf axils and combine quite harmoniously with the foliage in April and May. Fruit are ⅓-in.-wide, whitish to purple, globose to pear-shaped berries. Found in shade and sandy soils in the wild. I have walked through large, wild seedling populations with no two plants exactly alike. Excellent native shrub for naturalizing. Grows 2 to 10 ft. high (my observations). Zones 5 to 9. Massachusetts to Minnesota, south to Florida and Louisiana.

Vaccinium vitis-idaea
cowberry

Cowberry is an evergreen groundcover that seldom reaches more than 10 in. in height. The lustrous dark green leaves develop metallic mahogany winter color. White or pinkish flowers bloom in May and June and are fol-

Vaccinium vitis-idaea, cowberry

Vaccinium vitis-idaea var. minus

Vernicia fordii, tung-oil tree

Vernicia fordii

Vernicia fordii

lowed by ⅜-in.-wide, dark red fruit that ripen in August. Provide moist, peaty, acid, well-drained soils, in full sun or partial shade. Makes a handsome rock garden plant. Zones 4 and 5. Northern United States, Canada.

CULTIVARS AND VARIETIES

Variety *minus* has smaller fruit than var. *major*, lingonberry. The latter is utilized for tart (unless sugar is added) jellies, jams, juices, and sauces.

Vernicia fordii
syn. *Aleurites fordii*

tung-oil tree

Many years past, on the campus of Louisiana State University, Baton Rouge, I spied a completely unknown (to me) small tree with the glossiest dark green, deeply veined leaves. Detective work coupled with a worthy reference text pointed to tung-oil tree. Once experienced, it is impossible to forget. The habit is pyramidal to rounded with a dense canopy of foliage. Leaves may remain evergreen in warmer climates but turn brown and

abscise where freezes occur. The flowers are beautiful, white changing to rose in center, bell-shaped, and borne in 6- to 8-in.-long panicles during mid to late spring; flowers in early to mid April in Athens. Fruit are 2- to 3-in.-wide globular drupes, each with three to five seeds. Seeds are the source of tung oil, which is used in the paint and varnish industry. Site in any well-drained soil, sun to partial shade. Grows 10 to 20 ft. high, as wide at maturity. Consistently injured by cold in Athens; often killed back to various degrees but regenerates with gusto. Zones 8 to 10. China.

Viburnum acerifolium

mapleleaf viburnum

This suckering, colonizing denizen of the woods may be the most obscure of all the viburnums, but it offers tremendous shade tolerance and exquisite fall color. The dark green, three-lobed, 2- to 5-in.-long and -wide leaves resemble red maple leaves, hence, the epithet and common name.

The foliage turns fluorescent rose to grape-juice purple in fall. The 1- to 3-in.-wide, white, largely nonfragrant flower clusters open in May and June (April, Athens) and are followed by ⅓-in.-long, shiny black fruit that ripen in September and persist into winter. Adaptable to difficult dry and shady conditions. Use as a mass or filler.

MORE ▶

Vernicia fordii

Viburnum acerifolium fall color

Viburnum acerifolium

Viburnum acerifolium, mapleleaf viburnum

835

Viburnum acerifolium CONTINUED

Grows 4 to 6 ft. high, wider at maturity. Zones 3 to 8. New Brunswick to Minnesota, south to Georgia. Have collided with the species on numerous occasions, and a second take is necessary to confirm identification.

Viburnum awabuki

Viburnum awabuki

Viburnum awabuki

Forever called *Viburnum macrophyllum* or mistaken for *V. japonicum* and *V. odoratissimum* in the South but in recent years provided its correct name. The more I travel through the South, the more often this species surfaces, and an immense old specimen to the left of the number 10 hole at the Augusta National Golf Club reflects its true beauty. Almost pyramidal at maturity, the foliage is so thickly set that the outline resembles a solid green structure. The leaves are beyond leathery, lustrous and dark green, 3 to 7 in. long, ½ to 2 in. wide; they hold their color through the seasons. A plant in the Dirr garden, sited by the front door, was kept in check, pruned to 8 ft. annually. For more than 12 years it was assaulted yet returned quickly to its former glory. White flowers appear in June, in rounded cymose-panicles. Fruit are red, finally black,

Viburnum awabuki 'Variegata'

Viburnum awabuki

but for great numbers a cross-pollinator is necessary. Ubiquitously adaptable, growing in any soil except wet. Tolerates sun and shade with equal facility. Large specimen broadleaf evergreen for screens, borders, and heavy shade plantings. Grows 10 to 15 (to 20) ft. high. Zones (7)8 and 9. Japan.
CULTIVARS AND VARIETIES
'Chindo' was introduced by J. C. Raulston for its large, pendulous, red fruit clusters.

'Variegata' has white-margined leaves that are quite spectacular but do revert to green and white.

Viburnum ×bodnantense

Simply could not omit these early-flowering (December through March), fragrant viburnums from this work. Hybrids between *Viburnum farreri* and *V. grandiflorum*, they are suited to culture in warm climates if properly sited in shade and provided mois-

Viburnum ×bodnantense 'Dawn'

ture in hot, dry weather. The habit is ragged to rugged, upright-spreading with a rounded top. The leaves, 2 to 4 in. long, are heavily pleated with impressed veins, rich green with red petioles. Fall foliage color seldom develops. Flowers occur in small, 1- to 2-in.-wide panicles in winter, actually fall to spring depending on climate. Colors, depending on cultivar, are deep pink ('Charles Lamont'), rich pink ('Dawn'), and shell-pink buds to white ('Deben'). The fragrance is sweet with a slight edge. I observed fruit only once, ovoid, ⅓ in. long, red, finally black in fall. Adaptable species; provide protection from winter wind and sun. Flowers are often singed to browned (burned) by extreme cold. The smallest amount of warmth induces sporadic flowering. *Never* spectacular but always worth waiting for. Grows 8 to 10 (to 15) ft. high and wide. Zones 5 to 7, 8 and 9 on West Coast.

Viburnum bracteatum
bracted viburnum

A rare but singularly beautiful species that is often confused with *Viburnum dentatum* but offers more leathery, lustrous dark green, heat-resistant leaves and is self-fruitful, based on the heavy fruit that occurs on 'Emerald Luster'. Habit is oval-rounded with even-diameter, arrow-shaft stems that eventually arch to form a rounded outline. A 12-ft.-high behemoth grew in the shade of southern red oak, *Quercus falcata*, in the Dirr garden.

Leaves are coarsely dentate, with scalloped margins, 2 to 4 in. long and almost as wide, lustrous dark green turning bronze-yellow in fall. In May, the cream-white, malodorous flowers appear at the end of every shoot in 5-in.-wide, flat-topped cymes. Flowers are showy for a white-flowered viburnum. The beautiful rich blue-purple-black fruit ripen in late summer and are taken by the birds. Tougher-than-nails species that receives little press. Adaptable to anything but wet soil, in

MORE ▶

Viburnum bracteatum 'Emerald Luster'

Viburnum ×bodnantense

Viburnum bracteatum 'Emerald Luster'

Viburnum bracteatum 'Emerald Luster'

Viburnum bracteatum CONTINUED

sun to moderate shade; flowering is maximized in sun. Excellent for the border, in shade and groupings, and for screening. Stems are so thickly set that the plant serves as an effective screen even in winter. Grows 10 ft. high and wide, easily kept smaller by pruning. Zones 6 to 8. Southeastern United States.

CULTIVARS AND VARIETIES
'Emerald Luster', an introduction from my Georgia program, embodies all the traits just mentioned in a single genetic unit.

Viburnum ×burkwoodii
Burkwood viburnum

Viburnum popularity may ebb and flow like the tide, but this hybrid (of *Viburnum utile* and *V. carlesii*) species never goes out of fashion, principally because of its climatic and cultural adaptability. Burkwood viburnum develops into an oval-rounded shrub with a mass of rather fine stems. The 1½- to 4-in.-long, lustrous dark green leaves persist late in fall and may develop a burgundy to red color. In late March (Athens) and April, flower buds emerge pink, opening to 2- to 3-in.-wide, hemispherical, white flowers with the fragrance of winter daphne, *Daphne odora*. Flowers are effective for only seven to ten days. Fruit are red, changing to black, and sparsely produced. Site in moist, acid to neutral, well-drained soils, in full sun (for maximum flowering) to partial shade. A great plant for the shrub border. Grows 8 to 10 ft. high, slightly less in spread. Zones 4 to 8.

Viburnum ×burkwoodii

Viburnum ×burkwoodii

Viburnum ×burkwoodii 'Conoy'

Viburnum ×burkwoodii, Burkwood viburnum

Viburnum ×burkwoodii

Viburnum ×burkwoodii 'Mohawk'

CULTIVARS AND VARIETIES

American Spice™ ('Duvone') is a new introduction with lustrous foliage, spicy-fragrant flowers, and a compact habit; original selection was 4 ft. by 4½ ft. in 14 years. Observed in leaf but not in flower. Foliage is beautiful. Survived ten consecutive days of −20°F.

'Conoy', a densely branched ever-green shrub, 5 to 6 ft. by 6 to 8 ft., resulted from Dr. Egolf's crossing *Viburnum utile* and 'Park Farm Hybrid'. Flowers pink in bud, opening white without fragrance; abundant red to black fruit when cross-pollinated. Grew

successfully for many years in the Dirr garden.

'Mohawk', another Egolf hybrid, rates as one of my top five viburnums: brilliant dark red buds that open to white, deliciously fragrant flowers, glossy dark green leaves, orange-red to red-purple fall color, red to black fruit, and refined habit, 7 to 8 ft. high and wide. I grew many beautiful seedlings from 'Mohawk' seed; several are under evaluation for possible introduction.

'Park Farm Hybrid' is a beauty: large, shiny dark green leaves and

pink-budded, 3- to 5-in.-wide, fragrant flowers. About the largest-flowered *Viburnum* ×*burkwoodii* cultivar. Grows 8 to 10 ft. high and wide.

Viburnum ×*carlcephalum*
fragrant viburnum

This loose, often open shrub offers deliciously fragrant flowers in late April and May. Flowers open late March to early April in Athens. The flowers are pink in bud, finally white, in 5-in.-wide

MORE ▶

Viburnum ×*burkwoodii* 'Park Farm Hybrid'

Viburnum ×*carlcephalum*

Viburnum ×*burkwoodii* 'Park Farm Hybrid'

Viburnum ×*burkwoodii* 'Mohawk' fall color

Viburnum ×*carlcephalum* 'Cayuga'

Viburnum ×carlcephalum CONTINUED

Viburnum ×carlcephalum, fragrant viburnum

Viburnum carlesii, Koreanspice viburnum

clusters of half-snowball shape. The dark green leaves have a slight luster and may develop reddish purple fall color. Use in the border. Grows 6 to 10 (to 15) ft. high and wide. Zones (5)6 to 8.

CULTIVARS AND VARIETIES

'Cayuga' has sheeny, darker green foliage, large fragrant flowers to 5 in. in diameter, and overall improved habit. Original plant was 8½ ft. by 11 ft. after 20 years.

Viburnum carlesii

Koreanspice viburnum

Along with *Viburnum ×burkwoodii*, this is the most familiar *Viburnum* species because of the excellent spicy-sweet fragrance of its flowers. Koreanspice viburnum develops into a dense, rounded shrub with stiff, upright-spreading branches. The 2- to 4-in.-long, dull dark green leaves may develop reddish to wine-red fall color. Pink- to reddish budded flowers open white and offer a wonderful fragrance.

Viburnum carlesii

Viburnum carlesii 'Aurora'

The 2- to 3-in.-wide, semi-snowball inflorescences are at their best in April and May (late March to early April, Athens) when the leaves are about one-half to two-thirds their mature size. Use in a foundation planting, in the border, or in a grouping. Grows 4 to 8 ft. high and wide. Zones 4 to 7. Korea.

CULTIVARS AND VARIETIES
'Aurora' has deep pink-red buds that open to white fragrant flowers in inflorescences up to 5 in. across.

'Compactum' has exceptionally dark green leaves, and its flowers are about the same size as those of the species. Grows 2½ to 3½ ft. high and wide. Listed as 6 ft. by 4 ft. on the West Coast.

'Diana' offers bronze-purple tinged emerging leaves and red flower buds opening to fragrant pink flowers, turning to white. Compact habit, 6 ft. by 8 ft.

Spiced Bouquet™ ('J. N. Select'), Spice Island™ ('JNSA'), and Sugar n' Spice™ ('Select S') offer fragrant flowers, improved summer and fall foliage, and smaller stature (about 5 ft.) than the species. From Johnson's Nursery, Menomonee Falls, Wisconsin.

Viburnum cassinoides
witherod viburnum
A longtime favorite that has followed me from Georgia to Maine and back home again. Lovely, rounded shrub with spreading, arching branches and 1½- to 3½-in.-long, dull, dark green leaves, morphing into yellow, red, and purple in autumn. The new, early-emerging shoots are bronze to chocolate-tinted. The white flowers with yellow stamens are borne in 2- to 5-in.-wide, flat-topped cymes in May and June. The fruit are beautiful, transmogrifying themselves from green to pink-rose to blue to purple-black, often all colors in the same cluster. Fruit ripen in September and October. Adaptable species, growing along Panther Creek in north Georgia and in granite cracks and crevices on Cadillac Mountain, Maine, where it is quite common in moist to wet areas. More compact and heavy-fruiting in full sun but tolerates considerable shade. Beautiful in mass plantings, in borders, and as a filler in shade. Grows 6 to 10 (to 15) ft. high and wide. Zones 3 to 8. Canada to Georgia.

Viburnum cassinoides, witherod viburnum

Viburnum cassinoides

Viburnum cassinoides new growth

Viburnum cassinoides fall color

Viburnum davidii
David viburnum

A favored evergreen viburnum among the cognoscenti but temperamental and better suited to the Mediterranean climate around San Francisco and into British Columbia. In Europe, it is as common as privet and thrives with neglect. The habit is distinctly rounded to mounded, dense, and bulletproof. Possible to bounce a quarter off the tightly affixed foliage. The conspicuous, three-nerved leaves, leathery, lustrous dark green, are 2 to 6 in. long. The pink-budded flowers open dull white in dense, 2- to 3-in.-wide, convex cymes in April and May. Fragrance slight but pleasant. Plants

Viburnum cinnamomifolium

Viburnum davidii, David viburnum

Viburnum davidii

Viburnum davidii

Viburnum cinnamomifolium

Viburnum ×globosum 'Jermyns Globe'

are self-sterile and require cross-pollination for good fruit set. The ¼-in.-long, oval fruit are lustrous metallic blue and persist into winter. Requires moist, well-drained soil and shade protection, particularly in the South. Beautiful when properly grown. Use in groupings and masses and for textural accent. Grows 3 to 5 ft. high and wide. Zones (7)8 and 9. China.

Viburnum cinnamomifolium is a large version of *V. davidii*, reaching 6 to 10 (to 15) ft. high. Atlanta Botanical Garden houses a respectable 6- to 8-ft. specimen. Hardier than *V. davidii* and better adapted to the heat. Zones 6 and 7, 8 and 9 on West Coast. China.

CULTIVARS AND VARIETIES
'Jermyns Globe', a hybrid between *Viburnum davidii* and *V. calvum*, originated at Hillier Arboretum. Leaves are smaller, slightly twisted with an undulating surface, and not as lustrous as *V. davidii*. White flowers and blue fruit. Grows 10 to 12 ft. high and wide. Taxonomically categorized as a cultivar of *V. ×globosum*. Zones 6 and 7 in the East, into 9 and 10 on the West Coast.

Viburnum dentatum
arrowwood viburnum
In any landscape, arrowwood viburnum feels as comfortable as an old shoe, combining a durable nature with glossy dark green leaves, white flowers, and bluish fruit. It becomes a large, rounded shrub with spreading, finally arching branches. The lustrous dark green, 2- to 4½-in.-long leaves may turn yellow to red in fall. The white flowers, scentless to ill-odored, are borne in 2- to 4-in.-wide, flat-topped cymes in May and June. The bluish to blue-black fruit mature in September and October and are a favorite food of birds; plants can be stripped in short order. Valued for its durability and utility, it makes a good hedge or screen and is useful in groupings, masses, and barriers. Susceptible to viburnum leaf beetle feeding. Displays excellent salt tolerance and is evident in New England coastal areas. Variable in size. Grows 6 to 8 (to 15) ft. high, 6 to 15 ft. wide. Zones 2 to 8. New Brunswick to Minnesota, south to Georgia. In the wild, observed it growing in sand near the coast and in moist, swampy habitats.

CULTIVARS AND VARIETIES
Numerous selections, not all that different except for size. Tested many in Georgia, and none were as heat-toler-

MORE ▶

Viburnum dentatum, arrowwood viburnum

Viburnum dentatum

Viburnum dentatum Autumn Jazz®

Viburnum dentatum CONTINUED

ant as *Viburnum bracteatum* 'Emerald Luster'. In the northern states, I recommend Autumn Jazz® ('Ralph Senior') and Chicago Lustre® ('Synnesvedt'). Roy Klehm's Cardinal™, a brilliant red fall foliage selection, had *no* fall color in five years in the Georgia trials.

Blue Muffin™ ('Christom') has glossy dark green leaves, intense blue fruit, and though listed as 4 to 5 ft. high, grew 7 ft. high in five years in Georgia trials.

Variety *scabrellum* (*Viburnum ashei*) has been a pleasant surprise. Its shiny, refined foliage withstands the sun/heat, and it is the latest flowering of all *V. dentatum* selections, mid June in Athens, followed by blue fruit. Grows 5 to 8 ft. high and wide. Perhaps the best form for the South, i.e., zones 7 to 9.

Viburnum dentatum Cardinal™ fall color

Viburnum dilatatum
linden viburnum

Certainly one of the best fruiting shrubs for American gardens. Habit is variable; most often upright and somewhat stiff, occasionally densely rounded. The 2- to 5-in.-long, lustrous dark green leaves change to inconsistent russet-reds in fall. White, malodorous flowers are borne in 3- to 5-in.-wide, flat-topped cymes in May and June. The real show follows in September and October when the ⅔-in.-long, ovoid fruit ripen to bright red, cherry-red, or scarlet. Fruit often persist into winter. Several different seedlings or cultivars are required for cross-pollination and abundant fruit set. A great plant for groupings, borders, or large masses around com-

Viburnum dentatum Chicago Lustre®

Viburnum dentatum var. *scabrellum* fall color

Viburnum dilatatum

844

Viburnum dilatatum, linden viburnum

mercial buildings. Grows 8 to 10 ft. high, variable spread. Zones (4)5 to 7. Eastern Asia.

Viburnum wrightii, Wright viburnum, is similar *except* largely without hairs on stems, while *V. dilatatum* is flush with pubescence. Worth noting that flowers are fragrant, at least on 'Hessei'. Grows 6 to 10 ft. high. Zones 5 to 7. Japan.

CULTIVARS AND VARIETIES

Dr. Don Egolf's breeding work at the U.S. National Arboretum has resulted in several superior cultivars. His 'Catskill', 'Erie', and 'Iroquois' are excellent selections for contemporary landscapes. So is Don Shadow's 'Asian Beauty'. 'Catskill' is more compact than the others. All produce shiny red fruit.

Cardinal Candy™ ('Henneke') is a

MORE ▶

Viburnum dilatatum 'Erie'

Viburnum dilatatum 'Asian Beauty'

Viburnum dilatatum Cardinal Candy™

Viburnum dilatatum 'Michael Dodge'

Viburnum dilatatum CONTINUED
new introduction with lustrous dark green leaves, abundant glossy red fruit, and increased cold hardiness to −30°F.

'Michael Dodge' and 'Vernon Morris' are beautiful yellow-fruited forms. I observed both in gorgeous yellow fruit and was equally impressed.

'Ogon' is a yellow-gold leaf form that fades to green as leaves mature. Have grown for a number of years in Athens, and heat quickly diminishes color.

Viburnum farreri
fragrant viburnum

A delightfully fragrant, early-blooming shrub that foreshadows the advent of spring, yet it is nowhere common in gardens. The habit is loose, unkempt, and unruly, possibly a reason for the plant's scarcity. The leaves emerge bronzy green, turn dark green, and finally take on reddish purple hues in fall. The 1½- to 4-in.-long leaves have deeply pleated veins. Fragrant pink flowers occur in 1- to 2-in.-long panicles in March and April, before the leaves. The flowers are randomly produced, and the shrub never quite jumps out and says "hello." Fruit are ½ in. long, oval, red to black, ripening in early summer, but seldom produced in large quantities. Prefers moist, acid, well-drained soils, but the species did prosper in the higher pH soil of my Illinois garden. Use in the border; definitely not for single-specimen use. Grows 8 to 12 ft. high and wide. Zones (4)5 to 8. Northern China.
CULTIVARS AND VARIETIES
'Candidissimum' ('Album') has white flowers and bright green leaves. Not as vigorous or large as the species, although I noted a 10-ft.-high plant in England. Leaves have none of the red-purple color of the species.

Viburnum wrightii, Wright viburnum, fall color

Viburnum dilatatum 'Catskill'

Viburnum dilatatum 'Ogon'

Viburnum farreri, fragrant viburnum

'Nanum' is a compact form, smaller in all its parts, with pinkish buds that open to fragrant, pinkish white flowers. It is tidier than the species. Grows 2 to 3 (to 4) ft. high, 4 to 6 ft. wide.

Viburnum japonicum
Japanese viburnum

If a gardening friend tells you they have this species, provide the quizzical "are you sure?" look. Misidentified by pro and amateur, the true species is evergreen, white-flowered, and red-fruited, with broad-ovate leaves. Habit is rounded and relatively dense; leaves, each 2 to 5 in. long, about as wide, are leathery, lustrous dark green, with a few remote teeth toward the apex. The fragrant, white, 3/8-in.-wide flowers are produced in 2- to 4-in.-wide cymes in May. Beautiful red fruit, 1/3 in. long, oval-rounded, ripen in fall and persist into winter. Requires some shade protection, moist, acid, well-drained soil. Rare species, possibly for the collector. Grows 6 to 8 ft. high and wide. Zones 7 to 9. Japan.

CULTIVARS AND VARIETIES

Dr. Egolf used this species to breed 'Chippewa' (*Viburnum japonicum* × *V. dilatatum*) and 'Huron' (*V. lobophyllum* × *V. japonicum*), two 8- to 10-ft.-high

MORE ▶

Viburnum farreri 'Candidissimum'

Viburnum japonicum, Japanese viburnum

Viburnum farreri 'Nanum'

Viburnum farreri new growth

Viburnum japonicum

Viburnum japonicum CONTINUED
and -wide cultivars with leathery dark green foliage and red fruit. 'Chippewa' flowers seven to ten days ahead of 'Huron'. The white flowers of both are "stinky" and the red fruit are sparsely set.

'Fugitive' is another *Viburnum japonicum* hybrid of dense habit. Somewhat of a mystery as to origin.

Viburnum ×juddii
Judd viburnum
Gardeners have debated the fragrance of this hybrid species as compared to that of one of its parents, *Viburnum carlesii*, but to my olfactory senses, there is little difference. Judd viburnum does, however, display greater heat tolerance than *V. carlesii* and exhibits increased resistance to bacterial leaf spot. It is a full, rounded shrub with dark, almost blue-green leaves. Pink buds open to fragrant,

white flowers in 2½- to 3¼-in.-wide, semi-snowball inflorescences in April and May (late March to early April, Athens). Its other parent is *V. bitchiuense*, with pink-budded, fragrant, white flowers in late March to early April (Athens), and greater heat tolerance and better performance in Georgia trials than *V. carlesii*. Grows 6 to 8 ft. high and wide. Plants at the University's Botanical Garden were over 10 ft. high. Zones 4 to 8.

Viburnum lantana
wayfaringtree viburnum
An old standby in the Midwest and Northeast because of its ironclad

Viburnum lantana

Viburnum japonicum

Viburnum ×juddii, Judd viburnum

Viburnum ×juddii

Viburnum lantana 'Mohican'

848

adaptability and reliable performance over time. The habit is distinctly rounded with stout, coarse branches. The dull dark green, 2- to 5-in.-long leaves seldom develop good fall color. White, off-odor flowers are borne in 3- to 5-in.-wide cymes in May. The fruit are extremely handsome, beginning yellow and changing to red and black, often with all colors on the same infructescence. Fruiting is maximized when several different clones are in close proximity. One of the best viburnums for calcareous, clay-based soils. Use in the border, as a screen, or in groupings. It is coarse in winter and, for that reason, is best mixed with other shrubs. Grows 10 to 15 ft. high and wide. Zones 4 to 8. Europe, western Asia.

CULTIVARS AND VARIETIES
'Mohican' is more compact and has darker green leaves and heavy, orange-red fruit set. Original selection was 8½ ft. high and 9 ft. wide after 15 years. Definitely superior to run-of-the-mill *Viburnum lantana*.

Viburnum lentago
nannyberry viburnum

In its finest form, this is an attractive large shrub or small tree with 2- to 4-in.-long leaves that emerge soft yellow-green, turn glossy dark green, and may change to purplish red in fall. Bark is often scaly to blocky on old plants. The 3- to 4½-in.-wide, white inflorescences open in May. Flowers have been described as having "no real fragrance" to "agreeably fragrant." They are followed by green, yellow, rose, and pink fruit that mature to purplish black. Unfortunately, this

MORE ▶

Viburnum lantana, wayfaringtree viburnum

Viburnum lentago, nannyberry viburnum

Viburnum lantana

Viburnum lentago fall color

849

Viburnum lentago CONTINUED

species may be disfigured by mildew; plant where air movement is excellent to best deter mildew. Use in a naturalized planting. Grows 15 to 18 (to 30) ft. high, quite variable in spread. Zones 2 to 7. Hudson Bay to Manitoba, south to Georgia and Mississippi.

Viburnum macrocephalum
Chinese snowball viburnum

Visitors to the Dirr garden were intrigued and mystified by the large, white, poofy flowers that cover this plant in April and May. When I tell them it's a viburnum, the usual retort reverberates, "I thought it was a hydrangea!" Large, robust, dominating, vase-shaped shrub with a rounded top. The 2- to 4-in.-long leaves are dark green, hold late, and develop little fall color. The flower buds are naked (no covering scales), similar

to small cauliflower heads, and send forth apple-green florets that mature glistening white; nonfragrant. The entire process is stretched over six to eight weeks. Inflorescences are 5 to 8 in. in diameter. Fruit are not formed because the inflorescence is sterile. Site in full sun (partial shade acceptable), in moist, acid, well-drained soil. Have never witnessed any pest problems. A strong flowering element in the shrub border. Our lone plant, stationed in front of a large *Cedrus deodara*, captured the spotlight when in flower. Often overgrew its boundaries; I cut it to within 2 to 3 ft. of the

ground after flowering. The new growth does not flower the next year, but terrific rebloom occurs thereafter. Also possesses the curious and welcome initiative of flowering in autumn. Grows 12 to 15 (to 20) ft. high, about as wide. Zones 6 to 9. China.

CULTIVARS AND VARIETIES
Forma *keteleeri*, the reproductive member of the species, produces sterile, showy florets on the outside, fertile on the interior, in 4- to 5-in.-wide, flat-topped cymes. The brilliant red fruit that follow are spectacular and eventually age to black.

'Nantucket', a large (12 ft. by 7 ft.),

Viburnum macrocephalum f. *keteleeri*

Viburnum macrocephalum, Chinese snowball viburnum

Viburnum macrocephalum f. *keteleeri*

Viburnum macrocephalum

850

evergreen, slightly fragrant, white-flowered form, is a U.S. National Arboretum release; the original cross by Dr. Egolf utilized 'Eskimo' and f. *keteleeri*. Outstanding in Georgia trials: abundant flowers every year, superb heat tolerance, grew 6½ ft. by 4 ft. in five years. Utilized for breeding by the author with many exciting, heavily flowered seedlings. Nantucket-02-06 is fully evergreen, with 4-in.-wide, white, slightly fragrant flowers, abundant red to black fruit, and compact rounded habit, 4 ft. by 4 ft. after five years. Superior to 'Conoy'.

Viburnum nudum
smooth witherod

Considered by some authorities a subspecies of *Viburnum cassinoides* but logically a distinct entity based on leaf and habitat characteristics. Large shrub, similar to *V. cassinoides* in outline but with extremely lustrous dark green leaves that turn red to reddish purple in fall. The lustrous, sheeny, waxy cuticle accentuates the fall colors. Each leaf is 2 to 5 in. long, oval in outline, and usually entire, compared to those of *V. cassinoides*, which have serrated margins. The musky-scented, creamy white

flowers, in 3- to 5-in.-wide, flat-topped cymes, open in May and June. Fruit, much like those of *V. cassinoides*, start green on their way to waxy pink, rose, bluish, and purplish black. In the wild, it is found in wet soil areas, and near Mobile, Alabama, I witnessed the species at home in the swamps of Weeks Bay Reserve. Many nurseries produce splendid container-grown plants. Beautiful for foliage effect. Grows 6 to 10 ft. high and wide. Zones 5 to 9. Connecticut, Long Island to Florida, west to Kentucky and Louisiana.

MORE ▶

Viburnum 'Nantucket'

Viburnum Nantucket-02-06

Viburnum nudum

Viburnum nudum var. *angustifolium* fall color

851

Viburnum nudum CONTINUED

CULTIVARS AND VARIETIES

Variety *angustifolium* has smaller, narrower leaves and more open habit in youth, becoming denser and developing outstanding red fall color. Flowers and fruit similar to the species. Plant seems to improve with age as it becomes more dense and richly foliated.

'Pink Beauty' has beautiful lustrous dark green leaves and abundant, pink to blue fruit. More compact; I estimate 5 to 7 ft. high and wide. Appears self-fruitful based on performance in Chapel Hill and Athens. Truly one of the best *Viburnum nudum* selections, and I have grown most, including Brandywine™, 'Count Pulaski', 'Earthshade', 'Moonshine', and 'Winterthur'.

'Winterthur' has lustrous dark green foliage, reddish purple fall color, and typical flowers and fruit. Grows larger than I originally estimated: plants 10 ft. high and rather open have crossed my path.

Viburnum obovatum
small viburnum

Although considered a "small" viburnum, this is only from the standpoint of the ¾- to 2-in.-long, spatulate leaves, lustrous dark green, tardily deciduous, and early leafing. A plant in the University's Botanical Garden started petite and is now 12 ft. high and wide—a rounded, dense matrix of stems. The white, nonfragrant flowers, in 1¾- to 2¼-in.-wide cymes, open with the emerging leaves in April.

Viburnum nudum

Viburnum nudum 'Winterthur' fruit and fall color

Viburnum nudum, smooth witherod

Viburnum nudum 'Pink Beauty'

Viburnum obovatum

852

Flowers do not shout, so engage them at close quarters. The red, ellipsoidal, ⅓-in.-long fruit mature to black. Adapted to wet areas in nature but tolerant of dry soils once established. Found along stream banks and low woods. A worthy massing shrub, used in commercial landscapes in Tampa, Florida. More evergreen in the Deep South, progressing to deciduous in zones 6 and 7. Grows 10 to 12 ft. high and wide. Zones 6 to 9. South Carolina to Florida and Alabama.

CULTIVARS AND VARIETIES
Many dwarf forms have been introduced, with 'Reifler's Dwarf' and 'Mrs. Schiller's Delight' the best I observed. The first is less than 5 ft. high; the second, about 3 ft. high. Both injured by the cold winter of 2009–10 in Athens but regrew. The latter, the most cold sensitive, and 11°F killed all leaves.

'Lord Byron' is a unique hybrid (*Viburnum obovatum* × *V. rufidulum*),

MORE ▶

Viburnum obovatum 'Reifler's Dwarf'

Viburnum obovatum, small viburnum

Viburnum obovatum CONTINUED
an upright twiggy plant with smallish, lustrous dark green leaves, exuberant orange-red fall color, white flowers in March, and blackish fruit. Will reach 6 to 8 ft. high, and flowers are produced from most of the nodes up and down the stems.

Viburnum odoratissimum

The species that is most often misidentified as *Viburnum awabuki* and *V. japonicum*. Unique because of dull,

Viburnum odoratissimum

Viburnum opulus

Viburnum opulus

flat green leaves and stinky odor of bruised leaves, which recalls that of green peppers. Also minimally cold hardy, adapted only to zone 8 and higher. A large, broadleaf evergreen shrub or small tree, oval-rounded in habit. The 2- to 4-in.-long, elliptic-oval leaves are dull olive-green. The fragrant, cream-white flowers, late April to early May (Athens), are followed

Viburnum odoratissimum

Viburnum opulus, European cranberrybush viburnum

by red, maturing purple-black fruit. Extremely durable species for the Coastal Plain of the Southeast; large plants grow in Florida and Louisiana. Full sun and moderate shade adaptability. Good hedge plant. Grows 10 to 20 (to 30) ft. high. Witnessed a 40-ft.-high tree at Leu Gardens, Orlando. Zones 8 to 10. India, Myanmar, China to Japan and Philippines.

CULTIVARS AND VARIETIES
'Red Tip', with reddish green young foliage, is occasionally offered. Tested in Athens, where it was killed outright by the cold.

Viburnum opulus
European cranberrybush viburnum
An old favorite that is at home from Boston to Fargo to the West Coast.

It is a large, coarse, rounded shrub that is quite imposing in the winter landscape. In leaf, however, it is significantly less intense. The three-lobed, maple-like leaves average 2 to 4 in. long and wide. The lustrous dark green leaves may develop yellow-red to purplish red autumn tints. Flowers, April and May, occur in 2- to 3- (to 4-) in.-wide, flat-topped cymes. The

outer flowers are white and showy, the inner ones fertile (off-odor) and rather inconspicuous, and the entire effect is pinwheel-like. The ¼- to ⅜-in.-wide fruit change from yellow to bright red, giving the plant its common name. Fruit may persist into winter but will develop the appearance of red raisins. A February speaking engagement in

MORE ▶

Viburnum opulus 'Compactum'

Viburnum opulus 'Nanum'

Viburnum opulus 'Aureum'

V*Viburnum opulus* 'Roseum' fall color

Viburnum opulus 'Roseum', European snowball viburnum

Viburnum opulus CONTINUED

Midland, Michigan, landed me in Dow Gardens, where the only significant color resulted from *Viburnum opulus*. Excellent shrub for fruit effect. Use exclusively in borders. Tolerates wet or boggy areas better than many plants. Susceptible to viburnum leaf beetle. Grows 8 to 12 (to 15) ft. high and wide. Zones 3 to 7(8). Europe, northern Africa, northern Asia.

Viburnum plicatum

Viburnum plicatum Newport®

Viburnum plicatum 'Pink Sensation'

CULTIVARS AND VARIETIES

'Aureum', 'Harvest Gold', and 'Park Harvest' have yellow foliage fading to green. All are large plants in the 8- to 10-ft. range.

'Compactum' matures to about half the size of the species and offers similar flowers and fruit. Good choice where space is a problem. Observed 6-ft.-high and -wide plants.

'Nanum', a dwarf form with fine branches and smaller leaves, usually does not flower or fruit. Grows 1½ to 2 ft. high, 2 to 3 ft. wide; I have observed 4- to 5-ft.-high plants with flowers.

'Roseum', European snowball viburnum or Guilder-rose, has the same growth characteristics as the species, except its flowers are sterile and occur in 2½- to 3-in.-wide, white, snowball-shaped inflorescences. Large shrub, 10 to 12 ft. high and wide.

Viburnum plicatum
Japanese snowball viburnum

Much like doublefile viburnum, except this species typically has a more upright branching structure and the flowers open about two to three weeks later than those of some doublefile viburnums, although many exceptions occur. The sterile, semi-snowball, 2- to 3-in.-wide, white, carnation-like flowers last for two to three weeks in April (Athens) to May (Boston). Size ranges from 5 or 6 to 15 ft. high, and in some cultivars even greater width. Zones 5 to 8. China, Japan.

CULTIVARS AND VARIETIES

Excellent plants for about every garden niche.

Newport® ('Newzam') is a dwarf, compact form, 5 to 6 ft. high and wide, with dense branch structure. Flowers are meshed with the dark green foliage, which dampens their effect. Flowered seven to ten days later than 'Popcorn' in Georgia trials, typically late April (Athens) to early May (Chapel Hill).

'Pink Sensation' has pink-emerging flowers opening white, depending on degree of heat; not stable, and white-flowered reversions are common. New leaves of pink-flowerers are bronze-tinted; white, light green. 'Roseace' ('Kern's Pink') is probably the same;

Viburnum plicatum, Japanese snowball viburnum

Viburnum plicatum 'Popcorn'

'Mary Milton' is pink but weakly so. In the later case, everything I have witnessed is white. Grows 10 ft. high, 8 ft. wide.

'Popcorn' is the *best*: consistent white flowers in mid April (Athens); thickish, pleated, heat-tolerant dark green leaves; more upright, 8 to 10 ft. high; does not develop the wide-spreading outline, i.e., horizontal branching, of 'Grandiflorum' and 'Rotundifolium'; survived −23°F.

Viburnum plicatum f. *tomentosum*

doublefile viburnum

An aristocrat among flowering shrubs. In its finest form, doublefile viburnum is a graceful, horizontally branched shrub. The 2- to 4- (to 6-) in.-wide, white flower cymes, similar in appearance to those of *Viburnum opulus*, are raised on 2-in.-high stalks above the foliage, resulting in a Milky Way effect. The flowers open in April and May. The 2- to 4- (to 5-) in.-long, dark green

MORE ▶

Viburnum plicatum f. *tomentosum*, doublefile viburnum

Viburnum plicatum f. *tomentosum* CONTINUED leaves are deeply veined and appear pleated. Fall color is often a good wine-red. The bright cherry-red fruit ripen in July and August, changing to black, and are a favorite food of birds. In my experience, this form resents dry soil and heat stress more than most viburnums. Provide ample moisture. Surprisingly, plants flower as well in shade as in sun. Use as an understory shrub, in borders, or as a specimen. It is virtually impossible to err when utilizing this form or one of its excellent cultivars. Grows 8 to 10 ft. high, 9 to 12 ft. wide. Zones 5 to 8. China, Japan.

CULTIVARS AND VARIETIES

'Cascade', with large showy florets, is one of my favorites. Inflorescences are umbrella-shaped, 2½ to 4 in. across, with large showy sterile outer flowers that arch slightly at the middle, creating a cascading effect. Estimate 6 to 8 ft. high.

'Lanarth' is variable in size but typically wider than high with distinct horizontal branches; a memorable plant in the Arnold's collection was 8 ft. by 10 to 12 ft.

'Mariesii' is common in commerce but not well defined as far as characteristics; strong horizontal branches, abundant flowers, leaves with a long acuminate apex, and robust constitution, 10 to 15 ft. high, wider at maturity.

'Molly Schroeder' has pink florets that, depending on age and degree of heat, change to white. Flowered this in our Chapel Hill garden, and it was not impressive. Weak growing with smaller leaves compared to species.

'Pink Beauty' is somewhat upright in habit with pink flowers and, on occasion, abundant red fruit; consistency of pink varies but beautiful when at its best. Matures 6 to 10 ft. high, less in spread.

'Shasta' is an Egolf hybrid that grew in our Georgia garden, eventually removed because of size; 10 to 12 ft. high, wider at maturity. Certainly one of the hardiest doublefiles, surviving –27°F.

Viburnum plicatum f. *tomentosum*

Viburnum plicatum f. *tomentosum*

Viburnum plicatum f. *tomentosum* 'Lanarth'

Viburnum plicatum f. *tomentosum* 'Cascade'

'Shoshoni', with reduced stature, 5 ft. by 8 ft. in 17 years, offers flowers and fruit similar to 'Shasta'.

'Summer Snowflake' is a continuous-flowering selection, inflorescences smaller, habit more upright, 10 to 15 ft. high, 6 to 8 ft. wide. Not as cold hardy as 'Shasta'.

Viburnum 'Pragense'
syn. *Viburnum ×pragense*
Prague viburnum
Prague viburnum is a hybrid between *Viburnum rhytidophyllum* and *V. utile*, embodying the best features of both parents. It is an oval-rounded shrub with 2- to 4-in.-long, waxy, dark green

MORE ▶

Viburnum 'Pragense', Prague viburnum

Viburnum plicatum f. *tomentosum* 'Molly Schroeder'

Viburnum plicatum f. *tomentosum* 'Pink Beauty'

Viburnum plicatum f. *tomentosum* 'Mariesii'

Viburnum plicatum f. *tomentosum* 'Shasta'

Viburnum 'Pragense'

evergreen leaves. In April and May, pink buds open to white, pleasantly fragrant flowers. I have not observed fruit set. This species is extremely fast-growing and occasionally requires pruning to fatten it up. It makes a great foliage mass or screen and can serve as an excellent background shrub for other plants. This hybrid is more cold hardy than *V. rhytidophyllum*, by five to eight degrees Fahrenheit, and should remain evergreen at −10°F. Grows 10 ft. high or more, 8 to 10 ft. wide.

Zones 5 to 8. Utilized on the Georgia campus for grouping and screening and performed beyond expectations, surviving drought and heat.

Viburnum prunifolium
blackhaw viburnum

A great native species, described by Florence Robinson as a "puritan with a rigidity of character similar to some of the hawthorns." Blackhaw viburnum develops into a large, stiffly branched shrub or small tree. The 1½- to 3½-in.-

Viburnum 'Pragense'

Viburnum prunifolium fall color

Viburnum prunifolium

Viburnum prunifolium

Viburnum prunifolium, blackhaw viburnum

long, dark green leaves change to bronze, dull deep red, and shining red in fall. White, non-offensive flowers occur in 2- to 4-in.-wide, flat-topped cymes in April and May with the emerging leaves. The fruit are quite similar to those of *Viburnum lentago*, passing from pinkish rose to bluish black at maturity. Very adaptable. Much like *V. lentago*, but this species is preferable for its mildew resistance and superior foliage. At times, difficult to identify, but the flower buds of *V. lentago* are larger and the leaves have winged petioles compared to *V. prunifolium*. Grows 12 to 15 ft. high, 8 to 12 ft. wide; can grow to a 20-ft.-high tree. National champion is 26 ft. high, 35 ft. wide. Zones 3 to 9. Connecticut to Michigan, south to Florida and Texas.

Viburnum rafinesqueanum
downy arrowwood, rafinesque viburnum

What started as a small, rather forlorn shrub in the University's Botanical Garden matured into a broad-rounded meshwork of fine-textured stems and deeply veined, smallish leaves. Leaves are medium to dark green, 2 to 3 in. long, narrow-ovate with strong serrations; autumn coaxes a stubborn pale yellow to russet-red from them, just enough to notice. The dull white, malodorous flowers appear after the leaves in May in 2-in.-wide clusters and are followed by blue-black fruit. In the wild, grows in drier basic or neutral soils but is quite adaptable under cultivation. Full sun to partial shade prove ideal. A good wildlife plant, naturalizing shrub, grouping, or massing. Observed outstanding plants at Minnesota Landscape Arboretum. An enterprising nurseryman grew hundreds in the hopes of creating a market and still has hundreds. Grows 6

MORE ▶

Viburnum rafinesqueanum, downy arrowwood

Viburnum rafinesqueanum fall color

Viburnum rafinesqueanum

Viburnum rafinesqueanum 'Louise's Sunbeam'

Viburnum rafinesqueanum CONTINUED
to 10 ft. high and wide. Zones 5 to 8. Quebec to Manitoba, south to Georgia, Kentucky, and Missouri.
CULTIVARS AND VARIETIES
Discovered three yellow-leaf seedlings in Chapel Hill, North Carolina, in 2005 and with sustained evaluation have selected the best, which has shiny yellow leaves, turning yellow-green, then red-purple in fall. The parent plant was added to the new Dirr garden and is named 'Louise's Sunbeam' after Louise Quinlan, our Susy's organ donor. Royalties go to the Sweet Melissa Fund, University of North Carolina, which assists lung transplant patients and their families.

Viburnum ×rhytidophylloides

lantanaphyllum viburnum
This is another useful hybrid viburnum, with *Viburnum rhytidophyllum* and *V.*

Viburnum ×rhytidophylloides 'Alleghany'

lantana as parents. In my estimation, this plant and especially its cultivars are superior to either parent in ornamental quality and cultural adaptability. It is often confused with *V. rhytidophyllum*, but the leaves of the hybrid are much wider in the middle and are tardily deciduous. Flowers and fruit are similar to those of *V. lantana*. Flowers carry that characteristic "unpleasant" scent of *V. lantana*. Requires another clone for cross-pollination. Excellent large shrub for screens, groupings,

Viburnum ×rhytidophylloides 'Alleghany'

and backgrounds. Grows 10 to 15 ft. high and wide. Zones 4 to 8.
CULTIVARS AND VARIETIES
'Alleghany' is a superior selection, with dark green, coriaceous leaves, abundant inflorescences, and a vigorous, dense, globose growth habit. It is resistant to bacterial leaf spot. Appears slightly more cold hardy than the typical species. The original plant was 10½ ft. high, 11 ft. wide after 13 years.

'Emerald Triumph', a *Viburnum bure-*

Viburnum 'Emerald Triumph'

Viburnum 'Emerald Triumph' fall color

jaeticum × 'Alleghany' hybrid, grows 6 to 8 ft. high and wide, with lustrous dark green leaves that turn maroon in fall. White flowers and green to red to black fruit are attractive. Zone 4 adaptability; observed in Maine.

'Willowwood' offers excellent lustrous, rugose, dark green foliage and an arching habit. Leaves may be more persistent than those of 'Alleghany'. Has the odd trait of flowering in the fall. A good selection, but no match for 'Alleghany'.

Viburnum rhytidophyllum
leatherleaf viburnum

For textural quality, this large-leaved evergreen shrub is a fine addition to the border. Although somewhat out of place in modern gardens because of its massive, rounded outline and coarse texture, it still functions for screening or as a background shrub. The leathery, lustrous dark green leaves are 3 to 7½ in. long, 1 to 2½ in. wide, and heavily veined. Creamy, slightly fragrant flowers are borne in 4- to 8-in.-wide inflorescences in May. The flower buds are formed the previous summer and appear as small, brownish spheres in fall and winter. The fruit are spectacular and rival those of *Viburnum lantana* for effect and color. The oval, ⅓-in.-long fruit pass from yellow to red to black at maturity. For maximum fruiting, cross-pollinate with other clones or seedlings. This species grows best in heavy shade and should be sheltered

MORE ▶

Viburnum ×rhytidophylloides

Viburnum ×rhytidophylloides, lantanaphyllum viburnum

Viburnum rhytidophyllum

Viburnum rhytidophyllum, leatherleaf viburnum

Viburnum rhytidophyllum CONTINUED from winter wind and sun. Prefers a more organic-laden, moist, well-drained soil than many viburnums. Grows 10 to 15 ft. high and wide. Zones 6 to 8. Central and western China.

CULTIVARS AND VARIETIES
Several, including 'Cree' (more compact), Fenceline™ ('Hefline') (more upright), and 'Green Trump' (more compact with longer leaves).

Viburnum rufidulum
rusty blackhaw viburnum

A beautiful plant with creamy white flowers, pink to blue-black fruit, reddish purple fall color, and blocky, blackish bark. The habit is oval to rounded, and full-grown specimens are behemoths (in the wild, plants can grow 30 to 40 ft. tall). The 2- to 4-in.-long, leathery, glossy dark green leaves are exquisite. Flowers, slight to no fragrance, occur in 2- to 4-in.- wide, flat-topped cymes in April (Athens), May, and June. Tolerates heavy shade, but maximum flowering and fruiting occur in full sun. Adaptable to dry soils. Use in the border, for screening, or in large groupings. Grows 10 to 20 ft. high and wide. Zones 5 to 9. Virginia to Illinois, south to Florida and Texas.

CULTIVARS AND VARIETIES
Emerald Charm™ ('Morton') is more cold hardy and 'Royal Guard' has

Viburnum rhytidophyllum

Viburnum rhytidophyllum

Viburnum rufidulum

Viburnum rufidulum

Viburnum rufidulum, rusty blackhaw viburnum

improved glossy dark green leaves and rich burgundy fall color. As I viewed the latter, nothing impressed.

Viburnum sargentii
Sargent viburnum

Sargent viburnum is a robust, large, coarse shrub, not unlike *Viburnum opulus* or *V. trilobum* in general characteristics. The habit is distinctly upright-rounded to rounded. The three-lobed, 2- to 5-in.-long, dark green leaves are leathery in texture and assume yellowish to reddish hues in autumn. The leaves have a longer central (terminal) lobe than those of *V. opulus* and *V. trilobum*. The flowers have the same configuration as those of the other species, but the anthers are usually purple, compared to the yellow color of *V. opulus* and *V. trilobum*. Flowers, somewhat malodorous, more so than *V. opulus*, usually open in May, perhaps slightly later than *V. opulus*.

The scarlet, ½-in.-long fruit are effective from August into October. Sargent viburnum is definitely not heat-tolerant and should be reserved for the cooler northern states. Susceptible to viburnum leaf beetle. Uses are similar to those of *V. opulus*. Grows 12 to 15 ft. high and wide. Zones 3 to 6(7). Northeastern Asia.

CULTIVARS AND VARIETIES
'Onondaga' and 'Susquehanna' are

MORE ▶

Viburnum rufidulum fall color

Viburnum sargentii, Sargent viburnum

Viburnum sargentii 'Onondaga'

Viburnum sargentii 'Susquehanna'

Viburnum sargentii CONTINUED

two U.S. National Arboretum introductions, possibly better than the typical species. 'Onondaga' has dark maroon new growth, maroon-red flower buds, opening white, the fertile flowers maroon, and a more compact growth habit. 'Susquehanna' is a thickly branched, prolific fruiting form with corky bark and leathery, dark green foliage. Grows 12 to 15 ft. high and wide.

Viburnum setigerum
tea viburnum

Gardening aficionados rave about the supposed sculptural quality of the branches and the handsome, persistent red fruit. Try to sell this plant on the open market, however, and you probably wouldn't do too well. If used in a border where the bare stems can be masked by facer plants, it can serve a wonderful function. Typically, plants are upright-arching in habit, with foliage only on the upper half of the shrub. Inconspicuous white, slight to non-fragrant flowers occur in 1- to 2-in.-wide, flat-topped cymes in May and June, and one has to look pretty hard to see if plants are actually in flower. The ⅓-in.-long, egg-shaped, bright red fruit ripen in September and October and persist into late fall. This species prefers full sun for best fruit set, but reasonable fruiting does occur in shady environments. Grows 8

Viburnum sargentii

Viburnum setigerum, tea viburnum

Viburnum sargentii fall color

Viburnum setigerum

Viburnum setigerum 'Aurantiacum'

to 12 ft. high, 6 to 10 ft. wide. Zones 5 to 7. China.

CULTIVARS AND VARIETIES
'Aurantiacum' offers orange fruit and provides a pleasing color contrast to the typical red of the species.

Viburnum sieboldii
Siebold viburnum

Siebold viburnum is one of the largest *Viburnum* species, easily topping 20 ft. tall. The lustrous dark green, impressed-veined, corrrugated leaves average 2 to 6 in. long and have the odor of green pepper when bruised. Leaves hold late, and fall color seldom develops, although I have observed ashy purple. Creamy white, lemon-scented flowers open in May and June in 3- to 6-in.-long, cymose-paniculate inflorescences. The flowers are borne in great profusion and mask the bright green foliage. The fruit, which ripen from August through early October, can be spectacular, especially as they change from rose to red to black. The fruit stalks are a rich, almost fluorescent rose-red and remain effective for two to four weeks after the fruit have fallen. Requires sufficient moisture; leaf scorch will develop under stress of high heat and drought. Whether a large shrub or small tree, this viburnum, possibly more so than any other, is deserving of specimen use, against buildings, walls, fences or in the open. The rigidity of habit provides a texture different from that of dogwood or redbud. Grows 15 to 20 (to 30) ft. high, 10 to 15 ft. wide. Zones 4 to 7. Japan.

CULTIVARS AND VARIETIES
Ironclad™ ('KLMfour') is a cold hardy, zone 4 selection, 15 ft. by 12 ft., by Roy Klehm.

'Seneca' and 'Wavecrest' are improved fruiting forms, the latter with barn-red fall color.

Viburnum suspensum
Sandankwa viburnum

Broadleaf evergreen shrub, thickly set with branches and leaves—a perfect combination for hedge and screening uses. From the coast of Georgia to Key West, Florida, it increases in frequency. Leaves, 2 to 5 in. long, leathery, lustrous dark green, remain so through the seasons. In April, the white, faintly tinged pink, fragrant

MORE ▶

Viburnum sieboldii

Viburnum sieboldii

Viburnum sieboldii

Viburnum sieboldii, Siebold viburnum

Viburnum suspensum, Sandankwa viburnum

867

Viburnum suspensum CONTINUED
flowers open. Typically, they remain
an enigma, because the plants are
pruned for hedges and so flowers are
removed. The globose fruit start red,
maturing black. Appears well adapted
to full sun, moderate shade, heat,
drought, sandy soils, and maritime
conditions. Grows 6 to 12 ft. high
and wide. Zones (8)9 to 11. Ryukyu
Islands of Japan.

Viburnum tinus
laurustinus
Never have I observed so many variations on a *Viburnum* species as occur
within the genetic plasticity of *Vibur-*

num tinus. At Hillier Arboretum, from
my arrival in mid February to my return
on July 27, one cultivar or another still
produced the odd flower. Peak period
is late winter (England), January, February, March (Athens). Habit is upright-
rounded, evergreen, dense, thickly
branched, and wall-like. The leaves are
beautiful, lustrous dark, almost black-
green, 1½ to 4 in. long, maintaining
this beauty through the seasons. The
pink-budded flowers open white in 2- to
4-in.-wide cymes. Flower effect seems
forever because cool temperatures
prolong the effectiveness. Ever so
slightly fragrant, but especially pleasant to be around when thoughts of the

new gardening season are strong. The
metallic blue fruit mature blue-black to
black and persist into the next flowering cycle. This is a stalwart plant in
Europe, less so in the South and West.
Excellent shade plant, also tolerant
of full sun. Grows in gravel and clay;
pH adaptable and salt-tolerant. Great
plant for the winter garden. Serviceable, functional, and aesthetic in one
mass of green. Hedge, barrier, screen,
grouping, and shrub border use. Grows
6 to 12 ft. high, slightly less in spread.
Zones (8)9 and 10. In Athens, killed
to the ground at −3°F; in Washington, Georgia, 40 miles southeast, two
10-ft.-high shrubs were not injured dur-

Viburnum suspensum

Viburnum tinus 'Variegatum'

Viburnum tinus, laurustinus

Viburnum tinus 'Gwenllian'

ing the same winter. Southern Europe, northern Africa.

CULTIVARS AND VARIETIES

Many smaller in stature than the species, including 'Spring Bouquet' (dark red buds, white flowers), 'Eve Price' (red buds, pink-tinged flowers; described as compact, I experienced a 15 ft. by 10 ft. plant), and 'Compactum' (pink buds; about one-third to one-half the size of the species based on performance at JC Raulston Arboretum).

'Bewley's Variegated' and 'Variegatum' have cream-margined leaves and are less vigorous and cold hardy than the species.

'Clyne Castle', 'Gwenllian', and 'French White' are larger types with good foliage; all 10 ft. or greater.

Viburnum trilobum

syn. *Viburnum opulus* var. *americanum*

American cranberrybush viburnum

For the casual observer, separating this species from European cranberry-bush viburnum (*Viburnum opulus*) is exceedingly difficult. Habit, flowers, and fruit are all quite similar. Non-offensive floral odor. One major reliable difference is the stalked or raised petiolar glands of *V. trilobum*, as compared to the squatty, concave glands of *V. opulus*. For general landscape use in the northern states, *V. trilobum* is a better choice because of its superior fall color and greater resistance to aphids. Like *V. opulus* and *V. sargentii* it is susceptible to viburnum leaf

MORE ▶

Viburnum trilobum, American cranberrybush viburnum

Viburnum tinus

Viburnum tinus

Viburnum trilobum

Viburnum tinus 'Spring Bouquet'

Viburnum trilobum 'Hahs'

Viburnum trilobum 'Wentworth'

869

Viburnum trilobum CONTINUED

beetle; also susceptible to viburnum borer. Provide moist soils and a cool climate for best growth. I have seen it used to define property boundaries, as a hedge or screen, and in groupings. A handsome plant with multiseason ornamental characteristics. Grows 8 to 12 ft. high and wide. Zones 2 to 6(7). New Brunswick to British Columbia, south to New York and Oregon. Grows in moist to wet habitats in the wild.
CULTIVARS AND VARIETIES
'Andrews', 'Hahs', and 'Wentworth' are good fruiting forms selected for their edible fruit. 'Andrews' fruits early in the season, 'Hahs' in midseason, and 'Wentworth' late. 'Hahs' and 'Wentworth' are excellent ornamental shrubs and are preferable to the typical species.

'Compactum' offers fine-textured branches and smaller leaves. Flowering and fruiting characteristics are quite good. Grows 5 to 6 ft. high and wide. 'Alfredo' and 'Bailey Compact' are other compact forms.

Redwing™ ('J. N. Select') produces a red flush of new growth, red fall color, and typical flowers and fruit. Matures 8 to 12 ft. high and wide.

Viburnum utile
service viburnum

The great breeding partner that resulted in the *Viburnum* ×*burkwoodii* complex and superior cultivars like 'Conoy', 'Eskimo', and 'Chesapeake'. Multiplicity of ornamental traits—leaf, flower, fruit—are transmitted to its offspring. The species is a broadleaf evergreen shrub, somewhat loose

Viburnum trilobum Redwing™ fall color

Viburnum utile

Viburnum trilobum 'Bailey Compact'

Viburnum trilobum fall color

Viburnum utile

and open in habit, with 1- to 3-in.-long, lustrous black-green leaves, wavy-margined and -surfaced. The underside is covered with thickish gray-white pubescence. The slightly fragrant flowers appear in 2- to 3-in.-wide, rounded cymes in April. Buds are pink and open to white, five-petaled, nonfragrant flowers. Fruit is a flattened, ovoid, ¼-in.-long, red to black drupe. Durable and resilient, it displays drought and heat tolerance as well as shade and sun adaptability. Plants in our garden and the Georgia trials exhibited no drought stress in the recent spate of disastrously hot, dry summers. In some measure, a collector's and breeder's plant but quite beautiful in flower and foliage. Excellent shrub border plant. Grows 4 to 6 ft. high and wide. Zones 6 to 8. China.

Viburnum utile, service viburnum

Vinca major
large periwinkle

The standard window box or container plant, located in the front and allowed to trail over the edges. Such creativity! It is also a respectable, if rampageous, broadleaf evergreen groundcover: entire areas, bordered by walks, were eaten by the species at the University's Botanical Garden. I planted the variegated form in the heavily shaded area of the Dirr garden, and ten years later was still trying to eradicate it. With that said, the

MORE ▶

Vinca major, large periwinkle

Vinca major CONTINUED

plant forms a rolling sea of lustrous dark green, with 1½-in.-wide, five-petaled, lilac-blue flowers in March and April. Flowers are lovely but never overwhelming. Soils should be evenly moist, well-drained, and acid. Shade is preferred. Displays drought intolerance by flagging like a limp lasagne noodle. Less drought-tolerant than *Vinca minor*. For rapid cover in shade, a reasonable choice. Nooks and crannies on the east and north sides of houses and structures are good locations. Frisky when left to wide-open, shady places. Grows 12 to 18 in. high, rooting as it spreads, forming large colonies. Zones 6 to 9. France, Italy, former Yugoslavia.

CULTIVARS AND VARIETIES

'Alba' has white flowers.

'Pubescens' produces deep-purple, star-shaped flowers that show minimal resemblance to the species.

Variegated selections. Several known, with 'Variegata' the most common; its leaves are broadly margined with cream. 'Aureomaculata' has a central blotch of yellow-green that is not as visually potent as 'Variegata'. 'Wojo's Jem' has a large, cream-yellow center to the leaf; the margin is green bordered.

Vinca minor
common periwinkle

Along with *Liriope* species, *Pachysandra terminalis*, *Hedera helix*, and *Euonymus fortunei* 'Coloratus', one of the big five of American groundcovers. A low, ground-hugging, broadleaf evergreen, with ½- to 1½-in.-long, medium to dark green leaves, it forms a perfect carpet. Flowers are 1 in. in

Vinca major

Vinca major 'Pubescens'

Vinca minor, common periwinkle

Vinca major 'Variegata'

Vinca minor

diameter, lilac-blue, opening in March and April. Prefers moist, well-drained soil in shade. Discolors in full sun, especially in southern climes. More drought-tolerant than *Vinca major*. Blight, canker, and die-back are attributable to several fungi. I have observed significant infection in wet soils and with prevalent rainfall. Also, the species is invasive, and entire woodlands have been digested. At its best, a worthy groundcover in a garden situation. The clump you dig up and throw in the woods may some day own the woods. Grows 3 to 6 in. high, rooting at the nodes and spreading indefinitely. Zones 4 to 8. Europe, western Asia.

CULTIVARS AND VARIETIES
Many, several worth exploring for foliage and flower colors.

'Alba' represents the white-flowered types, which are not as vigorous as the typical species. 'Bowles White', 'Emily', and 'Gertrude Jekyll' are other white-flowered clones.

'Atropurpurea' bears deep plum-purple flowers and has always been one of my favorites.

'Bowles Variety' ('La Grave') produces large, 1½-in.-wide, lavender-blue flowers on a clump-forming plant.

Double-flowered forms include 'Azurea Flore Pleno' (sky blue), 'Florepleno' (purple-blue), and 'Rosea Plena' (violet-pink).

Variegated selections. Whether with blue or white flowers, these are common. 'Albovariegata' (white flowers, yellow-edged leaves), 'Argenteovariegata' (blue flowers, white-margined leaves), 'Illumination' (blue flowers, yellow-centered leaf, completely unstable), 'Ralph Shugert' (blue flowers, cream-white to white margins, dark green centers), and 'Sterling Silver' (pale violet-blue flower, cream-margined leaf) are available.

Vitex agnus-castus
chastetree

I never fully appreciated the merits of this species until I saw 20-ft.-high shrubs covered with lilac-purple flowers in June and July. Truly magnificent! In the North, the species is a dieback shrub, but it will flower on new growth of the season. The habit is rounded to broad-rounded. On old specimens, the gray-brown bark develops a blocky, alligator-hide texture. The

MORE ▶

Vitex agnus-castus 'Alba'

Vinca minor 'Alba'

Vinca minor 'Bowles Variety'

Vitex agnus-castus, chastetree

Vitex agnus-castus CONTINUED
dark gray-green, almost blue-green, aromatic leaves are composed of five to seven, 2- to 4- (to 5-) in.-long, digitate (finger-like) leaflets that hold late and are usually killed by the first heavy frost. Flowers occur in 12- to 18-in.-long and -wide panicles at the ends of the branches. Keep plants well fertilized and watered in the early part of the growing season to encourage vigorous shoots and, eventually, large flowers. Remove spent flowers to encourage new growth and repeat flowering. Plant in full sun. Use as a herbaceous perennial in Boston, a large shrub in Baltimore, or a small tree in Atlanta. Grows 6 to 10 ft. high or more, often wider at maturity. National champion is 28 ft. by 40 ft. Zones (6)7 and 8(9). Southern Europe, western Asia.

CULTIVARS AND VARIETIES
White- ('Alba', 'Silver Spire', 'Snow Spire', 'Woodlanders White') and pink- ('Rosea', 'Salinas Pink') flowered forms are known; however, the white forms are weaker growers, and the pink forms not very pink.

'Abbeville Blue' and 'Mississippi Blues' are deep blue-purple-flowered selections; 'Shoal Creek', from Shoal Creek Nursery, Athens, Georgia, has lilac flowers and shows high leaf spot resistance. Not much difference in color, as I observed them.

Vitex negundo
Chinese chastetree
This species is not as widely planted as *Vitex agnus-castus*, and based on my observations, it is not as robust or large-flowering. Larger plants are open, airy, and fine-textured and have smaller, 5- to 8-in.-long panicles of lilac or lavender flowers. Cultural requirements are similar to that of *V. agnus-castus*. This species is possibly cold hardy to one more zone. Grows 10 to 15 ft. high and wide. Zones (5)6 to 8(9). Southeast Africa, Madagascar, eastern and southeastern Asia, Philippines.

CULTIVARS AND VARIETIES
'Heterophylla' (var. *heterophylla*), with finely cut gray-green leaves, provides an excellent foliage effect. Ideally it should be cut to the ground in late winter to induce long shoot extensions. 'Incisa' (var. *incisa*), by some considered synonymous, may be the correct name.

Vitex rotundifolia
Unusual species that looks nothing like a vitex. The habit is sprawling-spreading: a single five-year-old plant in our test plots was about 2 ft. high and 12 ft. wide. The leaves are beau-

Vitex agnus-castus

Vitex agnus-castus

Vitex negundo 'Heterophylla'

874

tiful bluish green, about 2 in. long, 1½ in. wide, suborbicular in outline. The bluish purple flowers appear in short inflorescences from the leaf axils in May and thereafter on new growth of the season. Noted for its salt tolerance and ability to prosper in dry, sandy soils. Excellent for stabilizing oceanfront real estate but has become invasive along the coasts of the Carolinas: check Global Invasives website for a shocker. Also prospers in heavy soils. Requires full sun for best development. Utilize in rough areas of the garden or commercial landscape. Remember, it is deciduous and has an

overstated disheveled look in winter. Grows 1 to 2 ft. high, infinitely spreading. Hybrids with *Vitex agnus-castus* form a shrub-like outline with intermediate, rather pretty, foliage and blue-purple flowers. Zones 7 to 10. Asia to Australia.

Vitis
grape

Few gardeners in the United States consider grapes to be ornamental plants, but in Europe they are often used as wall plants to provide foliage color and texture. I will describe here a few species worthy of note. The two

I see most often are *Vitis coignetiae*, gloryvine, and *V. rotundifolia*, muscadine. Gloryvine has 4- to 10-in.-wide, dull green, leathery leaves that turn rich scarlet in fall. I was given a small dormant plant of this species, or so I was told, only to find out when the leaves emerged that it was,

MORE ▶

Vitis coignetiae, gloryvine

Vitex rotundifolia

Vitex rotundifolia

Vitis coignetiae fall color

Vitis CONTINUED

in fact, *V. rotundifolia* (see expanded discussion). *Vitis vinifera*, wine grape, is another common garden species. Its 3- to 6-in.-wide, rich green leaves have three to five lobes. *Vitis vinifera* 'Purpurea' has attractive new leaves that mature to dull reddish purple. Grape vines climb by means of tendrils and require support. Most prosper in moist, acid, well-drained soils, in sun or partial shade. Many *Vitis* species exist as understory vines in the wild. Zones 5 to 7(8).

Vitis rotundifolia
muscadine

Native throughout the Southeast and domesticated for garden and commercial fruit production. A phenomenally vigorous and long-lived vine that grows in the understory, almost groundcover-like, and can climb a tree like no creature on earth. Leaves are 2½ to 5 in. long and wide, glossy dark green, and coarsely serrate. In fall, leaves turn soft mellow yellow. The ⅓- to 1-in.-wide, rounded fruit are greenish to purplish with a thick skin.

Fruit are utilized for jellies, jams, and wine. Alternatively, pop in your mouth, extract the skin, savor the sweet juice in the interior, and remove the rest. Unbelievably adaptable, but best fruit set occurs in the sun. Use trellises and arbors in garden settings; requires considerable pruning to keep it in harmony with the structure and the rest of the garden. Grows 100 ft. high. Zones 5 to 9. Delaware to northern Florida, west to Missouri, Kansas, Texas, and Mexico.

Vitis vinifera 'Purpurea'

Vitis rotundifolia

Vitis rotundifolia, muscadine

Weigela florida
old-fashioned weigela

My negative sentiments toward this species were formed in my youth, when I saw the old, dirty, lavender-pink form haunting virtually every garden in the Midwest. Ugly! Times have changed, however, and breeders have improved upon the species by offering a variety of foliage and flower colors, more compact forms, and greater cold hardiness. I counted some 69 cultivars in the sixth edition of my *Manual* (2009) and missed another dozen or so that were lying in the weeds. The typical species is a spreading, dense, rounded shrub, with coarse branches that arch to the ground. The 2- to 4½-in.-long, oppositely arranged leaves are a nondescript green and are even worse in fall. The rosy pink flowers average 1 to 2 in. long, with an extended tubular corolla that flares at the mouth. The flowers occur in great profusion during April (Athens), May, and June and sporadically throughout the growing season. Provide well-drained soils of moderate fertility and full sun for best growth. Prune after flowering. Shrubs often retain dead branches and require tidying. Use in masses or in a shrub border. Grows 6 to 10 ft. high, 10 to 12 ft. wide. Zones (4)5 to 8. Japan.

Weigela coraeensis produces 1½-in.-long, cream-yellow, pink changing to carmine flowers in two- to eight-flowered cymes. Grows 5 to 6 ft. high and wide. Zones 6 and 7. Japan.

Weigela middendorffiana, Middendorf weigela, is similar to *W. florida*,

MORE ▶

Weigela middendorffiana, Middendorf weigela

Weigela florida

Weigela florida, old-fashioned weigela

Weigela florida

Weigela subsessilis

Weigela florida CONTINUED

with sulfur-yellow flowers and shining bright green leaves. Zones (4)5 to 7. Manchuria, northern China, Japan.

Weigela subsessilis carries its yellowish green flowers, changing to shades of pink and lavender, on a compact, twiggy shrub, 4 to 5 ft. by 4 to 6 ft. Zones 6 and 7. China.
CULTIVARS AND VARIETIES
Some of the better cold hardy selections include 'Minuet' and 'Newport Red' (with ruby-red flowers), 'Pink Princess' (lavender-pink), 'Polka' (pink outside, yellow inside), 'Red Prince' (red), 'Rumba' (dark red with a yellow throat), and 'Samba' and 'Tango' (red, yellow throat).

Purple, maroon-foliage types include 'Dark Horse', Fine Wine™ ('Bramwell'), 'Foliis Purpureis', Midnight Wine® ('Elvera'), Shining Sensation™, Wine & Roses® ('Alexandra'), and too many others.

Variegated selections. Insane number of white- and yellow-margined leaf types, including French Lace™ ('Brigela'), Magical Fantasy® ('Kolsunn'), My Monet™ ('Verweig'), 'Sunny Princess', 'Suzanne', 'Variegata', and 'Variegata Nana'.

Wisteria floribunda
Japanese wisteria

Gardeners in the North labor intensely to successfully flower this species, while southerners with pruning equipment attempt to eradicate it. One gardener's flower is another's weed. Japanese wisteria is a wild, twining vine that crushes any plant or wooden structure in its path in a boa constrictor–like fashion. The rich green leaves are composed of (11 to) 13 to 19 leaflets, each 1½ to 3 in. long. Fragrant, violet-blue, ½- to ¾-in.-long flowers are borne in 8- to 20-in.-long racemes that open from the base to the apex. The flowers open before or as the leaves develop in April and May. The fruit are borne in 4- to 6-in.-long velutinous pods that contain multiple green bean-like seeds. The species thrives with minimal care and is quite adaptable to soil conditions. Provide full sun to partial shade and a suitable structure, preferably one that is metal. Use with the knowledge that considerable pruning is necessary to keep it in bounds. It is sometimes trained as a small tree and then pruned to main-

MORE ▶

Weigela florida 'Variegata'

Weigela florida Wine & Roses®

Weigela florida Shining Sensation™

Weigela florida French Lace™

Weigela florida 'Newport Red'

Weigela florida 'Red Prince'

Wisteria floribunda

Wisteria floribunda 'Longissima Alba'

Wisteria floribunda, Japanese wisteria

879

Wisteria floribunda CONTINUED

tain this shape. Grows 30 to 50 ft. high and more. Unfortunately invasive, and I have observed out-of-control plants, 80- to 90-ft.-high vines in oak trees along the South Carolina coast. Zones 4 to 9. Japan.

CULTIVARS AND VARIETIES
Many cultivars are available in a variety of flower colors, from white to pink-rose, violet, deep purple, singles and doubles.

'Longissima Alba' is white-flowered, the racemes 2 to 3 ft. long. A favorite of the author.

'Macrobotrys' ('Multijuga'), lilac-tinged, blue-purple, fragrant flowers, on 1½- to 3- (to 4-) ft. racemes. A beauty.

Wisteria frutescens
American wisteria

Years past, the species was meshed into our garden and never really impressed. I experienced a plant in flower (late April, Athens) and was smitten. The great attributes over the Asiatic species like *Wisteria floribunda* and *W. sinensis* are lateness to leaf and flower, thus avoiding spring frosts, and less rambunctious growth habit. Still a vigorous, twining vine that requires support to look its best. Leaves consist of nine to 15, bright green leaflets, each 1½ to 2½ in. long, that turn yellowish in fall. The slightly fragrant flowers, pale lilac-purple, ¾ in. long, are compressed into 4- to 6-in.-long, dense, villous, grape-like racemes. Flowering is most pronounced in late April to May (in Athens) but sporadically continues on new growth into the summer. The flowers are not as impressive (or as large) as the Asiatic relatives but are more delicately beautiful and restrained. Fruit are 2- to 4-in.-long, glabrous pods with rounded, lima bean–like seeds. Best in moist soil in sun to partial shade. The plant in our garden was in dry soil and simply never performed. In the wild, it occurs naturally along moist shores of streams, ponds, and lakes, on the borders of wet woodlands and swamps, and in moist to wet thickets. This tells the gardener

Wisteria floribunda 'Macrobotrys'

Wisteria frutescens

Wisteria macrostachya 'Aunt Dee'

something about best siting in the garden. Grows 20 to 30 ft. high. Zones 5 to 9. Virginia to Florida and Texas.

Wisteria macrostachya, Kentucky wisteria, is similar and by taxonomists now treated as a variety of *W. frutescens*. Appears more cold hardy, flowering in June in Chicago, April and May in Raleigh, with the typical lilac-purple flowers. 'Aunt Dee' produces slightly fragrant, light purple flowers, in 7- to 12-in.-long racemes. 'Clara Mack' produces white, lightly fragrant flowers, later and in longer racemes than the species. Grows 15 to 25 ft. high. Zones (4)5 to 8(9). Kentucky, Tennessee, southern Illinois, Missouri, and Texas.

CULTIVARS AND VARIETIES
'Amethyst Falls', a selection of *Wisteria frutescens*, is appropriately named for the most beautiful, fragrant, lavender-blue flowers. Profuse flowering and perhaps more restrained than the species.

'Nivea' is a white-flowered form.

Wisteria sinensis
Chinese wisteria

Arguably, Chinese wisteria is superior to Japanese wisteria as a landscape vine because of its less rampant growth. The flowers open along the 6- to 12-in. length of the raceme at more or less the same time as those of *Wisteria floribunda*. Charted flowering times in early to late April (Athens). Leaves are composed of seven to 13 leaflets. Grows 20 to 30 ft. high. Zones 5 to 8. China.

MORE ▶

Wisteria sinensis

Wisteria sinensis 'Augusta's Pride'

Wisteria macrostachya 'Clara Mack'

Wisteria frutescens 'Amethyst Falls'

Wisteria frutescens, American wisteria

Wisteria sinensis CONTINUED
CULTIVARS AND VARIETIES
Variety *alba* ('Alba') is a pretty, white-flowered form.

'Augusta's Pride' is an early-flowering, light lavender-lilac selection from the Augusta National Golf Club; the original vine resides under an

Aphananthe aspera just outside the clubhouse.

Wollemia nobilis
Wollemi pine
Discovered by David Noble in 1994, growing in sandstone formations of Australia's Wollemi National Forest,

a rain-forest setting about 90 miles northwest of Sydney. Tree is pyramidal-conical, central-leadered, with spongy, bumpy bark. Evergreen leaves (needles) are 1¼ to 1¾ in. long, dark olive-green, and leathery pliable. Plant is another poster child for conservation as only 40 trees remain in nature. Now available and in cultivation in the United States. I have been unable to judge adaptability. Small plants at the JC Raulston Arboretum were toast at 15°F; at the Keith Arboretum, two plants, one no injury, the other slight, survived about 10°F under pine trees; and the West Coast reports top half

Wisteria sinensis var. *alba*

Wollemia nobilis, Wollemi pine

Wisteria sinensis, Chinese wisteria

of plant killed at 7°F, bottom half protected by snow. A feel-good story with no definite conclusions about garden worthiness. Zones (8)9 and 10 on West Coast.

Xanthoceras sorbifolium
yellowhorn

A virtual unknown in American gardens. The habit is not unlike that of *Koelreuteria paniculata*, panicled goldenraintree, developing an ultimately rounded outline of rather coarse branches. The lustrous dark green leaves are compound pinnate, with nine to 17 sharply serrated, 1½- to 2½-in.-long leaflets that remain late into fall. Fragrant white flowers, each ¾ to 1 in. in diameter, occur in 6- to 10-in.-long racemes in May. Each flower has a yellow basal blotch that matures to red. The fruit are three-valved, 2- to 4-in.-long capsules, each containing several dark brown, pea-sized seeds. Adaptable to any well-drained soil of acid or high pH. Requires full sun for maximum growth. Use as a small flowering tree, either freestanding or in a border. Grows 18 ft. high, 24 ft. wide. Zones (3)4 to 6(7). Northern China. CULTIVARS AND VARIETIES Clear Creek™ ('Psgan') produces fragrant white flowers, the centers aging yellow to red; 22 ft. by 15 ft. Introduced by the Plant Select® program at Colorado State University.

Xanthoceras sorbifolium

Xanthoceras sorbifolium

Xanthoceras sorbifolium

Xanthoceras sorbifolium, yellowhorn

Xanthocyparis nootka-tensis

syn. *Chamaecyparis nootkatensis*
Nootka falsecypress, Alaska cedar, yellow cypress

A common sight on the West Coast, especially plentiful in Washington and Oregon. The habit is softly pyramidal-conical with numerous drooping branches and long, flattened, pendulous sprays. The needles range from grayish green to bluish green. The ⅓- to ½-in.-wide, globose cones are composed of four (to six) scales. The species grows best when both atmospheric and soil moisture are abundant. Respectable performance in Midwest, East, and upper South. Grows 30 to 45 ft. high, 15 to 20 ft. wide; larger (100 ft. high) in the wild. Zones 4 to 7. Alaska to Oregon.

Xanthocyparis nootkatensis

Xanthocyparis nootkatensis, Nootka falsecypress

Xanthocyparis nootkatensis 'Pendula'

CULTIVARS AND VARIETIES
'Green Arrow' with green needles is a narrow weeping form.

'Pendula' is an attractive weeping form with graceful, elegantly arranged pendulous branches. It is reasonably common in the Mid-Atlantic states.

Xanthorhiza simplicissima
yellowroot

The absence of this fine native species in the American landscape has always been a mystery to me. In the wild, this robust, suckering, woody groundcover occurs along shady watercourses. Under cultivation, it develops into a full, dense groundcover mass, particularly when sited in full sun. The

leaves are composed of three to five, 1½- to 2¾-in.-long, lustrous bright green, deeply incised to sharply serrated leaflets that hold late and turn golden yellow to orange in fall. The purple flowers appear in March and April. Flowers and fruit are not showy. For best growth, provide moist, well-drained, acid soils, but magnificent plantings will develop under less-than-ideal conditions. Could be used effectively in shady nooks and crannies around buildings. Grows 2 to 3 ft.

high. Zones 3 to 9. New York to Kentucky and Florida.

Yucca
yucca

Although seldom considered as shrubs, the yuccas are acaulescent (no stem) or caulescent (stem) evergreen plants with sword-like leaves and reliable adaptability. The species are much confused taxonomically, but they are more or less the same for

MORE ▶

Xanthorhiza simplicissima

Xanthorhiza simplicissima, yellowroot

Xanthorhiza simplicissima fall color

Yucca glauca, small soapweed

Yucca CONTINUED

landscape considerations. They offer creamy white flowers in large inflorescences above the leaves in July and August. For textural effect, the 1- to 2½-ft.-long, 1½- to 3-in.-wide leaves provide a Desert Southwest atmosphere. Yuccas are hardy to at least –15 to –20°F and thrive in infertile, dry, sandy soils, in full sun. Transplant from a container.

Yucca filamentosa, Adam's-needle yucca; *Y. flaccida*, weakleaf yucca; *Y. glauca*, small soapweed; and *Y. smalliana*, small yucca, are the most cold hardy and the most landscape-worthy species. Grow 2 to 3 ft. high. Zones (4)5 to 9. Eastern and midwestern United States.

Yucca gloriosa, Spanish-dagger, and its variety *recurvifolia* (formerly *Y. recurvifolia*), curveleaf yucca, are larger caulescent types with stiff, sharp-pointed, almost lethal tips, the former with rigid, spine-tipped leaves, the latter with recurved leaves and less spiny tips. Have run (literally) into enough of these mean-spirited yuccas to know they need to be respected and planted into a "distant" relative's garden. Zones 6 to 9. Both found in Southeast.
CULTIVARS AND VARIETIES
'Golden Sword', with green-margined, yellow-centered leaves, and 'Bright Edge', just the opposite, are rather soul-stirring selections; both are probably selections of *Yucca filamentosa*.

Zamia pumila

syn. *Zamia floridana*

coontie

Delicate, elegant, spreading, broad-leaf evergreen "shrub" that is utilized throughout Florida in foundation and mass plantings. The deep green, lustrous, leathery leaflets are held on 3- to 5-ft.-long, compound pinnate leaves. Each leaflet is less than ½ in. wide and either planar along the rachis or twisted and curved. The species is dioecious; female plants develop cone-like structures with

Yucca filamentosa 'Bright Edge'

Yucca gloriosa, Spanish-dagger

Yucca filamentosa, Adam's-needle yucca

orange to scarlet seeds that mature in fall to winter. Adaptable, growing in any well-drained soil. Prefers partial shade, but I have observed plants in full sun in north Florida. Brought plants to Athens for testing, and they were burned beyond recognition by a single winter. Irresistibly beautiful, with many landscape uses. Grows 1 to 3 ft. high, wider at maturity. Zones 8 to 11. Florida, West Indies, Cuba.

Zamia furfuracea, cardboard palm, has 2- to 6-in.-long, 1- to 3-in.-wide leaflets with cardboard-like texture. Not as cold hardy as *Z. pumila* but unique for its foliage. Grows on sand dunes in its native habitat. Zones 9 to 11. Mexico.

Zanthoxylum americanum
prickly-ash, toothache tree

Seldom utilized for contrived landscapes but a worthy native for naturalizing and wildlife food. Almost always a colonizing shrub, rather unruly in outline, prominently armed with ⅓- to ½-in.-long prickles. The compound pinnate leaves, composed of five to 13, 1½- to 2½-in.-long, lustrous dark green leaflets, are insect- and disease-resistant. Yellowish green flowers open on naked stems in April and May. Fruit, on female plants, are ⅕-in.-long, red capsules that ripen in July and August and contain small, lustrous black seeds. Adaptable, tough, durable species for sun or partial shade. Could be utilized as a barrier plant in infertile soils. Might prove a respectable massing plant for cuts

MORE ▶

Zamia pumila, coontie

Zanthoxylum clava-herculis, Hercules'-club

Zamia furfuracea, cardboard palm

Zanthoxylum clava-herculis

887

Zanthoxylum americanum CONTINUED
or fills along highways. The bark was chewed to alleviate toothaches. Usually 10 ft. high and 15 to 25 ft. wide. Zones 3 to 7. Quebec to North Dakota, south to Georgia and Louisiana.

The related species *Zanthoxylum clava-herculis*, Hercules'-club, pepperwood, is a shrub or tree with glossy dark green leaves, white to yellow-green flowers, and thorn-like prickles on a platform base. Stems are coarse and chubby with prickles increasing in diameter and length. Grows on sand dunes along the coast and is quite salt-tolerant. Important source of butterfly-caterpillar food. Grows 25 to 30 ft. high. National champion is 36 ft. by 48 ft. Zones 7 to 10. Virginia, along coast to Texas and Oklahoma.

Zelkova schneideriana
Schneider zelkova
Included because of cultural similarity to *Zelkova serrata* but with at least one significant ornamental advantage. The dark green leaves, 1¾ to 4 in. long, ¾ to 2 in. wide, have seven to 14 indented vein pairs. The upper leaf surface is quite scabrous. Most rewarding trait is the brilliant wine-red to red fall color. I've observed it only a few times, but colleagues have confirmed the reliable, outstanding fall color. Estimate 30 to 50 ft. high under cultivation. Listed as 100 ft. or greater in China. Differs from *Z. serrata* in its much more pubescent gray-white new shoots and its much hairier leaves. I believe with expanded germplasm evaluation, superior cultivars could be introduced. Another sleeping beauty waiting for the plantsman's kiss. Zones 6 and 7.

Zelkova serrata
Japanese zelkova
The habit of this species, typically vase-shaped, with branches diverging at 45° angles to the central axis, is similar to that of American elm (*Ulmus americana*), but without the dignity and grace. Dark green, strongly serrated, 2- to 5-in.-long leaves give way to yellow, golden bronze, and reddish purple fall colors. The brown bark on young trees has a polished, almost cherry-

MORE ▶

Zanthoxylum americanum, prickly-ash

Zanthoxylum americanum

Zanthoxylum americanum fruit

Zelkova schneideriana, Schneider zelkova, fall color

Zelkova serrata, Japanese zelkova

Zelkova serrata 'Ogon'

Zelkova serrata 'Ogon'

Zelkova serrata CONTINUED

like quality, becoming gray and exfoliating with age, somewhat like that of Chinese elm (*U. parvifolia*). Adaptable to varied soils and climates. Displays reasonable tolerance to high heat and drought. Resistant to Dutch elm disease and the elm leaf beetle. Makes a fine street and park tree and is now a major player in the shade-tree market from Chicago to Atlanta to the West Coast, a success that in large part relates to the introduction of superior forms. Seedling zelkovas usually grow like a rabbit's hind legs—crooked and uneven; they are respectable trees, however, if properly pruned. Grows 50 to 80 ft. high, similar spread. Zones 5 to 8. Japan.

CULTIVARS AND VARIETIES

City Sprite™ ('JFS-KW1') is a compact

Zelkova serrata Village Green™ fall color

Zelkova serrata Green Vase® at Milliken Arboretum

oval- to vase-shaped outline; 24 ft. by 18 ft. J. Frank Schmidt & Son introduction. A diminutive form for underwire planting.

'Goshiki' has irregularly cream-marked, -speckled, and -splashed leaves. A collector's plant.

Green Vase® is a superior cultivar with upright-arching branches, resulting in a more graceful tree than Village Green™. Excellent dark green foliage turns orange-brown to bronzy red in fall. Faster growing than Village Green™. Grows 60 to 70 ft. high, 40 to 50 ft. wide.

'Musashino' is upright, narrow-columnar-vase-shaped; medium green leaves turn yellow in fall. Early leafing, the first zelkova to leaf at Milliken Arboretum, usually by mid to late March. Estimate 45 ft. by 15 ft. Good choice for tight planting areas.

'Ogon' ('Aurea', 'Bright Park') sports yellow leaves in spring, eventually green, and amber-gold-brown winter stems and trunk; attractive accent. Slow-growing in Georgia trials.

Village Green™, one of the first named selections, is still justifiably popular. The crown is more dense and stiff than that of Green Vase®. Old trees that I have observed were equal in height and width. The leathery, dark green foliage may develop a wine-red fall color. At maturity, probably smaller than Green Vase®.

Zelkova sinica
Chinese zelkova

Forever second fiddle to *Zelkova serrata* but a handsome genetic unit with uniform habit and unique bark. Rare in all but arboreta with notable trees in the Arnold and Morton (Massachusetts and Illinois, respectively), and the former USDA Bamboo Station, Savannah, Georgia. Vase-shaped habit, narrower than the average *Z. serrata*, 1- to 2½-in.-long, scabrous, dark green leaves, and multi-colored gray, orange, brown, exfoliating bark offer seasonal aesthetics. Leaves turn yellow-orange in fall but with no degree of certainty. A tough species, from Chicago to Boston to Savannah.

Zelkova sinica

Clay, sand, and drought present no problem to successful culture. Selection for desirable traits is necessary before it can become an everyday street and urban tree. Grows 20 to 40 ft. high. Zones (5)6 to 9. Eastern China.

Zenobia pulverulenta
dusty zenobia

Dusty zenobia is another underutilized native species that is more culturally adaptable than is generally believed. The habit is rounded-mounded with gracefully arching, slender branches. The typical bluish green to grayish green foliage is quite handsome and

MORE ▶

Zenobia pulverulenta

Zelkova serrata fall color

Zelkova sinica, Chinese zelkova

Zenobia pulverulenta CONTINUED
usually persists into winter; in autumn, leaves may turn yellowish with a tinge of red to red-purple. The white, ⅜-in.-wide, anise-scented flowers arrive in May and June. The standard cultural recommendation is for acid, moist, well-drained soils, but plantings in full sun, in moist sites, at the Arnold Arboretum were successful. Plants tend to sucker and colonize. Use in mass plantings, along streams, or in a perennial or shrub border. Variable in almost all characteristics. Grows 2 to 3 (to 6) ft. high and as wide. Zones 5 to 9. North Carolina to Florida.
CULTIVARS AND VARIETIES
Selections with almost silvery blue summer foliage are now popular plants. Such glaucous, powdery blue-foliage forms include 'Blue Sky', 'Misty Blue', and 'Woodlanders Blue'.

'Raspberry Ripple' produces beautiful, large white flowers marked with red-staining. Foliage tends toward gray-green.

Ziziphus jujuba
Chinese date

Beautiful, lustrous, mirror-reflective, dark green foliage seems sufficient reason to utilize the species. However, habit—upright-spreading to rounded—is often rumpled. The 1- to 2½-in.-long, strongly three-veined leaves are uniquely crenate-serrulate along the margin. The ¼-in.-wide, grape-soda fragrant, yellowish flowers occur two or three together from the leaf axils of the current season's growth. Flower effect is masked, for the leaves develop simultaneously. The egg-shaped, ½- to 1-in.-long fruit are brownish orange on the outside with a dried apple–like consistency on the inside. Several trees at the University's Horticulture Farm yielded tons of fruit. I sample a fruit each visit and still have not found a window of time when the taste is palatable, though they are prized in China as a commercial staple. I know, I know—to each their own. Concrete-like tenacity in heat. If paired stem spines and fruit could be removed, it might make a good street tree. Two 25- to 30-ft.-high trees grow on the south side of the U.S. Capitol. Grows 15 to 20 (to 25) ft. high. Zones 6 to 9. Southeastern Europe to southern and eastern Asia.

Zenobia pulverulenta, dusty zenobia

Zenobia pulverulenta 'Woodlanders Blue'

Zenobia pulverulenta 'Raspberry Ripple'

Ziziphus jujuba, Chinese date

Ziziphus jujuba

Ziziphus jujuba

Selecting Plants for Specific Characteristics or Purposes

Many readers require ready access to information on specific plants for specific purposes. In compiling the following lists, I limited the entries to those plants that are most appropriate. Entries in the A-to-Z offer full details. Certainly a tad of personal bias is evident, but in the main, I erred on the side of objectivity. Use these lists as ready references to possible solutions for planting design problems. Perhaps salt tolerance is a criterion for landscaping a beach house; *Agave* *americana* and ×*Cupressocyparis leylandii* appear in the list of salt-tolerant plants. Look them up in the main body of the book, read the text, peruse the photographs, and decide which plant will create the desired effect.

FLOWER COLOR

The following trees and shrubs bear showy flowers of notable color. Variations of the primary flower color(s) listed here will exist in certain cultivars or varieties of a given tree or shrub, and flowers can often be ornamented with stripes or blotches of a different color.

YELLOW

Abelia serrata
Abutilon pictum
Acacia dealbata
Acer platanoides
Acer rubrum
Acer saccharinum
Acer truncatum
Alangium platanifolium
Allamanda cathartica
Azara microphylla
Berberis
Bougainvillea glabra
Brugmansia ×*candida*
Buddleia
Butia capitata
Calycanthus chinensis
Campsis grandiflora
Caragana arborescens
Caragana frutex
Cassia

Chamaerops humilis
Chimonanthus praecox
Clematis
Colutea arborescens
Cornus mas
Cornus officinalis
Corokia cotoneaster
Corylopsis
Cytisus battandieri
Cytisus scoparius
Diervilla sessilifolia
Dipelta floribunda
Dirca palustris
Edgeworthia chrysantha
Elaeagnus angustifolia
Forsythia
Galphimia gracilis
Gelsemium sempervirens
Genista
Gleditsia triacanthos f. *inermis*

Grevillea juniperina
Hamamelis
Helianthemum nummularium
Hibiscus rosa-sinensis
Hypericum
Illicium parviflorum
Jasminum floridum
Jasminum humile
Jasminum mesnyi
Jasminum nudiflorum
Jasminum parkeri
Kerria japonica
Koelreuteria bipinnata
Koelreuteria paniculata
+*Laburnocytisus adamii*
Laburnum ×*watereri*
Lantana camara
Laurus nobilis
Lindera
Liriodendron tulipifera
Lonicera caprifolium
Lonicera flava
Lonicera japonica
Lonicera maackii
Lonicera nitida
Lonicera periclymenum
Lonicera pileata

Lonicera xylosteum
Magnolia acuminata
Magnolia figo
Mahonia
Nerium oleander
Parkinsonia aculeata
Phoenix canariensis
Pittosporum heterophyllum
Pittosporum tobira
Potentilla fruticosa
Prinsepia sinensis
Rhapidophyllum hystrix
Rhododendron austrinum
Rhododendron flammeum
Ribes aureum var. *villosum*
Rosa banksiae 'Lutea'
Rosa spinosissima
Santolina chamaecyparissus
Sapindus drummondii
Sarcandra glabra
Sassafras albidum
Shepherdia argentea
Stephanandra incisa
Sycopsis sinensis
Symphoricarpos orbiculatus
Symplocos tinctoria
Tecoma capensis
Tilia

Trachelospermum
Trachycarpus fortunei
Triadica sebifera
Ziziphus jujuba

YELLOW-GREEN

Acer buergerianum
Acer campestre
Acer carpinifolium
Acer cissifolium subsp.
   henryi
Acer griseum
Acer miyabei
Acer negundo
Acer pensylvanicum
Acer pseudoplatanus
Acer saccharum
Acer saccharum subsp. flori-
   danum
Acer saccharum subsp. leu-
   coderme
Aesculus flava
Aesculus glabra
Aesculus sylvatica
Agave americana
Ailanthus altissima
Alnus
Ampelopsis brevipeduncu-
   lata
Andrachne colchica
Aristolochia macrophylla
Broussonetia papyrifera
Buxus
Celastrus orbiculatus
Celastrus scandens
Celtis laevigata
Celtis occidentalis
Cocculus carolinus
Comptonia peregrina
Cotinus
Croton alabamensis
Danae racemosa
Decaisnea fargesii
Eleutherococcus sieboldia-
   nus
Eucommia ulmoides
Euonymus alatus
Euonymus americanus
Euonymus bungeanus
Euonymus carnosus
Euonymus europaeus

Euonymus fortunei
Fagus grandifolia
Fagus sylvatica
Firmiana simplex
Forestiera acuminata
Frangula alnus
Frangula caroliniana
Garrya elliptica
Ginkgo biloba
Hippophae rhamnoides
Idesia polycarpa
Juglans nigra
Juglans regia
Leitneria floridana
Liquidambar formosana
Liquidambar styraciflua
Maclura pomifera
Magnolia acuminata
Menispermum canadense
Morus
Myrica
Nyssa ogeche
Nyssa sylvatica
Orixa japonica
Ostrya virginiana
Parthenocissus
Paxistima canbyi
Phellodendron amurense
Picrasma quassioides
Pinckneya bracteata
Pistacia chinensis
Planera aquatica
Platanus ×acerifolia
Platanus occidentalis
Pseudolarix amabilis
Ptelea trifoliata
Pterocarya fraxinifolia
Rhamnus cathartica
Rhus
Ribes alpinum
Sambucus racemosa
Sarcococca saligna
Smilax
Stachyurus praecox
Trochodendron aralioides
Vitex rotundifolia
Vitis rotundifolia
Zanthoxylum americanum
Zelkova

ORANGE/RED

Abelia floribunda

Acer japonicum
Acer palmatum
Acer rubrum
Acer saccharinum
Aesculus ×carnea
Aesculus pavia
Bignonia capreolata
Bougainvillea glabra
Buddleia davidii
Callistemon citrinus
Calluna vulgaris
Calycanthus floridus
Calycanthus occidentalis
Camellia japonica
Camellia sasanqua
Camellia ×williamsii
Campsis grandiflora
Campsis radicans
Campsis ×tagliabuana
   'Madame Galen'
Chaenomeles japonica
Chaenomeles speciosa
Clematis
Daboecia cantabrica
Desfontainia spinosa
Distylium myricoides
Distylium racemosum
Enkianthus campanulatus
Erica carnea
Erythrina ×bidwillii
Escallonia rubra
Eucalyptus
Fuchsia magellanica
Grevillea robusta
Grevillea rosmarinifolia
Hamamelis ×intermedia
Hamamelis japonica
Hamamelis vernalis
Helianthemum nummu-
   larium
Hibiscus rosa-sinensis
Hibiscus syriacus
Hydrangea macrophylla
Hydrangea serrata
Illicium floridanum
Illicium mexicanum
Ixora coccinea
Lagerstroemia hybrids
Lantana camara
Liriodendron tulipifera
Lonicera ×brownii
Lonicera flava

Lonicera sempervirens
Magnolia liliiflora
Malvaviscus arboreus var.
   drummondii
Mandevilla splendens
Nerium oleander
Parrotia persica
Paxistima canbyi
Potentilla fruticosa
Prunus campanulata
Prunus mume
Prunus persica
Prunus tenella
Punica granatum
Rhododendron austrinum
Rhododendron calendula-
   ceum
Rhododendron flammeum
Rhododendron prunifolium
Ribes sanguineum
Rosa moyesii
Sesbania punicea
Sycopsis sinensis
Tecoma capensis
Vaccinium crassifolium
Weigela florida

PINK/ROSE

Abelia ×grandiflora
Abelia macrotera
Abelia parvifolia
Abelia spathulata
Abutilon vitifolium
Acer circinatum
Acer japonicum
Acer palmatum
Acer pseudosieboldianum
Actinidia pilosula
Aesculus ×carnea
Aesculus indica
Albizia julibrissin
Andromeda polifolia
Antigonon leptopus
Arbutus unedo
Arctostaphylos uva-ursi
Ardisia japonica
Bignonia capreolata
Brugmansia ×candida
Buddleia davidii
Callicarpa
Calluna vulgaris
Camellia japonica

Camellia reticulata
Camellia saluenensis
Camellia sasanqua
Camellia ×williamsii
Ceanothus ×pallidus
Cercis canadensis
Cercis chinensis
Chaenomeles japonica
Chaenomeles speciosa
Chilopsis linearis
Cistus
Clematis
Cotoneaster adpressus
Cotoneaster apiculatus
Cotoneaster divaricatus
Cotoneaster horizontalis
Cotoneaster lucidus
Daboecia cantabrica
Daphne bholua
Daphne ×burkwoodii
Daphne cneorum
Daphne mezereum
Daphne odora
Deutzia ×hybrida
Deutzia scabra
Dichroa febrifuga
Dipelta floribunda
Elsholtzia stauntonii
Enkianthus campanulatus
Epigaea repens
Erica carnea
Escallonia rubra
Gaylussacia brachycera
Gaylussacia ursina
Hebe
Helianthemum nummu-
    larium
Hibiscus
Hydrangea macrophylla
Hydrangea quercifolia
Hydrangea serrata
Illicium henryi
Indigofera
Jasminum officinale
Kalmia angustifolia
Kalmia latifolia
Kolkwitzia amabilis
+Laburnocytisus adamii
Lagerstroemia indica
Lagerstroemia limii
Lantana camara
Leiophyllum buxifolium

Leptospermum scoparium
Lespedeza bicolor
Lespedeza thunbergii
Leucophyllum frutescens
Lonicera alpigena
Lonicera fragrantissima
Lonicera ×heckrottii
Lonicera korolkowii
Lonicera tatarica
Loropetalum chinense var.
    rubrum
Lyonia lucida
Magnolia campbellii
Magnolia cylindrica
Magnolia kobus
Magnolia liliiflora
Magnolia ×loebneri
Magnolia ×soulangeana
Magnolia stellata
Magnolia zenii 'Pink Parch-
    ment'
Malus angustifolia
Malus floribunda
Malus hupehensis
Malus sargentii
Malus sieboldii var. zumi
    'Calocarpa'
Mandevilla splendens
Mespilus germanica
Mitchella repens
Musa
Nandina domestica
Neillia sinensis
Nerium oleander
Pachysandra procumbens
Potentilla fruticosa
Prunus campanulata
Prunus cerasifera
Prunus glandulosa 'Rosea
    Plena'
Prunus 'Hally Jolivette'
Prunus incisa
Prunus mume
Prunus 'Okame'
Prunus persica
Prunus sargentii
Prunus serrulata
Prunus subhirtella
Prunus tenella
Prunus triloba var. multiplex
Prunus ×yedoensis
Pseudocydonia sinensis

Rhaphiolepis umbellata
Rhododendron atlanticum
Rhododendron canescens
Rhododendron catawbiense
Rhododendron degronianum
    subsp. yakushimanum
Rhododendron hyperythrum
Rhododendron maximum
Rhododendron minus
Rhododendron minus var.
    chapmanii
Rhododendron mucronula-
    tum
Rhododendron periclymen-
    oides
Rhododendron 'PJM'
Rhododendron prinophyllum
Rhododendron schlippen-
    bachii
Rhododendron vaseyi
Rhododendron viscosum
Ribes sanguineum
Robinia hispida
Rosa carolina
Rosa glauca
Rosa rugosa
Rosa spinosissima
Rosa virginiana
Rostrinucula dependens
Spiraea alba var. latifolia
Spiraea tomentosa
Spiraea japonica
Symphoricarpos
Syringa ×chinensis
Syringa ×hyacinthiflora
Syringa pubescens subsp.
    microphylla
Syringa villosa
Syringa vulgaris
Tamarix ramosissima
Ungnadia speciosa
Vaccinium angustifolium
Vaccinium ashei
Vaccinium corymbosum
Vaccinium crassifolium
Vaccinium elliottii
Vaccinium vitis-idaea
Viburnum ×bodnantense
Viburnum ×burkwoodii
Viburnum ×carlcephalum
Viburnum carlesii
Viburnum farreri

Viburnum ×juddii
Viburnum 'Pragense'
Viburnum tinus
Viburnum utile
Weigela florida
Wisteria floribunda
Wisteria sinensis

BLUE/PURPLE
Abutilon vitifolium
Acer palmatum
Akebia quinata
Amorpha canescens
Amorpha fruticosa
Asimina triloba
Aucuba japonica
Bauhinia variegata
Bougainvillea glabra
Brunfelsia pauciflora
Buddleia alternifolia
Buddleia davidii
Buddleia lindleyana
Buddleia salviifolia
Calia secundiflora
Callicarpa
Calluna vulgaris
Camellia japonica
Camellia sasanqua
Caryopteris ×clandonensis
Catalpa bignonioides
Catalpa speciosa
Ceanothus ×delileanus
Cercidiphyllum japonicum
Chilopsis linearis
×Chitalpa tashkentensis
Cistus
Clematis
Daboecia cantabrica
Daphne genkwa
Daphniphyllum macropodum
Dichroa febrifuga
Disanthus cercidifolius
Duranta erecta
Fraxinus americana
Fraxinus pennsylvanica
Fuchsia magellanica
Hamamelis ×intermedia
Hamamelis japonica
Hebe
Hibiscus rosa-sinensis
Hibiscus syriacus
Holboellia latifolia

Hydrangea macrophylla
Hydrangea serrata
Illicium floridanum
Illicium mexicanum
Kalmia latifolia
Lagerstroemia indica
Lavandula angustifolia
Leptodermis oblonga
Leucophyllum frutescens
Magnolia ×soulangeana
Melia azedarach
Millettia reticulata
Parrotia persica
Passiflora incarnata
Paulownia tomentosa
Pittosporum tenuifolium
Plumbago auriculata
Rhododendron minus
Rhododendron minus var.
  chapmanii
Rhododendron 'PJM'
Rhododendron yedoense
  var. poukhanense
Rosmarinus officinalis
Syringa ×chinensis
Syringa ×hyacinthiflora
Syringa ×laciniata
Syringa meyeri
Syringa oblata var. dilatata
Syringa ×persica
Syringa pubescens subsp.
  microphylla
Syringa pubescens subsp.
  patula
Syringa vulgaris
Teucrium chamaedrys
Vinca major
Vinca minor
Vitex agnus-castus
Vitex negundo
Wisteria
Xanthorhiza simplicissima

WHITE

Abelia chinensis
Abelia ×grandiflora
Abelia macrotera
Abelia mosanensis
Abelia serrata
Abelia spathulata
Abeliophyllum distichum

Abutilon vitifolium
Acca sellowiana
Acer tataricum
Acer tataricum subsp. gin-
  nala
Actinidia arguta
Actinidia deliciosa
Actinidia kolomikta
Actinidia polygama
Adina rubella
Aesculus californica
Aesculus hippocastanum
Aesculus indica
Aesculus parviflora
Aesculus turbinata
Agarista populifolia
Alangium platanifolium
Amelanchier
Andromeda polifolia
Aralia elata
Aralia spinosa
Arbutus menziesii
Arbutus unedo
Arctostaphylos uva-ursi
Ardisia japonica
Aronia arbutifolia
Aronia melanocarpa
Bauhinia variegata
Bougainvillea glabra
Brugmansia ×candida
Buddleia davidii
Buddleia loricata
Butia capitata
Calluna vulgaris
Calycanthus chinensis
Camellia japonica
Camellia oleifera
Camellia sasanqua
Camellia sinensis
Camellia ×williamsii
Carissa macrocarpa
Castanea mollissima
Castanea pumila
Catalpa bignonioides
Catalpa speciosa
Ceanothus americanus
Cephalanthus occidentalis
Chaenomeles japonica
Chaenomeles speciosa
Chamaedaphne calyculata
Chilopsis linearis

Chionanthus retusus
Chionanthus virginicus
Choisya ternata
Cinnamomum camphora
Cistus
Cladrastis kentukea
Clematis
Clerodendrum trichotomum
Clethra
Cleyera japonica
Cliftonia monophylla
Cornus alba
Cornus alternifolia
Cornus amomum
Cornus capitata
Cornus florida
Cornus kousa
Cornus macrophylla
Cornus nuttallii
Cornus racemosa
Cornus sanguinea
Cornus sericea
Cotoneaster dammeri
Cotoneaster lacteus
Cotoneaster multiflorus
Cotoneaster salicifolius
Crataegus
Cyrilla racemiflora
Cytisus scoparius
Daboecia cantabrica
Daphne bholua
Daphne ×burkwoodii
Daphne ×transatlantica
Davidia involucrata
Decumaria barbara
Deutzia gracilis
Deutzia ×lemoinei
Deutzia scabra
Deutzia setchuenensis
Diospyros kaki
Diospyros virginiana
Edgeworthia chrysantha
Ehretia dicksonii
Elaeagnus ×ebbingei
Elaeagnus macrophylla
Elaeagnus multiflora
Elaeagnus pungens
Elaeagnus umbellata
Elliottia racemosa
Emmenopterys henryi
Enkianthus
Epigaea repens

Erica carnea
Eriobotrya japonica
Eubotrys racemosa
Eucalyptus
Eucryphia glutinosa
Euonymus japonicus
Euonymus kiautschovicus
Eurya japonica
Euscaphis japonica
Exochorda racemosa
Exochorda serratifolia
Fallopia baldschuanica
×Fatshedera lizei
Fatsia japonica
Ficus carica
Ficus pumila
Fontanesia philliraeoides
  subsp. fortunei
Fothergilla gardenii
Fothergilla major
Franklinia alatamaha
Fraxinus ornus
Gardenia jasminoides
Gaultheria mucronata
Gaultheria procumbens
Gaylussacia brachycera
Gaylussacia ursina
Gordonia lasianthus
Gymnocladus dioicus
Halesia carolina
Halesia diptera
Hebe
Hedera
Helianthemum nummu-
  larium
Heptacodium miconioides
Hibiscus
Hovenia dulcis
Hydrangea
Ilex
Illicium anisatum
Itea virginica
Jasminum officinale
Kadsura japonica
Kalmia latifolia
Kalopanax septemlobus
Lagerstroemia indica
Lagerstroemia limii
Lagerstroemia subcostata
  var. fauriei
Lantana camara
Leiophyllum buxifolium

Leucothoe axillaris
Leucothoe fontanesiana
Leycesteria formosa
Ligustrum
Lithocarpus henryi
Livistona chinensis
Lonicera caprifolium
Lonicera fragrantissima
Lonicera japonica
Lonicera maackii
Lonicera nitida
Lonicera periclymenum
Lonicera pileata
Lonicera tatarica
Lonicera xylosteum
Loropetalum chinense
Lyonia lucida
Maackia amurensis
Magnolia cylindrica
Magnolia denudata
Magnolia fraseri
Magnolia fraseri subsp.
  pyramidata
Magnolia grandiflora
Magnolia kobus
Magnolia ×loebneri
Magnolia macrophylla
Magnolia macrophylla
  subsp. ashei
Magnolia salicifolia
Magnolia sieboldii
Magnolia ×soulangeana
Magnolia stellata
Magnolia virginiana
Magnolia zenii 'Pink Parch-
  ment'
Malus floribunda
Malus hupehensis
Malus sargentii
Malus sieboldii var. zumi
  'Calocarpa'
Mespilus germanica
Mitchella repens
Myrtus communis
Nandina domestica
Nerium oleander
Neviusia alabamensis
Olea europaea

Osmanthus
Oxydendrum arboreum
Pachysandra procumbens
Pachysandra terminalis
Parrotiopsis jacquemontiana
Persea borbonia
Philadelphus coronarius
Philadelphus inodorus
Phillyrea angustifolia
Phoenix canariensis
Photinia
Physocarpus opulifolius
Pieris
Pittosporum heterophyllum
Pittosporum tobira
Poliothyrsis sinensis
Poncirus trifoliata
Prunus americana
Prunus avium
Prunus besseyi
Prunus caroliniana
Prunus cerasifera
Prunus 'Hally Jolivette'
Prunus incisa
Prunus laurocerasus
Prunus lusitanica
Prunus maackii
Prunus maritima
Prunus mume
Prunus padus
Prunus serotina
Prunus serrula
Prunus serrulata
Prunus tomentosa
Prunus virginiana
Prunus ×yedoensis
Pterostyrax hispida
Pyracantha coccinea
Pyracantha koidzumii
Pyrus
Rhaphiolepis umbellata
Rhapidophyllum hystrix
Rhapis excelsa
Rhododendron alabamense
Rhododendron atlanticum
Rhododendron canescens
Rhododendron degronianum
  subsp. yakushimanum

Rhododendron hyperythrum
Rhododendron maximum
Rhododendron viscosum
Rhodotypos scandens
Ribes sanguineum
Robinia pseudoacacia
Rosa laevigata
Rosa rugosa
Rosa spinosissima
Rubus pentalobus
Sabal
Sambucus canadensis
Sambucus nigra
Sapindus drummondii
Sarcococca confusa
Sarcococca hookeriana
Sarcococca orientalis
Sarcococca ruscifolia
Schizophragma hydrange-
  oides
Serenoa repens
Serissa japonica
Sinojackia rehderiana
Skimmia japonica
Skimmia japonica subsp.
  reevesiana
Sorbaria
Sorbus
Spiraea
Staphylea trifolia
Stephanandra incisa
Stewartia
Styphnolobium japonicum
Styrax
Syagrus romanzoffianum
Symphoricarpos orbiculatus
Symplocos paniculata
Syringa reticulata
Syringa reticulata subsp.
  pekinensis
Syringa vulgaris
Ternstroemia gymnanthera
Tetradium daniellii
Tilia
Toona sinensis
Trachelospermum asiaticum
Trachelospermum jasmin-
  oides

Vaccinium angustifolium
Vaccinium arboreum
Vaccinium ashei
Vaccinium corymbosum
Vaccinium elliottii
Vaccinium stamineum
Vaccinium vitis-idaea
Vernicia fordii
Viburnum acerifolium
Viburnum awabuki
Viburnum bracteatum
Viburnum ×burkwoodii
Viburnum ×carlcephalum
Viburnum carlesii
Viburnum cassinoides
Viburnum davidii
Viburnum dentatum
Viburnum dilatatum
Viburnum japonicum
Viburnum ×juddii
Viburnum lantana
Viburnum lentago
Viburnum macrocephalum
Viburnum nudum
Viburnum obovatum
Viburnum odoratissimum
Viburnum opulus
Viburnum plicatum
Viburnum plicatum f. tomen-
  tosum
Viburnum 'Pragense'
Viburnum prunifolium
Viburnum rafinesqueanum
Viburnum ×rhytidophylloides
Viburnum rhytidophyllum
Viburnum rufidulum
Viburnum sargentii
Viburnum setigerum
Viburnum sieboldii
Viburnum suspensum
Viburnum tinus
Viburnum trilobum
Viburnum utile
Washingtonia robusta
Weigela florida
Xanthoceras sorbifolium
Yucca
Zenobia pulverulenta

FLOWERING SEQUENCE

Trees and shrubs are listed for each season in which they are in bloom. These are approximations: in any given year, spring may come two weeks earlier or later than the norm, and bloom times will change accordingly. This list should be used as a guide only.

WINTER

Abeliophyllum distichum
Acacia dealbata
Acer rubrum
Acer saccharinum
Alnus
Arbutus menziesii
Arbutus unedo
Asimina triloba
Bauhinia variegata
Buxus
Callistemon citrinus
Camellia japonica
Camellia reticulata
Camellia saluenensis
Chaenomeles japonica
Chaenomeles speciosa
Chimonanthus praecox
Cliftonia monophylla
Cornus mas
Cornus officinalis
Corylopsis
Corylus
Croton alabamensis
Daphne bholua
Daphne mezereum
Daphne odora
Dirca palustris
Distylium myricoides
Distylium racemosum
Edgeworthia chrysantha
Epigaea repens
Erica carnea
×Fatshedera lizei
Fatsia japonica
Forestiera acuminata
Forestiera angustifolia
Forsythia
Garrya elliptica
Gelsemium sempervirens
Hamamelis ×intermedia
Hamamelis japonica
Hamamelis mollis
Hamamelis vernalis
Illicium anisatum

Illicium floridanum
Illicium mexicanum
Jasminum mesnyi
Jasminum nudiflorum
Leitneria floridana
Lindera
Lithocarpus henryi
Lonicera fragrantissima
Lyonia lucida
Magnolia campbellii
Magnolia cylindrica
Magnolia denudata
Magnolia kobus
Magnolia ×loebneri
Magnolia salicifolia
Magnolia ×soulangeana
Magnolia stellata
Magnolia zenii 'Pink Parchment'
Mahonia ×media
Metasequoia glyptostroboides
Osmanthus fragrans
Osmanthus serrulatus
Pachysandra procumbens
Pachysandra terminalis
Parrotia persica
Pieris japonica
Pieris phillyreifolia
Prunus campanulata
Prunus incisa
Prunus mume
Prunus 'Okame'
Prunus subhirtella
Rhododendron mucronulatum
Ribes sanguineum
Rosmarinus officinalis
Salix caprea
Sarcococca
Skimmia japonica
Skimmia japonica subsp. reevesiana
Spiraea thunbergii
Stachyurus praecox

Sycopsis sinensis
Taxodium distichum
Taxodium distichum var. imbricarium
Ulmus alata
Ulmus americana
Ulmus crassifolia
Ulmus glabra
Ulmus minor
Ulmus pumila
Viburnum ×bodnantense
Viburnum farreri
Viburnum obovatum
Viburnum tinus

SPRING

Abelia chinensis
Abelia floribunda
Abelia ×grandiflora
Abelia macrotera
Abelia mosanensis
Abelia parvifolia
Abelia serrata
Abelia spathulata
Abeliophyllum distichum
Abies
Abutilon vitifolium
Acacia dealbata
Acer
Actinidia
Aesculus californica
Aesculus ×carnea
Aesculus flava
Aesculus glabra
Aesculus hippocastanum
Aesculus indica
Aesculus pavia
Aesculus sylvatica
Aesculus turbinata
Agarista populifolia
Ailanthus altissima
Akebia quinata
Alangium platanifolium
Alnus
Amelanchier
Ampelopsis brevipedunculata
Andrachne colchica
Andromeda polifolia
Arctostaphylos uva-ursi
Aronia arbutifolia
Aronia melanocarpa

Asimina triloba
Aucuba japonica
Azara microphylla
Bauhinia variegata
Berberis
Betula
Bignonia capreolata
Broussonetia papyrifera
Brunfelsia pauciflora
Buddleia alternifolia
Buddleia davidii
Buddleia lindleyana
Buxus
Calia secundiflora
Callicarpa
Callistemon citrinus
Calocedrus decurrens
Calycanthus
Camellia reticulata
Camellia saluenensis
Camellia ×williamsii
Caragana arborescens
Caragana frutex
Carissa macrocarpa
Carpinus betulus
Carpinus caroliniana
Carya
Castanea mollissima
Castanea pumila
Catalpa bignonioides
Catalpa speciosa
Ceanothus americanus
Ceanothus ×delileanus
Ceanothus ×pallidus
Celastrus orbiculatus
Celastrus scandens
Celtis laevigata
Celtis occidentalis
Cephalotaxus fortunei
Cephalotaxus harringtonia
Cercidiphyllum japonicum
Cercis canadensis
Cercis chinensis
Chaenomeles japonica
Chaenomeles speciosa
Chamaecyparis
Chamaedaphne calyculata
Chionanthus retusus
Chionanthus virginicus
Choisya ternata
Cinnamomum camphora
Cladrastis kentukea

Clematis
Cleyera japonica
Cliftonia monophylla
Cocculus carolinus
Colutea arborescens
Comptonia peregrina
Cornus
Corokia cotoneaster
Corylopsis
Corylus
Cotoneaster
Crataegus
Croton alabamensis
Cryptomeria japonica
Cunninghamia lanceolata
×Cupressocyparis leylandii
×Cupressocyparis ovensii
Cupressus
Cytisus scoparius
Daphne bholua
Daphne ×burkwoodii
Daphne cneorum
Daphne genkwa
Daphne ×transatlantica
Daphniphyllum macropodum
Davidia involucrata
Decaisnea fargesii
Decumaria barbara
Deutzia
Diospyros kaki
Diospyros virginiana
Dipelta floribunda
Dirca palustris
Distylium myricoides
Distylium racemosum
Ehretia dicksonii
Elaeagnus angustifolia
Elaeagnus multiflora
Elaeagnus umbellata
Eleutherococcus sieboldianus
Enkianthus
Epigaea repens
Escallonia rubra
Eubotrys racemosa
Eucalyptus
Eucommia ulmoides
Euonymus
Eurya japonica
Euscaphis japonica
Exochorda racemosa
Exochorda serratifolia

Fagus grandifolia
Fagus sylvatica
Firmiana simplex
Fontanesia philliraeoides
    subsp. fortunei
Forestiera acuminata
Forestiera angustifolia
Forsythia
Fothergilla gardenii
Fothergilla major
Frangula alnus
Frangula caroliniana
Fraxinus americana
Fraxinus pennsylvanica
Fraxinus quadrangulata
Gardenia jasminoides
Gaultheria mucronata
Gaultheria procumbens
Gaylussacia brachycera
Gaylussacia ursina
Gelsemium sempervirens
Genista
Ginkgo biloba
Gleditsia triacanthos f. inermis
Gymnocladus dioicus
Halesia carolina
Halesia diptera
Heptacodium miconioides
Hibiscus syriacus
Hippophae rhamnoides
Holboellia latifolia
Hovenia dulcis
Hydrangea anomala subsp.
    petiolaris
Hydrangea arborescens
Hydrangea macrophylla
Hydrangea quercifolia
Hydrangea serrata
Idesia polycarpa
Ilex
Illicium anisatum
Illicium floridanum
Illicium henryi
Illicium mexicanum
Itea virginica
Jasminum humile
Jasminum mesnyi
Jasminum parkeri
Juglans nigra
Juglans regia
Juniperus

Kadsura japonica
Kalmia angustifolia
Kalmia latifolia
Kalopanax septemlobus
Kerria japonica
Koelreuteria paniculata
Kolkwitzia amabilis
+Laburnocytisus adamii
Laburnum ×watereri
Larix
Laurus nobilis
Leiophyllum buxifolium
Leitneria floridana
Leptospermum scoparium
Leucophyllum frutescens
Leucothoe axillaris
Leucothoe fontanesiana
Ligustrum
Lindera
Liquidambar formosana
Liquidambar styraciflua
Liriodendron tulipifera
Lonicera alpigena
Lonicera ×brownii
Lonicera flava
Lonicera ×heckrottii
Lonicera japonica
Lonicera korolkowii
Lonicera maackii
Lonicera nitida
Lonicera periclymenum
Lonicera pileata
Lonicera sempervirens
Lonicera tatarica
Lonicera xylosteum
Loropetalum chinense
Loropetalum chinense var.
    rubrum
Lyonia lucida
Maclura pomifera
Magnolia acuminata
Magnolia campbellii
Magnolia cylindrica
Magnolia denudata
Magnolia figo
Magnolia fraseri
Magnolia fraseri subsp.
    pyramidata
Magnolia kobus
Magnolia liliiflora
Magnolia ×loebneri
Magnolia macrophylla

Magnolia macrophylla
    subsp. ashei
Magnolia salicifolia
Magnolia sieboldii
Magnolia ×soulangeana
Magnolia stellata
Mahonia aquifolium
Mahonia bealei
Malus
Melia azedarach
Menispermum canadense
Mespilus germanica
Metasequoia glyptostroboides
Mitchella repens
Morus
Myrica
Myrtus communis
Nandina domestica
Neillia sinensis
Nerium oleander
Neviusia alabamensis
Nyssa ogeche
Nyssa sylvatica
Orixa japonica
Osmanthus americanus
Osmanthus ×burkwoodii
Osmanthus delavayi
Osmanthus fragrans
Ostrya virginiana
Pachysandra procumbens
Pachysandra terminalis
Parkinsonia aculeata
Parrotia persica
Parrotiopsis jacquemontiana
Parthenocissus
Paulownia tomentosa
Paxistima canbyi
Persea borbonia
Phellodendron amurense
Philadelphus coronarius
Philadelphus inodorus
Philadelphus pubescens
Phillyrea angustifolia
Photinia
Physocarpus opulifolius
Picea
Picrasma quassioides
Pieris floribunda
Pieris formosa var. forrestii
Pieris japonica
Pieris phillyreifolia

Pinus

Pistacia chinensis

Pittosporum

Planera aquatica

Platanus ×acerifolia

Platanus occidentalis

Poncirus trifoliata

Populus

Prinsepia sinensis

Prunus americana

Prunus angustifolia

Prunus avium

Prunus besseyi

Prunus caroliniana

Prunus cerasifera

Prunus glandulosa 'Rosea Plena'

Prunus 'Hally Jolivette'

Prunus incisa

Prunus laurocerasus

Prunus lusitanica

Prunus maackii

Prunus maritima

Prunus 'Okame'

Prunus padus

Prunus persica

Prunus sargentii

Prunus serotina

Prunus serrula

Prunus serrulata

Prunus subhirtella

Prunus tenella

Prunus tomentosa

Prunus triloba var. multiplex

Prunus virginiana

Prunus ×yedoensis

Pseudocydonia sinensis

Pseudolarix amabilis

Pseudotsuga menziesii

Ptelea trifoliata

Pterocarya fraxinifolia

Pterostyrax hispida

Pyracantha coccinea

Pyrus

Quercus

Rhamnus cathartica

Rhaphiolepis umbellata

Rhododendron alabamense

Rhododendron atlanticum

Rhododendron austrinum

Rhododendron calendula-ceum

Rhododendron canescens

Rhododendron catawbiense

Rhododendron degronianum subsp. yakushimanum

Rhododendron flammeum

Rhododendron hyperythrum

Rhododendron maximum

Rhododendron minus

Rhododendron minus var. chapmanii

Rhododendron mucronula-tum

Rhododendron periclymen-oides

Rhododendron 'PJM'

Rhododendron prinophyllum

Rhododendron schlippen-bachii

Rhododendron vaseyi

Rhododendron viscosum

Rhododendron yedoense var. poukhanense

Rhodotypos scandens

Rhus aromatica

Rhus

Ribes alpinum

Ribes aureum var. villosum

Ribes sanguineum

Robinia hispida

Robinia pseudoacacia

Rosa

Rosmarinus officinalis

Rubus pentalobus

Ruscus aculeatus

Salix

Sambucus racemosa

Sapindus drummondii

Sarcandra glabra

Sassafras albidum

Schizophragma hydrange-oides

Sciadopitys verticillata

Sequoia sempervirens

Sequoiadendron giganteum

Serissa japonica

Shepherdia argentea

Sinojackia rehderiana

Skimmia japonica

Skimmia japonica subsp. reevesiana

Smilax

Sorbus

Spiraea betulifolia var. aemiliana

Spiraea cantoniensis 'Lanceata'

Spiraea fritschiana

Spiraea japonica

Spiraea nipponica 'Snow-mound'

Spiraea prunifolia

Spiraea thunbergii

Spiraea ×vanhouttei

Spiraea virginiana

Stachyurus praecox

Staphylea trifolia

Stephanandra incisa

Stewartia

Styrax

Symphoricarpos

Symplocos paniculata

Symplocos tinctoria

Syringa

Taiwania cryptomerioides

Taxodium distichum

Taxodium distichum var. imbricarium

Taxus

Ternstroemia gymnanthera

Thuja

Thujopsis dolabrata

Tilia

Toona sinensis

Torreya taxifolia

Triadica sebifera

Trochodendron aralioides

Tsuga

Ulmus alata

Ulmus americana

Ulmus crassifolia

Ulmus glabra

Ulmus minor

Ulmus pumila

Ungnadia speciosa

Vaccinium

Vernicia fordii

Viburnum

Vinca major

Vinca minor

Vitis rotundifolia

Weigela florida

Wisteria

Wollemia nobilis

Xanthoceras sorbifolium

Xanthocyparis nootkatensis

Xanthorhiza simplicissima

Zamia pumila

Zanthoxylum americanum

Zelkova

Zenobia pulverulenta

Ziziphus jujuba

SUMMER

Abelia chinensis

Abelia ×grandiflora

Abelia macrotera

Abelia parvifolia

Abutilon pictum

Acca sellowiana

Adina rubella

Aesculus parviflora

Albizia julibrissin

Allamanda cathartica

Amorpha canescens

Amorpha fruticosa

Ampelopsis brevipeduncu-lata

Antigonon leptopus

Aralia elata

Aralia spinosa

Arctostaphylos uva-ursi

Ardisia japonica

Aristolochia macrophylla

Azara microphylla

Bignonia capreolata

Bougainvillea glabra

Brugmansia ×candida

Brunfelsia pauciflora

Buddleia davidii

Buddleia lindleyana

Buddleia loricata

Buddleia salviifolia

Butia capitata

Callicarpa

Callistemon citrinus

Calluna vulgaris

Campsis

Carissa macrocarpa

Caryopteris ×clandonensis

Cassia

Castanea mollissima
Castanea pumila
Catalpa bignonioides
Catalpa speciosa
Ceanothus ×delileanus
Ceanothus ×pallidus
Cedrus
Cephalanthus occidentalis
Chilopsis linearis
×Chitalpa tashkentensis
Cistus
Clematis
Clerodendrum trichotomum
Clethra
Cleyera japonica
Colutea arborescens
Cornus kousa
Cornus nuttallii
Cotinus
Cyrilla racemiflora
Cytisus battandieri
Daboecia cantabrica
Daphne ×transatlantica
Decumaria barbara
Desfontainia spinosa
Dichroa febrifuga
Dichroa versicolor
Diervilla sessilifolia
Duranta erecta
Ehretia dicksonii
Elaeagnus ×ebbingei
Elliottia racemosa
Elsholtzia stauntonii
Emmenopterys henryi
Erythrina ×bidwillii
Eucryphia glutinosa
Euonymus kiautschovicus
Euscaphis japonica
Fallopia baldschuanica
Ficus carica
Ficus pumila
Firmiana simplex
Franklinia alatamaha
Fraxinus ornus
Fuchsia magellanica
Galphimia gracilis
Gardenia jasminoides
Gordonia lasianthus
Grevillea robusta
Hebe

Helianthemum nummularium
Heptacodium miconioides
Hibiscus
Holboellia latifolia
Hydrangea anomala subsp.
    petiolaris
Hydrangea arborescens
Hydrangea macrophylla
Hydrangea paniculata 'Gran-
    diflora'
Hypericum
Illicium parviflorum
Indigofera amblyantha
Indigofera decora
Indigofera heterantha
Indigofera kirilowii
Itea virginica
Ixora coccinea
Jasminum floridum
Jasminum humile
Jasminum officinale
Kalopanax septemlobus
Koelreuteria bipinnata
Koelreuteria paniculata
Lagerstroemia
Lantana camara
Lavandula angustifolia
Leptodermis oblonga
Lespedeza bicolor
Lespedeza thunbergii
Leycesteria formosa
Liriodendron tulipifera
Lonicera ×brownii
Lonicera caprifolium
Lonicera flava
Lonicera ×heckrottii
Lonicera japonica
Lonicera periclymenum
Lonicera sempervirens
Maackia amurensis
Magnolia figo
Magnolia grandiflora
Magnolia macrophylla
Magnolia macrophylla
    subsp. ashei
Magnolia sieboldii
Magnolia virginiana
Mahonia fortunei
Malvaviscus arboreus var.
    drummondii

Mandevilla splendens
Millettia reticulata
Mitchella repens
Musa
Nerium oleander
Olea europaea
Osmanthus fragrans
Oxydendrum arboreum
Parkinsonia aculeata
Parthenocissus
Passiflora incarnata
Persea borbonia
Pinckneya bracteata
Plumbago auriculata
Poliothyrsis sinensis
Potentilla fruticosa
Punica granatum
Pyracantha koidzumii
Rhododendron prunifolium
Rhododendron viscosum
Rosa carolina
Rosa rugosa
Rostrinucula dependens
Sabal palmetto
Sambucus
Santolina chamaecyparissus
Sesbania punicea
Sorbaria
Spiraea alba var. latifolia
Spiraea tomentosa
Spiraea japonica
Stewartia
Styphnolobium japonicum
Syringa reticulata
Syringa reticulata subsp.
    pekinensis
Tamarix ramosissima
Tecoma capensis
Tetradium daniellii
Teucrium chamaedrys
Tilia cordata
Trachelospermum asiaticum
Trachelospermum jasmin-
    oides
Trachycarpus fortunei
Ulmus parvifolia
Vitex
Wisteria frutescens
Yucca

FALL
Abelia ×grandiflora
Abelia macrotera
Abelia parvifolia
Arbutus menziesii
Arbutus unedo
Ardisia japonica
Bignonia capreolata
Bougainvillea glabra
Callistemon citrinus
Calluna vulgaris
Camellia oleifera
Camellia sasanqua
Camellia sinensis
Caryopteris ×clandonensis
Cassia
Cedrus
Cephalanthus occidentalis
Disanthus cercidifolius
Elaeagnus ×ebbingei
Elaeagnus macrophylla
Elaeagnus pungens
Eriobotrya japonica
×Fatshedera lizei
Fatsia japonica
Franklinia alatamaha
Galphimia gracilis
Hamamelis virginiana
Hedera
Hydrangea macrophylla
Indigofera amblyantha
Indigofera decora
Lantana camara
Lespedeza thunbergii
Lithocarpus henryi
Mahonia fortunei
Mahonia ×media
Musa
Nerium oleander
Osmanthus armatus
Osmanthus ×fortunei
Osmanthus fragrans
Osmanthus heterophyllus
Rosmarinus officinalis
Rostrinucula dependens
Tamarix ramosissima
Viburnum ×bodnantense
Viburnum farreri

903

FRAGRANT FLOWERS

The following trees and shrubs bear flowers with notable—not necessarily pleasant—fragrance.

Abelia chinensis
Abelia ×grandiflora
Abelia macrotera
Abelia mosanensis
Abelia parvifolia
Abeliophyllum distichum
Acacia dealbata
Acer tataricum
Acer tataricum subsp. ginnala
Actinidia arguta
Actinidia deliciosa
Actinidia kolomikta
Actinidia polygama
Adina rubella
Aesculus californica
Aesculus indica
Agarista populifolia
Ailanthus altissima
Akebia quinata
Albizia julibrissin
Azara microphylla
Bignonia capreolata
Brugmansia ×candida
Buddleia alternifolia
Buddleia davidii
Buddleia loricata
Buddleia salviifolia
Calia secundiflora
Calycanthus floridus
Calycanthus occidentalis
Camellia sinensis
Carissa macrocarpa
Castanea mollissima
Castanea pumila
Ceanothus
Cephalanthus occidentalis
Chilopsis linearis
Chimonanthus praecox
Chionanthus retusus
Chionanthus virginicus
Choisya ternata
Cladrastis kentukea
Clematis terniflora
Clerodendrum trichotomum
Clethra acuminata
Clethra alnifolia
Clethra arborea

Clethra barbinervis
Cliftonia monophylla
Corylopsis
Cotoneaster lacteus
Cotoneaster multiflorus
Crataegus
Cyrilla racemiflora
Cytisus battandieri
Daphne bholua
Daphne ×burkwoodii
Daphne cneorum
Daphne mezereum
Daphne odora
Daphne ×transatlantica
Decumaria barbara
Diospyros kaki
Diospyros virginiana
Edgeworthia chrysantha
Ehretia dicksonii
Elaeagnus
Elliottia racemosa
Enkianthus campanulatus
Epigaea repens
Eriobotrya japonica
Eucryphia glutinosa
Euonymus japonicus
Euonymus kiautschovicus
Forsythia ×intermedia
Fothergilla gardenii
Fothergilla major
Franklinia alatamaha
Fraxinus ornus
Gardenia jasminoides
Gelsemium sempervirens
Gordonia lasianthus
Gymnocladus dioicus
Hamamelis
Heptacodium miconioides
Holboellia latifolia
Hydrangea anomala subsp. petiolaris
Hydrangea arborescens
Hydrangea paniculata 'Grandiflora'
Hydrangea quercifolia
Ilex ×altaclerensis
Ilex aquifolium
Ilex cassine

Ilex cornuta
Ilex 'Emily Bruner'
Ilex ×koehneana
Ilex latifolia
Ilex 'Nellie R. Stevens'
Ilex Red Hollies
Ilex rotunda
Ilex vomitoria
Illicium anisatum
Illicium floridanum
Illicium mexicanum
Itea virginica
Jasminum officinale
Kadsura japonica
+Laburnocytisus adamii
Laburnum ×watereri
Lagerstroemia
Lantana camara
Lavandula angustifolia
Leucothoe axillaris
Leucothoe fontanesiana
Ligustrum
Lindera benzoin
Lithocarpus henryi
Lonicera caprifolium
Lonicera fragrantissima
Lonicera ×heckrottii
Lonicera japonica
Lonicera periclymenum
Loropetalum chinense
Loropetalum chinense var. rubrum
Lyonia lucida
Maackia amurensis
Magnolia
Mahonia aquifolium
Mahonia bealei
Mahonia ×media
Malus
Melia azedarach
Millettia reticulata
Mitchella repens
Myrtus communis
Olea europaea
Osmanthus
Oxydendrum arboreum
Pachysandra procumbens
Parkinsonia aculeata
Paulownia tomentosa
Philadelphus coronarius
Phillyrea angustifolia
Photinia ×fraseri

Photinia glabra
Photinia serratifolia
Pieris formosa var. forrestii
Pieris japonica
Pieris phillyreifolia
Pittosporum heterophyllum
Pittosporum tobira
Poliothyrsis sinensis
Prunus americana
Prunus avium
Prunus caroliniana
Prunus cerasifera
Prunus laurocerasus
Prunus lusitanica
Prunus maackii
Prunus mume
Prunus 'Okame'
Prunus padus
Prunus sargentii
Prunus serotina
Prunus virginiana
Prunus ×yedoensis
Ptelea trifoliata
Pterostyrax hispida
Pyracantha coccinea
Pyracantha koidzumii
Pyrus calleryana
Pyrus communis
Pyrus pyrifolia
Pyrus ussuriensis
Rhaphiolepis umbellata
Rhododendron alabamense
Rhododendron atlanticum
Rhododendron austrinum
Rhododendron canescens
Rhododendron periclymenoides
Rhododendron prinophyllum
Rhododendron schlippenbachii
Rhododendron viscosum
Robinia pseudoacacia
Rosa
Sabal palmetto
Sarcococca confusa
Sarcococca hookeriana
Sarcococca orientalis
Sarcococca ruscifolia
Sinojackia rehderiana
Styphnolobium japonicum
Styrax grandifolius
Styrax japonicus

Styrax obassia
Symplocos paniculata
Symplocos tinctoria
Syringa ×chinensis
Syringa ×hyacinthiflora
Syringa ×laciniata
Syringa oblata var. dilatata
Syringa ×persica
Syringa pubescens subsp. microphylla
Syringa pubescens subsp. patula

Syringa reticulata
Syringa reticulata subsp. pekinensis
Syringa villosa
Syringa vulgaris
Ternstroemia gymnanthera
Tilia
Toona sinensis
Trachelospermum asiaticum
Trachelospermum jasminoides

Ungnadia speciosa
Vaccinium ashei
Vaccinium corymbosum
Vernicia fordii
Viburnum ×bodnantense
Viburnum ×burkwoodii
Viburnum ×carlcephalum
Viburnum carlesii
Viburnum farreri
Viburnum japonicum
Viburnum ×juddii

Viburnum 'Pragense'
Viburnum rafinesqueanum
Viburnum suspensum
Viburnum tinus
Viburnum trilobum
Viburnum utile
Wisteria
Xanthoceras sorbifolium
Zenobia pulverulenta
Ziziphus jujuba

FRUIT

Trees and shrubs listed offer ornamental or sizeable fruit. The primary fruit color is indicated for each plant, although variations occur within a species, and many fruit change color as they mature.

TAXON	COLOR/COMMENTS
Acca sellowiana	yellow-green
Acer japonicum	red
Acer palmatum	orange/red, pink/rose
Acer pseudosieboldianum	orange/red, pink/rose
Acer rubrum	orange/red
Acer saccharinum	orange/red
Acer tataricum	orange/red
Acer tataricum subsp. ginnala	orange/red
Actinidia arguta	yellow-green
Actinidia deliciosa	brown
Actinidia kolomikta	yellow-green
Actinidia pilosula	yellow-green
Actinidia polygama	yellow-green
Aesculus	brown, showy brown to black seeds
Akebia quinata	pink/rose, blue/purple
Alangium platanifolium	blue/purple
Alnus	brown, like small pine cones
Amelanchier	pink/rose, blue/purple
Ampelopsis brevipedunculata	yellow, pink/rose, blue/purple
Aralia elata	blue/purple, black
Aralia spinosa	blue/purple, black
Arbutus menziesii	orange/red
Arbutus unedo	orange/red
Arctostaphylos uva-ursi	orange/red
Ardisia japonica	orange/red
Aristolochia macrophylla	yellow-green, brown
Aronia arbutifolia	red
Aronia melanocarpa	blue/purple, black

TAXON	COLOR/COMMENTS
Asimina triloba	yellow, yellow-green, black
Aucuba japonica	orange/red
Baccharis halimifolia	white
Berberis candidula	gray-blue
Berberis ×gladwynensis 'William Penn'	gray-blue
Berberis julianae	gray-blue
Berberis koreana	orange/red
Berberis ×mentorensis	orange/red
Berberis thunbergii	orange/red
Broussonetia papyrifera	orange/red
Butia capitata	orange/red
Callicarpa	blue/purple, magenta
Carissa macrocarpa	red
Castanea mollissima	brown, spiny involucre
Castanea pumila	brown, spiny involucre
Ceanothus	red-bronze
Celastrus orbiculatus	yellow, orange/red
Celastrus scandens	yellow, orange/red
Celtis laevigata	orange/red, blue/purple
Celtis occidentalis	orange/red, blue/purple
Cephalotaxus fortunei	brown, olive-shaped
Cephalotaxus harringtonia	brown, olive-shaped
Chaenomeles japonica	yellow, sometimes blushed red
Chaenomeles speciosa	yellow, sometimes blushed red
Chionanthus retusus	blue/purple
Chionanthus virginicus	blue/purple
Cinnamomum camphora	blue/purple
Clematis	white, silky achene
Clerodendrum trichotomum	blue/purple, pink/rose calyx
Cleyera japonica	black
Cocculus carolinus	orange/red
Colutea arborescens	yellow-green, bronze

TAXON	COLOR/COMMENTS
Cornus alba	white, blue/purple
Cornus alternifolia	blue/purple, black
Cornus amomum	white, blue/purple
Cornus capitata	orange/red
Cornus florida	orange/red
Cornus kousa	orange/red
Cornus macrophylla	blue/purple
Cornus mas	orange/red
Cornus nuttallii	orange/red
Cornus officinalis	orange/red
Cornus racemosa	white, blue/purple
Cornus sanguinea	black
Cornus sericea	white, blue/purple
Corokia cotoneaster	orange/red
Corylus maxima 'Purpurea'	maroon, showy involucre
Cotoneaster adpressus	orange/red
Cotoneaster apiculatus	orange/red
Cotoneaster dammeri	orange/red
Cotoneaster divaricatus	orange/red
Cotoneaster horizontalis	orange/red
Cotoneaster lacteus	orange/red
Cotoneaster lucidus	black
Cotoneaster multiflorus	orange/red
Cotoneaster salicifolius	orange/red
Crataegus crus-galli	orange/red
Crataegus laevigata	orange/red
Crataegus ×lavalleei	orange/red
Crataegus ×mordenensis	orange/red
Crataegus nitida	orange/red
Crataegus phaenopyrum	orange/red
Crataegus punctata	orange/red
Crataegus viridis 'Winter King'	orange/red
Cycas revoluta	orange-brown seeds
Danae racemosa	orange/red
Daphne bholua	orange/red
Daphne ×burkwoodii	orange/red
Daphne cneorum	orange/red
Daphne genkwa	white, gray-white
Daphne mezereum	orange/red
Daphne odora	orange/red
Daphne ×transatlantica	orange/red, blue/purple, black
Daphniphyllum macropodum	blue/purple
Davidia involucrata	green with purplish bloom (wax)
Decaisnea fargesii	blue/purple
Dichroa febrifuga	pink/rose, blue/purple
Diospyros kaki	orange/red
Diospyros virginiana	orange/red, orange-brown

TAXON	COLOR/COMMENTS
Dirca palustris	green, orange/red
Duranta erecta	yellow
Elaeagnus	orange/red
Eleutherococcus sieboldianus	black
Eriobotrya japonica	yellow, yellow-orange
Euonymus alatus	pink/rose, orange/red
Euonymus americanus	orange/red
Euonymus bungeanus	pink/rose
Euonymus carnosus	pink/rose
Euonymus europaeus	pink/rose
Euonymus fortunei	pink/rose
Euonymus japonicus	pink/rose
Euonymus kiautschovicus	pink/rose
Eurya japonica	black
Euscaphis japonica	orange/red, black seeds
×Fatshedera lizei	black
Fatsia japonica	black
Ficus carica	green, brown, red
Forestiera acuminata	blue/purple, black
Frangula alnus	black
Frangula caroliniana	orange/red, black
Fuchsia magellanica	orange/red, blue/purple
Gardenia jasminoides	orange/red
Gaultheria mucronata	pink/rose, orange/red, blue/purple
Gaultheria procumbens	red
Gaylussacia brachycera	blue/purple
Gaylussacia ursina	black
Gelsemium sempervirens	yellow
Ginkgo biloba	yellow, orange/red
Gymnocladus dioicus	black
Hedera	black
Hippophae rhamnoides	orange/red
Holboellia latifolia	blue/purple
Hovenia dulcis	light gray-brown
Idesia polycarpa	orange/red
Ilex ×altaclerensis	orange/red
Ilex aquifolium	orange/red
Ilex ×aquipernyi	orange/red
Ilex ×attenuata	orange/red
Ilex cassine	orange/red
Ilex cornuta	orange/red
Ilex crenata	black
Ilex decidua	orange/red
Ilex 'Emily Bruner'	orange/red
Ilex glabra	black
Ilex ×koehneana	orange/red
Ilex latifolia	orange/red
Ilex ×meserveae	orange/red
Ilex mucronata	orange/red

TAXON	COLOR/COMMENTS
Ilex 'Nellie R. Stevens'	orange/red
Ilex opaca	orange/red
Ilex pedunculosa	orange/red
Ilex Red Hollies	orange/red
Ilex rotunda	orange/red
Ilex serrata	orange/red
Ilex verticillata	orange/red
Ilex vomitoria	orange/red
Ixora coccinea	blue/purple, black
Jasminum floridum	black
Jasminum humile	black
Jasminum nudiflorum	black
Jasminum parkeri	greenish white
Juniperus	green, silver, blue to blackish
Kadsura japonica	orange/red
Kalopanax septemlobus	black
Koelreuteria bipinnata	pink/rose
Koelreuteria paniculata	yellow-green to brown
Lantana camara	blue/purple, black
Laurus nobilis	black
Leitneria floridana	brown
Ligustrum amurense	black
Ligustrum japonicum	black
Ligustrum lucidum	blue/purple, black
Ligustrum obtusifolium	black
Ligustrum ovalifolium	black
Ligustrum sinense	black
Ligustrum 'Vicaryi'	black
Ligustrum vulgare	black
Lindera aggregata	black
Lindera benzoin	red
Lindera erythrocarpa	red
Lindera glauca	black
Lindera obtusiloba	orange/red to black
Livistona chinensis	blue/purple
Lonicera alpigena	orange/red
Lonicera ×brownii	orange/red
Lonicera caprifolium	orange/red
Lonicera flava	orange/red
Lonicera fragrantissima	orange/red
Lonicera ×heckrottii	orange/red
Lonicera japonica	black
Lonicera korolkowii	orange/red
Lonicera maackii	orange/red
Lonicera nitida	blue/purple
Lonicera periclymenum	orange/red
Lonicera pileata	blue/purple
Lonicera sempervirens	orange/red
Lonicera tatarica	orange/red
Lonicera xylosteum	orange/red

TAXON	COLOR/COMMENTS
Maclura pomifera	yellow-green
Magnolia	pink/rose, orange/red, aggregate of follicles
Mahonia aquifolium	blue/purple
Mahonia bealei	blue/purple
Mahonia fortunei	blue/purple, black
Mahonia ×media	blue/purple
Malus angustifolia	yellow-green
Malus floribunda	yellow, orange/red
Malus hupehensis	yellow, orange/red
Malus sargentii	orange/red
Malus sieboldii var. zumi 'Calocarpa'	orange/red
Melia azedarach	yellow
Menispermum canadense	purple-red to blue-black
Mespilus germanica	brown
Mitchella repens	orange/red
Morus alba	white, pink/rose, orange/red, purplish black
Morus rubra	orange/red, blue/purple
Musa	yellow
Myrica cerifera	gray-white
Myrica inodora	black
Myrica pensylvanica	gray-white
Myrtus communis	blue/purple, black
Nandina domestica	orange/red
Nyssa ogeche	orange/red
Nyssa sylvatica	blue/purple
Olea europaea	green/black
Osmanthus	blue/purple
Pachysandra terminalis	white
Parthenocissus	blue/purple
Passiflora incarnata	yellow-green
Persea borbonia	blue/purple, black
Phellodendron amurense	black
Phillyrea angustifolia	blue/purple, black
Phoenix canariensis	yellow, orange/red
Photinia	orange/red
Picrasma quassioides	orange/red
Pistacia chinensis	pink/rose, orange/red, blue/purple
Pittosporum tobira	yellow, orange/red seeds
Podocarpus macrophyllus 'Maki'	orange/red, blue/purple
Poncirus trifoliata	yellow
Prinsepia sinensis	orange/red
Prunus americana	yellow, orange/red
Prunus avium	blue/purple
Prunus besseyi	blue/purple, black
Prunus campanulata	orange/red

TAXON	COLOR/COMMENTS
Prunus caroliniana	black
Prunus cerasifera	orange/red, blue/purple
Prunus incisa	blue/purple, black
Prunus laurocerasus	orange/red, black
Prunus lusitanica	orange/red, black
Prunus maackii	orange/red, black
Prunus maritima	yellow, orange/red, blue/purple
Prunus mume	yellow
Prunus 'Okame'	orange/red, black
Prunus padus	black
Prunus persica	yellow, orange/red
Prunus sargentii	orange/red, blue/purple, black
Prunus serotina	orange/red, black
Prunus serrula	orange/red
Prunus subhirtella	orange/red, black
Prunus tomentosa	orange/red
Prunus virginiana	orange/red, blue/purple, black
Prunus ×yedoensis	orange/red, black
Pseudocydonia sinensis	yellow
Punica granatum	orange/red
Pyracantha coccinea	orange/red
Pyracantha koidzumii	orange/red
Pyrus calleryana	brown
Pyrus communis	yellow-brown
Pyrus ussuriensis	brown
Rhamnus cathartica	black
Rhaphiolepis umbellata	blue/purple
Rhapidophyllum hystrix	red-brown
Rhodotypos scandens	black
Rhus	orange/red
Ribes alpinum	orange/red
Ribes aureum var. villosum	black
Ribes sanguineum	blue/purple, black
Rosa carolina	orange/red
Rosa glauca	orange/red
Rosa laevigata	orange/red
Rosa moyesii	orange/red
Rosa rugosa	orange/red
Rosa spinosissima	dark brown to black
Rosa virginiana	orange/red
Rubus pentalobus	yellow, orange/red
Ruscus aculeatus	orange/red
Sabal palmetto	black
Sambucus canadensis	blue/purple
Sambucus nigra	blue/purple
Sambucus racemosa	orange/red
Sapindus drummondii	yellow

TAXON	COLOR/COMMENTS
Sarcandra glabra	orange/red
Sarcococca confusa	black
Sarcococca hookeriana	black
Sarcococca orientalis	black
Sarcococca ruscifolia	orange/red
Sarcococca saligna	black, blue/purple
Sassafras albidum	dark blue, red calyx
Shepherdia argentea	orange/red
Skimmia japonica	orange/red
Skimmia japonica subsp. reevesiana	orange/red
Smilax	orange/red, black
Sorbus alnifolia	pink/rose
Sorbus americana	orange/red
Sorbus aria	orange/red
Sorbus aucuparia	orange/red
Staphylea trifolia	yellow-green, inflated capsules
Styphnolobium japonicum	yellow-green pods
Styrax	gray-white ovoid drupe
Symphoricarpos albus	white
Symphoricarpos ×chenaultii	pink/rose
Symphoricarpos orbiculatus	pink/rose
Symplocos paniculata	blue/purple
Symplocos tinctoria	orange/brown
Taxus	orange/red aril
Ternstroemia gymnanthera	orange/red
Tetradium daniellii	orange/red, black seeds
Torreya taxifolia	orange/red
Trachycarpus fortunei	black
Triadica sebifera	brown, waxy white seeds
Ungnadia speciosa	brown, black seeds
Vaccinium angustifolium	blue/purple
Vaccinium arboreum	black
Vaccinium ashei	blue/purple
Vaccinium corymbosum	blue/purple
Vaccinium elliottii	black
Vaccinium stamineum	white, blue/purple
Vaccinium vitis-idaea	orange/red
Viburnum acerifolium	black
Viburnum awabuki	orange/red, black
Viburnum ×bodnantense	orange/red
Viburnum bracteatum	blue/purple
Viburnum ×burkwoodii	orange/red, black
Viburnum ×carlcephalum	orange/red, black
Viburnum carlesii	orange/red, black
Viburnum cassinoides	pink/rose, blue/purple
Viburnum davidii	blue/purple
Viburnum dentatum	blue/purple
Viburnum dilatatum	orange/red
Viburnum farreri	orange/red

TAXON	COLOR/COMMENTS	TAXON	COLOR/COMMENTS
Viburnum japonicum	orange/red	*Viburnum rufidulum*	pink/rose, blue/purple, black
Viburnum ×*juddii*	orange/red, black		
Viburnum lantana	yellow, orange/red, black	*Viburnum sargentii*	orange/red
Viburnum lentago	pink/rose, blue/purple	*Viburnum setigerum*	orange/red
Viburnum nudum	pink/rose, blue/purple	*Viburnum sieboldii*	orange/red, black
Viburnum obovatum	blue/purple, black	*Viburnum suspensum*	orange/red, black
Viburnum odoratissimum	orange/red, blue/purple	*Viburnum tinus*	blue/purple
Viburnum opulus	orange/red	*Viburnum trilobum*	orange/red
Viburnum plicatum f. tomentosum	orange/red, black	*Viburnum utile*	orange/red, black
		Vitis rotundifolia	green, yellow, blue/purple
Viburnum 'Pragense'	orange/red, black	*Xanthoceras sorbifolium*	brown, dark brown seeds
Viburnum prunifolium	pink/rose, blue/purple	*Zamia pumila*	brown, orange/red seeds
Viburnum rafinesqueanum	black	*Zanthoxylum americanum*	orange/red, black
Viburnum ×*rhytidophylloides*	yellow, orange/red, black	*Ziziphus jujuba*	brown
Viburnum rhytidophyllum	orange/red, black		

FALL COLOR

Trees and shrubs listed exhibit attractive fall foliage color. Many will display the full range of fall colors, often on the same tree or even on the same leaf. Some will not develop the color fully until winter. For the purposes of this list, colors have been broken into broad categories; "red," for example, can signify anything from pinks to deep maroon tints.

YELLOW

Abelia chinensis
Acer buergerianum
Acer campestre
Acer carpinifolium
Acer circinatum
Acer cissifolium subsp. henryi
Acer japonicum
Acer miyabei
Acer palmatum
Acer pensylvanicum
Acer platanoides
Acer pseudosieboldianum
Acer rubrum
Acer saccharinum
Acer saccharum
Acer saccharum subsp. *floridanum*
Acer saccharum subsp. *leucoderme*
Acer tataricum
Acer tataricum subsp. *ginnala*
Acer truncatum

Aesculus flava
Aesculus glabra
Aesculus parviflora
Alangium platanifolium
Amelanchier arborea
Amelanchier canadensis
Amelanchier ×*grandiflora*
Amelanchier laevis
Aralia elata
Aralia spinosa
Asimina triloba
Betula albosinensis var. septentrionalis
Betula alleghaniensis
Betula lenta
Betula maximowicziana
Betula nigra
Betula papyrifera
Betula pendula
Betula platyphylla var. *japonica*
Betula populifolia
Betula utilis var. *jacquemontii*

Calycanthus chinensis
Calycanthus floridus
Calycanthus occidentalis
Carpinus betulus
Carpinus caroliniana
Carya aquatica
Carya cordiformis
Carya glabra
Carya illinoinensis
Carya ovata
Castanea mollissima
Castanea pumila
Celastrus orbiculatus
Celastrus scandens
Cercidiphyllum japonicum
Cercis canadensis
Cercis chinensis
Chimonanthus praecox
Chionanthus retusus
Chionanthus virginicus
Cladrastis kentukea
Clethra acuminata
Clethra alnifolia
Cornus kousa
Cotinus coggygria
Cotinus obovatus
Cotinus szechuanensis
Decumaria barbara
Diervilla sessilifolia
Dirca palustris
Edgeworthia chrysantha
Enkianthus campanulatus

Enkianthus serrulatus
Euonymus americanus
Fagus grandifolia
Fagus sylvatica
Firmiana simplex
Fothergilla gardenii
Fothergilla major
Fraxinus americana
Fraxinus pennsylvanica
Ginkgo biloba
Gleditsia triacanthos f. *inermis*
Gymnocladus dioicus
Halesia diptera
Hamamelis ×*intermedia*
Hamamelis japonica
Hamamelis mollis
Hamamelis vernalis
Hamamelis virginiana
Hydrangea anomala subsp. petiolaris
Hydrangea arborescens
Hydrangea macrophylla
Hydrangea serrata
Kalopanax septemlobus
Kerria japonica
Koelreuteria bipinnata
Koelreuteria paniculata
Lagerstroemia indica
Lagerstroemia subcostata var. *fauriei*
Larix decidua

Larix kaempferi
Larix laricina
Lindera benzoin
Lindera erythrocarpa
Lindera glauca
Lindera obtusiloba
Liquidambar formosana
Liquidambar styraciflua
Liriodendron tulipifera
Maclura pomifera
Magnolia kobus
Magnolia liliiflora
Magnolia ×loebneri
Magnolia macrophylla
Magnolia macrophylla
    subsp. ashei
Magnolia salicifolia
Magnolia sieboldii
Magnolia stellata
Morus alba
Morus australis 'Unryu'
Morus rubra
Nyssa sylvatica
Oxydendrum arboreum
Parrotia persica
Phellodendron amurense
Photinia villosa
Pistacia chinensis
Poncirus trifoliata
Populus deltoides
Populus grandidentata
Populus nigra 'Italica'
Populus tremuloides
Prunus avium
Prunus campanulata
Prunus incisa
Prunus maritima
Prunus mume
Prunus subhirtella
Prunus tenella
Prunus ×yedoensis
Pseudolarix amabilis
Punica granatum
Pyrus pyrifolia
Pyrus ussuriensis
Quercus acutissima
Quercus falcata
Quercus imbricaria
Quercus lyrata
Quercus macrocarpa

Quercus muehlenbergii
Quercus phellos
Rhododendron alabamense
Rhododendron atlanticum
Rhododendron austrinum
Rhododendron canescens
Rhododendron flammeum
Rhododendron periclymen-
    oides
Rhododendron prinophyllum
Rhododendron prunifolium
Rhododendron schlippen-
    bachii
Rhododendron vaseyi
Rhododendron viscosum
Salix alba 'Tristis'
Salix babylonica
Salix matsudana
Salix udensis 'Sekka'
Sambucus canadensis
Sambucus nigra
Sambucus racemosa
Sapindus drummondii
Sassafras albidum
Sorbus alnifolia
Spiraea japonica
Spiraea thunbergii
Stephanandra incisa
Stewartia koreana
Stewartia pseudocamellia
Styphnolobium japonicum
Styrax obassia
Symplocos paniculata
Tamarix ramosissima
Taxodium distichum
Taxodium distichum var.
    imbricarium
Tilia americana
Tilia cordata
Tilia ×euchlora
Tilia kiusiana
Tilia 'Petiolaris'
Tilia platyphyllos
Tilia tomentosa
Ulmus americana
Ulmus parvifolia
Ungnadia speciosa
Viburnum bracteatum
Viburnum cassinoides
Viburnum dentatum
Viburnum dilatatum

Viburnum farreri
Viburnum nudum
Viburnum opulus
Vitis rotundifolia
Wisteria floribunda
Wisteria frutescens
Wisteria sinensis
Xanthoceras sorbifolium
Xanthorhiza simplicissima
Zelkova schneideriana
Ziziphus jujuba

ORANGE

Acer buergerianum
Acer carpinifolium
Acer circinatum
Acer cissifolium subsp.
    henryi
Acer japonicum
Acer palmatum
Acer pseudosieboldianum
Acer rubrum
Acer saccharum
Acer saccharum subsp. flori-
    danum
Acer saccharum subsp. leu-
    coderme
Acer tataricum
Acer tataricum subsp. gin-
    nala
Aesculus flava
Aesculus glabra
Amelanchier alnifolia
Amelanchier arborea
Amelanchier canadensis
Amelanchier ×grandiflora
Amelanchier laevis
Berberis ×mentorensis
Berberis thunbergii
Carpinus caroliniana
Cercidiphyllum japonicum
Clethra barbinervis
Corylus americana
Cotinus coggygria
Cotinus obovatus
Cotinus szechuanensis
Crataegus crus-galli
Crataegus nitida
Crataegus phaenopyrum
Croton alabamensis
Cyrilla racemiflora

Diospyros kaki
Diospyros virginiana
Disanthus cercidifolius
Enkianthus campanulatus
Enkianthus cernuus
Enkianthus perulatus
Fothergilla gardenii
Fothergilla major
Franklinia alatamaha
Hamamelis ×intermedia
Hamamelis japonica
Hamamelis vernalis
Itea virginica
Lagerstroemia indica
Lagerstroemia limii
Lagerstroemia subcostata
    var. fauriei
Lindera glauca
Liquidambar formosana
Liquidambar styraciflua
Metasequoia glyptostroboi-
    des
Nyssa sylvatica
Oxydendrum arboreum
Parrotia persica
Photinia villosa
Pistacia chinensis
Prunus americana
Prunus avium
Prunus campanulata
Prunus 'Hally Jolivette'
Prunus incisa
Prunus maritima
Prunus mume
Prunus 'Okame'
Prunus sargentii
Prunus serotina
Prunus serrula
Prunus serrulata
Prunus ×yedoensis
Pseudocydonia sinensis
Pyrus calleryana
Pyrus pyrifolia
Pyrus ussuriensis
Quercus falcata
Quercus nuttallii
Quercus palustris
Quercus shumardii
Rhododendron calendula-
    ceum
Rhododendron mucronulatum

Rhododendron schlippen-
   bachii
Rhus chinensis
Rhus copallina
Rhus glabra
Rhus typhina
Sassafras albidum
Sorbus americana
Sorbus aucuparia
Stewartia koreana
Stewartia pseudocamellia
Stewartia sinensis
Taxodium distichum
Taxodium distichum var.
   imbricarium
Viburnum cassinoides
Viburnum nudum
Zenobia pulverulenta

RED
Acer buergerianum
Acer circinatum
Acer griseum
Acer japonicum
Acer palmatum
Acer pseudosieboldianum
Acer rubrum
Acer saccharum
Acer saccharum subsp. flori-
   danum
Acer saccharum subsp. leu-
   coderme
Acer tataricum subsp. ginnala
Aesculus glabra
Amelanchier alnifolia
Amelanchier arborea
Amelanchier canadensis
Amelanchier ×grandiflora
Amelanchier laevis
Aronia arbutifolia
Aronia melanocarpa
Berberis koreana
Berberis ×mentorensis
Berberis thunbergii
Bignonia capreolata
Carpinus caroliniana
Cercidiphyllum japonicum
Clethra barbinervis
Cornus alba
Cornus alternifolia
Cornus amomum

Cornus florida
Cornus kousa
Cornus macrophylla
Cornus mas
Cornus officinalis
Cornus racemosa
Cornus sanguinea
Cornus sericea
Corylus americana
Cotinus coggygria
Cotinus obovatus
Cotinus szechuanensis
Cotoneaster adpressus
Cotoneaster apiculatus
Cotoneaster divaricatus
Cotoneaster horizontalis
Cotoneaster lucidus
Crataegus crus-galli
Crataegus ×lavalleei
Crataegus nitida
Crataegus phaenopyrum
Crataegus viridis 'Winter
   King'
Cyrilla racemiflora
Diervilla sessilifolia
Diospyros kaki
Diospyros virginiana
Disanthus cercidifolius
Enkianthus campanulatus
Enkianthus cernuus
Enkianthus perulatus
Enkianthus serrulatus
Euonymus alatus
Euonymus carnosus
Euonymus europaeus
Fothergilla gardenii
Fothergilla major
Franklinia alatamaha
Fraxinus americana
Gaylussacia ursina
Hamamelis ×intermedia
Hamamelis japonica
Hydrangea macrophylla
Hydrangea quercifolia
Hydrangea serrata
Itea virginica
Lagerstroemia indica
Lagerstroemia limii
Lagerstroemia subcostata
   var. fauriei
Leucothoe axillaris

Lindera glauca
Liquidambar formosana
Liquidambar styraciflua
Nandina domestica
Nyssa sylvatica
Oxydendrum arboreum
Parrotia persica
Parrotia subaequalis
Parthenocissus henryana
Parthenocissus quinquefolia
Parthenocissus tricuspidata
Photinia villosa
Pistacia chinensis
Prunus americana
Prunus avium
Prunus campanulata
Prunus 'Hally Jolivette'
Prunus incisa
Prunus 'Okame'
Prunus sargentii
Prunus serotina
Prunus serrula
Prunus serrulata
Prunus ×yedoensis
Pseudocydonia sinensis
Pyrus calleryana
Pyrus communis
Quercus alba
Quercus coccinea
Quercus ellipsoidalis
Quercus georgiana
Quercus michauxii
Quercus nuttallii
Quercus palustris
Quercus rubra
Quercus shumardii
Quercus velutina
Rhododendron calendula-
   ceum
Rhododendron mucronula-
   tum
Rhododendron schlippen-
   bachii
Rhus aromatica
Rhus chinensis
Rhus copallina
Rhus glabra
Rhus michauxii
Rhus typhina
Rosa carolina
Rosa virginiana

Sassafras albidum
Sorbus americana
Sorbus aucuparia
Stewartia koreana
Stewartia monadelpha
Stewartia pseudocamellia
Stewartia sinensis
Syringa pubescens subsp.
   patula
Vaccinium angustifolium
Vaccinium arboreum
Vaccinium ashei
Vaccinium corymbosum
Vaccinium elliottii
Viburnum acerifolium
Viburnum ×bodnantense
Viburnum ×burkwoodii
Viburnum ×carlcephalum
Viburnum carlesii
Viburnum cassinoides
Viburnum dentatum
Viburnum dilatatum
Viburnum ×juddii
Viburnum lentago
Viburnum nudum
Viburnum opulus
Viburnum plicatum
Viburnum plicatum f. tomen-
   tosum
Viburnum prunifolium
Viburnum rufidulum
Viburnum sargentii
Viburnum setigerum
Viburnum sieboldii
Viburnum trilobum
Zelkova schneideriana
Zelkova serrata
Zenobia pulverulenta

PURPLE
Acer circinatum
Acer palmatum
Aralia elata
Aralia spinosa
Callicarpa bodinieri
Callicarpa dichotoma
Callicarpa japonica
Cornus alba
Cornus alternifolia
Cornus amomum
Cornus florida

911

Cornus kousa
Cornus macrophylla
Cornus mas
Cornus officinalis
Cornus racemosa
Cornus sanguinea
Cornus sericea
Corylus maxima 'Purpurea'
Cotinus coggygria
Cotinus obovatus
Cotinus szechuanensis
Cotoneaster adpressus
Cotoneaster apiculatus
Cotoneaster divaricatus
Cotoneaster horizontalis
Crataegus ×lavalleei
Cryptomeria japonica
Deutzia gracilis
Disanthus cercidifolius
Euonymus carnosus
Euonymus europaeus
Euonymus fortunei
Forsythia ×intermedia
Fothergilla gardenii
Fothergilla major
Fraxinus americana
Gaylussacia ursina
Hamamelis ×intermedia
Hamamelis japonica
Hydrangea macrophylla
Hydrangea quercifolia
Itea virginica
Juniperus horizontalis
Leucothoe axillaris
Liquidambar formosana
Liquidambar styraciflua
Mahonia aquifolium
Microbiota decussata
Nandina domestica
Nyssa sylvatica
Oxydendrum arboreum
Parrotia persica
Pyrus calleryana
Pyrus communis
Rhododendron 'PJM'
Stewartia koreana
Stewartia pseudocamellia
Syringa oblata var. dilatata
Syringa pubescens subsp.
    patula

Vaccinium arboreum
Vaccinium ashei
Vaccinium corymbosum
Viburnum acerifolium
Viburnum lentago
Viburnum plicatum
Viburnum plicatum f. tomen-
    tosum
Viburnum prunifolium
Viburnum rufidulum
Viburnum sargentii
Viburnum setigerum
Viburnum sieboldii
Viburnum trilobum

BRONZE

Abelia ×grandiflora
Abelia parvifolia
Arctostaphylos uva-ursi
Berberis ×gladwynensis 'Wil-
    liam Penn'
Berberis julianae
Bignonia capreolata
Callistemon citrinus
Calluna vulgaris
Castanea mollissima
Castanea pumila
Clethra barbinervis
Corylus americana
Corylus maxima 'Purpurea'
Cotoneaster dammeri
Cotoneaster lacteus
Cotoneaster salicifolius
Crataegus viridis 'Winter King'
Cryptomeria japonica
Elliottia racemosa
Enkianthus serrulatus
Epigaea repens
Eubotrys racemosa
Euonymus fortunei
Fagus grandifolia
Fagus sylvatica
Gaultheria procumbens
Gaylussacia brachycera
Juniperus horizontalis
Leucothoe axillaris
Magnolia kobus
Magnolia ×loebneri
Magnolia macrophylla
Magnolia macrophylla
    subsp. ashei

Magnolia stellata
Mahonia aquifolium
Mespilus germanica
Metasequoia glyptostroboi-
    des
Microbiota decussata
Pachysandra procumbens
Prunus 'Hally Jolivette'
Prunus mume
Prunus subhirtella
Prunus tenella
Prunus triloba var. multiplex
Quercus bicolor
Quercus falcata
Quercus lyrata
Quercus marilandica
Quercus michauxii
Quercus montana
Quercus phellos
Rhododendron alabamense
Rhododendron atlanticum
Rhododendron austrinum
Rhododendron calendula-
    ceum
Rhododendron canescens
Rhododendron flammeum
Rhododendron periclymen-
    oides
Rhododendron 'PJM'
Rhododendron prinophyllum
Rhododendron prunifolium
Rhododendron vaseyi
Rhododendron viscosum
Rhus chinensis
Rhus michauxii
Rosa carolina
Rosa rugosa
Rosa virginiana
Rubus pentalobus
Spiraea betulifolia var.
    aemiliana
Spiraea japonica
Spiraea prunifolia
Spiraea thunbergii
Stephanandra incisa
Stewartia monadelpha
Syringa oblata var. dilatata
Syringa pubescens subsp.
    patula
Tamarix ramosissima
Taxodium distichum

Taxodium distichum var.
    imbricarium
Trachelospermum asiaticum
Ulmus parvifolia
Vaccinium vitis-idaea
Viburnum ×bodnantense
Viburnum bracteatum
Viburnum farreri
Viburnum ×juddii
Viburnum obovatum
Viburnum rafinesqueanum
Viburnum setigerum
Zenobia pulverulenta

YELLOW-GREEN

Abelia macrotera
Abelia mosanensis
Abelia serrata
Abelia spathulata
Abeliophyllum distichum
Abutilon vitifolium
Acer negundo
Acer pseudoplatanus
Actinidia arguta
Actinidia deliciosa
Actinidia kolomikta
Actinidia pilosula
Actinidia polygama
Adina rubella
Aesculus californica
Aesculus ×carnea
Aesculus hippocastanum
Aesculus indica
Aesculus pavia
Aesculus sylvatica
Aesculus turbinata
Ailanthus altissima
Albizia julibrissin
Alnus cordata
Alnus glutinosa
Alnus serrulata
Amorpha canescens
Amorpha fruticosa
Ampelopsis brevipeduncu-
    lata
Andrachne colchica
Aristolochia macrophylla
Baccharis halimifolia
Broussonetia papyrifera
Callicarpa americana
Callicarpa bodinieri

Callicarpa dichotoma
Callicarpa japonica
Campsis grandiflora
Campsis radicans
Campsis ×tagliabuana
  'Madame Galen'
Caragana arborescens
Caragana frutex
Carissa macrocarpa
Cassia
Catalpa bignonioides
Catalpa speciosa
Ceanothus americanus
Celtis laevigata
Celtis occidentalis
Cephalanthus occidentalis
Chaenomeles japonica
Chaenomeles speciosa
Chilopsis linearis
Chimonanthus praecox
×Chitalpa tashkentensis
Clematis
Clerodendrum trichotomum
Cocculus carolinus
Colutea arborescens
Corylopsis glabrescens
Corylopsis pauciflora
Corylopsis sinensis var. cal-
  vescens
Corylopsis spicata
Corylus americana
Corylus avellana
Corylus colurna
Corylus fargesii
Cotoneaster multiflorus
Crataegus laevigata
Crataegus ×mordenensis
Crataegus punctata
Cytisus battandieri
Cytisus scoparius
Davidia involucrata
Decaisnea fargesii
Deutzia gracilis
Deutzia ×hybrida
Deutzia ×lemoinei
Deutzia scabra

Deutzia setchuenensis
Dipelta floribunda
Duranta erecta
Elsholtzia stauntonii
Euonymus bungeanus
Euscaphis japonica
Exochorda racemosa
Exochorda serratifolia
Fallopia baldschuanica
Fontanesia philliraeoides
  subsp. fortunei
Forestiera acuminata
Forsythia 'Arnold Dwarf'
Forsythia ×intermedia
Forsythia suspensa var.
  sieboldii
Forsythia viridissima 'Bronx-
  ensis'
Frangula alnus
Frangula caroliniana
Fraxinus ornus
Fraxinus quadrangulata
Genista pilosa
Genista tinctoria
Gymnocladus dioicus
Halesia carolina
Heptacodium miconioides
Hibiscus syriacus
Hovenia dulcis
Hydrangea arborescens
Hydrangea paniculata 'Gran-
  diflora'
Hypericum brachyphyllum
Hypericum densiflorum
Hypericum fasciculatum
Hypericum frondosum
Hypericum galioides
Hypericum kalmianum
Hypericum lissophloeus
Hypericum prolificum
Idesia polycarpa
Ilex decidua
Ilex serrata
Ilex verticillata
Indigofera amblyantha
Indigofera decora

Indigofera heterantha
Indigofera kirilowii
Kalopanax septemlobus
Kolkwitzia amabilis
Leitneria floridana
Leptodermis oblonga
Lespedeza bicolor
Lespedeza thunbergii
Leycesteria formosa
Ligustrum amurense
Ligustrum obtusifolium
Maackia amurensis
Magnolia acuminata
Magnolia campbellii
Magnolia cylindrica
Magnolia denudata
Magnolia ×soulangeana
Magnolia virginiana
Magnolia zenii 'Pink Parch-
  ment'
Malus angustifolia
Malus floribunda
Malus hupehensis
Malus sargentii
Malus sieboldii var. zumi
  'Calocarpa'
Melia azedarach
Neillia sinensis
Neviusia alabamensis
Orixa japonica
Ostrya virginiana
Paulownia tomentosa
Philadelphus coronarius
Philadelphus inodorus
Physocarpus opulifolius
Picrasma quassioides
Planera aquatica
Platanus ×acerifolia
Platanus occidentalis
Poliothyrsis sinensis
Populus alba
Potentilla fruticosa
Prinsepia sinensis
Prunus cerasifera
Prunus glandulosa 'Rosea
  Plena'

Prunus maackii
Prunus padus
Prunus persica
Prunus tomentosa
Prunus virginiana
Ptelea trifoliata
Pterocarya fraxinifolia
Pterostyrax hispida
Quercus nigra
Quercus robur
Quercus stellata
Rhamnus cathartica
Rhodotypos scandens
Ribes alpinum
Salix caprea
Salix gracilistyla
Schizophragma hydrange-
  oides
Sinojackia rehderiana
Smilax
Sorbaria kirilowii
Sorbaria tomentosa
Sorbaria sorbifolia
Spiraea alba var. latifolia
Spiraea tomentosa
Spiraea fritschiana
Spiraea virginiana
Staphylea trifolia
Styrax americanus
Styrax grandifolius
Styrax japonicus
Syringa reticulata
Syringa reticulata subsp.
  pekinensis
Tetradium daniellii
Triadica sebifera
Ulmus crassifolia
Ulmus glabra
Ulmus minor
Ulmus pumila
Viburnum macrocephalum
Vitex agnus-castus
Vitex negundo
Weigela florida
Zanthoxylum americanum

WINTER INTEREST

The following shrubs and trees bring something to the winter months. Some have bark or stems with unusual texture or color that is especially notable during that season; others flower in winter, or have persistent sepals or fruit.

Abelia floribunda
Abelia ×grandiflora
Abeliophyllum distichum
Abies
Acacia dealbata
Acca sellowiana
Acer buergerianum
Acer griseum
Acer palmatum
Acer pensylvanicum
Acer pseudosieboldianum
Acer rubrum
Acer saccharinum
Aesculus californica
Agarista populifolia
Agave americana
Amelanchier arborea
Amelanchier canadensis
Amelanchier ×grandiflora
Amelanchier laevis
Andromeda polifolia
Aralia elata
Aralia spinosa
Araucaria araucana
Arbutus menziesii
Arbutus unedo
Arctostaphylos uva-ursi
Ardisia japonica
Aronia arbutifolia
Aucuba japonica
Azara microphylla
Berberis candidula
Berberis ×gladwynensis 'William Penn'
Berberis julianae
Betula albosinensis var. septentrionalis
Betula alleghaniensis
Betula maximowicziana
Betula nigra
Betula papyrifera
Betula pendula
Betula platyphylla var. japonica
Betula populifolia
Betula utilis var. jacquemontii

Bignonia capreolata
Bougainvillea glabra
Buddleia loricata
Butia capitata
Buxus
Callistemon citrinus
Calluna vulgaris
Calocedrus decurrens
Camellia
Carissa macrocarpa
Carpinus betulus
Carpinus caroliniana
Carya ovata
Cedrus
Celastrus orbiculatus
Celastrus scandens
Cephalotaxus fortunei
Cephalotaxus harringtonia
Cercidiphyllum japonicum
Chaenomeles japonica
Chaenomeles speciosa
Chamaecyparis
Chamaerops humilis
Chimonanthus praecox
Choisya ternata
Cinnamomum camphora
Cistus
Cladrastis kentukea
Clethra acuminata
Clethra arborea
Clethra barbinervis
Cleyera japonica
Cliftonia monophylla
Cocculus carolinus
Cornus alba
Cornus alternifolia
Cornus amomum
Cornus florida
Cornus kousa
Cornus officinalis
Cornus sanguinea
Cornus sericea
Corokia cotoneaster
Corylus fargesii
Cotinus obovatus
Crataegus crus-galli

Crataegus nitida
Crataegus phaenopyrum
Crataegus viridis 'Winter King'
Cryptomeria japonica
Cunninghamia lanceolata
×Cupressocyparis leylandii
×Cupressocyparis ovensii
Cupressus
Cycas revoluta
Cyrtomium falcatum
Cytisus scoparius
Daboecia cantabrica
Danae racemosa
Daphne bholua
Daphne ×burkwoodii
Daphne mezereum
Daphne odora
Daphniphyllum macropodum
Davidia involucrata
Desfontainia spinosa
Dichroa febrifuga
Dicksonia antarctica
Diospyros virginiana
Distylium myricoides
Distylium racemosum
Edgeworthia chrysantha
Elaeagnus ×ebbingei
Elaeagnus macrophylla
Elaeagnus pungens
Epigaea repens
Erica carnea
Eriobotrya japonica
Escallonia rubra
Eucalyptus
Euonymus alatus
Euonymus americanus
Euonymus fortunei
Euonymus japonicus
Euonymus kiautschovicus
Eurya japonica
Fagus grandifolia
Fagus sylvatica
×Fatshedera lizei
Fatsia japonica
Ficus pumila
Firmiana simplex
Franklinia alatamaha
Gardenia jasminoides
Garrya elliptica
Gaultheria mucronata
Gaultheria procumbens

Gaylussacia brachycera
Gelsemium sempervirens
Genista
Gordonia lasianthus
Grevillea robusta
Gymnocladus dioicus
Hamamelis
Hebe
Hedera
Holboellia latifolia
Hypericum
Idesia polycarpa
Ilex
Illicium
Itea virginica
Ixora coccinea
Jasminum floridum
Jasminum humile
Jasminum mesnyi
Jasminum nudiflorum
Jasminum parkeri
Juniperus
Kerria japonica
Lagerstroemia indica
Lagerstroemia limii
Lagerstroemia subcostata var. fauriei
Laurus nobilis
Leiophyllum buxifolium
Leptospermum scoparium
Leucophyllum frutescens
Leucothoe axillaris
Leucothoe fontanesiana
Ligustrum japonicum
Ligustrum lucidum
Lindera aggregata
Liriodendron tulipifera
Lithocarpus henryi
Livistona chinensis
Lonicera nitida
Lonicera pileata
Loropetalum chinense
Loropetalum chinense var. rubrum
Lyonia lucida
Maackia amurensis
Magnolia grandiflora
Magnolia virginiana
Magnolia zenii 'Pink Parchment'
Mahonia
Melia azedarach

Metasequoia glyptostroboides
Microbiota decussata
Millettia reticulata
Morus australis 'Unryu'
Myrica cerifera
Myrica inodora
Myrtus communis
Nageia nagi
Nandina domestica
Nerium oleander
Nyssa sylvatica
Olea europaea
Osmanthus
Ostrya virginiana
Oxydendrum arboreum
Pachysandra procumbens
Pachysandra terminalis
Parrotia persica
Paxistima canbyi
Persea borbonia
Phellodendron amurense
Phillyrea angustifolia
Phoenix canariensis
Photinia davidiana
Photinia ×fraseri
Photinia glabra
Photinia serratifolia
Physocarpus opulifolius
Picea
Pieris
Pinus
Pittosporum
Platanus ×acerifolia
Platanus occidentalis
Podocarpus macrophyllus 'Maki'
Poncirus trifoliata
Populus alba

Populus grandidentata
Populus nigra 'Italica'
Populus tremuloides
Potentilla fruticosa
Prunus campanulata
Prunus caroliniana
Prunus laurocerasus
Prunus lusitanica
Prunus maackii
Prunus mume
Prunus 'Okame'
Prunus sargentii
Prunus serrula
Prunus serrulata
Pseudocydonia sinensis
Pseudotsuga menziesii
Pyracantha coccinea
Pyracantha koidzumii
Quercus acuta
Quercus glauca
Quercus myrsinifolia
Quercus phillyraeoides
Quercus virginiana
Rhaphiolepis umbellata
Rhapidophyllum hystrix
Rhapis excelsa
Rhododendron catawbiense
Rhododendron degronianum subsp. yakushimanum
Rhododendron hyperythrum
Rhododendron maximum
Rhododendron minus
Rhododendron minus var. chapmanii
Rhododendron 'PJM'
Rhododendron yedoense var. poukhanense
Rhodotypos scandens
Rosa carolina

Rosa glauca
Rosa moyesii
Rosa rugosa
Rosa virginiana
Rosmarinus officinalis
Rubus pentalobus
Ruscus aculeatus
Sabal palmetto
Salix alba 'Tristis'
Salix babylonica
Salix caprea
Salix gracilistyla
Salix matsudana
Salix purpurea
Salix udensis 'Sekka'
Santolina chamaecyparissus
Sarcandra glabra
Sarcococca
Sciadopitys verticillata
Sequoia sempervirens
Sequoiadendron giganteum
Serenoa repens
Skimmia japonica
Skimmia japonica subsp. reevesiana
Smilax
Stachyurus praecox
Stewartia koreana
Stewartia monadelpha
Stewartia pseudocamellia
Stewartia sinensis
Styrax grandifolius
Styrax japonicus
Styrax obassia
Syagrus romanzoffianum
Sycopsis sinensis
Symplocos tinctoria
Syringa reticulata subsp. pekinensis

Taiwania cryptomerioides
Taxodium distichum
Taxus
Ternstroemia gymnanthera
Tetradium daniellii
Thuja
Thujopsis dolabrata
Tilia kiusiana
Torreya taxifolia
Trachelospermum asiaticum
Trachelospermum jasminoides
Trachycarpus fortunei
Trochodendron aralioides
Tsuga
Ulmus parvifolia
Vaccinium vitis-idaea
Viburnum awabuki
Viburnum ×bodnantense
Viburnum davidii
Viburnum farreri
Viburnum japonicum
Viburnum obovatum
Viburnum odoratissimum
Viburnum 'Pragense'
Viburnum rhytidophyllum
Viburnum suspensum
Viburnum tinus
Viburnum utile
Vinca major
Vinca minor
Washingtonia robusta
Wollemia nobilis
Xanthocyparis nootkatensis
Yucca
Zamia pumila
Zelkova serrata
Zelkova sinica

SHADE TOLERANCE

Plants listed are tolerant of conditions of light shade or greater. Some will produce diminished flowers or fruit in shady environments.

Abelia chinensis
Abelia ×grandiflora
Abelia serrata
Acer carpinifolium

Acer circinatum
Acer japonicum
Acer palmatum
Acer pensylvanicum

Acer pseudosieboldianum
Acer saccharum
Acer saccharum subsp. floridanum
Acer saccharum subsp. leucoderme
Aesculus parviflora
Aesculus pavia
Aesculus sylvatica

Agarista populifolia
Akebia quinata
Amelanchier
Ardisia japonica
Asimina triloba
Aucuba japonica
Bignonia capreolata
Buxus
Callicarpa americana

Calycanthus
Camellia
Carpinus betulus
Carpinus caroliniana
Cephalotaxus fortunei
Cephalotaxus harringtonia
Cercidiphyllum japonicum
Chamaerops humilis
Chionanthus retusus
Chionanthus virginicus
Choisya ternata
Clethra acuminata
Cleyera japonica
Cliftonia monophylla
Cornus alba
Cornus alternifolia
Cornus amomum
Cornus florida
Cornus kousa
Cornus racemosa
Cornus sericea
Croton alabamensis
Cryptomeria japonica
Cunninghamia lanceolata
Cycas revoluta
Cyrtomium falcatum
Danae racemosa
Daphne
Daphniphyllum macropodum
Decumaria barbara
Desfontainia spinosa
Diervilla sessilifolia
Dirca palustris
Disanthus cercidifolius
Distylium myricoides
Distylium racemosum
Edgeworthia chrysantha
Elaeagnus ×ebbingei
Elaeagnus macrophylla
Elaeagnus pungens
Eleutherococcus sieboldianus
Enkianthus
Epigaea repens
Eriobotrya japonica
Eubotrys racemosa
Euonymus alatus
Euonymus americanus
Euonymus fortunei
Euonymus japonicus
Euonymus kiautschovicus

Eurya japonica
Fagus grandifolia
Fagus sylvatica
×Fatshedera lizei
Fatsia japonica
Ficus pumila
Fothergilla gardenii
Fothergilla major
Frangula caroliniana
Franklinia alatamaha
Gardenia jasminoides
Garrya elliptica
Gaultheria procumbens
Gaylussacia brachycera
Gaylussacia ursina
Halesia carolina
Halesia diptera
Hamamelis
Hedera
Holboellia latifolia
Hydrangea anomala subsp.
    petiolaris
Hydrangea arborescens
Hydrangea macrophylla
Hydrangea quercifolia
Hydrangea serrata
Ilex ×altaclerensis
Ilex aquifolium
Ilex ×aquipernyi
Ilex ×attenuata
Ilex cassine
Ilex cornuta
Ilex crenata
Ilex 'Emily Bruner'
Ilex glabra
Ilex ×koehneana
Ilex latifolia
Ilex ×meserveae
Ilex 'Nellie R. Stevens'
Ilex opaca
Ilex pedunculosa
Ilex Red Hollies
Ilex rotunda
Illicium
Itea virginica
Ixora coccinea
Jasminum nudiflorum
Kadsura japonica
Kalmia latifolia
Kerria japonica
Laurus nobilis

Leitneria floridana
Leucothoe axillaris
Leucothoe fontanesiana
Ligustrum japonicum
Ligustrum lucidum
Lindera
Livistona chinensis
Lonicera
Loropetalum chinense
Loropetalum chinense var.
    rubrum
Magnolia figo
Magnolia grandiflora
Mahonia
Myrtus communis
Nandina domestica
Neviusia alabamensis
Orixa japonica
Osmanthus
Ostrya virginiana
Pachysandra procumbens
Pachysandra terminalis
Parrotia persica
Parthenocissus
Phillyrea angustifolia
Photinia davidiana
Photinia ×fraseri
Photinia glabra
Photinia serratifolia
Pieris
Pittosporum
Podocarpus macrophyllus
    'Maki'
Prunus caroliniana
Prunus laurocerasus
Prunus lusitanica
Pseudocydonia sinensis
Ptelea trifoliata
Quercus acuta
Quercus glauca
Quercus myrsinifolia
Quercus phillyraeoides
Quercus virginiana
Rhamnus cathartica
Rhaphiolepis umbellata
Rhapidophyllum hystrix
Rhapis excelsa
Rhododendron
Rhodotypos scandens
Ribes
Rubus pentalobus

Ruscus aculeatus
Sarcandra glabra
Sarcococca
Schizophragma hydrange-
    oides
Sequoia sempervirens
Serenoa repens
Serissa japonica
Sinojackia rehderiana
Skimmia japonica
Skimmia japonica subsp.
    reevesiana
Smilax
Stachyurus praecox
Staphylea trifolia
Stewartia
Styrax
Sycopsis sinensis
Symphoricarpos
Symplocos tinctoria
Taxus
Ternstroemia gymnanthera
Trachelospermum asiaticum
Trachelospermum jasmin-
    oides
Trachycarpus fortunei
Trochodendron aralioides
Tsuga
Vaccinium
Viburnum acerifolium
Viburnum awabuki
Viburnum cassinoides
Viburnum davidii
Viburnum nudum
Viburnum obovatum
Viburnum odoratissimum
Viburnum plicatum
Viburnum plicatum f. tomen-
    tosum
Viburnum 'Pragense'
Viburnum prunifolium
Viburnum rafinesqueanum
Viburnum rhytidophyllum
Viburnum rufidulum
Viburnum suspensum
Viburnum tinus
Viburnum utile
Vinca major
Vinca minor
Xanthorhiza simplicissima

SALT TOLERANCE

Plants listed show various degrees of tolerance to aerial- and/or soil-deposited salts. Very few plants are truly salt tolerant.

Acca sellowiana
Acer campestre
Acer platanoides
Acer pseudoplatanus
Acer saccharinum
Aesculus hippocastanum
Agave americana
Ailanthus altissima
Amelanchier canadensis
Amorpha canescens
Amorpha fruticosa
Araucaria araucana
Ardisia japonica
Baccharis halimifolia
Broussonetia papyrifera
Butia capitata
Calia secundiflora
Callistemon citrinus
Caragana arborescens
Caragana frutex
Carissa macrocarpa
Catalpa speciosa
Cedrus atlantica var. glauca
Chamaecyparis thyoides
Chamaerops humilis
Chilopsis linearis
Cinnamomum camphora
Crataegus crus-galli
Cunninghamia lanceolata
×Cupressocyparis leylandii
Cupressus
Cycas revoluta
Cyrtomium falcatum
Cytisus battandieri
Cytisus scoparius
Diospyros kaki
Duranta erecta
Elaeagnus
Eriobotrya japonica

Escallonia rubra
Euonymus japonicus
×Fatshedera lizei
Fatsia japonica
Frangula alnus
Fuchsia magellanica
Gleditsia triacanthos f. inermis
Hedera canariensis
Hippophae rhamnoides
Hydrangea macrophylla
Ilex ×altaclerensis
Ilex aquifolium
Ilex cassine
Ilex cornuta
Ilex 'Emily Bruner'
Ilex glabra
Ilex ×koehneana
Ilex latifolia
Ilex 'Nellie R. Stevens'
Ilex opaca
Ilex Red Hollies
Ilex rotunda
Ilex vomitoria
Ixora coccinea
Juniperus
Lantana camara
Laurus nobilis
Lavandula angustifolia
Leptospermum scoparium
Leucophyllum frutescens
Ligustrum
Livistona chinensis
Lonicera
Magnolia grandiflora
Melia azedarach
Morus alba
Myrica
Myrtus communis

Nageia nagi
Nandina domestica
Nerium oleander
Parkinsonia aculeata
Persea borbonia
Phoenix canariensis
Photinia ×fraseri
Picea glauca
Picea pungens
Pinus banksiana
Pinus cembra
Pinus clausa
Pinus echinata
Pinus elliottii
Pinus glabra
Pinus heldreichii
Pinus mugo
Pinus nigra
Pinus palustris
Pinus parviflora
Pinus rigida
Pinus sylvestris
Pinus taeda
Pinus thunbergii
Pistacia chinensis
Pittosporum tenuifolium
Pittosporum tobira
Podocarpus macrophyllus 'Maki'
Populus alba
Populus deltoides
Populus grandidentata
Populus tremuloides
Prunus caroliniana
Prunus maritima
Prunus padus
Prunus serotina
Prunus virginiana
Pyracantha koidzumii
Quercus alba
Quercus macrocarpa
Quercus marilandica
Quercus robur

Quercus rubra
Quercus virginiana
Rhamnus cathartica
Rhaphiolepis ×delacourii
Rhaphiolepis umbellata
Rhapis excelsa
Rhus
Robinia pseudoacacia
Rosa laevigata
Rosa rugosa
Rosa virginiana
Rosmarinus officinalis
Sabal palmetto
Salix alba 'Tristis'
Salix matsudana
Santolina chamaecyparissus
Sapindus drummondii
Serenoa repens
Sesbania punicea
Shepherdia argentea
Sorbaria
Styphnolobium japonicum
Syagrus romanzoffianum
Tamarix ramosissima
Tecoma capensis
Trachycarpus fortunei
Triadica sebifera
Ulmus alata
Ulmus americana
Ulmus crassifolia
Ulmus glabra
Ulmus parvifolia
Ulmus pumila
Viburnum awabuki
Viburnum dentatum
Viburnum suspensum
Viburnum tinus
Vitex rotundifolia
Washingtonia robusta
Yucca
Zamia pumila
Zanthoxylum americanum
Zelkova sinica

TOLERANCE TO MOIST OR WET SOILS

The following plants are good for moist to wet soil conditions.

Acer negundo
Acer rubrum
Acer saccharinum
Alnus
Amorpha fruticosa
Andromeda polifolia
Aralia spinosa
Aronia arbutifolia
Aronia melanocarpa
Baccharis halimifolia
Betula nigra
Carpinus caroliniana
Carya aquatica
Carya illinoinensis
Celtis laevigata
Celtis occidentalis
Cephalanthus occidentalis
Chamaecyparis thyoides
Chamaedaphne calyculata
Clethra alnifolia
Cornus alba
Cornus amomum
Cornus sanguinea
Cornus sericea
Cyrilla racemiflora
Decumaria barbara
Distylium myricoides
Distylium racemosum

Forestiera acuminata
Frangula alnus
Fraxinus pennsylvanica
Gleditsia triacanthos f. inermis
Gordonia lasianthus
Hypericum brachyphyllum
Hypericum densiflorum
Hypericum fasciculatum
Hypericum galioides
Hypericum lissophloeus
Ilex cassine
Ilex decidua
Ilex glabra
Ilex mucronata
Ilex opaca
Ilex verticillata
Ilex vomitoria
Illicium floridanum
Illicium parviflorum
Itea virginica
Larix laricina
Leitneria floridana
Ligustrum lucidum
Ligustrum sinense
Lindera benzoin
Liquidambar styraciflua
Lyonia lucida

Magnolia grandiflora
Magnolia virginiana
Metasequoia glyptostroboides
Morus alba
Myrica
Nyssa aquatica
Nyssa ogeche
Nyssa sylvatica
Osmanthus americanus
Persea borbonia
Physocarpus opulifolius
Pieris phillyreifolia
Pinckneya bracteata
Pinus glabra
Pinus taeda
Planera aquatica
Platanus ×acerifolia
Platanus occidentalis
Populus deltoides
Pterocarya fraxinifolia
Quercus bicolor
Quercus lyrata
Quercus michauxii
Quercus nigra
Quercus nuttallii
Quercus palustris
Quercus phellos
Quercus virginiana
Rhododendron atlanticum
Rhododendron viscosum

Rosa carolina
Rosa virginiana
Sabal palmetto
Salix
Sambucus canadensis
Sambucus nigra
Serenoa repens
Sesbania punicea
Smilax
Spiraea alba var. latifolia
Spiraea tomentosa
Spiraea virginiana
Taxodium distichum
Taxodium distichum var. imbricarium
Thuja occidentalis
Thuja plicata
Triadica sebifera
Ulmus americana
Vaccinium ashei
Vaccinium corymbosum
Viburnum cassinoides
Viburnum dentatum
Viburnum nudum
Viburnum obovatum
Viburnum opulus
Viburnum sargentii
Viburnum trilobum
Wisteria frutescens
Xanthorhiza simplicissima
Zenobia pulverulenta

TOLERANCE TO DRY SOILS

The following plants are good for dry soil conditions. Plants require time to establish extensive root systems before acclimating to dry soils.

Abelia chinensis
Abelia ×grandiflora
Abelia macrotera
Abelia parvifolia
Abelia serrata
Abelia spathulata
Abeliophyllum distichum
Abies cilicica
Abies concolor
Abies firma
Abies pinsapo

Acca sellowiana
Acer buergerianum
Acer campestre
Acer miyabei
Acer platanoides
Acer pseudoplatanus
Acer truncatum
Actinidia arguta
Agave americana
Ailanthus altissima
Akebia quinata

Albizia julibrissin
Amorpha canescens
Ampelopsis brevipedunculata
Andrachne colchica
Antigonon leptopus
Araucaria araucana
Arbutus menziesii
Arctostaphylos uva-ursi
Azara microphylla
Bauhinia variegata
Berberis candidula
Berberis ×gladwynensis 'William Penn'
Berberis julianae
Betula populifolia

Bougainvillea glabra
Broussonetia papyrifera
Brunfelsia pauciflora
Buddleia lindleyana
Buddleia loricata
Buddleia salviifolia
Butia capitata
Buxus harlandii
Calia secundiflora
Callistemon citrinus
Calocedrus decurrens
Campsis radicans
Campsis ×tagliabuana 'Madame Galen'
Caragana arborescens
Caragana frutex

Carissa macrocarpa
Carya glabra
Carya ovata
Caryopteris ×clandonensis
Cassia
Castanea mollissima
Castanea pumila
Catalpa bignonioides
Catalpa speciosa
Cedrus atlantica
Cedrus deodara
Cedrus libani
Celastrus orbiculatus
Celastrus scandens
Celtis laevigata
Celtis occidentalis
Chilopsis linearis
Chionanthus retusus
Cistus
Cleyera japonica
Cocculus carolinus
Colutea arborescens
Comptonia peregrina
Cornus mas
Cornus officinalis
Cotinus obovatus
Crataegus crus-galli
Crataegus nitida
Crataegus punctata
Cupressus arizonica var.
   glabra
Cupressus macrocarpa
Cupressus sempervirens
Cytisus scoparius
Diospyros kaki
Diospyros virginiana
Distylium myricoides
Distylium racemosum
Elaeagnus angustifolia
Elaeagnus ×ebbingei
Elaeagnus macrophylla
Elaeagnus multiflora
Elaeagnus pungens
Elaeagnus umbellata
Eleutherococcus sieboldianus

Eucalyptus
Fallopia baldschuanica
Ficus carica
Ficus pumila
Firmiana simplex
Fontanesia philliraeoides
   subsp. fortunei
Genista lydia
Genista pilosa
Genista tinctoria
Ginkgo biloba
Hebe
Helianthemum nummu-
   larium
Hippophae rhamnoides
Idesia polycarpa
Ilex cornuta
Ilex 'Emily Bruner'
Ilex ×koehneana
Ilex latifolia
Ilex 'Nellie R. Stevens'
Ilex Red Hollies
Ilex rotunda
Ilex vomitoria
Ixora coccinea
Jasminum floridum
Jasminum nudiflorum
Juniperus chinensis
Juniperus chinensis 'Par-
   sonii'
Juniperus chinensis var. pro-
   cumbens
Juniperus communis
Juniperus horizontalis
Juniperus rigida subsp. con-
   ferta
Juniperus sabina
Juniperus scopulorum
Juniperus squamata
Juniperus virginiana
Juniperus virginiana var.
   silicicola
Lantana camara
Lavandula angustifolia

Leptospermum scoparium
Leucophyllum frutescens
Ligustrum japonicum
Ligustrum lucidum
Ligustrum ovalifolium
Lithocarpus henryi
Maackia amurensis
Maclura pomifera
Mahonia bealei
Mahonia ×media
Melia azedarach
Morus alba
Morus australis 'Unryu'
Morus rubra
Myrica cerifera
Myrica pensylvanica
Nageia nagi
Nandina domestica
Nerium oleander
Olea europaea
Osmanthus ×fortunei
Osmanthus fragrans
Osmanthus heterophyllus
Photinia ×fraseri
Photinia serratifolia
Pinus banksiana
Pinus clausa
Pinus echinata
Pinus rigida
Pinus taeda
Pinus virginiana
Pistacia chinensis
Pittosporum tobira
Prunus maritima
Punica granatum
Pyracantha coccinea
Pyracantha koidzumii
Pyrus calleryana
Pyrus pyrifolia
Pyrus ussuriensis
Quercus acutissima
Quercus ellipsoidalis
Quercus falcata
Quercus georgiana

Quercus hemisphaerica
Quercus marilandica
Quercus montana
Quercus muehlenbergii
Quercus phillyraeoides
Quercus stellata
Rhaphiolepis umbellata
Rhodotypos scandens
Rhus aromatica
Rhus copallina
Rhus glabra
Rhus typhina
Ribes sanguineum
Robinia hispida
Rosa laevigata
Rosa rugosa
Rosmarinus officinalis
Ruscus aculeatus
Santolina chamaecyparissus
Sapindus drummondii
Serissa japonica
Shepherdia argentea
Spiraea cantoniensis
   'Lanceata'
Spiraea ×vanhouttei
Symphoricarpos orbiculatus
Taiwania cryptomerioides
Tamarix ramosissima
Triadica sebifera
Ulmus alata
Ulmus crassifolia
Ulmus parvifolia
Ulmus pumila
Vernicia fordii
Viburnum obovatum
Viburnum utile
Vitex agnus-castus
Washingtonia robusta
Yucca
Zamia pumila
Zanthoxylum americanum
Zelkova serrata
Zelkova sinica
Ziziphus jujuba

STREET AND URBAN PLANTING

The following plants adapt exceptionally well to a variety of environmental and/or urban stresses, such as heat, drought, and compacted, infertile soils.

Abelia chinensis
Abelia ×grandiflora
Abelia parvifolia
Acca sellowiana
Acer buergerianum
Acer campestre
Acer miyabei
Acer platanoides
Acer pseudoplatanus
Acer tataricum
Acer tataricum subsp. ginnala
Actinidia arguta
Agave americana
Ailanthus altissima
Akebia quinata
Albizia julibrissin
Ampelopsis brevipedunculata
Antigonon leptopus
Aucuba japonica
Berberis
Bougainvillea glabra
Broussonetia papyrifera
Butia capitata
Calia secundiflora
Callistemon citrinus
Caragana arborescens
Carissa macrocarpa
Catalpa bignonioides
Catalpa speciosa
Cedrus
Celastrus orbiculatus
Celastrus scandens
Celtis laevigata
Celtis occidentalis
Chamaerops humilis
Chilopsis linearis
Chionanthus retusus
Cinnamomum camphora

Cotinus obovatus
Crataegus
Cunninghamia lanceolata
Cupressus arizonica var. glabra
Cupressus sempervirens
Deutzia gracilis
Diospyros kaki
Diospyros virginiana
Distylium myricoides
Distylium racemosum
Elaeagnus
Eleutherococcus sieboldianus
Eriobotrya japonica
Erythrina ×bidwillii
Eucalyptus
Eucommia ulmoides
Euonymus fortunei
Euonymus japonicus
Fallopia baldschuanica
Ficus carica
Ficus pumila
Firmiana simplex
Fontanesia philliraeoides subsp. fortunei
Ginkgo biloba
Gleditsia triacanthos f. inermis
Gymnocladus dioicus
Hedera helix
Hippophae rhamnoides
Ilex cornuta
Ilex 'Emily Bruner'
Ilex ×koehneana
Ilex 'Nellie R. Stevens'
Ilex Red Hollies
Ilex vomitoria
Ixora coccinea
Juniperus chinensis

Juniperus chinensis 'Parsonii'
Juniperus chinensis var. procumbens
Juniperus communis
Juniperus horizontalis
Juniperus sabina
Juniperus scopulorum
Juniperus squamata
Juniperus virginiana
Juniperus virginiana var. silicicola
Koelreuteria bipinnata
Lespedeza thunbergii
Leucophyllum frutescens
Ligustrum amurense
Ligustrum japonicum
Ligustrum lucidum
Ligustrum obtusifolium
Ligustrum ovalifolium
Ligustrum vulgare
Lonicera fragrantissima
Maackia amurensis
Maclura pomifera
Mahonia bealei
Mahonia ×media
Melia azedarach
Morus alba
Myrica cerifera
Myrica pensylvanica
Nageia nagi
Nandina domestica
Nerium oleander
Olea europaea
Osmanthus ×fortunei
Osmanthus heterophyllus
Paulownia tomentosa
Photinia ×fraseri
Photinia glabra
Photinia serratifolia
Pistacia chinensis
Pittosporum heterophyllum
Pittosporum tobira
Poncirus trifoliata
Punica granatum

Pyracantha coccinea
Pyracantha koidzumii
Pyrus calleryana
Pyrus pyrifolia
Pyrus ussuriensis
Quercus bicolor
Quercus ellipsoidalis
Quercus falcata
Quercus glauca
Quercus lyrata
Quercus michauxii
Quercus myrsinifolia
Quercus nuttallii
Quercus palustris
Quercus phellos
Quercus shumardii
Quercus virginiana
Rhamnus cathartica
Rhaphiolepis umbellata
Rhus glabra
Rhus typhina
Ruscus aculeatus
Sabal palmetto
Sapindus drummondii
Sorbaria sorbifolia
Spiraea cantoniensis 'Lanceata'
Spiraea ×vanhouttei
Taiwania cryptomerioides
Taxodium distichum
Taxodium distichum var. imbricarium
Tetradium daniellii
Thuja orientalis
Triadica sebifera
Ulmus alata
Ulmus crassifolia
Ulmus parvifolia
Ulmus pumila
Viburnum awabuki
Viburnum obovatum
Viburnum odoratissimum
Yucca
Zelkova serrata
Ziziphus jujuba

HEDGING

Plants listed are particularly amenable to pruning and are among the better choices for hedging and parterres.

Abelia chinensis
Abelia ×grandiflora
Acer campestre
Acer platanoides
Acer tataricum subsp. ginnala
Agarista populifolia
Aucuba japonica
Berberis julianae
Berberis koreana
Berberis ×mentorensis
Berberis thunbergii
Buxus
Camellia sasanqua
Carpinus betulus
Carpinus caroliniana
Cephalotaxus harringtonia
Cleyera japonica
Cotoneaster divaricatus
Cotoneaster lucidus
Cotoneaster multiflorus
Crataegus phaenopyrum
Cryptomeria japonica
×Cupressocyparis leylandii
×Cupressocyparis ovensii
Cupressus
Distylium racemosum
Elaeagnus ×ebbingei
Elaeagnus macrophylla
Elaeagnus multiflora

Elaeagnus pungens
Elaeagnus umbellata
Eleutherococcus sieboldianus
Euonymus alatus
Euonymus japonicus
Euonymus kiautschovicus
Eurya japonica
Fagus grandifolia
Fagus sylvatica
Fontanesia philliraeoides subsp. fortunei
Frangula alnus
Gardenia jasminoides
Gaultheria mucronata
Ilex ×altaclerensis
Ilex aquifolium
Ilex ×aquipernyi
Ilex ×attenuata
Ilex cornuta
Ilex crenata
Ilex 'Emily Bruner'
Ilex glabra
Ilex ×koehneana
Ilex 'Nellie R. Stevens'
Ilex opaca
Ilex Red Hollies
Ilex vomitoria
Illicium henryi

Illicium parviflorum
Ixora coccinea
Jasminum mesnyi
Juniperus chinensis
Juniperus communis
Juniperus sabina
Juniperus scopulorum
Juniperus virginiana
Juniperus virginiana var. silicicola
Laurus nobilis
Ligustrum
Lonicera fragrantissima
Lonicera korolkowii
Lonicera maackii
Lonicera nitida
Lonicera pileata
Lonicera tatarica
Lonicera xylosteum
Loropetalum chinense
Loropetalum chinense var. rubrum
Myrica
Myrtus communis
Olea europaea
Osmanthus armatus
Osmanthus ×burkwoodii
Osmanthus delavayi
Osmanthus ×fortunei
Osmanthus fragrans
Osmanthus heterophyllus
Osmanthus serrulatus
Phillyrea angustifolia

Photinia davidiana
Photinia ×fraseri
Photinia glabra
Photinia serratifolia
Pinus strobus
Pittosporum
Podocarpus macrophyllus 'Maki'
Poncirus trifoliata
Prunus caroliniana
Prunus laurocerasus
Prunus lusitanica
Pyracantha coccinea
Pyracantha koidzumii
Rhaphiolepis umbellata
Ribes alpinum
Serissa japonica
Sycopsis sinensis
Taxus baccata
Taxus chinensis
Taxus cuspidata
Taxus ×media
Ternstroemia gymnanthera
Teucrium chamaedrys
Thuja
Tilia cordata
Tsuga
Viburnum awabuki
Viburnum dentatum
Viburnum obovatum
Viburnum odoratissimum
Viburnum suspensum
Viburnum tinus

EVERGREENS FOR SPECIMENS, GROUPINGS, SCREENS, AND GROVES

In many landscapes, a grouping of three or more needle or broadleaf evergreens provides both visual privacy and a more aesthetically pleasing feeling than tightly pruned hedges. When positioning these trees and shrubs, be sure to provide them with ample space to spread.

Abies
Acca sellowiana
Agarista populifolia
Araucaria araucana
Arbutus menziesii

Arbutus unedo
Aucuba japonica
Azara microphylla
Berberis julianae
Buxus sempervirens

Calocedrus decurrens
Camellia
Cedrus
Cephalotaxus fortunei
Cephalotaxus harringtonia
Chamaecyparis
Clethra arborea
Cliftonia monophylla
Cotoneaster lacteus
Cotoneaster salicifolius
Cryptomeria japonica
Cunninghamia lanceolata
×Cupressocyparis leylandii

×Cupressocyparis ovensii
Cupressus
Daphniphyllum macropodum
Distylium racemosum
Elaeagnus ×ebbingei
Elaeagnus macrophylla
Elaeagnus pungens
Eriobotrya japonica
Escallonia rubra
Fatsia japonica
Garrya elliptica
Gordonia lasianthus
Ilex ×altaclerensis

Evergreens for Specimens, Groupings, Screens, and Groves CONTINUED

Ilex aquifolium
Ilex ×aquipernyi
Ilex ×attenuata
Ilex 'Emily Bruner'
Ilex ×koehneana
Ilex latifolia
Ilex 'Nellie R. Stevens'
Ilex opaca
Ilex Red Hollies
Ilex rotunda
Illicium anisatum
Illicium floridanum
Illicium henryi
Illicium parviflorum
Jasminum mesnyi
Juniperus chinensis
Juniperus communis
Juniperus sabina
Juniperus scopulorum
Juniperus virginiana

Juniperus virginiana var. silicicola
Kalmia latifolia
Laurus nobilis
Ligustrum japonicum
Ligustrum lucidum
Lindera aggregata
Lithocarpus henryi
Livistona chinensis
Loropetalum chinense
Loropetalum chinense var. rubrum
Magnolia grandiflora
Magnolia virginiana
Mahonia ×media
Myrica cerifera
Nerium oleander
Olea europaea
Osmanthus
Persea borbonia

Phillyrea angustifolia
Photinia ×fraseri
Photinia glabra
Photinia serratifolia
Picea
Pinus
Pittosporum
Podocarpus macrophyllus 'Maki'
Prunus caroliniana
Prunus laurocerasus
Prunus lusitanica
Pseudotsuga menziesii
Quercus acuta
Quercus glauca
Quercus myrsinifolia
Quercus phillyraeoides
Rhapidophyllum hystrix
Rhapis excelsa
Rhododendron catawbiense

Rhododendron maximum
Sciadopitys verticillata
Sequoia sempervirens
Sequoiadendron giganteum
Sycopsis sinensis
Taiwania cryptomerioides
Taxus baccata
Taxus cuspidata
Ternstroemia gymnanthera
Thuja
Thujopsis dolabrata
Trochodendron aralioides
Tsuga
Viburnum awabuki
Viburnum odoratissimum
Viburnum 'Pragense'
Viburnum rhytidophyllum
Viburnum suspensum
Viburnum tinus
Xanthocyparis nootkatensis

WEEPING OR COLUMNAR HABIT

The following trees are either weeping or fastigiate/columnar in habit, whether by nature or as selected/bred.

WEEPING

Acer buergerianum 'Angyo Weeping'
Acer palmatum 'Ryusen'
Albizia julibrissin 'Pendula'
Alnus incana 'Pendula'
Betula nigra 'Summer Cascade'
Betula pendula 'Youngii'
Carpinus betulus 'Pendula'
Cedrus atlantica 'Glauca Pendula'
Cedrus libani 'Pendula'
Cercidiphyllum japonicum 'Amazing Grace'
Cercidiphyllum japonicum 'Morioka Weeping'
Cercis canadensis Lavender Twist™
Cercis canadensis 'Ruby Falls'
Corylus avellana 'Pendula'
Fagus sylvatica 'Aurea Pendula'
Fagus sylvatica 'Pendula'

Halesia carolina 'Lady Catherine'
Larix decidua 'Pendula'
Morus alba 'Chaparral'
Morus alba 'Urbana'
Nyssa sylvatica 'Autumn Cascades'
Parrotia persica 'Pendula'
Prunus subhirtella 'Pendula'
Prunus ×yedoensis 'Shidare Yoshino'
Salix alba 'Tristis'
Salix babylonica
Salix caprea 'Pendula'
Sequoiadendron giganteum 'Pendulum'
Sorbus aucuparia 'Pendula'
Styphnolobium japonicum 'Pendula'
Styrax japonicus 'Fragrant Fountains'
Styrax japonicus 'Pendula'
Taxodium distichum 'Cascade Falls'

Taxodium distichum 'Falling-water'
Thuja occidentalis 'Pendula'
Tilia 'Petiolaris'
Tsuga canadensis 'Sargentii'
Ulmus alata 'Lace Parasol'

FASTIGIATE/COLUMNAR

Acer rubrum 'Armstrong'
Acer rubrum 'Columnare'
Acer saccharum 'Monumentale'
Alnus cordata
Betula pendula 'Fastigiata'
Carpinus betulus 'Fastigiata'
Celtis occidentalis 'Prairie Sentinel'
Chionanthus retusus 'Tokyo Tower'
×Cupressocyparis leylandii
×Cupressocyparis ovensii
Cupressus sempervirens 'Stricta'
Fagus sylvatica 'Dawyck Gold'
Fagus sylvatica 'Dawyck Purple'
Fagus sylvatica 'Fastigiata'
Frangula alnus 'Columnaris'

Ginkgo biloba Golden Colonnade™
Ginkgo biloba 'Princeton Sentry'
Koelreuteria paniculata 'Fastigiata'
Koelreuteria paniculata Golden Candle™
Liquidambar styraciflua 'Slender Silhouette'
Liriodendron tulipifera 'Fastigiatum'
Parrotia persica 'Jennifer Teates'
Parrotia persica 'Vanessa'
Populus nigra 'Italica'
Populus tremuloides Mountain Sentinel™
Quercus Crimson Spire™
Quercus Regal Prince®
Quercus palustris Green Pillar®
Quercus robur 'Fastigiata'
Quercus robur Skyrocket®
Taxodium distichum var. imbricarium 'Prairie Sentinel'
Ulmus parvifolia Everclear®
Zelkova serrata 'Musashino'

VINES FOR FLOWERS, FRUIT, AND FALL COLOR

The vines listed have notably colorful or fragrant flowers, attractive fruit, and/or interesting fall color.

Actinidia
Akebia quinata
Allamanda cathartica
Ampelopsis brevipeduncu-
    lata
Antigonon leptopus
Aristolochia macrophylla
Campsis
Celastrus orbiculatus
Celastrus scandens

Clematis
Cocculus carolinus
Decumaria barbara
Euonymus fortunei
Fallopia baldschuanica
×Fatshedera lizei
Ficus pumila
Gelsemium sempervirens
Hedera
Holboellia latifolia

Hydrangea anomala subsp.
    petiolaris
Jasminum officinale
Kadsura japonica
Lonicera ×brownii
Lonicera caprifolium
Lonicera flava
Lonicera ×heckrottii
Lonicera japonica
Lonicera periclymenum
Lonicera sempervirens
Mandevilla splendens
Menispermum canadense
Millettia reticulata

Parthenocissus
Passiflora incarnata
Plumbago auriculata
Rosa banksiae 'Lutea'
Schizophragma hydrange-
    oides
Smilax
Tecoma capensis
Trachelospermum asiaticum
Trachelospermum jasmin-
    oides
Vinca major
Vitis rotundifolia
Wisteria

Conversion Table for Metric Measurements

INCHES	CENTIMETERS		FEET	METERS
1/8	0.3		1/4	0.08
1/6	0.4		1/3	0.1
1/5	0.5		1/2	0.15
1/4	0.6		1	0.3
1/3	0.8		1½	0.5
3/8	0.9		2	0.6
2/5	1.0		2½	0.8
1/2	1.25		3	0.9
3/5	1.5		4	1.2
5/8	1.6		5	1.5
2/3	1.7		6	1.8
3/4	1.9		7	2.1
7/8	2.2		8	2.4
1	2.5		9	2.7
1¼	3.1		10	3.0
1⅓	3.3		12	3.6
1½	3.8		15	4.5
1¾	4.4		18	5.4
2	5.0		20	6.0
3	7.5		25	7.5
4	10		30	9.0
5	12.5		35	10.5
6	15		40	12
7	18		45	13.5
8	20		50	15
9	23		60	18
10	25		70	21
12	30		75	22.5
15	38		80	24
18	45		90	27
20	50		100	30
24	60		125	37.5
30	75		150	45
32	80		175	52.5
36	90		200	60

Hardiness Zones

AVERAGE ANNUAL MINIMUM TEMPERATURE

ZONE	TEMPERATURE (°F)	TEMPERATURE (°C)
1	Below −50	Below −46
2	−50 to −40	−46 to −40
3	−40 to −30	−40 to −34
4	−30 to −20	−34 to −29
5	−20 to −10	−29 to −23
6	−10 to 0	−23 to −18
7	0 to 10	−18 to −12
8	10 to 20	−12 to −7
9	20 to 30	−7 to −1
10	30 to 40	−1 to 4
11	40 and above	4 and above

TEMPERATURES

$$°C = 5/9 \times (°F - 32)$$
$$°F = (9/5 \times °C) + 32$$

To see the U.S. Department of Agriculture Hardiness Zone Map, go to the U.S. National Arboretum site at http://www.usna.usda.gov/Hardzone/ushzmap.html.

Acknowledgments

To Timber Press staff, old and new: Neal Maillet, for first suggesting I combine and update the *Hardy* and *Warm Climate* books; Andrew Beckman, for his seamless leadership and belief that a quality reference tome would prove worthy; and Franni Bertolino, for staying the course and softening the rough spots.

To Margie Boccieri and Hillary Barber, equally integral to the process of shaping this book, from researching, typing, proofing, and slide-pulling to determining the minute (niggling) details of taxonomic *truth*.

To Sweet Bonnie, who patiently perused 1,500 pages of edited text as we answered the many questions that always surface in the stretch run.

To all the people and their gardens, private and public, who allowed me to walk, talk, photograph, and assimilate. And to gardeners everywhere, who have supported the Dirr lectures, writings, and plant introductions.

Appreciation to all, and may your garden be enriched.

Index of Common Names